FOOD AND BEVERAGE COST CONTROL

Fifth Edition

FOOD AND BEVERAGE COST CONTROL

Fifth Edition

LEA R. DOPSON

DAVID K. HAYES

WILEY

John Wiley & Sons, Inc.

For general information on our other products and services, or technical support, please contact our Customer Care Department within the United States at 800-762-2974, outside the United States at 317-572-3993 or fax 317-572-4002.

Wiley also publishes its books in a variety of electronic formats. Some content that appears in print may not be available in electronic books.

For more information about Wiley products, visit our Web site at http://www.wiley.com.

Library of Congress Cataloging-in-Publication Data:

Dopson, Lea R.
  Food and beverage cost control / Lea R. Dopson, David K. Hayes — Fifth ed. p. cm.
  ISBN 978-0-470-25138-6
1. Food service—Cost control.   I. Hayes, David K. II. Title.
  TX911.3.C65D66 2011
  647.95068'l—dc22

                                                                2009026533

Printed in the United States of America

10 9 8 7 6 5 4 3 2

**This edition is dedicated to the memory
of Jack E. and Anita Miller.**

CONTENTS

CHAPTER 3   MANAGING THE COST OF FOOD   55

CHAPTER 4   MANAGING THE COST OF BEVERAGES   132

CHAPTER 5   MANAGING THE FOOD AND BEVERAGE PRODUCTION PROCESS   177

CHAPTER 6   MANAGING FOOD AND BEVERAGE PRICING   236

CHAPTER 7 MANAGING THE COST OF LABOR 275

CHAPTER 8 CONTROLLING OTHER EXPENSES 340

CHAPTER 11   MAINTAINING AND IMPROVING THE REVENUE CONTROL SYSTEM   458

CHAPTER 12   GLOBAL DIMENSIONS OF COST CONTROL   491

PREFACE

*P*revious editions of *Food and Beverage Cost Control* have met with tremendous success in great part because the authors recognized that all foodservice managers, regardless of the type of foodservice business with which they are involved, must effectively manage the costs of operating their businesses.

Today's professional managers know that guiding their operating units to profitability is a constant challenge. These managers are faced daily with a variety of responsibilities, from accounting, marketing, human relations, facilities maintenance, and legal issues to sanitation, production, and service methods, just to name a few.

To be successful, talented foodservice managers must know where they want to take their operations and then apply their training and expertise to get there. In that regard, a professional hospitality manager is much like an airline pilot. Both utilize highly specialized skills and equipment. Both depend on other team members to reach their goals. Both must master a highly specialized area of study.

Regardless of the type of plane they fly, all airline pilots must be well-trained professionals. Regardless of the type of operation for which they are responsible, all foodservice managers must understand the logic and the complex systems involved with managing their costs. An additional similarity between foodservice managers and airline pilots is especially important to recognize. It is this: airline pilot performance improves with experience. So does the performance of foodservice managers. As readers of this new edition will find, added experience also improves the performance of authors! As a result, this newly revised and updated *Food and Beverage Cost Control* is the authors' best ever. It should be held in a professional manager's personal library for reference throughout his or her entire career. It is intended to provide students with the first step in what will be a lifelong and financially rewarding study of how to reach new heights in their management of food and beverage costs.

TO THE STUDENT

Learning about cost control by reading *Food and Beverage Cost Control* will be exciting. We can promise you that because the book was written to present a realistic view of managing a food and beverage operation. And like flying a plane, managing food and beverage operations is exciting... but only if you know what you are doing!

Ask any airplane pilot why they love to fly and one of the answers you will likely get is "It's great fun!" Ask experienced hospitality managers why they love their industry and you get the same answer, "It's great fun!" The hospitality industry is an exciting one. Those professionals who have the skills to effectively manage in it can see their careers soar. The purpose of this book is to provide you all the cost control-related information and tools you will need to achieve success levels that match your own highest career goals.

If you work hard and do your best, we know you will find you have the ability to master all of the information in this text. When you do, you will have gained an invaluable set of management skills and tools that will enhance your knowledge of the hospitality management industry. These skills and tools will ensure that your hospitality career will really take off, allowing you to go wherever you want to go and as high as you want to go!

TO THE INSTRUCTOR

Food and Beverage professionals and airline pilots are remarkably similar. Perhaps the most important similarity, however, is simply this: Great pilots are taught, not born. Unlike some painters, song writers, or basketball players who seem to have been born with an instinctive ability to excel in their areas of interest, no one is born with the innate ability to fly a Boeing 747. Learning to do so requires a motivated student, but more importantly, it requires the skill of highly talented and dedicated instructors. The same is true of professional foodservice managers. They also must be taught by talented and dedicated professionals.

Before a person earns the right to take over the controls of an aircraft, he or she must first learn how those controls work, and how to use them at the proper time. The same is true of professional foodservice managers. Like student pilots, if your students are to learn all they need to take complete control of their own foodservice units, we believe *four* essential learner-related conditions must be satisfied. When these conditions are present, instructors consistently achieve success. As a result, these four areas were clearly identified and enthusiastically addressed by the authors in all phases of this revision. To produce trained professionals capable of confidently taking control of their areas of responsibility and their careers, both flight instructors and their foodservice counterparts require:

1.   Students Who Are Motivated

Hospitality management instructors are fortunate because most of their students are *already* motivated to learn more about this exciting industry. Whether they see themselves as *people* persons or *numbers* persons, most students readily recognize the value of learning to monitor and control their food, beverage, and labor costs. As authors, our goal was to ensure this edition of *Food and*

Beverage Cost Control built upon and enhanced this high level of student motivation by presenting cost-related information in a format that is:

- Easy to read
- Easy to understand
- Easy to remember

Like learning to pilot a plane, learning to manage foodservice costs to ensure profitability can be complex. It does **not** follow, however, that the materials used to teach must be complex. In fact, for both instructors and their students, the best teaching materials are clearly written, easy to understand and easy to use. We believe we have achieved these goals with the publication of this *Fifth Edition*.

2. Students Who Can Be Properly Trained

When they encounter motivated students, talented instructors can apply the best available teaching practices, and they can freely draw from their own experiences to produce outstanding hospitality professionals. In such a setting, the role of a text book should be one of aiding teachers and students through a clear and logical presentation of information. Based on extensive student and instructor feedback received over many years since its introduction, *Food and Beverage Cost Control* has been continually modified, revised, and updated. Its arrangement of material maximizes instructor flexibility in presentation while painstakingly incorporating all of the core topics that must be addressed. It does this in a way that aids students' comprehension and their ability to retain information.

3. Students Who Can Be Properly Equipped

Trained pilots rely on a properly equipped and functioning aircraft to get them to their destinations safely. In a similar manner, hospitality managers must be well equipped. Their equipment is the information gathering and analysis tools used by foodservice professionals. This means they must learn and be able to apply the many procedures, formulas and strategies related to successful food and beverage cost control. Perhaps no area is more important in a book about cost control than the accuracy of the formulas and mathematical solutions used to demonstrate important cost concepts. In addition to the extensive analysis by text reviewers, the authors have conscientiously checked and rechecked to ensure that the formulas, examples, and answers provided in this text are indeed accurate and clarified to the greatest possible degree.

4. Student's Whose Performance Can Be Accurately Assessed

Flight instructors are justifiably proud when their students successfully complete their first solo flights. Prior to that first flight, however, those students' knowledge and skill levels must have been subject to thorough assessment to ensure they were ready to fly. In a similar manner, hospitality instructors know that quality assessment tools must be used to measure their own students' progress.

Professional instructors also know the importance of student assessment goes far beyond the mere assignment of a grade at semester's end. As a result, easy identification of areas in which students may need further instruction, ease of administration and exam quality were all factors meticulously incorporated into the large number of assessment tools developed for this book. These tools include an extensive number of true-to-life case studies *(Consider the Cost)* that are presented in the text at precisely the point where they are most meaningful.

Additional assessment tools include end-of-chapter cases studies *(Apply What You Have Learned)* and an expanded number of end-of-chapter problems *(Test Your Skills)*. Instructors who choose to utilize these tools or the extensive *Test Bank* provided in the **Instructor's Manual** will find that each of these assessment devices will be perceived by students as fair and have been meticulously checked for accuracy. When you use these tools, you will know exactly which of your own students are prepared to take control and solo!

The authors were committed to the careful consideration of these four pedagogically relevant areas during each phase of this revision. Combining this emphasis with accurate and up-to-date cost management tools has resulted, we believe, in what is easily our most useful and student/instructor-friendly edition of *Food and Beverage Cost Control*.

NEW IN THE FIFTH EDITION

As always, input from students and instructors, industry professionals, our colleagues at Wiley, and our own experiences have provided ample material for the new edition. We are extremely happy with the final result. In this *Fifth Edition*, readers will be pleased to find the following significant text enhancements.

NEW "CONSIDER THE COST" FEATURE   One of the most exciting things about learning any new skill is the ability to directly apply what has been learned to situations the learners will actually encounter. To give students an opportunity to do just that, "Consider the Cost" micro case studies have been developed to present students with common cost control-related challenges they will likely encounter at work. Each case study poses questions that allow readers to apply information learned in the chapter to these

Consider The Cost

"We have to lower our price or we'll just get killed," said Hoyt Jones, director of operations for the seven-unit Binky's Sub shops. Binky's was known for its modestly priced, but very high-quality, sandwiches and soups. Business and profits were good, but now Hoyt and Rachel, who served as Binky's director of marketing, were discussing the new $4.99 "*Foot Long Deal*" sandwich promotion that had just been rolled out by their major competitor, an extremely large chain of sub shops that operated over 5,000 units nationally and internationally.

"They just decided to lower their prices to appeal to value-conscious customers," said Hoyt.
"But how can they do that and still make money?" asked Rachel.

"real world" work situations and problems. Instructors will also find these cases are fun for their students to read and discuss in class.

NEW "GREEN AND GROWING" FEATURE   Today's student recognizes that environmental consciousness is as important at work as it is at home. Customers recognize this fact as well. As a result, hospitality professionals are increasingly being asked to adopt practices and policies that aid the planet as well as their own bottom lines. In this new feature, students will become familiar with the "Why's" and the "How's" of responsibly growing their businesses by implementing earth-friendly business practices that are specific to the hospitality industry.

In this edition, the authors have sought to emphasize the importance of sustainability and environmental responsibility as it relates to foodservice cost control. Anyone can talk the green talk, but it takes more than empty eco-labels to convince today's savvy restaurant customers that an operation is doing its part to help preserve the environment. As a result, students must know what they can do, as well as what they should do, to employ environmentally responsible foodservice management practices. This new feature directly addresses these important issues.

Green and Growing!

Increasingly, foodservice managers are finding that creative "green" initiatives benefit their operations in many ways, including those that reduce other expenses. "Trayless dining" is just such an example. In study after study, college foodservice operators find that when serving trays are removed from cafeteria lines, diners take less food (because they only want to carry what they know they will eat). In typical cases, trayless operations experience a 30–50% reduction in food and beverage waste (and in the long run, a likely reduction in the "waist" lines of students!).

ENHANCED TECHNOLOGY FOCUS   This edition, like the previous editions, has been painstakingly designed to present important information in a style that is easy to teach, read, and understand. However, the hospitality industry continues to evolve and, as a result, become more complex. This is especially so in the important area of technology. Because this is true, this edition of *Food and Beverage Cost Control* has again been carefully updated to ensure that readers are aware of the most advanced technological applications of cost control methods available today. In the time between this and the previous edition, the advances in hospitality related computer hardware, software, communication devices, and cost control systems integration have been nothing short of breathtaking. Staying current in the field of cost control requires continual learning and relearning on the part of those who teach and those who practice hospitality cost management.

ENHANCED GLOBAL FOCUS   The changes affecting costs management are varied and become significantly more rapid than ever. The authors' response to new cost control-related issues can be readily found in each of the applicable text chapters and especially in modifications to Chapter 12, "Global Dimensions of Cost Control." This chapter demonstrates to students the specific challenges associated with the management of costs in international foodservice operations. Foodservice operators are increasingly expanding internationally. As a result, the importance to all students of understanding the global implications of what they do daily is increasing swiftly.

SPECIAL EMPHASIS AREAS IN THE FIFTH EDITION

Simplification of Presentation One driving force behind this revision was the continued commitment to fully utilize the computer and the Internet as teaching tools. It was also important that we review each line of type, chart, graph, and figure to ensure that we did not lose sight of one fact—that a text's main function should be to enhance student learning. Students have always been our primary focus and we were delighted to find that, again and again, creative graphics and simply written narrative help to enhance the book's reader friendliness and, as a result, present complex ideas in easily understandable ways. For example, in this edition, we implemented feedback from instructors that we "shorten" Chapter 3 "Managing the Cost of Food" by separating it into two main parts. As a result, Part One of Chapter 3 now addresses menu item forecasting, standardized recipes, inventory control, and purchasing. Part Two addresses receiving, storage, and the determination of actual food expense.

"TEST YOUR SKILLS" ENHANCEMENTS One of the book's most popular features is the end-of-chapter Test Your Skills resource. The decision to include computerized application tools has proved extremely popular; and as was true in previous editions, the authors have again taken the opportunity to maximize their utilization by increasing the number of student exercises (and providing answers in the *Instructor's Manual* and on the book's *Website*) as well as building greater diversity in the difficulty level of these popular exercises. As a result, students will quickly see how the skills they acquire can be easily adapted to the study of cost control, and practicing managers will find the book useful as a reference as well as a source for ready-to-use forms and formulas that can be easily applied to their own operations. Exercises that use Excel spreadsheets for calculations are indicated by the icon that appears in

Test Your Skills

Complete the Test Your Skills exercises by placing your answers in the shaded boxes and answering the questions as indicated.

1. Gil Bloom is planning for the wedding of the mayor's daughter in his hotel. The reception, to be held in the grand ballroom, will be attended by 1,000 people. From his sales histories of similar events, Gil knows that the average drinking habits of those attending receptions of this type are as follows:

    25 percent select champagne
    50 percent select white wine
    25 percent select spirits

    Assuming three drinks per person and a portion size of 3 ounces for champagne, 4 ounces for wine, and 1 ounce for spirits, how much of each product, in 750-ml bottles, should Gil order? (Multiply fluid ounces by 29.57 to convert to milliliters.) Spreadsheet hint: Use the ROUNDUP function in the **Total Bottles** column to determine number of full bottles to order.

    If you were Gil, would you order more than you think you would need? Why or why not? If so, how much more would you order?

Beverage Selection	Percent Selecting	Total Guests	# of Guests Selecting	# of Drinks per Guest	Total # of Portions	Portion Size (oz.)	Amount Needed (oz.)	Total Milliliters	Total Bottles (750 ml)
Champagne	0.25	1000							
Wine	0.50	1000							
Spirits	0.25	1000							

the margin and can be downloaded at the student companion website at www.wiley.com/college/dopson.

These exercises have been extensively reviewed and updated for accuracy and clarity. For this edition, this segment has been expanded in each chapter. The emphasis of the new exercises is on developing student spreadsheet skills in cost control problem solving as well as considering what they would do in the future when faced with real-world cost control-related challenges.

ESSENTIAL ELEMENTS OF THE TEXT

Overviews

Each chapter begins with a brief narrative overview. This is simply a quick and easy guide to the chapter's contents. Overviews make it easy for readers to see what the chapter is about and what they will learn by reading it.

Chapter Outlines

The chapter outline that follows the overview helps teachers as well as students to see how each topic follows the next and provides a simple way to quickly find material within the chapter.

Learning Outcomes

Each chapter of this text was written with specific learning outcomes in mind. The Learning Outcomes feature of this edition is placed at the beginning of each chapter. It clearly informs readers about what they will be able to do, know or apply when they have successfully mastered the chapter's content.

Fun on the Web!

This important feature of the text adds to student learning by integrating the use of technology—in this case, the Internet—to the study of cost control. Students will quickly realize the power of the Web when gathering information related to cost control. This feature also provides Web-based resources that help managers more effectively do their jobs.

Green and Growing!

This new element provides readers with information about the importance of environmentally responsible management actions related to cost control, profits, and guest expectations. In many cases, carefully chosen website references direct students to web sources they can use when implementing planet-friendly cost control activities in their own facilities.

Consider the Cost

This new micro-case element allows students to easily put themselves in the position of decision maker when addressing cost control-related challenges. In each hospitality specific case, students will be presented with a real-world cost control challenge and are then asked how they themselves would respond to it. Suggested answers to the cases presented in this new feature are included in the *Instructor's Manual*.

Technology Tools

These updated listings of real-life application examples demonstrate to students that they can utilize computer hardware, advanced applications software, sophisticated communication devices, and much more to help manage their costs and improve their operating efficiency. While not all managers will use all of the tools suggested, it is important for students to understand the many technological resources available to them today.

Apply What You Have Learned

This pedagogical feature, placed near the end of each chapter, allows students to draw on their own problem-solving skills, ideas, and opinions using the concepts explored within each chapter. Challenging and realistic, yet purposely brief, these industry-specific scenarios provide excellent starting points for class discussions or, if the instructor prefers, outstanding written homework assignments.

Key Terms and Concepts

Students often need help in identifying key concepts that should be mastered after reading a section of a book. These are listed at the conclusion of each chapter and are invaluable as study aids.

Test Your Skills Exercises

This popular feature has, of course, been retained and again expanded in size. As was true in previous editions, predesigned Microsoft Excel spreadsheets are employed to allow students to practice problem-solving, thus improving the instructor's ability to evaluate mastery of the actual cost control concepts as well as spreadsheet building ability. These exercises are highlighted by the icon at the left of this paragraph. The Excel spreadsheets are downloadable from the student companion website at www.wiley.com/college/dopson.

"Test Your Skills" exercises allow the reader to conclusively determine if he or she has mastered the chapter's content. The answer set layouts for the problems have been redesigned to make them more user-friendly. Again, the intent is to allow the reader to immediately practice the skills acquired in the chapter. Through these exercises, the authors seek to reinforce the concepts presented in the chapters.

Spreadsheets on the Web

Students may download Excel spreadsheets that introduce then to the important skill of spreadsheet development. Using the supplied spreadsheets, students can immediately see how their answers to "Test Your Skills" problems translate into cost control solutions via spreadsheet formula development and manipulation. The spreadsheets are available for download at the student companion website at www.wiley.com/college/dopson, and will assist students in understanding the how and why of building spreadsheet solutions for the cost control–related hospitality problems they will face in the classroom and in their careers. Instructors will find that the grading of problem sets becomes much easier when all students use a consistent spreadsheet approach to classroom assignments.

Study Guide

A newly revised *Study Guide* (978-0-470-25139-3) provides several additional resources to help students review the material and exercises to test their knowledge of key concepts and topics. Study guides are popular with students and instructors alike because they provide yet another tool for those professionals seeking to maximize their learning of this text's important material.

MANAGERIAL TOOLS

It is the authors' hope that readers find the book as helpful to use as we found it exciting to develop. To that end, appendices are provided that we believe will be of great value.

Appendix A: Frequently Used Formulas for Managing Costs is included on the student companion website (www.wiley.com/college/dopson) as an easy reference guide. This feature allows readers to look up mathematical formulas for any of the computations presented in the text. We have intentionally chosen the simplest formulas that have the widest use.

Appendix B: Management Control Forms provides simplified cost control–related forms. This popular appendix has been retained from previous editions of this text. Included on the student companion website at www.wiley.com/college/dopson, these forms can be used as guideposts in the development of property specific forms. They may be implemented as-is or modified as the manager sees fit.

Appendix C: Fun on the Web! Sites is designed to give readers the Internet addresses of those sites identified in the text as being helpful in learning more about cost control. Included For download on the student companion website at www.wiley.com/college/dopson, the sites are listed as they appear in the chapters in this appendix.

A *Glossary* of industry terms is included in the back of the text to help the reader with the operational vocabulary necessary to understand the language of hospitality cost control management. Finally, a *Bibliography* is provided for the reader who wishes to pursue his or her study by referring to a variety of excellent books.

INSTRUCTOR'S MATERIALS

To help instructors effectively manage their time and to enhance student learning opportunities, several significant educational tools have been developed specifically for this text: An *Instructor's Manual* (978-0-470-25738-8) and, on the book's companion website at www.wiley.com/college/dopson, PowerPoint slides, a test bank, and spreadsheet answer key.

Instructor's Manual

As an additional aid to instructors, an *Instructor's Manual* (978-0-470-25738-8) has been painstakingly developed and classroom tested for this text. The manual includes:

- Lecture outlines for each chapter
- Suggested answers to each chapter's Consider the Cost micro cases
- Suggested answers for Apply What You Have Learned for each chapter
- Answers to chapter-ending Test Your Skills problems
- A Test Bank including exam questions developed for each chapter

Respondus Test Bank

The *Test Bank* for this text has been specifically formatted for Respondus, an easy-to-use software for creating and managing exams that can be printed to paper or published directly to Blackboard, WebCT, Desire2Learn, eCollege, ANGEL, and other eLearning systems. Instructors who adopt *Food and Beverage Cost Control, Fifth Edition* can download the *Test Bank* for free. Additional Wiley resources also can be uploaded into your LMS course at no charge. To view and access these resources and the *Test Bank*, visit www.wiley.com/college/dopson, select the correct title, and click on the "Instructor Companion Website" link, then click on "LMS Course Student Resources."

Companion Website

The Website (www.wiley.com/college/dopson) devoted entirely to this book includes the *Instructor's Manual* and expanded instructor aids that can immediately be used to enhance student learning. These are:

PowerPoint slides:

These easy-to-read and graphically sophisticated teaching aids are excellent tools for instructors presenting their lectures via computer, or for those who wish to download the graphics and present them as overhead transparencies. These slides can also serve as a chapter review aid.

Respondus Test Bank: Instructors utilizing the website will find a password-protected, expanded bank of exam questions that includes each question's correct and classroom-tested answer.

Test Your Skills spreadsheet answers: Instructors will be able to access answers and formulas to the "Test Your Skills" spreadsheet exercises at the end of each chapter within the password-protected portion of the instructor's page of the site.

Appendices: The three appendices, *Frequently Used Formulas for Managing Costs, Management Control Forms,* and *Fun on the Web! Sites* are also available for download on the Instructor Companion site.

One thing that has not changed in this new edition is that the authors continue to find the topic of cost management to be one of creativity, excitement, and, in many cases, outright fun. In contrast to the prevalent perception of cost control as drudgery, in this text cost management becomes an engaging challenge for the foodservice manager who wishes to reach new heights of career and personal success.

It has been said that there are three kinds of managers: those who know what has happened in the past, those who know what is happening now, and those who know what will happen in the future. Clearly, the manager who possesses all three traits is best prepared to manage effectively and efficiently. This text will give the reader the tools required to maintain sales and cost histories (the past), develop systems for monitoring current activities (the present), and learn the techniques required to anticipate what is to come (the future).

As was true in previous editions, the authors hope that the study of cost management creates in the reader the same interest and excitement for the topic that the authors experience. If that is the case, we will have been successful in our attempt to be true to this text's original vision of creating an outstanding learning tool that prepares students to be successful and responsible managers in the exciting hospitality industry.

We know the value of a quality publisher in the development of an outstanding text revision. We are continually impressed with the high standards exhibited by JoAnna Turtletaub, Wiley Vice President and Publisher, and the patient support provided by her staff. Julie Kerr, the text's developmental editor, deserves special recognition because of her exceptional efforts to improve this work. Julie's efforts helped ensure that this text met the high standards Wiley sets for its own publications and by doing so, helped us contribute our very best efforts as well. We are deeply grateful, as will be the students who read this text, for all of the staff at Wiley for their intellect, patience, and faithfulness in producing this fifth, and best-ever version of *Food and Beverage Cost Control*.

Lea Dopson, Ed.D.   David K. Hayes, Ph.D.
Denton, TX   Okemos, MI

ACKNOWLEDGMENTS

The first four editions of this text were very popular, for which we are deeply grateful. As a result, this book has now become the market leader among hospitality cost control texts. This success has stemmed in large part from the testing of its concepts and materials in classes at the University of North Texas, Purdue University, Texas Tech University, the University of Houston, and California State Polytechnic University at Pomona, as well as from those original St. Louis Community College students who received their instruction under Jack Miller. Students today will indeed benefit from the insight and input of students in our past classes. In addition, the industry focus of this edition is exceptionally strong. This is due in large part to the various professionals in institutional, commercial and hotel foodservice operations who so freely gave of their time and advice in this endeavor. A special thanks goes to Allisha Miller of PandaPros Hospitality Training for her effort and support.

As with the first four editions, we appreciate all the assistance and comments we have received in bringing this book to fruition. We are extremely grateful to those who contributed to the original concept and idea for the book.

For comment, collaboration, and constructive criticism on the manuscript, we thank our reviewers: Victor Moruzzi, Hudson County Community College; Nancy Swanger, Washington State University; and Don Wilson, The Chef's Academy

They continually improved the text by reminding us of our original goal: providing a text full of information that is easy to read, easy to understand, and easy to retain.

We especially would like to thank our Wiley publisher, JoAnna Turtletaub, who has supported this text for so long and whose continual support and constant attention helped encourage us to make this edition a reality. In addition, we would like to recognize Rachel Livsey, Senior Editor and Julie Kerr, Senior Developmental Editor with Wiley, for their special attention to detail in this edition.

We also want to thank those colleagues and family and friends who have been so supportive of us throughout our careers: Loralei, Terry, Laurie, Tutti, and Thandi, as well as Peggy, Scott, Trish, Joshua, Pauline, M.D. and JJC. We appreciate all of you!

Most important of all, we wish to thank our former colleague Jack Miller, who conceived the text. We believe he would be proud of this extension of his original textbook concept. It is the authors' hope that this edition lives up to the high standards Jack Miller exhibited in his personal and professional life as well as demonstrates our admiration both for him and for his initial vision of this text.

Lea R. Dopson
David K. Hayes

FOOD AND BEVERAGE COST CONTROL

Fifth Edition

Chapter 1

MANAGING REVENUE AND EXPENSE

OVERVIEW

This chapter presents the relationship among foodservice revenue, expense, and profit. As a professional foodservice manager, you must understand the relationship that exists between controlling these three areas and the resulting success of your operation. In addition, the chapter presents the mathematical foundation you must know to express your operating results as a percentage of your revenue or budget, a method that is standard within the hospitality industry.

Chapter Outline

▦ Professional Foodservice Manager
▦ Profit: The Reward for Service
▦ Getting Started
▦ Understanding the Income (Profit and Loss) Statement
▦ Understanding the Budget
▦ Apply What You Have Learned
▦ Key Terms and Concepts
▦ Test Your Skills

LEARNING OUTCOMES

At the conclusion of this chapter, you will be able to:
- Apply the basic formula used to determine profit.
- Express both expenses and profit as a percentage of revenue.
- Compare actual operating results with budgeted operating results.

PROFESSIONAL FOODSERVICE MANAGER

*T*here is no doubt that to be a successful foodservice manager you must be a talented individual. Consider, for a moment, your role in the operation of a profitable facility. As a foodservice manager, you are both a manufacturer and a retailer. A professional foodservice manager is unique because all of the functions of a product's sale, from item conceptualization to product delivery, are in the hands of the same individual. As a manager, you are in charge of securing raw materials, producing a product, and selling it—all under the same roof. Few other managers are required to have the breadth of skills that effective foodservice operators must have. Because foodservice operators are in the service sector of business, many aspects of management are more difficult for them than for their manufacturing or retailing management counterparts.

A foodservice manager is one of the few types of managers who actually have contact with the ultimate customer. This is not true of the manager of a tire factory or automobile production line. These individuals produce a product, but they do not sell it to the person who will actually use it. In a like manner, grocery store or computer store managers will sell their product lines, but they have had no role in actually producing their goods. The face-to-face guest contact in the hospitality industry requires that you assume the responsibility of standing behind your own work and that of your staff, in a one-on-one situation with the ultimate consumer, or end user of your products and services.

The management task checklist in Figure 1.1 shows just some of the areas in which foodservice, manufacturing, and retailing managers differ in responsibilities.

In addition to your role as a food factory supervisor, you must serve as a cost control manager, because, if you fail to perform this vital role, your business might cease to exist. Foodservice management provides the opportunity for creativity in a variety of settings. The control of revenue and expense is just one more area in which the effective foodservice operator can excel. In most areas of foodservice, excellence in operation is measured in terms of producing and delivering quality products in a way that ensures an appropriate operating profit for the owners of the business.

■ FIGURE 1.1 Management Task Checklist

Task	Foodservice Manager	Manufacturing Manager	Retail Manager
1. Secure raw materials	Yes	Yes	No
2. Manufacture product	Yes	Yes	No
3. Distribute to end user	Yes	No	Yes
4. Market to end user	Yes	No	Yes
5. Reconcile problems with end user	Yes	No	Yes

PROFIT: THE REWARD FOR SERVICE

*T*here is an inherent problem in the study of cost control or, more accurately, cost management. The simple fact is that management's primary responsibility is to deliver a quality product or service to guests, at a price mutually agreeable to both parties. In addition, the quality must be such that the buyer of the product or service feels that excellent value was received for the money spent on the transaction. When this level of service is achieved, the business prospers. If management focuses on controlling costs more than on servicing guests, problems will certainly occur.

It is important to remember that guests cause businesses to incur costs. You do not want to get yourself in the mind-set of thinking that "low" costs are good and "high" costs are bad. A restaurant with $5 million in revenue per year will undoubtedly have higher "costs" than the same size restaurant achieving $500,000 in revenue per year. The reason is quite clear. The amount of food products, labor, and equipment needed to sell $5 million worth of food is greater than that required to produce a smaller amount of revenue. Remember, if there are fewer guests, there are likely to be lower costs, but less profit as well! Because that is true, the business will surely suffer if management attempts to reduce costs with no regard for the impact on the balance between managing costs and guest satisfaction. In addition, efforts to reduce costs that result in unsafe physical conditions for guests or employees are never wise. Although some short-term savings may result, the expense of a lawsuit resulting from a guest or employee injury can be very high. Managers who, for example, neglect to spend the money to shovel and salt a snowy restaurant entrance area may find that they spend thousands more dollars defending themselves in a lawsuit brought by an individual who slipped and fell on the ice.

For an effective manager, the question to be considered is not whether costs are high or low. The question is whether costs are too high or too low, given management's view of the value it hopes to deliver to the guest and the goals of the foodservice operation's owners. Managers can eliminate nearly all costs by closing the operation's doors. Obviously, however, when you close the doors to expense, you close the doors to profits. Expenses, then, must be incurred, and they must be managed in a way that allows the operation to achieve its desired profit levels.

It is important for you to understand profits. Some people assume that if a business purchases an item for $1.00 and sells it for $3.00, the profit generated equals $2.00. In fact, this is not true. As a business operator, you must realize that the difference between what you have paid for the goods you sell and the price at which you sell them does not represent your actual profit. Instead, all expenses, including advertising, the building that houses your operation, management salaries, and the labor required to generate the sale, to name but a few, are expenses that must be subtracted before you can determine your profits accurately.

Every foodservice operator is faced with the following profit-oriented formula:

Revenue − Expenses = Profit

Thus, when you manage your facility, you will receive **revenue**—the money you take in—and you will incur **expenses**—the cost of the items required to operate the business. The dollars that remain after all expenses have been paid represent your **profit.** For the purposes of this book, the authors will use the following terms interchangeably: revenues and sales; expenses and costs.

This formula holds true even in the "nonprofit" sector of foodservice management. For example, consider the situation of Hector Bentevina. Hector is the foodservice manager at the headquarters of a large corporation. Hector supplies the foodservice to a large group of office workers, each of whom is employed by the corporation that owns the facility Hector manages. In this situation, Hector's employer does not have "profit" as its primary motive. In most **business dining** situations, food is provided as a service to the company's employees either as a no-cost (to the employee) benefit or at a greatly reduced price. In some cases, executive dining rooms may be operated for the convenience of management. In all cases, however, some provision for profit must be made. Figure 1.2 shows the flow of business for the typical foodservice operation. Note that profit must be taken out at some point in the process, or management is in a position of simply trading cash for cash.

In your own operation, if you find that revenue is less than or equal to your expense, with no reserve for the future, you will also find that there is no money for new equipment; needed facility maintenance may not be performed; employee raises (as well as your own) may be few and far between; and, in general, your facility will eventually become outdated due to a lack of funds for remodeling and upgrading. The fact is, all foodservice operations need revenue in excess of expenses if they are to thrive. If you manage a foodservice operation in a profit or a nonprofit setting, it will be your responsibility to communicate this message to your own staff.

Profit is the result of solid planning, sound management, and careful decision making. The purpose of this text is to give you the information and tools you need to make informed decisions with regard to managing your operation's revenue and expenses. If these tools are utilized properly, the potential for achieving the profits you desire is greatly enhanced.

■ **FIGURE 1.2** Foodservice Business Flowchart

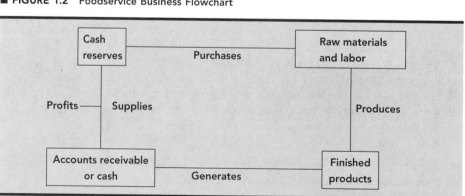

Profit should not be viewed as what is left over after the bills are paid. In fact, careful planning is necessary to earn a profit. In most cases, investors will not invest in businesses that do not generate enough profit to make their investment worthwhile. The restaurant business can be very profitable; however, there is no guarantee that an individual restaurant will make a profit. Some restaurants do, and others do not. Because that is true, a more appropriate formula, which recognizes and rewards the business owner for the risk associated with business ownership or investment, is as follows:

> Revenue − Desired Profit = Ideal Expense

Ideal expense, in this case, is defined as management's view of the correct or appropriate amount of expense necessary to generate a given quantity of revenue. **Desired profit** is defined as the profit that the owner wants to achieve on that predicted quantity of revenue. This formula clearly places profit as a reward for providing service, not a leftover. When foodservice managers deliver quality and value to their guests, anticipated revenue levels can be achieved and desired profit is attainable. Desired profit and ideal expense levels are not, however, easily achieved. It takes a talented foodservice operator to consistently make decisions that will maximize revenue while holding expenses to the ideal or appropriate amount. This book will teach you how to do just that.

■ REVENUE

To some degree, you can manage your revenue levels. Revenue dollars are the result of units sold. These units may consist of individual menu items, lunches, dinners, drinks, or any other item produced by your operation. Revenue varies with both the number of guests frequenting your business and the amount of money spent by each guest. You can increase revenue by increasing the number of guests you serve, by increasing the amount each guest spends, or by a combination of both approaches. Adding seating or drive-through windows, extending operating hours, and building additional foodservice units are all examples of management's efforts to increase the number of guests served. Suggestive selling by service staff, creative menu pricing techniques, and discounts for very large purchases are examples of efforts to increase the amount of money each guest spends.

Management's primary task is to take the steps necessary to bring guests to the foodservice operation. This is true because the profit formula begins with revenue. Experienced foodservice operators know that adding guests and selling more to each guest are extremely effective ways of increasing overall profitability, but *only* if effective cost management systems are also in place.

The focus of this text is on managing and controlling expenses, not on generating additional revenue. While the two topics are related, they are different. Marketing efforts, restaurant design and site selection, employee training, and food preparation methods are critical links in the revenue-producing chain. No amount of effective expense control can solve the profit problems caused by inadequate revenue resulting from inferior food quality or service levels.

Effective cost control, however, when coupled with management's aggressive attitude toward meeting and exceeding guests' expectations, can result in outstanding revenue and profit performance.

Green and Growing!

Good food and service will attract foodservice customers. So will other important factors customers care about, including location, unusual décor, and, increasingly, how "green" an operation is perceived to be. "Green" is the term used to describe those foodservice operations that incorporate environmentally conscious activities into the design, construction, and operation of their businesses. These activities can be related to packaging and shipping materials reduction, energy conservation, or **environmental sustainability**, a term used to describe a variety of earth-friendly practices and policies designed to meet the needs of the present population without compromising the ability of future generations to meet their own needs.

The positive benefits that accrue when businesses incorporate green activities are significant, and they are increasing. Managers of green operations help protect the environment. For example, did you know that every ton of 100 percent post-consumer waste recycled paper saves 12 trees, 1,976 pounds of greenhouse gases, and 390 gallons of oil? Green is also gaining because more and more guests seek out and frequent green restaurants simply because they are committed to preserving the environment.

The Green Restaurant Association^{SM} (GRA) is a nonprofit, national environmental organization founded in 1990 to help restaurants and their customers become more "green" (environmentally sustainable) in ways that are convenient and cost-effective. The GRA's agenda includes issues related to:

Research
Environmental consulting
Education
Public relations and marketing
Community organizing and consumer activism

To learn more about this increasingly high profile group, visit the GRA's Web site at **www. dinegreen.com.**

To learn more about how your foodservice operation can profit by implementing environmentally sustainable activities, watch for the "Green and Growing" feature in each upcoming chapter of this book.

FUN ON THE WEB!

www.restaurant.org. Click on "Industry Research" to see the National Restaurant Association's revenue projections for the restaurant industry, which has annual sales of over $500 billion.

■ EXPENSES

There are four major foodservice expense categories that you must learn to control:

  1. Food costs
  2. Beverage costs
  3. Labor costs
  4. Other expenses

FOOD COSTS

Food costs are the costs associated with actually producing the menu items a guest selects. They include the expense of meats, dairy, fruits, vegetables, and other categories of food items produced by the foodservice operation. When computing food costs, many operators include the cost of minor paper and plastic items, such as the paper wrappers used to wrap sandwiches. In most cases, food costs will make up the largest or second-largest expense category you must learn to manage.

BEVERAGE COSTS

Beverage costs are those related to the sale of alcoholic beverages. It is interesting to note that it is common practice in the hospitality industry to consider beverage costs of a nonalcoholic nature as an expense in the food cost category. Thus, milk, tea, coffee, waters, carbonated beverages, and other nonalcoholic beverage items are not generally considered a beverage cost. Alcoholic beverages accounted for in the beverage cost category include beer, wine, and liquor. This category may also include the costs of ingredients necessary to produce these drinks, such as cherries, lemons, olives, limes, mixers like carbonated beverages and juices, and other items commonly used in the production and service of alcoholic beverages.

LABOR COSTS

Labor costs include the cost of all employees necessary to run the business. This expense category also includes the amount of any taxes you are required to pay when you have employees on your payroll. Some operators find it helpful to include the cost of management in this category. Others prefer to place the cost of managers in the category of Other Expenses. In most operations labor costs are an operator's highest cost, or they are second only to food costs in total dollars spent. If management is included as a labor cost, then this category will frequently be even larger than the food cost category.

Consider The Costs

"I'm feeling pretty good about our cost management efforts," said Rachel. "Our labor cost is higher than our food cost."

"I'm pleased with our efforts too," said Julie. "Our food cost is higher than our labor cost."

"That's great, Julie" said Joseph. "I just calculated our monthly costs, and our food and labor expenses are just about equal. Sounds like we are all doing well!"

Rachel, Julie, and Joseph had all attended hospitality school together. Each had taken a job in the same large city, so they often got together over coffee to talk about their businesses and their jobs. One manages "Chez Paul's," a fine dining French-style restaurant know for impeccable service. Another manages "Fuby's," a family-style cafeteria known for its tasty, home-style cooking, and one had taken a job with "Gardinos," a national restaurant chain that offered mid-priced Italian foods in a beautiful Tuscan-style decor.

1. Which foodservice operation do you think Rachel manages? Why?
2. Which foodservice operation do you think Julie manages? Why?
3. Which foodservice operation do you think Joseph manages? Why?

OTHER EXPENSES

Other expenses include all expenses that are not covered under food, beverage, or labor costs. Examples include franchise fees, utilities, rent, linen, and such items as china, glassware, kitchen knives, and pots and pans. Although this expense category is sometimes incorrectly referred to as "minor expenses," your ability to successfully control this expense area is especially critical to the overall profitability of your foodservice unit.

GETTING STARTED

Good managers learn to understand, control, and manage their expenses. Consider the case of Tabreshia Larson, the food and beverage director of the 200-room Renaud Hotel, located in a college town and built near an interstate highway. Tabreshia has just received her end-of-the-year operating reports for the current year. She is interested in comparing these results to those of the prior year. The numbers she received are shown in Figure 1.3.

Tabreshia is concerned, but she is not sure if she should be. Revenue is higher than last year, so she feels her guests must like the products and services they receive. In fact, repeat business from corporate meetings and special-events meals is really

■ **FIGURE 1.3** Renaud Hotel Operating Results

	This Year	Last Year
Revenue	$1,106,040	$850,100
Expense	1,017,557	773,591
Profits	88,483	76,509

beginning to develop. Profits are greater than last year also, but Tabreshia has the uneasy feeling that things are not going as well as they could. The kitchen appears to run smoothly. The staff, however, often runs out of needed items, and there seems to be a large amount of leftover food thrown away on a regular basis. Sometimes, there seem to be too many staff members on the property; at other times, guests have to wait too long to get served. Tabreshia also feels that employee theft may be occurring, but she certainly doesn't have the time to watch every storage area within her operation. She would really like to get a handle on the problems (if there are any), but how and where should she start?

The answer for Tabreshia, and for you, if you want to develop a serious expense control system, is very simple. You start with basic mathematics skills that you must have to properly analyze your expenses. The mathematics required, and used in this text, consist only of addition, subtraction, multiplication, and division. These tools will be sufficient to build a cost control system that will help you professionally manage the expenses you incur.

What would it mean if a fellow foodservice manager told you that he spent $500 on food yesterday? Obviously, it means little unless you know more about his operation. Should he have spent $500 yesterday? Was that too much? Too little? Was it a "good" day? These questions raise a difficult problem. How can you equitably compare your expenses today with those of yesterday, or your foodservice unit with another, so that you can see how well you are doing? We know that the value of dollars has changed over time. A restaurant with revenue of $1,000 per day in 1954 is very different from the same restaurant with daily revenue of $1,000 today because the value of the dollar today is quite different from what it was in 1954. Generally, inflation causes the purchasing power of a dollar today to be less than that of a dollar from a previous time period. While this concept of changing value is useful in the area of finance, it is vexing when one wants to answer the simple question, "Am I doing as well today as I was doing five years ago?"

Alternatively, consider the problem of a multiunit manager. She manages two units that sell tacos on either side of a large city. One uses $500 worth of food products each day; the other unit uses $600 worth of food products each day. Does the second unit use an additional $100 worth of food each day because it has more guests or because it is less efficient in utilizing the food?

The answer to all of the preceding questions, and many more, can be determined if we use percentages to relate expenses incurred to revenue generated. Percentage calculations are important for at least two major reasons. First and foremost, percentages are the most common standard used for evaluating costs in the foodservice industry. Therefore, knowledge of what a percent is and how it is calculated is vital. Second, as a manager in the foodservice industry, you will be evaluated primarily on your ability to compute, analyze, and control these percent figures. Although it is true that many basic management tools such as Microsoft Excel, Lotus, and other software programs will "compute" percentages for you, it is important that you understand what the percentages mean and how they should be interpreted. Percent calculations are used extensively in this text and are a cornerstone of any effective cost control system.

■ PERCENT REVIEW

Understanding percents and how they are mathematically computed is important. The following review may be helpful for some readers. If you thoroughly understand the percent concept, you may skip this section and the Computing Percent section and proceed directly to the Using Percent section.

Percent (%) means "out of each hundred." Thus, 10 percent would mean 10 out of each 100. If we asked how many guests would buy blueberry pie on a given day, and the answer is 10 percent, then 10 people out of each 100 we serve will select blueberry pie. If 52 percent of your employees are female, then 52 out of each 100 employees are female. If 15 percent of your employees will receive a raise this month, then 15 out of 100 employees will get their raise. Figure 1.4 shows three ways to write a percent.

COMMON FORM

In its common form, the % sign is used to express the percentage. If we say 10 percent, then we mean "10 out of each 100" and no further explanation is necessary. The common form, the percent, is equivalent to the same amount expressed in either the fraction or the decimal form.

■ FIGURE 1.4 Forms of Expressing Percent

Form	Percent		
	1%	10%	100%
Common	1%	10%	100%
Fraction	1/100	10/100	100/100
Decimal	0.01	0.10	1.00

FRACTION FORM

In fraction form, the percent is expressed as the part, or a portion of 100. Thus, 10 percent is written as 10 "over" 100 (10/100). This is simply another way of expressing the relationship between the part (10) and the whole (100).

DECIMAL FORM

A decimal is a number developed from the counting system we use. It is based on the fact that we count to 10, then start over again. In other words, each of our major units—10s, 100s, 1,000s, and so on—is based on the use of 10s, and each number can easily be divided by 10. Instead of using the % sign, the decimal form uses the (.), or decimal point, to express the percent relationship. Thus, 10 percent is expressed as 0.10 in decimal form. The numbers to the right of the decimal point express the percentage.

Each of these three methods of expressing percentages is used in the foodservice industry, and to be successful you must develop a clear understanding of how a percentage is computed. Once that is known, you can express the percentage in any form that is required or that is useful to you.

■ COMPUTING PERCENT

To determine what percent one number is of another number, divide the number that is the part by the number that is the whole. Usually, but not always, this means dividing the smaller number by the larger number. For example, assume that 840 guests were served during a banquet at your hotel and that 420 of them asked for coffee with their meal. To find what percent of your guests ordered coffee, divide the part (420) by the whole (840).

The process looks like this:

$$\frac{\text{Part}}{\text{Whole}} = \text{Percent} \quad or \quad \frac{420}{840} = 0.50$$

Thus, 50% (common form), 50/100 (fraction form), and 0.50 (decimal form) represent the proportion of people at the banquet who ordered coffee. A large number of new foodservice managers have difficulty computing percent figures. It is easy to forget which number goes "on the top" and which number goes "on the bottom." In general, if you attempt to compute a percentage and get a whole number (a number larger than 1), either a mistake has been made or costs are extremely high!

Many people also become confused when converting from one form of percent to another. If that is a problem, remember the following conversion rules:

1. To convert from common form to decimal form, move the decimal two places to the left; that is, 50.00% = 0.50.

2. To convert from decimal form to common form, move the decimal two places to the right; that is, 0.40 = 40.00%.

■ **FIGURE 1.5** Percent Computation

Possibilities	Examples	Results
Part is smaller than the whole	$\frac{61}{100} = 61\%$	Always less than 100%
Part is equal to the whole	$\frac{35}{35} = 100\%$	Always equals 100%
Part is larger than the whole	$\frac{125}{50} = 250\%$	Always greater than 100%

In a restaurant, the "whole" is usually a revenue figure. Expenses and profits are the "parts," which are usually expressed in terms of a percent. It is interesting to note that, in the United States, the same system in use for our numbers is in use for our money. Each dime contains 10 pennies, each dollar contains 10 dimes, and so on. Thus in discussions of money, it is true that a percent refers to "cents out of each dollar" as well as "out of each 100 dollars." When we say 10 percent of a dollar, we mean 10 cents, or "10 cents out of each dollar." Likewise, 25 percent of a dollar represents 25 cents, 50 percent of a dollar represents 50 cents, and 100 percent of a dollar represents $1.00.

Sometimes, when using percent to express the relationship between portions of a dollar and the whole, we find that the part is indeed larger than the whole. Figure 1.5 demonstrates the three possibilities associated with computing a percentage. Great care must always be taken when computing percents, so that the percent arrived at is of help to you in your work and does not represent an error in mathematics.

■ USING PERCENT

Consider a restaurant that you are operating. Imagine that your revenues for a week are in the amount of $1,600. Expenses for the same week are $1,200. Given these facts and the information presented earlier in this chapter, your profit formula for the week would be as follows:

Revenue − Expenses = Profit
or
$1,600 − $1,200 = $400

If you had planned for a $500 profit for the week, you would have been "short." Using the alternative profit formula presented earlier, you would find:

$$\text{Revenue} - \text{Desired Profit} = \text{Ideal Expense}$$
$$\text{or}$$
$$\$1,600 - \$500 = \$1,100$$

Note that expense in this example ($1,200) exceeds ideal expense ($1,100), and thus too little profit was achieved.

These numbers can also be expressed in terms of percent. If we want to know what percent of our revenue went to pay for our expenses, we would compute it as follows:

$$\frac{\text{Expense}}{\text{Revenue}} = \text{Expense \%}$$
$$\text{or}$$
$$\frac{\$1,200}{\$1,600} = 0.75, \text{ or } 75\%$$

Another way to state this relationship is to say that each dollar of revenue costs 75 cents to produce. Also, each revenue dollar taken in results in 25 cents profit:

$$\$1.00 \text{ Revenue} - \$0.75 \text{ Expense} = \$0.25 \text{ Profit}$$

As long as expense is smaller than revenue, some profit will be generated, even if it is not as much as you had planned. You can compute profit percent using the following formula:

$$\frac{\text{Profit}}{\text{Revenue}} = \text{Profit \%}$$

In our example:

$$\frac{\$400 \text{ Profit}}{\$1,600 \text{ Revenue}} = 25\% \text{ Profit}$$

We can compute what we had planned our profit percent to be by dividing desired profit ($500) by revenue ($1,600):

$$\frac{\$500 \text{ Desired Profit}}{\$1,600 \text{ Revenue}} = 31.25\% \text{ Desired Profit}$$

In simple terms, we had hoped to make 31.25 percent profit, but instead made only 25 percent profit. Excess costs could account for the difference. If these costs could be identified and corrected, we could perhaps achieve the desired profit percentage. Most foodservice operators compute many cost percentages, not just one. The major cost divisions used in foodservice are:

1. Food and beverage cost
2. Labor cost
3. Other expense

A modified profit formula, therefore, is as follows:

Revenue − (Food and Beverage Cost + Labor Cost + Other Expenses) = Profit

Put in another format, the equation looks like this:

Revenue (100%)
− Food and Beverage Cost %
− Labor Cost %
− Other Expense %
= Profit %

Regardless of the approach used, foodservice managers must evaluate their expenses, and they use percents to do so.

UNDERSTANDING THE INCOME (PROFIT AND LOSS) STATEMENT

Consider Figure 1.6, an example from Pat's Steakhouse. All of Pat's expenses and profits can be computed as percents by using the revenue figure, $400,000, as the whole, with expenses and profit representing the parts as follows:

$$\frac{\text{Food and Beverage Cost}}{\text{Revenue}} = \text{Food Beverage Cost \%}$$

or

$$\frac{\$150,000}{\$400,000} = 37.50\%$$

$$\frac{\text{Labor Cost}}{\text{Revenue}} = \text{Labor Cost \%}$$

or

$$\frac{\$175,000}{\$400,000} = 43.75\%$$

$$\frac{\text{Other Expenses}}{\text{Revenue}} = \text{Other Expense \%}$$

or

$$\frac{\$25,000}{\$400,000} = 6.25\%$$

$$\frac{\text{Total Expense}}{\text{Revenue}} = \text{Total Expense \%}$$

or

$$\frac{\$350,000}{\$400,000} = 87.50\%$$

$$\frac{\text{Profit}}{\text{Revenue}} = \text{Profit \%}$$

or

$$\frac{\$50,000}{\$400,000} = 12.50\%$$

■ **FIGURE 1.6** Pat's Steakhouse

Revenue		$400,000
Expenses		
Food and Beverage Cost	$150,000	
Labor Cost	175,000	
Other Expense	25,000	
Total Expenses		$350,000
Profit		$ 50,000

■ **FIGURE 1.7** Pat's Steakhouse P&L

Revenue		$400,000		100%
Food and Beverage Cost	$150,000		37.50%	
Labor Cost	175,000		43.75%	
Other Expense	25,000		6.25%	
Total Expenses		$350,000		87.50%
Profit		$ 50,000		12.50%

An accounting tool that details revenue, expenses, and profit for a given period of time, is called the **income statement,** which is commonly called the **profit-and-loss statement (P&L).** It lists revenue, food and beverage cost, labor cost, and other expense. The P&L also identifies profits since, as you recall, profits are generated by the formula:

$$\text{Revenue} - \text{Expense} = \text{Profit}$$

Figure 1.7 is a simplified P&L statement for Pat's Steakhouse. Note the similarity to Figure 1.6. This time, however, expenses and profit are expressed in terms of both dollar amount and percent of revenue.

Another way of looking at Pat's P&L is shown in Figure 1.8. The pieces of the pie represent Pat's cost and profit categories. Costs and profit total 100 percent, which is equal to Pat's total revenues. Put another way, out of every revenue dollar that Pat generates, 100 percent is designated as either costs or profit.

Pat knows from the P&L that revenues represent 100 percent of the total dollars available to cover expenses and provide for a profit. Food and beverage cost is 37.50 percent, and labor cost percentage in the steakhouse equals 43.75 percent.

■ **FIGURE 1.8** Pat's Steakhouse Costs and Profit as a Percentage of Revenues

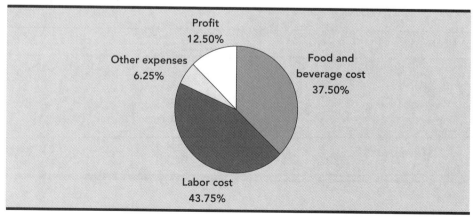

Other expense percentage equals 6.25 percent, and her total expense percent is 87.50 percent (37.50 + 43.75 + 6.25 = 87.50 percent). The steakhouse profit equals 12.50 percent. Thus, for each dollar in revenue, Pat earns a profit of 12.50 cents. Pat's revenue, expense, and profit information is contained in the steakhouse's P&L.

In restaurants that serve alcohol, food costs and beverage costs are most often separated into two categories in the P&L. Likewise, food revenues and beverage revenues are reported separately. This is done so that the food cost can be compared to food revenues, and the beverage cost can be compared to beverage revenues. This is helpful when, for example, one manager is responsible for controlling food cost percent in the restaurant and another manager is responsible for controlling beverage cost percent in the bar.

The P&L is important because it indicates the efficiency and profitability of an operation. Because so many individuals and groups are interested in a food facility's performance, it is important that the P&L and other financial statements are prepared in a manner that is consistent with other facilities. If, for example, you own two Italian restaurants, it would be very confusing if the units' two managers used different methods for preparing their P&Ls. You, your investors, your accountant, governmental taxing entities, and your creditors will all be interested in your operational results, and unless you report and account for these in a manner they can easily understand, confusion may result.

To avoid such a set of circumstances, the **Uniform System of Accounts** is used to report financial results in most foodservice units. This system was created to ensure uniform reporting of financial results. A Uniform System of Accounts exists for restaurants, another for hotels, and another for clubs. The Uniform System of Accounts will be discussed in greater detail later in this text.

The primary purpose of preparing a P&L is to identify revenue, expenses, and profits for a specific time period. As a manager, your efforts will greatly influence your operation's profitability. Good managers provide excellent value to their guests, which causes guests to return and thus increases revenue. In addition, good managers know how to analyze, manage, and control their costs. For these managers, expenses are held to the amount that was preplanned. The result is the desired profit level. Good managers influence the success of their units and their own employees. The results for them personally are promotions, added responsibilities, and salary increases. If you wish to succeed in the hospitality industry, it is important to remember that your performance will be evaluated primarily on your ability to achieve the profit levels your operation has planned for.

In addition to your own efforts, many factors influence profit dollars and profit percent, and you must be aware, and in control, of all of them. All of the factors that impact profit percent are discussed in later chapters of this text.

FUN ON THE WEB!

www.restaurant.org. Link to "Industry Research," then "Reports" to see how you can get industry averages for P&Ls.

UNDERSTANDING THE BUDGET

*S*ome foodservice managers do not generate revenue on a daily basis. Consider, for a moment, the foodservice manager at a summer camp run for children. In this case, parents pay a fixed fee to cover housing, activities, and meals for a set period of time. The foodservice director, in this situation, is just one of several managers who must share this revenue. If too many dollars are spent on providing housing or play activities, too few dollars may be available to provide an adequate quantity or quality of meals. On the other hand, if too many dollars are spent on providing foodservice, there may not be enough left to cover other needed expense areas. In a case like this, foodservice operators must prepare a budget. A **budget** is simply an estimate of projected revenue, expense, and profit. In some hospitality companies, the budget is known as **the plan,** referring to the fact that the budget details the operation's estimated, or "planned for," revenue and expense for a given accounting period. An **accounting period** is an hour, day, week, or month in which an operator wishes to analyze revenue and expenses.

All effective managers, whether in the commercial (for-profit) or nonprofit sector, use budgets. Budgeting is simply planning for revenue, expense, and profit. If these items are planned for, you can determine how close your actual performance is to your plan or budget. In the summer camp example, the following information is known:

1. Number of campers: 180
2. Number of meals served to each camper per day: 3
3. Length of campers' stay: 7 days

With 180 campers eating 3 meals each day for 7 days, 3,780 meals will be served (180 campers × 3 meals per day × 7 days = 3,780 meals).

Generally, in a case such as the summer camp, the foodservice director is given a dollar amount that represents the allowed expense for each meal to be served. For example, if $1.85 per meal is the amount budgeted for this director, the total revenue budget would equal $6,993 ($1.85 per meal × 3,780 meals = $6,993).

From this figure, an expense budget can begin to be developed. In this case, we are interested in the amount of expenses budgeted and the amount actually spent on those expenses. Equally important, we are interested in the percent of the budget actually used, a concept known as **performance to budget.**

A simple example may help to explain the idea of budget and performance to budget. Assume that a child has $1.00 per day to spend on candy. On Monday morning, the child's parents give the child $1.00 for each day of the week, or $7.00 total ($1.00 × 7 days = $7.00). If the child spends exactly $1.00 per day, he or she will be able to buy candy all week. If, however, too much is spent in any one day, there may not be any money left at the end of the week. To ensure a week of candy eating, a good "candy purchasing" pattern could be created, such as the one in Figure 1.9. The "% of Total" column is computed by dividing $1.00 (the part) by $7.00 (the whole). Notice that we can determine the percent of total that should have been spent by any given day; that is, each day equals 14.28 percent, or 1/7 of the total.

■ **FIGURE 1.9** Candy Purchases

Weekday	Budgeted Amount	% of Total
Monday	$1.00	14.28%
Tuesday	$1.00	14.28%
Wednesday	$1.00	14.28%
Thursday	$1.00	14.28%
Friday	$1.00	14.28%
Saturday	$1.00	14.28%
Sunday	$1.00	14.28%
Total	$7.00	100.00%

This same logic applies to the foodservice operation. Figure 1.10 represents commonly used budget periods and their accompanying proportion amounts.

Many foodservice operations are changing from "one month" budget periods to periods of 28 days. The **28-day-period approach** divides a year into 13 equal periods of 28 days each. Therefore, each period has four Mondays, four Tuesdays, four Wednesdays, and so on. This helps the manager compare performance from one period to the next without having to compensate for "extra days" in any one period. The downside of this approach is that you can no longer talk about the month of March, for example, because "period 3" would occur during part of February and part of March. Although using the 28-day-period approach takes a while to get used to, it is an effective way to measure performance and plan from period to period.

■ **FIGURE 1.10** Common Foodservice Budget Periods

Budget Period	Portion	% of Total
One week	One day	1/7, or 14.3%
Two-week period	One day	1/14, or 7.1%
	One week	1/2, or 50.0%
One month	One week	1/4, or 25.0%
28 days	One day	1/28, or 3.6%
30 days	One day	1/30, or 3.3%
31 days	One day	1/31, or 3.2%
Six months	One month	1/6, or 16.7%
One year	One day	1/365, or 0.3%
	One week	1/52, or 1.9%
	One month	1/12, or 8.3%

■ **FIGURE 1.11** Camp Eureka One-Week Budget

Item	Budget	Actual
Meals Served	3,780	3,700
Revenue	$6,993	$6,993
Food Expense	$2,600	$2,400
Labor Expense	$2,800	$2,900
Other Expense	$ 700	$ 965
Profit	$ 893	$ 728

For example, in Camp Eureka, after one week's camping was completed, we found the results shown in Figure 1.11.

We can use the expense records from the previous summer as well as our solid industry knowledge and experience to develop expense budget figures for this summer. In this case, we are interested in both our plan (budget) and our actual performance. Figure 1.12 shows a performance-to-budget summary with revenue and expenses presented in terms of both the budget amount and the actual amount. In all cases, percentages are used to compare actual expense with the budgeted amount, using the formula:

$$\frac{\text{Actual}}{\text{Budget}} = \% \text{ of Budget}$$

In this example, revenue remained the same although some campers skipped (or slept through!) some of their meals. This is often the case when one fee or price buys a number of meals, whether they are eaten or not. In some other cases, managers will receive revenue only for meals actually served. This, of course, is true in a traditional restaurant setting. In either case, budgeted amount, actual expense, and the concept of percent of budget, or performance to budget, are important management tools. In

■ **FIGURE 1.12** Camp Eureka Performance-to-Budget Summary

Item	Budget	Actual	% of Budget
Meals Served	3,780	3,700	97.9%
Revenue	$6,993	$6,993	100.0%
Food Expense	$2,600	$2,400	92.3%
Labor Expense	$2,800	$2,900	103.6%
Other Expense	$ 700	$ 965	137.9%
Total Expenses	$6,100	$6,265	102.7%
Profit	$ 893	$ 728	81.5%

looking at the Camp Eureka performance-to-budget summary, we can see that the manager served fewer meals than planned and, thus, spent less on food than estimated, but spent more on labor than originally thought necessary. In addition, much more was spent than estimated for other expenses (137.9 percent of the budgeted amount). As a result, profit dollars were lower than planned. This manager has some problems, but note that there are not problems everywhere in the operation.

How do we know that? If our budget is accurate and we are within reasonable limits of our budget, we are said to be "in line," or in compliance, with our budget. It is difficult to budget exact revenue and expenses, so if we determine that plus (more than) or minus (less than) 10 percent of budget in each category is considered in line, or acceptable, then an examination of Figure 1.12 shows we are in line with regard to meals served, food expense, labor expense, and total expense. We are not in line with other expenses, however, because they were 137.9 percent of the amount originally planned. Thus, they far exceed the 10 percent variation that was reasonably allowed. Profit was also outside the acceptable boundary we established because it was only 81.5 percent of the amount budgeted. Note that figures over 100 percent mean too much (other expense), and figures below 100 percent mean too little (profit).

Many operators use the concept of "significant" variation to determine whether a cost control problem exists. In this case, a significant variation is any variation in expected costs that management feels is an area of concern. This variation can be caused by costs that were either higher or lower than the amount originally budgeted or planned for.

When you manage a foodservice operation and you find that significant variations from your planned results occur, you must:

1. Identify the problem.
2. Determine the cause.
3. Take corrective action.

It is crucial to know the kind of problem you have if you are to be an effective problem solver. Management's attention must be focused on the proper place. In this case, the proper areas for concern are other expense and profit. If, in the future, food expense became *too* low, it too would be an area of concern. Why? Remember that expenses create revenue; thus, it is not your goal to eliminate expense. In fact, managers who focus too much on eliminating expense, instead of building revenue, often find that their expenses are completely eliminated when they are forced to close their operation's doors permanently because guests did not feel they received good value for the money spent at that restaurant! Control and management of revenue and expense are important. Elimination of either is not desired.

As you have seen, revenue and expense directly impact profit. Your important role as a hospitality manager is to analyze, manage, and control your costs so that you achieve planned results. It can be done, and it can be fun.

The remainder of this text discusses how you can best manage and account for foodservice revenue and expense. With a good understanding of the relationship among revenue, expense, and profit, and your ability to analyze using percentages, you are ready to begin the cost control and cost management process.

Technology Tools

Most hospitality managers would agree that an accurate and timely income statement (P&L) is an invaluable aid to their management efforts. There are a variety of software programs on the market that can be used to develop this statement for you. You simply fill in the revenue and expense portions of the program, and a P&L is produced. Variations include programs that compare your actual results to budgeted figures or forecasts, to prior-month performance, or to prior-year performance. In addition, P&Ls can be produced for any time period, including months, quarters, or years. Most income statement programs will have a budgeting feature and the ability to maintain historical sales and cost records. Some of these have been developed specifically for restaurants, but cost-effective generic products are also available.

A second issue, and one that must be kept foremost in mind, is that of information accessibility. An executive chef, for example, would certainly need to have information on food cost available to him or her. At the same time, it may not be wise to allow servers or cooks access to payroll information about others that, while it certainly affects costs, should be shared only with those who need to know. Thus, as you examine (in this chapter and others) the cost control technology tools available to you, keep in mind that not all information should be accessible to all parties, and that security of your cost and customer information can be just as critical as accuracy.

FUN ON THE WEB!

Peachtree creates a variety of accounting software programs that will help you create a monthly income statement (P&L) and do much more. To view its product offerings, go to **www. peachtree.com.** Click on "Help me choose the right Peachtree product" to see the features available in the newest products.

Apply What You Have Learned

Jennifer Caratini has recently accepted the job as the foodservice director for Techmar Industries, a corporation with 1,000 employees. As foodservice director, Jennifer's role is to operate a company cafeteria, serving 800 to 900 meals per day, as well as an executive dining room, serving 100 to 200 meals per day. All of the meals are provided "free of charge" to the employees of Techmar. One of Jennifer's first jobs is to prepare a budget for next year's operations.

1. In addition to food products and foodservice employees, what other expenses will Techmar incur by providing free meals to its employees?

2. Since employees do not pay for their food directly, what will Jennifer use as the "revenue" portion of her budget? How do you think this number should be determined?

3. In addition to her know-how as a foodservice manager, what skills will Jennifer need as she interacts with the executives at Techmar who must approve her budget?

Key Terms and Concepts

The following are terms and concepts discussed in the chapter that are important for you as a manager. To help you review, please define the following terms:

Revenue
Expenses
Profit
Business dining
Ideal expense
Desired profit
Environmental
   sustainability

Food costs
Beverage costs
Labor costs
Other expenses
Percent
Income statement
Profit and loss
   statement (P&L)

Uniform System
   of Accounts
Budget/Plan
Accounting period
Performance
   to budget
28-day-period
   approach

Test Your Skills

Complete the Test Your Skills exercises by placing your answers in the shaded boxes and answering the questions as indicated.

1. At the conclusion of her first month of operating Val's Donut Shop, Val computed the following revenue and expense figures:

Week	Revenue	Expense	Profit/Loss
1	$ 894.50	$ 761.80	
2	1,147.60	522.46	
3	1,261.80	879.14	
4	1,345.11	1,486.20	
Month			
To Receive $1,200.00 Profit for the Month			
Month			

Prepare both weekly and monthly profit formulas so that Val has a good idea about her current profit situation. Also, given her sales for the month, tell her how much her ideal expense should have been to realize her desired profit of $1,200.

2. Su Chan manages a Chinese restaurant called the Bungalow. Her P&L for the month of March is as follows:

The Bungalow's March P&L		
Revenue	$100,000.00	100.0%
F&B Expense	34,000.00	34.0%
Labor Expense	40,000.00	40.0%
Other Expense	21,000.00	21.0%
Total Expenses	95,000.00	95.0%
Profit	5,000.00	5.0%

Su has a meeting with the owner of the Bungalow next week, so she decided to create a pie chart showing the percentage of her costs in relation to her total sales (see the following diagram).

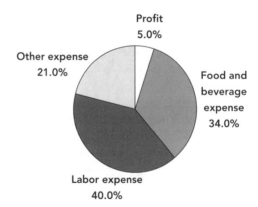

At the meeting with the owner, Su is asked to change the information on the pie chart to reflect the next month's projections. The owner suggests that April revenues and costs should be as follows:

April Revenues = $120,000.
Food and Beverage Expense = $44,000.
Labor and Other Expenses remain constant.

Using these numbers, is the owner's profit percentage going to be higher or lower than that in March? By how much?

After looking at the owner's projections, she thinks it might be too difficult (and not so good for her guests) if she cannot increase labor costs along with sales. She proposes a compromise and tells the owner that if he will agree to increase labor costs, she will try to decrease other expenses. So Su proposes the following:

April Revenues = $120,000.
Food and Beverage Expense = $44,000.
Labor Expense = $50,000.
Other Expense = $19,000.

Using these numbers, is the owner's profit percentage going to be higher or lower than that in March? By how much?

Which set of projections has more reasonable goals?

Note: If you use the Excel spreadsheets on your student disk, the changes you make to the numbers should be reflected on the pie charts as well.

3. The dining room at the Roadrock Inn is extremely popular. Terry Ray, the food and beverage director, is pleased to see that his revenue is higher than last year's. Of course, expenses are higher also. Express Terry's expenses and profit as a percentage of total revenue, for both this year and last year (fill in all empty blanks).

	This Year	%	Last Year	%
Revenue	$965,971.00		$875,421.00	
F&B Expense	367,069.00		350,168.00	
Labor Expense	338,090.00		315,151.00	
Other Expense	144,896.00		140,068.00	
Total Expenses				
Profit				

How is Terry doing in managing his expenses this year compared to last year? How do changes in revenue affect his performance?

4. Pamela Cantu operates a school foodservice department in a small, rural community. She feeds approximately 1,000 students per day in three different locations. She receives an average of $1.20 in revenues per meal. Her budget, set at the beginning of the school year by the superintendent, is developed in such a way that a small amount is to be reserved for future equipment purchases and dining-room renovation. These funds are available, however, only if Pamela meets her budget. She hopes to use this year's reserve (profit) to buy a $5,000 refrigerated salad bar for the high school. Because it is the midpoint of her school year, help her determine her "performance to budget" thus far (fill in all blanks).

Item	Budget	Actual	% of Budget
Meals Served	300,000	149,800	
Revenue			
Food Expense	$170,000	$ 84,961	
Labor Expense	125,000	63,752	
Other Expense	60,000	31,460	
Total Expenses	355,000		
Reserve		5,000	

Assuming that the year is 50 percent completed and Pamela continues doing what she is doing, is she likely to meet the reserve requirement and thus be able to purchase the salad bar by the end of the year? If not, what changes should she make over the next six months to ensure that she will have the $5,000 in reserve?

5. Sam Guild operates a dining room reserved for doctors in a large hospital in the Northeast. Sam's boss has given Sam a target of a 33 percent food cost but has indicated that the target may be adjusted. Currently, the doctors' meals sell for $15.00. Sam knows he currently can spend $4.95 for the food required to produce each meal. Fill out the chart below to help Sam find out how much he will be able to spend on each meal at various food cost percent levels if his boss adjusts his target.

Meal Selling Price	Food Cost %	Amount That Can Be Spent for Food
$15.00	20%	
$15.00	25%	
$15.00	30%	
$15.00	33%	$4.95
$15.00	35%	
$15.00	40%	

How will the doctors' meals likely be affected if the target cost percentage is reduced? What if it is increased?

6. Dawne Juan is the food and beverage director for a mid-size hotel in a beach destination area. The general manager of the hotel has given Dawne a target of 10 percent profit for this year. Dawne's staff is predominantly composed of her beach buddies. Although she is good at controlling most of her costs, she has a hard time telling her friends to go home when business slows down and she needs to reduce her staff. If she doesn't make her profit goal, her general manager will likely reprimand her, and she could possibly lose her job. Express

Dawne's expenses and profit as a percentage of total revenue, both this year and last year, to determine if she met her profit goal (fill in all blanks).

	This Year	%	Last Year	%
Revenue	$1,448,956		$1,094,276	
F&B Expense	463,666			35%
Labor Expense	652,030			40%
Other Expense		15%	186,027	
Total Expenses				
Profit				8%

Was Dawne effective at controlling her expenses? Did she meet the profit goal set by the general manager? If not, what could Dawne do in the future to help her make her target profit?

7. Lee Ray operates the Champs Steak and Seafood restaurant. Last month, Lee budgeted $10,000 for food, in the specific categories listed below. It was a busy month, but Lee thought he did a good job managing his costs. Imagine his surprise when, at the end of the month, Lee calculated his actual expenses and entered them in the chart below. He found he was way over budget! Calculate Lee's % of Budget in each category listed on the chart, as well as the total.

	Budget	Actual	% of Budget
Meats and Poultry	$ 1,500	$ 1,600	
Seafood	1,200	1,500	
Fruits and Vegetables	350	370	
Dairy Products	200	210	
Groceries	250	270	
Total			

By how much money was Lee over his total budget? In which categories did Lee's costs vary more than 10 percent from the amount he had originally budgeted? Lee said it was a busy month. Would the number of customers he served affect his actual costs? What would you recommend he do next to further analyze the reasons for his restaurant's budget performance last month?

8. Some foodservice professionals feel the best way to improve profits is to reduce costs. Others feel that increasing revenue is the best way to increase profits. Name three specific steps a manager can take to reduce current costs. Name three specific steps a manager can take to increase revenues. Which approach do you feel would be best for the type of operation you want to manage in the future?

Chapter 2

DETERMINING SALES FORECASTS

OVERVIEW

This chapter presents the methods and procedures you must learn to create accurate histories of what you have sold in the past as well as projections of how much you will sell in the future. This includes the total revenue you will generate, the number of guests you will serve, and the amount of money each guest will spend. Knowledge of these techniques is critical for analyzing sales trends in the facility you manage and preparing to serve your future guests well.

Chapter Outline

- Importance of Forecasting Sales
- Sales History
- Maintaining Sales Histories
- Sales Variances
- Predicting Future Sales
- Technology Tools
- Apply What You Have Learned
- Key Terms and Concepts
- Test Your Skills

LEARNING OUTCOMES

At the conclusion of this chapter, you will be able to:

- Develop a procedure to record current sales.
- Compute percentage increases or decreases in sales over time.
- Develop a procedure to predict future sales.

IMPORTANCE OF FORECASTING SALES

*W*hen they open their facility's doors at the beginning of the day, the first questions operating managers must ask themselves are very simple: "How many guests will I serve today?—This week?—This year?" The answers to questions such as these are critical because the guests you serve will provide the revenue from which you will pay basic operating expenses and create a profit. Simply put, if too few guests are served, total revenue may be insufficient to cover your costs, even if these costs are well managed. In addition, decisions regarding the kind and quantity of food or beverages to purchase are dependent on knowing the number of guests who will be coming to buy those products. The labor required to serve guests is also determined based on the manager's "best guess" of the projected number of guests to arrive as well as what these guests will buy. In an ongoing operation, it is often true that future sales estimates, or projected sales, will be heavily based on sales history because what has happened in the past in your operation is often the best predictor of what will happen in the future. Those managers who can best predict the future are those who are most prepared to control how it will affect them.

In the hospitality industry, we have many ways of counting or defining sales. In the simplest case, sales are the dollar (or other currency) amount of revenue collected during some predetermined time period. The time period may be an hour, a shift of various lengths, a day, a week, a month, or a year. When used in this manner, sales and revenue are considered interchangeable terms. When you predict the number of guests you will serve and the revenues they will generate in a given future time period, you have created a **sales forecast.** You can determine your actual sales for a current time period in a variety of ways; however, many foodservice managers utilize a computerized system called a **point of sales (POS) system,** which is designed to provide specific sales information. Alternatively, manually produced guest checks or head counts will help you establish how many sales were completed. Today, however, even the smallest of foodservice operations should take advantage of the speed and accuracy provided by computerized programs for recording sales.

FUN ON THE WEB!

Look at the following sites to see examples of POS systems used to record historical sales information:

www.micros.com.   Click "Industries" and continue from there to see product descriptions.

www.squirrelsystems.com.   Click "Squirrelone" to find product information.

www.datatrakpos.com.   Click "Products," "DataTrakPOS," and then "Screenshots" to see how sales are displayed on the system.

It is important to remember that a distinction is made in the hospitality industry between sales (revenue) and **sales volume.** Sales volume is the number of units sold. Consider Manuel, a bagel shop manager, whose Monday business consists of $2,000 in sales (revenue) because he actually sold 3,000 bagels (sales volume). Obviously, it is important for Manuel to know how much revenue is taken in, so he can evaluate the expenses required to generate his revenue and the number of units that have been sold. With this information, he can properly prepare to serve additional guests the next day.

In many areas of the hospitality industry, for example, in college and university dormitory foodservice, it is customary that no cash actually changes hands during a particular meal period. Of course, the manager of such a facility still created sales and would be interested in sales volume, that is, how much food was actually consumed by the students on that day. This is critical information because, as we have seen, a manager must be prepared to answer the questions, "How many individuals did I serve today, and how many should I expect tomorrow?" In some cases, a food and beverage operation may be a blend of cash and noncash sales.

Consider Tonya Brown, a hospital foodservice director. It is very likely that Tonya will be involved in serving both cash-paying guests (in a public cafeteria) and noncash patients (tray line assembled meals that are then delivered to rooms). In addition, meals for hospital employees may be cash sales but at a reduced or subsidized rate. Clearly, Tonya's operation will create sales each day, and it will be important to her and her staff to know, as accurately as possible, how many of each type of guest she will serve.

An understanding of anticipated sales, in terms of revenue dollars, guest counts, or both, will help you have the right number of workers, with the right amounts of product available, at the right time. In this way, you can begin to effectively manage your costs. In addition to the importance of accurate sales records for purchasing and staffing, sales records are valuable to the operator when developing labor standards that improve efficiency. Consider, for example, managing a large restaurant with 400 seats. If an individual server can serve 25 guests at lunch, you would need 400/25, or 8, servers per lunch shift if all your seats were filled. If management keeps no accurate sales histories or forecasts, too few or too many servers could be scheduled. With accurate sales records, a sales history can be developed for each foodservice outlet you operate, and better decisions will be reached with regard to planning for each unit's operation. Figure 2.1 lists some of the advantages that you gain when you can accurately predict the number of people you will serve in a future time period.

SALES HISTORY

A **sales history** is the systematic recording of all sales achieved during a predetermined time period. It is an accurate record of what your operation has sold. Before you can develop a sales history, however, you must think about the definition

■ **FIGURE 2.1** Advantages of Precise Sales Forecasts

1. Accurate revenue estimates
2. Improved ability to predict expenses
3. Greater efficiency in scheduling needed workers
4. Greater efficiency in scheduling menu item production schedules
5. Better accuracy in purchasing the correct amount of food for immediate use
6. Improved ability to maintain proper levels of nonperishable food inventories
7. Improved budgeting ability
8. Lower selling prices for guests because of increased operational efficiencies
9. Increased dollars available for current facility maintenance and future growth
10. Increased profit levels and stockholder value

of sales that is most helpful to you and your understanding of how your facility functions. The simplest type of sales history records revenue only. The sales history format used by Rae's Restaurant and shown in Figure 2.2 is a typical one for recording sales revenue on a weekly basis.

Notice that, in this most basic of cases, you determine daily sales either from your POS system or from adding the information recorded on your guest checks. You then transfer that number on a daily basis to your sales history by entering the amount of your daily sales in the column titled Daily Sales. Sales to date is the cumulative total of sales reported in the unit. **Sales to date** is the number you will get when you add today's Daily Sales to the sales of all prior days in the **reporting period,** the time period for which sales records are being maintained.

■ **FIGURE 2.2** Sales History

Rae's Restaurant			
Sales Period	Date	Daily Sales	Sales to Date
Monday	1/1	$ 851.90	$ 851.90
Tuesday	1/2	974.37	1,826.27
Wednesday	1/3	1,004.22	2,830.49
Thursday	1/4	976.01	3,806.50
Friday	1/5	856.54	4,663.04
Saturday	1/6	1,428.22	6,091.26
Sunday	1/7	1,241.70	7,332.96
Week's Total			7,332.96

To illustrate, Sales to Date on Tuesday, January 2, is computed by adding Tuesday's sales to those of the prior day ($851.90 + $974.37 = $1,826.27). As a result, the Sales to Date column is a running total of the sales achieved by Rae's Restaurant for the week. Should Rae's manager prefer it, the sales period could be defined in time blocks other than one week. Common alternatives are meal periods (breakfast, lunch, dinner, and so forth), days, weeks, two-week periods, four-week (28 day) periods, months, quarters (three-month periods), or any other unit of time that helps managers better understand their business. Most modern POS systems allow you to choose the specific reporting period of most interest to you.

In some situations, you will not have the ability to consider your sales in terms of revenue generated. Figure 2.3 is the type of sales history you can use when no cash sales are typically reported. Notice that, in this case, the manager is interested in recording sales based on serving periods rather than some alternative time frame such as a 24-hour (one-day) period. This approach is often used in such settings as all-inclusive hotels and resorts, extended care facilities for senior citizens, nursing homes, college dormitories, correctional facilities, hospitals, camps, or any other situation where knowledge of the number of actual guests served during a given period is critical for planning purposes.

Given the data in Figure 2.3, the implications for staffing service personnel at the camp are very clear. Fewer service personnel are needed from 9:00 to 11:00 a.m. than from 7:00 to 9:00 a.m. The reason is obvious. Fewer campers eat between 9:00 and 11:00 a.m. (40) than between 7:00 and 9:00 a.m. (121). As a knowledgeable manager, if you were operating this camp, you could either reduce staff during the slower service period or move those workers to some other necessary task. You might also decide not to produce as many menu items for consumption during the 9:00 to 11:00 a.m. period. In that way you could make more efficient use of both labor and food products. It is simply easier to manage well when you know the answer to the question "How many guests will I serve?"

■ **FIGURE 2.3** Sales History

Eureka Summer Camp								
	Guests Served							
Serving Period	Mon	Tues	Wed	Thurs	Fri	Sat	Sun	Total
7:00–9:00 A.M.	121							
9:00–11:00 A.M.	40							
11:00–1:00 P.M.	131							
1:00–3:00 P.M.	11							
3:00–5:00 P.M.	42							
5:00–7:00 P.M.	161							
Total Served	506							

Sales histories can be created to record revenue, guests served, or both. It is important, however, that you keep good records of how much you have sold because doing so is the key to accurately predicting the amount of sales you will achieve in the future.

■ COMPUTING AVERAGES FOR SALES HISTORIES

In some cases, knowing the average number of revenue dollars generated in a past time period, or the average number of guests served in that period, may be a real benefit to you. This is because it may be helpful to know, for example, the number of dollar sales achieved on a typical day last week or the number of guests served on that same typical day. Future guest activity can often be expected to be very similar to past guest activity, and thus using historical averages from your operation can be quite useful in helping you project future guest sales and counts.

An **average** is a value computed by adding the quantities in a series and dividing the sum of the quantities by the number of items in the series. Thus, 11 is the average of 6 + 9 + 18. The sum of the quantities in this case equals 33 (6 + 9 + 18 = 33). The number of items in the series is three, that is, 6, 9, and 18. Thus, 33/3 = 11, the average of the numbers. Sometimes, an average is referred to as the **mean**. The two major types of averages you are likely to encounter as a foodservice manager are:

1. Fixed average
2. Rolling average

FIXED AVERAGE

A **fixed average** is an average for a specific (fixed) time period, for example, the first 14 days of a given month, and you compute the average amount of sales or guest activity for that period. Note that this average is called fixed because the first 14 days of the month will always consist of the same days (the 1st thru the 14th) as shown in Figure 2.4, the sales activity of Dan's Take-Out Coffee. The calculation of this average (total revenue/number of days) is fixed, or constant, because Dan's management has identified the 14 specific days used to make up the average. The number $427.14 may be very useful because it might, if management wishes, be used as a good predictor of the revenue volume that should be expected for the first 14 days of next month.

ROLLING AVERAGE

A **rolling average** is the average amount of sales or volume over a changing time period. A fixed average is computed using a specific or constant set of data but a rolling average is computed using data that will change. To illustrate, consider the case of Ubalda Salas, who operates a sports bar. Ubalda is interested in knowing

---

■ **FIGURE 2.4** 14-Day Fixed Average

Dan's Take-Out Coffee

Day of Month	Daily Sales
1	$ 350.00
2	320.00
3	390.00
4	440.00
5	420.00
6	458.00
7	450.00
8	460.00
9	410.00
10	440.00
11	470.00
12	460.00
13	418.00
14	494.00
14-day total	$5,980.00

$$\frac{\$5,980}{14} = \$427.14 \text{ per day}$$

---

what the average revenue dollars were in her operation for each prior seven-day period. Obviously, in this case, the prior seven-day period changes, or rolls forward by one day, as each day passes. It is important to note that Ubalda could have been interested in her average daily revenue last week (fixed average), but she prefers to know her average sales for the last seven days. This means that she will, at times, be using data from both last week and this week to compute the last seven-day average. Using the sales data recorded in Figure 2.5, the seven-day rolling average for Ubalda's Sports Bar is computed as shown in Figure 2.6.

Note that each seven-day period is made up of a group of daily revenue numbers that changes over time. The first seven-day rolling average is computed by summing the first seven days' revenue (revenue on days 1–7 = $28,280) and dividing that number by seven to arrive at a seven-day rolling average of $4,040.00 ($28,280/7 = $4,040.00).

Each day, Ubalda adds her daily revenue to that of the prior seven-day total and drops the day that is now eight days past. This gives her the effect of continually rolling the most current seven days' data forward. The rolling average, although more complex and time-consuming than a fixed average, can be extremely useful in recording data to help you make effective predictions about the sales levels you can expect in the future. This is true because, in many cases, rolling data are more

■ **FIGURE 2.5** 14-Day Sales Levels

Ubalda's Sports Bar

Day	Sales	Day	Sales
1	$3,500	8	$4,600
2	3,200	9	4,100
3	3,900	10	4,400
4	4,400	11	4,700
5	4,200	12	4,600
6	4,580	13	4,180
7	4,500	14	4,940

■ **FIGURE 2.6** Seven-Day Rolling Average

Ubalda's Sports Bar

Day	Seven-Day Period							
	1–7	2–8	3–9	4–10	5–11	6–12	7–13	8–14
1	$ 3,500	—						
2	3,200	$ 3,200	—					
3	3,900	3,900	$ 3,900	—				
4	4,400	4,400	4,400	$ 4,400	—			
5	4,200	4,200	4,200	4,200	$ 4,200	—		
6	4,580	4,580	4,580	4,580	4,580	$ 4,580	—	
7	4,500	4,500	4,500	4,500	4,500	4,500	$ 4,500	—
8		4,600	4,600	4,600	4,600	4,600	4,600	$ 4,600
9			4,100	4,100	4,100	4,100	4,100	4,100
10				4,400	4,400	4,400	4,400	4,400
11					4,700	4,700	4,700	4,700
12						4,600	4,600	4,600
13							4,180	4,180
14								4,940
Total	28,280	29,380	30,280	30,780	31,080	31,480	31,080	31,520
7-Day Rolling Average	4,040.00	4,197.14	4,325.71	4,397.14	4,440.00	4,497.14	4,440.00	4,502.86

current and, thus, more relevant than some fixed historical averages. You may choose to compute fixed averages for some time periods and rolling averages for others. For example, it may be helpful to know your average daily sales for the first 14 days of last month as well as your average sales for the last 14 days. If, for example, these two numbers are very different, you know if the number of sales you can expect in the future is increasing or declining. Regardless of the type of average you feel is best for your operation, you should always document your sales history because it is from your sales history that you will be better able to predict future sales levels.

■ RECORDING REVENUE, GUEST COUNTS, OR BOTH

As you have learned, some foodservice operations do not record revenue as a measure of their sales activity. For them, developing sales histories by recording the number of individuals they serve each day makes the most sense. Thus, **guest count,** the term used in the hospitality industry to indicate the number of people served, is recorded on a regular basis. You may decide that your operation is best managed by tracking both revenue and guest counts. In fact, if you do decide to record both revenue and guest counts, you have the information you need to compute **average sales per guest,** a term commonly known as **check average.**

Average sales per guest is determined by the following formula:

$$\frac{\text{Total Sales}}{\text{Number of Guests Served}} = \text{Average Sales per Guest}$$

Consider the information in Figure 2.7 in which the manager of Brothers' Family Restaurant has decided to monitor and record the following:

1. Sales
2. Guests served
3. Average sales per guest

■ **FIGURE 2.7** Sales History

Brothers' Family Restaurant				
Sales Period	Date	Sales	Guests Served	Average Sales per Guest
Monday	1/1	$1,365.00	190	$7.18
Tuesday	1/2	2,750.00	314	8.76
Two-Day Average		2,057.50	252	8.16

Most POS systems report the amount of revenue you have generated in a selected time period, the number of guests you have served, and the average sales per guest. Of course, the same data could be compiled manually. In the case of Brothers' Family Restaurant, Monday's revenue was $1,365, the number of guests served was 190, and the average sales per guest for Monday, January 1, was determined to be $7.18 ($1,365/190 = $7.18). On Tuesday, the average sales per guest was $8.76 ($2,750/314 = $8.76).

To compute the two-day revenue average, the Brothers' manager would add Monday's revenue and Tuesday's revenue and divide by 2, yielding a two-day revenue average of $2,057.50 [($1,365 + $2,750)/2 = $2,057.50]. In a like manner, the two-day guests-served average is computed by adding the number of guests served on Monday to the number served on Tuesday and dividing by 2, yielding a two-day average guests-served number of 252 [(190 + 314)/2 = 252].

It might be logical to think that the manager of Brothers' could compute the Monday and Tuesday combined average sales per guest by adding the averages from each day and dividing by 2. It is important to understand that this would *not* be correct. A formula consisting of Monday's average sales per guest plus Tuesday's average sales per guest divided by 2 [($7.18 + $8.76)/2] yields $7.97. In fact, the two-day average sales per guest is $8.16 [($1,365 + $2,750)/(190 + 314) = ($4,115/504) = $8.16].

Although the difference of $0.19 might, at first glance, appear to be an inconsequential amount, assume that you are the chief executive officer (CEO) of a restaurant chain with 4,000 units worldwide. If each unit served 1,000 guests per day and you miscalculated average sales per guest by $0.19, your daily revenue assumption would be "off" by $760,000 per day [(4,000 × 1,000 × $0.19) = $760,000]!

Returning to the Brothers' Family Restaurant example, the correct procedure for computing the two-day sales per guest average is as follows:

$$\frac{\text{Monday Sales} + \text{Tuesday Sales}}{\text{Monday Guests} + \text{Tuesday Guests}} = \text{Two-Day Average Sales per Guest}$$

or

$$\frac{\$1,365 + \$2,750}{190 + 314} = \$8.16$$

The correct computation is a **weighted average,** that is, an average that weights the number of guests with how much they spend in a given time period.

To demonstrate further, assume that you want to answer the question "What is the combined average sales per guest?" using the data in Figure 2.8. From the data in Figure 2.8, it is easy to see that the two-day average would not be $7.50 [($5.00 + $10.00)/2] because many more guests were served at a $10.00 average than were served at the $5.00 average. Obviously, with so many guests spending an average of $10.00, and so few spending an average of $5.00, the overall average

■ **FIGURE 2.8** Weighted Average

	Sales	Guests Served	Average Sales per Guest
Day 1	$ 100	20	$ 5.00
Day 2	4,000	400	10.00
Two-Day Average	2,050	210	???

should be quite close to $10.00. In fact, the correct weighted average sales per guest would be $9.76, as follows:

$$\frac{\text{Day 1 Sales} + \text{Day 2 Sales}}{\text{Day 1 Guests} + \text{Day 2 Guests}} = \text{Two-Day Average Sales per Guest}$$

or

$$\frac{\$100 + \$4,000}{20 + 400} = \$9.76$$

MAINTAINING SALES HISTORIES

Although a sales history may consist of revenue, number of guests served, and average sales per guest, you may want to use even more detailed information, such as the number of a particular menu item or menu type served, the number of guests served in a specific meal or time period (for example, breakfast, lunch, or dinner), or the method of meal delivery (e.g., drive-through sales vs. counter sales). The important concept to remember is that you have the power to choose the information that best suits your operation. That information should be updated at least daily, and a cumulative total for the appropriate time period should also be maintained. In most cases, your sales histories should be kept for a period of at least two years. This allows you to have a good sense of what has happened to your business in the recent past. Of course, if you are the manager of a new operation, or one that has recently undergone a major concept change, you may not have the advantage of reviewing meaningful sales histories. If you find yourself in such a situation, it is imperative that you begin to build and maintain your sales histories as soon as possible so you will have good sales information on which to base your future managerial decisions.

SALES VARIANCES

After an accurate sales history system has been established, you may begin to see that your operation, if it is like most, will experience some level of sales variation. These **sales variances,** or changes from previously experienced sales levels, will give you an indication of whether your sales are improving, declining, or staying the same. Because that information is so important to predicting future sales levels, many foodservice managers improve their sales history information by including sales variance as an additional component of the history. Figure 2.9 details a portion of a sales history that has been modified to include a Variance column, which allows the manager to see how sales are different from a prior period. In this case, the manager of Quick Wok wants to compare sales for the first three months of this year to sales for the first three months of last year. Note, of course, that the manager would find this revenue information in the sales histories regularly maintained by the operation.

The variance in Figure 2.9 is determined by subtracting sales last year from sales this year. In January, the variance figure is obtained as follows:

Sales This Year − Sales Last Year = Variance

or

$54,000 − $51,200 = $2,800

Thus, the manager of Quick Wok can see that sales are greater than last year. In fact, all three months in the first quarter of the year showed revenue increases over the prior year. The total improvement for the first quarter was $13,250 ($172,700 − $159,450 = $13,250). The format used in Figure 2.9 lets a manager know the dollar value of revenue variance, but good managers want to know even more. Simply knowing the dollar value of a variance has limitations. Consider two restaurant managers. One manager's restaurant had revenue of $1,000,000 last year. The second manager's restaurant generated one-half as much revenue, or

■ **FIGURE 2.9** Sales History and Variance

Quick Wok			
Month	Sales This Year	Sales Last Year	Variance
January	$ 54,000	$ 51,200	$ 2,800
February	57,500	50,750	6,750
March	61,200	57,500	3,700
First-Quarter Total	172,700	159,450	13,250

■ **FIGURE 2.10** Sales History, Variance, and Percentage Variance

Quick Wok				
Month	Sales This Year	Sales Last Year	Variance	Percentage Variance
January	$ 54,000	$ 51,200	$ 2,800	5.5%
February	57,500	50,750	6,750	13.3
March	61,200	57,500	3,700	6.4
First-Quarter Total	172,700	159,450	13,250	8.3

$500,000. This year both had sales increases of $50,000. It is clear that a $50,000 sales increase represents a much greater improvement in the second restaurant than in the first. Because that is true, effective managers are interested in the **percentage variance,** or percentage change, in their sales from one time period to the next.

Figure 2.10 shows how the sales history at Quick Wok can be expanded to include percentage variance as part of that operation's complete sales history.

Percentage variance is obtained by subtracting sales last year from sales this year and dividing the resulting number by sales last year. Thus, in the month of January, the percentage variance is determined as follows:

$$\frac{\text{Sales This Year} - \text{Sales Last Year}}{\text{Sales Last Year}} = \text{Percentage Variance}$$

or

$$\frac{\$54,000 - \$51,200}{\$51,200} = 0.055$$

(in common form, 5.5%)

Note that the resulting decimal-form percentage can be converted to the more frequently used common form discussed in Chapter 1 by moving the decimal point two places to the right (or multiplying by 100).

An alternative, and shorter, formula for computing the percentage variance is as follows:

$$\frac{\text{Variance}}{\text{Sales Last Year}} = \text{Percentage Variance}$$

or

$$\frac{\$2,800}{\$51,200} = 0.055$$

(in common form, 5.5%)

Another way to compute the percentage variance is to use a math shortcut, as follows:

$$\frac{\text{Sales This Year}}{\text{Sales Last Year}} - 1 = \text{Percentage Variance}$$

or

$$\frac{\$54,000}{\$51,200} - 1 = 0.055$$

(in common form, 5.5%)

Calculating percentage variance is invaluable when you want to compare the operating results of two foodservice operations of different sizes. Return to our previous example of the two restaurant managers, each of whom achieved $50,000 revenue increases. Using the first percentage variance formula presented before, you will see that the restaurant with higher sales increased its revenue by 5.0 percent [($1,050,000 − $1,000,000)/$1,000,000 = 5.0%], whereas the restaurant with lower revenue achieved a 10 percent increase [($550,000 − $500,000)/$500,000 = 10.0%]. As your level of expertise increases, you will find additional areas in which knowing the percentage variance in revenue and in expense areas (introduced later in this text) will help your management decision making.

PREDICTING FUTURE SALES

It has been pointed out that truly outstanding managers have an ability to see the future in regard to the revenue figures they will achieve and the number of guests they expect to serve. You, too, can learn to do this when you apply the knowledge of percentage variances you now have to estimating your own operation's future sales. Depending on the type of facility you manage, you may be interested in predicting, or forecasting, future revenues, guest counts, or average sales per guest levels. We will examine the procedures for all three of these in detail.

■ FUTURE REVENUES

Erica Tullstein is the manager of Rock's Pizza Pub on the campus of State College. Her guests consist of college students, most of whom come to the Rock to talk, surf the web, eat, and study. Erica has done a good job in maintaining sales histories in the two years she has managed the Rock. She records the revenue dollars she achieves on a daily basis, as well as the number of students frequenting the Rock. Revenue data for the last three months of the year are recorded in Figure 2.11.

■ FIGURE 2.11 Revenue History

Rock's Pizza Pub				
Month	Sales This Year	Sales Last Year	Variance	Percentage Variance
October	$ 75,000	$ 72,500	$ 2,500	3.4%
November	64,250	60,000	4,250	7.1
December	57,500	50,500	7,000	13.9
Fourth-Quarter Total	196,750	183,000	13,750	7.5

As can easily be seen, fourth-quarter revenues for Erica's operation have increased from the previous year. Of course, there could be a variety of reasons for this. Erica may have extended her hours of operation to attract more students. She may have increased the size of pizzas and held her prices constant, thus creating more value for her guests. She may have raised the price of pizza but kept the pizzas the same size. Or perhaps a competing pizza parlor was closed during this time period. Using all of her knowledge of her own operation and her market, Erica would like to predict the sales level she will experience in the first three months of next year. This sales forecast will be most helpful as she plans for next year's anticipated expenses, staffing levels, and profits.

The first question Erica must address is the amount her sales have actually increased. Revenue increases range from a low in October of 3.4 percent, to a high in December of 13.9 percent. The overall quarter average of 7.5 percent is the figure that Erica elects to use as she predicts her sales revenue for the first quarter of the coming year. She feels it is neither too conservative, as would be the case if she used the October percentage increase, nor too aggressive, as would be the case if she used the December figure.

If Erica were to use the 7.5 percent average increase from the fourth quarter of last year to predict her revenues for the first quarter of this year, a planning sheet for the first quarter of this year could be developed as presented in Figure 2.12.

■ FIGURE 2.12 First-Quarter Revenue Forecast

Rock's Pizza Pub				
Month	Sales Last Year	% Increase Estimate	Increase Amount	Revenue Forecast
January	$ 68,500	7.5%	$ 5,137.50	$ 73,637.50
February	72,000	7.5	5,400.00	77,400.00
March	77,000	7.5	5,775.00	82,775.00
First-Quarter Total	217,500	7.5	16,312.50	233,812.50

Revenue forecast for this time period is determined by multiplying sales last year by the percent increase estimate and then adding sales last year. In the month of January, revenue forecast is calculated using the following formula:

Sales Last Year + (Sales Last Year × % Increase Estimate) = Revenue Forecast

or

$68,500 + ($68,500 × 0.075) = $73,637.50

An alternative way to compute the revenue forecast is to use a math shortcut, as follows:

Sales Last Year × (1 + % Increase Estimate) = Revenue Forecast

or

$68,500 × (1 + 0.075) = $73,637.50

Erica is using the increases she has experienced in the past to predict increases she may experience in the future. Monthly revenue figures from last year's sales history plus percent increase estimates based on those histories give Erica a very good idea of the revenue levels she may achieve in January, February, and March of the coming year.

■ FUTURE GUEST COUNTS

Using the same techniques employed in estimating increases in sales, the noncash operator or any manager interested in guest counts can estimate increases or decreases in the number of guests served. Figure 2.13 shows how Erica, the manager

■ **FIGURE 2.13** Guest Count History

Rock's Pizza Pub				
Month	Guests This Year	Guests Last Year	Variance	Percentage Variance
October	14,200	13,700	+ 500	3.6%
November	15,250	14,500	+ 750	5.2
December	16,900	15,500	+1,400	9.0
Fourth-Quarter Total	46,350	43,700	+2,650	6.1

■ **FIGURE 2.14** First-Quarter Guest Count Forecast

Rock's Pizza Pub

Month	Guests Last Year	% Increase Estimate	Guest Increase Estimate	Guest Count Forecast
January	12,620	6.1%	770	13,390
February	13,120	6.1	800	13,920
March	13,241	6.1	808	14,049
First-Quarter Total	38,981	6.1	2,378	41,359

of Rock's Pizza Pub, used a sales history to determine the percentage of guest count increases achieved in her facility in the fourth quarter of last year.

If Erica were to use the 6.1 percent average increase from the fourth quarter of last year to predict her guest count for the first quarter of the coming year, a planning sheet could be developed as presented in Figure 2.14. It is important to note that Erica is not required to use the same percentage increase estimate for each month. Any forecasted increase management feels is appropriate can be used to predict future sales.

Notice that in January, for example, the guest increase estimate is rounded from 769.82 to 770. This is because you cannot serve "0.82" people!

The guest count forecast is determined by multiplying guest count last year by the percent increase estimate and then adding the guest count last year. In the month of January, guest count forecast is calculated using the following formula:

Guest Count Last Year
+ (Guest Count Last Year × % Increase Estimate)
= Guest Count Forecast

or

12,620 + (12,620 × 0.061) = 13,390

This process can be simplified by using a math shortcut, as follows:

Guests Last Year × (1.00 + % Increase Estimate) = Guest Count Forecast

or

12,620 × (1.00 + 0.061) = 13,390

You should choose the formula you feel most comfortable with.

Consider The Costs

"A 60-minute wait! You've got to be kidding!" said the guest.

"I'm sorry sir," replied Romy. "We'll seat your party as quickly as possible."

Romy was the dining room host at the Al-Amir restaurant. The Al-Amir featured Middle Eastern and North African Cuisine. Guests loved the Al-Amir's baba gannouj, tabouleh, and kibbeh. As a result, the restaurant often was very busy. When that happened, the waiting lists for tables got long and customers sometimes got upset.

"Listen" replied the guest, "I understand when places are busy. It can take a while to serve everyone. But look, nearly half your dining room is empty. The tables just need to be cleared and reset."

"Yes sir," replied Romy. "But the workers we do have are clearing tables as fast as they can."

"Then you need more dining room help. We'll just come back another time," said the guest, as he left the restaurant along with his female dining companion, two small children in hand.

"I'm really very sorry, sir," said Romy to the guest's back as he watched him leave. Romy thought to himself, "This happens way too often!"

Assume the Al-Amir does not have an effective sales forecast system in place.

1. What will be the likely long-term impact on the revenue-generating ability of the restaurant of understaffing its dining room?

2. What would be the long-term impact on Al-Amir's staff?

3. Sometimes even the best sales forecasts are inaccurate. What steps can managers take to ease the difficulties encountered when their sales forecasts prove to be incorrect?

■ FUTURE AVERAGE SALES PER GUEST

Recall that average sales per guest (check average) is simply the average amount of money each guest spends during a visit. The same formula is used to forecast average sales per guest as was used in forecasting total revenue and guest counts. Using data taken from the sales history, the following formula is employed:

> Last Year's Average Sales per Guest
> + Estimated Increase in Sales per Guest
> = Sales per Guest Forecast

Alternatively, you can compute average sales per guest using the data collected from revenue forecasts (Figure 2.12) and combining that data with the guest count forecast (Figure 2.14). If that is done, the data presented in Figure 2.15 will result.

An average sales per guest forecast is obtained by dividing the revenue forecast by the guest count forecast. Thus, in the month of January, the average sales per guest forecast is determined by the following formula:

$$\frac{\text{Revenue Forecast}}{\text{Guest Count Forecast}} = \text{Average Sales per Guest Forecast}$$

or

$$\frac{\$73,637.50}{13,390} = \$5.50$$

■ **FIGURE 2.15** First-Quarter Average Sales per Guest Forecast

Rock's Pizza Pub

Month	Revenue Forecast	Guest Count Forecast	Average Sales per Guest Forecast
January	$ 73,637.50	13,390	$5.50
February	77,400.00	13,920	5.56
March	82,775.00	14,049	5.89
First-Quarter Total	233,812.50	41,359	5.65

Increasingly, sophisticated POS systems analyze not only how many persons were served on a given day in the past, but what these guests ordered as well. Even historical weather patterns can be analyzed to discover, for example, if rainy days affect total sales volume (and thus perhaps indicate that a forecast adjustment should be made on a day on which rain is predicted). Weather, day of the month, and day of the week are just some of the many factors that may affect sales volume and thus should be carefully considered by sophisticated food-service managers.

It is important to note that sales histories, regardless of how well they have been developed and maintained, are not sufficient alone to accurately predict future sales. Your knowledge of potential price changes, new competitors, facility renovations, and improved selling programs are additional factors that you may need to consider when predicting future sales. There is no question, however, that a sales history report is easily developed and will serve as the cornerstone of other management systems you will design. Without accurate sales data, the control systems you implement, regardless of their sophistication, are very likely to fail.

When added to your knowledge of the unique factors that impact your unit, properly maintained histories will help you answer two important control questions, namely, "How many people are coming tomorrow?" and "How much is each person likely to spend?" The judgment of management is critical in forecasting answers to these questions. Since you can now answer those questions, you are ready to develop systems that will allow you to prepare an efficient and cost-effective way of serving your guests. You want to be ready to provide them with quality food and beverage products and enough staff to serve them properly. You have done your homework with regard to the number of individuals who may be coming and how much they are likely to spend; now you must prepare for their arrival!

Green and Growing!

If your operation is "Going Green" and your customer counts are going up, don't be surprised. In increasing numbers, customers are concerned about the quality of their environment. These customers also prefer to frequent foodservice operations that share their concerns and act on them. As a result, guest counts can be increased by undertaking green initiatives and then proudly letting customers know about what you are doing. It is important to market your products and services directly to the rapidly growing market segment of educated, savvy customers who care about the food they eat and their impact on the world around them. Implementing sustainable practices that focus on conservation as well as utilizing organic, seasonal, and locally grown products can help build customer and employee loyalty, as well as boost profits.

Technology Tools

The importance of accurate sales histories for use in forecasting future sales is unquestionable. Your POS system can be invaluable in this effort. Many systems today can be utilized to:

1. Track sales by guest count
2. Track sales by date
3. Monitor cash vs. credit sales
4. Maintain products sold histories
5. Maintain check average data
6. Compare actual sales to prior-period sales
7. Maintain rolling sales averages
8. Forecast future sales in increments:
   a. Monthly
   b. Weekly
   c. Daily
   d. By meal period
   e. Hourly
   f. Portions of an hour (i.e., 15 min., 30 min., etc.)
9. Maintain actual sales to forecasted sales variance reports

(*continued on next page*)

(continued from previous page)
10. Maintain reservations systems:

      a. Automate advanced bookings up to two years in advance

      b. Track no-shows and cancellations

      c. Build a guest database for mailings and e-mailings

      d. Track guest birthdays, favorite tables, food preferences, etc.

For those operations that rely on reservations to control bookings, software of this type is available to instantly identify repeat guests, giving the operator a display screen that can include such information as frequency of visit, purchase preferences, and total dollars spent in the operation. In addition, reservations software makes it possible for operators to reward repeat guests by developing their own "frequent dining" programs, similar to a hotel or airline's frequent-traveler program. In addition, customer complaints can be tracked and, if desired, coupons to compensate guests for difficulties can be printed and distributed. Also, reservations-related programs such as these can store information on reservation demand, predict optimal reservation patterns, identify frequent no-show guests, and even allow guests to make their own reservations via on-line Internet connections.

FUN ON THE WEB!

Digital Dining, a product created by Menusoft Systems Corporation (in conjunction with Microsoft) is one of the most innovative high-volume restaurant software programs available today. Its Web site is **www.digitaldining.com.**

    Start at "Products," and then follow the prompts to get an overview of the system. When you arrive, pay especially close attention to the features related to the maintenance of sales histories.

Apply What You Have Learned

*P*auline Cooper is a registered dietitian and the foodservice director at Memorial Hospital. Increasingly, the hospital's marketing efforts have emphasized its skill in treating diabetic patients. As a result, the number of diabetic meals served by Pauline's staff has been increasing. As a professional member of the hospital's management team, Pauline has been asked to report on how the hospital's diabetic treatment marketing efforts have affected her area.

1. How important is it that Pauline have historical records of the "type" of meals served by her staff and not merely the number of meals served? Why?

2. Assume that Pauline's "per meal" cost has been increasing because diabetic meals are more expensive to produce than regular meals. Could Pauline use sales histories to estimate the financial impact of serving additional diabetic meals in the future? How?

3. What are other reasons managers in a foodservice operation might keep detailed records of meal "types" (i.e., vegetarian, low-sodium, etc.) served, as well as total number of meals served?

Key Terms and Concepts

*T*he following are terms and concepts discussed in the chapter that are important for you as a manager. To help you review, please define the terms below:

Sales forecast/projected
   sales
Point of sales (POS)
   system
Sales volume
Sales history

Sales to date
Reporting period
Average (mean)
Fixed average
Rolling average
Guest count

Average sales per guest
   (check average)
Weighted average
Sales variance
Percentage variance

Test Your Skills

Complete the Test Your Skills exercises by placing your answers in the shaded boxes and answering the questions as indicated.

1. Laurie Fitsin owns a small sandwich shop called Laurie's Lunch Box. She has developed a sales history for the first week of March using total sales and guests served. Help Laurie calculate her average sales per guest for each day of the week and calculate her totals. Laurie has decided that she could take a shortcut and calculate the average sales per guest for the week by adding Monday through Sunday's average sales per guest and dividing by seven. Would this shortcut make a difference in her total average sales per guest for the week? If so, how much of a difference? Should she take this shortcut? Why or why not?

Laurie's Lunch Box				
Sales Period	**Date**	**Sales**	**Guests Served**	**Average Sales per Guest**
Monday	3/1	$1,248.44	200	
Tuesday	3/2	1,686.25	360	
Wednesday	3/3	1,700.00	350	
Thursday	3/4	1,555.65	300	
Friday	3/5	1,966.31	380	
Saturday	3/6	2,134.65	400	
Sunday	3/7	2,215.77	420	
Total				

2. Peggy Richey operates Peggy's Pizza Place in southern California. She has maintained a sales history for January through June, and she wants to compare this year's sales with last year's sales. Calculate her sales variances and percentage variances for the first six months of the year.

Peggy's Pizza Place				
Month	Sales This Year	Sales Last Year	Variance	Percentage Variance
January	$37,702.73	$34,861.51		
February	33,472.03	31,485.60		
March	36,492.98	33,707.79		
April	35,550.12	32,557.85		
May	36,890.12	37,852.42		
June	37,482.52	37,256.36		
6-Month Total				

3. Peggy (from the preceding exercise) wants to use the sales and variance information from her first six months of the year to forecast her revenues for the last six months of the year. She decides to use her six-month total percentage variance of 4.75 percent to predict her changes in sales. Help her calculate the projected sales increases and revenue forecasts for the last six months of the year.

Peggy's Pizza Place				
Month	Sales Last Year	Predicted Change	Projected Sales Increase	Revenue Forecast
July	$36,587.91	4.75%		
August	36,989.73	4.75%		
September	40,896.32	4.75%		
October	37,858.63	4.75%		
November	37,122.45	4.75%		
December	37,188.71	4.75%		
6-Month Total				

4. The Lopez brothers, Victor, Tony, and Soren, own the Lopez Cantina. Victor is in charge of marketing, and he is developing his sales forecast for next year. Because of his marketing efforts, he predicts a 5 percent increase in his monthly guest counts. Victor is not aware of any anticipated menu price increases and assumes, therefore, that his weighted check average will remain stable.

    A. Using last year's sales and guest counts, estimate Victor's weighted check average (average sales per guest) for the year. (Spreadsheet hint: Use the

ROUND function to two decimal places on weighted check average, cell D18, because it will be used in another formula in part B.)

Month	Sales Last Year	Guest Count Last Year	Check Average
January	$45,216.00	4,800	
February	48,538.00	5,120	
March	50,009.00	5,006	
April	45,979.00	4,960	
May	49,703.00	5,140	
June	48,813.00	5,300	
July	55,142.00	5,621	
August	59,119.00	6,002	
September	55,257.00	5,780	
October	50,900.00	5,341	
November	54,054.00	5,460	
December	50,998.00	5,400	
Total			

B. Using the weighted check average calculated in part A, determine Victor's projected sales assuming a 5 percent increase in guest counts. (Spreadsheet hint: Use the ROUND function to zero decimal places in the Guest Count Forecast column, cells C23:C34. Use the SUM function for the total, cell C35. Otherwise, your answers will not be correct.)

Month	Guest Count Last Year	Guest Count Forecast	Weighted Check Average	Projected Sales
January	4,800			
February	5,120			
March	5,006			
April	4,960			
May	5,140			
June	5,300			
July	5,621			
August	6,002			
September	5,780			
October	5,341			
November	5,460			
December	5,400			
Total				

5. Donna Berger is a hotel food and beverage director at a 500-room hotel. Donna knows that as the number of rooms sold in the hotel increases, the number of guests she serves for breakfast increases also. Based on historical records, Donna will serve breakfast to 55 percent of the hotel's registered guests. Help Donna plan for the number of breakfasts she will serve by completing the following chart:

Number of Guests in Hotel	Historical % of Guests Eating Breakfast	Estimated Number of Guests to Be Served
100	55	
175	55	
225	55	
275	55	
325	55	
375	55	
425	55	
475	55	
500	55	

What information will Donna need to determine the historical percentage of guests who eat breakfast?

6. Amy Pelletier operates Hall's House, an upscale restaurant with a $30.00 check average in mid-town Manhattan. Her clientele consists of business persons and tourists visiting the city. Based on the historical sales records she keeps, Amy believes her business will achieve a food sales increase next year of 4 percent per month for each of the first six months of the year. She feels this increase will be the result of increases in guest counts (not check average).

At mid-year (July 1), Amy intends to increase her menu prices (and thus, her check average) by 2 percent. She feels that although these price increases could result in a slight, short-term reduction in her guest counts, the restaurant's guest counts will still increase 3 percent for the last six months of the year.

Taking into account her guest count growth estimates and mid-year price increases, Amy would like to estimate her predicted year-end food revenues. Prepare the revenue estimates for Hall's House. (Spreadsheet hint: Use the ROUND function to zero decimal places in the Guest Count Forecast columns, cells D5 thru D10 (D5:D10) and D15 thru D20 (D15:D20). Use the SUM function for the totals, cells D11 and D21. Otherwise, your answers will not be correct.)

Months January Through June					
Month	Guest Count Last Year	Guest Count % Increase Estimate	Guest Count Forecast	Original Check Average	Revenue Forecast
January	6,270				
February	6,798				
March	6,336				
April	6,400				
May	6,930				
June	6,864				
6-Month Total					

Months July Through December					
Month	Guest Count Last Year	Guest Count % Increase Estimate	Guest Count Forecast	New Check Average	Revenue Forecast
July	6,845				
August	6,430				
September	6,283				
October	6,402				
November	6,938				
December	7,128				
6-Month Total					

7. Raktida is the manger of a popular Italian Restaurant on Mott Street, and she is trying to predict guest counts for the first week of November so that she can estimate an accurate number of servers to schedule. Business is very good, but her sales history from last month indicates that fewer guests are served during the first few days of the week compared to last year, whereas more guests per day are served in the later part of the week. Raktida has entered the guest counts from last year and the estimated percentage change in guest counts for this year in the chart below. Because good service is so important to her, she wants to ensure that enough servers are scheduled to work each day. One server can provide excellent service to 50 guests. Help Raktida calculate how many servers to schedule each day by completing the following chart. Note: Raktida always rounds the number of servers required **up** to the next whole number to ensure the best service possible for her guests! (Spreadsheet hint: Use ROUNDUP to 0

Raktida's Guest Forecast and Server Scheduling Workheet for the First Week of November				
	Guest Count Last Year	Estimated Change This Year	Estimate Guest Count This Year	Number of Servers Needed This Year
Sunday	625	−5%		
Monday	750	−5%		
Tuesday	825	0		
Wednesday	850	5%		
Thursday	775	5%		
Friday	1250	10%		
Saturday	1400	10%		

decimal places in the Estimated Guest Count This Year column and in the Number of Servers Needed This Year columns.)

How would Raktida's server scheduling efforts this year be affected if last year she had recorded only her weekly (not daily) guest counts?

8. Sales forecasts are important because knowing how many people you will serve is important. What are three specific problems that will occur when managers *underestimate* the number of guests they will serve on a given day? What are three specific difficulties that will likely result if managers *overestimate* the number they will serve?

Chapter 3

MANAGING THE COST OF FOOD

OVERVIEW

In Part One of this chapter, you will learn the professional techniques and methods used to effectively purchase food products. In Part Two, you will learn how to receive and store food products. You will also master the formulas used to compute the true cost of the food you provide your guests, as well as a process for estimating the value of food you have used on a daily or weekly basis, by applying the food cost percentage method, which is the standard in the hospitality industry.

Chapter Outline

At the conclusion of this chapter, you will be able to:

- Use sales histories and standardized recipes to determine the amount of food products to buy in anticipation of forecasted sales.
- Purchase, receive, and store food products in a cost-effective manner.
- Compute the cost of food sold and food cost percentage.

PART ONE

MENU ITEM FORECASTING

*W*hen they get hungry, many potential guests ask the question, "What do you feel like eating?" For many, the answer is "a meal prepared away from home!" Currently the U.S. Bureau of Labor Statistics consumer expenditure survey reports that sales of food consumed away from home exceed 48 percent of total food purchases and are growing by more than 5 percent per year. According to the National Restaurant Association's current forecasts, continued economic growth, gains in consumers' real disposable income, and changes in the lifestyles of today's busy American families are all spurring the sustained rise in the number of meals served away from home. This is good news for your career as a hospitality manager.

All this growth, activity, and consumer demand, however, will also create challenges for you. Consider the situation you would encounter if you used sales histories (Chapter 2) to project 300 guests for lunch today at the restaurant you own or manage. Your restaurant serves only three entrée items: roast chicken, roast pork, and roast beef. The question you face is this: "How many servings of each item should we produce so that we do not run out of any one item?"

If you were to run out of one of your three menu items, guests who wanted that item would undoubtedly become upset. They might even leave your restaurant (and perhaps take with them dining companions who would have ordered the other items you had plenty of!). Producing too much of any one item would, on the other hand, result in unsold items that could cause costs to rise to unacceptable levels unless these items could be sold for their full price at a later time.

Clearly, in this situation, it would be unwise to produce 300 portions of each item. Although you would never run out of any one item (each of your 300 estimated guests could order the same item and you would still have produced enough), you would also have 600 carryovers (leftovers) at the end of your lunch period. What you would really like to do, of course, is instruct your staff to make the "right" amount of each menu item. The right amount would be the number of servings that minimizes your chances of running out of an item before lunch is over as well as your chance of having excessive carryovers.

Just as estimating the number of guests who will arrive at your restaurant depends upon an accurate forecast of guest counts, the answer to the question of how

■ FIGURE 3.1 Menu Item Sales History

Date: 1/1–1/5				Menu Items Sold			
Menu Item	Mon	Tues	Wed	Thurs	Fri	Total	Week's Average
Roast Chicken	70	72	61	85	77	365	73
Roast Pork	110	108	144	109	102	573	115
Roast Beef	100	140	95	121	106	562	112
Total	280	320	300	315	285	1,500	300

many servings of roast chicken, pork, and beef you should prepare lies in accurate menu forecasting.

Let us return to the example cited previously. This time, however, assume that you were wise enough to have recorded last week's menu item sales on a form similar to the one presented in Figure 3.1.

An estimate of 300 guests for next Monday makes sense because the weekly sales total last week of 1,500 guests served averages 300 guests per day (1,500/5 days = 300/day). You also know that on an average day, you sold 73 roast chicken (365 sold/5 days = 73/day), 115 roast pork (573 sold/5 days = 115/day), and 112 roast beef (562 sold/5 days = 112/day).

Once you know the average number of people selecting a given menu item, and you know the total number of guests who made the selections, you can compute the **popularity index**, which is defined as the percentage of total guests choosing a given menu item from a list of menu alternatives. In this example, you can improve your "guess" about the quantity of each item to prepare if you use the sales history to help guide your decision. If you assume that future guests will select menu items much as past guests have done, given that the list of menu items remains the same, that information can be used to improve your predictions with the following formula:

$$\text{Popularity Index} = \frac{\text{Total Number of a Specific Menu Item Sold}}{\text{Total Number of All Menu Items Sold}}$$

In this example, the popularity index for roast chicken last week was 24.3 percent (365 roast chicken sold/1,500 total guests = 0.243, or 24.3 percent). Similarly, 38.2 percent (573 roast pork sold/1,500 total guests = 38.20 percent) preferred roast pork, whereas 37.50 percent (562 roast beef sold/1,500 total guests = 37.50 percent) selected roast beef.

If you know, even in a general way, what you can expect your guests to select, you are better prepared to make good decisions about the quantity of each item that should be produced. In this example, Figure 3.2 illustrates your best guess of what your 300 guests are likely to order when they arrive.

■ **FIGURE 3.2** Forecasting Item Sales

Menu Item	Guest Forecast	Popularity Index	Predicted Number to Be Sold
Roast Chicken	300	0.243	73
Roast Pork	300	0.382	115
Roast Beef	300	0.375	112
Total			300

The basic formula for individual menu item forecasting, based on an item's individual sales history, is as follows:

$$\text{Number of Guests Expected} \times \text{Item Popularity Index} = \text{Predicted Number of That Item to Be Sold}$$

The **predicted number to be sold** is simply the quantity of a specific menu item likely to be sold given an estimate of the total number of guests expected.

Once you know what your guests are likely to select, you can determine how many of each menu item your production staff should be instructed to prepare. Foodservice managers face a great deal of uncertainty when attempting to estimate the number of guests who will arrive on a given day because a variety of factors influence that number. Among these are:

1. Competition
2. Weather
3. Special events in your area
4. Holidays
5. Facility occupancy (in hospitals, dormitories, hotels, and the like) and/or the availability of parking (in selected situations such as shopping malls and strip shopping centers)
6. Your own advertising and promotional offers
7. Your competitor's advertising and promotional offerings
8. Quality of service
9. Changes in operating hours
10. Operational consistency

These factors, as well as other situations that affect sales volume, can make accurate guest count prediction very challenging.

In addition, remember that sales histories track only the general trends of an operation. They are not able to estimate precisely the number of guests who may arrive on any given day. Sales histories, then, are a guide to what can be expected. In our example, last week's guest counts range from a low of 280 (Monday) to a high of 320 (Tuesday). In addition, the percentage of people selecting each menu item changes somewhat on a daily basis. As a professional foodservice manager, you must take into account possible increases or decreases in guest count and possible fluctuations in your predicted number-to-be-sold computations when planning how many of each menu item you should prepare.

In Chapter 2, we examined the concept of sales forecasting. Forecasting can involve estimating the number of guests you expect, the dollar amount of sales you expect, or even what guests may want to purchase. This forecasting is crucial if you are to effectively manage your food expenses. In addition, consistency in food production and guest service will positively influence your operation's overall financial success.

STANDARDIZED RECIPES

Although it is the menu that determines what is to be sold and at what price, the **standardized recipe** controls both the quantity and the quality of what your kitchen will produce. A standardized recipe details the procedures to be used in preparing and serving each of your menu items. The standardized recipe ensures that each time guests order an item from your menu they receive exactly what you intended them to receive.

Critical factors in a standardized recipe, such as cooking times and serving size, must remain constant so the menu items produced are always consistent. Guests expect to get what they pay for. The standardized recipe helps you make sure that they do. Inconsistency is the enemy of any quality foodservice operation. It will make little difference to the unhappy guest, for instance, if you tell him or her that although the menu item he or she purchased today is not up to your normal standard, it will be tomorrow, or it was the last time the guest visited your operation.

Good standardized recipes contain the following information:

1. Menu item name
2. Total yield (number of servings)
3. Portion size
4. Ingredient list
5. Preparation/method section
6. Cooking time and temperature
7. Special instructions, if necessary
8. Recipe cost (optional)*

*This information is optional. If the recipe cost is *not* included in the standardized recipe, a standardized cost sheet must be developed for each recipe item (see Chapter 5).

■ **FIGURE 3.3** Standardized Recipe

Roast Chicken

Special Instructions: Serve with _____   Recipe Yield: 48

Crabapple Garnish (see Crabapple Garnish) _____   Portion Size: $^1/_4$ chicken

Standardized Recipe). _____   Portion Cost: See cost sheet

Serve on 10-in. plate. _____

Ingredients	Amount	Method
Chicken Quarters (twelve 3–3$^1/_2$-lb. chickens)	48 ea.	Step 1. Wash chicken; check for pinfeathers; tray on 24 in. × 20 in. baking pans.
Butter (melted)	1 lb. 4 oz.	Step 2. Clarify butter; brush liberally on chicken quarters; combine all seasonings; mix well; sprinkle all over chicken quarters.
Salt	$^1/_4$ C	
Pepper	2 T	
Paprika	3 T	
Poultry Seasoning	2 t	
Ginger	1$^1/_2$ t	
Garlic Powder	1 T	Step 3. Roast at 325°F in oven for 2$^1/_2$ hours, to an internal temperature of at least 165°F.

Figure 3.3 shows a standardized recipe for roast chicken. If this standardized recipe represents the quality and quantity management wishes its guests to have and if it is followed carefully each time, then guests will indeed receive the value management intended.

Interestingly, despite their tremendous advantages, some managers refuse to take the time to develop standardized recipes. The excuses used are many, but the following list contains arguments often used against standardized recipes:

1. They take too long to use.
2. My employees don't need recipes; they know how we do things here.
3. My chef refuses to reveal his or her secrets.
4. They take too long to write up.
5. We tried them but lost some, so we stopped using them.
6. They are too hard to read, or many of my employees cannot read English.

Of the preceding arguments, only the last one, an inability to read English, has any validity. Even in that case, the effective operator should have recipes printed in the language of his or her production employees. Standardized recipes have far more advantages than disadvantages. Reasons for incorporating a system of standardized recipes include the following:

1. Accurate purchasing is impossible without the existence and use of standardized recipes.

2. Dietary concerns require some foodservice operators to know the exact ingredients and the correct amount of nutrients in each serving of a menu item.

3. Accuracy in menu laws require that foodservice operators be able to tell guests about the type and amount of ingredients in their recipes.

4. Accurate recipe costing and menu pricing is impossible without standardized recipes.

5. Matching food used to cash sales is impossible to do without standardized recipes.

6. New employees can be better trained with standardized recipes.

7. The computerization of a foodservice operation is impossible unless the elements of standardized recipes are in place; thus, the advantages of advanced technological tools available to the operation are restricted or even eliminated.

Standardized recipes are the cornerstone of any serious effort to produce consistent, high-quality food products at an established cost. Without them, cost control efforts become nothing more than raising selling prices, reducing portion sizes, or lessening quality. Any recipe can be standardized. The process can sometimes be complicated, however, especially in the areas of baking and sauce production. It is always best to begin with a recipe of proven quality. Frequently, you may have a recipe designed for 10 servings, but you want to expand it to serve 100 people. In cases like this, it may not be possible to simply multiply the amount of each ingredient by 10. A great deal has been written regarding various techniques used to expand recipes. Computer software designed for that purpose is also now on the market. As a general rule, however, any item that can be produced in quantity can be standardized in recipe form and can be adjusted, up or down, in quantity.

When adjusting recipes, it is important that measurement standards be consistent. Weighing with a pound or an ounce scale is the most accurate method of measuring many ingredients. The food item to be measured must be **recipe-ready**. That is, it must be cleaned, trimmed, cooked, and generally completed, save for its addition to the recipe. For liquid items, measurement of volume (i.e., cup, quart, or gallon, etc.) may be preferred. Some operators like to weigh all ingredients, even liquids, for improved accuracy.

When adjusting recipes for quantity (total yield), two general methods may be employed:

1. Factor method

2. Percentage technique

■ FACTOR METHOD

When using the factor method, you utilize the following formula to arrive at a recipe conversion factor:

$$\frac{\text{Yield Desired}}{\text{Current Yield}} = \text{Conversion Factor}$$

If, for example, our current recipe makes 50 portions, and the number of portions we wish to make is 125, the formula would be as follows:

$$\frac{125}{50} = 2.5$$

Thus, 2.5 would be the conversion factor. To produce 125 portions, we would multiply each ingredient in the recipe by 2.5 to arrive at the required amount of that ingredient. Figure 3.4 illustrates the use of this method for a three-ingredient recipe.

■ PERCENTAGE METHOD

The percentage method deals with recipe weight rather than with a conversion factor. It is sometimes more accurate than using a conversion factor alone. Essentially, the percentage method involves weighing all ingredients and then computing the percentage weight of each recipe ingredient in relation to the total weight of all ingredients.

To facilitate the computation, many operators convert pounds to ounces prior to making their percentage calculations. These are converted back to standard pounds and ounces when the conversion is completed. To illustrate the use of the percentage method, assume that you have a recipe with a total weight of 10 pounds and 8 ounces, or 168 ounces. If the portion size is 4 ounces, the total recipe yield would be 168/4, or 42, servings. If you want your kitchen to prepare 75 servings, you would need to supply it with a standardized recipe consisting of the following total recipe weight:

■ **FIGURE 3.4** Factor Method

Ingredient	Original Amount	Conversion Factor	New Amount
A	4 lb.	2.5	10 lb.
B	1 qt.	2.5	$2^{1}/_{2}$ qt.
C	$1^{1}/_{2}$ T	2.5	$3^{3}/_{4}$ T

$$75 \text{ Servings} \times 4 \text{ oz./Serving} = 300 \text{ oz.}$$

You now have all the information necessary to use the percentage method of recipe conversion. Figure 3.5 details how the process would be accomplished. Note that percent of total is computed as ingredient weight/total recipe weight. Thus, for example, ingredient A's percent of total is computed as follows:

$$\frac{\text{Item A Ingredient Weight}}{\text{Total Recipe Weight}} = \% \text{ of Total}$$

or

$$\frac{104 \text{ oz.}}{168 \text{ oz.}} = 0.619 \ (61.9\%)$$

To compute the new recipe amount, we multiply the percent of total figure by the total amount required. For example, with ingredient A, the process is as follows:

$$\text{Item A \% of Total} \times \text{Total Amount Required} = \text{New Recipe Amount}$$

or

$$61.9\% \times 300 \text{ oz.} = 185.70 \text{ oz.}$$

The proper conversion of weights and measures is important in recipe expansion or reduction. The judgment of the recipe writer is critical, however, because such factors as cooking time, cooking temperature, and utensil selection may vary as recipe sizes are increased or decreased. In addition, some recipe ingredients, such as spices or flavorings, may not respond well to mathematical conversions. In the final analysis, it is your assessment of product taste that should ultimately determine ingredient ratios in standardized recipes. All recipes should be standardized and used as written. It is your responsibility to see that this is done.

■ **Figure 3.5 Percentage Method**

Ingredient	Original Amount	Ounces	% of Total	Total Amount Required	% of Total	New Recipe Amount
A	6 lb. 8 oz.	104	61.9%	300 oz.	61.9%	185.7 oz.
B	12 oz.	12	7.1	300 oz.	7.1	21.3 oz.
C	1 lb.	16	9.5	300 oz.	9.5	28.5 oz.
D	2 lb. 4 oz.	36	21.5	300 oz.	21.5	64.5 oz.
Total	10 lb. 8 oz.	168	100.0	300 oz.	100.0	300.0 oz.

INVENTORY CONTROL

*W*ith knowledge of what is likely to be purchased by your guests (sales forecast) and a firm idea of the ingredients necessary to produce these items (standardized recipes), you must make decisions about desired inventory levels. A desired inventory level is simply the answer to the question, "How much of each needed ingredient should I have on hand at any one time?"

It is clear that this question can only be properly answered if your sales forecast is of good quality and your standardized recipes are in place so you do not "forget" to stock a necessary recipe ingredient. Inventory management seeks to provide appropriate **working stock**, which is the amount of an ingredient you anticipate using before purchasing that item again, and a minimal **safety stock**, the extra amount of that ingredient you decide to keep on hand to meet higher than anticipated demand. Demand for a given menu item can fluctuate greatly between delivery periods, even when the delivery occurs daily. With too little inventory, you may run out of products and, therefore, reduce guest satisfaction. With too much inventory, waste, theft, and spoilage can become excessive. The ability to effectively manage the inventory process is one of the best skills a foodservice manager can acquire.

■ DETERMINING INVENTORY LEVELS

Inventory levels are determined by a variety of factors. Some of the most important ones are as follows:

1. Storage capacity
2. Item perishability
3. Vendor delivery schedule
4. Potential savings from increased purchase size
5. Operating calendar
6. Relative importance of stock outages
7. Value of inventory dollars to the operator

STORAGE CAPACITY

Inventory items must be purchased in quantities that can be adequately stored and secured. Many times, kitchens lack adequate storage facilities. This may mean more frequent deliveries and holding less of each product on hand than would otherwise be desired. When storage space is too great, however, the tendency by some managers is to fill the space. It is important that this not be done because increased inventory of items generally leads to greater spoilage and loss due to theft. Moreover, large quantities of goods on the shelf tend to send a message to employees that there is "plenty" of everything. This may result in the careless use of valuable and expensive products. It is also unwise to overload refrigerators or freezers. This can not only result in difficulty in finding items quickly but may also cause **carryovers** (items produced for a meal period but not sold) to be "lost" in the storage process.

ITEM PERISHABILITY

If all food products had the same **shelf life**—that is, the amount of time a food item retains its maximum freshness, flavor, and quality while in storage—you would have less difficulty in determining the quantity of each item you should keep on hand. The shelf life of food products, however, varies greatly.

Figure 3.6 lists the difference in shelf life of some common foodservice items when properly stored in a dry storeroom or refrigerator. Figure 3.7 lists the difference in shelf life of some common foodservice items when properly stored in a freezer.

■ **Figure 3.6** Shelf Life

Item	Storage	Shelf Life
Milk	Refrigerator	5–7 days
Butter	Refrigerator	14 days
Ground Beef	Refrigerator	2–3 days
Steaks (fresh)	Refrigerator	14 days
Bacon	Refrigerator	30 days
Canned Vegetables	Dry Storeroom	12 months
Flour	Dry Storeroom	3 months
Sugar	Dry Storeroom	3 months
Lettuce	Refrigerator	3–5 days
Tomatoes	Refrigerator	5–7 days
Potatoes	Dry Storeroom	14–21 days

■ **Figure 3.7** Recommended Refrigeration and Freezer Storage Period Maximums

Cold Storage Chart		
These short, but safe, time limits will help keep refrigerated food from spoiling or becoming dangerous to eat. Because freezing keeps food safe indefinitely, recommended storage times are for quality only.		
Product	Refrigerator (40°F, 4.5°C)	Freezer (0°F, –18°C)
Eggs		
Fresh, in shell	3 to 5 weeks	Do not freeze
Raw yolks & whites	2 to 4 days	1 year
Hard cooked	1 week	Does not freeze well
Liquid pasteurized eggs, egg substitutes		
Opened	3 days	Does not freeze well
Unopened	10 days	1 year
Mayonnaise		
Commercial, refrigerate after opening	2 months	Do not freeze
Frozen Dinners & Entrées		
Keep frozen until ready to heat	—	3 to 4 months
Deli & vacuum-packed products		
Store-prepared (or homemade) egg, chicken, ham, tuna, & macaroni salads	3 to 5 days	Does not freeze well
Hot dogs & luncheon meats		
Hot dogs		
Opened package	1 week	1 to 2 months
Unopened package	2 weeks	1 to 2 months
Luncheon meat		
Opened package	3 to 5 days	1 to 2 months
Unopened package	2 weeks	1 to 2 months
Bacon & Sausage		
Bacon	7 days	1 month
Sausage, raw—from chicken, turkey, pork, beef	1 to 2 days	1 to 2 months
Smoked breakfast links, patties	7 days	1 to 2 months
Hard sausage—pepperoni, jerky sticks	2 to 3 weeks	1 to 2 months
Summer sausage labeled "Keep Refrigerated"		
Opened	3 weeks	1 to 2 months
Unopened	3 months	1 to 2 months
Ham, Corned Beef		
Corned beef, in pouch with pickling juices	5 to 7 days	Drained, 1 month

Product	Refrigerator (40°F, 4.5°C)	Freezer (0°F, −18°C)
Ham, canned		
labeled "Keep Refrigerated"		
Opened	3 to 5 days	1 to 2 months
Unopened	6 to 9 months	Do not freeze
Ham, fully cooked		
vacuum sealed at plant, undated, unopened	2 weeks	1 to 2 months
Ham, fully cooked		
vacuum sealed at plant, dated, unopened	"Use-By" date on package	1 to 2 months
Ham, fully cooked		
Whole	7 days	1 to 2 months
Half	3 to 5 days	1 to 2 months
Slices	3 to 4 days	1 to 2 months
Hamburger, ground, & stew meat		
Hamburger & stew meat	1 to 2 days	3 to 4 months
Ground turkey, veal, pork, lamb, & mixtures of them	1 to 2 days	3 to 4 months
Fresh beef, veal, lamb, pork		
Steaks	3 to 5 days	6 to 12 months
Chops	3 to 5 days	4 to 6 months
Roasts	3 to 5 days	4 to 12 months
Variety meats—tongue, liver, heart, kidneys, chitterlings	1 to 2 days	3 to 4 months
Pre-stuffed, uncooked pork chops, lamb chops, or chicken breasts stuffed with dressing	1 day	Does not freeze well
Soups & stews		
Vegetable or meat added	3 to 4 days	2 to 3 months
Cooked meat leftovers		
Cooked meat & meat casseroles	3 to 4 days	2 to 3 months
Gravy & meat broth	1 to 2 days	2 to 3 months
Fresh poultry		
Chicken or turkey, whole	1 to 2 days	1 year
Chicken or turkey, pieces	1 to 2 days	9 months
Giblets	1 to 2 days	3 to 4 months
Cooked poultry leftovers		
Fried chicken	3 to 4 days	4 months
Cooked poultry casseroles	3 to 4 days	4 to 6 months

(continued)

■ **Figure 3.7** Recommended Refrigeration and Freezer Storage Period Maximums (*continued*)

Product	Refrigerator (40°F, 4.5°C)	Freezer (0°F, –18°C)
Pieces, plain	3 to 4 days	4 months
Pieces covered with broth, gravy	1 to 2 days	6 months
Chicken nuggets, patties	1 to 2 days	1 to 3 months
Pizza, cooked	3 to 4 days	1 to 2 months
Stuffing, cooked	3 to 4 days	1 month

Because food items have varying shelf lives, you must balance the need for a particular product with the optimal shelf life of that product. Serving items that are "too old" is a sure way to incur guest complaints. In fact, one of the quickest ways to determine the overall effectiveness of a foodservice manager is to "walk the boxes." This means to take a tour of a facility's storage area. If many products, particularly in the refrigerated area, are moldy, soft, overripe, or rotten, it is a good indication of a foodservice operation that does not have a feel for proper inventory levels based on the shelf lives of the items kept in inventory. It is also a sign that sales forecasting methods either are not in place or are not working well.

VENDOR DELIVERY SCHEDULE

It is the fortunate foodservice operator who lives in a large city with many vendors, some of whom may offer the same service and all of whom would like to have the operator's business. In many cases, however, you will not have the luxury of daily delivery. Your operation may be too small to warrant such frequent stops by a vendor, or the operation may be in such a remote location that daily delivery is simply not possible. Consider, for a moment, the difficulty you would face if you were the manager of a foodservice operation located on an offshore oil rig. Clearly, in a case like that, a vendor willing to provide daily doughnut delivery is going to be hard to find! In all cases, it is important to remember that the cost to the vendor for frequent deliveries will be reflected in the cost of the goods to you.

POTENTIAL SAVINGS FROM INCREASED PURCHASE SIZE

Sometimes you will find that you can realize substantial savings by purchasing needed items in large quantities. This certainly makes sense if the total savings actually outweigh the added costs of receiving and storing the larger quantity.

Remember, however, that there are costs associated with extraordinarily large purchases. These may include storage costs, spoilage, deterioration, insect or rodent infestation, or theft. As a general rule, you should determine your ideal product inventory levels and then maintain your stock within that needs range. Only when the advantages of placing an extraordinarily large order are very clear should such a purchase be undertaken.

OPERATING CALENDAR

When an operation is involved in serving meals seven days a week to a relatively stable number of guests, the operating calendar makes little difference to inventory level decision making. If, however, the operation opens on Monday and closes on Friday for two days, as is the case in many school foodservice accounts, the operating calendar plays a large part in determining desired inventory levels. In general, it can be said that an operator who is closing down either for a weekend or for a season (as in the operation of a summer camp or seasonal hotel) should attempt to greatly reduce overall inventory levels as the closing period approaches.

RELATIVE IMPORTANCE OF STOCK OUTAGES

In many foodservice operations, not having enough of a single food ingredient or menu item is simply not that important. In other operations, the shortage of even one menu item might spell disaster. For example, it may be all right for the local French restaurant to run out of one of the specials on Saturday night, but it is not difficult to imagine the problem of the McDonald's restaurant manager who runs out of French fried potatoes on that same Saturday night!

For the small operator, a mistake in the inventory level of a minor ingredient that results in an outage can often be corrected by a quick run to the grocery store. For the larger facility, such an outage may well represent a substantial loss of sales or guest goodwill. In the restaurant industry, when an item is no longer available on the menu, you "86" the item, a reference to restaurant slang originating in the early 1920s (86 rhymed with "nix," a Cockney term meaning "to eliminate"). If you, as a manager, "86" too many items on any given night, the reputation of your restaurant as well as your ability to manage it will suffer.

A strong awareness and knowledge of how critical this outage factor is will help you determine the appropriate inventory level. A word of caution is, however, necessary. The foodservice operator who is determined never to run out of anything must be careful not to set inventory levels so high as to actually end up costing the operation more than if realistic levels were maintained.

VALUE OF INVENTORY DOLLARS TO THE OPERATOR

In some cases, operators elect to remove dollars from their bank accounts and convert them to product inventory. When this is done, the operator is making the decision to value product more than dollars. When it is expected that the value of the inventory will rise faster than the value of the banked dollar, this is a good strategy. All too often, however, operators overbuy or "stockpile" inventory, causing too many dollars to be tied up in non–interest-bearing food products. When this is done, managers incur opportunity costs. An **opportunity cost** is the cost of forgoing the next best alternative when making a decision. For example, suppose you have two choices, A and B, both having potential benefits or returns for you. If you choose A, then you lose the potential benefits from choosing B (opportunity cost). In other words, you could choose to use your money to buy food inventory that will sit in your storeroom until it is sold, or you could choose not to stockpile food inventory and invest the money. If you stockpile the inventory, then the opportunity cost is the amount of money you would have made if you had invested the money rather than held the excess inventory.

If the dollars used to purchase inventory must be borrowed from the bank, rather than being available from operating revenue, an even greater cost to carry the inventory is incurred because interest must be paid on the borrowed funds. In addition, a foodservice company of many units that invests too much of its money in inventory may find that funds for acquisition, renovation, or marketing are not readily available. In contrast, a state institution that is given its entire annual budget at the start of its **fiscal year** (a year that is 12 months long but may not follow the calendar year) may find it advantageous to use its purchasing power to acquire large amounts of inventory at the beginning of the year and at very low prices.

■ SETTING THE PURCHASE POINT

A *purchase point,* as it relates to inventory levels, is that point in time when an item should be reordered. This point is typically designated by one of two methods:

1. As needed (just in time)
2. Par level

AS NEEDED

When you elect to use the **as-needed,** or **just-in-time,** method of determining inventory level, you are basically purchasing food based on your prediction of unit sales and the sum of the ingredients (from standardized recipes) necessary to produce those sales. Then, no more than the absolute minimum of needed inventory level is secured from the vendor. When this system is used, the buyer compiles a list of needed ingredients and submits it to management for approval to purchase. For example, in a hotel foodservice operation, the demand for 500 servings of a raspberries and cream torte dessert, to be served to a group in the hotel next week, would cause the responsible person to check the standardized recipe for this item and, thus, determine the amount of raspberries that should be ordered. Then that amount, and no more, would be ordered from the vendor.

PAR LEVEL

Foodservice operators may set predetermined purchase points, called **par levels,** for some items. In the case of the raspberries and cream torte dessert referred to previously, it is likely that the torte will require vanilla extract. It does not make sense, however, to expect your food production manager to order vanilla extract by the tablespoon! In fact, you are likely to find that you are restricted in the quantity you could buy due to the vendor's delivery minimum, namely, bottle or case, or the manufacturer's packaging methods. In cases such as this, or when demand for a product is relatively constant, you may decide to set needed inventory levels for some items by determining purchase points based on appropriate par levels.

When determining par levels, you must establish both minimum and maximum amounts required. Many foodservice managers establish a minimum par level by computing working stock and then adding 25 to 50 percent more for safety stock. Then, an appropriate purchase point, or point at which additional stock is purchased, is determined. If, for example, you have decided that the inventory level for coffee should be based on a par system, the decision may be made that the minimum (given your usage) amount that should be on hand at all times is four cases. This would be the minimum par level. Assume that you set the maximum par level at ten cases. Although the inventory level in this situation would vary from a low of four cases to a high of ten cases, you would be assured that you would never have too little or too much of this particular menu item.

If cases of coffee were to be ordered under this system, you would always attempt to keep the number of cases between the minimum par level (four cases) and the maximum par level (ten cases). The purchase point in this example might be six cases; that is, when your operation had six cases of coffee on hand, an order would be placed with the coffee vendor. The intention would be to get the total stock up to ten cases before your supply got below four cases. Delivery might take one or two days, so six cases might be an appropriate purchase point.

Whether you use an as-needed, a par-level, or, as in the case of most operators, a combination purchase point, each ingredient or menu item should have a management-designated inventory level. As a rule, highly perishable items should be ordered on an as-needed basis, whereas items with a longer shelf life can often have their inventory levels set using a par-level system. The answer to the question "How much of each ingredient should I have on hand at any point in time?" must come from you, and compliance with your decision should be monitored on a regular basis.

PURCHASING

Regardless of the method used to determine inventory levels, once the quantity needed on hand has been determined, you must turn your attention to the extremely important area of purchasing. Purchasing is essentially a matter of determining the following:

1. What should be purchased?
2. What is the best price to pay?
3. How can a steady supply be ensured?

■ WHAT SHOULD BE PURCHASED?

Just as it is not possible to determine inventory levels or items to be purchased without standardized recipes, it is not possible to manage costs where purchasing is concerned without the use of product specifications, or "specs." A **product specification** is simply a detailed description of an ingredient or menu item. A spec is a way for you to communicate in a very precise way with a vendor so that your operation receives the exact item requested every time. A foodservice specification generally consists of the following information:

1. Product name or specification number
2. Pricing unit
3. Standard or grade
4. Weight range/size
5. Processing and/or packaging
6. Container size
7. Intended use
8. Other information such as product yield

It is very important to note that the product specification determines neither the "best" product to buy nor the product that costs the least. It is the product that you have determined to be the *most appropriate product* for its intended use in terms of both quality and cost.

A product specification that is written too loosely can be a problem because the needed level of item quality may not be delivered. On the other hand, if your product specifications are too tight (that is, overly and unnecessarily specific), too few vendors may be able to supply the product, resulting in your paying excessively high costs for that item.

The necessity of specifications will become clear if we listen in on a telephone call made by Louie, a manager who is about to place an order for bread with a new vendor, Sam's Uptown Bakery:

Louie: "Sam, I need bread for sandwiches."

Sam: "Louie, you know I have the best bread in town!"

Louie: "Well, send me 50 loaves as soon as possible."

Sam: "No problem, Louie. We will deliver this afternoon!"

Little does Louie know that Sam's definition of bread for sandwiches is quite different from his own. Louie is expecting $1\frac{1}{4}$-pound, white, split, thin-sliced, 45-slices-to-the-bag bread. From Sam's exotic shop, however, he may well receive a 2-pound, thick-sliced, sesame seed-topped Italian loaf. Thus, even for a product as common as bread, a product specification must be developed. Fortunately, the process is relatively simple because it depends mainly on your own view of appropriate product quality.

Figure 3.8 demonstrates a form used to develop product specifications. Each menu item or ingredient should have its own spec. In fact, management should make it a habit to ensure that only telephone conversations such as the following take place:

Louie: "Sam, I need fifty loaves of my spec #617 as soon as possible."

Sam: "Spec #617? Let's see, I've got it right here. That's your white bread for sandwiches spec, right?"

Louie: "That's right, Sam."

Sam: "No problem, Louie. We will deliver this afternoon!"

■ Figure 3.8 Product Specification

Product Name:	Bacon, Sliced	**Spec #: 117**
Pricing Unit:	lb.	
Standard/Grade:	Select No. 1	
	Moderately thick slice	
	Oscar Mayer item 2040 or equal	
Weight Range:	14–16 slices per pound	
Packaging:	2/10 lb. Cryovac packed	
Container Size:	Not to exceed 20 lb.	
Intended Use:	Bacon, lettuce, and tomato sandwiches	
Other Information:	Flat packed on oven-proofed paper	
	Never frozen	
Product Yield:	60% Yield	

PRODUCT NAME

This may seem self-explanatory, but, in reality, it is not. Mangos are a fruit to those in the southwestern United States but may mean a bell pepper to those in the Midwest. Bell peppers do not just come in green, their most common color, but can also be purchased in yellow and red forms. Thus, the product name must be specific enough to clearly and precisely identify the item you wish to buy.

Many canned hams are pear shaped, but a Pullman canned ham is square. You may be requesting 100 percent maple syrup when you place a syrup order, but your vendor could assume "maple-flavored" syrup is the item you desire. Purchasing food becomes even more difficult when you realize that, especially in the area of meats and seafood, different regions in the country may have different names for the same product.

When developing the product specification, you may find it helpful to assign a number to the item as well as its name. This can be useful when, for example, many forms of the same ingredient or menu item may be purchased. A deli-restaurant may use 10 to 20 different types of bread, depending on the intended use of the bread; thus, in our product specification example, bacon, which this operation uses in many forms, has both a name and a number assigned to the specification. The same may be true with a number of items, such as cheese, which may come in a brick, sliced, shredded, or in a variety of other forms as well as several types (Colby, cheddar, Swiss, etc.).

PRICING UNIT

A pricing unit may be established in terms of pounds, quarts, gallons, cases, or any other commonly used unit. Parsley, for example, is typically sold in the United States by the bunch. Thus, it is also priced by the bunch. How much is a bunch? You must know. Grapes are sold by the "lug." Unless you are familiar with the term, you may not be able to buy that product in an effective way. Again, knowledge of the pricing unit, whether it is a gallon, pound, case, bunch, or lug, is critical when developing a product specification. Figure 3.9 lists some of the more common pricing units for produce in the United States. You should insist that all your vendors supply you with definitions of each pricing unit upon which they base their selling prices.

■ **Figure 3.9** Selected Producer Container Net Weights

Items Purchased	Container	Approximate Net Weight (lb.)
Apples	Cartons, tray pack	40–45
Asparagus	Pyramid crates, loose pack	32
Beets, bunched	$1/2$ crate, 2 dozen bunches	36–40
Cabbage, green	Flat crates ($1^1/3$ bushels)	50–60
Cantaloupe	$1/2$ wirebound crate	38–41
Corn, sweet	Cartons, packed 5 dozen ears	50
Cucumbers, field grown	Bushel cartons	47–55
Grapefruit, FL	$4/5$-bushel cartons and wirebound crates	$42^1/2$
Grapes, table	Lugs and cartons, plain pack	23–24
Lettuce, loose leaf	$4/5$-bushel crates	8–10
Limes	Pony cartons	10
Onions, green	$4/5$-bushel crates (36 bunches)	11
Oranges, FL	$4/5$-bushel cartons	45
Parsley	Cartons, wax treated, 5 dozen bunches	21
Peaches	2-layer cartons and lugs, tray pack	22
Shallots	Bags	5
Squash	1-layer flats, place pack	16
Strawberries, CA	12 one-pint trays	11–14
Tangerines	$4/5$-bushel cartons	$47^1/2$
Tomatoes, pink and ripe	3-layer lugs and cartons, place pack	24–33

STANDARD OR GRADE

Many food items are sold with varying degrees of quality or desirability. Because that is true, the U.S. Department of Agriculture, the Bureau of Fisheries, and the Food and Drug Administration have developed standards for many food items. In addition, grading programs are in place for many commonly used foodservice items. Trade groups such as the National Association of Meat Purveyors publish item descriptions for many of these products. Consumers also are aware of many of these distinctions. Prime beef, in the consumer's mind, may be superior to choice beef. In a similar manner, you may wish to purchase and serve Coca-Cola rather than a lower-cost generic fountain soda. When developing a specification, a specific brand name or product source (A-1 Steak Sauce, Maine lobster) may be included in this section. You should be cautious, however, about specifying a brand name unless it is actually critical to your operation. Unless several vendors are able to supply you with the product you need, the price you may pay to the vendor who does have that item may be too high.

WEIGHT RANGE/SIZE

Weight range or size is important when referring to meats, fish, poultry, and some vegetables. In our standardized recipe example of roast chicken, the quarters were to have come from chickens in the 3- to $3^1/_2$-pound range. This will make them very different than if they came from chickens in the 4- to $4^1/_2$ -pound range. In the case of products requiring specific trim or maximum fat covering, that should be designated also, such as 10-ounce strip steak, maximum tail 1 inch, fat covering 1/2 inch.

Four-ounce hamburger patties, 16-ounce T-bones, and $^1/_4$-pound hot dogs are additional examples of items of the type that require an exact size, not a weight range. *Count,* in the hospitality industry, is a term that is used to designate size. For example, 16- to 20-count shrimp refers to the fact that, for this size shrimp, 16 to 20 of the individual shrimp would be required to make 1 pound. In a like manner, 30- to 40-count shrimp means that it takes 30 to 40 of this size shrimp to make a pound. Many fruits and vegetables are also sold by count. For example, 48-count avocados mean that 48 individual avocados will fit in a standard case. In general, the larger the count, the smaller the size of the individual food items.

PROCESSING AND/OR PACKAGING

Processing and packaging refers to the product's state when you buy it. Apples, for example, may be purchased fresh, canned, or frozen. Each form will carry a price appropriate for its processed or packaged state. It is important to note that the term "fresh" is one with varying degrees of meaning. Fish that has been frozen and then thawed should be identified as such. Packaging is also extremely important when determining product yield. For example, 3 pounds of canned corn will not yield the same number of 3-ounce servings as 3 pounds of fresh ear corn. Fresh fruits and vegetables may be of excellent quality and low in cost per pound, but the effective foodservice operator must consider actual usable product when computing the price

Green and Growing!

"Farm to Fork" is a term increasingly important to those in foodservice. It refers to the path food follows from those who grow or raise it to those who will prepare and serve it. Ideally, this path is short, to maximize freshness, minimize health risks, and be environmentally friendly. For that reason many foodservice operators prefer to seek out and buy locally grown foods whenever possible. In addition to their freshness, locally grown foods are good for the environment because less storing, shipping, and packaging results in less energy to transport and less solid waste from excessive packing materials. Reduced transportation and packaging costs often translate into lower prices charged to foodservice operators.

Locally grown and organic products also help support the same local economies from which many foodservice operations draw their customers. Buying locally is an option that all foodservice managers should thoroughly examine for its benefits to their communities and the environment, as well as the health of their customers and their own bottom lines!

per pound. Also, the labor cost of washing, trimming, and otherwise preparing fresh products must be considered when comparing their price to that of a canned or frozen product. The world's food supply is one of great variety and quality. Food can come packed in a large number of forms and styles, including slab packed, layered cell packed, fiberboard divided, shrink packed, individually wrapped, and bulk packed. Although it is beyond the scope of this text to detail all of the many varieties of food processing and packing styles, it is important for you to know about them. Your vendors will be pleased to explain to you all the types of item processing and packaging they offer.

CONTAINER SIZE

This term refers to the can size, number of cans per case, or weight of the container in which the product is delivered. Most operators know that a 50-pound bag of flour should contain 50 pounds of flour. Some may not be sure, however, what the appropriate weight for a "lug" of tomatoes would be (see Figure 3.9).

INTENDED USE

Different types of the same item are often used in the same foodservice operation but in a variety of ways. Consider, for example, the operator who uses strawberries in a variety of ways. Obviously, perfect, large berries are best for chocolate-dipped strawberries served on a buffet table. Less-than-perfect berries, however, may cost less and be a perfectly acceptable form for sliced strawberries on strawberry shortcake. Frozen berries may make a good choice for a baked strawberry pie and would be much more cost effective. Breads, milk products, apples, and other fruits are additional examples of foods that come in a variety of forms; the "best" form of a food product is not necessarily the most expensive.

OTHER INFORMATION SUCH AS PRODUCT YIELD

Additional information may be included in a specification if it helps the vendor understand exactly what you have in mind when your order is placed. An example is product yield. *Product yield* is simply the amount of product that you will have remaining after cooking, trimming, portioning, or cleaning. Product yield will help you and your vendor determine how much product you will have to purchase in order to have the desired product quantity after waste is removed. You will learn how to calculate product yield in Chapter 5.

■ WHAT IS THE BEST PRICE TO PAY?

Once purchase specifications have been developed and quantities to be purchased have been established, your next step is to determine how to buy these items at the best price. Some would say that determining the best price should be a simple matter of finding the vendor with the lowest-cost product and placing an order with that person. In fact, that is almost always a sure sign of a manager who lacks understanding of the way business, and vendors, operate. The **best price**, in fact, is more accurately stated as the lowest price that meets the long-term goals of both the foodservice operation and its vendor.

When you have a choice of vendors, each supplying the same product (your specification), it is possible to engage in comparison shopping. The vehicle used to do this is called the *bid sheet* (see Figure 3.10). The bid sheet includes vendor information, buyer information, item description, unit of bid, bid price, salesperson's signature, and date. It also includes the dates that the bid prices will be "fixed," which means the dates that the supplier agrees to keep the bid price in effect. Using our example in Figure 3.10, the bid sheet would be sent to all meat vendors each week on Friday to be returned Monday for the weekly bid prices. Then you would compare the item prices to see from which vendor you would buy.

After you have received bids from your suppliers, you can compare those bids on a *price comparison sheet* (Figure 3.11). A price comparison sheet typically has a place to list the category being bid, namely, produce, dairy products, meats, and so on; the name of the vendors available to bid; bid date; item description; unit of purchase; best bid price; best company quote; and last price paid. This information may then be used to select a vendor based on the best price. Once the best price is determined for each item, then a purchase order (discussed later in this chapter) using the best prices can be developed for each vendor.

Bid sheets and price comparison sheets may be used to determine the specific vendor who can supply the lowest price, but they do not give enough information to determine the best price. This makes sense when you realize that your own guests do not necessarily go to the lowest-priced restaurants for all of their meals. If they did, there would be no hope of success for the operator who tried to provide a better food product, in a better environment, with better service. In fact, most foodservice operators would resent guests who came into their operation and

■ **FIGURE 3.10** Bid Sheet

Vendor: _____   Buyer: _____

Vendor's Address: _____   Buyer's Address: _____

Vendor's Telephone #: _____   Buyer's Telephone #: _____

Vendor's Fax #: _____   Buyer's Fax #: _____

Vendor's E-Mail: _____   Buyer's E-Mail: _____

Item Description	Unit	Bid Price
109 Rib, 19–22#, Choice	Pound	
110 Rib, 16–19#, Choice	Pound	
112A Rib eye Lip on 9–11#, Choice	Pound	
120 Brisket, 10–12# Deckle off, Choice	Pound	
164 Steamship Round, 60#, Square bottom, Choice	Pound	
168 Inside Round, 17–20#, Choice	Pound	
184 Top Butt, 9–11#, Choice	Pound	
189A Tender, 5# Avg.	Pound	
193 Flank Steak, 2# Avg., Choice	Pound	
1184b Top Butt Steak, 8 oz., Choice	Pound	
1190a Tenderloin Steak, 8 oz., Choice	Pound	
109 Rib, 19–22#, Certified Angus Beef, Choice	Pound	
123 Short Ribs, 10#	Pound	
180 Strip, 10–12#, Choice	Pound	

Bid Prices Fixed From: _____ to _____
Salesperson Signature: _____   Date: _____

complained they could get the exact same item for a lower price at a competitor's restaurant.

It is a truism that any product can be sold a little cheaper if quality is allowed to vary. Even with the use of product specifications, vendor dependability, ease of order placement, ability to access important account information via the Internet, the quality of vendor service, accuracy in delivery, and payment terms can all be determining factors when attempting to determine the "best price" from a supplier.

In Figure 3.11, Bill's Produce has the lowest price for several items. Bill's Produce may be the preferred vendor for these items if price alone is the issue. If, however, Bill's Produce is frequently late in delivery, has questionable sanitary habits,

■ **FIGURE 3.11** Price Comparison Sheet

Vendors   Category: Produce
  A. Bill's Produce   Date Bid: 1/1
  B. Davis Foods
  C. Ready Boy

Price Comparison Sheet							
Item Description	Unit	A	B	C	Best Bid ($)	Best Company	Last Price Paid
Lettuce, Iceberg, 24 ct.	case	$ 9.70	$10.20	$ 9.95	$ 9.70	A	$ 9.50
Lettuce, Red Leaf, 24 ct.	case	10.50	10.25	10.75	10.25	B	10.10
Mushroom, Button, 10 lb.	bag	15.50	15.75	16.10	15.50	A	15.75
Mushroom, Portobello, 5 lb.	bag	19.00	19.80	18.90	18.90	C	19.00
Onion, White, Medium, 50 lb.	bag	20.25	20.00	20.50	20.00	B	19.80
Pepper, Green Bell, 85 ct.	case	28.90	29.50	30.10	28.90	A	27.00
Potato, Russet Idaho, 60 ct.	case	12.75	12.50	12.20	12.20	C	12.85

Reviewed By: M. Hayes

and is frequently short or unable to deliver the promised product, the lower price may be no bargain. Davis Foods, on the other hand, may have a reputation for quality products and service that make it the vendor of choice. Any foodservice operator who uses price as the *only* criterion when shopping will find it very difficult to develop any meaningful relationship with a supplier.

For the smaller operation, the manager may be interested in comparing the total price from each supplier rather than the price of individual items. That is, each ordering day, the manager would multiply the quantity of an item needed by the best price. An approach such as this when buying strictly from the price comparison sheet may result in orders too small to meet a supplier's **minimum order requirement**, that is, the smallest order that can be placed with a vendor who delivers. If the minimum order requirement cannot be met using the lowest prices, then the manager may have to choose the supplier with the next highest price to fill a complete order.

In some cases, the vendor to be used by the foodservice operator has been determined in advance. This is often true in a large corporate organization or in a franchise situation. Contracts to provide goods may be established by the central purchasing department of these organizations. When that happens, the designated vendor may have a national or a long-term contract to supply, at a predetermined price, items that meet the operation's specifications.

FUN ON THE WEB!

Houston, Texas, is home to one of the nation's largest foodservice suppliers. Sysco Foods, or one of its regional operational partners, delivers a wide array of foodservice products to virtually every part of the United States and, as a result, is often chosen to fill national food supplier contracts. An innovative company, Sysco was one of the first to utilize the Internet to simplify an operator's ordering processes. To learn more about Sysco and its product lines, go to www.sysco.com.

■ HOW CAN A STEADY SUPPLY BE ENSURED?

Unfortunately, very little has been written in the field of foodservice about managing costs through cooperation with vendors. Your food salesperson can be one of your most important allies in controlling costs. Operators who determine their supplier only on the basis of cost will find that they receive only the product they have purchased, whereas their competitors may be buying more than just food! Or, as one food salesperson said when asked why he should be selected as the primary food vendor, "With my products, you also get me!" And so it is; just as good foodservice operators know that guests respond to both products and personal service levels, so, too, do effective food suppliers. Ensuring a steady supply of quality products at a fair price is extremely important to the long-term success of a foodservice operator, yet many operators treat their suppliers as if they were the enemy. In fact, suppliers can be of immense value in ensuring a steady supply of quality products at a fair price if you remember the following points.

SUPPLIERS HAVE MANY PRICES, NOT JUST ONE

Unlike the restaurant business, which tends to hold its prices steady between menu reprints and generally charges the same price to all who come in the door, suppliers have a variety of prices based on the customer to whom they are quoting them. Therefore, when an operator gets a quote on a case of lettuce, the telephone conversation may sound like this:

Foodservice Manager:	"Hello, is this Ready Boy Produce?"
Ready Boy:	"Yes, how can I help you?"
Foodservice Operator:	"What is your price on lettuce today?"
Ready Boy:	"$28.50 per case."

This conversation should really be interpreted, as follows:

Foodservice Operator:	"Hello, is this Ready Boy produce?"
Ready Boy:	"Yes, how can I help you?"
Foodservice Operator:	"What is *my* price on lettuce today?"
Ready Boy:	"Based on our current relationship, *your* price is $28.50 per case."

The "current relationship" referred to in the above conversion will be based upon a variety of factors, including the total amount of food and other products you buy from the vendor and even the promptness with which you pay your bills!

SUPPLIERS REWARD VOLUME GUESTS

It is simply in the best interest of a supplier to give a better price to a high-volume customer. The cost to deliver a $1,000 food order is not that much different from the cost to deliver a $100 order. They both take one truck and one driver. Those operators who decide to concentrate their business in the hands of fewer suppliers will, as a general rule, pay a lower price.

CHERRY PICKERS ARE SERVICED LAST

Cherry pickers is the term used by suppliers to describe the customer who gets bids from multiple vendors and then buys only the items that each vendor has "on sale" or for the lowest price. If an operator buys only a vendor's "on sale" items, the vendor will usually respond by providing limited service. It is a natural reaction to the foodservice operator's failure to take into account varying service levels, long-term relationships, dependability, or any other vendor characteristic except cheapest price. It is important to remember, however, that a foodservice manager who meets minimum delivery requirements and buys regularly from the same vendor is not seen as a cherry picker just because he or she buys items from the vendor with the lowest price.

SLOW PAY MEANS HIGH PAY

Those operators who do not pay their bills in a timely manner may be surprised to know what their competitors are paying for similar products. In most cases, operators who are slow to pay will find that the vendor has decided to add the extra cost of carrying the "loan charges" related to their account to the price those operators pay for their products.

VENDORS CAN HELP REDUCE COSTS

Frequently vendors have a knowledge of the products they sell that exceeds that of the average foodservice operator. This skill can be used to help the competition, or it can be harnessed for your own good use. Vendors can be a great source of information related to new products, cooking techniques, menu trends, and alternative product usage.

■ ONE VENDOR VERSUS MANY VENDORS

Every operator is faced with the decision of whether to buy from one vendor or many vendors. In general, the more vendors there are, the more time must be spent in ordering, receiving, and paying invoices. Many operators, however, fear that if they give all their business to one supplier, their costs may rise because of a lack of competition. In reality, the likelihood of this occurring is extremely small. Just as foodservice operators are unlikely to take advantage of their best guests (and, in fact, would tend to offer additional services not available to the occasional guest) so, too, does the vendor tend to behave in a manner that is preferential to the operator who does most of his or her buying from that vendor. In fact, it makes good business sense for the vendor to do so.

Using one or perhaps two primary vendors tends to bring the average delivery size up and should result in lower per-item prices. On the other hand, giving one vendor all of the operation's business can be dangerous and costly if the items to be purchased vary widely in quality and price. Staples and nonperishables are best purchased in bulk from one vendor. Orders for meats, produce, and some bakery products are best split among several vendors, perhaps with a primary and a secondary vendor in each category so that you have a second alternative should the need arise. If you are using bid buying as a purchasing method, having three vendors is advisable so that you have an adequate choice of prices and services.

■ PURCHASING ETHICS

Purchasing food products is an area that can test the ethics of even the most conscientious manager. **Ethics** have been defined as the choices of proper conduct made by an individual in his or her relationships with others. Ethics come into play in purchasing products because of the tendency for some suppliers to seek an unfair advantage over the competition by providing "personal" favors to the buyer. These favors can range from small holiday gifts given in appreciation for another year's partnership to outright offers of cash bribes or kickbacks to the buyer in exchange for volume purchases. Some suppliers have been known to offer buyers computers, monthly cash payments, trips to Hawaii, and other such "big ticket" items to guarantee business. Although you, as a buyer, might personally benefit from these items, the foodservice operation, your employer, will ultimately "pay" for these kickbacks through higher product prices. Should you get caught accepting these items, it is possible that you will be fired. It is the wise manager who knows the boundaries of appropriate behavior with suppliers. Some large foodservice organizations have formal codes of conduct for their buyers. When these are in place, they should, of course, be carefully reviewed and followed. If your organization does not have a formal set of ethical guidelines for buying, the following self-tests can be helpful in determining whether a considered course of action with your supplier is indeed ethical.

Ethical Guidelines

1. Is it legal?
   Any course of action that violates written law or company policy and procedure is wrong.

2. Does it hurt anyone?
   Are benefits that rightfully belong to the owner of the business accruing to the buyer? Discounts, rebates, and free products are the property of the business, not the buyer.

3. Am I being honest?
   Is the activity one that you can comfortably say reflects well on your integrity as a professional, or will the activity actually diminish your reputation with other suppliers?

4. Would I care if it happened to me?
   If you owned the business, would you be in favor of your buyer behaving in the manner you are considering? If you owned multiple units, would it be good for the business if all of your buyers followed the considered course of action?

5. Does it compromise my freedom as a buyer?
   If your action negatively influences the way you perform as a buyer, then you shouldn't do it. For example, you accept a gift from a supplier and then the supplier provides you poor service. Will you feel comfortable reprimanding the supplier even though he has given you a gift? If you do feel uncomfortable, then maybe you shouldn't accept the gift.

6. Would I publicize my action?
   A quick way to review the ethical merit of a situation is to consider whom you would tell about it. If you are comfortable telling your boss and your other suppliers about the considered course of action, it is likely ethical. If you would prefer that your actions go undetected, you are probably on shaky ethical ground. If you wouldn't want your action to be read aloud in a court of law (even if your action is legal), you probably shouldn't do it.

Part One: Consider the Cost

Billy DeGates is the new President of Big B's coffee shops, a chain of 15 units that competes directly with Starbucks. At this year's first quarterly meeting with his unit managers, he is surprised to find that one of the reasons they are having difficulty tracking their purchasing costs and easily reporting them on a weekly basis is that not all of their office computers have Microsoft Excel software installed on them.

"It would cost $200 per computer to buy it," says one manger, "so we were never authorized to purchase it."

"It doesn't have to cost that much," said another manager. "I have a real 'techie' kind of employee at my store who made a copy of Excel for me and loaded it on my computer. He's a whiz and it works great. It didn't cost me anything. I can just have him make discs for everyone, and you can all install it yourself. Why should we buy 15 copies of Excel when we don't need to?"

1. Assume you were Billy. Would you allow the pirated software program to be illegally installed on the manager's computers?
2. Assume, for this illustration, that the action suggested by the unit manager was not actually illegal, and that it would not be detected by Microsoft. Utilizing the six-step questioning process introduced in this chapter, would you personally, at some point in the questioning process, decide the purchasing action proposed was unethical? If so, at which step?

■ DAILY INVENTORY SHEET

Before you can place an order, you will need to find out what you need! The process is much like going through your house and making a shopping list before you go to the store. Some managers say that they intuitively "know" what they need without looking at their storage areas. If you have ever gone grocery shopping without a list, however, you know that you will inevitably miss a few items. We have all been in a situation in which we went to the store, purchased what we thought we needed to prepare a great meal but ultimately found that we forgot an important ingredient or item!

Making a detailed assessment of your present inventory prior to placing orders is always a good idea. A good way to make sure that you have checked all your in-storage items is to use a **daily inventory sheet** (Figure 3.12). A daily inventory sheet will have the items listed in your storage areas, their unit of purchase, and their par values preprinted on the sheet. In addition, the form will have the following columns: on hand, special order, and order amount.

Having a preprinted list of all your items in storage and units of purchase is important so that you will not have to write down the items every time you check the inventory. The list should be arranged in the same order that you store the items so that you can quickly and easily locate your products. The par value should be listed so that you know how much inventory you should have in storage at any given time. You may also want to list the purchase point, if appropriate.

■ **Figure 3.12:** Daily Inventory Sheet

Item	Description	Unit	Par Value	On Hand	Special Order	Order Amount
Hot Wings	15# IQF	Case	6	2	3	7
Babyback Ribs	2–2 ½ #	Case	3	1.5	1	3
Sausage Links	96, 1 oz.	Case	5			
Drummies	2–5#	Case	4			
Bologna	10# avg.	Each	3			
Beef Pastrami	10# avg.	Each	4			
Slice Pepperoni	10# avg.	Each	6			
All-Beef Franks	8/1, 10#	Case	7			

To use the daily inventory sheet, you would physically walk through your storage areas to determine which items (and amounts) you should order. Under the On-Hand column, you would list how many of each item you have on hand, that is, sitting on the shelf. You also need to list any "special order" amounts needed above the par level. An example of this would be extra cases of perishables, such as strawberries, ordered for a banquet. Then you must calculate the order amount as follows:

Par Value − On Hand × Special Order = Order Amount

In Figure 3.12, the order amount for hot wings would be calculated as follows:

Order Amount for Hot Wings
6 − 2 + 3 = 7

If you have less than a whole purchase unit on hand, for example, $^1/_2$ case of babyback ribs as in Figure 3.12, you may need to round the order amount up to a full case as follows:

Order Amount for Babyback Ribs
3 − 1.5 + 1 = 2.5, Round Up to 3

Although the form in Figure 3.12 is called the daily inventory sheet, this does not mean that you have to check your inventory or place orders on a daily basis. You should make your "grocery lists" for your normal ordering days.

■ PREPARING THE PURCHASE ORDER

Some items are purchased daily, others weekly, and some, perhaps, monthly. In addition, you may be able to choose from a variety of ways to communicate with your supplier, including the Internet, via ordering software provided by your vendors, by fax or by telephone. Regardless of your communication method, however, it is critical that you prepare a written **purchase order**, or record of what you have decided to buy. The purchase order (PO) should be made out in triplicate (three copies). One copy goes to the receiving area for use by the receiving clerk. One copy is retained by management for the bookkeeping area. The original is, of course, sent to the vendor. If the purchase order is developed by telephone, management retains the original copy, with a notation (in the Comments section in the example in Figure 3.13), stating that the vendor has not seen the PO. In all cases, however, it is important to place all orders using a purchase order form. If this is not done, the receiving clerk will have no record of what should be coming in on the delivery. Figure 3.13 is an example of a simple yet effective purchase order form.

Purchase order preparation can be simple or complex, but, in all cases, the written purchase order form should contain space for the following information:

Purchase Order Information

1. Item name
2. Spec #, if appropriate
3. Quantity ordered
4. Quoted price per unit
5. Extension price
6. Total price of order
7. Vendor information
8. Purchase order number
9. Date ordered
10. Delivery date
11. Name of person who placed order
12. Name of person who received order
13. Delivery instructions
14. Comments

Each order you place should result in the preparation of a PO. This is true even if the vendor is delivering a standing order on a daily basis. The advantages of a written purchase order are many and include the following:

■ **Figure 3.13** Purchase Order

Vendor: _____   Purchase Order #: _____

Vendor's Address: _____   Delivery Date: _____

Vendor's Telephone #: _____

Vendor's Fax #: _____

Vendor's E-Mail: _____

Item Pirchased	Spec #	Quantity Ordered	Quoted Price	Extended Price
1.				
2.				
3.				
4.				
5.				
6.				
7.				
8.				
9.				
10.				
11.				
12.				
13.				
14.				
15.				
16.				
Total				

Order Date: _____   Comments: _____

Ordered By: _____   _____

Received By: _____   _____

Delivery Instructions: _____   _____

■ **Figure 3.14** Purchase Order

Vendor: Scooter's Produce _____   Purchase Order #: 56 _____

Vendor's Address: 123 Anywhere _____   Delivery Date: 1/3 _____

Vendor's Telephone #: 999-0000 _____

Vendor's Fax #: 999-0001 _____

Vendor's E-Mail: Scootersproduce@lsp.Org_

Vendor's Web Site: Scootersproduce.Org ___

Item Purchased	Spec #	Quantity Ordered	Quoted Price	Extended Price
1. Bananas	81	30 lb.	$0.24 lb.	$ 7.20
2. Parsley	107	4 bunches	0.80/bunch	3.20
3. Oranges	101	3 cases	31.50/case	94.50
4. Lemons	35	6 cases	29.20/case	175.20
5. Cabbages	85	2 bags	13.80/bag	27.60
6.				
7.				
8.				
9.				
10.				
11.				
12.				
13.				
14.				
15.				
16.				
Total				$307.70

Order Date: 1/1 _____   Comments: _____

Ordered by: Joshua David _____   Entered on 1/1 _____

Received by: _____   Transmitted by Joshua David

Delivery Instructions: After 1:00 P.M. _____

1. Written verification of quoted price
2. Written verification of quantity ordered
3. Written verification of the receipt of all goods ordered
4. Written and special instructions to the receiving clerk, as needed
5. Written verification of conformance to product specification
6. Written authorization to prepare vendor invoice for payment

Figure 3.14 shows the completed purchase order following a thorough inspection of a produce walk-in at a mid-sized hotel. The chef has used a sales forecast to determine the quantity of products needed for next Thursday's delivery. A check of the produce walk-in lets the chef know what is on hand and the quantity of each product required. This information allows for the accurate preparation of the PO. In this case, the order is then placed using the vendor's Web site. The receiving clerk at the hotel is now prepared with the information necessary to effectively receive the product from Scooter's.

FUN ON THE WEB!

Look up the following to see examples of sites that will help you learn more about food and nonfood products when purchasing.

www.uffva.org. United Fresh Fruit and Vegetable Association. Look up product news and search for your favorite fruit or vegetable.

www.namp.com. North American Meat Processors Association. Look up information on beef, pork, lamb, veal, and poultry. Also, order the Meat Buyer's Guide and Poultry Buyer's Guide online.

www.seafood.com. Search for your favorite seafood items. Buy wholesale or retail.

www.thomasregister.com. Find listings of companies that carry nonfood items and equipment.

www.recipegoldmine.com. Find recipes of your favorite menu items.

www.usda.gov. United States Department of Agriculture. Look up government reports on food legislation and news.

PART TWO

RECEIVING

*O*nce the PO has been submitted to the vendor, it is time to prepare for the acceptance or receiving of the order. This function is performed by the receiving clerk in a large operation, or it may be performed by you, as the manager, or by a staff member you designate. In all cases, however, it is wise for you to establish the purchasing and receiving functions so that one individual places the order and another individual is responsible for verifying delivery and acceptance of the product. When this is not done, the potential for fraud or theft is substantial.

Auditors, those individuals responsible for reviewing and evaluating proper operational procedures, frequently find that the purchasing agent in an operation ordered a product, signed for its acceptance, and authorized payment for it when, in fact, no product was ever delivered! In this case, the purchasing agent could be getting cash payment from the purveyor or supplier without the manager's knowledge. When purchasing duties are split among individuals in the purchasing chain, this is much less likely to happen. If it is not possible to have more than one person involved in the buying process, the work of the purchasing agent/receiving clerk must be carefully monitored by management to prevent fraud.

There is probably no area of the foodservice establishment more ignored than the physical area in which receiving takes place. This is unfortunate because this is the area where you ensure the quality and quantity of ordered products. Here are the proper receiving requirements:

1. Proper location
2. Proper tools and equipment
3. Proper delivery schedules
4. Proper training

■ PROPER LOCATION

The "back door," which is usually reserved for receiving, is often no more than that, just an entrance to the kitchen. In fact, the receiving area must be adequate to handle the job of receiving, or product loss and inconsistency will result.

First, the receiving area must be large enough to allow for checking products delivered against both the delivery invoice (the seller's record) and the PO (the buyer's record). In addition to space required to count and weigh incoming items, accessibility to equipment required to move products to their proper storage area and to dispose of excess packaging is important. A location near refrigerated storage areas is essential in maintaining refrigerated and frozen products at their desired temperatures.

You should make sure the area stays free of trash and clutter; these things make it too easy to hide delivered food items that may be taken home at the end of a dishonest employee's shift. It is important to remember that the delivery person is also a potential thief. Although most suppliers are extremely careful to screen their delivery personnel for honesty, it is a fact that a delivery person has access to products and has a truck available to remove as well as deliver goods. For this reason, it is important that the receiving clerk work in an area that has a clear view of delivery personnel and their vehicles.

The receiving area should be kept extremely clean; you do not want to contaminate incoming food or provide a carrying vehicle for pests. Often suppliers deliver goods that can harbor roach eggs or other insects. A clean receiving area makes it easier to both prevent and detect this type of problem. The area should be well lit and properly ventilated. Excessive heat in the receiving area can quickly damage delivered goods, especially if they are refrigerated or frozen products. Too little light may cause product defects to go unnoticed; therefore, the receiving area should be well lit. Flooring should be light in color and of a type that is easily cleaned. In colder climates, it is important that the receiving area be warm enough to allow the receiving clerk to carefully inspect products. The outside dock area in February, if the outside temperature is below freezing, is no place for an employee to conduct a thorough inspection of incoming products!

■ PROPER TOOLS AND EQUIPMENT

Although the tools and equipment needed for effective receiving vary by type and size of operation, some items are standard in any receiving operation. These include the following items.

SCALES

Scales should be of two types: those accurate to the fraction of a pound (for large items) and those accurate to the fraction of an ounce (for smaller items and pre-portioned meats). Scales should be calibrated regularly to ensure accuracy.

WHEELED EQUIPMENT

These items, whether hand trucks or carts, should be available so that goods can be moved quickly and efficiently to their proper storage areas.

BOX CUTTER

This item, properly maintained and used, allows the receiving clerk to quickly remove excess packaging and thus accurately verify the quality of delivered products. Of course, care must be taken when using this tool, so proper training is essential.

THERMOMETER

Foods must be delivered at their proper storage temperatures. You must establish the range of temperatures you deem acceptable for product delivery. For many operators, those temperatures would be the following:

	Acceptable Temperature Range	
Item	°F	°C
Frozen Foods	10°F or less	−12°C or less
Refrigerated Foods	30 to 45°F	−1 to 7°C

CALCULATOR

Vendor calculations should always be checked, especially if the invoice has been prepared by hand. It is especially useful if the calculator has a physical tape (as on an adding machine) that can be used by the receiving clerk when needed. The calculator should also be available in case the original invoice is either increased or decreased in amount because of incorrect vendor pricing or because items listed on the invoice were not delivered. In addition, invoice totals will change when all or a portion of the delivery was rejected because the items were of substandard quality.

RECORDS AREA

The records area should, in the best of cases, include a desk, telephone, computer/ fax, copy machine, file cabinet, and ample office supplies such as pens, pencils, and a stapler. Obviously, larger operations are more likely to have such an area. In a smaller operation, however, the need for basic equipment still exists. In all cases, the records area should include a copy of all product specifications, so there is no confusion about whether a delivered food or supply item meets the spec and, thus, should be accepted or rejected.

■ PROPER DELIVERY SCHEDULES

In an ideal world, you would accept delivery of products only during designated hours. These times would be scheduled during your slow periods, when there would be plenty of time for a thorough checking of the products delivered. In fact, some operators are able to demand that deliveries be made only at certain times, say between 9:00 a.m. and 10:30 a.m. These are called **acceptance hours**. The operation may refuse to accept delivery at any other time. Some large operations prefer to establish times in which they will not accept deliveries, say between 11:00 a.m. and 1:00 p.m. These are called **refusal hours**. A busy lunchtime may make it inconvenient to accept deliveries at this time, and some operators will simply not take deliveries then. In both cases, however, the assumption is that the operator is either a large enough or a good enough customer to make demands such as these.

You may find yourself in a situation, however, where the supplier will determine when goods are delivered. Although this may seem inconvenient (and often is), remember that all foodservice units would like to have their deliveries made during the slow periods, between peak meal times. In many cases, it is simply not possible for the supplier to stop his or her trucks for several hours to wait for a good delivery time. In fact, in remote locations, some foodservice operators will be told only the day a delivery will be made, not a specific time!

The key to establishing a successful delivery schedule with suppliers is, quite simply, to work with them. Although every relationship between operator and supplier is somewhat different, both sides, working together, can generally come to an acceptable solution on delivery hours. If you do decide to post either acceptance hours or refusal hours, these should be enforced equally with all vendors.

■ PROPER TRAINING

Receiving clerks should be properly trained to verify the following product characteristics:

1. Weight
2. Quantity
3. Quality
4. Price

WEIGHT

One of the most important items to verify when receiving food products is, of course, their weight. It is simply true that 14 pounds of ground beef in a box looks exactly like 15 pounds. There is no way to tell the difference without putting the product on the scale. Receiving clerks should be required to weigh all meat, fish, and poultry delivered. The only exception to this rule would be unopened Cryovac (sealed) packages containing items such as hot dogs, bacon, and the like. In this situation, the entire case should be weighed to detect shortages in content. Often, meat deliveries consist of several items, all of which are packaged together. When the receiving clerk or supplier is very busy, the temptation exists to weigh all of the products together. The following example shows why it is important to weigh each item rather than the entire group of items as a whole.

Assume that you ordered 40 pounds of product from Bruno's Meats. The PO that was prepared showed the information in Figure 3.15.

When the Bruno's delivery person arrived, all three items were in one box and the deliverer was in a hurry. He, therefore, suggested that your receiving clerk simply weigh the entire box. Your receiving clerk did just that and found that the contents weighed 40.5 pounds. Since the box itself weighed about 1/2 pound, she signed for delivery. When she began to put the meat away, however, she weighed each item individually and found the information in Figure 3.16.

If you called the supplier to complain about the overcharge ($248.50 total price − $232.75 actual value = $15.75 overcharge), you would likely be told that the misdelivery was simply a mistake caused by human error. It may well have been, but the lesson here is to always instruct your receiving personnel to weigh delivered items individually, even if they are in a hurry.

When an item is ordered by weight, its delivery should be verified by weight. It is up to the operator to train the receiving clerk to always verify that the operation

■ **FIGURE 3.15** Ordered

Item Ordered	Unit Price	Total Ordered	Total Price
Hamburger	$2.25/lb.	10 lb.	$ 22.50
New York Strip Steak	7.00/lb.	20 lb.	140.00
Corned Beef	8.60/lb.	10 lb.	86.00
Total		40 lb.	248.50

■ FIGURE 3.16 Delivered

Item Ordered	Unit Price	Total Delivered	Actual Value
Hamburger	$2.25/lb.	15 lb.	$ 33.75
New York Strip Steak	7.00/lb.	10 lb.	70.00
Corned Beef	8.60/lb.	15 lb.	129.00
Total		40 lb.	232.75

is charged only for the product weight delivered. Excess packaging, ice, or water in the case of produce can all serve to increase the delivered weight. The effective receiving clerk must be aware of and be on guard against deceptive delivery practices.

QUANTITY

The counting of products is as important as weighing them. Suppliers make more mistakes in not delivering products than they do in excessive delivery. Products delivered but not charged for cost the supplier money. Products not delivered but charged for cost you money. If you order five cases of green beans, then, of course, you want to receive and pay for five cases. This is important for two reasons. First, you only want to pay for products that have been delivered. Second, and just as important, if you have prepared your purchase order correctly, you truly need five cases of green beans. If only three are delivered, you may not be able to prepare the menu items that are necessary to service your guests. If this means you will run out of an item or have to make a substitute, you may be forced to deal with unhappy diners.

Shorting is the term used in the industry to indicate that an ordered item has not been delivered as promised. When a vendor shorts the delivery of an item you ordered, that item may or may not appear on the invoice. If it does not appear, it must be noted so that management knows that the item is missing and appropriate reorder action can be taken. If the item is listed on the invoice, the delivery driver should sign a **credit memo**. The credit memo should be filled out in triplicate (three copies). One copy goes to the receiving area to be filed. One copy is retained by management for the bookkeeping area. The original is, of course, sent to the vendor. Figure 3.17 is an example of such a form that, in this case, documents the shortage of two cases of green beans from a delivery invoice. Note that the credit memo has a place for the signature of not only a representative from your operation but also that of the vendor. It must be signed by both. The credit memo is simply a formal way of notifying the vendor that an item listed on the original invoice is missing, and, thus, the value of that item should be reduced from the invoice total. If a supplier consistently shorts your operation, that supplier is suspect in terms of both honesty and lack of concern for your operation's long-term success.

The counting of boxes, cases, bags, and the like must be routine behavior for the receiving clerk. Counting items such as the number of lemons or oranges in a box should be done on a periodic basis, but the value of counting items such as

■ **FIGURE 3.17** Credit Memo

CREDIT MEMO

Unit Name: _____

Vendor: _____ Delivery Date: _____

Invoice #: _____ Credit Memo #: _____

		Correction			
Item	Quantity	Short	Refused	Price	Credit Amount
Total					

Original Invoice Total: _____

Less: Credit Memo Total: _____

Adjusted Invoice Total: _____

Additional Information: _____

_____

_____

Vendor Representative: _____

Vendor Representative Telephone #: _____

Operation Representative: _____

Operation Representative Telephone #: _____

these on a regular basis is questionable. Although an unscrupulous supplier might be able to remove one or two lemons from each box delivered, the time it would take for an employee to detect such behavior is hardly worth the effort expended. It is preferable to do a periodic check and to work with reputable vendors.

The direct delivery of products to a foodservice operator's storeroom or holding area is another area for concern. The delivery person may deliver some items, such as bread, milk, and carbonated beverage mixes, directly to the storage areas, thus bypassing the receiving clerk. This should not be allowed. After such an activity, it may simply be impossible to verify the accurate quantity of items delivered. If this process must be used, product dates on each item can help ensure that all products listed on the invoice were indeed delivered.

QUALITY

No area of your operation should be of greater concern to you than that of the appropriate quality of product delivered. If you go to the trouble of developing product specifications but then accept delivery of products that do not match these specifications, you are simply wasting time and effort. Without product specifications, verification of quality is difficult because management itself is unsure of the quality level that is desired. Suppliers know their products. They also know their customers. Some customers will accept only those items they have specified. Others will accept virtually anything because they do not inspect or verify deliveries. If you were a supplier and you had a sack of onions that was getting a bit old, which customer would you deliver it to?

Unscrupulous suppliers can cost your operation guests because of both overcharging and shortchanging. Imagine, for example, a restaurant manager who requests a $1/4$-inch fat cover on all New York strip steaks ordered. Instead, the meat company delivers steaks with a $1/2$-inch fat cover. The operation will, of course, pay too much for the product because steaks with a $1/4$-inch fat covering sell at a higher price per pound than those with a $1/2$-inch covering. Guests, however, will hold the operator responsible for steaks that suddenly seem to be a little "fatter" than they used to be. Coincidentally, the guests who eat the fatter steaks may tend to be a bit fatter themselves in the future!

Checking for quality means checking the entire shipment for conformance to specifications. If only the top row of tomatoes in the box conforms to spec, it is up to the receiving clerk or manager to point that out to the vendor. If the balance of the box does not meet the specification, it should be refused. The credit memo can then be used to reduce the total on the invoice to the proper amount.

Sometimes, quality deficiencies are not discovered until after a delivery driver has left your establishment. When that is the case, you should notify the vendor that a thorough inspection has uncovered substandard product. The vendor is then instructed to pick up the nonconforming items. Many managers use the Additional Information section of the credit memo form shown in Figure 3.17 to record this requested pickup. When the product is picked up, the pickup information is recorded. Alternatively, a separate memo to the vendor requesting a product pickup could be produced. It is best, however, to keep the number of cost control forms to a minimum whenever possible, especially when minor modifications of one form will allow that form to serve two purposes.

Vendors are sometimes out of a product, just as you may sometimes run out of a menu item. In cases such as these, the receiving clerk must know whether it is management's preference to accept a product of higher quality, lower quality, or no product at all as a substitute. If this information is not known, one can expect that suppliers will be able to downgrade quality simply by saying that they were "out" of the requested product and did not want the operator to be "shorted" on the delivery. Training to assess and evaluate quality products is a continuous process. The effective receiving clerk should develop a keen eye for quality. This is done to ensure that both the operation and those guests it serves receive the quality products intended by management.

PRICE

In the area of training for price, two major concerns should be addressed:

1. Matching PO unit price to invoice unit price
2. Verifying price extensions and total

MATCHING PURCHASE ORDER UNIT PRICE TO INVOICE UNIT PRICE

When the person responsible for purchasing food for the operation places an order, the confirmed quoted price should be recorded on the purchase order because it is never safe to assume that the delivered price will match the price on the purchase order. As an ethical manager, you should not be happy with either an overcharge or an undercharge for a purchased product. Just as you would hope that a guest would inform you if a waiter forgot to add the price of a bottle of wine to the dinner check, a good receiving clerk works with the supplier to ensure that the operation is fairly charged for all items delivered. The proper acceptance of products puts the integrity of both supplier and operator on the line. Honesty and fair play must govern the actions of both parties.

If the receiving clerk has access to the purchase order, it is a simple matter to verify the quoted price and the delivered price. If these two do not match, management should be notified immediately. If management notification is not possible, both the driver and the receiving clerk should initial the Comments section of the purchase order, showing the difference in the two prices, and a credit memo should be prepared. Obviously, if the receiving clerk has no record of the quoted price, from either a purchase order or an equivalent document, price verification of this type is not possible. An inability to verify the quoted price and the delivered price at the time of delivery is a sure indication of a poorly designed food cost control system.

Some operators deal with suppliers in such a way that a contract price is established. A **contract price** is simply an agreement between buyer and seller to hold the price of a product constant over a defined period of time. For example, Bernardo uses Dairy O Milk. Dairy O agrees to supply Bernardo with milk at the price of $2.55 per gallon for three months from January 1 through March 31. Bernardo is free to buy as much or as little as he needs. The milk will always be billed at $2.55 per gallon; $2.55, then, is the contract price. The advantage to Bernardo is that he knows exactly what his per-gallon milk cost will be for the three-month period. The advantage to Dairy O is that it can offer a lower price in the hope of securing all of Bernardo's milk business. Even in the case of a contract price, however, the receiving clerk must verify the invoice delivery price against the established contract price.

VERIFYING PRICE EXTENSIONS AND TOTAL

Price extension is just as important for you to monitor as is the ordered/delivered price. Price extension is the process by which you compute extended price. **Extended price** is simply the unit price multiplied by the number of units delivered. If the price for a case of lettuce is $18.00 and the number of cases delivered is six, the extended price is calculated as follows:

Unit Price × Number of Units = Extended Price
$18.00 × 6 = $108.00

Extended price verification is extremely important. It is critical that the receiving clerk verify:

- Unit prices
- Number of units delivered
- Extended price computations (unit price × number of units delivered)
- Invoice totals

There seem to be two major reasons why operators do not always insist that the receiving clerk verify the extended prices and invoice totals. The most common reason is the belief that there is not enough time to do so. The driver may be in a hurry and the operation may be very busy. If that is the case, the process of verifying the extended price can be moved to a slower time. Why? Because there is a written record provided by the vendor of both the unit price and the number of units delivered. Thus, extension errors are vendor errors, in the vendor's own handwriting! Or, more accurately, today they are in the vendor's own computer.

The second reason operators sometimes ignore price extensions is related to these same computers. Some operators believe that if an invoice is computer generated, the mathematics of price extension must be correct. Nothing could be further from the truth. Anyone familiar with the process of using computers knows that there are many possible entry errors that can result in extension errors (even formulas entered into Excel-type spreadsheets can be entered in error). Once all extensions have been verified, it is always a good idea to check the invoice total against the sum of the individual, correct price extensions.

Managers must ensure that delivery clerks verify both extension prices and invoice totals. If this cannot be done at the time of delivery, it must be done as soon thereafter as possible. Errors are made, and they can cost your operation greatly if they go undetected.

■ RECEIVING RECORD OR DAILY RECEIVING SHEET

Some large operations use a receiving record when receiving food. This method, although taking administrative time to both prepare and monitor, does have some advantages.

A receiving record generally contains the following information:

1. Name of supplier
2. Invoice number

3. Item description

4. Unit price

5. Number of units delivered

6. Total cost

7. Storage area (unit distribution)

8. Date of activity

Figure 3.18 is an example of a receiving record, specifically designed for the receiving area of a large hotel. Note that some items are placed directly into production areas (direct use), whereas others may be used in specific units or sent to the storeroom. Sundry items, such as paper products, ashtrays, matches, and cleaning supplies, may be stored in specific nonfood areas. Note also that subtotals for storage areas can be determined in terms of either units or dollars, as the operator prefers. In all cases, the sums for each distribution area should equal the total for all items received during the day.

Receiving reports can be useful to management if it is important to record where items are to be delivered or where they have been delivered. Although some food-service operators will find the receiving report useful, many will not because most of the information it contains is also included in the receiving clerk's copy of the purchase order.

Part Two: Consider the Cost

"Come on Gloria, give me a break. I'm already behind because my truck broke down this morning, and I've got people all over town calling my boss to scream about their deliveries. It wasn't my fault I'm late. I'm just the driver," said Monte.

Monte, who makes deliveries for Raider Produce, was talking to Gloria, the receiving clerk for the High-Five Restaurant. The delivery he was making was a big one, and it was two hours late.

"You know, Gloria," Monte continued, "you guys take longer to accept a delivery than any other restaurant on my route. Nobody else inspects and weighs like you do. And you hardly ever find any problems. Look, I know it's a big delivery, but just this once can't you just sign the invoice and let me get going? I want to see my son's ball game, and I won't make it if you take forever to inspect this load."

"I don't know Monte," replied Gloria. "We've got procedures to follow here, and I'm supposed to use them every time."

"Look, just sign the ticket. If you find a problem later, I'll take care of it. I promise you," said Monte, who seemed to be increasingly flustered.

1. What do you think Gloria will most likely do about Monte's request that she speed up?

2. Assume you were this restaurant's owner. If you were personally accepting the delivery, what would you say to Monte?

■ **FIGURE 3.18** Hotel Pennycuff

Supplier	Invoice #	Item	Unit Price	No. of Units	Total Cost	A	B	C	Distribution D	E
					Receiving Report				Date: 1/1	
Dairy O	T-16841	½ pt. milk	$ 0.24	800	$192.00	75	600	125	—	
Tom's Rice	12785	Rice (bags)	12.00	3	36.00	—	1	—	2	—
Barry's Bread	J-165	Rye	0.62	25	15.50	—	25	—	—	—
		Wheat	0.51	40	20.40	20	—	20	—	—
		White	0.48	90	43.20	40	10	—	40	—
Total units				958		135	636	145	42	0
Total cost					$307.10					

Distribution Key:

A = Coffee Shop D = Storeroom

B = Banquet Kitchen E = Sundry (nonfood items)

C = Direct Use

Comments: _____

STORAGE

*T*he ideal situation for you and your operation would be for you to store only the food you will use between the time of a vendor's delivery and the time of that vendor's next delivery. This is true because storage costs money, in terms of providing both the storage space for inventory items and the money that is tied up in inventory items and thus unavailable for use elsewhere. It is always best, whenever possible, to order only the products that are absolutely needed by the operation. In that way, the vendor's storeroom actually becomes your storeroom. The vendor then absorbs the costs of storing your needed products. In all cases, however, you must have an adequate supply of products on hand to service your guests. They are your main concern. If you are doing your job well, you will have many guests and will need many items in storage!

Once the receiving clerk has properly accepted the food products you have purchased, the next step in the control of food costs is that of storing those items. The storage process, in most foodservice establishments, consists of essentially four main parts:

1. Placing products in storage
2. Maintaining product quality and safety
3. Maintaining product security
4. Determining inventory value

■ PLACING PRODUCTS IN STORAGE

Food products are highly perishable items. As such, they must be moved quickly from your receiving area to the area selected for storage. This is especially true for refrigerated and frozen items. An item such as ice cream, for example, can deteriorate substantially if it is at room temperature for only a few minutes. Most often, in foodservice, this high perishability dictates that the same individual responsible for receiving the items is the individual responsible for their storage.

Consider the situation of Kathryn, the receiving clerk at Fairview Estates, an extended care facility with 400 residents. She has just taken delivery of seven loaves of bread. They were delivered in accordance with the purchase order and now must be put away. When Kathryn stores these items, she must know whether management requires her to use the *LIFO* (last in, first out) or *FIFO* (first in, first out) method of product rotation.

LIFO SYSTEM

When using the **LIFO** storage system, the storeroom operator intends to use the most recently delivered product (last in) before he or she uses any part of that same product previously on hand. If Kathryn decides, for example, to use the new bread first, she would be using the LIFO system. In all cases, you must strive to maintain a consistent product standard. In the case of some bread, pastry, fruit, and vegetable items, the storeroom clerk could be instructed to utilize the LIFO system. With LIFO, you will need to take great care to order only the quantity of product needed between deliveries. If too much product is ordered, loss rates will be very high. Costs can rise dramatically when older LIFO items must eventually be discarded or used in a way that reduces their revenue-producing ability. For most of the items you will buy, the best storage system to use is the FIFO system.

FIFO SYSTEM

First in, first out (**FIFO**) means that you intend to rotate your stock in such a way that product already on hand is sold prior to the sale of more recently delivered product. If this is the case, the storeroom clerk must take great care to place new stock behind or at the bottom of old stock. It is the tendency of employees not to do this. Consider, for example, the storeroom clerk who must put away six cases of tomato sauce. The cases weigh about 40 pounds. The FIFO method dictates that these six cases be placed *under* the five cases already stacked in the storeroom. Will the clerk place the six newly delivered cases underneath the five older cases? In many instances, the answer is no. Unless management strictly enforces the FIFO rule, employees may be tempted to take the easy way out. Figure 3.19 demonstrates the difference between LIFO and FIFO when dealing with cases of food products.

FIFO is the preferred storage technique for most perishable and nonperishable items. Failure to implement a FIFO system of storage management can result in excessive product loss due to spoilage, shrinkage, and deterioration of quality. All of these must be avoided if you are to effectively manage food expenses.

Decisions about storing food items according to the LIFO or FIFO method are your decisions. Once these decisions have been made, they should be communicated to the storeroom clerk and monitored on a regular basis to ensure compliance. To ensure that this is so, some foodservice managers require the storeroom clerk to mark or tag each delivered item with the date of delivery. These markings provide a visual aid in determining which product should be used first. This is especially critical in the area of highly perishable and greater cost items such as fresh meats and seafood. Special meat and seafood date tags will be available from your vendor. These tags contain a space for writing in the item name, quantity, and delivery date. The use of these tags or an alternative date tracking system is strongly recommended. If the supplier has computerized his or her delivery, the box or case may already bear a bar code strip identifying both the product and the delivery date. When this is not the case, however, the storeroom clerk should assume this function.

■ FIGURE 3.19 FIFO and LIFO Storage Systems

Oldest		Newest
Oldest		Newest
Oldest		Newest
Newest		Oldest
Newest		Oldest
Newest		Oldest
FIFO		LIFO

■ **FIGURE 3.20** FIFO Stocking System

Tomato Sauce	2/10	Beets	2/10	Egg Noodles	2/18
Tomato Sauce	2/18	Beets	2/10	Egg Noodles	2/18
Tomato Sauce	2/18	Beets	2/18	Egg Noodles	2/22
Tomato Sauce	2/22	Beets	2/22	Egg Noodles	2/22

Figure 3.20 demonstrates the visual aspect of products in a dry-storage area when management requires that the storeroom clerk mark each item with its date of delivery.

Some operators prefer to go even further when labeling some products for storage. These operators date the item and then also indicate the day (or hour) in which the product should be pulled from storage, thawed, or even discarded. Figure 3.21 is an example of a typical storage label utilized for this process.

FUN ON THE WEB!

Daydots is a company that specializes in providing product date labels for the restaurant industry. To learn more about how the company's food labeling and bagging systems save money go to **www.daydots.com**.

■ STORAGE AREAS

The food and related products you buy will generally be placed in one of the following three major storage areas within your facility:

1. Dry storage
2. Refrigerated storage
3. Frozen storage

■ **FIGURE 3.21** Product Storage Label

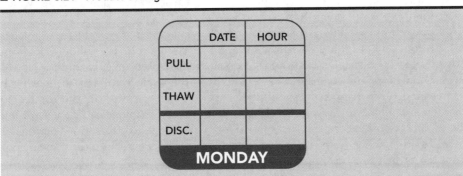

DRY STORAGE

Dry-storage areas should generally be maintained at a temperature ranging between 65°F and 75°F (18°C and 24°C). Temperatures below that range can be harmful to food products. More often, however, dry-storage temperatures can get very high, exceeding by far the upper limit of temperature acceptability. This is because storage areas are frequently in poorly ventilated closed-in areas of the building. Excessive temperatures damage dry-storage products.

Shelving in dry-storage areas must be easily cleaned and sturdy enough to hold the weight of dry products. Shelving should be placed at least six inches above the ground to allow for proper cleaning beneath the shelving and to ensure proper ventilation. Dry-goods products should never be stored directly on the floor. Slotted shelving is generally preferred over solid shelving when storing food, because slotted shelving allows for better air circulation around the product.

Can labels should face out for easy identification. Bulk items such as flour or sugar should be stored in wheeled bins whenever possible so that heavy lifting and resulting employee injuries can be avoided. Most important, dry-storage space must be sufficient in size to handle your operation's needs. Cramped and cluttered dry-storage areas tend to increase costs because inventory cannot be easily rotated, maintained, and counted. Theft can go undetected, and you may find yourself accidentally using the FIST (first in, still there!) method of inventory storage because products get "lost" in the storeroom.

REFRIGERATED STORAGE

Refrigerator temperatures should generally be maintained between 32°F (0°C) and 36°F (2°C). In fact, the refrigerator itself will vary as much as four degrees (F) between its coldest spot (near the bottom) and its warmest spot. In most cases, the bottom tends to be coldest in a refrigerator because warm air rises and cold air falls. Refrigerators actually work by removing heat from the contents, rather than "making" food cold. This is an important point to remember when refrigerating food. Foods that are boiling hot should be precooled to 160°F before placing them in the refrigerator. This results in lower operating costs for the refrigerator, but the temperature is still well above the potentially hazardous food danger zone, which most food experts place at 40°F to 140°F (4°C to 60°C).

Refrigerators should have easily cleaned shelving units that are at least six inches off the floor and are slotted to allow for good air circulation. They should be properly cleaned on a regular basis and be opened and closed quickly, both to lower operational costs and to ensure that the items in the refrigerator stay at their peak of freshness. Carryover items should be properly labeled, wrapped, and rotated so that items can be found easily, resulting in both greater employee efficiency and reduced energy costs because refrigerator doors will be opened for shorter periods of time. Many managers find that requiring foods to be stored in clear plastic containers also helps in this regard.

FREEZER STORAGE

Freezer temperatures should be maintained between 0°F and –10°F (–18°C and –23°C). What is usually called a freezer, however, is more properly a "frozen-food storage unit." The distinction is an important one. To be frozen at its peak of freshness, a food item must be frozen very quickly. This involves temperatures of –20°F (–29°C) or lower. Freezer units in a foodservice operation do not generally operate at these temperatures; thus, they are best at "holding" foods that are already frozen, rather than freezing food.

Frozen foods comprise an increasingly large portion of the foods you are likely to buy. Frozen foods should be wrapped securely to reduce moisture loss, and newly delivered products should be carefully checked with a thermometer when received to ensure that they are at the proper temperature. In addition, these items should be carefully inspected to ensure that they have not been thawed and refrozen.

Frozen-food holding units must be regularly maintained, a process that includes cleaning inside and out and constant temperature monitoring to detect possible improper operation. A thermometer permanently placed in the unit or one easily read from outside the unit is best. It is also a good idea to periodically check that gaskets on freezers, as well as on refrigerators, tightly seal the food cabinet. This will not only reduce operating costs but will also maintain food quality for a longer period of time.

■ STORAGE BASICS

Regardless of the storage type, food and related products should be stored neatly in some logical order. This makes them easier to find and to count when the need arises. You may decide, for example, to arrange your stored products on the basis of how often your staff uses them. That is, frequently used items are placed near the front of the storage area. When a few items constitute a majority of the sales volume in your unit, this can be an effective storage technique.

Regardless of the storage system you choose, inventory sheets should match the physical order of items in storage. This saves time in taking inventory and results in fewer errors. It is also important to note that the objective of a neat storage area is to both maximize storage space and minimize the time it takes to locate the item in storage. To save employee time, storage areas should be in close proximity to the areas in which the stored products will be used.

■ MAINTAINING PRODUCT QUALITY AND SAFETY

It is a fact that food product quality rarely improves with increased storage time. In most cases, the quality of ingredients you buy is at its peak when the product you ordered is delivered to you. From then on, most products can only decline in freshness, quality, and nutrition. In most cases, the primary method for ensuring the quality of stored products is through proper product rotation and high standards of storeroom sanitation. Storage areas are excellent breeding grounds for insects, some bacteria, and also rodents. To protect against these hazards, you should insist on a regular cleaning of all storage areas. Compressor units on refrigerators and frozen-food holding units should be checked regularly for the buildup of dust and dirt. Interior storage racks should be kept free of spills and soil.

Refrigerators and frozen-food holding units remove significant amounts of stored product moisture, causing shrinkage in meats and produce and **freezer burn**. Freezer burn refers to deterioration in product quality resulting from poorly wrapped or stored items kept at freezing temperatures. Unless they are built in, refrigerators and frozen-food holding units should be high enough off the ground to allow for easy cleaning around and under them to prevent cockroaches and other insects from living beneath them. Both refrigerators and frozen-food holding units should be kept six to ten inches from walls to allow for the free circulation of air around, and efficient operation of, the units. Drainage systems in refrigerators should be checked at least weekly. In larger storage areas, hallways should be kept clear and empty of storage materials or boxes. This helps both in finding items in the storage area and in reducing the number of hiding places for insects and rodents.

■ MAINTAINING PRODUCT SECURITY

Food products are the same as money to you. In fact, you should think of food inventory items in exactly that way. The apple in a produce walk-in is not just an apple. It represents, at a selling price of $2.00, that amount in revenue to the airport foodservice director, who hopes to sell a crisp, fresh apple to a weary traveler. If the apple disappears, revenue of $2.00 will disappear also. When you think of inventory items in terms of their sales value, it becomes clear why product security is of the utmost importance. All foodservice establishments will experience some amount of theft, in its strictest sense. The reason is very simple. Some employee theft is impossible to detect. Even the most sophisticated, computerized control system is not able to determine if an employee or vendor's employee walked into the produce walk-in and ate one green grape. Similarly, an employee who takes home two small sugar packets per night will likely go undetected for a great length of time. In neither of these cases, however, is the amount of loss significant, and certainly not enough to install security cameras in the walk-in or to search employees as they leave for home at the end of their shifts. What you do want to do, however, is to make it difficult to remove significant amounts of food from storage without authorization, so that you can know when that food has been removed. Good cost control systems must be in place if you are to achieve this goal.

It is amazing how large the impact of theft can be on profitability. Consider the following example. Jesse is the receiving clerk at the Irish Voice sports bar. On a daily basis, Jesse takes home $2.00 worth of food products. How much, then, does Jesse cost the bar in one year? The answer is a surprising $14,600 in sales revenue! If Jesse or others pilfer $2.00 per day for 365 days, the total theft amount is $730 (365 days $\times$ $2.00 per day = $730). If the bar makes an after-tax profit of 5 percent on each dollar of food products sold, to recover the lost $730, the operation must sell $1.00/0.05 $\times$ $730 = $14,600! To recover the dollar amount of Jesse's theft, the sports bar must sell $14,600 of food per year and make five cents per dollar sold on these sales. In the case of a smaller bar, $14,600 may well represent several days' sales revenue. Clearly, small thefts can add up to large dollar losses!

Most foodservice operators attempt to control access to the location of stored products. In some areas, this may be done by a process as simple as keeping the dry-storage area locked and requiring employees to "get the keys" from the manager or supervisor. In other situations, cameras may be mounted in both storage areas and employee exit areas. Sometimes the physical layout of the foodservice operation may prevent management from being able to effectively lock and secure all storage areas, but too much traffic is sure to cause theft problems. This is not because employees are basically dishonest. Most are not. Theft problems develop because of the few employees who feel either that management will not miss a few of whatever is being stolen or that they "deserve" to take a few things because they work so hard and are paid so little!

It is your responsibility to see to it that the storeroom clerk maintains good habits in securing product inventory. As a general rule, if storerooms are to be locked, only one individual should have access during any shift. In reality, however, it is difficult to keep all inventory items under lock and key. Some items must be received and immediately sent to the kitchen for processing or use. Also, what would happen if you or another designated "key holder" were gone from the operation for a few minutes? Most operators find that it is impossible to operate under a system where all food products are locked away from the employees. Storage areas should, however, not be accessible to guests or vendor employees. If proper control procedures are in place, employees will know that you can determine if theft has occurred. Without such control, employees are aware that theft can go undetected. This must, and can, be avoided.

■ DETERMINING INVENTORY VALUE

The inventory you have on hand should be maintained in a way that makes it easy to **issue** (place into production) as well as to count and to determine its monetary value. This is because you must be able to answer this fundamental question, "What is the value of the products I currently have on hand?"

The answer to this question is critical because it is simply not possible to know your actual food expense without an accurate inventory. In fact, the mathematical formula used to determine the cost of food sold (food expense) requires you to know the dollar value of all food products in your inventory. The process of determining inventory value is quite simple, even if the actual task can be very time consuming.

Valuing, or establishing a dollar value for your entire inventory, is achieved by using the following inventory value formula:

Item Amount × Item Value = Item Inventory Value

ITEM AMOUNT

Item amount may be determined by counting the item, as in the case of cans, or by weighing items, as in the case of meats. Volume, that is, gallons, quarts, and the like, is another method of establishing product amounts. If an item is purchased by the pound, it is generally weighed to determine item amount. If it is purchased by the piece or case, the appropriate unit to determine the item amount may be either pieces or cases. If, for example, canned pears are purchased by the case, with six cans per case, management might decide to consider the item either as case or as can. That is, three cases of the canned pears might be considered as three items (by the case) or as 18 items (by the can). Any method you use to accurately establish the amount of product you have on hand is acceptable. As you will learn, if products are undercounted, your food expenses will appear higher than they actually are. If, on the other hand, you erroneously (or on purpose) overstate inventory, or **pad inventory,** costs will appear artificially low.

ITEM VALUE

An item's actual value can be more complicated to determine than its amount. This is because the price you pay for an item may vary slightly each time you buy it. Assume, for example, that you bought curly endive for $2.20 per pound on Monday, but the same item was $2.50 per pound on Wednesday. On Friday, you see that you have one pound of the curly endive in your refrigerated walk-in. Is the value of the item $2.20 or $2.50?

Item value must be determined by using either the LIFO or the FIFO method. When the LIFO method is in use, the item's value is said to be the price paid for the least recent (oldest) addition to item amount. If the FIFO method is in use, the item value is said to be the price paid for the most recent (newest) product on hand. In the hospitality industry, most operators value inventory at its most recently known value; thus, FIFO is the more common method.

A simple illustration may help. Peggy purchased grapes on Monday and paid $30.00 per lug. On Friday, she again purchased grapes, but paid $40.00 per lug. On Saturday morning, she took inventory and found that she had 1½ lugs of grapes. What is their inventory value? The LIFO system says that Peggy's grapes have an inventory value of $45.00 ($30.00 LIFO price × 1.5 lugs = $45.00). The FIFO method places a value of $60.00 on the grapes ($40.00 FIFO price × 1.5 lugs = $60.00). Because it is closest to the actual replacement cost of the inventory item, choosing to value inventory at the most recently paid price (FIFO) is the best method for establishing item value for the majority of hospitality operators.

Inventory value is determined using a form similar to the **inventory valuation sheet** shown in Figure 3.22. This inventory valuation sheet has a place for all

■ **FIGURE 3.22** Inventory Valuation Sheet

| Unit Name: _____ | | | Inventory Date: _____ | |
| Counted By: _____ | | | Extended By: _____ | |

Item	Unit	Item Amount	Item Value	Inventory Value
			Page Total	

Page _____ of _____

inventory items, the quantity on hand, and the unit value of each item. There is also a place for the date the inventory was taken, a spot for the name of the person who counted the product, and another space for the person who extends or establishes the value of the inventory. It is recommended that these two be different individuals to reduce the risk of inventory valuation fraud.

The inventory valuation sheet should be completed each time the inventory is counted. It can be manually prepared or produced as part of an inventory evaluation software program. Regardless of the form used, the item's inventory value is determined using the inventory value formula presented earlier in this section. Thus, if we have five cases of fresh beets in our inventory and each case has a value of $20.00, the inventory value of our beets is

Item Amount 3 Item Value 5 Inventory Value

or

$$5 \times \$20 = \$100$$

The process of determining inventory value requires that you or a member of your staff count all food products on hand and multiply the value of the item by the number of units on hand. The process becomes more difficult when one realizes that the average foodservice operation has hundreds of items in inventory. Thus, "taking the inventory" can be a very time-consuming task. A **physical inventory**, one in which the food products are actually counted, must, however, be taken to determine your actual food usage. Some operators take this inventory monthly, others weekly or even daily! Some, unfortunately, feel that there is no need to ever take inventory. These operators cannot effectively control their costs because they do not know what their costs are.

DETERMINING ACTUAL FOOD EXPENSE

Assume that you own and manage a small ice cream store that makes its own products. You have reviewed your records for the past month and found the following:

January Revenue and Expense

Ice Cream Sales = $98,000

Food Expense = $39,000

You have determined your revenue figure from the sales history you maintained (see Chapter 2). You have determined your food expense by adding the dollar value of all the properly corrected delivery invoices that you accumulated for the month. That is, you totaled the value of all food purchased and delivered between the first day of the month and the last. Would it be correct to say that your food expense for the month of January is $39,000? The answer is No. Why not? Because you may have more, or less, of the food products required to make your

■ **FIGURE 3.23**   Formula for Cost of Food Sold

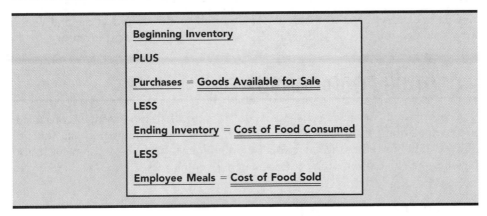

ice cream in inventory on the last day of January than you had on the first day. If you have more food products in inventory on January 31 than you had on January 1, your food expense is less than $39,000. If you have fewer products in inventory on January 31 than you had on January 1, your food expense is higher than $39,000. To understand why this is so, you must understand the formula for calculating your actual food expense. The correct formula is shown in Figure 3.23. **Cost of food sold** is the dollar amount of all food actually sold, thrown away, wasted, or stolen.

■ BEGINNING INVENTORY

Beginning inventory is the dollar value of all food on hand at the beginning of the accounting period. It is determined by completing an actual count and valuation of your food inventory.

■ PURCHASES

Purchases are the sum cost of all food purchased during the accounting period. Purchases are determined by adding all properly tabulated invoices for the accounting period.

■ GOODS AVAILABLE FOR SALE

Goods available for sale is the sum of the beginning inventory and purchases. It represents the value of all food that was available for sale during the accounting period.

▪ ENDING INVENTORY

Ending inventory refers to the dollar value of all food on hand at the end of the accounting period. It also is determined by completing a physical inventory.

▪ COST OF FOOD CONSUMED

The **cost of food consumed** is the actual dollar value of all food used, or consumed, by the operation. Again, it is important to note that this is not merely the value of all food sold but rather the value of all food no longer in the establishment. It also includes the value of any food (meals) eaten by employees.

▪ EMPLOYEE MEALS

Employee meal cost is actually a labor-related, not food-related, cost. Free or reduced-cost employee meals are a benefit much in the same manner as medical insurance or paid vacation. Therefore, the value of this benefit, if provided, should be transferred and charged not as a cost of food but as a cost of labor. The dollar value of food eaten by employees is subtracted from the cost of food consumed to yield the cost of food sold.

▪ COST OF FOOD SOLD

As stated earlier, the cost of food sold is the actual dollar value of all food expenses incurred by the operation except for those related to employee meals. It is not possible to determine this number unless a beginning inventory has been taken at the start of the accounting period, followed by another inventory taken at the end of the accounting period. Without these two numbers, it is impossible to accurately determine the cost of food sold. Figure 3.24 illustrates a recap sheet used to determine the cost of food sold.

In the ice cream store example, had you completed such a form, you would have known your actual cost of food sold. Every manager should, on a regular basis, compute the actual cost of food sold because it is not possible to improve your cost picture unless you first know what your costs are.

▪ VARIATIONS ON THE BASIC COST OF FOOD SOLD FORMULA

Figure 3.24 demonstrates the format most commonly used to determine cost of food sold, but some operators prefer slightly different formulas, depending on the unique aspects of their units. The important point to remember, however, is that all of

■ **FIGURE 3.24** Recap Sheet

Cost of Food Sold	
Accounting Period: to _____	
Unit Name: _____	
Beginning Inventory	$ _____
PLUS	
Purchases	$ _____
Goods Available for Sale	$ _____
LESS	
Ending Inventory	$ _____
Cost of Food Consumed	$ _____
LESS	
Employee Meals	$ _____
Cost of Food Sold	$ _____

these formulas should seek to accurately reflect actual cost of food sold by the operation for a given time period. Two variations of the formula follow.

FOOD OR BEVERAGE PRODUCTS ARE TRANSFERRED FROM ONE FOODSERVICE UNIT TO ANOTHER

This is the case when, for example, an operator seeks to compute one cost of food sold figure for a bar and another for the bar's companion restaurant. In this situation, it is likely that fruits, juices, vegetables, and similar items are taken from the kitchen for use in the bar, whereas wine, sherry, and similar items may be taken from the bar for use in the kitchen. This concept of transferability is covered in detail in Chapter 4. The formula for cost of food sold in this situation would be as follows:

Beginning inventory	$ _____	
PLUS		
Purchases	$ _____	
= Goods Available for Sale		$ _____
LESS		
Ending Inventory		$ _____
LESS		
Value of Transfers Out		$ _____
PLUS		

Value of Transfers In	$ _____
= Cost of Food Consumed	$ _____
LESS	
Employee Meals	$ _____
= Cost of Food Sold	$ _____

NO EMPLOYEE MEALS ARE PROVIDED

When an operation provides no employee meals at all, the computation of cost of food sold is as follows:

Beginning inventory	$	
PLUS		
Purchases	$	
Goods Available for Sale		$ _____
LESS		
Ending Inventory		$
Cost of Food Sold		$ _____

It is important for you to know exactly which formula or variation is in use when analyzing cost of food sold. The variations, although slight, can make big differences in the interpretation of your cost information. In all cases, it is critical that accurate beginning and ending inventory figures be maintained if accurate cost data are to be computed.

In the ice cream store example, both beginning and ending inventory, transfers, and employee meals are known, thus enabling you to determine your actual cost of food sold.

Beginning Inventory	$23,225
Purchases	$39,000
Ending Inventory	$27,500
Transfers Out	$ 4,500
Transfers In	$ 3,775
Employee Meals	$ 725

You are now able to complete your recap sheet as illustrated in Figure 3.25.

In this example, employee meals were determined by assigning a food value of $1.00 per employee ice cream treat consumed. It is important to note that food products do not have to be consumed as a meal in order to be valued as an employee benefit. Soft drinks, snacks, and other food items consumed by employees are all considered employee meals for the purpose of computing cost of food sold. If records are kept on the number of employees eating per day, monthly employee meal costs are easily determined. Some operators prefer to estimate the dollar value of employee meals each month rather than record actual employee meals. This is not a good practice, both from a control point of view and in terms of developing accurate cost data.

■ **FIGURE 3.25** Recap Sheet

Cost of Food Sold	
Accounting Period: 1/1 to 1/31	
Unit Name: Your Ice Cream Store	
Beginning Inventory $23,225	
PLUS	
Purchases $39,000	
Goods Available for Sale	$62,225
LESS	
Ending Inventory	$27,500
LESS	
Transfers Out	$ 4,500
PLUS	
Transfers In	$ 3,775
Cost of Food Consumed	$34,000
LESS	
Employee Meals	$ 725
Cost of Food Sold	$33,275

It is important to note that ending inventory for one accounting period becomes the beginning inventory figure for the next period. For example, in the case of your ice cream store, the January 31 ending inventory figure of $27,500 will become the February 1 beginning inventory figure. In this manner, it is clear that physical inventory need only be taken one time per accounting period, not twice. Although there is no reliable method for replacing the actual counting of inventory items on hand, there are many computer programs on the market programmed to allow an individual to scan the bar codes on products using a handheld scanning device and, thus, perform both the counting and the price extension process necessary to develop actual inventory valuations. Using technology in this manner can make a time-consuming task much less tedious and more efficient.

FUN ON THE WEB!

Counting food and beverage inventories has traditionally been a very time-consuming task. However, advances in inventory-counting systems are occurring regularly. To see an example of how one company is utilizing handheld devices to assist restaurateurs in speeding up their inventory taking, go to **www.stevenscreek.com/palm/onhand.html.**

Green and Growing!

A foodservice operation's cost of food consumed is affected by a variety of factors. One such factor relates to the source reduction decisions made by the operation's suppliers. Where recycling occurs within the foodservice operation and seeks to reuse materials, **source reduction** is utilized by suppliers to minimize the amount of resources initially required to package, store, and ship the items they sell. The result of effective source reduction is a lessened impact on the environment and lower product costs!

Consider, for example, the difference in the producer's cost between packaging, storing, and shipping frozen orange juice concentrate (which foodservice operators will reconstitute on-site) and "ready-to-serve" juice. Not only will packaging costs be higher in the second case (because of the greater volume), but the item's greater weight will also mean higher transportation costs. Storage costs, too, will be greater with the "ready-to-serve" item, as will the cost of disposing of used product containers. Packaging and energy costs add up, and these costs will inevitably be passed on from the manufacturer to the foodservice operation. The result is higher food costs and lowered profits. Creative source reduction efforts, however, result in fewer wasted natural resources and lower food costs. Foodservice operators should encourage these efforts by purchasing quality products from those suppliers who take their source reduction responsibilities seriously and act upon them.

FOOD COST PERCENTAGE

You know from Chapter 1 that food expense is often expressed as a percentage of total revenue or sales. Since you can now determine your actual cost of food sold, you can also learn to compute and evaluate your operation's food cost percentage. Again, this is the traditional way of looking at food expense and generally the method used by most operators when preparing the profit and loss statement.

The formula used to compute actual food cost percentage is as follows:

$$\frac{\text{Cost of Food Sold}}{\text{Food Sales}} = \text{Food Cost \%}$$

Food cost percent represents that portion of food sales that was spent on food expenses.

In the case of the ice cream store example discussed previously, you know that cost of food sold equals $33,275 (Figure 3.25). If the store experienced $98,000 in food sales for the period of January 1 to January 31, the food cost percentage for the period would be

$$\frac{\text{Cost of Food Sold}}{\text{Food Sales}} = \frac{\$33,275}{\$98,000} = 34\% \text{ Food Cost}$$

Thus, 34 percent of the dollars in sales revenue taken in was needed to buy the food used to generate that revenue. Put another way, 34 cents of each dollar in sales were used to buy the products needed to make the ice cream.

■ ESTIMATING DAILY COST OF FOOD SOLD

Many operators would like to know their food usage on a much more regular basis than once per month. When this is the case, the physical inventory may be taken as often as desired. Again, however, physical inventories are time consuming.

It would be convenient if you could have a close estimate of your food usage on a weekly or daily basis without the effort of a daily inventory count. Fortunately, such an approximation exists. Figure 3.26 illustrates a six-column form, which you can use for a variety of purposes. One of them is to estimate food cost percent on a daily or weekly basis.

■ **FIGURE 3.26** Six-Column Form

Date: _____

Weekday	Today	To Date	Today	To Date	Today	To Date

As an example, assume that you own an Italian restaurant that serves no liquor and caters to a family-oriented clientele. You would like to monitor your food cost percentage on a more regular basis than once per month, which is your regular accounting period. You have decided to use a six-column form to estimate your food cost percentage. Since you keep track of both daily sales and daily purchases, you can easily do so. In the space above the first two columns, write the word "Sales." Above the middle two columns, write "Purchases," and above the last two columns, enter the words "Cost %."

You then proceed each day to enter your daily sales revenue in the column labeled Sales Today. Your invoices for food deliveries are totaled daily and entered in the column titled Purchases Today. Dividing the Purchases Today column by the Sales Today column yields the figure that is placed in the Cost % Today column. Purchases to Date (the cumulative purchases amount) is divided by Sales to Date (the cumulative sales amount) to yield the Cost % to Date figure. A quick summary is as follows:

Six-Column Food Cost % Estimate

$$1. \quad \frac{\text{Purchases Today}}{\text{Sales Today}} = \text{Cost \% Today}$$

$$2. \quad \frac{\text{Purchases to Date}}{\text{Sales to Date}} = \text{Cost \% to Date}$$

Figure 3.27 shows this information for your operation for the time period January 1 to January 7.

As you can see, you buy most of your food at the beginning of the week, whereas sales are strongest in the later part of the week. This is a common occurrence at many foodservice establishments. As can also be seen, your daily cost percent ranges from a high of 130 percent (Monday) to a low of 0 percent (Sunday), when no deliveries are made. In the Cost % to Date column, however, the range is only from a high of 130 percent (Monday) to a low of 39.20 percent (Sunday).

In order for the six-column food cost to be an accurate estimate, you must make one important assumption: *for any time period you are evaluating, the beginning inventory and ending inventory amounts are the same.* In other words, over any given time period, you will have approximately the same amount of food on hand at all times. If this assumption is correct, the six-column food cost estimate is, in fact, a good indicator of your food usage. If you assume that your inventory is constant, your cost of food sold for the one-week period is a little less than $4,034.21, or 39.20 percent of sales. Why a little less? Because we must still subtract the value of employee meals, if any are provided, because they are an employee benefit and not a food expense.

How accurate is the six-column form? For most operators, it is quite accurate and has the following advantages:

1. It is very simple to compute, requiring 10 minutes or less of data entry per day for most operations (the cells in a 6-column excel spreadsheet can be formulated to do the math for you).

■ **FIGURE 3.27**   Six-Column Food Cost Estimate

Date: 1/1–1/7

	Sales		Purchases		Cost %	
Weekday	Today	To Date	Today	To Date	Today	To Date
Monday	$ 850.40	$ 850.40	$1,106.20	$1,106.20	130.0%	130.0%
Tuesday	920.63	1,771.03	841.40	1,947.60	91.4	110.0
Wednesday	1,185.00	2,956.03	519.60	2,467.20	43.8	83.5
Thursday	971.20	3,927.23	488.50	2,955.70	50.3	75.3
Friday	1,947.58	5,874.81	792.31	3,748.01	40.7	63.8
Saturday	2,006.41	7,881.22	286.20	4,034.21	14.3	51.2
Sunday	2,404.20	10,285.42	0	4,034.21	0	39.2
Total	10,285.42		4,034.21		39.2	

2. It records both sales history and purchasing patterns.

3. It identifies problems before the end of the monthly accounting period.

4. By the ninth or tenth day, the degree of accuracy in the To Date column is very high.

5. It is a daily reminder to both management and employees that there is a very definite relationship between sales and expenses.

The use of a six-column food cost estimator is highly recommended for the operator who elects to conduct a physical inventory less often than every two weeks.

The control of food expense is critical to all foodservice operations. From the purchase of the raw ingredient to its receiving and storage, the effective foodservice operator strives to have the proper quality and quantity of product on hand at all times. Food represents a large part of your overall expense budget. Protecting this product and accounting for its usage are extremely important in helping to manage overall costs.

Technology Tools

This chapter focused on managing food-related costs by controlling the areas of purchasing, receiving, storage, and issuing. In addition, computing food costs through the use of the food cost percentage was introduced. A variety of software programs are available that can assist in these areas.

Recipe Software

1. Maintain standardized recipes.
2. Cost standardized recipes.
3. Allow for computer-assisted recipe quantity conversion.
4. Maintain and supply dietary information by portion.
5. Create ingredient lists for purchase or issue from storeroom.
6. Suggest alternative cooking methods.
7. Supply color pictures of the finished product.
8. Create purchase orders based on production forecasts.
9. Create suggested selling price based on cost.

Menu Programs

1. Create and print physical menus.
2. Create cycle menus based on management-supplied parameters.
3. Produce production schedules based on selected menus.
4. Produce equipment usage plans based on selected menus.
5. Produce purchase orders based on selected menus.
6. Create and cost catering/special-event menus.
7. Forecast revenue and expense based on selected menu and forecasted sales.

Purchasing Software

1. Create vendor bid sheets based on forecasted ingredient needs.
2. Compare bids and make purchase recommendations based on best cost/best value.
3. Maintain vendor price histories.
4. Establish minimum and maximum par values by ingredient.
5. Create purchase orders and auto-order based on established par levels with automatic electronic order confirmation.
6. Interface (if desirable) with other systems to create aggregate purchase orders (in multiunit settings).
7. Create purchase recap by item and/or vendor.

8. Maintain a "red-flag" system for product purchasing variances that exceed forecasted usage.

9. Utilize purchase orders to predict actual profitability.

10. Purchase directly from vendor using vendor-supplied software.

Receiving Software

1. Prepare a daily receiving report.

2. Compare product received (receiving records) with purchase orders (PO) in areas of:
   a. Weight
   b. Quantity
   c. Quality
   d. Price

3. Maintain outage and shortage records by vendor.

4. Verify vendor price extensions.

5. Maintain receiving histories.

Storage/Inventory Assessment Programs

1. Maintain product inventory values by food category (i.e., produce, meat, dairy, etc.).

2. Create "shopping lists" through production of daily inventory and comparison with production schedules.

3. Report par stock levels, daily storeroom issues and daily product usage.

4. Maintain perpetual inventory.

5. Compute LIFO or FIFO inventory values.

6. Maintain inventory products database by vendor, storeroom location, product type, alpha order, etc.

7. Report below-par inventory levels.

8. Report daily cost of goods issued or sold.

9. Report product usage variances based on actual sales.

10. Interface with handheld bar code readers for accurate inventory count and price extension.

11. Compute inventory loss rates.

Cost of Goods Sold Programs

1. Compare forecasted to actual cost of goods sold.

2. Maintain employee meal records.

3. Compute cost of goods sold by menu category (i.e., salad, entrée, dessert, etc.).

4. Compare current cost of goods sold with:

   a. Same unit historical data

   b. Same unit budgeted cost data

   c. Multiunit operation averages (for multiunit operations)

   d. Industry- or management-generated standards

Perhaps it is in the area of managing food products, from their purchase to usage, that you can most effectively utilize the rapidly advancing technological tools available today. Remember, however, that the amount of information that can be generated in this case is vast, and you should elect to gather and maintain only information that is of real value to you.

FUN ON THE WEB!

Eatec Corp. is another company that creates innovative software products that really speed up the process of taking inventory. To view its product offerings go to **www.eatec.com.**

Apply What You Have Learned

*T*onya Johnson is the Regional Manager for Old Town Buffets. Each of the five units she supervises is in a different town. Produce for each unit is purchased locally by each buffet manager. One day, Tonya gets a call from Danny Trevino, one of the buffet managers reporting to her. Danny states that one of the local produce suppliers he uses has offered Danny the use of season tickets to the local university's football games. Danny likes football and would like to accept them.

1. Would you allow Danny to accept the tickets? Why or why not?

2. Would you allow your managers to accept a gift of any kind (including holiday gifts) from a vendor?

3. Draft a "gifts" policy that you would implement in your region. Would you be subject to the same policy?

Key Terms and Concepts

*T*he following are terms and concepts discussed in the chapter that are important for you as a manager. To help you review, please define the terms below.

Popularity index	Standardized recipe	Safety stock
Predicted number to be sold	Recipe ready	Carryovers
	Working stock	Shelf life

Opportunity cost	Ethics	Padded inventory
Fiscal year	Daily inventory sheet	Inventory valuation sheet
Purchase point	Purchase order	Physical inventory
As needed/just in time	Auditors	Cost of food sold
Par level	Acceptance hours	Beginning inventory
Product specification/spec	Refusal hours	Purchases
Count	Shorting	Goods available for sale
Product yield	Credit memo	Ending inventory
Best price	Contract price	Cost of food consumed
Bid sheet	Extended price	Employee meal cost
Price comparison sheet	LIFO	Source reduction
Minimum order	FIFO	Food cost percent
requirement	Freezer burn	
Cherry picker	Issue	

Test Your Skills

Complete the Test Your Skills exercises by placing your answers in the shaded boxes and answering the questions as indicated.

1. Saint John's Hospital foodservice director, Herman Zindu, has a problem. He has the following information about his operation for the month of April, but has forgotten how to compute cost of food sold for the month. Use Herman's figures to compute actual cost of food sold for his operation.

Inventory on March 31	<u>$22,184.50</u>
April Purchases	

Meats	$11,501.00
Dairy	$ 6,300.00
Fruits and Vegetables	$ 9,641.00
All Other Foods	$32,384.00
Number of Employees Eating Daily	85
Cost per Employee for Employee Meals	$1.25
Inventory on April 30	<u>$23,942.06</u>

   Could Herman have computed this figure if he had not taken a physical inventory on April 30? Why or why not?

2. "Fast Eddie" Green operates a restaurant in the casino town of Taloona. He is checking over the work of his assistant manager who has been newly hired. One of the jobs of the assistant manager is to complete daily the six column food cost estimate. "Fast Eddie" finds that, although the data are there for the first 10 days of the accounting period, the form has not been completed. Complete the form for "Fast Eddie" so that he can go home.

| Weekday | PURCHASES | | SALES | | COST % | |
	Today	Todate	Today	To Date	Today	To Date
1/1	$1,645.80		$3,842.50			
1/2	2,006.40		2,970.05			
1/3	1,107.20		2,855.20			
1/4	986.24		3,001.45			
1/5	1,245.60		3,645.20			
1/6	2,006.40		4,850.22			
1/7	0.00		6,701.55			
1/8	1,799.90		3,609.20			
1/9	851.95		2,966.60			
1/10	924.50		3,105.25			
Total						

3. Billie Mendoza is the purchasing manager for a medium-sized all-suite hotel with a restaurant and a banquet hall. She needs to create the food purchase orders for tomorrow, and she wants to make sure that she is getting the best price for the best quality and service. At the beginning of this week, Billie received bids on produce items from Village Produce, City Produce, and Country Produce. She has listed these prices in the following price comparison sheet.

   a. Identify the best bid price and best company for each of Billie's produce items. (Spreadsheet hint: Use the MIN function in the Best Bid $ column.)

Price Comparison Sheet								
Item	Description	Unit	Village Produce	City Produce	Country Produce	Best Bid $	Best Company Quote	Last Price Paid
Avocados	48 ct.	Case	$61.80	$60.30	$59.46			$57.94
Cauliflower	12 ct.	Case	12.80	12.90	13.27			13.26
Cucumbers	Medium	Case	11.10	11.52	10.91			11.34
Grapes	Red Seedless	Lug	19.32	19.50	19.14			18.72
Lettuce	Green Leaf, 24 ct.	Case	9.53	9.84	10.27			10.02
Lettuce	Romaine, 24 ct.	Case	17.75	17.82	18.22			18.10
Pears	D'Anjou	Case	20.82	20.58	20.64			20.62
Peppers	Green Bell, Med.	Case	8.30	8.38	9.28			9.02
Pineapples	7 ct.	Case	10.50	10.38	10.68			10.08
Potatoes	B Reds	50# Bag	15.06	14.82	14.88			14.98
Potatoes	Peeled, Large	25# Bag	17.52	17.22	17.28			17.18
Squash	Yellow #2	30# Case	8.55	8.71	8.98			9.10
Strawberries	Driscoll	Flat	18.29	18.06	17.10			18.30

b. Now that Billie knows which vendors have the best prices, she decides to take the daily inventory to find out what she needs to order for tomorrow. Her par value, on-hand, and special-order requirements are as follows. Help Billie determine the amount of each item she needs to order. (Spreadsheet hint: Use the ROUNDUP function in the Order Amount column.)

Item	Description	Unit	Par Value	On Hand	Special Order	Order Amount
Avocados	48 ct.	Case	6	2	3	
Cauliflower	12 ct.	Case	5	1		
Cucumbers	Medium	Case	3	0		
Grapes	Red Seedless	Lug	4	1		
Lettuce	Green Leaf, 24 ct.	Case	5	2	4	
Lettuce	Romaine, 24 ct.	Case	3	0.5		
Pears	D'Anjou	Case	3	1		
Peppers	Green Bell, Med.	Case	7	2	5	
Pineapples	7 ct.	Case	4	0		
Potatoes	B Reds	50# Bag	3	0.5		
Potatoes	Peeled, Large	25# Bag	4	1	4	
Squash	Yellow #2	30# Case	5	2	2	
Strawberries	Driscoll	Flat	3	1.5		

c. Next, Billie needs to create the purchase order for tomorrow. Help her create the correct purchase order for Village Produce based on her inventory needs (part b.) and the bid prices for Village Produce located on the price comparison worksheet (part a).

Purchase Order							
Supplier					**Purchase Order**		
Company Name:	Village Produce				P.O. Number		456
Street Address:	123 Somewhere				Order Date:		1/1
City, State, Zip:	Village, CA 12345				Delivery Date:		1/2
Phone Number:	555-5555				Phone Number:		555-5557
Fax Number:	555-5556				Fax Number:		555-5558
E-Mail:	Village@isp.org				E-Mail:		Billie@isp.org
Contact:	Mr. Green				Buyer:		Ms. Mendoza
Item	**Description**	**Unit**	**Quantity**		**Unit Price $**		**Extension**
Total							

4. Loralei operates the foodservice for a large elementary school. She buys produce from Shady Tree Produce Company. Wayne, Shady Tree's owner, makes many errors when he prepares invoices for his customers, but he is the only vendor who has the ability to deliver daily. Loralei needs daily delivery. Because she knows Wayne is careless with the invoices, Loralei checks each one carefully. For Monday, Loralei needs the items listed below.

Monday Order		
Item	**Unit Price**	**Number of Cases Needed**
Tomatoes	$18.50	3
Potatoes	$12.90	6
Carrots	$18.29	4

Using this information, complete her Purchase Order for Monday below.

Purchase Order						
Supplier				**Purchase Order**		
Company Name:	Shady Tree			P.O. Number	123	
Street Address:	123 Somewhere			Order Date:	1/1	
City, State, Zip:	Village, TX 12345			Delivery Date:	1/2	
Phone Number:	555-5555			Phone Number:	555-5557	
Fax Number:	555-5556			Fax Number:	555-5558	
E-Mail:	Shady@isp.org			E-Mail:	Lora@isp.org	
Contact:	Wayne			Buyer:	Loralei	
Item	**Description**	**Unit**	**Quantity**	**Unit Price $**	**Extension**	
Tomatoes	4 × 5, Layered	Case				
Potatoes	Peeled, Large	Case				
Carrots	Julienne, 5# bags	Case				
Total						

Upon delivery, Loralei checks her invoice from Wayne to see if he has, once again, made any errors.

Review the following invoice totals.

Shady Tree Produce Company Invoice for Monday Order			
Item	**Unit price**	**Number Delivered**	**Extended Price**
Tomatoes	$18.50	3	$ 55.55
Potatoes	$19.20	6	$115.20
Carrots	$18.92	4	$ 75.68
Total Amount Due			$256.43

Does the invoice contain errors? If so, what are they? What is the total amount of "error" on the invoice, if any? How can Loralei detect such errors in the future?

5. Barry Stiller is the assistant manager of the Pine Tree Grill. The Pine Tree is one food outlet located at the Great Bear Water Park and Resort. Each Sunday morning he is required to submit the dollar value of his inventory to his Food and Beverage Director. These data form the basis for the F&B department's cost of food sold for the previous week. The Food and Beverage Director has given Barry a weekly food cost percent goal of 28 percent. She has promised Barry a monthly bonus if he can stay at or under his food cost percent goal. Complete Barry's Inventory Valuation Sheet below and calculate his food cost percent.

Inventory Valuation Sheet				
Unit Name: Pine Tree Grill Counted By: Barry Stiller			Inventory Date: Sunday 3/8 Extended By: Barry Stiller	
Item	Unit	Item Amount	Item Value	Inventory Value
Rib Eye Steaks (10 oz.)	units	44	$ 8.50	
Rib Eye Steaks (16 oz.)	units	34	$11.50	
New York Strip Steak	lb.	28	$ 7.75	
Corned Beef	lb.	22.5	$ 8.25	
Rib Roast	lb.	60	$ 6.75	
Hamburger	lb.	15	$ 2.75	
Chicken Breasts	lb.	53	$ 2.50	
Sausage Links	pound	25.5	$ 2.40	
Bacon	case	3.5	$62.00	
Beef Base	jar	17	$ 8.00	
Tomatoes (4x5)	case	2	$25.00	
Bananas	case	3	$15.00	
Oranges	case	2.5	$30.00	
Lemons	case	2	$28.00	
Lettuce	case	3.5	$26.30	
Bread	unit	7	$ 2.50	
Rice	bags	4	$12.00	
Total				

Beginning Inventory 3/1	$ 2,735.70
Purchases	$ 5,348.53
Goods Available for Sale	
Ending Inventory 3/8	
Transfers Out	$ 470.40
Transfers In	$ 336.60
Cost of Food Consumed	
Employee Meals	$ 740.00
Cost of Food Sold	
Sales	$17,538.46
Food Cost %	

Did Barry meet his food cost percentage goal for the week? Is he doing a good job at controlling his costs and managing his inventory? Is Barry likely to reach his monthly goal and receive his bonus?

6. Spike Dykes operates the student foodservice in a dormitory at Clairmont College. Spike is interested in calculating his "Food Cost per Student Meal Served." Data about his costs and meals served for the spring semester can be found in the table below; but some of it is missing. Help Spike complete the table, and then answer the questions he has about his operation.

	Jan	Feb	March	April	May	Total
Beginning Inventory	$ 22,500			$25,500		
Purchases	$ 65,000		$63,000	$64,500	$64,300	
Goods Available for Sale		$86,500				
Ending Inventory	$ 21,750			$16,000	$12,000	
Cost of Food Consumed		$60,000				
Employee Meals		$5,500	$5,250		$4,850	
Cost of Food Sold	$ 60,000			$69,000		
Meals Served	20,750	20,100	21,500	21,250	19,000	
Cost Per Meal						

What was Spike's:

a. Cost of Food Sold in:

> February
> March
> May

b. Cost per Meal in:

> January
> February
> March
> April
> May

c. Total Cost of Employee Meals for the spring semester?

d. Total Cost of Food Sold for the spring semester?

e. Average Cost per Meal Served for the spring semester?

7. Because drive-through, take-away, and delivery service constitute increasingly large proportions of many foodservice operations' sales, more managers are considering adding paper and packaging costs to cost of food calculations. Assume you were managing a foodservice operation with significantly increasing "off-premise" food sales.

   a. What would be some advantages of including "packaging" (containers, wrappings, and the like) as a cost of food?

   b. What could be some disadvantages of such an approach?

   c. In addition, what are some specific steps you could take to ensure that you are following "green" practices with regard to the packaging of carryout items?

Chapter 4

MANAGING THE COST OF BEVERAGES

OVERVIEW

This chapter begins with an overview of the special responsibilities you assume when your operation serves alcoholic beverages. It then details the various types of beverage products you may sell and the techniques used to purchase them, as well as the specific knowledge you must have to store them properly. Important topics in this chapter include the use of standardized drink recipes and the procedures used to monitor and forecast beverage sales. Lastly, the chapter explains how your guests' beverage choices influence the beverage cost percentages that you will compute as you evaluate the cost efficiency of your beverage unit.

Chapter Outline

- Serving Alcoholic Beverages
- Forecasting Beverage Sales
- Standardized Drink Recipes and Portions
- Purchasing Beverage Products
- Receiving Beverage Products
- Storing Beverage Products
- Bar Transfers
- Computing Cost of Beverages
- Special Features of Liquor Inventory
- Sales Mix
- Technology Tools
- Apply What You Have Learned
- Key Terms and Concepts
- Test Your Skills

At the conclusion of this chapter, you will be able to:

- Use sales histories and standardized drink recipes to develop a beverage purchase order.
- Compute the dollar value of bar transfers both to and from the kitchen.
- Compute an accurate cost of goods sold percentage for beer, wine, and spirits.

SERVING ALCOHOLIC BEVERAGES

*I*t might seem unusual that a book about cost management would separate the study of cost control into a segment dealing with food and another one dealing with alcoholic beverage products. In fact, it might seem unusual that the very term "beverages" in this chapter will always refer to beverages containing alcohol. In fact, if you have the skill to serve alcoholic beverages responsibly and can properly account for the cost of serving these beverages, you are better prepared to manage a variety of foodservice operations than managers who do not have those skills. The reason is simple. Many operations include alcohol as a major component of the products they offer to guests. There are three types of operations that serve alcoholic beverages. These can be grouped as:

1. Beverage only
2. Beverage and food
3. Beverage and entertainment/activity

■ BEVERAGE ONLY

The beverage only operation has been in existence in the United States for a little more than a hundred years. Prior to that, alcohol was generally sold only in conjunction with food and lodging services. Actually, in these facilities, snacks such as pretzels, chips, and nuts are often served, but beverage service is clearly most important. Beverage only bars are often neighborhood gathering places. Some are frequented by businesspeople who work in the vicinity, whereas travelers may drop in when they are in the area. Decor can be anything from comfortably casual to upscale. When provided, entertainment may include television, recorded music, a pool table, pinball, trivia, Internet-delivered juke box music and videos, lottery games, and, increasingly, sophisticated video games. In some cases, an outdoor setting may also be an attractive customer draw.

Beverage only bars usually have a predictable traffic flow. Because they deal only in beverages, these are usually the easiest service operations to manage. Beverage only operations can include:

1. Neighborhood bars
2. Taverns
3. Hotel bars
4. Airport bars
5. Breweries
6. Wineries

■ BEVERAGE AND FOOD

Beverage and food operations are the predominant type of beverage operation in the United States and a major industry in the world today. Restaurants serving wine, beer, and liquor and bars serving limited menus are examples of this type of service.

It is important to remember that the profit margins on alcoholic beverages are generally much higher than those on food; thus, it makes good business sense to add the service of alcoholic beverages to the service of providing food whenever possible. Although it is impossible to state the appropriate profit levels for alcoholic beverages, profits are generally two to five times greater for beverage products than for food products. Thus, it is highly likely that the profit in the pitcher of beer that you may sell in a pizza restaurant you own will exceed that of its accompanying pizza by a great deal, even though the beer may be sold for half the price of the pizza.

Many alcoholic beverages were created because they are enjoyed most when combined with food; thus, it is only natural for professional food and beverage managers to seek out and promote these combinations. Beverage and food operations can include:

1. Quick-service restaurants
2. Full-service restaurants
3. Self-service and cafeterias
4. Airport bars
5. Sports complexes such as areas and stadiums
6. Grocery/convenience store carryout
7. Brew pubs
8. Hotel room service
9. Banquet halls
10. Country clubs

■ BEVERAGE AND ENTERTAINMENT/ACTIVITY

Beverage and entertainment/activity operations exist because many people want to do something while they consume their favorite alcoholic beverage. As discussed earlier, eating is one of those favorite activities. This segment of the beverage business, however, can offer even more.

There is enormous variety in the types of entertainment and activities that can accompany beverage service, ranging from dartboards and pool tables to elaborate stage shows in nightclubs and cabarets. Dance clubs can provide live or recorded music while guests enjoy dancing. Piano bars and small clubs provide quiet, intimate places to enjoy music and conversation. There are high-tech clubs where the entertainment comes from giant video screens and computerized games, and old-fashioned ballparks where your guests can enjoy a game. Beverage and entertainment/activity operations can include:

1. Comedy clubs
2. Taverns
3. Entertainment clubs
4. Full-service restaurants
5. Sports complexes
6. Brew pubs
7. Nightclubs
8. Country clubs
9. Dance/music clubs
10. Bowling alleys

■ CLASSIFICATIONS OF ALCOHOLIC BEVERAGES

Alcoholic beverages are those products that are meant for consumption as a beverage and that contain a significant amount of ethyl alcohol. These products are generally classified as:

1. **Beer:** A fermented beverage made from grain and flavored with hops
2. **Wine:** A fermented beverage made from grapes, fruits, or berries
3. **Spirits:** Fermented beverages that are distilled to increase the alcohol content of the product

Whether you combine the sale of food products with that of beverages or manage a facility that sells beverages exclusively, you face a set of challenges that deserve special attention. In many ways, you will treat beverage products in a manner similar to that of food products. The beverage products you buy will be specified, ordered, received, and stored in a fashion that is very close to that of food products. In other ways, however, when you are responsible for the sale and service of alcohol, you take on a responsibility that society views as extremely critical.

■ RESPONSIBLE ALCOHOLIC BEVERAGE SERVICE

People have long been fond of alcoholic beverages regardless of where they are consumed because they add greatly to the enjoyment of food and friends. In moderate doses, ethyl alcohol, the type found in beverage products, acts as a mild tranquilizer. In excessive doses, it can become toxic, causing impaired judgment and, in some cases, death. Clearly, a foodservice manager whose establishment serves alcoholic beverages must take great care in the serving of alcohols beverages and monitoring of guests' alcohol intake.

Many states have now enacted third-party liability legislation, which, under certain conditions, holds your business and, in some cases, you, personally, responsible for the actions of your guests who consume excessive amounts of alcoholic beverages. This series of legislative acts, commonly called **dramshop laws,** shifts the liability for acts committed by an individual under the influence of alcohol from that individual to the server or operation that supplied the intoxicating beverage. (*Dramshop* is derived from the word *dram*, which refers to a small drink, and *shop* where such a drink was sold.)

Because of these laws, managers are becoming increasingly concerned about alcohol awareness and the importance of safely serving their guests. In addition, as states continue to move to lower the allowable **blood alcohol content (BAC)** of motor vehicle drivers, good managers simply want to help guests obey the law. This means training employees to serve alcoholic beverages properly and to notice telltale signs of possible guest intoxication.

Through passage of dramshop and related laws, it is very clear that society holds the seller of alcoholic beverages to a very high standard. In all states, the sale of these products is regulated either by the licensing of establishments that are allowed to sell alcoholic beverages (**license states**) or by direct control and sale of the products by the state (**control states**).

Although the special requirements involved in serving alcoholic beverages are many—including licensing, age restrictions, promotional limitations, drinking and driving issues, and social responsibility, to name just a few—the control of beverage costs is similar, in many respects, to the control of food-related costs.

This chapter details the unique aspects of sales forecasting, purchasing, receiving, and storage of beverage products. In some areas, beverage control is no different from that of nonalcoholic food products reviewed in the last chapter. In others, the differences are pronounced.

FORECASTING BEVERAGE SALES

*T*he number of possible "menu items" in the average bar or lounge is staggering. Human imagination has few limits; thus, the number of different alcoholic beverage mixtures a skilled bartender can concoct makes forecasting guest item selection a difficult process, indeed. Of course, you now know how to track the number of guests served and the items these guests will buy. This is done exactly as previously discussed (Chapter 2). **Percent selecting**—the proportion of people who will buy a particular drink, given a choice of many different drink types—must be modified somewhat if it is to be applied to forecasting beverage sales. In fact, beverage sales forecasting varies also by the type of beverage sold.

■ FORECASTING BEER SALES

Forecasting beer sales is essentially the same as forecasting any regular menu item. That is, given a choice of beverage products, some percentage of your guests will likely choose beer. However, the questions you must answer to effectively manage your costs are, "What percentage of my guests will choose beer?" and "Which kind of beer?" and "In what packaging format will they choose that beer?"

To illustrate, assume that you are the owner of LeRae, a small bar in a trendy section of a large West Coast city. Your clientele generally consists of upscale office and managerial professionals. For the time period 1/1 to 1/8, you served an alcoholic beverage to a total of 1,600 guests: 400, or 25 percent, selected a beer product; 160, or 10 percent, selected a wine product; and 1,040, or 65 percent, selected some type of spirit-based drink.

Using your sales history, you have a good idea of how many people will be coming to your bar on any given day. You have monitored your percent selecting data and found that one out of four guests coming to LeRae's will order beer. You need to determine, however, which specific brand of beer your guests will buy, given the several brands of beer that you do, or can, offer. In addition, it is very likely that at least some of the beer you serve will come packaged in more than one form. That is, a specific beer brand might be sold in individual cans or bottles or in kegs. **Keg beer** is also known as **draft beer**, or beer in a form of packaging in which the beer is shipped to you in multigallon units for bulk sale. By charting current beer sales, you can know what your guests' beer preferences are. Figure 4.1 demonstrates that, for the period 1/1 to 1/8, LeRae's served 400 beers to guests. It also details which specific beer those guests ordered.

By reviewing data from your point of sales (POS) system, you will know exactly which beers, by brand and packaging form, you have sold in the bar on a daily basis. A tally of guest checks would also furnish you with the same information, but such a system is labor intensive, time-consuming, and subject to inaccuracy. Regardless of the tracking method used, the goal is the same as that of tracking a food item sale. That is, with a good idea of what guests have purchased in the past,

■ **FIGURE 4.1**   LeRae's Bar Beer Sales

Beverage Sales		Date: 1/1–1/8
Product: Beer	Number Sold	Percentage Sold
Budweiser Bottles	45	11.25%
Coors Bottles	18	4.50
Miller Cans	61	15.25
Coors Cans	68	17.00
Budweiser Draft	115	28.75
Harp's Draft	93	23.25
Total	400	100.00

FUN ON THE WEB!

Americans love their beer and have for many years. The nation's oldest continuously operating brewery opened in 1829 when David G. Yuengling established the Eagle Brewery on Centre Street in Pottsville, Pennsylvania. It survived the 18th Amendment (Prohibition) and today sells seven different brewed beers. To learn more about this (still!) family-run brewery, go to **www.yuengling.com.**

we are better prepared to order the products, in their proper packaging form, that we believe guests will purchase in the future.

■ FORECASTING WINE SALES

The forecasting of wine sales is similar to that of beer sales in that it must be divided into two parts:

1. Forecasting bottled-wine sales
2. Forecasting wine-by-the-glass sales

FORECASTING BOTTLED-WINE SALES

When forecasting wine sales by the bottle, you treat an individual type of bottled wine exactly as you would treat a menu item. A wine list or wine menu detailing the selections of wines available is presented to the guest, who then makes a choice. Percent selecting figures are computed exactly as they would be when analyzing food item sales. You may find, however, that it is possible and quite desirable to offer wines with very small percent selecting figures because wines in a bottle are not highly perishable. Thus, many operators develop extensive wine lists consisting of a large number of wines, many of which sell only infrequently. Although this selling strategy has its place because some restaurants consider an extensive wine list as an integral part of their marketing strategy, you must remember that excessive product inventory, whether food or beverage, must be avoided. Dollars invested in extravagant inventory are not available for use in other areas of the foodservice organization. Even though bottled wine is not highly perishable, all wine products are perishable to some degree; thus, excessive inventory of some wine types can result in increased product loss through oxidation (deterioration), theft, or both.

FORECASTING WINE-BY-THE-GLASS SALES

Generally, forecasting the sale of **house wines** includes those wines served to a guest who does not stipulate a specific brand when ordering, as well as those named wines offered by the glass. Once you have estimated the number of guests who will select wine, the type of wine they will select can be forecasted. The popularity of different wine types changes frequently, as newer styles and varieties gain in popularity and newer wine producing regions (such as Argentina, Australia, and South Africa) improve the quality and marketing of their locally produced wines. As a result, you must continually monitor the wines your guests prefer to drink "now," rather than attempt to sell what they preferred "back then"!

Figure 4.2 details the by-the-glass sales of wine at LeRae's for the period 1/1 to 1/8. From the data, you know that one out of ten guests will buy wine by the glass. Thus, 160 (from a total of 1,600 guests) will select this beverage.

If your guests remain consistent in their buying habits, you will have a good idea of the total demand for your wine-by-the-glass products and will be better able to ascertain the amount that must be on hand on any given day.

■ FIGURE 4.2 LeRae's Bar Wine-by-the-Glass Sales

Beverage Sales		Date: 1/1–1/8
Product: Wine by The Glass	Number Sold	Percentage Sold
Fabiano Chardonnay	30	18.75%
House Merlot	16	10.00
Bolla Soave	62	38.75
House Zinfandel	52	32.50
Total	160	100.00

■ FORECASTING SPIRIT SALES

Like beer and wine, the number of guests who order a mixed drink can be tracked. Unlike beer and wine, however, the exact item the guests will request is very difficult to determine. When ordering spirits, tracking sales can become complicated. For example, assume that two guests order bourbon and soda; one guest specifies Jack Daniel's brand of bourbon, whereas the other one prefers Heaven Hill brand. From the guests' point of view, they both ordered bourbon and soda. From the operator's point of view, two distinct items were selected. To make matters a bit more complicated, a third guest arrives and orders bourbon and soda without preference as to the type of bourbon used. Obviously, a different method of sales forecasting is necessary in a situation such as this, and, in fact, several are available. One method requires that the operator view guest selection not in terms of the drink requested, such as bourbon and water, gin and tonic, Sea Breeze, and so on, but rather in terms of the particular spirit that forms the base of the drink. Consider a table of four guests who order the following:

1. Kahlúa on the rocks
2. Kahlúa and coffee
3. Kahlúa and cream
4. Kahlúa and Coke

Each guest could be considered as having ordered the same item: a drink in which Kahlúa, a coffee-flavored liqueur from Mexico, forms the base of the drink. The purpose of this method is, of course, to simplify the process of recording guests' preferences.

Depending on the degree of accuracy desired by the operator, tracking spirit sales can be done by any of the following methods:

1. Generic product name:
   a. Coffee liqueur
   b. Bourbon
   c. Vodka
   d. Gin
2. Specific product name:
   a. Kahlúa
   b. Jack Daniel's Black Label
   c. Absolut
   d. Bombay
3. Specific drink requested:
   a. Kahlúa on the rocks
   b. Kahlúa and coffee
   c. Kahlúa and cream
   d. Kahlúa and Coke

■ **FIGURE 4.3** LeRae's Bar Spirit Sales

Beverage Sales		Date: 1/1–1/8
Product: Spirits	Number Sold	Percentage Sold
Scotch	210	13.1%
Bourbon	175	10.9
Vodka	580	36.3
Gin	375	23.4
Kahlúa	175	10.9
Tequila	85	5.3
Total	1,600	100.0

Figure 4.3 demonstrates the system you would use to track spirit sales using the generic product method illustrated previously. It also is an excellent example of the power of an effective beverage POS system to help track sales in a manner that is far more effective than can be done manually. The number of different spirit drinks that can be made numbers in the hundreds. A POS system programmed specifically for your operation can be a great asset in helping you develop the sales histories you need to purchase spirit products effectively because it can easily track this large number of drink combinations.

As the amount of time and effort required to track specific drink sales increases, so does accuracy. Each operator must determine the level of control appropriate for his or her own operation. This is due to the simple fact that there must be a relationship between the time, money, and effort required to maintain a control system and its cost effectiveness.

STANDARDIZED DRINK RECIPES AND PORTIONS

*I*f a beverage operation is even moderately busy, it is simply unrealistic to assume that the bartender can stop each time an order comes in, consult a written standardized recipe as discussed in Chapter 3, and then prepare the drink requested. Imagine the resulting confusion, chaos, and time delay if such a system were in place! The demand for control in the bar, however, is even greater than that required in the kitchen. The reason is simple. The potential for employee inefficiency, theft, or waste is often greater in the bar than in the kitchen. Consider, for a moment, just a few of the unique aspects of beverage operations that require strict adherence to control procedures:

1. Beverage operations are subject to tax audits to verify sales revenue. In some states, these audits are unannounced.

2. Beverage operations can be closed down "on the spot" for the violation of a liquor law.

3. Employees in a bar may deceptively seek to become operational "partners" by bringing in their own beverage products to sell and then keeping sales revenue.

4. Detecting the disappearance of small amounts of beverage products is extremely difficult, as, for example, the loss of 8 ounces of beer from a multigallon keg.

For these reasons and others, using standardized recipes is an absolute must for the beverage operation, even if using written standardized recipes for each drink is not a viable option. Consider the case of Paul, the bar manager at a full-service restaurant. He knows that each bourbon and water he produces should consist of 95 cents in beverage product cost. His selling price is $8.50. He uses the beverage cost percent formula to determine his beverage cost percentage. The following beverage cost percent formula, as you can easily see, is nearly identical to the food cost percent formula presented in Chapter 3:

$$\frac{\text{Cost of Beverage Sold}}{\text{Beverage Sales}} = \text{Beverage Cost \%}$$

Thus, Paul's beverage cost percent should be as follows:

$$\frac{\$0.95}{\$8.50} = 11.2\%$$

Yet his actual beverage cost percent on this item could be much higher. How can this be, on an item as uncomplicated as bourbon and water? The answer is simple. The bartender did not follow the standardized recipe. Even on an item as commonplace as bourbon and water, the bartender must know exactly the amount of product to use. It is not simply a matter of combining bourbon and water, but rather a matter of how much bourbon to add to how much water. This ratio affects both the drink's cost and its taste. Figure 4.4 shows the beverage cost that would be achieved with different drink sizes and a standard 1-liter bottle of spirits.

As shown, the difference in the drink recipe can make a big difference in total beverage cost percent. For purposes of accuracy, assume approximately a

■ **FIGURE 4.4** Beverage Cost Competition

Beverage: Bourbon			Container Size: One Liter (33.8 OZ.)			
Product Cost: $24.80/Liter						
Portion Size	Number of Portions	Liter Cost	Portion Cost	Selling Price	Total Beverage Sales	Beverage Cost %
1.00 oz.	33	$24.80	$0.75	$8.50	$280.50	8.8%
1.25 oz.	26	24.80	0.95	8.50	221.00	11.2
1.50 oz.	22	24.80	1.13	8.50	187.00	13.3
1.75 oz.	19	24.80	1.31	8.50	161.50	15.4

0.8-ounce-per-liter evaporation loss, thus leaving Paul with 33 ounces of usable product from this liter of bourbon. Also, assume a product cost of $24.80 per liter, with an $8.50 per drink selling price and a normal portion size of 1 and 1/4 ounce of bourbon. Obviously, the quantity of alcohol actually used makes the liquor cost percent vary greatly.

Stated in another way, assume that you manage a large convention hotel that has a beverage sales volume in spirit drinks of $4,000,000 per year. If your bartenders consistently pour 1.75-ounce drinks rather than 1.25-ounce drinks, and you assume average costs and selling prices as shown in Figure 4.4, then beverage costs will be 15.4 percent rather than the planned 11.2 percent. The difference is 4.2 percent (15.4 − 11.2 = 4.2). The loss represents $4,000,000 × 0.042 = $168,000 for this one operation in just one year! A loss as sizable as this is certainly career threatening for any manager!

Although standardized recipes, which include step-by-step methods of preparation, may be necessary for only a few types of drinks, standardized recipes that detail the quantity of beverage product management has predetermined as appropriate should be strictly adhered to. That is, if management has determined that bourbon and water should be a 1-ounce portion of bourbon and a 2-ounce portion of water, then both items should be measured by a **jigger,** a tool for measuring liquid, or by an automated device programmed to dispense these predetermined amounts.

Regardless of method of measurement (manual or automated), both bourbon and water, in this case, must be delivered to the guest in the proper ratio if product quality is to be maintained. Consider, for a moment, the case of a manager who determines that a particular blend of bourbon, although expensive, can be sold at a premium price. The manager sets the drink price and instructs the bartender that the portion size is to be 1 ounce of spirit with 2 ounces of water. Consider the following guest reactions when the bartender varies the quantity of water added to the bourbon:

Drink Ratio	Possible Guest Response
A. 1 oz. bourbon	1. Gee, the drinks sure are small here!
1 oz. water	2. Gee, this sure is strong! Can you add a splash of water?
B. 1 oz. bourbon	1. Gee, this sure tastes good! It's just right!
2 oz. water	
C. 1 oz. bourbon	1. Gee, this tastes watered down. Can you add a splash of bourbon?
3 oz. water	2. Gee, these drinks cost a lot for such a small amount of alcohol!

Remember that the quantity of spirit used and, thus, the product cost percentage, did not change under scenario A, B, or C. In this case, the bartender was very careful not to use more product than he or she had been instructed to do. In effect, the bartender put the profitability of the operation before guest satisfaction. It is important to remember that happy guests provide profits; profits do not provide happy guests. The manager of this operation might be pleased with the bartender's precise product control because the cost of 1 ounce versus 3 ounces of water is minuscule. Guests, however, will react to sloppy drink preparation in the same way they do to sloppy food preparation.

In summary, each drink in the bar must have a standardized recipe or, if the preparation of the drink is simple, a standardized portion size. These recipes affect the planned profitability of the operation as well as guest satisfaction.

Since it is necessary to cost beverage recipes just as it is necessary to cost food item recipes, a standardized recipe sheet (see Chapter 3) should be prepared for each drink item to be sold. A record of these recipes should be available at each beverage outlet. If questions about portion size or preparation arise, the standardized recipe should be referred to.

FUN ON THE WEB!

Loss of beverage products through theft, shrinkage, breakage, and overpouring can cost a restaurant a lot of money in lost profits. To view the Web site of a company that works with restaurateurs to increase beverage profits by controlling loss of beverage inventory, go to **www.bevinco.com**.

PURCHASING BEVERAGE PRODUCTS

*M*ost foodservice operators select only one quality level for food products. Once a determination on necessary quality level has been made and a product specification written, then only that quality of meat, lettuce, milk, bread, and so on is selected. In the area of alcoholic beverage products, however, several levels of quality are generally chosen. This ensures that a beverage product is available for those guests who wish to purchase the very best, and a product is also offered for those guests who prefer to spend less. Thus, the beverage manager is faced, for example, with deciding not only whether to carry wine on the menu but also how many different kinds of wine and their quality levels. The same process is necessary for spirits and, to a lesser degree, for beers

■ DETERMINING BEER PRODUCTS TO CARRY

Beer is the most highly perishable of beverage products. The **pull date**, or expiration date, on these products can be as short as a few months. Because of this, it is important that the beverage operator only stock those items that will sell relatively well. This generally means selecting both appropriate brands and appropriate packaging methods.

BRAND SELECTION

Beverage operators typically carry between 3 and 10 types of beer. Some operations, however, stock as many as 50 or more! Generally speaking, geographic location, clientele, ambience, and menu help determine the beer product that will be selected. Obviously, we would not expect to see the same beer products at Hunan Gardens Chinese Restaurant that we would at Three Pesos Mexican Restaurant. Most foodservice operators find that one or two brands of light beer, two or three national domestic brands, and one or two quality import beers meet the great majority of their guests' demand. One must be very careful in this area not to stock excessive amounts of products that sell poorly. Again, beer is perishable, and great care must be taken to ensure proper product movement. It is important, however, to train bartenders to make a notation on a **product request log** (see Figure 4.5) so

■ FIGURE 4.5 Beverage Product Request Log

Date	Item Requested	Entry By
1/1	Lowenbrau Beer	P. J.
1/1	Cherry Schnapps	L. T.
1/2	Rolling Rock Beer on Draft	T. R.
1/4	Lowenbrau Beer	P. J.
1/5	Soave Wine	L. D.
1/6	Any Texas Wine	S. H.
1/6	Lowenbrau Beer	T. R.

that guest requests that cannot be filled are noted and monitored by management. This log should be easily accessible to service personnel. Its purpose is to maintain a record of guest product requests that are not currently available. In the case of beverages, those items that guests wish to purchase that are not available are nearly as important to track as the sales of the items that are available.

If you were managing the operation that generated the requests documented in Figure 4.5, you might, for example, wish to investigate the possibility of stocking Lowenbrau beer.

PACKAGING

Beer typically is sold to foodservice operators in cans, bottles, or kegs. Although each of these containers has its advantages and disadvantages, most foodservice operators with active beverage operations will select some of each of these packaging methods. It makes little sense to carry the same beer product in both bottles and cans; however, many operators choose to serve some brands of their bottled or canned beer in draft form as well.

Many beer drinkers prefer draft beer (beer from kegs) over bottled or canned beer, and the cost to you per glass served is lower with beer from a keg. Special equipment and serving techniques are, however, required if quality draft beer is to be sold to guests. Also, the shelf life of keg beer is the shortest of all packaging types, ranging from 30 to 45 days for an untapped keg, that is, one that has not yet been opened by the bartender, and even fewer days for a **tapped** (opened) *keg*. Full kegs can be difficult to handle because of their weight, and it is hard to keep an exact count of the product served without special metering equipment. Despite these drawbacks, many operators serve draft beer. Draft beer is sold in a variety of keg and barrel sizes, as listed in Figure 4.6.

■ **FIGURE 4.6** Draft Beer Containers

Size (Us Gal)	Size (Liters)	No. of 12 - Oz. Drinks	No. of 16- Oz. Drinks	No. of 20- Oz. Drinks	Weight	Common Name
1.32	5	14	10	8	-	Mini-Keg/(single-use/recyclable)
5	18.9	53	40	32		Home Keg
5.23	19.8	55	41	33		Sixth Barrel
6.6	25	70	52	42		"Half Barrel" (Europe)
7.75	29.3	82	62	49	90 lb.	Quarter Barrel/Pony Keg
13.2	50	140	105	84		Import Keg (standard European "Barrel")
15.5	58.7	165	124	99	140–170 lb.	Half Barrel/Full Keg

FUN ON THE WEB!

Look up the following to see examples of sites that will help you learn more about beers and breweries:

www.beerweek.com. This site is a beer "news" site. Instead of *Newsweek*, explore *Beerweek*. Also, play a beer game for fun!

www.alestreetnews.com. This is another beer "news" site. It prides itself on being a "brewspaper."

www.beerhistory.com. Explore the history of beer and breweries. This site includes brewer profiles and a beer library.

www.allaboutbeer.com. *All About Beer* is a beer magazine in print. This Web site is its dot.com venue.

■ DETERMINING WINE PRODUCTS TO CARRY

Determining which wines to carry is, like beer, a matter of selecting both product and packaging. Typically, you must determine if you will sell wine by the:

1. Glass
2. Split or half-bottle
3. Carafe
4. Bottle

Wines sold by the glass or carafe can be served from bottles opened specifically for that purpose or they can be drawn from specially boxed wine containers. Wines in a box typically are house wines sold to the beverage manager in multiliter-sized boxes to ease handling, speed, and service and to reduce packaging costs. Bottled wines of many sizes and varieties can also be purchased. Common wine bottle sizes are shown in Figure 4.7

In addition, you may find that you must purchase wine for cooking. In general, these products will be secured from your beverage wholesaler rather than your grocery wholesaler. It makes little sense to use extraordinarily fine wine in cooking. Again, the guiding principle for you should be to select the appropriate quality food or beverage product for its intended use. Some operators add salt to their cooking wines in an effort to discourage the kitchen staff from drinking them. This method, if used, should be clearly communicated to kitchen personnel if the operator is to avoid potential liability.

■ **FIGURE 4.7** Wine Bottle Sizes

Bottle Size (Capacity)	Common Name	Description
0.100 Liters	Miniature (mini)	A single serving bottle
0.187 Liters	*Split*	1/4 a standard bottle
0.375 Liters	*Half-bottle*	1/2 a standard bottle.
0.750 Liters	Bottle	A standard wine bottle
1.5 Liters	Magnum	Two bottles in one
3.0 Liters	Double Magnum	Four bottles in one

Note:

1 U.S. quart = 0.946 liters

1 U.S. gallon = 3.785 liters

WINE LISTS

As a good manager, you will build a **wine list,** the term used to describe your menu of wine offerings selected for your own particular operation and guest expectations. Figure 4.8 is an example of a wine list used at Toliver's Terrace, a mid-priced fast casual restaurant.

At Toliver's Terrace, the wine list is first divided by types of wines/grape varietals: Sparkling Wine and Champagne, Chardonnay, Other White Wines, Cabernet Sauvignon, Merlot, and Pinot Noir. Each category of wines is then numbered as follows: 100s for sparkling wine and champagne, 200s for white wines (Chardonnay and other white wines), and 300s for red wines (Cabernet Sauvignon, Merlot, and Pinot Noir). The numbering system is used to assist the guest in ordering and to help the server identify the correct wine in storage. Guests may feel intimidated by the French, Italian, or German names of wines and, thus, might not order them for fear of pronouncing the words incorrectly. A numbering system allows guests to choose a number rather than a name and so reduces the amount of anxiety they may have in ordering.

The second column in Figure 4.8 lists the name and place of the **vintner,** or wine producer. The third column lists the price by the glass and/or the price per bottle. Usually, it is the less expensive wines that are available by the glass because more people are likely to order the less expensive wines than the most expensive wines, especially at a mid-priced restaurant. It is much more cost-effective to offer wine by the glass from a $20.00 bottle of wine than from an $80.00 bottle of wine because, once the bottle is opened, it has a relatively short shelf life and if any product remains unsold, it may have to be discarded.

■ **FIGURE 4.8** Sample Wine List

Toliver's Terrace

	Sparkling Wine and Champagne	Dollars Per Glass/ Dollars Per Bottle
101	Gloria Ferrer, Brut, Sonoma County	$7.00/$26.00
102	Pommery, Reims, France	$43.00
103	Jordan "J," Sonoma	$48.00
104	Moët & Chandon, Epernay, France	$55.00
105	Dom Perignon, Epernay, France	$125.00
	Chardonnay	
201	Kendall-Jackson, California	$5.00/$20.00
202	Camelot, California	$6.00/$22.00
203	St. Francis, Sonoma	$7.00/$26.00
204	Cartlidge & Browne, California	$30.00
205	Stag's Leap, Napa Valley	$52.00
	Other White Wines	
206	Fall Creek, Chenin Blanc, Texas	$5.00/$18.00
207	Max Richter, Riesling, Germany	$6.00/$22.00
208	Honig, Sauvignon Blanc, Napa Valley	$7.00/$25.00
209	Tommasi, Pinot Grigio, Italy	$7.00/$25.00
210	Santa Margherita, Pinot Grigio, Italy	$34.00
	Cabernet Sauvignon	
301	Tessera, California	$5.00/$20.00
302	Guenoc, California	$7.00/$27.00
303	Sebastiani Cask, Sonoma	$35.00
304	Franciscan, Napa Valley	$38.00
305	Chateau Ste. Michelle, Cold Creek, Washington	$45.00
	Merlot	
306	Talus, California	$5.00/$20.00
307	Tapiz, Argentina	$6.00/$22.00
308	Ironstone, Sierra Foothills	$7.00/$26.00
309	Solis, Santa Clara County	$35.00
	Pinot Noir	
310	Firesteed, Oregon	$6.00/$23.00
311	Carneros Creek, Carneros	$31.00
312	Iron Horse, Sonoma	$39.00
313	Domain Drouhin, Willamette Valley, Oregon	$55.00

In wine list development, several points must be kept in mind. First, you must seek to provide alternatives for the guest who wants the best, as well as the guest who prefers to spend less. Second, wines that either complement the food or, in the case of a bar, are popular with the guests must be available. Tastes in wines change, and you must keep up with these changes. Subscribing to at least one wine journal in the hospitality field is a good way to do so. You must also avoid the temptation to offer too many wines on a wine list. Excess inventory and use of valuable storage space make this a poor idea. In addition, when selling wine by the glass, those items that sell poorly can lose quality and flavor rapidly. Third, wine sales can be diminished due to the complexity of the product itself. You should strive to make the purchase of wine by the bottle a pleasant, nonthreatening experience. Wait staff, who help in selling wine, should be knowledgeable but not pretentious.

In general, when foodservice managers have trouble selling wine (the world's most popular beverage), the difficulty more often lies in the delivery of the product rather than with the product itself. Sometimes operators make the ordering, presentation, and service of wine so pretentious as to intimidate many guests into not purchasing wine at all. This is unfortunate, because wine is perceived as a beverage of moderation and is enjoyed the world over by many guests. You can enlist the aid of your own wine supplier to help you train your staff in the effective marketing of wine, either by the bottle or by the glass. Far too few operators use this valuable resource to their advantage.

Consider The Cost

"You really need to add the Merlot, the Cabernet Franc, and the Chenin Blanc," said Guy Smiley, the salesperson for Abboit Wines. "Look, you have a Texas theme. These are Texas wines from Pheasant Ridge winery. We just got them in. They are really modestly priced. Your customers will love them. You add these wines and you'll see your wine sales increase, I'll promise you that!"

Guy was attempting to convince Judith Fornes, manager of the Austin Limits steakhouse, that she should significantly increase the number of wines offered to the guests of the restaurant, which was located in a suburb of Atlanta, Georgia.

"I don't know, Guy," replied Judith. "We already have nine good reds, six whites, and two blush wines on the menu now. Additional choices may just confuse our guests. Or those that want wine with dinner may just switch from their current wine selection to a different wine. That doesn't mean increased sales, just increased inventory."

Assume that you were Judith:

1. Other than recommendations of your salesperson, what factors would you assess regularly to determine if a new product should be added to your wine list?

2. What signs might suggest to you that the number of wines offered on your menu is already too large, and thus the list's size should be reduced?

3. Would you question the wisdom of Guy's advice in this case? Explain your answer.

■ DETERMINING SPIRIT PRODUCTS TO CARRY

Distilled spirits have an extremely long shelf life. Thus, you can make a "mistake" and purchase the wrong spirit product without disastrous results, if that product can be sold over a reasonable period of time. Guest preference will dictate the types of liquors that are appropriate for a given operation, but it is your responsibility to determine product quality levels in the beverage area. Nowhere is this more important than in the area of distilled spirits.

Consumer preferences concerning alcoholic beverages can change rapidly. The wise beverage manager stays abreast of changing consumption trends by reading professional journals and staying active in his or her professional associations. These associations can be major providers of information related to changes in consumer buying behavior as far as beer, wine, and spirits are concerned. What is extremely popular one year may be out of fashion the next! It is important to spot these trends and respond to them quickly.

Packaging is not a particular issue, as it is for beer and wine, in the selection of spirits for an establishment's use. In the United States, as in most parts of the world, bottle sizes for spirits are standard. Since the early 1980s, the bottle sizes shown in Figure 4.9 represent those most commonly offered for sale to the hospitality market.

The miniature, or "mini-bottle" (50 ml), is typically offered for sale on airlines and in some situations, such as in-room minibars and room service, in the hotel segment of the hospitality industry. In some areas of the country, it can even be purchased individually in bars. The most common spirit bottle size used in the hospitality industry is the 1-liter size.

Although packaging is not a major concern of the operator selecting a spirit product, brand quality is crucial. As a comparison, consider a product such as Budweiser Light beer, a standard product, which tastes the same from coast to coast. An operator who chooses to carry that beer need only decide whether it will be sold in bottles, in cans, or on draft. Should that same operator elect to carry scotch, however, an extremely wide selection of products at widely varying prices is

■ **FIGURE 4.9** Spirit Bottle Sizes and Capacities

Common Bottle Name	Metric Capacity	Fluid Ounce Capacity
Miniature	50 ml	1.7
Half-pint	200 ml	6.8
Pint	500 ml	16.9
Fifth	750 ml	25.4
Quart	1.0 Liter	33.8
Half-gallon	1.75 Liters	59.2
1 Liter equals 1,000 milliliters		

available for purchase. In general, restaurant operators will select spirits in two major categories. These are well liquors and call liquors.

WELL LIQUORS

Well liquors are those spirits that are poured when the guest does not specify a particular brand name when ordering. The name stems from the concept of the "well," or the bottle holding area in the bar. The wise operator will choose well liquors very carefully. Guests who order well liquors may be price conscious, but that does not mean they are not quality conscious also. It is fairly easy to tell the difference between a well liquor of average quality and one of very poor quality. Managers who shop for well liquors considering only price as a criterion for selection will find that guest reaction is extremely negative. Conversely, if exceptionally high-quality products are chosen as well items, liquor costs may be excessive unless an adequate price structure is maintained.

CALL LIQUORS

Call liquors are those spirits that are requested by name, such as Jack Daniel's, Kahlúa, and Chivas Regal. Extremely expensive call liquors are sometimes referred to as **premium liquors**.

You will generally charge a higher price for those drinks prepared with call or premium liquors. Guests understand this and, in fact, by specifying call liquors indicate their preference to pay the price required for these special products.

Figures 4.10 and 4.11 illustrate the effect of changes in the selection of well liquors. In Figure 4.10, 50 well drinks and 50 call drinks are sold. Total beverage cost percentage, in this example, equals 19.1 percent.

In Figure 4.11, the portion cost of our well brand is reduced from 90 cents to 60 cents, because of a reduction in the quality of product selected for this purpose. This results in a decrease in overall beverage cost percentage to 16.4 percent.

Although the decision to lower the quality of well liquor used did, in this case, reduce overall liquor cost percentage, the question of the long-term effect on guest satisfaction and loyalty is not addressed. In fact, changes in guest behavior may

■ **FIGURE 4.10** Spirit Cost Percentage

Original Portion Cost						
Spirit	Number Sold	Portion Cost	Total Cost	Selling Price	Total Sales	Beverage Cost %
Well	50	$0.90	$ 45	$5	$250	18.0%
Call	50	1.20	60	6	300	20.0
Total	100		105		550	19.1

seem negligible in the short run. Successful foodservice operators, however, remember that you cannot fool all of the people all of the time. Quality products at fair prices build guest loyalty. Because that is true, you are wise to select well products that are in keeping with your clientele, price structure, and desired image. Anything less cheats both you and your guests.

FUN ON THE WEB!

Look up the following to see examples of sites that will help you learn more about spirits and cocktails.

www.cocktails.com. Go to this site to learn about bartending, cocktail recipes, cocktail culture, and much more!

www.epicurious.com. This site approaches food, wine, and liquor from an epicurean perspective. Click on "Beverages" to find out more about cocktails.

www.extremebartending.com. This site provides training tools to improve bartending skills, as well as a variety of great bartending related links.

If you are 21 or over, you can explore numerous sites developed by liquor companies. Go to the Google or MSN search engine, and enter "Liquor & Spirits." From there, you will be launched into a world of spirits companies.

■ **FIGURE 4.11** Spirit Cost Percentage

Reduced Portion Cost						
Spirit	Number Sold	Portion Cost	Total Cost	Selling Price	Total Sales	Beverage Cost %
Well	50	$0.60	$30	$5	$250	12.0%
Call	50	1.20	60	6	300	20.0
Total	100		90		550	16.4

Green and Growing!

Eco-oriented drink programs present challenges and opportunities for restaurant and bar owners. Increasingly, customers ask for (or even demand!) organic beverages. Available organic spirits products include vodka, gin, tequila, scotch, and rum. Although more expensive than non-organic versions of the same product, these items are increasingly available for purchase from main-line beverage distributors. Organic wines and beers are also becoming increasingly common.

Concerns about costs can plague green beverage initiatives because organic product costs are historically higher, and in the past, the number of interested customers has been smaller. Today, however, using seasonal and local produce and juices for drink production can help moderate every operation's costs while increasing quality. In addition, consumers are increasingly willing to pay the extra costs incurred by operations that choose to go green. The result? Delighted guests and increased profit margins.

■ BEVERAGE PURCHASE ORDERS

The form in Figure 3.13 can be used to document the beverage purchase order in the same way it is used for food purchases. Special laws, depending on the state and county, may influence how beverage purchases are to be made or paid for. One of the first responsibilities you have is to become familiar with all applicable state and local laws regarding beverage purchases. As with food, the goal in purchasing is to have an adequate, but not excessive, amount of product on hand at all times. Unlike most food products, however, beverage distributors will sometimes sell products in less than one-case lots. This is called a **broken case** and occurs when several different brands or products are used to completely fill the case. For example, assume that an operator orders a case of scotch, consisting of 12 bottles. The case, however, might contain four bottles of Scotch Brand A, four bottles of Brand B, and four bottles of Brand C.

As a general rule, wine, beer, and spirits are purchased by the case. Beer, of course, may also be bought by full- or reduced-size kegs. As with food products, a smaller container size usually results in higher costs per servable ounce. It is important to remember that both product quality and container size are critical when determining what to buy.

RECEIVING BEVERAGE PRODUCTS

*T*he skill required to receive beverage products is somewhat less than what is needed for receiving food. The reason is that beverage products do not vary in quality in the same manner food products do. As with food, the receiving clerk needs a proper location, tools, and equipment. In addition, proper delivery schedules must be maintained. The training required in beverage receiving, however, is reduced due to the consistent nature of the product received. A case of freshly produced Coors beer, for example, will be consistent in quality regardless of the vendor. And if the product is **fresh dated**, that is, a date is stamped on the product to indicate its freshness, very little inspection is required to ensure that the product is exactly what was ordered. In fact, when matching the purchase order to the vendor invoice, only quantity ordered and price must be verified, unlike food deliveries that require the verification of weight, quantity, quality, and price.

It is possible, however, that the goods delivered will not match those ordered. Or, in fact, the goods delivered may be defective in some manner. Thus, appropriate receiving procedures must still be in place.

When receiving beverage products, the following items are of concern and should be verified:

Key Beverage Receiving Checkpoints

1. Correct brand
2. Correct bottle size
3. No broken bottles or bottle seals
4. Freshness dates (beer)
5. Correct vintage or year produced (wine)
6. Refrigerated state (if appropriate)
7. Correct unit price
8. Correct price extension
9. Correct invoice total

If errors are detected, a credit memo (see Figure 3.17) should be filled out and signed by both the delivery person and the receiving clerk.

STORING BEVERAGE PRODUCTS

Although the shelf life of most beverage products is relatively long, alcoholic beverages, especially wine, must be treated in a very careful manner. Beverage storage rooms should be easily secured because beverages are often expensive items and are a favorite target for both employee and guest theft. These storage areas should, of course, be kept clean and free of insect or rodent infestations, and they should be large enough to allow for easy rotation of stock. Many beverage managers use a **two-key system** to control access to beverage storage areas. In this system, one key (or, in the case of electronic locks, one preprogrammed, coded key) is in the possession of the individual responsible for the beverage area. The other key, used when the beverage manager is not readily available, is kept in a sealed envelope in the safe or other secured area of the operation. Should this key be needed, management will be aware of its use because the envelope will be opened. Of course, it is up to management to ascertain the validity of the use of this key should the envelope be opened. **Recodable electronic locks** (which are highly recommended) include features that allow management to issue multiple keys and to identify precisely the time an issued key was used to access the lock and to whom that key was issued.

FUN ON THE WEB!

The recodable electronic lock was introduced by VingCard in 1979. Today, VingCard's locks are popular in hotels, where guest security is extremely important, as well as in many other situations (such as liquor storeroom access), where traceable access and high levels of security are critical. To view its current product offerings, go to: **www.vingcard.com.**

■ BEER STORAGE

Beer in kegs should be stored at refrigeration temperatures of 36 to 38°F (2 to 3°C) because keg beer is unpasteurized and, thus, must be handled carefully to avoid spoilage. When receiving and storing canned and bottled beer, it is also important to examine freshness dates. If these dates are not easily discernible, you should demand that the vendor explain to you the date-coding system that is being used. Pasteurized beer in either cans or bottles should be stored in a cool, dark room at 50 to 70°F (10 to 21°C) and does not require refrigeration.

Storage areas should be kept clean and dust free. Canned beer, especially, should be covered when stored to eliminate the chance of dust or dirt settling on the rims of the cans. Nothing is quite as disturbing to a beer drinker than to find the top of a cold beer can covered with dust, dirt, or other foreign material that cannot be removed. It is a good idea for the individual issuing canned beer to the bar to thoroughly rinse beer can tops prior to delivering these products for use in the bar.

Product rotation is critical if beer is to be served at its maximum freshness, and it is important that you and your team devise a system to ensure that this happens. The best method is to date each case or six-pack as it comes in. In this manner, you can, at a glance, determine whether proper FIFO (see Chapter 3) product rotation has occurred.

■ WINE STORAGE

Wine storage is the most complex and time-consuming activity required of beverage storeroom personnel. Depending on the type and volume of the restaurant, extremely large quantities of wine may be stored.

In general, the finer wines in the United States are sold in bottles of 750 ml (see Figure 4.7). Foreign wines are generally sold in bottles of approximately this size, but the contents may vary by a few milliliters more or less. Sometimes, larger bottle sizes may be sold, especially of sparkling wine, such as champagne. Increasingly, quality wines in bottles smaller than 750 ml are being offered for sale. If you find that large numbers of couples or two-person groups are coming to your restaurant, it is simply unrealistic to assume that they will have before-dinner drinks, a full 750-ml bottle of wine with dinner, and then finish the meal with coffee and after-dinner drinks. In today's age of caution about drinking and driving, the trend is away from this kind of consumption, and if wine sales are to be maintained at their current levels, operators would do well to provide the option of the half-bottle to their guests.

Regardless of bottle size stored, the techniques for proper wine storage must be followed in all circumstances if the quality of the product is to be maintained and product losses are to be kept at a minimum. Despite the mystery associated with wine storage, the effective manager will find that proper wine storage can be achieved if the following factors are monitored:

1. Temperature
2. Light
3. Cork condition

TEMPERATURE

A great deal of debate has centered on the proper temperature at which to store wine. All can agree that red wine should be served at cellar temperature. There is, however, less agreement about what exactly is meant by "cellar temperature." When serving white wine by the glass, we may find that the proper storage temperature, at least for the containers currently being used, is refrigerator temperature. Obviously, this would not do for a case of fine red wine. But, generally speaking, most experts would agree that wines should be stored at a temperature of 50 to 65°F (10 to 18°C). If you find, however, that wines must be stored at higher temperatures than this, the wine storage area should be as cool as can reasonably be achieved, and it is important to remember that, although wine may improve with age, it improves only if it is properly stored. Heat is an enemy of effective wine storage.

LIGHT

Just as wine must be protected from excess heat, it must also be protected from direct sunlight. In olden times, this was achieved by storing wines in underground cellars or caves. In your own foodservice establishment, this means using a storage area where sunlight cannot penetrate and where the wine will not be subject to excessive fluorescent or incandescent lighting. With regard to light, the rule of thumb for storing wine is that it should be exposed only to the minimum amount necessary.

CORK CONDITION

It is the wine's cork that protects it from oxygen, its greatest enemy, and from the effects of oxidation. **Oxidation** occurs when oxygen comes in contact with bottled wine; you can detect a wine that has been overly oxidized because it smells somewhat like vinegar. Oxidation deteriorates the quality of bottled wines; thus, keeping oxygen out of the wine is a prime consideration of the vintner and should be important to you as well.

Cork has proven, over the years, to be the bottle sealer of choice for most wine producers. Quality wines demand quality corks, and the best wines are fitted with cork sealers that should last many years if they are not allowed to dry out. This is the reason wine should be stored in such a manner that the cork remains in contact with the wine and, thus, stays moist. In an effort to accomplish this, most foodservice managers store wines on their sides, usually on specially built wine racks. Corks should be inspected at the time the wine is received and periodically thereafter to ensure that there are no leaks resulting in oxidation and, thus, damaged products. If a leak is discovered, the wine should be refused; if the leak occurs during storage, the wine should be examined for quality and then either consumed or discarded, as appropriate. In general, you can effectively manage the storage of wines if you think about how you should treat the cork protecting the wine. The wine the cork is protecting is likely to be properly stored if the cork is always kept:

1. Cool
2. In the dark
3. Moist

Proper beverage storage techniques are important if you hope to have the desired amount of product ready and available for service during the beverage production process. In most instances, wine and beer will be consumed directly from their original containers. With spirits, on the other hand, the bartender will probably find that the guest prefers the spirit mixed with some other product to make the beverage fit their personal preference.

■ LIQUOR STORAGE

Spirits should be stored in a relatively dry storage area between 70 and 80°F (21 to 27°C). Since these products do not generally require refrigeration, they may be stored along with food products, if necessary. An organized, well-maintained area for spirits will also ensure that purchasing decisions will be simplified because no product is likely to be overlooked or lost. In addition, care should be taken that access to liquor storage areas is strictly limited.

BAR TRANSFERS

Although the great majority of product cost related to bar operations is alcoholic beverages, you must also manage the cost of those items associated with the preparation and service of beverage products. In the case of wine and beer, there are, in general, no additions to the beverage prior to serving and, thus, no additional product costs. As far as spirits are concerned, however, a great number of nonalcoholic food products may be served as a part of the drink order. To illustrate this, assume that a guest in your bar orders Irish coffee. This popular drink has, as its two primary ingredients, Irish whiskey and brewed coffee. The cost of the spirit itself should clearly be charged to the cost of operating the bar. A question arises, however, on how to account for the coffee. In this case, coffee is as central to the preparation of the drink as the whiskey itself. If your operation is a stand-alone bar, accounting for the cost of purchasing the coffee is not complex. If the bar is, however, operated as part of a larger foodservice operation, the ground coffee used to make the brewed coffee in the bar may have to come from the restaurant's portion of the foods storeroom. When that is the case, the transfer of the product, and its associated costs, from the kitchen to the bar must be controlled and recorded to accurately track revenue and expense. If this is not done, the food cost percentage in the restaurant will be artificially inflated (overstated), and the total cost of beverage sold percentage in the bar will be understated. This would be the inevitable result if revenues from alcoholic drinks utilizing coffee were reported as bar sales, but the expense of generating those sales (the coffee) was considered a restaurant expense.

This same issue exists with products such as cherries, limes, lemons, cream, coffee, sugar, and a host of other items, which may be ordered as regular food products for the kitchen but are needed by and transferred to the bar area. Similarly, many foodservice operators use items from the bar when preparing menu items for service in the dining room. Using a bottle of beer from the bar for steaming bratwurst in the kitchen would be an example of a transfer of products from the bar to the kitchen. Wines may frequently be used by the kitchen to produce some sauces. In fact, a close working relationship between kitchen and bar management is helpful as both areas attempt to assist each other to the best of their ability in providing needed ingredients and in helping to utilize any carryover products.

The control procedure for kitchen and bar transfers is quite simple. To be effective, it requires nothing but consistency. Assume that you manage the Surfside Bar, on the beach in Florida. Figure 4.12 is an example of what your transfer record for the first week of January might be. It is the type of form that you can use to monitor product flow either to or from the bar. Should you prefer it, a separate form can be used for each transfer area, but, for most operators, Figure 4.12 is sufficient. Note that the form requires the initials of both the person receiving and the person issuing the product. In addition, space is available to compute the sum total of all product values at the end of the accounting period. These figures would then be used to adjust, as needed, either cost of food sold data or cost of beverage sold data.

In this example, when calculating your actual beverage costs, they would be increased by $66.88 (the value of food products transferred to the bar from the kitchen) and decreased by $17.80 (the value of beverage products transferred from the bar to the kitchen). The kitchen's food cost would be increased by adding

■ **FIGURE 4.12** Transfer Record

Location: **Surfside Bar**					Month/Date: **1/1–1/7**	
			Product Value			
Date	Item	Quality	To Bar	From Bar	Issued By	Received By
1/1	Lemons	6	$ 0.72		T. S.	B. H.
	Limes	2	0.28		T. S.	B. H.
	Cream	2 qt.	4.62		T. S.	B. H.
1/2	Chablis	1 gal.		$11.10	B. H.	T. S.
1/3	Coffee	2 lb.	10.70		T. S.	B. H.
1/4	Cherries	1/2 gal.	12.94		T. S.	B. H.
1/4	Lemons	4	0.48		T. S.	B. H.
	Limes	2	0.28		T. S.	B. H.
	Ice Cream (vanilla)	1 gal.	13.32		T. S.	B. H.
1/5	Pineapple Juice	1/2 gal.	3.00		T. S.	B. H.
1/6	Tomato Juice	1 case	20.00		T. S.	B. H.
1/6	Sherry	750 ml		6.70	B. H.	T. S.
1/7	Celery	1 bunch	0.54		T. S.	B. H.
Total Product Value			**$66.88**	**$17.80**		

transfers from the bar to the kitchen ($17.80) and decreased by subtracting transfers to the bar from the kitchen ($66.80). The principle is that all product costs should be assigned to the area of the operation that is reporting the sale of that product.

COMPUTING COST OF BEVERAGES

*T*he proper computation of beverage cost percentage is identical to that of food cost percentage with one important difference. Typically, there is no equivalent for employee meals because the consumption of alcoholic beverage products by employees who are working should be strictly prohibited. Thus, "employee drinks" would never be considered as a reduction from overall beverage cost.

Consider the situation you would face as manager of Rio Lobo's, a popular Tex-Mex style restaurant that does a high volume of alcoholic beverage sales. To prepare your drinks, your bartenders use limes, lemons, and fruit juices from the kitchen. You would, of course, like your beverage cost percentage to reflect all the costs associated with the actual ingredients used in drink preparation. You keep excellent daily records of the number of food products transferred from the kitchen to the bar and the dollar value of these transfers. In this operation, there are no transfers from the bar to the kitchen as there might be, for instance, in a French restaurant that uses wine extensively in its recipes. Figure 4.13 details how you would compute your actual cost of beverage sold for a month where the following data represent your operating results:

■ **FIGURE 4.13** Co st of Beverage Sold

	Accounting Period: 1/1 – 2/1	
	Unit Name: Rio Lobo's	
Beginning Inventory	$24,405.00	
PLUS		
Purchases	21,986.40	
Goods Available for Sale		$46,391.40
LESS		
Ending Inventory		18,741.25
LESS		
Transfers from Bar		1,572.00
PLUS		
Transfers to Bar		2,140.00
Cost of Beverages Sold		$28,218.15

	Operating Data—Rio Lobo's
Beverage sales	$100,000.00
Beginning inventory	24,405.00
Ending inventory	18,741.25
Purchases	21,986.40
Transfers to bar	2,140.00
Transfers from bar	1,572.00

Note, again, that beginning inventory for this accounting period is the ending inventory figure from the prior accounting period.

SPECIAL FEATURES OF LIQUOR INVENTORY

Determining beginning and ending inventory levels for beverage products is generally more difficult than determining these same levels for food. Food items can most often be weighed, counted, or measured for inventory purposes. Of course, any of these methods may be used for liquor inventory, should you choose to do so. Unopened containers of beer, wine, and spirits can, of course, be counted. Opened containers, however, must be valued also. It is the process of valuing these opened containers that will present a challenge to you. Three inventory methods are commonly used to accomplish this goal:

1. Weight
2. Count
3. Measure

■ LIQUOR INVENTORY BY WEIGHT

The weight method uses a scale to weigh open bottles of liquor. This system is effective if you remember to subtract the weight of the empty bottle itself from the total product's weight and if you remember that each liquor, due to its unique specific gravity (density), must be weighed separately. Because some liquors are heavier than others, 3 "fluid" ounces of each, for example, would not weigh the same amount. Figure 4.14 lists the specific gravity of some common products used to make the colorful pousse-café, a layered drink that relies on the fact that differing spirit products have different weights (the more dense liquids will fall to the bottom of the glass).

■ FIGURE 4.14 **Specific Gravity of Selected Liqueurs**

Liqueur Or Cordial	Color	Specific Gravity
Kirsch	Clear	0.940
Sloe Gin	Red	1.040
Rock and Rye	Amber	1.065
Triple Sec	Clear	1.075
Peach Brandy	Peach	1.085
Blue Caraçao	Blue	1.120
Crème de Cacao	Brown	1.150
Crème de Cassis	Purple	1.170
Crème de Banana	Yellow	1.180

Just as your bartenders will use their knowledge of specific gravity to create drinks, you can use that same knowledge to weigh the amount of product in an opened bottle and, thus, establish its inventory value.

■ LIQUOR INVENTORY BY COUNT

Counting full bottles is easy; valuing partial bottles is more difficult. You can do it rather quickly and fairly accurately, however, if you use the tenths system. This system requires that the inventory taker assign a value of 10/10 to a full bottle, 5/10 to a half bottle, and so on. Then, when inventory is taken, the partial bottle is examined and the appropriate "tenth" is assigned, based on the amount left in the bottle. Although this system results in an approximation of the actual amount in a bottle, many managers feel the tenths system is accurate enough for their purposes. It does have the advantage of being a rather quick method of determining inventory levels of open bottles.

■ LIQUOR INVENTORY BY MEASURE

Some beverage managers determine product levels of open bottles by using a ruler to determine the amount the bottle contains. Dollar values are then assigned to each inch or portion of an inch for inventory evaluation purposes. This method has a high degree of accuracy and is favored by many.

In general, it is important to take liquor inventories at a time when the operation is closed so that product quantities on hand do not change when the inventory is being taken. It is also important that product contained in the lines of mechanical drink-dispensing systems be counted if the quantity of product in these lines is deemed to be significant.

Returning to the Rio Lobo example, regardless of the method used to determine the actual value of ending inventory, with sales of $100,000 and a cost of beverage sold of $28,218.15, you would apply the beverage cost percentage formula as follows:

$$\frac{\text{Cost of Beverage Sold}}{\text{Beverage Sales}} = \text{Beverage Cost \%}$$

$$\text{or}$$

$$\frac{\$28,218.15}{\$100,000} = 28.22\%$$

Again, it is important to note that transfers both to and from the bar must be accounted for if they occur. These adjustments will affect the overall product cost percentages in the kitchen and the bar. In addition, computing transfers to the bar will help your bar staff remember that the use of fruit juices, milk, cherries, lemons, limes, and the like do impact the total cost effectiveness of the bar.

There are a large number of factors that can influence the actual beverage cost percentage you achieve. Many of these factors are discussed in Chapter 5. Note, however, that guests themselves can contribute to relatively major changes (up or down) in food or beverage cost percentages. This is due to the concept that food and beverage operators call the sales mix, or product mix. Our preferred term is the former.

SALES MIX

*S*ales mix is defined as the series of guest purchasing decisions that result in a specific food or beverage cost percentage. Sales mix affects overall product cost percentage anytime guests have a choice among several menu selections, each one having its own unique product cost percentage.

To illustrate the effect of sales mix on beverage cost percentage, assume that you are the food and beverage director at the Raider Resort, a 400-room beachfront hotel property on the Gulf Coast of Texas. In addition to your regular restaurant, you serve beverages in three basic locations. They are as follows:

1. Banquet beverages for receptions prior to meal events, typically served in your grand ballroom, foyer, or outdoors; banquet beverages are also served during banquet meal functions.

■ FIGURE 4.15   Raider Resort

Monthly Beverage Percentage Report			
Location	Cost of Beverages	Beverage Sales	Beverage Cost %
Banquets	$20,500	$ 80,000	25.6%
Starlight Bar	10,350	45,500	22.7
Harry O's	16,350	67,000	24.4
Total	47,200	192,500	24.5

2. The Starlight Bar, an upscale bar with soft piano music that typically appeals to guests who are 55 years and older.

3. Harry O's, a bar with indoor and poolside seating. Contemporary Top 40 music in the evenings draws a younger crowd interested in dancing.

You compute a separate beverage cost percentage for each of these beverage outlets. Figure 4.15 details the separate operating results for each outlet and an overall percentage for the three units using the standard beverage cost percentage formula.

You know that each beverage location uses the same portion size for all standard drinks. Well and call liquors, as well as wine-by-the-glass brands, are constant in all three locations. In this resort setting, you dislike the difficulty associated with serving draft beer, thus beer is sold in cans or bottles only. In addition, bartenders are typically rotated on a regular basis through every serving location. Should you be concerned that your beverage cost percentage varies so greatly by service location? The answer, in this case, is that you have no cause for concern. In this situation, it is sales mix, and not poor control that governs your overall beverage cost percentage in each individual location. A close examination of the three outlets in Figure 4.16 will reveal how this can happen.

Although product cost percentages are constant in each location for beer, wine, and spirits, the overall beverage cost percentage is not. The reason that each unit varies in total beverage cost percentage is due to sales mix, or the guests' selection of product. In other words, guests, and not management alone, have helped to determine your final beverage cost percent. You can certainly help shape guest selection by such techniques as cost controls, effective pricing, menu design, and marketing, but to some degree it is the guest who will determine overall cost percentage through sales mix. This is true in both the beverage and the food areas. In the case of the Raider Resort, it is easy to analyze the sales mix by examining Figure 4.17, a detailing of the beverage products guests selected in each beverage outlet.

■ **FIGURE 4.16**   Raider Beverage Outlets

Monthly Beverage Percentage Recap

#1 Outlet Name: <u>Banquets</u>   Month: <u>January</u>

Product	Cost of Beverages	Beverage Sales	Beverage Cost %
Beer	$ 2,500	$10,000	25.0%
Wine	12,000	40,000	30.0
Spirits	6,000	30,000	20.0
Total	20,500	80,000	25.6

#2 Outlet Name: <u>Starlight Bar</u>

Product	Cost of Beverages	Beverage Sales	Beverage Cost %
Beer	$ 3,750	$15,000	25.0%
Wine	1,500	5,000	30.0
Spirits	5,100	25,500	20.0
Total	10,350	45,500	22.7

#3 Outlet Name: <u>Harry O's</u>

Product	Cost of Beverages	Beverage Sales	Beverage Cost %
Beer	$11,250	$45,000	25.0%
Wine	2,100	7,000	30.0
Spirits	3,000	15,000	20.0
Total	16,350	67,000	24.4

■ **FIGURE 4.17**   Raider Resort

Beverage Sales Percentage Recap

Unit	Beer	Wine	Spirits	Total Sales
Banquets	12.5%	50.0%	37.5%	100%
Starlight Bar	33.0%	11.0%	56.0%	100%
Harry O's	67.0%	10.5%	22.5%	100%

Each sales percent in Figure 4.17 was computed using this formula:

$$\frac{\text{Item Dollar Sales}}{\text{Total Beverage Sales}} = \text{Item \% of Total Beverage Sales}$$

Therefore, in the case of beer sales in the banquet area, using the data from Figure 4.16:

$$\frac{\text{Banquet Beer Sales}}{\text{Total Banquet Beverage Sales}} = \text{\% Banquet Beer Sales}$$

or

$$\frac{\$10,000}{\$80,000} = 12.5\%$$

As indicated, each beverage outlet operates with a unique sales mix. Figure 4.17 shows that in the banquet area the mix is heavy in wines and spirits, the choice of many guests when they are at a reception or dining out. The Starlight Bar clientele is older, and their preferred drink tends to be spirits. Harry O's, on the other hand, caters to a younger crowd that, in this case, prefers beer. It is important to remember that, despite controls that are in place, costs that are in line, and effective management policies, variations in beverage cost percentages can still occur due to sales mix, rather than other confounding factors. Experienced managers recognize this fact, and as a result, they monitor sales mix carefully.

Beverages are, and will remain, an important part of the hospitality industry. Marketed and consumed properly, they enhance many an occasion. In the hands of the thoughtful and conscientious manager, they are a powerful profit center.

Now that we know who is coming (Chapter 2) and we have enough food (Chapter 3) and beverages (Chapter 4) available to be served, we turn to one of the most challenging aspects of foodservice management, namely, managing the food and beverage production process (Chapter 5).

FUN ON THE WEB!

In the United States (at the federal government level) alcohol sales are regulated by the Bureau of Alcohol, Tobacco, Firearms and Explosives (ATF), which is part of the Department of Treasury. The ATF maintains a Web site that details most of its requirements related to alcohol service. To view the regulations posted on the site, go to: **www.atf.gov.**

Technology Tools

In this chapter you learned about cost control concepts related to the service of alcoholic beverages. For those operations that sell a significant amount of alcoholic beverage products, there are a variety of programs designed to discourage theft and carefully monitor product sales and expenses. In fact, the software and hardware available to help you in the beverage service area is generally more sophisticated than that found in most food-related areas. Programs available include those that can help you:

1. Monitor product sales
2. Monitor product (inventory) usage
3. Calculate actual and targeted pour percentages
4. Adjust product costs for happy hours and specials, as well as product transfers to and from the kitchen
5. Maintain adequate levels of product inventory
6. Establish par stock quantities and values
7. Generate purchase orders
8. Schedule employees based on forecasted sales levels
9. Create and print customized wine lists and specials menus
10. Maintain sales histories
11. Maintain drink recipe files
12. Project the impact of sales mix on beverage cost percentages

It is important to realize that some bar-related software may be dependent on specific and sometimes expensive automated beverage dispensing systems. Other software is either stand-alone or designed to operate in conjunction with many of the basic POS systems currently on the market.

FUN ON THE WEB!

The Internet is one of the best resources for drink recipes. To view comprehensive sites related to drink production, go to:

www.webtender.com.   Click on "Search for Drinks" to see how quickly bartenders could get a recipe for a drink they have not made before.

www.barmedia.com.   This is another helpful site.

Apply What You Have Learned

Assume you are the manager of a restaurant (serving casual Italian food) that is part of a national chain. Beverage sales account for 35 percent of your total sales with one-half of those sales coming from diners and one-half from guests drinking in the bar area. An e-mail message from your supervisor arrives asking your opinion about the company converting from the manual bartending system currently in use to one that is fully automated. The system (similar to the one you can see at www.easybar.com) essentially controls and accounts for the quantity of alcohol poured when making drinks or serving beer or wine. Your written response to the following questions is requested.

1. How would such a system specifically affect the controls procedures in place at your restaurant?

2. How would guests sitting at the bar likely perceive the system?

3. How would the system likely be perceived by your bartenders?

Key Terms and Concepts

The following are terms and concepts discussed in the chapter that are important for you as a manager. To help you review, please define the terms below.

Alcoholic beverages	Keg beer/draft beer	Well liquors
Beer	House wine	Call liquors
Wine	Jigger	Premium liquors
Spirits	Pull date	Broken case
Dramshop laws	Product request log	Fresh dated
Blood alcohol	Tapped keg	Two-key system
content (BAC)	Split (wine)	Recodable
License states	Half bottle (wine)	electronic locks
Control states	Wine list	Oxidation
Percent selecting	Vintner	Sales mix

Test Your Skills

Complete the Test Your Skills exercises by placing your answers in the shaded boxes and answering the questions as indicated.

1. Gil Bloom is planning for the wedding of the mayor's daughter in his hotel. The reception, to be held in the grand ballroom, will be attended by 1,000

people. From his sales histories of similar events, Gil knows that the average drinking habits of those attending receptions of this type are as follows:

25 percent select champagne
50 percent select white wine
25 percent select spirits

Assuming three drinks per person and a portion size of 3 ounces for champagne, 4 ounces for wine, and 1 ounce for spirits, how much of each product, in 750-ml bottles, should Gil order? (Multiply fluid ounces by 29.57 to convert to milliliters.) Spreadsheet hint: Use the ROUNDUP function in the **Total Bottles** column to determine number of full bottles to order.

If you were Gil, would you order more than you think you would need? Why or why not? If so, how much more would you order?

Beverage Selection	Percent Selecting	Total Guests	# of Guests Selecting	# of Drinks per Guest	Total # of Portions	Portion Size (oz.)	Amount Needed (oz.)	Total Milliliters	Total Bottles (750 ml)
Champagne	0.25	1000							
Wine	0.50	1000							
Spirits	0.25	1000							

2. Jim Heeb operates a magical restaurant called Shazam! In it, he features both excellent food and magic shows. The lounge is popular because that is where the magic is viewed. Help Jim first calculate his transfers to and from the bar and then help him compute his cost of beverage sold percentage using the following data for the month of January:

Beverage Sales $52,214
Beginning inventory   15,000
Purchases   11,000
Ending inventory   13,500

Product Value						
Date	Item	Quantity	To Bar	From Bar	Issued By	Received By
1/1	Lemons	200	$ 12.00		T. A.	B. P.
1/6	Coffee	60 lb.	126.00		T. A.	B. P.
	Cream	10 qt.	8.00		T. A.	B. P.
1/11	Chablis	5 gal.		$31.20	B. P.	T. A.
	Ice Cream	3 gal.	16.65		T. A.	B. P.
1/13	Pineapple Juice	5 gal.	15.00		T. A.	B. P.
	Sherry	3 gal.		42.60	B. P.	T. A.
1/17	Celery	5 cs.	48.60		T. A.	B. P.
1/22	Olives	5 gal.	42.50		T. A.	B. P.
1/27	Brandy	5 btl. (750 ml)		60.00	B. P.	T. A.
Total						

Beverage Sales =	

Beginning Inventory	Purchases	Ending Inventory	Transfers to Bar	Transfers from Bar	Cost of Beverage Sold	Beverage Cost %

3. Mary Louise operates a popular French restaurant in a large Midwestern city of the United States. Her establishment is a favorite both for its cozy cocktail area and for its superb cuisine, patterned after that of the Nantes area of France. Mary Louise keeps excellent records on all of her product usage. She wishes to compute, for the month of January, cost of goods sold in the food, beer, wine, and spirits areas. In effect, she desires a separate product cost percentage for each of these four areas. In addition, she has determined that the value of all transfers from the kitchen to the bar will be assigned to the "spirits" area for cost purposes.

a. Given the following data, compute these four cost percentages.

Sales

Food	$175,000
Beer	$ 12,000
Wine	$ 45,000
Spirits	$ 51,000

Employee Meals $ 3,500

Transfers from Bar

Beer	$ 125
Wine	$ 1,800
Spirits	$ 425

Transfers to Bar $ 960

Beginning Inventory

Food	$ 45,800
Beer	$ 4,500
Wine	$ 65,000
Spirits	$ 6,400

Ending Inventory

Food	$ 41,200
Beer	$ 4,400
Wine	$ 66,900
Spirits	$ 8,050

Purchases

Food	$ 65,400
Beer	$ 2,900
Wine	$ 15,400
Spirits	$ 11,850

	Beginning Inventory	Purchases	Ending Inventory	Employee Meals	Transfers from Bar	Transfers to Bar	Cost of Goods Sold	Cost %
Food								
Beer								
Wine								
Spirits								
Total Beverage								

b. Calculate Mary Louise's Sales Mix (sales percentages) for beer, wine, and spirits. Then create, either manually or electronically, a pie chart like the following that shows these percentages.

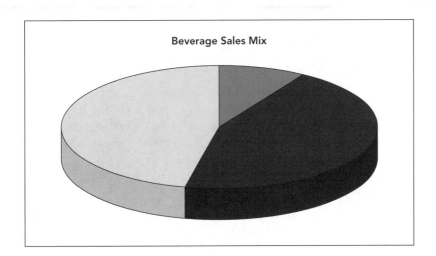

Beverage Sales Mix

4. Maureen is the manager of a very popular nightspot. She and her bartender, Leon, have created a new drink called "The Midnight Triple." It includes Gin, pineapple juice, and soda. Assume Maureen wants to sell the drink for $7.00. Using the data below, compute her beverage cost percentage if she and Leon make the drink according to the following recipes. (Spreadsheet hint: Use the ROUND function to two decimals in the **Cost per Ounce** column and the **Total Cost** column.)

Recipe 1: 1 oz. gin, 3 oz. pineapple juice, 2 oz. soda water
Recipe 2: 2 oz. gin, 3 oz. pineapple juice, 2 oz. soda water
Recipe 3: 1 oz. gin, 1 oz. pineapple juice, 4 oz. soda water
Recipe 4: 1.5 oz. gin, 1.5 oz. pineapple juice, 2 oz. soda water
Recipe 5: 2 oz. gin, 1 oz. pineapple juice, 3 oz. soda water

Cost of Gin: $9.50 per 750 ml (750 ml = 25.35 oz.)
Cost of Pineapple juice: $2.50 per quart
Cost of Soda water: $0.06 per ounce

Product	Unit	Cost	Cost Per Ounce
Gin	750 ml	$9.50	
Pineapple Juice	Quart	$2.50	
Soda Water	Ounce	$0.06	

Recipe	Ounces of Gin	Ounces of Pineapple Juice	Ounces of Soda Water	Total Cost	Selling Price	Beverage Cost %
1						
2						
3						
4						
5						

Which recipe has the lowest beverage cost percent? If Maureen chooses the recipe with the lowest beverage cost percent, would the recipe be likely to make her guests happy? If not, what other recipe(s) might most satisfy her guests and still prove to be cost effective for Maureen?

How would Maureen's decision be affected by the sizes of glassware she has available to her?

5. Jana Foster is the General Manager for a new restaurant in the Champos Restaurants chain. This new facility is located in a beachfront resort town, and sales there are excellent. The problem, according to Jana's Regional Manager, is that the new operation is consistently operating at a beverage cost percentage higher than the company average. Jana's Regional Manager has flown to Jana's town to see why her beverage cost percentage is too high. The prices set by the company for all restaurants are $3.00 for beer, $3.50 for wine, $5.00 for spirits (nonfrozen specialty drinks), and $7.00 for frozen specialty drinks.

Help Jana compare her beverage cost percentages with the company averages below.

Company Averages				
Product	Product Mix	Cost of Beverages	Beverage Sales	Beverage Cost %
Beer	30%	24,336	121,680	
Wine	20%	20,280	81,120	
Spirits (nonfrozen specialty drinks)	30%	30,420	121,680	
Spirits (frozen specialty drinks)	20%	24,336	81,120	
Total				

Jana's Beachfront Restaurant				
Product	Product Mix	Cost of Beverages	Beverage Sales	Beverage Cost %
Beer	15%	14,700	73,500	
Wine	5%	6,125	24,500	
Spirits (nonfrozen specialty drinks)	15%	18,375	73,500	
Spirits (frozen specialty drinks)	65%	95,550	318,500	
Total				

Look at the sales mixes and the beverage cost percentages of both the company and the beachfront restaurant. Explain why Jana's total beverage cost percentages are consistently higher than the company averages. What would you advise Jana to tell her regional manager?

6. Jack Stills operates the Spartan Restaurant. He is taking the month-end inventory in the restaurant's bar. When calculating the value of his spirits, he uses the "tenths" method of estimating product value. He has accounted for all of the spirits product held in his liquor storage area and is now calculating the value of his "behind the bar" inventory. He has completed this process for all of the products he serves except gin. Help him arrive at the ending inventory value for gin by completing the following portion of his Spirits inventory value sheet.

Product	Cost Per 750-mL Bottle	Amount on Hand (750 mL)	Product Value
Seagram's	$11.50	2.3	
Well Gin	$7.50	4.6	
Bombay	$17.50	2.2	
Bombay Sapphire	$19.50	2.9	
Tanqueray	$16.50	1.0	
Tanqueray Ten	$19.00	1.7	
Tanqueray Rangpur	$19.00	2.3	
Gordon's	$10.75	1.5	
White Satin	$22.50	0.8	
Total Value			

7. Increasingly, some local and state governments are defining the phrase "drinking and driving" in a way that would prevent any individual who has consumed an alcoholic beverage from operating a motor vehicle. In Massachusetts, legislation has been proposed that would reduce the current 0.08 blood-alcohol limit recognized nationwide as the standard for being legally intoxicated to 0.02. Federal government research indicates a 160- to 240-pound man would register 0.02 sipping one glass of wine over the course of an hour. As a hospitality professional, would you support the proposed legislation? What specific operating cost–related beverage issues would be affected if such proposed laws became widely adopted?

Chapter 5

MANAGING THE FOOD AND BEVERAGE PRODUCTION PROCESS

OVERVIEW

This chapter teaches you the methods used to issue and prepare food and beverage products in a cost-effective manner, including steps you can take to minimize theft and spoilage. It also shows how to estimate the cost of producing the menu items you plan to sell. In addition, you will learn how to compare the cost results you actually achieve with those you planned to achieve and discover methods to reduce your costs if they are too high.

Chapter Outline

- Managing the Food and Beverage Production Process
- Product Issuing
- Inventory Control
- Managing the Food Production Area
- Managing the Beverage Production Area
- Employee Theft
- Determining Actual and Attainable Product Costs
- Reducing Overall Product Cost Percentage
- Technology Tools
- Apply What You Have Learned
- Key Terms and Concepts
- Test Your Skills

At the conclusion of this chapter, you will be able to:

- Use management techniques to control the costs of preparing food and beverages for guests.
- Compute the actual cost of producing a menu item and compare that cost against the cost you planned to achieve.
- Recognize and be able to apply various methods to reduce the cost of goods sold percentage.

MANAGING THE FOOD AND BEVERAGE PRODUCTION PROCESS

*W*hen you have ordered and received the food and beverage products you believe will be purchased by your guests, your concern turns toward the most important function of all, controlling the food and beverage production process. If any one activity stands at the heart of foodservice management and control, this is it. To study this process, assume that you are the manager of Scotto's Supper Club. Scotto's is a high-volume steakhouse with an upscale clientele. Business is good both during the lunch period and in the evenings. Volume is especially heavy on Friday and Saturday nights, and at Sunday brunch. As you prepare for another week of business, you review your sales history, forecasts, purchase orders, and menu specials. You do these things to take the first step in the production process: developing your kitchen production schedules.

■ PRODUCTION SCHEDULES

Each foodservice manager is in charge of kitchen production. How much of each item to prepare may be a joint decision between you and your chef or production manager, but it is you who must ultimately take the responsibility for proper production decisions. The complete production process involves the following steps:

1. Maintain sales histories.
2. Forecast future sales levels.
3. Purchase and store needed food and beverage supplies.
4. Plan daily production schedules.
5. Issue needed products to production areas.
6. Manage the food and beverage production process.

Planning daily production schedules is important because you will want to have both the products and the staff needed to properly service your guests. If, for example, you forecast that 50 chocolate cakes will be needed on a given day for the college residence hall you manage, then you must have both the products and the staff necessary to produce the cakes. In a similar manner, if you know that 500 pounds of ground beef patties must be cooked for your burger restaurant, then the ground beef patties and the staff to prepare them must be secured. In this chapter, we examine the food and beverage production process; in Chapter 7, we consider the planning required to secure the labor needed to produce these products.

Ideally, the process of determining how much of each menu item to prepare on a given day would look as follows:

Prior Day's Carryover + Today's Production
= Today's Sales Forecast ± Margin of Error

The margin of error amount should be small; however, projecting sales and guest counts is an imprecise science at best, thus most foodservice managers will find that they must produce a small amount more than they anticipate selling each day. This minimizes the chances of running out of an important menu item. Of course, with some menu items, preparation does not begin until the sale is made. For example, in most cases a New York strip steak will not actually be cooked until it is ordered by the guest. An order for coconut cream pie, however, cannot be filled in the same manner. It is because of items like coconut cream pie that production sheets are necessary. Figure 5.1 demonstrates the production sheet in use at Scotto's.

From Figure 5.1 you can see that you had 15 servings of prime rib left over from the prior day's operation. You would know that by looking at the carryover section of the prior day's production sheet. You anticipate sales of 85 servings of prime rib, and so it might seem that only 70 servings should be prepared (70 new servings plus 15 carryovers from the prior day equals 85). In fact, you would prepare a number of new servings that is slightly higher than anticipated demand. The reason is simple: If you have more guests come in than anticipated or if more of the guests than you forecast select prime rib, you do not want to run out of the item. There is no industry-wide standard percentage that should be overproduced for a given item. The amount you plan to make will depend on a variety of factors, including your own knowledge of your guests and the importance of running out of a given item. Standard overages tend to run 5 to 10% above normal forecasts. For purposes of this example, assume that five extra servings of prime rib is the amount of overproduction you feel is appropriate for this item.

In the case of broccoli, you make the decision not to carry over any broccoli that was not sold on the prior day. If any such product exists, it could be used to make soup or, if there is no appropriate use for it, discarded because the quality of previously cooked broccoli is not likely to be at the same high level as that of freshly cooked broccoli. Regardless of the type of operation you manage, you will likely find that some of your menu items simply do not retain their quality well when they are carried over. These generally must be discarded or utilized as an ingredient in a different dish. Again, in the case of broccoli, proposed production exceeds anticipated demand by a small margin (10 servings). In the case of the coconut cream pie, you make the decision to produce none on this particular day. This is because this item

■ **FIGURE 5.1** Production Schedule

Unit Name: Scotto's Supper Club   **Date: 1/1**

Menu Item	Sales Forecast	Prior-Day Carryover	New Production	Total Available	Number Sold	Carryover
1. Prime Rib	85	15	75	90		
2. Broccoli	160	0	170	170		
3. Coconut Cream Pie	41	70	0	70		
4.						
5.						
6.						
7.						
8.						
9.						
10.						
11.						
12.						
13.						
14.						
15.						
16.						
17.						
18.						

Special Instructions: <u>Thaw turkeys for Sunday preparation</u>

Production Manager: <u>S. Antony</u>

is made in large quantities, but not each day. With 70 servings available and an anticipated demand of 41, you have enough to sustain your operation through this day and, perhaps, the next as well, if the quality of the carried-over pies remains high.

At the end of the evening service period, you would enter the number sold in the appropriate column and make a determination on how much, if any, of each product you will carry over to the next day. Some foodservice managers preprint their production sheets listing all menu items and, thus, ensure that production

Consider the Cost

"How many dozen should I put in the proofer?" asked Elizabeth, the new baker at the Sands Cafeteria.

Rami El-Hussieny was the day shift operations manager and, unfortunately, he did not know how to answer Elizabeth's question. What she wanted to know was simple enough: How many dozen rolls should be placed in the proofer in anticipation of the night's dinner business?

The problem was that the frozen dinner roll dough used at the Sands Cafeteria needed to proof for at least two hours prior to being baked for 15 minutes. If too many rolls were proofed, they would never be needed, but they would still have to be baked and made into bread dressing or even tossed out. If too few dozen were proofed and the night was busier than anticipated, they would run out of "Fresh Baked Rolls" (one of the restaurant's signature items), and Rami knew that the night manager would be really upset. It was a daily guess, and sometimes Rami missed the guess!

He wondered if a prebaked roll with a shelf life of three or four days would, despite not having been baked on site, be the best solution to this problem.

1. What do you think is the main cause of Rami's difficulty?

2. Most foodservice managers would agree that fresh baked goods are very high quality and greatly enjoyed by their guests, yet many of these bake few, if any, products on-site. What are two specific reasons why higher-quality, made-on-site items are often not produced?

3. What is the relationship between product quality and product cost in this case study? Which product characteristic do you think is more important from the guest's point of view?

levels for each major menu item are considered on a daily basis. Others prefer to use the production sheet on an "as-needed" basis. When this is the case, it is used daily but only for the items to be prepared that day. Either method is acceptable, but production schedules are always critical to operational efficiency.

When your kitchen production staff knows what you want them to produce for a given meal period, they can move to the next logical step, which is to **requisition**, or request, the inventory items they must have to produce the menu items indicated on your production schedule. These inventory items are then **issued**, that is, taken from storage and placed into the food and beverage production areas. In both the food and the beverage production process, the issuing of products from the storage area is a critical part of the cost control process.

PRODUCT ISSUING

Getting necessary beverage, food, and supply products from the storage area in smaller properties may be as simple as entering the locked storeroom, selecting the product, and locking the door behind you. In a more complex operation, especially one that serves alcoholic beverages, this method is simply inadequate to achieve appropriate control.

The act of requisitioning products from the storage area need not be unduly complex. Often, however, foodservice managers create difficulties for their workers by developing a requisition system that is far too time-consuming and complicated. The difficulty in such an approach usually arises because management hopes to equate products issued with products sold without taking a physical inventory. In reality, this process is difficult, if not impossible, to carry out.

Consider, for example, the bar area of Scotto's Supper Club. If, on a given night, you attempt to match liquor issued to liquor sold, you would need to assume that all liquor issued on a given day is sold on the same day and that no liquor issued on a prior day was sold on the given day. This will, generally, not be the case. In the kitchen, some items issued today, for example, coconut cream pie, will be sold over several days; thus, in the same way as for liquor, food products issued will not relate exactly to products sold. It is simply good management to see an issuing system as one of providing basic product security and an inventory control/cost system as a separate entity entirely. Given that approach, let us examine how Scotto's issuing system can be designed to protect the security of food and beverage products, and then move to the process of inventory control, with a view toward achieving effective cost control and purchasing.

The process of requisitioning and issuing food, beverages, and supplies to employees need not be tremendously complicated. Remember that employees should requisition food and beverage items based on management-approved production schedules. Although special care must be taken to ensure that employees use the products for their intended purpose, maintaining product security can be achieved with relative ease if a few principles are observed:

1. Food, beverages, and supplies should be requisitioned only as needed based on approved production schedules.
2. Required items (issues) should be issued only with management approval.
3. If a written record of issues is to be kept, each person removing food, beverages, or supplies from the storage area must sign, acknowledging receipt of the products.
4. Products that do not ultimately get used should be returned to the storage area, and their return should be recorded.

Some larger foodservice operators who employ a full-time storeroom person prefer to operate with advance requisition schedules. This process can sometimes be helpful because requisition schedules for tomorrow's food, for instance, can be submitted today, thus allowing storeroom personnel the time to gather the items prior to delivering them to the kitchen. Occasionally, products are even weighed and measured for kitchen personnel, according to the standardized recipes to be prepared. When this system is in place, the storeroom is often called an **ingredient room**. Figure 5.2 illustrates the kind of food and supplies requisition form you might use at Scotto's.

■ **FIGURE 5.2** Storeroom Requisition

Unit Name: Scotto's Supper Club			Requisition #: 0221		
			Date: 1/15		

Item	Storage Unit	Requested Amount	Issued Amount	Unit Cost	Total Cost
Rice	1 lb.	5 lb.	5 lb.	$ 0.25/lb.	$ 1.25
Broccoli	1 lb.	30 lb.	28.5 lb.	$ 0.90/lb.	$ 25.65
Rib Roast	1 lb.	100 lb.	103.5 lb.	$ 8.40/lb.	$ 869.40
Total					$ 896.30

To: Kitchen X		Requisition Approved By: S.A.R.
Bar		Requisition Filled By: T.A.P.

Note that the requested amounts and issued amounts may vary somewhat. In the case of rice, it is relatively easy to issue exactly the amount requisitioned because the rice can be weighed. In the cases of broccoli and rib roast, however, the nature of the product itself may make it impossible to exactly match the amount issued with the amount requisitioned. In other cases, the storeroom may be out of a requested item completely.

Note also that the total cost is arrived at by computing the value of the issued amount, not the requisitioned amount. This is so because it is the value of the issued amount that has actually been removed from inventory and, thus, will ultimately be reflected in the cost of food sold computations.

Some managers omit the Unit Cost and Total Cost columns from their Storeroom Requisition forms. If they are to be included, it is important to remember that their primary role is to remind employees that all food items have a cost. It is not recommended that these dollar amounts be considered as being equal to the cost of goods sold. That system might work in a manufacturing or shipping company but is not sufficiently accurate for use in foodservice.

It is vital that a copy of the storeroom requisition form be sent to the purchasing agent after it has been prepared so that this individual will know about the movement of products in and out of the storage areas. The form in Figure 5.2, or one similar to it, could also be used by the bar manager at Scotto's to serve as a record of the product requisitions and issues to the bar from the kitchen. As you learned in Chapter 4, you must know the dollar value of these transfers to accurately compute the cost of beverages sold.

■ SPECIAL CONCERNS FOR ISSUING BEVERAGES

The basic principles of product issuing that apply to food and supplies also apply to beverages. There are, however, special concerns that must be addressed when issuing beverage products:

1. Liquor storeroom issues
2. Wine cellar issues

LIQUOR STOREROOM ISSUES

Although several methods of liquor issues could be in place, one choice you would have as a manager, and the system favored by the authors, is to implement the **empty for full system** of liquor replacement. In this system, each bartender is required to hold empty liquor bottles in the bar or a closely adjacent area. At the conclusion of the shift, or at the start of the next shift, each empty liquor bottle is replaced with a full one. The empty bottles are then either broken or disposed of, as local beverage law requires.

Figure 5.3 illustrates the requisition form you would use to issue liquor products with the empty for full system. Note that this requisition form does not include unit or total price on product issued; monitoring those costs should be a function of the liquor storeroom personnel or management, not the bartender. You could, of course, elect to include the unit and total costs on the liquor requisition form should you so desire.

It is important to note that all liquor bottles issued from the liquor storage area should be visibly marked in a manner that is not easily duplicated. This allows management to ensure, at a glance, that all liquor sold is the property of the foodservice operation, and not that of a bartender who has produced his or her own bottle for the purpose of going into an illicit partnership with the operation. In a "partnership" of this type, the operation supplies the guest while the bartender provides the liquor and then pockets the product sales and profit! Although bottle marking will not completely prevent dishonest bartenders from bringing in their own liquor, it will force them to pour their product into the operation's bottles and to dispose of their own empties, which make the process quite difficult.

Occasionally, it may be necessary for a bartender or supervisor to enter the liquor storeroom area during a shift. Typically, when this need arises, a manager will be available to meet the bartender's product needs. There may be occasions, however, when the bartenders themselves must enter the beverage storage area. In preparation for this possibility, management should (if a recodable electronic

■ **FIGURE 5.3** Liquor Requisition

		Unit Name: Scotto's Supper Club		

Shift: P.M.

Date: 1/15

Service Area: Cocktail Lounge

Verified By: Management

Product	Number of Empties	Bottle Size	Bartender	Management
Old Crow	6	750 ml	P.O.F.	S.A.R.
Tanqueray	4	750 ml	P.O.F.	S.A.R.
Peach Schnapps	2	1,000 ml	P.O.F.	S.A.R.
Seagram's 7	3	750 ml	P.O.F.	S.A.R.
Jack Daniel's	2	750 ml	P.O.F.	S.A.R.
Absolut Vodka	8	1,000 ml	P.O.F.	S.A.R.
Total Empties	25			

locking system is not in place) have a key, sealed in an envelope and then signed over the seal so that it cannot be opened without detection. This key should only be used if the manager or supervisor is not immediately available. When it is used, management should be notified immediately of its use. If the key is used, it should be made clear that an adequate explanation of this occurrence will be expected. It is wrong not to give employees controlled access to the products desired by your guests, but it is equally wrong to allow employees this access without your knowledge.

WINE CELLAR ISSUES

The issuing of wine from a wine cellar is a special case of product issuing because these sales cannot be predicted as accurately as sales of other alcoholic beverage products. That is, you may know that a given percentage of your guests are likely to select wine, but you are not likely to know the specific wines they will select. This is especially true in an operation where a large number of wines are routinely stored. If the wine storage area contains products valuable enough to remain locked, it is reasonable to assume that each bottled wine issued should be noted. You can use a form such as the one shown in Figure 5.4 to record your operation's wine-issuing activity.

This form may be used to secure wine for either the bar or the kitchen, as well as for dining room sales. In the case of transfers to the kitchen or the bar, it should be noted that the product has been directed to one of these two locations rather than having been assigned to a guest transaction number (maintained by the POS system) or a guest check number (when using a manual system). Forcing servers to identify the guest served when requesting wine will ensure that, at the conclusion of the shift, wine issues will match wine sales. If the wine is to be sent to a guest as "complimentary," or "**comp**" that can be noted as well, along with the initials of the management personnel authorizing the comp. In the case of the wine cellar

■ **FIGURE 5.4** Wine Cellar Issues

Product	Vintage	Number of Bottles	Check #	Removed By
1. Bolla Soave	2004	2	60485 L	T.A.
2. Glen Ellen Cabernet Sauvignon	2003	1	60486 L	S.J.
3. Barton & Guestier Medoc	1999	1	Manager "comp"	S.A.R.
4. Copperridge Cabernet	Current Stock	1	Kitchen	S.A.R.
5. Bolla Soave	2006	1	60500 M	S.J.
6. Copperridge Cabernet	Current Stock	1	Bar stock	S.A.R.
7.				
8.				
9.				
10.				
11.				
12.				

Remarks: #4 Requested by Chef 1/1

#6 House Wine Sent to Bar Area 1/1

issue, the form itself should remain in the wine cellar for use by the wine-purchasing agent, and a copy should, on a daily basis, be sent to management for review.

■ ESTIMATING DAILY COSTS USING THE ISSUES SYSTEM

For operations that prefer to use a strict issue and requisition system, it is still possible to estimate product usage on a daily basis. This is done using the six-column estimate but not by using "purchases" as discussed in Chapter 3. Rather, in an issues system, the dollar amount of "issues" is used to form the basis of the estimate. To illustrate, consider the case of Shondra Jackson. Shondra operates a busy Irish pub in a large hotel and would like to have a daily estimate of her beverage costs. She completes her physical inventory on the last day of each month, yet, because of the time it takes for her corporate office to produce and distribute a final month-end profit-and-loss statement, it is after the seventh or eighth day of the next month before she is informed of the prior month's beverage cost percentage. At that point, of course, the previous month has come and gone. Shondra has been "surprised" by high costs in this process more than she can bear! In an effort to generate more current data about her operation, Shondra analyzes her daily beverage issues (not purchases!) and finds them to be as shown in Figure 5.5 for the first 10 days of January.

■ **FIGURE 5.5** Beverage Issues Recap

The Irish Pub	Date: 1/1–1/10
Date	Total Issues
1/1	$ 945.00
1/2	785.00
1/3	816.50
1/4	975.40
1/5	1,595.50
1/6	1,100.20
1/7	18.40
1/8	906.50
1/9	1,145.25
1/10	546.25
Total	**$8,834.00**

■ **FIGURE 5.6**   Six-Column Beverage Cost Estimate

Unit Name: <u>The Irish Pub</u>   Date: <u>1/1–1/31</u>

Date	Issues Today	Issues To Date	Sales Today	Sales To Date	Beverage Cost Estimate Today	Beverage Cost Estimate To Date
1/1	$ 945.00	$ 945.00	$1,450.22	$ 1,450.22	65.2%	65.2%
1/2	785.00	1,730.00	1,688.40	3,138.62	46.5%	55.1%
1/3	816.50	2,546.50	2,003.45	5,142.07	40.8%	49.5%
1/4	975.40	3,521.90	1,920.41	7,062.48	50.8%	49.9%
1/5	1,595.50	5,117.40	5,546.50	12,608.98	28.8%	40.6%
1/6	1,100.20	6,217.60	5,921.27	18,530.25	18.6%	33.6%
1/7	18.40	6,236.00	495.20	19,025.45	3.7%	32.8%
1/8	906.50	7,142.50	1,292.20	20,317.65	70.2%	35.2%
1/9	1,145.25	8,287.75	1,381.51	21,699.16	82.9%	38.2%
1/10	546.25	8,834.00	1,548.21	23,247.37	35.3%	38.0%
Subtotal		$8,834.00		$23,247.37		38.0%
+/–		-$1,000.00				
Total		$7,834.00		$23,247.37		33.7%

Shondra determines her daily issues amount by simply adding the total of all beverage requisitions she has filled during the day. That is, she reviews all requisition/issue forms that resulted in product going into the bar and determines their total dollar value. At the end of each day, Shondra records total operational sales and, using her beverage issues totals, fills in the six-column beverage estimate form shown in Figure 5.6. Data for the period 1/1 to 1/10 have been entered.

As can be seen, the six-column form requires only that Shondra divide today's issues by today's sales to arrive at the estimate for today. The formula for day 1/1 is as follows:

$$\frac{\text{Issues Today}}{\text{Sales Today}} = \text{Beverage Cost Estimate Today}$$

or

$$\frac{\$945.00}{\$1,450.22} = 65.2\%$$

The To Date columns represent cumulative totals of both issues and sales. Therefore, Shondra adds today's issues to the issues total of the prior day. She does the same with the sales figure. Thus, on 1/2, the To Date estimate would be as follows:

$$\frac{\text{Issues to Date}}{\text{Sales to Date}} = \text{Beverage Cost Estimate to Date}$$

or

$$\frac{\$1,730.00}{\$3,138.62} = 55.1\%$$

Shondra's 10-day beverage cost estimate is 38%. Notice that her daily cost estimate varies greatly. Notice also, however, that the To Date column is beginning to settle in the mid- to high-30 range and that it remains there, despite rather major changes in the daily cost estimates. This is true because each passing day adds to both the issues and the sales cumulative total. By the tenth or eleventh day, it is unlikely that normal changes in daily issues activity will change the To Date figure in a substantial way.

It is important to note that Shondra does not know, at this point, what her actual cost of beverage sold really is for this 10-day period. That, of course, can only be determined by a physical inventory and the application of the Cost of Beverage Sold formula presented in Chapter 4 of this text. Shondra's estimate, however, will be extremely close to her actual cost of goods sold percentage, if one assumption she makes is either true or nearly true. That assumption is that Shondra's bar inventory remains constant or nearly constant in total dollar value from month to month. If this assumption is true, then Shondra's estimate will be quite accurate.

It is unlikely, however, that bar inventory levels will be exactly the same from month to month or from accounting period to accounting period. It is true, however, that these values should not vary a great deal. If variation in inventory values is slight, the monthly estimate will be extremely close to the actual cost of beverage sold figure. Note that Figure 5.6 has, at the bottom, an entry point to adjust issues back to actual inventory levels at the end of the accounting period. If, for example, ending inventory is lower than beginning inventory, the difference between the two numbers is added to the issues total. If ending inventory is higher than beginning inventory, the difference between these two numbers will be subtracted from the issues total. In this way, management can determine actual cost of beverage sold if all issues have been accounted for and an ending physical inventory has been taken.

In this example, Shondra's ending inventory is $1,000 higher than her beginning inventory. Thus, this amount is subtracted from the issues To Date total to give an accurate estimate of her true cost of beverage sold. As can be seen in Figure 5.6, when the $1,000 is subtracted from issues to date, Shondra's cost can be computed as:

$$\frac{\text{Issues to Date} + \text{Inventory Adjustment}}{\text{Sales to Date}} = \text{Cost of Beverage Sold}$$

or, in this example,

$$\frac{\$8,834.00 - \$1,000.00}{\$23,247.36} = 33.7\%$$

Inventory levels can vary based on the delivery days of vendors, the day of the week inventory is taken, and even the seasonality of some businesses. Because of this variability, it is critical that users of this estimate technique perform the month-end inventory adjustment. Because it keeps costs uppermost in the minds of managers and employees alike, it is recommended that the issues cost estimate be posted where all employees can see it. It daily communicates to employees both sales and the costs required to generate those sales and lets them see the importance of controlling product usage.

INVENTORY CONTROL

*R*egardless of the methods used by employees to requisition food and beverage products, or the systems management uses to issue these products, inventory levels will change. It will be your responsibility and that of your purchasing agent to monitor this movement and purchase additional products as needed. Restocking the inventory is critical if product shortages are to be avoided and if product necessary for menu item preparation is to be available. Nothing is quite as traumatic for the foodservice manager as being in the middle of a busy meal period and finding that the operation is "out" of a necessary ingredient or frequently requested menu item. Therefore, you must carefully monitor inventory levels. It would obviously be very expensive and time-consuming to monitor each ingredient, food product, and all supplies on an individual daily basis. The average foodservice operation stocks hundreds of items, each of which may or may not be used every day. The task could be overwhelming.

Imagine, for example, the difficulty associated with monitoring, on a daily basis, the use of each sugar packet in a high-volume restaurant. Taking a daily inventory of the use of such a product would be akin to spending $10 to watch a penny! The effective foodservice manager knows that proper control involves spending time and effort where it is most needed and can do the most good. It is for this reason that many operators practice the ABC method of inventory control, which will be explained in the next section. To fully understand the principles of ABC inventory control, however, you first must be very familiar with the concepts of physical inventory and perpetual inventory.

■ PHYSICAL AND PERPETUAL INVENTORY

A **physical inventory** is a system in which an actual physical count and valuation of all inventory on hand is taken at the close of each accounting period. A **perpetual inventory** system is one in which the entire inventory is counted and recorded, and then additions to and deletions from total inventory are recorded as they occur. Both physical and perpetual inventories have advantages and disadvantages for the foodservice operator. The physical inventory, properly taken, is the most accurate of all because each item is actually counted and then valued. It is the physical inventory, taken at the end of the accounting period (ending inventory), that is used in conjunction with the beginning inventory (the ending inventory value from the prior accounting period) to compute the cost of food (or beverage) sold. In turn, the cost of food sold determines actual product usage and is used to compute the food cost percentage (see Chapter 3). Despite its accuracy, however, the physical inventory suffers from a significant disadvantage: It is extremely time-consuming. Even with the use of software programs that can extend inventory (multiply number of units by unit cost) or handheld bar code scanners that assist in the process, counting each food and beverage item in storage can be a cumbersome and time-consuming task. This is so even for the well-trained individuals who will carefully count and weigh the inventoried items.

Perpetual inventory seeks to eliminate the need for frequent counting by adding to the inventory when appropriate (via receiving slips) and subtracting from inventory when appropriate (via requisitions or issues). Perpetual inventory is especially popular in the area of liquor and wine, where each product may have its own inventory sheet or, in some cases, a bin card.

A **bin card** is simply an index card (or line on a spreadsheet) that details additions to and deletions from a given product's inventory level. Figure 5.7 illustrates the use of such a card. Bin cards are especially useful for food products such as staples and dry goods. Of course, the accurate use of a bin card, or any other perpetual inventory system, requires that each addition to, or subtraction from, the products in inventory be carefully noted.

As bar-code-reading hardware and software programs become more popular, additions and deletions to and from inventory are increasingly recorded electronically. In the ideal situation, perpetual inventory systems, regardless of the form they take, are verified, on some regular basis, by the physical inventory for costing purposes.

Some managers prefer to use the same form for recording both the quantity and the price of an inventory item. This can be done by using a perpetual inventory

■ FIGURE 5.7   Bin Card

Product Name: <u>Canadian Club</u>		Bottle Size: <u>750 ml</u>	
Balance Brought Forward: <u>24</u>		Date: <u>12/31</u>	
Date	In	Out	Total on Hand
1/1	4		28
1/2		6	22
1/3		5	17
1/4	12		29

card. **Perpetual inventory cards** are simply bin cards, similar to the one in Figure 5.7, that include the product's price. A new perpetual inventory card or spreadsheet line is created each time the product's purchase price changes, with the quantity of product on hand entered on the new card. This system allows for continual tracking of quantity of items on hand and their prices. At month-end, a physical inventory can be taken and the actual prices of items can be applied to inventory value. For example, if six cases of canned corn are sitting on the shelf at month-end, three cases purchased this week at $10.00 per case (3 × $10 = $30) and three cases purchased last week at $11.00 per case (3 × $11 = $33), then the inventory value would equal $30 + $33 = $63. By using perpetual inventory cards, the manager can determine the actual value of the inventory instead of using the last price paid for the month, which is often the case with physical inventories.

Today, managers increasingly use computer spreadsheets and specialized inventory software to maintain perpetual inventories. In addition, some POS systems include inventory components that can be as simple as maintaining an electronic perpetual inventory system with accurate prices or as complex as a complete scanner system that is used to electronically record additions to and subtractions from inventory.

Of course, the accurate use of a perpetual inventory system requires that each change in product quantity be noted. However, employees, when in a hurry, may simply forget to update the perpetual system as they add or remove inventory items. Obviously, mistakes such as these begin to wear at the accuracy of the perpetual inventory. For this reason, it is not wise to depend solely on a perpetual inventory system for accurate cost calculations. There are, however, several advantages to the perpetual inventory system, among them the ability of the purchasing agent to quickly note quantity of product on hand without resorting to a daily physical inventory count.

The question of which of the two systems is best arises when making the decision about whether to use a physical or perpetual inventory system. Experienced managers know that neither is best, so they use the best of both.

■ ABC INVENTORY CONTROL

This is exactly what the ABC inventory system was designed to do. It separates inventory items into three main categories:

Category A items are those that require tight control and the most accurate record keeping. These are typically high-value items, and though few in number, they can make up 70 to 80% of the total inventory value.

Category B items are those that make up 10 to 15% of the inventory value and require only routine control and record keeping.

Category C items make up only 5 to 10% of the inventory value. These items require only the simplest of inventory control systems.

Returning to the hypothetical example of Scotto's Supper Club, assume that the following 10 items are routinely held in your inventory:

1. Precut New York strip steak
2. Prepared horseradish
3. Eight-ounce chicken breasts (fresh)
4. Garlic salt
5. Onion rings
6. Crushed red pepper
7. Dried parsley
8. Lime juice
9. Fresh tomatoes
10. Rosemary sprigs

As can be seen, even with this short list, you have a variety of items in inventory. Some, like the New York strip steak, are very valuable, highly perishable, and critical for the execution of your menu. Others, like the crushed red pepper, are much less costly, not highly perishable, and may not dramatically affect the operation if you ran out between deliveries. Clearly, these two example items should not be treated the same for inventory purposes. The simple fact is that they are not equally critical to the operation's success. The ABC system helps you distinguish between those items that deserve special, perhaps daily, attention, and those items that you can safely spend less time managing.

To develop the A, B, and C categories, you simply follow these steps:

1. Calculate monthly usage in units (pounds, gallons, cases, etc.) for each inventory item.
2. Multiply total unit usage times purchase price to arrive at the total monthly dollar value of product usage.
3. Rank items from highest dollar usage to lowest.

In a typical ABC analysis, 20% of the items will account for about 70 to 80% of the total monthly product cost. These represent the A product category. It is not necessary that the line separating A, B, and C products be drawn the same for every operation. Many operators use the following guide, but it can be adapted as you see fit:

Category A—Top 20% of items

Category B—Next 30% of items

Category C—Next 50% of items

It is important to note that, although the percentage of items in category A is small, the percentage of total monthly product cost the items account for is large. Conversely, the number of items in category C is large, but the total dollar value of product cost that the items account for is small. It is important to note that the ABC inventory system is concerned with monetary value of products, not number of items. Returning to the Scotto's example may help make this distinction of the ABC system clear. One item on your menu is New York strip steak. The preparation of this item is simple. Your cook sprinkles the steak with seasoning salt and cooks it to the guest's specification. The steak is then garnished with one large deep-fried onion ring (which you buy frozen). In this example, these inventory items would likely be grouped as follows:

Scotto's Strip Steak	
Ingredient	**Inventory Category**
New York Strip Steak	A
Onion Ring	B
Garlic Salt	C

Figure 5.8 shows the complete result of performing an ABC analysis on the 10 menu items listed previously and then ranking those items in terms of their inventory value.

The ABC inventory system specifically directs your attention to the areas where it is most needed. Reducing product costs, especially for category A items, is extremely important and is discussed more fully later in this chapter. Figure 5.9 details the differences in handling items in the A, B, and C categories.

The ABC system will focus management's attention on the essential few items in inventory, while focusing less attention on the many low-cost, slow-moving items. Again, it is important to note that management's time is best spent on the items of

■ **FIGURE 5.8** ABC Inventory Analysis on Selected Items

Item	Monthly Usage	Purchase Price	Monthly Value	Category
Precut New York Strip Steak	300 lb.	$ 7.50/lb.	$2,250.00	A
8-Ounce Chicken Breasts (Fresh)	450 lb.	2.10/lb.	945.00	A
Fresh Tomatoes	115 lb.	0.95/lb.	109.25	B
Onion Rings	30 lb.	2.20/lb.	66.00	B
Rosemary Sprigs	10 lb.	4.50/lb.	45.00	B
Prepared Horseradish	4 lb.	2.85/lb.	11.40	C
Lime Juice	2 qt.	4.10/qt.	8.20	C
Garlic Salt	2 lb.	2.95/lb.	5.90	C
Crushed Red Pepper	1 oz.	16.00/lb.	1.00	C
Dried Parsley	4 oz.	4.00/lb.	1.00	C

■ FIGURE 5.9   Guide to Managing ABC Inventory Items

Category	Inventory Management Techniques
A	1. Order only on an as-needed basis.
	2. Conduct perpetual inventory on a daily or, at least, weekly basis.
	3. Have clear idea of purchase point and estimated delivery time.
	4. Conduct monthly physical inventory.
B	1. Maintain normal control systems; order predetermined inventory (par) levels.
	2. Monitor more closely if sale of this item is tied to sale of an item in category A.
	3. Review status quarterly for movement to category A or C.
	4. Conduct monthly physical inventory.
C	1. Order in large quantity to take advantage of discounts if item is not perishable.
	2. Stock constant levels of product.
	3. Conduct monthly physical inventory.

most importance. In the case of inventory management, these are the category A and, to a lesser degree, category B items.

The ABC system can also be used to arrange storerooms or to determine which items should be stored in the most secure area. Regardless of the inventory management system used, however, whether it is the physical, perpetual, or ABC inventory, management must be strict in monitoring both withdrawals from inventory and the process by which inventory is replenished. The reasoning behind this is quite simple. Although it is critical that you know how to compute your cost of goods sold and your food cost percentage, accurate inventory records allow you to know much more about your operation. To illustrate, consider Figure 5.10, which details Scotto's food usage in five major inventory categories. In this case, you have decided to categorize your product usage in terms of broad categories of food. In other words, although you are interested in your overall food cost percentage, you are also interested in your meat cost percentage, produce cost percentage, and so on. When the storeroom inventory is set up as a series of mini-inventories, this approach is possible. It simply requires you to determine desired subcategories and then use inventory valuation sheets that match these groups.

Product subcategories can be determined in any manner management feels is appropriate. At Scotto's, meat, seafood, dairy, produce, and "other" items are the five major categories. Figure 5.11 details food usage at Scotto's when monthly food sales are $190,000 and total cost of food sold equals $65,000, yielding a food cost percentage for the month of 34.2% ($65,000/$190,000).

Given sales of $190,000 for the month of January, you can now determine both food cost percentages by category and product usage ratios. You compute your **category food cost %**, that is, a food cost percentage computed on a portion of total food usage, by using the cost of food sold/sales formula. This is illustrated in Figure 5.11.

■ **FIGURE 5.10** Inventory Recap

Unit Name: Scotto's Supper Club						Date: January 31
	Meat	Seafood	Dairy	Produce	Other	Total
Beginning Inventory	$26,500	$ 4,600	$ 7,300	$ 2,250	$23,000	$ 63,650
Purchases	33,800	17,700	4,400	15,550	1,800	73,250
Goods Available	60,300	22,300	11,700	17,800	24,800	136,900
Ending Inventory	28,000	10,900	6,000	4,500	21,000	70,400
Cost of Food Consumed	32,300	11,400	5,700	13,300	3,800	66,500
Employee Meals	900	200	100	250	50	1,500
Cost of Food Sold	31,400	11,200	5,600	13,050	3,750	65,000

■ **FIGURE 5.11** Food Cost Category %/Proportion

Scotto's			Sales: $190,000
Category	Cost of Food Sold	Food Cost%	Proporation of Total Cost
Meat	$31,400	16.5%	48.3%
Seafood	11,200	5.9	17.2
Dairy	5,600	2.9	8.6
Produce	13,050	6.9	20.1
Other	3,750	2.0	5.8
Total	65,000	34.2	100.0

In each category group, including the total, you would use $190,000 as the denominator in your food cost percentage equation and the cost of food sold in each category as the numerator. The proportion of total cost percentages is developed by the formula:

$$\frac{\text{Cost in Product Category}}{\text{Total Cost in All Categories}} = \text{Proportion of Total Product Cost}$$

Thus:

$$\frac{\text{Cost in Meat Category}}{\text{Total Cost in All Categories}} = \text{Meat Cost Proportion of Total Cost}$$

In this example:

$$\frac{\$31,400}{\$65,000} = 48.3\%$$

By using the categories listed in Figure 5.11, you are better able to determine when your costs are above those you would expect. Using the category food cost percentage, you know, for example, that meats accounted for 48.3% of your total food usage in the month of January. You can compare this figure to the meat expense of prior months to determine whether your meat cost percentage is rising, declining, or staying constant. If your category or overall percentages are higher than you anticipated, you must find out why. One possible reason for costs that are higher than you expect may be the food and beverage production process itself. This production process is also one of the most complex and difficult to manage unless you truly understand it and how it influences your total operation and costs.

MANAGING THE FOOD PRODUCTION AREA

*O*ften, those individuals who manage restaurants do so because they relish managing the **back of the house,** or kitchen production area, of the food facility. Managing food production to produce tasty, nutritious, and cost-effective meals is one of the most challenging and enjoyable aspects of foodservice management. Managing the food production process entails control of the following five areas:

1. Waste
2. Overcooking
3. Overportioning
4. Improper carryover utilization
5. Inappropriate make or buy decisions

■ WASTE

Food losses through simple product waste can play a large role in overall excessive cost situations. This waste may be simple to observe, such as when an employee does not use a rubber spatula to get all of the salad dressing out of a 1-gallon jar, or as difficult to detect as the shoddy work of the salad preparation person who trims the lettuce just a bit more than management would prefer, resulting in a reduced amount of usable lettuce available to make salads and in higher salad costs.

Management must demonstrate its concern for the value of products on a daily basis. Each employee should be made to realize that wasting food affects the profitability of the operation and, thus, his or her own economic well-being. In general, food waste is the result of poor training or management inattentiveness. Unfortunately, some managers and employees feel that small amounts of food waste are unimportant. Your primary goal in reducing waste in the food production area should be to maximize product utilization and minimize the "it's only a few pennies worth" syndrome.

■ OVERCOOKING

Cooking is simply the process of exposing food to heat. It is a truism that prolonged cooking reduces product volume, whether the item cooked is roast beef or vegetable soup! This is so because most foods have a high moisture content and heating usually results in moisture loss. To minimize cooking loss, cooking times on standardized recipes must be carefully calculated and meticulously followed. It is important to remember that, in many ways, excess heat is the enemy of well-prepared foods. Too much time on the steam table line or in the holding oven extracts moisture from products and, thus, fewer portions are available for service. Figure 5.12 details the change in portion cost when ending weight is reduced in a roast prime rib of beef due to overcooking.

■ **FIGURE 5.12** Prime Ribs

Effect of Overcooking on Portion Cost of 50 Pounds (800 Ounces) of Roast Beef			
		50# Cost = $400	
Preparation State	Ending Weight (oz.)	Number of 8-Ounce Portions	Portion Cost
Properly prepared	800	100	$4.00
Overcooked 15 min.	775	97	4.12
Overcooked 30 min.	750	94	4.26
Overcooked 45 min.	735	92	4.35
Overcooked 60 min.	720	90	4.44
Overcooked 90 min.	700	88	4.55
Overcooked 120 min.	680	85	4.71

If we assume that a properly cooked pan of roast beef yields 50 lb. at a cost of $8.00 per pound, the total product cost equals $400.00 (50 lb. + $8.00/lb. = $400.00). In its properly cooked state, the roast beef would yield 100 eight-ounce portions, for a cost of $4.00 per portion. As you see, increased cooking time or temperature can cause product shrinkage that increases average portion cost.

Although the difference between a portion cost of $4.00 and $4.71 may seem small, it is the control of this type of production issue that separates the good food-service manager from the outstanding one.

In attempting to control loss due to overcooking, you must strictly enforce standardized recipe cooking times. This is especially true for meats, soups, stews, baked goods, and the like. Moreover, extended cooking times can result in total product loss if items are placed in an oven, fryer, steam equipment, or broiler and then "forgotten." It is, therefore, advisable to supply kitchen production personnel with small, easily cleanable timers for which they are responsible. This can help, substantially, in reducing product loss due to overcooking.

■ OVERPORTIONING

No other area of food and beverage cost control has been analyzed and described as fully through articles, speeches, and even books as the control of portion size. There are two reasons for this. First, overportioning on the part of service personnel has the effect of increasing operational costs and may cause the operation to mismatch its production schedule with anticipated demand. For example, assume that 100 guests are expected and 100 products are produced, yet overportioning causes you to be out of product after only 80 guests have been served. The remaining 20 guests will be left clamoring for "their" portions, which, of course, have already been served to others. Also, overportioning must be avoided because guests want to feel that they have received fair value for their money. If portions are large one day and small the next, guests may feel that they have been cheated on the second day. Consistency is a key to operational success in foodservice. Guests want to know exactly what they will get for their money.

It is not possible to set standard portion sizes for all foodservice operations. The proper portion size of an entrée in a college dormitory feeding male athletes should clearly be different from that of an extended-care facility whose typical resident might be over 75 years old. It is important for you to consider clientele, ambiance, pricing structure, and desired quality standards prior to establishing an appropriate portion size for your own operation.

Once portion size has been established, it is up to you to strictly enforce it. Often, employees resist management's efforts. When this is the case, it is a clear indication that management has failed in its mission to provide employees with a basic understanding that underlines the foodservice industry. Employees must be made to see that strict adherence to predetermined portion size is a benefit both to the guest and to the operation. Management must be sensitive, also, to the fact that it is the line, or dining room, server who often must deal with the guest who complains about the inadequacy of portion size. Therefore, servers must be made to feel comfortable about predetermined portion sizes so that management, along with the employees, will want to maintain them.

In most cases, tools are available that will help employees serve the proper portion size. Whether these are scales, scoops, ladles, dishes, or spoons, employees must have an adequate number of easily accessible portion control devices if they are to use them. Scoops, for example, are sized based on the number of servings per guest. Thus, a #12 scoop will yield 12 servings per quart, or 48 servings per gallon; a #20 scoop will yield 20 servings per quart; and so on.

Many portion sizes are closely tied to the purchasing function. To serve a 1/4-pound hot dog, for instance, one must begin with 1/4-pound hot dogs. In a similar vein, if one full banana is sliced for addition to breakfast cereals, the purchasing agent must have been diligent in ordering and accepting only the banana size for which management has developed a specification.

Constant checking of portion size is an essential task of management. When incorrect portion sizes are noticed, they must be promptly corrected. If not, considerable cost increases can be incurred. Returning again to our example of Scotto's Supper Club, consider that you purchase, on occasion, and in accordance with your menu plan, 3-pound boxes of frozen yellow corn to be served as your vegetable of the day. Each box costs $2.80. With a total of 48 ounces (3 pounds × 16 ounces = 48 ounces) and an established portion size of 3 ounces, you know that you should average 48 ounces/3 ounces = 16 servings per box. Figure 5.13 demonstrates the effect on total portion cost if one, two, or three servings are lost to overportioning.

As Figure 5.13 demonstrates, a small amount of overportioning on an item as inexpensive as corn costs the operation only a few cents per serving. Those few cents per serving, however, multiplied time after time, can mean the difference between a profitable operation and one that is only marginally successful. If your portion cost for corn should have been 17.5 cents ($2.80/16 portions = 17.5 cents), but, due to overportioning, it rises to 21.5 cents ($2.80/13 portions = 21.5 cents), then your costs are 4.0 cents higher than they should be on this item. If Scotto's is open seven days a week and serves an average of 200 portions of corn per day,

■ **FIGURE 5.13** Frozen Corn

Corn Portion Cost Chart @ $2.80 per 3-lb. Box		
Number of Portions per 3-lb. Box	Portion Size (oz.)	Portion Cost (cents)
16	3.0	17.5
15	3.2	18.7
14	3.4	20.0
13	3.7	21.5

your total "loss" for a year would be $365 \times 200 \times 0.04 = \$2,920$, enough to buy your operation proper portioning tools. It is also an amount worthy of your attention and correction.

■ IMPROPER CARRYOVER UTILIZATION

As discussed earlier in this text, predicting guest counts is an inexact science at best. Because this is true, and because most foodservice operators want to offer the same broad menu to the evening's last diner as was offered to its first, it is inevitable that some food that has been prepared will remain unsold at the end of the operational day. These items are called **carryovers**, or in some operations, leftovers. In some areas of the hospitality industry, this is a particular problem; in others, it is less of a concern. Consider, for example, the operation of a shaved ice or snow cone facility. At the end of the day, any unsold ice is simply held until the next day with no measurable loss of either product quantity or quality. Contrast that situation, however, with a full-service cafeteria. If closing time is 8:00 p.m., management wishes to have a full product line, or at least some of each item, available to the guest who walks in the door at 7:55 p.m. Obviously, in five more minutes a large number of items will become carryover items. This cannot be avoided. Your ability to effectively integrate carryover items on subsequent days can make the difference between profits and losses. In almost every case, food products are at their peak of quality when they are delivered to the restaurant's back door. From then on, storage, preparation, and holding activities often work against product quality. These forces are especially at work in the area of carryovers. It is for this reason that production schedules must note carryover items on a daily basis. If this is not done, these items tend to get stored and then "lost" in walk-in refrigerators or freezer units.

You should have a clear use in mind for each menu item that may have to be carried over. Broiled or sautéed fish may be used to prepare seafood chowder or bisque. Today's prime rib roast may be the key ingredient in tomorrow's beef Stroganoff, and so on. Menu specials, substitutions, and employee meals can be sources of utilization for products like these. This utilization process can be creative and, if you involve your staff, quite effective.

It is important to understand that carryover foods seldom can be sold for their original value. Today's beef stew made from yesterday's prime rib will not likely be sold at prime rib price. Carryovers generally mean reduced income relative to product value, and less profits; thus, it is critical that you strive for minimal carryovers.

■ INAPPROPRIATE MAKE
OR BUY DECISIONS

Many foodservice operators elect to buy some food products that are preprepared in some fashion. These items, called **convenience** or **ready foods**, can be of great value to your operation. Often, they can save dollars spent on labor, equipment, and hard-to-secure food products. They can also add menu variety beyond the skill level of the average kitchen crew. A disadvantage, however, is that these items tend to cost more on a per-portion basis. This is to be expected because these items include a charge for labor and packaging, as well as for the food itself.

Convenience items are not, of course, an all-or-nothing operational decision. Nearly all foodservice operations today use canned products, sliced bread, precut produce, and the like—items that would have been considered convenience items years ago. Therefore, the question is not whether to use convenience items but, rather, how many of a certain kind of convenience item to use. In general, the following guidelines are of value when determining whether to adopt the use of a convenience product:

1. Is the quality acceptable? This question must be answered from the point of view of the guest, not management alone.

2. Will the product save labor? Identifiable labor savings must be discovered if management is to agree that the convenience item will indeed save labor costs.

3. Would it matter if the guest knew? If an operation has built its image on made-on-premise items, guests may react negatively if they know that an item has been prepared from a "boil in a bag" package or in a microwave oven.

4. Does the product come in an acceptable package size? If convenience items are not sold in a size that complements the operation, excessive waste can result.

5. Is the appropriate storage space available? Many convenience items must be stored in a refrigerated or frozen form. Your facility must have the needed storage capacity for these items or product quality can be diminished.

MANAGING THE BEVERAGE PRODUCTION AREA

Control in the beverage area is just as important as control in the food production area. In some regards, beverage production is easier than that of food because the variability of product in the beverage area is so much less than that of food. On the other hand, controlling the amount of the product that actually is served to the guest is more complex with alcoholic beverages than with food. As a beverage manager, you will generally have several choices to consider when you decide exactly how you will control your beverage production area.

In its simplest, but least desired form, beverage production can consist of a bartender **free-pouring**, which is pouring liquor from a bottle without carefully measuring the poured amount. In a situation such as this, it is very difficult to control product costs. At the other end of the control spectrum are automated beverage-dispensing systems that are extremely sophisticated control devices. The following are various beverage control systems that you can use, based on the amount of control you feel is appropriate in a specific operation or physical setting.

■ FREE-POUR

The lack of control resulting from free-pouring alcohol is significant. It should never be allowed in the preparation of the majority of drinks your bartenders will serve. It is appropriate in some settings, however, for example, in wine-by-the-glass sales. In this situation, the wine glass itself serves as a type of control device. Large operations, however, may even elect to utilize a dispensing system for their "wines by the glass." Also, it is most often necessary for a bartender to free-pour when he or she must add extremely small amounts of a product as an ingredient in a drink recipe. An example would be a bartender who must add a very small amount of dry vermouth to a larger martini recipe.

■ JIGGER POUR

A **jigger** is a device (like a small cup) used to measure alcoholic beverages, typically in ounces and fraction of ounce quantities. Because jiggers are inexpensive, this control approach is also inexpensive. It is also quite portable. It is a good system to use in remote serving locations, such as a pool area, beach, guest suite, or banquet room. The disadvantage, of course, is that there is still room for employee over-pouring error and the potential for fraud.

■ METERED BOTTLE/DISPENSER

In some situations, you may determine that a **metered bottle** or other metered dispensing unit makes sense. In this case, a predetermined portion of product is dispensed whenever the bartender is called upon to serve that product. A metered draft beer system, for example, may be preset to dispense 12 ounces of beer whenever the bartender uses the draft system to serve a beer. In a like manner, a bottle of vodka may have a metering device (spout) attached to it so that, upon pouring, a preset amount of the product is dispensed.

■ BEVERAGE GUN

In some large operations, beverage guns are connected directly to liquor products. The gun may be activated by pushing a mechanical or electronic button built into the gun or POS. In either case, the bartender may find, for example, that pushing a gin and tonic button on a gun device will result in the dispensing of a predetermined amount of both gin and tonic. Although the control inherent in such a system is great, the cost, lack of portability, and possible negative guest reaction are limiting factors in its selection.

■ TOTAL BAR SYSTEM

The most expensive, but also the most complete, solution, a **total bar system**, combines sales information with product dispensing information to create a complete revenue and product management system. Depending on the level of sophistication and cost, the total bar system can perform one or all of the following tasks:

1. Record beverage sale by brand.
2. Record who made the sale.
3. Record sales dollars and/or post the sale to a guest room folio (bill) in a hotel.
4. Measure liquor.
5. Add predetermined mixes to drink.
6. Reduce liquor from inventory.
7. Prepare liquor requisition.
8. Compute liquor cost by brand sold.
9. Calculate gratuity on check.
10. Identify payment method, that is, cash, check, or credit/debit card.
11. Record guest sale (check) number.
12. Record date and time of sales.

FUN ON THE WEB!

There are a variety of companies selling advanced automatic beverage-dispensing systems. One of the best known is the Berg company. To see their products, go to **www.berg-controls.com**. When you arrive, click "Why Liquor Control?"

You must establish in each location that sells alcohol exactly how much control over the production process you desire. At a supper club such as Scotto's, you may elect to use a relatively simple beverage production control system. In the bar area, metering devices used on liquor bottles will allow the bartender to pour only a predetermined amount of liquor, yet give each guest the sense of a drink made to order by the bartender. Larger beverage operations that serve greater amounts of product may find that investing in more sophisticated and costly production control systems can be beneficial. The point to remember here is that you should establish and enforce the level of control you feel is appropriate.

Although the control of product cost is critical, it is also very important to designate a proper glass size and ice quantity for each drink. This ensures that the portion size of the drink is consistent with the guest's visual perception of a full glass. What does ice have to do with standardized beverage production? A lot! Large ice cubes will leave space between them when scooped into a glass. This will permit a larger amount of mixers to be added which may dilute the drink more than intended. By contrast, smaller cubes or (especially) shaved ice will pack a glass and permit less mixer to be added. This may, in turn, give the impression of a stronger drink.

Another difference created by ice size is that large cubes have, relative to their smaller counterparts, less exposed surface area and will melt (and dilute the drink) at a slower pace than smaller cubes. As a result, in the bar area, you should select an ice machine that makes ice in a form that you feel best fits your view of proper spacing in the glass and that possesses desirable melting characteristics.

It is also important to remember that not all alcohol sales take place in a traditional, designated bar area. This creates special beverage production management issues. These include:

1. In-room minibars
2. Bottle sales
3. Open bars
4. Banquet operations

■ MINIBARS

Minibars, serving 50-ml bottles, are popular in hotels that cater to the upscale business traveler. The control issue here is one of matching requests by housekeeping for replenishment bottles with guest usage of product. Some large hotels deal with this issue by having a single individual or department charged with the responsibility of filling the minibars. Modern minibars record liquor sales electronically but such records must be carefully monitored to ensure that items issued from storage are indeed used to restock the minibars and are not lost to theft.

■ BOTTLE SALES

When liquor sales are made by the bottle, either through room service, in the case of a hotel, or at a reception area, the control issue is one of verifying bottle count. The guest and the operation must both be treated fairly in such a transaction. In the case of full-bottle sales to a guest room, the guest should be required to sign a receipt confirming acceptance of the product. This is the only way to avoid potential misunderstandings about cost. In the case of receptions or banquets, guests should be charged only for empty bottles, or, in the case of a purchase of a specified number of bottles, should be shown both full and empty bottles equal to the number used and charged for the event. In an effort to protect both the establishment and the guest from employee theft, the thoughtful beverage manager will mark the bottles for that reception or banquet in a way that is not easily duplicated, thus preventing employees from bringing in their own empty bottles and then removing full ones at the guest's expense.

■ OPEN BARS

Open bars, or hosted bars, are those in which no charge is made to guests for the individual drinks the guests select at the time they are served because, when the open bar is closed, one total bar charge is assessed against the host or sponsor of the open bar. Unfortunately, because the individual drinker is not paying for each drink, the open-bar situation can, unless you are vigilant, create an "all you can drink environment" And so consumption by individual drinkers must be carefully monitored. Open bars are common, especially in cases such as weddings, special-occasion parties, and cocktail receptions.

The production control issues associated with open bars fall into one of two main categories: namely, portion size and accountability. In this environment, guests can sometimes cajole bartenders into pouring larger than normal portion drinks. This must, of course, be prevented. Bartenders, as well as guests, must understand that, although it may be an open bar, someone will be paying the bill at the end of the event. The hosts have the right to expect reasonable portion control if they are paying on a per-drink or per-bottle-used basis. If the foodservice operation has established a per-person charge for the open bar, overportioning costs will have to be absorbed by the operation. This, obviously, necessitates strict control of portion size and total liquor consumption per guest.

As great an issue as overportioning is, accountability looms larger and larger on the horizon as an area of legitimate cost control concern for the effective beverage manager. With states holding liquor sellers responsible for the actions of their patrons through the enactment of dram shop legislation, the entire concept of reasonable and prudent care in beverage operations is called into question. Bartenders who work open bars should be specially trained to spot signs of guest intoxication. As difficult as it may sometimes be, guests should be made aware that it is illegal, in all states, to serve an intoxicated guest. To do so puts the entire food and beverage operation at risk. Some managers have virtually eliminated the open-bar concept, preferring to go to a coupon system where each coupon issued is good for one drink, and the number of coupons issued, rather than the number of drinks, can be controlled. Although the possibility exists that coupons can be shared and, thus, given to an intoxicated guest, the coupon system does demonstrate an attempt by you to exercise reasonable care, an effort that may prove vital in your defense in the event of dram shop–related litigation.

■ BANQUET OPERATIONS

The sale of alcoholic beverages during a seated banquet usually takes the form of bottled-wine sales. Guests may be provided with a set number of bottles on the table, to be shared by those seated at the table. Alternatively, as they consume their wine, they can be served by the waitstaff. It is the latter method that presents cost control problems because the host of the event will be charged by either the number of bottles served or the number of guests served. If the payment is based on the number of bottles served, the bottles should be marked and the empties made available for inspection by either the guest or the banquet captain. If the sale is based on the number of glasses poured, then both the host of the event and the beverage operation must be in agreement as to the desired portion size and the total number of portions allowed to be served to each guest or to the entire group.

EMPLOYEE THEFT

*L*oss of product can happen when control systems do not prevent employee theft. Although all kitchens and beverage operations can expect to experience small amounts of product slippage, such as an apple eaten in secret or a carrot nibbled where the supervisor cannot see it, extensive loss of product must be prevented. Employee theft can occur in either the bar or the kitchen production areas, but it is typically more prevalent in the bar areas.

■ REDUCING BAR-RELATED THEFT

Experienced food and beverage managers seem to have an endless supply of stories related to theft in bar operations. Indeed, bar theft is one of the most frequent types of thefts in the foodservice industry. Although it may well be impossible to halt all kinds of bar theft, the following are areas that you should check periodically to ensure proper safeguards.

ORDER FILLED BUT NOT RUNG UP

In this case, the bartender delivers the drink as requested by the guest or server, but the drink is never recorded in the POS system, and the bartender simply pockets the sale. All drinks should be recorded by the POS system to prevent this type of theft. Management's vigilance is critical to ensure that no drink is prepared until after the order is properly recorded (rung up).

BRINGING IN EXTRA PRODUCT

In this scenario bartenders sell products that they have brought in and, of course, pocket the sales. Bottle stamps or markings help prevent this type of theft because nonmarked bottles can be easily detected by management.

OVER- AND UNDERPOURING

When bartenders overpour, they are stealing from the operation; when they underpour, they are shortchanging the guest. Remember that your bartenders will pour the appropriate amount if you always insist that they do so. When bartenders underpour, they may be making up for drinks they have given away or sold but have not rung up. When they overpour, they may be doing so for their friends or for the extra tips this activity may yield. In either case, management must prevent such behavior.

Proper portion size in the spirits area is ensured through the enforced use of jiggers, metered devices, or other mechanical or electronic equipment. In the case of draft beer, **head size**, that is, the amount of foam on top of the glass, directly affects portion size and portion cost, and, thus, it too must be controlled.

INCORRECT CHANGE MAKING

If a bar is extremely busy, and if guests are paying little attention, bartenders may be greatly tempted to give incorrect change for drinks that are sold. This can be as simple as "forgetting" that a guest paid with a $20 bill, and returning change from a $10 bill, or as clever as maintaining that the change was returned to an inattentive guest, when, in fact, no change was returned at all!

DILUTION OF PRODUCT

Often called "watering down the drinks," this method of bar or storeroom theft involves adding water to the product to make up for spirits that have either been stolen or given away. It is especially easy to water down products such as gin, vodka, rum, or tequila because these clear spirits will not change color with the addition of water. Detection of this type of theft is difficult. Periodic sampling of a known-proof alcohol against bar stock by a knowledgeable food and beverage director is one of the few defenses against such bartender fraud. Since each alcohol product has a particular specific gravity or weight associated with it, you may also check for product dilution through the use of a **hydrometer**, which identifies specific gravity. If water has been added to the bottle of liquor, the specific gravity will change from the value originally associated with that liquor.

PRODUCT THEFT

Alcohol is a highly desirable product; therefore, its theft is always a possibility. This is especially true in a beverage service area that is secluded or in which the bartender has access to inventory and ease of exit. Proper controls as well as strict rules limiting the access of employees to beer, wine, and liquor storage areas should help deter and detect this sort of theft.

PRODUCT SUBSTITUTION

If a call brand liquor has been ordered and paid for, it should, of course, be served. If the bartender, however, substitutes a less expensive well liquor for the call brand, he or she may keep the difference in prices paid for the two items. This has the effect of shortchanging guests, who have paid a premium for something they did not receive. Conversely, if guests have ordered a well drink, but the bartender serves them from the premium or super premium stock, guests have received more value than they have paid for and the operation is shortchanged.

Although it is impossible to list all types of bar thefts, it is important to note that they can and do occur. Conscientious managers should hire honest bartenders, train them well, and demand that they follow all house policies. Perhaps the best advice of all is simply to be vigilant. Watch the bar area carefully, or enlist the aid of a **spotter**, a professional who, for a fee, will observe the bar operation with an eye toward reporting any unusual or inappropriate behavior by the bartender.

Although theft may occur during the normal operation of the bar, it may also occur in the area of receptions and special events. Consider, for a moment, the case of a bride and groom who wish to serve champagne to their guests at their wedding reception, which is to be held in a local hotel. It is estimated that 10 cases of champagne will be used. The food and beverage director orders 12 cases because it would not be appropriate to run out of champagne. The newlyweds will pay for each bottle used. Potential difficulties loom in two areas, neither of which bode well for the couple. In one scenario, more champagne is used than should have been because the bartenders use larger than normal glasses or pour larger than normal portions. Obviously, this could also happen when serving spirits. In the second scenario, 10 cases are served, as predicted, yet one case ends up in the bartender's automobile trunk. The result is that 11 cases are gone. The bartender maintains that all 11 cases were used. Management, trusting the integrity of the bartender, calls upon the guests to pay for one extra case. Imagine, however, the embarrassment if management is asked by the bride and groom to produce the empty bottles from 11 cases!

Bartenders may suffer from a poor reputation in many parts of the foodservice industry, but it is important for you to remember that any time the same individual is responsible for both the preparation of a product and the collection of money for its sale, the opportunity for theft is greatly increased. In a small beverage operation, this situation is common. When you manage an operation such as this, your vigilance is critical, and the quality of your control system is crucial.

FUN ON THE WEB!

Product loss related to draft beer can be due to either employee theft or improper dispensing issues (i.e., too much carbonation, improperly cleaned beer lines, and the like). Importers of Beck and Bass draft beer products, InBev USA, based in Norwalk, Connecticut, offer their "Online Beer Training Course" delivered via the Web. An interactive program, it can be utilized by beverage mangers to train employees in the proper serving of draft beer and for dispensing equipment troubleshooting. You can view their course at **www.inbev.com**.

■ REDUCING KITCHEN-RELATED THEFT

Most kitchen-related theft deals with the removal of products from the premises; unlike bartenders, few kitchen production workers also handle cash. Kitchen workers can, however, work with service personnel to defraud the operation (see Chapter 11). In addition, kitchen workers have access to valuable food and beverage products. The following product security tips are helpful when designing control systems to ensure the safety and security of food (and beverage) products:

Product Security Tips

1. Keep all storage areas locked and secure.
2. Issue food only with proper authorization and management approval.
3. Monitor the use of all carryovers.
4. Do not allow food to be prepared unless a guest check or written request precedes the preparation.
5. Maintain an active inventory management system.
6. Ensure that all food received is signed for by the appropriate receiving clerk.
7. Do not pay suppliers for food products without an appropriate and signed invoice.
8. Do not use "petty cash" to pay for food items unless a receipt and the product can be produced.
9. Conduct systematic physical inventories of all level A, B, and C products.
10. Do not allow employees to remove food from the premises without management's specific approval.

DETERMINING ACTUAL AND ATTAINABLE PRODUCT COSTS

*W*hen you have implemented proper control procedures, you can create accurate product cost data. As we have seen, it is important to know and control your overall cost of food sold and your food cost percentage. Truly effective management of the food and beverage production process, however, requires you to know more. For this reason, we now turn our attention to answering an important series of questions:

1. What are our actual product costs?
2. What should our product costs be?
3. How close are we to this attainable goal?

■ DETERMINING ACTUAL PRODUCT COST

Knowledge of actual product cost begins with a standardized recipe cost for each menu item. Because each menu item should have a standardized recipe, it should also have a standardized cost. The **standardized recipe cost sheet** is a record of the ingredient costs required to produce an item sold by your operation. This standardized cost sheet can be created using any basic spreadsheet software. Standard spreadsheet programs are an excellent means of creating these records and keeping them current. Properly maintained, cost sheets provide you with up-to-date information that can help with pricing decisions in addition to assisting in comparing your actual costs with those you should incur.

Figure 5.14 shows the format you might use for recipes if you operate Steamer's, a small soup and sandwich carryout kiosk. The recipe in this example is for beef stew, which yields a cost per portion of $1.09. A standard recipe cost sheet can be produced in seconds today using a personal computer. This formerly tedious task has become so simplified there is just no reason for management not to have accurate, up-to-date costing sheets on all its recipes. To do any less means selling items for a set price when you have no idea what you paid for that item! The point to remember here is that it is easy to know exactly what it should cost to produce a menu item if you begin the process with a standardized recipe. Note that all ingredients are weighed as edible portion (EP), which is discussed in detail later in this chapter.

FUN ON THE WEB!

Look up the following sites to view several companies that sell software designed for recipe costing and much more!

www.foodsoftware.com. Click "Foodservice Software Catalog," and then scroll down to "Ipro Foodservice Program" and click it. Scroll down to read about one of the industry's most comprehensive inventory management programs.

www.restaurantplus.com. Scroll down and click "Specifications" to learn about the features and reports available with this software.

www.foodtrak.com. Click "Food-Trak for Windows," and then click "Product Information" or "Sample Reports" to see what this comprehensive food and beverage management software has to offer.

Some managers have difficulty computing recipe costs because recipes often contain ingredient amounts that are used in a different quantity than they are purchased. For example, you may purchase soy sauce by the gallon, but your recipes may call for it to be added by the cup or tablespoon. When situations such as this arise, the ingredient conversion table presented in Figure 5.15 can be of great value in calculating recipe costs. Weights, measures, and sizes must be accurately computed if your recipe costs are to be precise.

■ **FIGURE 5.14** Standardized Recipe Cost Sheet

Unit Name: <u>Steamer's</u>

Menu Item: <u>Beef Stew</u>	Recipe Number: 146
Special Notes: _____	Recipe Yield: 40
All Ingredients Weighted As Edible	Portion Size: 8 OZ.
Portion (EP)	Portion Cost: $1.09

Ingredients		Ingredient Cost	
Item	Amount	Unit Cost	Total Cost
Corn, Frozen	3 lb.	0.60 lb.	$ 1.80
Tomatoes	3 lb.	1.40 lb.	4.20
Potatoes	5 lb.	0.40 lb.	2.00
Beef Cubes	5 lb.	5.76 lb.	28.80
Carrots	2 lb.	0.36 lb.	0.72
Water	2 gal.	N/A	—
Salt	2 T	0.30 lb.	0.02
Pepper	2 t	12.00 lb.	0.12
Garlic	1 clove	0.80/clove	0.80
Tomato Juice	1 qt.	4.00 gal.	1.00
Onions	4 lb.	1.00 lb.	4.00
Total Cost			**$ 43.46**

Total Recipe Cost: $43.46	Recipe Type: Soups/Stews
Portion Cost: $ 1.09	Date Costed: 4/1
Previous Portion Cost: $ 1.01	Previous Dated Costed: 1/1

FUN ON THE WEB!

To calculate a variety of recipe conversions, go to **www.chefdesk.com.** First, check out "Book of Yields" to learn about a book that would be useful in any kitchen. Next, click "Free Online Foodservice Calculators," and then click "Conversion Calculator." This is a useful site that will help you cost out almost any recipe!

■ **FIGURE 5.15** Ingredient Conversion Table

Weight and Measure Equivalents	
Item	**Equivalent**
60 drops	1 teaspoon
3 teaspoons	1 tablespoon
2 tablespoons	1 liquid ounce
4 tablespoons	1/4 cup
16 tablespoons	1 cup
2 cups	1 pint
2 pints	1 quart
4 quarts	1 gallon
4 pecks	1 bushel
16 ounces	1 pound
Select Spices*	
Pepper: 4.20 tablespoons	1 ounce
Salt: 1.55 tablespoons	1 ounce
Common Can Sizes	
Can Size	**Quantity**
No. 303	$1\,^1/_4$ cups
No. 2	$2\,^1/_2$ cups
No. $2\,^1/_2$	$3\,^1/_2$ cups
No. 5	$7^1/_3$ cups
No. 10	13 cups

Conversion Formulas		
To Convert	**Multiply By**	
Ounces to Grams	Ounces	28.35
Grams to Ounces	Grams	0.035
Liters to Quarts	Liters	0.950
Quarts to Liters	Quarts	1.057
Pounds to Kilos	Pounds	0.45
Kilos to Pounds	Kilos	2.20

*Spices have different conversions based on their individual weights.

When costing standardized recipes, many foodservice managers prefer to use whole cent figures rather than fractions of a cent. In addition, many elect to omit seasoning costs completely. They prefer to add a predetermined standard cost to those standardized recipes that contain seasonings. This amount, a percentage of total recipe cost, is determined annually. Thus, if 3% represents the total product category of seasoning cost per year, then 3% would be added to the total ingredient cost to account for seasonings. Still others prefer to identify spices as high or low cost. In the example in Figure 5.14, salt, which is considered a low-cost spice, has a $0.02 cost assigned to its 2 tablespoons of product. Pepper, which is considered a high-cost spice, has a cost assigned to its 2 teaspoons of $0.12 to account for its usage.

If costs are to be correctly calculated, you must thoroughly understand the concept of product yield and the effect of that yield on costs. It is to this matter that you must turn your attention if you want to be sure that your standardized recipe cost data are accurate.

■ PRODUCT YIELD

Most foodservice products are delivered in the **AP** or **As Purchased** state. This refers to the weight or count of a product, as delivered to the foodservice operator. **Edible Portion (EP)** refers to the weight of a product after it has been cleaned, trimmed, cooked, and portioned. Thus, AP refers to food products as the operator receives them, and EP refers to food products as the guest receives them.

Yield % is important in the area of recipe costing. This is true because a recipe cost must take into account the difference in price of products in their AP or EP state. Foodservice buyers purchase at AP costs, but items are served in their EP state. To determine actual recipe costs, it is often necessary to conduct a yield test to determine actual EP ingredient costs. A **yield test** is a procedure used for computing your actual EP costs on a product that will experience weight or volume loss during preparation. In our beef stew example (Figure 5.14), you would need to compute the EP cost of the beef cubes used in the stew preparation. Beef is a major portion of the total recipe cost; thus, you would want to make sure that you computed the cost of the beef cubes accurately. As-purchased meat prices do not include any losses you will incur due to trimming, cooking, or carving. These activities, if undertaken, will of course affect the EP cost of the meat products. The same is true for many vegetables, fruits, seafood, and other products.

To illustrate how a yield test results in the determination of actual product cost, assume you purchased 8 pounds of beef chuck from which you will cut the beef cubes for your stew recipe. You know that you will have losses because of bone and fat removal, but unlike some other products, such as roast beef, you will have no cooking or slicing loss. You can use a form such as the one presented in Figure 5.16 to determine your EP meat yields and, thus, your cost per portion. The yield test for our beef chuck for beef stew is shown in Figure 5.16.

Waste % is the percentage of product lost due to cooking, trimming, portioning, or cleaning. For example, assume that the yield test (Figure 5.16) shows you

■ **FIGURE 5.16**   Butcher's Yield Test Results

Unit Name: Steamer's   Item: Beef Cubes   Date Tested: 1/1

Specification: # 842   Item Description: Beef Chuck

AP Amount Tested: 8 lb.

Price per Pound AP: $3.60

Loss Detail	Weight	Use % of Original
AP	8 lb. 0 oz.	100.0%
Fat Loss	1 lb. 2 oz.	14.1%
Bone Loss	1 lb. 14 oz.	23.4%
Cooking Loss	0	0%
Carving Loss	0	0%
Total Product Loss (Waste)	3 lb. 0 oz.	37.5%

Product yield: 62.5%   EP Cost per Pound: $5.76

Yield test performed by: L. D.

that 8 pounds, or 128 ounces (8 lb. × 16 oz. = 128 oz.), of beef chuck will lose 3 pounds, or 48 ounces (3 lb. × 16 oz. = 48 oz.), during the preparation and cooking process. You can compute your waste % using the following formula:

$$\text{Waste \%} = \frac{\text{Product Loss}}{\text{AP Weight}}$$

In this example, therefore:

$$\text{Waste \%} = \frac{48 \text{ oz.}}{128 \text{ oz.}} = 0.375, \text{ or } 37.5\%$$

Once waste % has been determined, it is possible to compute the yield %. **Yield %** is the percentage of product you will have remaining after cooking, trimming, portioning, or cleaning. Waste % + Yield % = 1.00, so yield % is calculated as shown in the following formula:

$$\text{Yield \%} = 1.00 - \text{Waste \%}$$

In this example, our yield % is computed as follows:

$$\text{Yield \%} = 1.00 - 0.375 = 0.625, \text{ or } 62.5\%$$

If we know the yield %, we can compute the AP weight needed to yield the appropriate EP weight required by using the following formula:

$$\frac{\text{EP Required}}{\text{Yield \%}} = \text{AP Required}$$

In this example, with an EP required of 5 pounds, or 80 ounces (5 lb. × 16 oz. = 80 oz.), and a yield % of 62.5%, or 0.625, the computation to determine the appropriate AP required is as follows:

$$\frac{80 \text{ oz.}}{0.625} = 128 \text{ oz.}$$
$$= 128 \text{ oz.}/16 \text{ oz.}$$
$$= 8 \text{ lb. AP Required}$$

To check the preceding figures to see if you should use a yield % of 0.625 when purchasing this item, you can proceed as follows:

$$\text{EP Required} = \text{AP Required} \times \text{Yield \%}$$

In this example,

$$\text{EP Required} = 8 \text{ lb.} \times 0.625 = 5 \text{ lb.}$$

Another way to determine product yield % is to compute it directly using the following formula:

$$\frac{\text{EP Weight}}{\text{AP Weight}} = \text{Product Yield \%}$$

In this example, EP weight is equal to AP weight of 8 lb. less the product loss of 3 lb. Thus, EP weight equals 5 lb., and product yield % is computed as follows:

$$\frac{5 \text{ lb.}}{8 \text{ lb.}} = 62.5 \text{ \%}$$

Edible portion cost (EP cost) is the cost of the item after cooking, trimming, portioning, or cleaning. The EP cost is useful to know because it represents the cost to you based on product yield. The same product may have different yields from different suppliers, and you can use EP cost to compare AP prices from suppliers. In general, you want to choose the supplier that offers the lowest EP cost for the same product, assuming the same specification or quality is being purchased. To compute actual EP cost, you must simply divide the AP price per pound by the product yield %.

In our example, with AP price per pound of beef chuck at $3.60 and a product yield of 0.625, the EP cost would be $5.76, which is computed using the EP cost formula:

$$\frac{\text{AP Price per Pound}}{\text{Product Yield \%}} = \text{EP Cost (per Pound)}$$

or

$$\frac{\$3.60}{0.625} = \$5.76$$

You know now that your actual EP cost when buying beef chuck with this particular specification is $5.76. You should conduct additional Butcher Yield Tests if you are considering changing suppliers, beef chuck specifications, or the quality level of the beef you are using. In addition, you should conduct yield tests on all of your meat items at least twice per year.

Waste % and yield % can be determined if records are kept on meat cookery, the cleaning and processing of vegetables and fruits, and the losses that occur during portioning. Most recipes assume some consistency in these areas, and good foodservice managers take the losses into account when making purchasing decisions. In our beef chuck example, knowing that you will experience a yield % of 0.625 will help you determine exactly the right amount of product to purchase. Good vendors are an excellent source for providing tabled information related to trim and loss rates for standard products they sell. Some operators even go so far as to add a minimum or required yield % as an additional component of their product specifications.

Many items, including meats, fruits, vegetables, and the like, should be periodically yield tested. Computer programs on the market today, including those mentioned previously in this chapter, have components that will quickly conduct yield calculations and compute EP costs for you based on your inputted AP prices and known product yields.

■ DETERMINING ATTAINABLE PRODUCT COST

If you are to draw reasonable conclusions regarding your facility's operational efficiency, you must be able to compare how well you are doing with how well you *should* be doing. This process begins with determining attainable product cost. **Attainable product** *cost* is defined as the cost of goods sold figure that should be achievable given the product sales mix of a particular operation. Simply put, when you compare attainable product cost to actual product cost, you get a measure of operational efficiency. The formula for this operational efficiency ratio is as follows:

Green and Growing!

Increasingly, foodservice operators recognize that most human activity, including their own businesses, leaves a "carbon footprint" on the planet. A **carbon footprint** is a measure of the impact human activities have on the environment in terms of the amount of greenhouse gases (carbon dioxide) produced. The term is useful for individuals and organizations to conceptualize their personal (or organizational) impact in contributing to global warming.

Examples of activities in which foodservice operations engage to help reduce their carbon footprint include:

- Buying food products locally.
- Monitoring efficient energy usage regularly.
- Avoiding the sale of bottled waters where the packaging and shipping of these items result in the unnecessary production of carbon dioxide.
- Using cold water for cleaning when practical and sanitary.
- Reducing, reusing, and recycling!

Reduction of a business's carbon footprint is good for the environment and for business. Keep watching the hospitality trade press for an ever-increasing number of new strategies you can consider for reducing your own operation's carbon footprint!

$$\frac{\text{Actual Product Cost}}{\text{Attainable Product Cost}} = \text{Operational Efficiency Ratio}$$

To illustrate, assume again that you own Steamer's, the small soup and sandwich carryout kiosk referred to in the previous example. You determine your attainable product cost for a week to be $850, and you actually achieve a product cost of $850 for that week. Applying the operational efficiency ratio, your results would be evaluated as follows:

$$\frac{\$850 \text{ Actual Product Cost}}{\$850 \text{ Attainable Product Cost}} = 100\%$$

These results represent perfection in the relationship between attainable and actual operational results. However, actual product cost might be higher than attainable product cost, say $900. In this case, the formula would be computed as:

$$\frac{\$900 \text{ Actual Product Cost}}{\$850 \text{ Attainable Product Cost}} = 105.9\%$$

In this case, you would know that your actual product usage, and thus cost, is 5.9% higher than your attainable product cost goal.

■ **FIGURE 5.17** Attainable Food Cost

Unit Name: <u>Steamer's</u>

Date Prepared: <u>1/8</u>   Time Period: <u>1/1–1/7</u>

Prepared by: <u>J. M.</u>

Item	Number Sold	Attainable Portion Cost	Total Cost	Menu Price	Total Sales
Beef Stew	150	$1.09	$ 163.50	$ 1.90	$ 285.00
Corn Chowder	140	.44	61.60	1.90	266.00
Ham & Bean Soup	160	.82	131.20	1.90	304.00
Turkey Sandwich	130	1.02	132.60	5.90	767.00
Ham Sandwich	190	1.20	228.00	5.20	988.00
Roast Beef Sandwich	125	1.74	217.50	5.90	737.50
Coffee	175	.20	35.00	1.85	323.75
Soda	525	.46	241.50	1.75	918.75
Total			**$1,210.90**		**$4,590.00**

Chapter 3 described the method used to determine actual product usage through the cost of goods sold formula. Attainable product cost is determined through the use of a form, as illustrated in Figure 5.17.

As is evident, total product cost for this week, as determined by the standardized recipes, should have been $1,210.90. Sales were $4,590. You would know your attainable product cost percentage through the use of the following formula:

$$\frac{\text{Cost as per Standardized Recipes}}{\text{Total Sales}} = \text{Attainable Product Cost \%}$$

In our example, then,

$$\frac{\$1,210.90}{\$4,590} = 26.4\%$$

Note that this cost excludes any losses due to overcooking, overportioning, waste, theft, and the like. Therefore, the attainable food cost is rarely achieved. Consider, for example, the cost of a product such as fresh brewed coffee. Although you may be able to compute the cost of producing an 8-ounce cup of coffee, it is much more difficult to estimate the amount of product that must be discarded on a regular basis to ensure guests are getting only freshly brewed coffee. In addition, every foodservice operation employs people, and people make errors at work. Some managers prefer to compute attainable cost data on specific items, for example, steaks in a steakhouse restaurant. In this manner, data collection and analysis is simplified, but, at the same time, management can maintain close control over its most important items. In all cases, the use of the operational efficiency ratio can help management answer the question made famous by the former mayor of New York City, Ed Koch: "How'm I doing?"

The attainable food cost and, thus, the operation a efficiency ratio, is designed to address just that issue. In general, operational efficiency ratings in the range of 100 to 110% are attainable. Variance beyond that, however, can indicate serious control problems. Ratios that are too high, that is, ratios above 110%, could be an indication of excessive waste, ingredient theft, spoilage, overportioning, or inaccurate recipe cost sheet computation. Operating efficiency ratings that are too low, that is, ratings in the 80 to 90% range, could be the result of miscalculation of the number of items sold, inaccurate ingredient costing, underportioning, incorrect standardized cost sheets, or errors in valuing inventory. Many managers find that it is helpful to share the operational efficiency results with employees because they also are interested in the question: "How are we doing?"

ACCEPTABLE AND UNACCEPTABLE VARIANCE

It is important to realize that you will not treat all variances from your expected results in the same manner. For example, a variance of one or two dollars from an expected result of several thousand dollars is small enough that it constitutes a very acceptable level of variation. A variance of one or two dollars from an expected result of ten dollars might well be cause for concern and, thus, is likely unacceptable. Figure 5.18 displays the operational efficiency ratios, dollar variances, and percentage variances that might result if you were to compute individual efficiency ratios on a variety of individual products in a steakhouse. The important concept

■ FIGURE 5.18 Acceptable and Unacceptable Variance

Item	Actual Cost	Attainable Cost	Efficiency Ratio	Dollar Variance	Percentage Variance
Steaks	$1,010	$1,000	1.01	$10	1%
Coffee	20	10	2.00	10	100
Bolla Soave	550	500	1.10	50	10
Horseradish	22	20	1.10	2	10
Parsley	45	50	0.90	5	10

here is a simple one: Your attention, as a manager, should be directed toward those areas where the need is greatest. In most cases it makes little sense to devote the same amount of time addressing a 1% variance as it does a variance of 10%.

As can be seen, results such as those in Figure 5.18 call upon you to make decisions about the acceptability of the variances you may encounter. Efficiency ratings in this example range from 0.90 to 2.00. The $10.00 variance in actual steak cost is likely within an acceptable range. The $10.00 variance in coffee costs is likely unacceptable. In a similar manner, the 10% variance in the cost of Bolla Soave wine may well be worth investigating, whereas the 10% variation in horseradish and parsley costs may be too small to merit your immediate attention. Although it is not possible to determine one range of variance acceptability that is appropriate for all food facilities, it is important for you to establish acceptability ranges for your own facility.

REDUCING OVERALL PRODUCT COST PERCENTAGE

*O*nce management has determined what costs actually are and has compared them to what costs should be, it may often be found that Walt Kelly's Pogo comic character was correct when he said, "We have met the enemy, and he is us!"

Foodservice managers (and their bosses) seem to be on a never-ending quest to reduce food and beverage production costs. Although you must remember to guard against inappropriate cost cutting, you will, on occasion, find yourself in a position where food and beverage production costs are deemed to be too high and, thus, must be reduced. When that is the case, effective managers turn to the solutions inherent in the product cost equation.

The food cost percentage equation is deceptively easy to understand. In its simplest form, it can be represented as:

$$\frac{A}{B} = C$$

where:

A = Cost of Goods Sold

B = Sales

C = Cost Percentage

This formula can, however, become extremely complex. Its analysis occupies many a food organization staff meeting and can give the foodservice operator many sleepless nights! Essentially, only six reduction strategies are available to influence this rather simple formula. A quick algebra lesson, however, prior to our discussion of these six approaches may be useful. In general, the rules of algebra reveal the following things about the A/B = C formula:

1. If A is unchanged and B increases, C decreases.
2. If A is unchanged and B decreases, C increases.
3. If A increases at the same proportional rate B increases, C remains unchanged.
4. If A decreases and B is unchanged, C decreases.
5. If A increases and B is unchanged, C increases.

Put into foodservice management terms, these five algebraic statements can be translated as follows:

1. If costs can be kept constant while sales increase, the cost percentage goes down.
2. If costs remain constant but sales decline, the cost percentage increases.
3. If costs go up at the same rate sales go up, the cost of goods sold percentage will remain unchanged.
4. If costs can be reduced while sales remain constant, the cost percentage goes down.
5. If costs increase with no increase in sales, the cost percentage will go up.

In general, foodservice managers work to control the variables that impact product cost percentage and, thus, strive to reduce the overall value of C in the equation. The six approaches to reducing overall product cost percentage, along with a summary of each, are presented here to help you devise your own cost reduction strategies:

Reducing Overall Product Cost Percentage

1. Decrease portion size relative to price.
2. Vary recipe composition.
3. Adjust product quality.
4. Achieve a more favorable sales mix.
5. Ensure that all product purchased is sold.
6. Increase price relative to portion size.

To reduce your food costs, you will ultimately select an appropriate strategy from this relatively small number of alternatives. It is the judicious selection and mixing of these approaches that differentiate the successful operator from the unsuccessful one.

For instance, assume that you own and operate a nightclub. You compute your actual liquor cost percentage and determine that it is 4 percentage points higher than you have budgeted for. If you have approximately six cost-reducing options available to you, by the mathematics law of permutations, this yields (6 × 5 × 4 ×

3 × 2), or 720 possible combinations of these differing cost reduction methods. No wonder, then, there is so much information written about reducing product costs!

It is not the authors' contention that all product cost reduction methods are exhausted by these six points, but rather they are presented here as a means of systematically analyzing the various alternatives available.

■ DECREASE PORTION SIZE RELATIVE TO PRICE

Too often, foodservice managers and bar operators assume that their standard portion sizes must conform to some unwritten rule of uniformity. This is simply not the case. Most guests would prefer a smaller portion size of higher quality ingredients than the reverse. In fact, one problem restaurants have is that portion sizes, in many cases, are too large. The point to remember here is that portion size is set by the foodservice manager and is variable.

For example, the table in Figure 5.19 represents the significant effect on liquor cost percentage of varying the standard drink size served in an operation using $16.00 per liter as the standard cost of liquor and assuming 0.8-ounce evaporation per 33.8-ounce (1-liter, or 1,000-ml) bottle and a standard $5.00 selling price per drink. When establishing portion size, you should take all the variables affecting your operation into account. These may include location, price structure, competition, requirements or regulations, and clientele, to name just a few.

■ VARY RECIPE COMPOSITION

Even the simplest recipes can be varied somewhat. For example, what is the proper amount of beef to use when making 100 servings of quality beef stew? The answer

---

■ **FIGURE 5.19** Impact of Drink Size on Liquor Cost Percentage at Constant Selling Price of $5.00 per Drink

Drink Size	Drinks Per Liter	Cost Per Liter	Cost Per Drink (Cents)	Sales Per Liter	Liquor Cost % Per Liter
2 oz.	16.5	$16.00	97.0	$ 82.50	19.4%
1³/₄ oz.	18.9	16.00	84.7	94.50	16.9
1¹/₂ oz.	22.0	16.00	72.7	110.00	14.5
1¹/₄ oz.	26.4	16.00	60.6	132.00	12.1
1 oz.	33.0	16.00	48.5	165.00	9.7

is up to management, and the answer to that question and others like it help determine overall food cost percentage. Similarly, the proportion of alcohol to mixer has a profound effect on liquor cost percentage. Indeed, overall drink sizes can actually be increased by the additional use of lower cost bar extenders such as milk, juices, and soda. This often contributes to a feeling of satisfaction by the guest, while allowing the operator to increase profitability. A second way to vary the recipe composition of a drink and, thus, reduce beverage costs is simply to reduce the amount of alcohol served in each drink. For example, a 2-ounce portion of Kahlua in a Kahlua and cream may simply become $1^3/_4$ ounces instead, or a $^1/_4$-ounce increase in the amount of cream may be used in the drink's preparation. As with all cost reduction strategies, this one must be carefully considered before implementation.

■ ADJUST PRODUCT QUALITY

This area must be approached with caution because you should strive to use the quality of product appropriate for its intended use. For example, less expensive canned asparagus may be excellent for a baked casserole dish but unacceptable for the freshly cooked asparagus accompanying a $25.00 steak. A specific coffee liqueur and cream, when called for, must, of course, include that name-brand liqueur and cream! It may be wise, however, to use an alternative brand for the many specialty drinks (black Russian, brave bull, black magic, sombrero, etc.) that include coffee liqueur as a major or minor ingredient. In this example, a generic-type coffee liqueur might be used with totally satisfactory results.

With appropriate care, you can determine the quality of ingredients necessary for your operation and then purchase that quality. This is a case where the appropriate ingredient, rather than the highest-cost ingredient, is actually the best possible ingredient.

■ ACHIEVE A MORE FAVORABLE SALES MIX

Typically, each beverage (and food) item you sell will carry a unique cost percentage. This is true because most operators set standard drink prices and ignore minor variances in the cost of differing types of liquor. Most operators, for example, set a particular price for each type of drink they sell. One and one-half ounce of all well liquors plus cola, for example, may sell for the same price. The various spirits ingredients that make up these drinks, however, do not all represent the exact same cost to the operator. Thus, there exist small differences in liquor cost percentages for these various drinks. The weighted sum total of these various percentages, due to the sales mix concept, yields the overall liquor cost percentage.

Figure 5.20 illustrates the effect of a shift in consumer buying habits away from a high-cost item to a lower-cost one, demonstrating how the sales mix

■ FIGURE 5.20 Impact of Sales Mix on Beverage Cost %

	Sales Per Drink	Number Sold	Total Sales	Cost Per Drink	Total Cost	Liqor Cost %
Rum/Cola	$5	60	$300	$1.04	$62.40	20.80%
Fruit Brandy/Cola	5	40	200	0.68	27.20	13.60
Combination 1 Total		100	500	0.896	89.60	17.92
Rum/Cola	5	40	200	1.04	41.60	20.80
Fruit Brandy/Cola	5	60	300	0.68	40.80	13.60
Combination 2 Total		100	500	0.824	82.40	16.48

affects profitability. Although the difference in overall liquor cost percentage in this illustration is only 1.44% (17.92 − 16.48 = 1.44), it represents an increase in cost savings per drink of 7.2 cents (89.6 cents cost − 82.4 cents cost = 7.2 cents). In cost control, it's the little things that add up. If you are open 365 days a year, serve 100 drinks per day, and each drink costs 7.2 cents less than it would ordinarily, the net result is an additional annual profit of $2,628 (365 × 100 × $0.072 = $2,628).

The effective merchandising and promotion of "good" cost items has a positive effect on profitability while allowing the portion size, recipe composition, and product quality of your items to remain constant.

■ ENSURE THAT ALL PRODUCT PURCHASED IS SOLD

These seven words have tremendous implications. They include all phases of purchasing, receiving, storage, inventory, issuing, and cash control. Perhaps the hospitality industry's greatest challenge in the area of cost control is ensuring that all products, once purchased, do indeed generate cash sales that make it to the operation's bank account!

■ INCREASE PRICE RELATIVE TO PORTION SIZE

This area must be approached with the greatest caution of all. There is no greater temptation in foodservice than to raise prices in an effort to conceal ineffectiveness at controlling costs. This temptation must be resisted. There are times, of course, when prices on selected items must be increased. This is especially true in inflationary times. Price increases should be considered, however, only when all necessary steps to control costs have been effectively implemented. Any price increases should reflect only increases in your costs, not your inefficiency.

On the other hand, many operators are afraid to be 25 or 50 cents higher per menu item than their competition. In some instances, keeping prices in line with competitors' prices is a good strategy. Frequently, however, decor, quality of product, and service allow you to be slightly higher in price than your competition. Given the proper ambiance, most guests will not react negatively to small variances in prices because it is perceived value, not price alone, that drives a guest's purchase decision.

Managing the food and beverage production process effectively is indeed at the heart of all foodservice operations. The combination of equipment, product, employee, and guest makes the foodservice industry one of the most fascinating professions in the world. If you find joy and a challenge in this process, you are well on your way to a successful foodservice management career. All of the preplanning, ordering, receiving, storing, and issuing systems in the world are for naught if the product cannot be produced well and delivered to the guest with a sense of style and hospitality. Cost control systems can never take the place of the sense of welcome you must impart to your guests. The latter must remain a priority; the former are additions to the personal attention you give your guests and not substitutions for it!

Managing the food and beverage production process is a complex task, and it must be accomplished with the utmost grace and skill. It is important that your food and beverages are prepared correctly and at an appropriate cost to you, but it is just as important to ensure that these products are sold for the proper price. It is this task that we examine in the next chapter.

Technology Tools

In the past, restaurants were slow to install working computer terminals and other technological tools in kitchen areas where production staff could easily use them. Increasingly, however, these installations are being made. In a professional kitchen, cost control efforts are often shared between management and the production staff. Advanced technology programs available for kitchen production use include those that can help both you and your production staff members:

1. Perform nutrition-related analysis of menu items, including:

   a. Recipe nutrient analysis
   b. Diet analysis

  c. FDA (Food and Drug Administration) food labels

  d. Diabetic exchange

  e. Weight management components

2. Develop production schedules based on forecasted sales:

  a. Weekly

  b. Daily

  c. By meal period

3. Create product requisition (issues) lists based on forecasted sales.

4. Compute actual versus ideal costs based on product issues.

5. Estimate and compute daily food cost.

6. Maintain physical or perpetual inventory; compute inventory turnover rates.

7. Maintain product usage record by:

  a. Vendor

  b. Product

  c. Food category

  d. Menu item

8. Compare portions served to portions produced to monitor overportioning.

9. Suggest usage for carryover products.

10. Conduct "make versus buy" calculations to optimize employee productivity and minimize costs.

FUN ON THE WEB!

Many of the software programs available for assisting in foodservice operations are geared toward commercial restaurants. Some of the very best, however, were developed for the institutional foodservice market. To view the features of two of these, go to:

www.computrition.com. Link to "Products," and click any category you desire.

www.cbord.com. First, link to "Products." Then try out "NetRecipe" and its online demo. Or, click any of the other products offered.

Apply What You Have Learned

*T*handi Tye is the manager of a cafeteria chain that serves a variety of menu items but is famous for its cream gravy and chicken fried steak (a beef steak, seasoned, breaded, and then pan fried). As food and labor costs on the item have risen, Thandi is considering whether this dish, which has previously been made onsite at each cafeteria, should be purchased prebreaded and frozen. The cost of the same sized convenience item is 15% more than the prepared on-site item.

1. What issues should Thandi consider prior to making this decision?

2. What would you advise Thandi to do?

3. If the decision were made to use the convenience item, how would guests likely respond to the change if it were known? Should it be made known?

Key Terms and Concepts

*T*he following are terms and concepts discussed in the chapter that are important for you as a manager. To help you review, please define the terms below.

Requisition	Carryovers	Standardized recipe cost
Issued	Convenience/	sheet
Ingredient room	ready foods	As Purchased (AP)
Empty for full system	Free-pouring	Edible Portion (EP)
Comp	Jigger	Yield test
Physical inventory	Metered bottle	Waste %
Perpetual inventory	Total bar system	Yield %
Bin card	Open bar	Edible portion
Perpetual inventory card	Head size	cost (EP cost)
Category food cost %	Hydrometer	Attainable product cost
Back of the house	Spotter	Carbon footprint

Test Your Skills

*C*omplete the Test Your Skills exercises by placing your answers in the shaded boxes and answering the questions as indicated.

1. Loralei owns Loralei's Electra Club, a nightclub in a midsized coastal city. She has set a standard beverage cost of 27% for her club, and she wants to make sure that her beverage costs are in line with her standard. Loralei wants to estimate her beverage cost after the first 10 days of the month. Since she doesn't have time to take a physical inventory, she decides to use her issues to estimate her costs. Help Loralei complete her six-column beverage cost estimate. Based on the first 10 days of the month, is her beverage cost within acceptable limits?

Six-Column Beverage Cost Estimate

Unit Name: Loralei's Electra Club   Date: 1/1–1/10

Date	Issues		Sales		Beverage Cost Estimate	
	Today	To Date	Today	To Date	Today	To Date
1/1	$ 701.89		$2,232.56			
1/2	650.21		2,536.56			
1/3	857.96		2,764.23			
1/4	852.65		2,656.82			
1/5	1,223.35		6,123.54			
1/6	1,300.50		6,445.36			
1/7	785.56		2,545.87			
1/8	1,200.80		3,568.91			
1/9	655.85		2,258.75			
1/10	601.25		2,379.96			
Total						

2. Guests come from all over the county to sample the surf and turf special at Mike's Seaside Café. However, Mike is concerned about his food cost %. He thinks that his seafood costs may be causing the problem. Help him calculate his category food cost percentages and his product usage ratios (portion of total cost). Then list six suggestions for Mike to help him lower his food cost %.

Monthly Food Cost Category Percentage/Proportion

Unit Name: Mike's Seaside Cafe

Sales: $271,795

Category	Cost of Food Consumed	Food Cost %	Proportion of Total Cost
Seafood	$38,500		
Meat	25,850		
Dairy	6,145		
Produce	12,500		
Other	4,315		
Total			

3. Dave would like to add a new menu item to his standard menu. Upper management has approved such an addition if his total product cost percentage does not exceed 31.5% of his allowable selling price. The selling price allowed is $9.75. Using the standardized recipe cost sheet below, can Dave add the new menu item?

Standardized Recipe Cost Sheet

Menu Item: **Dave's Pork Surprise**	Recipe Number: **15**
Special Notes:	Recipe Yield: **24**
Boston butt net	Portion Size: **5 oz**
All ingredients weighed as EP	Portion Cost:

	Ingredients			Ingredient Cost		
Item	Amount	Unit	Unit Cost	Unit	Total Cost	
Boston Butt	10	lb.	$5.90	lb.		
Sweet Baby Ray's Sauce	4	oz.	8.00	lb.		
Onion	8	oz.	1.20	lb.		
Water	1/4	C	N/A	N/A		
Salt	2	T	0.40	lb.		
Pepper	1	t	12.00	lb.		
Garlic	1	clove	0.60	clove		
Pineapple Juice	1/2	C	3.78	gal.		
Total						

Total Recipe Cost:

Portion Cost: Date Costed: 4/13

Previous Portion Cost: N/A Previous Date Costed: N/A

Selling Price: $9.75

Food Cost Percentage (by portion):

Food Cost Percentage Goal: 31.5%

4. Elaine is the Director of Foodservice at a large retirement center, and she has asked Jerry, one of her managers, to investigate the costs involved in adding a carving station to the regular Sunday brunch menu. Jerry is trying to decide which carved meats could be served. He must first determine the EP costs and yields of the various kinds of meats. Help him calculate the EP cost and yield of an inside round of beef.

Butcher's Yield Test Results

Unit Name: <u>Elaine's</u> Date Tested: <u>May 20</u>

Item: <u>Inside Round</u>

Specification: <u># 138</u>

AP Amount Tested: <u>20 lb.</u>

Price per Pound AP: <u>$6.00</u>

Loss Detail	Lb.	oz.	Total Ounces	% of Original
AP Weight	20	0		
Fat Loss	3	6		
Bone Loss	2	4		
Cooking Loss	1	12		
Carving Loss	0	8		
Total Production Loss				
EP Weight				

Net Product Yield %:

Yield Test Performed by: <u>GW</u>

EP Cost per Pound:

5. Liza operates a lunchroom in a large, exclusive health club. The members demand high-quality service and are especially concerned about reducing fat in their diets. They like high-protein items for their lunches, which are light and generally consumed prior to or immediately after a workout. The menu in Liza's restaurant consists of five main lunch specials. Each meat, poultry, or fish item is purchased by the pound (using product specifications) and then prepared and served in a 4-ounce portion (EP), according to the standardized recipe. Liza keeps excellent sales records and, thus, knows her % selecting figures, which are tabulated as follows. She also carefully monitors waste % data, which are tabulated for each item. How much of each item should Liza order for next week, given that she expects 500 customers for lunch next week, each of whom will order one of her five menu items?

What should the total of Liza's purchases for these items be next week if she buys at the purchase prices listed?

Do you think Liza should buy these items on a par or as-needed basis? Why?

Item	Percent Selecting	Waste	Purchase Price/lb.
Beef	0.21	0.30	$3.20
Pork	0.18	0.25	1.70
Chicken	0.15	0.10	0.89
Sole	0.30	0.10	3.20
Tuna	0.16	0.05	4.10

Item	Total Served	Percent Selected	Number of Servings	Ounces per Serving	Total Weight of Servings (oz.)	Yield	Purchase Weight (oz.)	Ounces per Pound	Purchase Weight (lb.)	Purchase Price	Total Purchases
Beef	500							16			
Pork	500							16			
Chicken	500							16			
Sole	500							16			
Tuna	500							16			

6. Kathey operates a takeout cookie store in the mall. Business is good, and guests seem to enjoy the products. Her employees, mostly young teens, are a problem because they seem to like the products also. Kathey takes a physical inventory on a weekly basis. This week, her total cost of goods sold figure was $725.58. Kathey has determined that this week she will also compute her attainable food cost and her operational efficiency ratio. Help Kathey by completing the following information using the attainable food cost form. After completing the form, give Kathey five suggestions to keep her employees from eating all of her profits.

Attainable Food Cost

Unit Name: <u>Kathey's</u>

Date Prepared: <u>1/8</u>   Time Period: <u>1/1 to 1/7</u>

Prepared By: <u>S.L.</u>

Item	Number Sold in Dozens	Cost per Dozen	Total Cost	Menu Price per Dozen	Total Sales
Chocolate Chip	85	$1.32		$3.40	
Macadamia	60	$1.61		$4.10	
Coconut Chip	70	$0.83		$2.95	
Fudge	141	$1.42		$3.80	
M & M	68	$1.39		$3.40	
Soft Drinks	295	$0.16		$0.85	
Coffee	160	$0.09		$0.75	
Attainable Product Cost					

Actual Product Cost: _____

Attainable Product Cost: _____

Operational Efficiency Ratio: _____

Attainable Food Cost %: _____

---

7. Shingi Rukunia operates a small home-style restaurant with a limited menu but extremely good food. Given the data below, help Shingi compute her entire food cost % in the first and second weeks of the month.

Item	Item Cost	Selling Price	Week One Number Sold	Week Two Number Sold
Sirloin Steak	$5.50	$18.95	25	20
Grilled Chicken	$2.50	$12.50	20	25
Broiled Cod	$3.95	$17.95	45	30
Beef Ragout	$1.95	$11.50	10	25
Total			100	100

Week One Food Cost %

	Number Sold	Item Cost	Total Cost	Selling Price	Total Sales	Food Cost %
Sirloin Steak						
Grilled Chicken						
Broiled Cod						
Beef Ragout						
Total						

Week Two Food Cost %

	Number Sold	Item Cost	Total Cost	Selling Price	Total Sales	Food Cost %
Sirloin Steak						
Grilled Chicken						
Broiled Cod						
Beef Ragout						
Total						

Shingi served the same total number of guests and used the same standardized recipes and portion sizes both weeks. Why did her total food cost % change from week one to week two?

8. Lebron operates "Ham From Heaven," a sandwich shop specializing in slow roasted spicy ham sandwiches. Currently, Lebron buys bone-in hams and roasts them in-house. These hams cost $2.99 per pound and produce a 58% usable yield. Semi-boneless hams of the same quality cost $3.99 per pound with a 78% yield. Boneless hams of the same quality would cost $6.99 per pound and produce a 96% yield. Calculate the EP cost per pound of each alternative. Then, choose the alternative you would recommend to Lebron and explain your reason for choosing it. Specifically, what factors would influence your decision?

Ham From Heaven

	Ap Price per lb.	Yield	Ep Cost per lb.
Bone-in Ham			
Semi-boneless Ham			
Boneless Ham			

9. This chapter introduced six different action steps managers could take to reduce their cost of food and cost of food percentages when they encounter rising costs. In some foodservice settings, such as schools, colleges, and correctional and health care facilities, however, managers are allotted a fixed amount of money to spend per meal served and this amount may only be adjusted on an annual basis. Thus, managers of these facility types cannot readily increase their prices in the face of rising costs. Review the six alternative cost reduction strategies presented in the chapter and identify three specific actions you would recommend noncommercial foodservice managers could take to stay within their budgets during times of rapidly rising product costs.

Chapter 6

MANAGING FOOD AND BEVERAGE PRICING

OVERVIEW

This chapter teaches you about the kinds of menus you will most often encounter as a hospitality manager. Knowledge of these formats will help you reduce costs through effective utilization of food and beverage products as well as better utilization of your staff. In addition, the chapter examines and analyzes the factors that influence the prices you will charge for the menu items you will sell. Finally, the chapter explains the procedures used to assign individual menu item prices based on cost and collected sales data. By fully understanding the hospitality pricing process, you can help ensure that your menu items will generate the sales revenue you need to meet your profit goals.

Chapter Outline

- Menu Formats
- Factors Affecting Menu Pricing
- Assigning Menu Prices
- Special Pricing Situations
- Technology Tools
- Apply What You Have Learned
- Key Terms and Concepts
- Test Your Skills

LEARNING OUTCOMES

At the conclusion of this chapter, you will be able to:
- Choose and apply the best menu format to an operation.
- Identify the variables to be considered when establishing menu prices.
- Assign menu prices to menu items based on their cost, popularity, and ultimate profitability.

MENU FORMATS

*I*f you have determined that your purchasing, receiving, storing, issuing, and production controls are well in line, you have an excellent chance of reaching your profit goals. It is possible to find, however, that even when these areas are well managed, food and beverage costs are still too high to achieve your profit projections. When this is the case, the problem may well lie in the fundamental areas of menu format, product pricing, or both.

Menus are one of the most effective ways managers can communicate with their guests. In a foodservice operation, the term "menu" actually means two things. Of course, the "menu" refers to the items available for sale to guests. In addition, however, the term "menu" refers to the specific method in which items available for sale are presented or communicated to guests. Alternatives for menu presentation include printed paper menus, menu display boards, blackboards, and even oral recitation by servers.

Some facilities create separate menus for food and beverage products. Other operators find it more appropriate to have menus that combine both their food and beverage offerings. Regardless of the choice the business makes, the menu is an excellent opportunity to build impulse sales or to communicate special sales and services the facility has to offer. With the advent of computers and inexpensive on-premise color printing, many operators find that they can create their own menus for a very low cost and change their menus more frequently than they would have been able to in the past. In addition, menu **tip-ons,** which are smaller menu segments clipped to more permanent menus, can prove very effective in influencing impulse buying. Menus and their design can vary greatly; thus, it makes good sense to analyze menu format first because menu design decisions drive most pricing decisions.

Menus in foodservice establishments generally fall into one of the following three major categories:

1. Standard menu

2. Daily menu

3. Cycle menu

Any of these can be an asset to your effort to control food costs if it is used in the proper setting. The menu most commonly used by commercial foodservice operations is the standard menu.

■ STANDARD MENU

The **standard menu** is printed, displayed, recited by service staff, or otherwise communicated to the guest. Examples of chain restaurants that utilize the standard menu include Cracker Barrel, Red Lobster, Applebee's, Outback Steakhouse, and

Starbucks. The standard menu is fixed day after day. You may periodically add or delete a menu item, but the standard menu remains virtually constant. There are many operational advantages to such a menu format. First, the standard menu simplifies your ordering process. The menu remains constant each day, thus it is easy to know which products must be purchased to produce these specific items. Second, guests tend to have a good number of choices when selecting from a standard menu. This is true because virtually every item that can be produced by the kitchen is available for selection by each guest entering the operation.

A third advantage of the standard menu is that guest preference data are easily obtained because the total number of menu items that will be served stays constant and, thus, is generally smaller than in some alternative menu formats. As you learned in Chapter 3, menu item sales histories can be used to accurately compute percent selecting data and, thus, production schedules and purchasing requirements. In addition, standard menus often become marketing tools for your operation because guests soon become familiar with and return for their favorite menu items.

The standard menu is most typically found in the traditional restaurant or hotel segment of the hospitality industry. It tends to dominate those segments of the business where the guest selects the location of the dining experience, as contrasted with situations where a guest's choice is restricted. Examples of restricted-choice situations include a college dormitory cafeteria where students are required to dine in one location, a hospital where patients during their stay must choose their menu selections from that hospital only, or an elementary school cafeteria.

Despite its many advantages, the standard menu does have drawbacks from a control standpoint. First, standard menus are often not developed to utilize carryovers effectively. In fact, in many cases, items that are produced for a standard menu and remain unsold must be discarded; the next day their quality will not be acceptable. An example is a quick-service restaurant that produces too many hamburgers for a busy lunch period and does not sell all of them. Indeed, for some quick-service restaurants, a burger that is made but not sold within five minutes (or less) is discarded. Contrast that cost control strategy with one that says that cooked burgers not sold within five minutes will be chopped and added to the house specialty chili, and it is easy to see how menu design and the items placed on the menu directly affect food cost and food cost control.

A second disadvantage of the standard menu is its lack of ability to respond quickly to market changes and product cost changes. For example, a restaurant that does not list green beans on the menu cannot take advantage of the seasonal harvest of green beans, a time when they can be purchased extremely inexpensively. Conversely, if management has decided that its two house vegetables will be broccoli and corn, even considerable price increases in these two items will have to be absorbed by the operation because these two menu items are listed on the permanent menu. An extreme example of this kind of problem was found in a quick-service seafood restaurant chain that found it was paying almost three times what it had the previous year for a seafood item that constituted approximately 80% of its menu sales. A foreign government had restricted fishing for this product off its shores, and the price skyrocketed. This chain was nearly devastated by this turn of events. Needless to say, management quickly moved to add chicken and different seafood products to the menu to dilute the effect of this incredible price increase.

Whenever possible, you should monitor food prices with an eye to making seasonal adjustments. The standard menu, however, makes this quite difficult. Some restaurant groups respond to this problem by changing their standard menu on a regular basis: that is, they develop a standard menu for the summer, for example, and another for the winter. In this manner, they can take advantage of seasonal cost savings, add some variety to their menus (by introducing new items and removing less popular ones), but still maintain the core menu items for which they are known and enjoy the cost-related benefits of a standard menu.

■ DAILY MENU

In some restaurants, you might elect to operate without a standard menu and, instead, implement a **daily menu,** that is, a menu that changes every day. This concept is especially popular in some upscale restaurants where the chef's daily creations are viewed with great anticipation, and even some awe, by the eager guest. The daily menu offers some advantages over the standard menu; for example, management can respond very quickly to changes in ingredient or item prices. In fact, that is one of the daily menu's great advantages. In addition, carryovers are less of a problem because any product unsold from the previous day has at least the potential of being incorporated, often as a new dish, into the present day's menu.

Every silver lining has its cloud, however. For all its flexibility, the daily menu is recommended only for very special situations due to the tremendous control drawbacks associated with its implementation. First, item popularity data are difficult to obtain because the items on any given day's menu may never have been served in that particular combination in that restaurant. Thus, the preparation of specific items in certain quantities is pure guesswork, and this is a dangerous way of determining production schedules. Second, it may be difficult to plan to have the necessary ingredients on hand to prepare the daily menu if the menu is not known well ahead of time. How does one decide on Monday whether one should order tuna or sirloin steak for the menu on Thursday? Obviously, this situation requires that even the daily menu be planned far enough in advance to allow the purchasing agent to select and order the items necessary to produce the menu. Third, the daily menu may sometimes serve as a marketing tool, but it can just as often serve as a disappointment to guests who had a wonderful menu item the last time they dined at this particular establishment and have now returned only to find that their favorite item is not being served. On a positive note, it is very unlikely that any guest will get bored with a routine at a daily menu restaurant because the routine is, in fact, no routine at all.

Both the standard and the daily menus have advantages and disadvantages. The cycle menu is an effort by management to enjoy the best aspects of both of these approaches and minimize their respective disadvantages.

■ CYCLE MENU

A **cycle menu** is a menu in effect for a specific time period. The length of the cycle refers to the length of time the menu is in effect. Thus, we refer to a 7-day cycle menu, a 21-day cycle menu, a 30-day cycle menu, or one of any other length of time. Cycle menus are utilized by institutions such as colleges and universities, hospitals, assisted living facilities, correctional facilities, and other settings where the guest (or type of guest) is served on an established basis each day.

Typically, a cycle menu is repeated on a regular basis. Thus, for example, a particular cycle menu could consist of four 7-day periods. If each of the four periods were labeled as A, B, C, and D, the cycle periods could rotate as illustrated in Figure 6.1.

■ **FIGURE 6.1**   Sample Cycle Menu Rotation

Days	Cycle
1–7	A
8–14	B
15–21	C
22–28	D
29–35	A
36–42	B
43–49	C
50–56	D
57–63	A

Within each cycle, the individual menu items vary on a daily basis. For example, cycle menu A might consist of the following seven dinner items:

Day 1	Monday	Cheese Enchiladas
Day 2	Tuesday	Turkey and Bread Dressing
Day 3	Wednesday	Corned Beef and Cabbage
Day 4	Thursday	Fried Chicken Strips
Day 5	Friday	Stir Fried Lobster
Day 6	Saturday	Lasagna
Day 7	Sunday	Beef Pot Roast

These menu items will be served again when cycle menu A repeats itself on days 29 through 35.

Day 29	Monday	Cheese Enchiladas
Day 30	Tuesday	Turkey and Bread Dressing
Day 31	Wednesday	Corned Beef and Cabbage
Day 32	Thursday	Fried Chicken Strips
Day 33	Friday	Stir-Fried Lobster
Day 34	Saturday	Lasagna
Day 35	Sunday	Beef Pot Roast

In the typical case, cycle menus B, C, and D consist of many (or all) different menu items. In this manner, no menu item will be repeated more frequently than desired by management.

Cycle menus make the most sense when guests dine with you on a very regular basis, either through the choice of the individual, such as a college student or summer camper eating in a dining hall, or through the choice of an institution, such as a hospital or correctional facility feeding situation. In cases like this, menu variety is very important. The cycle menu provides a systematic method for incorporating that variety into the menu. At a glance, the foodservice manager can determine how often, for example, fried chicken strips will be served per week, month, or year, and how frequently bread dressing rather than saffron rice is served with baked chicken. In this respect, the cycle menu offers more choice to the guest than does the standard menu. With cycle menus, production personnel can be trained to produce a wider variety of foods than with the standard menu, thus improving their skills, but requiring fewer skills than might be needed with a daily menu concept.

Cycle menus also have the advantage of being able to systematically incorporate today's carryovers into tomorrow's finished product. This is an extremely important cost-related advantage. Also, because of its cyclical nature, management should have a good idea of guest preferences and, thus, be able to schedule and control production to a greater degree than with the daily menu.

Purchasing, too, is simplified because the menu is known ahead of time, and menu ingredients that will appear on all the different cycles can be ordered with plenty of lead time. Inventory levels are easier to maintain as well because, as is the case with the standard menu, product usage is well known. Even price reductions in item costs (for example, incorporating the use of locally grown produce during peak production periods) can be incorporated into cycle menu planning, thus lowering costs and maximizing product quality.

To illustrate the differences and the impact of operating under the three different menu systems, consider the case of Larry, Moe, and Curly Jo, three foodservice operators who wish to serve roast turkey and dressing for their dinner entrée on a Saturday night in April. Larry operates a restaurant with a standard menu. If he is to print a standard menu that allows him to serve turkey in April, he may be required to have it available in January and June also. If he is to utilize any carryover parts of the turkey, he must incorporate a second turkey item, which also must be made available every day. Larry is not sure all the trouble and cost is worth it! In addition, consider the expense involved in a national chain restaurant with thousands of outlets. Reprints of menus in this situation are very costly. If Larry is the CEO (chief executive officer) of a national or international foodservice organization such as this, any decision to change the standard menu is indeed a major undertaking.

Moe operates a restaurant with a daily menu. For him, roast turkey and dressing on a Saturday in April is quite easy. His problem, however, is that he has no idea how much to produce because he has never before served this item at this time of the year on this specific evening in his restaurant. Also, few of the guests he has served in the past year are likely to know about his decision to serve the menu item. What if no one orders it?

Curly Jo operates on a cycle menu. She can indeed put roast turkey and dressing on the cycle. If it sells well, she will keep it on the cycle. If it does not, it will be removed from the next cycle. Curly Jo makes a note to herself that she should record how well it sells and leave a space in the cycle for the utilization of any carryover product that might exist within the next few days. The advantages of the cycle menu, in this specific situation, are apparent.

■ MENU SPECIALS

Regardless of the menu type used, you can generally incorporate relatively minor menu changes on a regular basis. This is accomplished through the offering of daily or weekly **menu specials,** that is, menu items that will appear on the menu as you desire and be removed when they are either consumed or discontinued. These daily or weekly specials are an effort to provide variety, take advantage of low-cost raw ingredients, utilize carryover products, or test-market potential new menu items. The menu special is a powerful cost control tool. Properly utilized, it helps shape the future menu by testing guest acceptance of new menu items while providing opportunities for you to respond to the challenges of using carryover or new food and beverage products you have in inventory.

FACTORS AFFECTING MENU PRICING

A great deal of important information has been written in the area of menu pricing and strategy. A great deal of nonsense has also been written. For the serious foodservice operator, menu pricing is a topic that deserves its own significant research and study. Pricing is related to cost control by virtue of the basic formula from Chapter 1:

Revenue − Expense = Profit

When foodservice operators find that profits are too low, they frequently question whether their prices (revenues) are too low. It is important to remember, however, that revenue and price are not synonymous terms. **Revenue** means the amount spent by all guests, and price refers to the amount charged to one guest. Thus, total revenue is generated by the following formula:

$$\text{Price} \times \text{Number Sold} = \text{Total Revenue}$$

From this formula, it can be seen that there are two components of total revenue. **Price** is one component, and the other is the number of items sold. It is most often a truism that as price increases, the number of items sold will generally decrease. For this reason, price increases must be evaluated based on their impact on total revenue and not on price alone.

Assume, for example, that you own a quick-service restaurant chain. You are considering raising the price of small drinks from $1.00 to $1.25. Figure 6.2 illustrates the possible effects of this price increase on total revenue in a single unit. Note especially that, in at least one alternative result, increasing price has the effect of actually decreasing total revenue. Experienced foodservice managers know that increasing prices without giving added value can result in higher prices but, frequently, lower revenue because of reduced guest counts. This is true because guests demand a good **price/value relationship** when making a purchase. The price/value relationship simply reflects guests' view of how much value they are receiving for the price they are paying.

Perhaps no area of hospitality management is less understood than the area of pricing. This is not surprising when you consider the many factors that play a part in the pricing decision. For some foodservice operators, inefficiency in cost control is passed on to guests in the form of higher prices. In fact, sound pricing decisions should be based on establishing a positive price/value relationship in the mind of the guest.

Most foodservice operators face fairly similar product costs when selecting their goods on the open market. Whether the product is oranges or beer, wholesale prices may vary only slightly from one supplier to the next. In some cases, this variation is due to volume buying, whereas in others, it is the result of the relationship established with the vendor. Regardless of the source, the fact remains that the variations are often small relative to variations in menu pricing. This becomes easier to understand when you realize that a menu item's selling price is often a function

■ **FIGURE 6.2** Alternative Results of Price Increases

Old Price	New Price	Number Served	Total Revenue	Revenue Result
$1.00		200	$200.00	
	$1.25	250	$312.50	Increase
	$1.25	200	$250.00	Increase
	$1.25	160	$200.00	No Change
	$1.25	150	$187.50	Decrease

of much more than its product cost. In fact, menu prices are significantly affected by all of the following factors:

Factors Influencing Menu Price

1. Local competition
2. Service levels
3. Guest type
4. Product quality
5. Portion size
6. Ambience
7. Meal period
8. Location
9. Sales mix

■ LOCAL COMPETITION

This factor is often too closely monitored by the typical foodservice operator. It may seem to some that the average guest is vitally concerned with price and nothing more. In reality, small variations in price generally make little difference to the average guest. If a group of young professionals goes out for pizza and beer after work, the major determinant will not be whether the selling price for the beer is $3.00 in one establishment or $3.25 in another. Your competition's selling price is somewhat important when establishing price, but it is a well-known fact in foodservice that someone can always sell a lesser quality product for a lesser price. The price competitors charge for their products can be useful information in helping you arrive at your own selling price. It should not, however, be the only determining factor in your pricing decision. Successful foodservice operators spend their time focusing on building guest value in their own operation and not in attempting to mimic the efforts of the competition. In fact, in the consumer's mind, higher prices are most often associated with higher quality products and thus a better price/value relationship.

■ SERVICE LEVELS

Guests expect to pay more for the same product when service levels are higher. The can of soda sold from a vending machine is generally less expensive than a soda served by a human being. In a like manner, many pizza chains charge a lower price, for example, for a large pizza that is picked up by the guest than for that same pizza when it is delivered to the guest's door. This is as it should be. The hospitality industry is, in fact, a service industry. As the personal level of service increases, prices may also be increased. This personal service may range from the delivery of products, as in the pizza example, to simply increasing the number of servers in a dining room and, thus, reducing the number of guests each must serve. This is not to imply that menu price increases based on service levels are reserved exclusively to pay for the labor required to increase those service levels. Guests are willing to pay more for increased service levels, but this higher price should provide for extra profit as well. In the hospitality industry, those companies that have been able to survive and thrive over the years have done so because of their uncompromising commitment to high levels of guest service.

∎ GUEST TYPE

Some guests are simply less price sensitive than others. All guests, however, want value for their money. The question of what represents value varies by the type of clientele. An example of this can clearly be seen in the pricing decisions of convenience stores across the United States. In these facilities, food products such as sandwiches, fruit, drinks, cookies, and the like are sold at relatively high prices. The guests these stores cater to, however, value speed and convenience above all else. For this speed and convenience they are willing to pay a premium price. In a like manner, guests at an expensive steakhouse restaurant are less likely to respond negatively to small variations in drink prices than are guests at a corner tavern. A thorough analysis of who their guests are and what they value most is critical to the ongoing success of foodservice operators.

∎ PRODUCT QUALITY

In nearly every instance, the guest's quality perception of any specific product offered for sale in the foodservice business can range from very low to very high. This is not to say that the wholesomeness or safety of the product will vary. They should not. But a guest's perception of quality is based on a variety of factors. As the product itself and those quality-influencing factors vary, so, too, does the guest's perception of quality. For example, when average foodservice guests think of a "hamburger" they actually think, not of one product, but of a range of products. A hamburger may be a rather small burger patty on a regular bun, wrapped in paper and served in a sack. If so, its price will be low and so perhaps may service levels and, thus, perceived quality. If, however, the guest's thoughts turn to an 8-ounce gourmet burger with avocado slices and alfalfa sprouts on a toasted whole-grain bun served in a white-tablecloth restaurant, the price will be much higher and so, probably, will service levels and perceived quality.

As an effective foodservice manager, you will choose from a variety of quality levels when developing product specifications and, consequently, planning menus and establishing prices. If you select the market's cheapest bourbon as your well brand, you will likely be able to charge less for drinks made from it than your competitor who selects a better brand. Your drink quality levels, however, may also be perceived by your guests as lower. To be successful, you should select the quality level that best represents your guests' anticipated desire as well as your own goals and then price your products accordingly.

■ PORTION SIZE

Portion size plays a large role in determining menu pricing. It is a relatively misunderstood concept, yet it is probably the second most significant factor (next to sales mix) in overall pricing. The great chefs know that people "eat with their eyes first!" This relates to presenting food that is visually appealing. It also relates to portion size. A burger and fries that fill an 8-inch plate may well be lost on an 11-inch plate. Portion size, then, is a function of both product quantity and presentation. It is no secret why successful cafeteria chains use smaller than average dishes to plate their food. For their guests, the image of price to value comes across loud and clear.

In some dining situations, particularly in an "all you care to eat" operation, the previously mentioned principle again holds true. The proper dish size is just as critical as the proper size scoop or ladle when serving the food. Of course, in a traditional table service operation, management controls (or should control!) portion size. Simply put, the larger the portion size, the higher your costs. One very good way to determine whether portion sizes are too large is simply to watch the dishwashing area and see what comes back from the dining room as uneaten. In this regard, the dishroom operator becomes an important player in the cost control team.

Many of today's consumers prefer lighter food with more choices in fruits and vegetables. The portion sizes of these items can be increased at a fairly low increase in cost. At the same time, average beverage sizes are increasing, as are the size of side items such as French fries. Again, these tend to be lower-cost items. This can be good news for the foodservice operator if prices can be increased to adequately cover the costs of the larger portion sizes.

Every menu item should be analyzed with an eye toward determining if the quantity being served is the "optimum" quantity. You would like to serve this amount, of course, but no more. The effect of portion size on menu price is significant, and it will be your job to establish and maintain strict control over proper portion sizes.

■ AMBIENCE

If people ate only because they were hungry, few restaurants would be open today. People eat out for a variety of reasons, some of which have little to do with food. Fun, companionship, time limitations, adventure, and variety are just a few reasons diners cite for eating out rather than eating at home. For the foodservice operator who provides an attractive ambience, menu prices can reflect this. In fact, the operator in such a situation is selling much more than food and, thus, justly deserves an increased price. In most cases, however, foodservice operations that count too heavily on ambience alone to carry their business generally start out well but are not ultimately successful. Excellent product quality with outstanding service goes much further over the long run than do clever restaurant designs. Ambience may draw guests to a location the first time. When this is true, prices may be somewhat higher if the quality of products also supports the price structure.

■ MEAL PERIOD

In some cases, diners expect to pay more for an item served in the evening than for that same item served at a lunch period. Sometimes this is the result of a smaller "luncheon" portion size, but in other cases the portion size, as well as service levels, may be the same in the evening as earlier in the day. You must exercise caution in this area. Guests should clearly understand why a menu item's price changes with the time of day. If this cannot be answered to the guest's satisfaction, it may not be wise to implement a time-sensitive pricing structure.

■ LOCATION

Location can be a major factor in determining price. One needs look no further than America's many themed amusement parks or sports arenas to see evidence of this. Foodservice operators in these locations are able to charge premium prices because they have, in effect, a monopoly on food sold to the visitors. The only all-night diner on the interstate highway exit is in much the same situation. Contrast that with an operator who is one of 10 seafood restaurants on restaurant row. It used to be said of restaurants that success was due to three things: location, location, and location! This may have been true before so many operations opened in the United States. There is, of course, no discounting the value of a prime restaurant location, and location alone can influence price. It does not, however, guarantee success. Location can be an asset or a liability. If it is an asset, menu prices may reflect that fact. If location is indeed a liability, menu prices may need to be lower to attract a sufficient clientele to ensure the operation's total revenue requirements.

■ SALES MIX

Of all the factors mentioned thus far, sales mix most heavily influences the menu pricing decision, just as guest purchase decisions will influence total product costs. Recall that sales mix refers to the specific menu items selected by guests. Managers can respond to this situation by employing a concept called price blending. **Price blending** refers to the process of pricing products with very different individual cost percentages in groups with the intent of achieving a favorable overall cost situation. The ability to knowledgeably blend prices is a useful skill and one that is well worth mastering. As an example, assume that you are the operations vice president

■ **FIGURE 6.3** Unblended Price Structure

Texas Red's Burgers

Item	Item Cost	Desired Food Cost	Proposed Selling Price
Hamburger	$1.50	40%	$3.75
French Fries	0.32	40%	0.80
Soft Drinks (12 oz.)	0.18	40%	0.45
Total	2.00	40%	5.00

for a chain of upscale hamburger restaurants known as Texas Red's. Assume also that you hope to achieve an overall food cost of 40% in your units. For purposes of simplicity, assume that Figure 6.3 illustrates the three products you sell and their corresponding selling price if each is priced to achieve a 40% food cost.

In Chapter 3, you learned that the formula for computing food cost percentage is as follows:

$$\frac{\text{Cost of Food Sold}}{\text{Food Sales}} = \text{Food Cost \%}$$

This formula can be worded somewhat differently for a single menu item without changing its accuracy:

$$\frac{\text{Cost of a Specific Food Item Sold}}{\text{Food Sales of That Item}} = \text{Food Cost \% of That Item}$$

It is important to understand that the food sales value in the preceding formula is a synonymous term to the selling price when evaluating the menu price of a single menu item. The principles of algebra allow you to rearrange the formula as follows:

$$\frac{\text{Cost of a Specific Food Item Sold}}{\text{Food Cost \% of That Item}} = \text{Food Sales(Selling Price)of That Item}$$

Thus, in Figure 6.3, the hamburger's selling price is established as:

$$\frac{\$1.50}{0.40} = \$3.75$$

Notice that in Figure 6.3 all products are priced to sell at a price that results in a 40% food cost. Certainly, under this system, sales mix, that is, the individual menu selections of guests, does not affect overall food cost %. The sales mix resulting from this pricing strategy could, however, have very damaging results on your profitability.

■ **FIGURE 6.4** Blended Price Structure

Texas Red's Burgers			
Item	Item Cost	Proposed Food Cost%	Proposed Selling Price
Hamburger	$1.50	60.2%	$2.49
French Fries	0.32	21.5	1.49
Soft Drinks (12 oz.)	0.18	16.5	1.09
Total	2.00	39.4	5.07

The reason is very simple. If you use the price structure indicated, your drink prices are too low. Most guests expect to pay far in excess of 45 cents for a soft drink at a quick-service restaurant. You run the risk, in this example, of attracting many guests who are interested in buying only soft drinks at your restaurants. Your French fries may also be priced too low. Your burger itself, however, may be priced too high relative to your competitors. However, if you use the price-blending concept, and if you assume that each guest coming into your restaurants will buy a burger, French fries, and a soft drink, you can create a different menu price structure and still achieve your overall cost objective, as seen in Figure 6.4.

Note that, in this example, you actually achieve a total food cost slightly lower than 40%. Your hamburger price is now less than $2.50 and in line with local competitors. Note also, however, that you have assumed each guest coming to Texas Red's will buy one of each item. In reality, of course, not all guests will select one of each item. Some guests will not elect fries, whereas others may stop in only for a soft drink. It is for this reason that guest selection data, discussed in Chapter 3, are so critical. These histories let you know exactly what your guests are buying when they visit your outlets. You can then apply percent selecting figures to your pricing strategy. To illustrate how this works, assume that you monitored a sample of 100 guests who came into one of your units and found the results presented in Figure 6.5.

As you can see from Figure 6.5, you can use the price-blending concept to achieve your overall cost objectives if you have a good understanding of how many people buy each menu item. In this example, you have achieved the 40% food cost you sought. It matters little if the burger has a 60.2% food cost if the burger is sold in conjunction with the sample number of soft drinks and fries. Obviously, there may be a danger if your guests begin to order nothing but hamburgers when they come to your establishment. That, however, is unlikely. Again, careful monitoring of guest preferences will allow you to make price adjustments, as needed, to keep your overall costs and prices in line. A word of caution regarding the manipulation of sales mix and price blending is in order, however. Because price itself is one of the factors that impact percent selecting figures, a change in menu price may cause a change in item popularity. If, in an effort to reduce overall product cost percentage, you were to increase the price of soft drinks at Texas Red's, for example, you might find that a higher percentage of

■ FIGURE 6.5 Sample Sales Mix Data

Texas Red's Burgers						
Total Sales: $449.25			Guests Served: 100			
Total Food Cost: $180.20			Food Cost %: 40.1%			

Item	Number Sold	Item Cost	Total Food Cost	Selling Price	Total Sales	Food Cost %
Hamburger	92	$1.50	$138.00	$2.49	$229.08	60.2%
French Fries	79	0.32	25.28	1.49	117.71	21.5
Soft Drink (12 oz.)	94	0.18	16.92	1.09	102.46	16.5
Total			180.20		449.25	40.1

guests would elect not to purchase a soft drink. This could have the effect of actually increasing your overall product cost percentage, because fewer guests would choose to buy the one item with an extremely low food cost percentage. The sales mix and the concept of price blending will have a major impact on your overall menu pricing philosophy and strategy.

Green and Growing!

You have now been introduced to at least nine factors that may influence the prices you charge for the items you sell. In the future, the level of Leadership in Energy and Environmental Design (LEED) certification achieved by your operation may well constitute another such factor. The LEED rating system developed by the U.S. Green Building Council (USGBC) evaluates facilities on a variety of standards. The rating system considers sustainability, water use efficiency, energy usage, air quality, construction and materials, and innovation. Currently, the maximum LEED score that can be achieved is 69 points, and operations scoring 26 or more points earn one of the following ratings:

Certified: 26–32 points
Silver: 33–38 points
Gold: 39–51 points
Platinum: 52–69 points

In many cases, when LEED certification is pursued, the initial construction cost of a building will be higher than the current industry standard. However, these costs are recovered by the savings incurred over time due to the lower-than-industry-standard operational costs that are typical of a LEED-certified building. In the foodservice business, these initial costs may also be mitigated by the fact that, increasingly, consumers are willing to pay more to dine in LEED-certified operations. In addition, LEED-certified buildings are healthier for workers and for diners. The LEED certification creates benefits for building owners, employees, and guests. Look for a continuing increase in its importance to your guests.

ASSIGNING MENU PRICES

*T*he methods used to assign menu prices are as varied as foodservice managers themselves. In general, however, menu prices have historically been assigned on the basis of one of the following two concepts:

1. Product cost percentage
2. Product contribution margin

■ PRODUCT COST PERCENTAGE

This method of pricing is based on the idea that product cost should be a predetermined percentage of selling price. As was illustrated earlier in this chapter, if you have a menu item that costs $1.50 (EP) to produce, and your desired cost percentage equals 40%, the following formula can be used to determine what the item's menu price should be:

$$\frac{\text{Cost of a Specific Food Item Sold}}{\text{Food Cost \% of That Item}} = \text{Food Sales (Selling Price) of That Item}$$

or

$$\frac{\$1.50}{0.40} = \$3.75$$

Thus, the recommended selling price, given a $1.50 product cost, is $3.75. If the item is sold for $3.75, then a 40% food cost should be achieved for that item. A check on this work can also be done using the food cost percentage formula:

$$\frac{\$1.50}{\$3.75} = 40\%$$

■ **FIGURE 6.6**   Pricing-Factor Table

Desired Product Cost %	Factor
20	5.000
23	4.348
25	4.000
28	3.571
30	3.333
$33\frac{1}{3}$	3.000
35	2.857
38	2.632
40	2.500
43	2.326
45	2.222

When management uses a predetermined food cost percentage to price menu items, it is stating its belief that product cost in relationship to selling price is of great importance. Experienced foodservice managers know that a second method of calculating prices based on predetermined food cost % goals can be used. This method uses a cost factor or multiplier that can be assigned to each desired food cost percentage. This factor, when multiplied by the item's EP cost, will result in a selling price that yields the desired food cost percentage. Figure 6.6 details such a factor table.

In each case, the factor is calculated by the following formula:

$$\frac{1.00}{\text{Desired Product Cost \%}} = \text{Pricing Factor}$$

Thus, if you were attempting to price a product to achieve a product cost of 40%, the computation is:

$$\frac{1.00}{0.40} = 2.5$$

This pricing factor of 2.5, when multiplied by any product cost, will result in a selling price that yields a 40% product cost. The formula is as follows:

$$\text{Pricing Factor} \times \text{Product Cost} = \text{Menu Price}$$

To return to our example, you could use the previous version of the formula to establish your selling price if you want to achieve a 40% product cost and if your item costs $1.50 to produce. The computation is as follows:

$$2.5 \times 1.50 = \$3.75$$

As can be seen, these two methods of arriving at the proposed selling price yield identical results. One formula simply relies on division, whereas the other relies on multiplication. The decision about which formula to use is completely up to you. With either approach, the selling price will be determined with a goal of achieving a specified product cost percentage for each item.

In many settings, such as "all-you-can-eat" buffets and banquet-style meals, foodservice managers must calculate their selling prices based upon their **plate costs.** A plate cost is simply the sum of all product costs included in a single meal (or "plate") served to a guest. In such settings, prices are determined in exactly the same manner as they are for an individual menu item. To illustrate, assume you managed the foodservice operation at an exclusive Country Club. The club specializes in wedding receptions. Assume a couple holding their reception at your facility selected a meal from your menu offerings that resulted in your incurring the following plate cost:

Pre-meal Reception	$ 4.50
Dinner	$ 11.00
Dessert	$ 2.00
Beverages (nonalcoholic)	$ 3.00
Total plate cost	$ 20.50

Assume also that you sought to achieve a 40% product cost on each of your banquet meals. Utilizing the factor method, the computation is as follows:

$$2.5 \times 20.50 = \$51.25$$

In this example, with a plate cost of $20.50 and a desired food cost of 40%, the selling price of your banquet meal would be $51.25.

■ PRODUCT CONTRIBUTION MARGIN

Some foodservice managers prefer an approach to menu pricing that is focused not on product cost percentage but rather on a menu item's contribution margin. **Contribution margin** is defined as the amount that remains after the product cost of the menu item is subtracted from the item's selling price. Contribution margin, then, is the amount that a menu item "contributes" to paying for your labor and other expenses and providing a profit. Thus, if an item sells for $3.75

and the product cost for this item is $1.50, the contribution margin is computed as follows:

$$\text{Selling Price} - \text{Product Cost} = \text{Contribution Margin}$$

or

$$\$3.75 - \$1.50 = \$2.25$$

When this approach is used, the formula for determining selling price is:

$$\text{Product Cost} + \text{Contribution Margin Desired} = \text{Selling Price}$$

Establishing menu price using this philosophy is a matter of combining product cost with a predetermined contribution margin. Management's role here is to determine the desired contribution margin for each menu item. When using this approach, you are likely to establish different contribution margins for various menu items or groups of items. For example, in a cafeteria where items are priced separately, entrées might be priced with a contribution margin of $2.50 each, desserts with a contribution margin of $1.25, and drinks, perhaps, with a contribution margin of $0.75. Those managers who rely on the contribution margin approach to pricing do so in the belief that the average contribution margin per item is a more important consideration in pricing decisions than is food cost percentage.

■ PRODUCT COST PERCENTAGE OR PRODUCT CONTRIBUTION MARGIN

Proponents exist for both of these approaches to menu pricing. Indeed, there are additional methods that have been proposed for menu pricing, but a thorough analysis of these is beyond the scope of a basic introduction to menu pricing theory. Some large foodservice organizations have established highly complex computer-driven formulas for determining appropriate menu prices. For the average foodservice operator, however, utilizing product cost percentage, contribution margin, or a combination of both will usually suffice when attempting to arrive at appropriate pricing decisions.

Although the debate over the "best" pricing method is likely to continue for some time, you should remember to view pricing as an important process that has as its end goal the establishment of a desirable price/value relationship in the mind of your guest.

Regardless of whether the pricing method used is based on food cost percentage or contribution margin, the selling price selected must provide for a predetermined operational profit. For this reason, it is important that the menu not be priced so low that no profit is possible or so high that you will not be able to sell a sufficient number of items to make a profit. In the final analysis, it is the market that will eventually determine what your sales will be on any given item. Being sensitive to both required profit and your guests—their needs, wants, and desires—is very critical to an effective pricing strategy.

Consider The Cost

"We have to lower our price or we'll just get killed," said Hoyt Jones, director of operations for the seven-unit Binky's Sub shops. Binky's was known for its modestly priced, but very high-quality, sandwiches and soups. Business and profits were good, but now Hoyt and Rachel, who served as Binky's director of marketing, were discussing the new $4.99 "*Foot Long Deal*" sandwich promotion that had just been rolled out by their major competitor, an extremely large chain of sub shops that operated over 5,000 units nationally and internationally.

"They just decided to lower their prices to appeal to value-conscious customers," said Hoyt.

"But how can they do that and still make money?" asked Rachel.

"There's always a less expensive variety of ham and cheese on the market," replied Hoyt. "They use lower-quality ingredients than we do. We charge $6.99 for our foot-long sub. That wasn't bad when they sold theirs at $5.99. Our customers know we are worth the extra dollar. Now that they are at $4.99 . . . I don't know, but I think they are going to kill us in the market. We need to do something—fast."

1. How large a role do you believe "cost" likely played into the decision of this competitor to reduce its sandwich prices? Explain your answer.

2. Do you think the typical foodservice customer will consistently pay a higher price for better-quality food and beverage products? Give a specific example to support your answer.

3. Assume you were the president of Binky's Subs. What steps would you instruct Hoyt and Rachel to take to address this specific pricing challenge?

SPECIAL PRICING SITUATIONS

Some pricing decisions faced by foodservice managers call for a unique approach. In many cases, pricing is used as a way to influence guests' purchasing decisions or to respond to particularly complex situations. The following are examples of special pricing situations:

1. Coupons
2. Value pricing
3. Bundling
4. Salad bars and buffets
5. Bottled wine
6. Beverages at receptions and parties

■ COUPONS

Coupons are a popular way to vary menu price. Essentially, there are two types of coupons in use in the hospitality industry. The first type generally allows guests to get a free item when they buy an additional item. This has the effect of reducing by 50% the menu price of the couponed item. With the second type, some form of restriction is placed on the coupon's use. For example, the coupon may only be accepted at a certain time of day, or the reduction in price may be available only if the guest purchases a specific designated menu item. Whichever type is offered, coupons have the effect of reducing sales revenue from individual guests in the hope that the total number of guests will increase to the point that total sales revenue increases. Coupons are a popular marketing tool, but their use should be carefully evaluated in terms of effect on menu price, product cost percentage, and product contribution margin.

■ VALUE PRICING

Value pricing refers to the practice of reducing prices on selected menu items in the belief that, as in couponing, total guest counts will increase to the point that total sales revenue also increases. A potential danger, of course, with value pricing is that if guest counts do not increase significantly, total sales revenue may, in fact, decline rather than increase. Many credit the Wendy's chain with establishing value pricing, but currently its use is widespread, as is evident by the large number of 99-cent and $1.00 menu items for sale in the major quick-service restaurant segment chains.

■ BUNDLING

Bundling refers to the practice of selecting specific menu items and pricing them as a group in such a manner that the single menu price of the group is lower than if the items in the group were purchased individually. The most common example is the combination meals offered by many quick-service restaurants. In many cases, these bundled meals consist of a sandwich, French fries, and a drink. These bundled meals, often promoted as "value meals" or "combo" meals, encourage guests to buy one of each menu item rather than only one or two of them. The bundled meal generally is priced so competitively that a strong value perception is established in the guest's mind.

When bundling, as in couponing or value pricing, lower menu prices are accepted by management in the belief that this pricing strategy will increase total sales revenue and, thus, profit by increasing the number of guests served.

■ SALAD BARS AND BUFFETS

The difficulty in establishing a set price for either a salad bar or a buffet is that total portion cost can and will vary greatly from one guest to the next. A person weighing 100 pounds will, most likely, consume fewer products from a buffet or an all-you-can-eat line than a 300-pound person will. The general rule, however, is that each of these guests will pay the same price to go through the salad bar or buffet line. Short of charging guests for the amount they actually consume (a technique that has been tried by some operators but with limited success), a method of determining a single selling price must be established. This price must be based on a known "average" plate cost for the diner who selects the all-you-can-eat option.

Consider the costs incurred by a foodservice manager whose operation daily feeds those attending a National Football League (NFL) training camp compared to a manager feeding an equal number of individuals attending a school for beginning ballerinas! The point is that the selling price for most restaurants open to the public must be established and monitored so that either guest could be accommodated at a price you find acceptable. This can be accomplished rather easily if record keeping is accurate and timely. The secret to keeping the selling price low in a salad bar or buffet situation is to apply the ABC inventory approach. That is, A items, which are expensive, should comprise no more than 20% of the total product available. The B items, which are moderate in price, should comprise about 30% of the item offerings, and C items, which are inexpensive, should comprise 50% of the offerings. Using this approach, a menu listing of items can be prepared to ensure that only items that stay within these predetermined ranges are offered for sale.

Regardless of the buffet items to be sold, their usage must be accurately recorded. Consider the situation of Mei, the manager of Lotus Gardens, a Chinese restaurant where patrons pay one price but may return as often as they like to a buffet line. Mei finds that a form like the one presented in Figure 6.7 is helpful in recording both product usage and guests served. Note that Mei uses the ABC method to determine her menu items. She does so because total food costs on a buffet line or salad bar are a function of both how much is eaten and what is eaten. She also notes the amount of product she puts on the buffet to begin the dinner meal period (Beginning Amount), any additions during the meal period (Additions), and the amount of usable product left at the conclusion of the meal period (Ending Amount). From this information, Mei can compute her total product usage and, thus, her total product cost.

Based on the data in Figure 6.7, Mei knows that her total product cost for dinner on January 1 was $305.28. She can then use the following formula to determine her buffet product cost per guest:

$$\frac{\text{Total Buffet Product Cost}}{\text{Guests Served}} = \text{Buffet Product Cost per Guest}$$

or

$$\frac{\$305.28}{125} = \$2.44$$

Thus, on her buffet, Mei had a portion cost (plate cost) per guest of $2.44. She can use this information to establish a menu price that she feels is appropriate.

■ **FIGURE 6.7** Salad Bar or Buffet Product Usage

Unit Name: <u>Lotus Gardens</u>   Date: <u>1/1 (Dinner)</u>

Item	Category	Beginning Amount	Additions	Ending Amount	Total Usage	Unit Cost	Total Cost
Sweet and Sour Pork	A	6 lb.	44 lb.	13 lb.	37 lb.	$4.40/lb.	$162.80
Bean Sprouts	B	3 lb.	17 lb.	2 lb.	18 lb.	1.60/lb.	28.80
Egg Rolls	B	40 each	85 each	17 each	108 each	0.56 each	60.48
Fried Rice	C	10 lb.	21.5 lb.	8.5 lb.	23 lb.	0.60/lb.	13.80
Steamed Rice	C	10 lb.	30 lb.	6.5 lb.	33.5 lb.	0.40/lb.	13.40
Wonton Soup	C	2 gal.	6 gal.	1.5 gal.	6.5 gal.	4.00/gal.	26.00
Total Product Cost							305.28

Total Product Cost: <u>$305.28</u>

Guests Served: <u>125</u>   Cost per Guest (plate cost): <u>$2.44</u>

Assume, for example, that Mei uses the food cost percentage approach to establishing menu price and that she has determined a 25% food cost to be her goal. Using the pricing factor table in Figure 6.6, Mei would use the following formula to establish her per-person buffet price:

$$\$2.44 \text{ (Per Person Cost)} \times 4.00 \text{ (Pricing Factor)} = \$9.76$$

For marketing purposes, and to ensure her desired food cost percentage, Mei may well round her buffet selling price up to, say, $9.99 per person. The significant point to remember here is that the amount consumed by any individual guest is relatively unimportant. It is the consumption of the average, or typical, guest that is used to establish menu price.

It is to be expected that Mei's buffet product cost per guest will vary somewhat each day. This is not a cause for great concern. Minor variations in product cost per guest should be covered if selling price is properly established. By monitoring buffet costs on a regular basis, you can be assured that you can keep good control over both costs per guest and your most appropriate selling price.

■ BOTTLED WINE

Few areas of menu pricing create more controversy than that of pricing wines by the bottle. The reason for this may be the incredible variance in cost among different **vintages,** or years of production, as well as the quality of alternative wine offerings. If your foodservice operation will sell wine by the bottle, it is likely that you will have some wine products that appeal to value-oriented guests and other, higher priced wines that are preferred by guests seeking these superior wines. An additional element that affects wine pricing is the fact that many wines that are sold by the bottle in restaurants are also sold in retail grocery or liquor stores. Thus, guests have a good idea of what a similar bottle of wine would cost them if it were purchased in either of these locations. How you decide to price the bottled-wine offerings on your own menu will definitely affect your guest's perception of the price/value relationship offered by your operation.

Properly pricing wine by the bottle calls for skill and insight. Consider the case of Claudia, who owns and manages a fine-dining Armenian restaurant. Using the product cost percentage method of pricing, Claudia attempts to achieve an overall wine product cost in her restaurant of 25%. Thus, when pricing her wines and using the pricing factor table in Figure 6.6, Claudia multiplies the cost of each bottled wine she sells by four to arrive at her desired selling price. Following are the four wines she sells and the costs and prices associated with each type:

Wine	Product Cost	Selling Price	Product Cost %
1	$ 4.00	$16.00	25%
2	6.00	24.00	25%
3	15.00	60.00	25%
4	20.00	80.00	25%

Claudia decides that she would like to explore the contribution margin approach to wine pricing. She therefore computes the contribution margin (Selling Price − Product Cost = Contribution Margin) for each wine she sells and finds the following results:

Wine	Selling Price	Product Cost	Contribution Margin
1	$16.00	$ 4.00	$12.00
2	24.00	6.00	18.00
3	60.00	15.00	45.00
4	80.00	20.00	60.00

Her conclusion, after evaluating the contribution margin approach to pricing and what she believes to be her customers' perception of the price/value relationship she offers, is that she may be hurting sales of wines 3 and 4 by pricing these products too high, even though they are currently priced to achieve the same 25% product cost as wines 1 and 2. In the case of bottled wine, the contribution margin approach to price can often be used to your advantage. Guests are often quite price conscious when it comes to bottled wine. When operators seek to achieve profits guests feel are inappropriate, bottled-wine sales may decline. Following is an alternative pricing structure that Claudia has developed for use in her restaurant. She must, however, give this price structure a test run and monitor its effect on overall product sales and profitability if she is to determine whether the pricing strategy will be effective.

Wine	Product Cost	Selling Price	Contribution Margin	Product Cost %
1	$ 4.00	$19.00	$15.00	21.1%
2	6.00	22.00	16.00	27.3%
3	15.00	33.00	18.00	45.5%
4	20.00	39.00	19.00	51.3%

Note that, although selling price has been increased in the case of wine 1, it has been reduced for wines 2, 3, and 4. Contribution margin still is higher for wine 4 than for wine 1. The difference, however, is not as dramatic as before. Product cost percentages have, of course, been altered due to the price changes Claudia is proposing. Note also that the **price spread,** defined as the range between the lowest and the highest priced menu item, has been drastically reduced. Whereas the price spread was previously $16.00 to $80.00, it is now $19.00 to $39.00. This reduction in price spread may assist Claudia in selling more of the higher-priced wine because her guests may be more comfortable with the price/value relationship perceived under this new pricing approach. It is important to remember, however, that Claudia must monitor sales and determine if her new strategy is successful. In general, it may be stated that pricing bottled wine only by the product percentage method is a strategy that may result in overall decreased bottled-wine sales. In this specific pricing situation, the best approach to establishing selling price calls for you to evaluate both your product cost percentage and your contribution margin.

■ BEVERAGES AT RECEPTIONS AND PARTIES

Pricing beverages for open-bar receptions and special events can be very difficult, and the reason for this is very simple. Each consumer group can be expected to behave somewhat differently when attending an open-bar or hosted-bar function. Clearly, we would not expect the guests at a formal political fund-raising cocktail reception to consume as many drinks during a one-hour reception as a group of fun-loving individuals celebrating a favorite team's victory in a championship game.

Establishing a price per person in these two situations may well result in quite different numbers. One way to solve this problem is to charge each of the guests for what they actually consume. In reality, however, many party hosts want their guests to consume beverage products without having to pay for each drink. When this is the case, you could elect to charge the host on a per-drink-consumed basis, or charge on a per-person (served), per-hour basis. When charging on a per-person, per-hour basis, you must have a good idea of how much the average attendee will consume during the length of the party or reception so that an appropriate price can be established.

For example, assume that you are the food and beverage director at the Carlton, a luxury hotel. Ms. Swan, a potential food and beverage guest, approaches you with the idea of providing a one-hour champagne reception for 100 guests prior to an important dinner that she is considering booking at your facility. The guest would like all of the attendees to drink as much champagne during the reception as they care to. Ms. Swan's specific question is: "How much will I be charged for the reception if 100 guests attend?" Clearly, an answer of "I don't know" or "It depends on how much they drink" is inappropriate. It is, of course, your business to know the answer to such questions, and you can know. If you are aware from past events and records you have kept on such events of what the average consumption for a group of this type has been previously, you can establish an appropriate price. To do so, records for this purpose must be maintained.

Figure 6.8 is an example of one such device that can be used. Note that average consumption of any product type can be recorded. In this example, assume that you had recently recorded the data from the Gulley wedding, an event very similar to the one requested by Ms. Swan. In this case, a wedding reception, which also requested champagne, was held for 97 guests. The product cost per guest for that event, based on your records in Figure 6.8, equaled $3.37.

Based on what you know about the drinking pattern of a similar group, you could use either the product cost percentage method or the contribution margin pricing method to establish your reception price. For purpose of illustration, assume that you used the product contribution margin approach to pricing alcoholic beverage receptions. Further assume that the contribution margin desired per person served is $15.00. The computation of selling price using the contribution margin formula is as follows:

Product Cost + Desired Contribution Margin = Selling Price

In this example:

$ 3.37	(Per-Person Product Cost)
+ $15.00	(Desired Contribution Margin)
= $18.37	Selling Price Per Person

Armed with this historical information, as well as that from other similar events, you are well prepared to answer Ms. Swan's question: "How much will I be charged for the reception if 100 guests attend?"

■ **FIGURE 6.8** Beverage Consumption Report

Event: <u>Gulley Wedding</u>   Date: <u>1/1</u>

Unit Name: <u>The Carlton Hotel</u>

Beverage Type	Beginning Amount	Additions	Ending Amount	Total Usage	Unit Cost	Total Cost
Liquor A						
B						
C						
D						
E						
F						
G						
Beer A						
B						
C						
D						
E						
Wine A						
B						
C						
D						
Other: Champagne: A. Sparkling	8 bottles	24	9	23	6.00/btl.	$138.00
B. Sparkling Pink	8 bottles	24	11	21	9.00/btl.	$189.00
Total Product Cost						327.00

Total Product Cost: <u>$327.00</u>

Guests Served: <u>97</u>   Cost per Guest: <u>$3.37</u>

Remarks: <u>Mild group; very orderly; no problems.</u>

Establishing product costs and then assigning reasonable menu prices based on these costs is a major component of your job as a foodservice manager. You must be able to perform this task well. Increasingly, however, the cost of labor, rather than the cost of products, has occupied a significant portion of the typical foodservice manager's cost control efforts. In fact, in some foodservice facilities, the costs of labor and employee benefits provided exceed that of the food and beverage products sold. Because this area of cost control is so important, in the next chapter we turn our attention to the unique set of skills and knowledge you must acquire to adequately manage and control your labor costs.

Technology Tools

In this chapter you learned about the menu formats you most often encounter as a hospitality manager, as well as the factors affecting menu prices and the procedures used to assign individual menu item prices based on cost and sales data. The mathematical computations required to evaluate the effectiveness of individual menu items and to establish their prices can be complex, but there are a wide range of software products available that can help you to do the following:

1. Develop menus and cost recipes.
2. Design and print menu "specials" for meal periods or happy hours.
3. Compute and analyze item contribution margin.
4. Compute and analyze item and overall food cost percentage.
5. Price banquet menus and bars based on known product costs.
6. Evaluate the profitability of individual menu items.
7. Estimate future item demand based on past purchase patterns.
8. Assign individual menu item prices based on management-supplied parameters.

Menu analysis and pricing software is often packaged as part of a larger software program. Its importance, however, is great. It is an area that will continue to see rapid development in the future as software makers seek additional ways to improve their products.

FUN ON THE WEB!

Advances in menu management software continue to occur rapidly. Increasingly, restaurateurs are looking for programs that will give them many options to choose from when designing their own sales tracking (and pricing) processes. The Point Of Success (POS) company is one such maker of advanced software programs designed specifically for the food service industry. You can visit its Web site at www.pointofsuccess.com, where you will be able to compare the features of the "Standard" and "Premium" Point of Success (POS) software programs. Which would you choose?

Apply What You Have Learned

Dominic Carbonne owns Hungry Henry's pizza, a four-unit chain of take-out pizza shops in a city of 60,000 people (with an additional 25,000 college students attending the local state university). Recently, a new chain of pizza restaurants has opened in town. The products sold by this new chain have lesser quality and use lesser quantity of ingredients (cheese, meat, and vegetable toppings, etc.), and are also priced 25% less than Hungry Henry's equivalent size. Dominic has seen his business decline somewhat since the new chain opened. This is especially true with the college students.

1. How would you evaluate the new competitor's pricing strategy?

2. What steps would you advise Dominic to take to counter this competitor?

3. Describe three specific strategies restaurants can use to communicate "quality, rather than low price," to potential guests.

Key Terms and Concepts

The following are terms and concepts discussed in the chapter that are important for you as a manager. To help you review, please define the terms below:

Tip-on (menu)	Revenue versus price	Contribution margin
Standard menu	Price/value	Value pricing
Daily menu	relationship	Bundling
Cycle menu	Price blending	Vintage
Menu specials	Plate cost	Price spread

Test Your Skills

Complete the Test Your Skills exercises by placing your answers in the shaded boxes and answering the questions as indicated.

1. Bill owns Bill's Burger Barn, and he is dissatisfied with his consistently high food cost percentage. In an effort to drop his food cost % below 35%, he has decided to incorporate price blending into his pricing strategy. He has developed three combo items, and he wants to find out if his food cost % has been lowered after the first week of sales. Help Bill calculate the food cost % for his combo items.

Bill's Burger Barn Combo

Item	Number Sold	Item Cost	Total Cost	Selling Price	Total Sales	Food Cost %
Hamburger	200	$1.50		$3.49		
French Fries (large)	185	0.40		1.60		
Soft Drink (16 oz.)	190	0.20		1.35		
Total						

Bill's Bacon Cheeseburger Combo

Item	Number Sold	Item Cost	Total Cost	Selling Price	Total Sales	Food Cost %
Bacon Cheeseburger	160	$1.65		$4.29		
Onion Rings	135	0.30		1.40		
Soft Drink (16 oz.)	155	0.20		1.35		
Total						

Bill's Chicken Sandwich Combo

Item	Number Sold	Item Cost	Total Cost	Selling Price	Total Sales	Food Cost %
Chicken Sandwich	75	$1.10		$3.15		
French Fries (large)	75	0.40		1.60		
Soft Drink (16 oz.)	75	0.20		1.35		
Total						

Should Bill continue with this pricing strategy?

2. Tonekwa has priced her menu items using the product cost percentage method in the past. She has asked her evening shift manager to price new menu items, and she believes that he will feel more comfortable using the factor method to price the new items. Help Tonekwa convert her desired product cost percentages to factors. (Spreadsheet hint: Use the ROUND function for the "Factor" column to three decimal places.)

Pricing Factor Table	
Desired Product Cost %	Factor
18%	
21%	
22%	
24%	
26%	
31%	
32%	
36%	
37%	
41%	
42%	
44%	
46%	

3. Bess and David own two small diners in a midsize city in Oklahoma. Bess has primary responsibility for the diner in the suburbs, and David has primary responsibility for the diner in the inner city. The menu items and product costs are the same in both diners, but the market in the inner city demands lower menu prices than that in the suburbs. So Bess has set her desired product cost percentage at 40%, and David's desired product cost percentage is 42% because he can't charge as much as Bess. Bess likes to use the product cost percentage method to price menu items, and David likes to use the factor method. Help both of them determine their selling prices. (Spreadsheet hint: Use the ROUND function for "Factor" column to three decimal places.)

Bess and David's Diner–Suburbs (Bess)

Desired Product Cost Percentage: 40%

Product Cost Percentage

Item	Cost of Product	Desired Product Cost Percentage	Selling Price
Chicken Breast Dinner	$2.25		
Seafood Platter	3.45		
Steak Dinner	4.99		
Turkey Sandwich	1.25		
Pork Chop	2.45		
Hamburger	1.50		
Cheeseburger	1.75		
Fries	0.45		
Meat Loaf	1.25		
Small Drink	0.35		

Bess and David's Diner–Inner City (David)

Desired Product Cost Percentage: 42%

Factor Method

Item	Cost of Product	Factor	Selling Price
Chicken Breast Dinner	$2.25		
Seafood Platter	3.45		
Steak Dinner	4.99		
Turkey Sandwich	1.25		
Pork Chop	2.45		
Hamburger	1.50		
Cheeseburger	1.75		
Fries	0.45		
Meat Loaf	1.25		
Small Drink	0.35		

4. Frankie Marie owns Frankie's Cafeteria in a small southern town. She has decided to price her menu items using the contribution margin method. She has determined the following contribution margins for her food categories:

Contribution Margins

Salad: $1.20
Entrées: $4.25
Desserts: $1.50
Drinks: $1.10

Help her price her menu items.

Contribution Margin Approach			
Item	Product Cost	Desired Contribution Margin	Selling Price
Salads			
Dinner Salad	$0.30		
Macaroni Salad	$0.55		
Potato Salad	$0.65		
Carrot and Raisin Salad	$0.40		
Bavarian Salad	$0.60		
Entrées			
Liver and Onions	$2.50		
Steak Kabob	$2.75		
Meatloaf	$2.85		
Chicken Fried Steak	$2.10		
Fried Catfish	$2.35		
Chicken Casserole	$2.25		
Turkey and Dressing	$2.55		
Desserts			
Chocolate Cream Pie	$0.75		
Coconut Cream Pie	$0.75		
Pecan Pie	$1.25		
Chocolate Cake	$0.60		
Pudding	$0.20		
Jello	$0.20		
Carrot Cake	$0.70		
Drinks			
Coffee	$0.15		
Tea	$0.15		
Soft Drink	$0.15		

5. Gabriel Hinojosa owns Gabriel's Tex-Mex Restaurant, an extremely popular, 250-seat establishment in a large California city. Gabriel has decided to offer a 4-hour Sunday brunch buffet for his guests because he thinks he can achieve a guest count of 625 ($2^1/_2$ turns). Last Sunday, June 1, he offered the buffet for the first time, and he charged $12.00 per guest. However, he only served 400 people. He thinks that maybe he could attract more guests if he offered the buffet at a lower price. He collected information on last Sunday's buffet product usage, and he used the ABC method to put his menu items into categories. His desired food cost percentage is 40%. Help him complete the buffet product usage report. (Spreadsheet hint: Use the ROUND function for "Cost per Guest" and "Desired Selling Price Based on Cost" to two decimal places.)

   After completing this analysis, what should be Gabriel's selling price? If he uses this new selling price and he serves 625 guests next Sunday, June 8, will his total revenue increase? If so, how much?

Buffet Product Usage (Sunday, June 1): Gabriel's Tex-Mex Restaurant

Item	Category	Unit	Beginning Amount	Additions	Ending Amount	Total Usage	Unit Cost	Total Cost
Steak Fajitas	A	lb.	20	60	6	74	$4.50	$ 333.00
Chicken Fajitas	A	lb.	15	70	10	75	4.00	300.00
Carne Asada	A	lb.	10	50	4	56	4.25	238.00
Cheese Enchiladas	B	lb.	2	80	15	67	2.00	134.00
Beef Enchiladas	B	lb.	3	60	10	53	2.50	132.50
Enchiladas Verde	B	lb.	1	70	8	63	2.00	126.00
Chili Rellenos	B	lb.	10	45	5	50	2.75	137.50
Tacos	C	each	0	150	20	130	0.30	39.00
Bean Chalupas	C	each	0	175	5	170	0.25	42.50
Tortilla Soup	C	gal.	2	10	4	8	0.30	2.40
Spanish Rice	C	lb.	5	70	12	63	0.20	12.60
Refried Beans	C	lb.	15	75	6	84	0.20	16.80
Sopapillas	C	each	25	200	30	195	0.15	29.25
Total Product Cost								$1,543.55

Guests Served: 400

Total Product Cost: $1,543.55

Cost Per Guest: $3.86

Desired Food Cost %: 40%

Desired Selling Price Based on Cost: $9.65

Revenues, June 1: $4,800.00 ———— Projected Revenues, June 8: $6,031.25 ———— Difference: $1,231.25

271

6. JoAnna is the foodservice director at Reading Hospital. She has just started a new menu program to offer guests visiting hospitalized patients "guest trays" so the patients and their guests can eat together. She has been offering her guest-tray program for one month, and it has been popular. She would like to know her average selling price per guest (check average) to see if she needs to change the price of her menu items. She would like to keep her average selling price above $11.50. Given the following information, and the fact that JoAnna has determined that she should achieve an $8.00 per guest tray contribution margin, calculate her average selling price for the month.

Menu Item	Number Sold	Product Cost	Contribution Margin	Selling Price	Total Sales
Hunter's Chicken	2,560	$3.50			
Jambalaya	750			$11.75	
Grilled Salmon	1,200	$4.50			
Beef Tenderloin	500			$16.50	
Vegetarian Cheese Bake	1,210	$2.75			
Total					

Average Selling
Price _____

Did JoAnna achieve her desired average selling price per guest? Does she need to change her prices?

7. Ming has recently inherited the Quick Wok restaurant started by her parents. It is located in a busy strip shopping area surrounded by many office complexes, but it is also near many quick-service restaurants. The Quick Wok has been successful because of the quality of its food, but Ming feels that it could do even better at lunchtime if she could create a "Value Meal" option to appeal to the price conscious consumer. Because both a McDonald's and a Wendy's are within a quarter-mile of her store, she has determined that her own Value Meal menu item needs to be priced at $1.00. She creates a stir-fry dish that, when served with white rice, has a portion cost of 65 cents. Her beverages have a cost of 20 cents. The beverages already sell for $1.00 each, and she does not want to raise this price.

She believes she could sell 75 of the new Value Meals per day if she offers the stir-fry dish at $1.00. As well, she seeks an overall product cost percentage of 35%. From historical data she knows that 80% of her customers purchase a drink with their meals.

Based on the information given, calculate the overall product cost percentage of the Value Meals and beverages. Would you advise Ming to "go for it"? Why or why not?

Value Meal and Beverage						
Item	Number Sold	Item Cost	Total Cost	Selling Price	Total Sales	Food Cost %
Stir Fry Dish	75					
Beverage						
Total						

How many beverages must be sold in addition to the Value Meals if Ming is to achieve her target food cost percentage goal? Is this number feasible? Spreadsheet hint: You will have to arrive at the number sold of beverages by trial and error. Specifically, start with 60 and increase or decrease the number until you reach a Total Food Cost % of 35%. This Test Your Skills problem is designed to show you how changes in the number of items (beverages) sold affect total food cost %.

Number of Beverages to Achieve Target Overall Product Cost Percentage						
Item	Number Sold	Item Cost	Total Cost	Selling Price	Total Sales	Food Cost %
Stir Fry Dish	75					
Beverage						
Total						

8. Jackson Daniels is the director of food and beverage at the Foxfire Country Club. In June, Jackson's club hosted three weddings. Each wedding featured a 4-hour hosted bar paid for by the bride and groom. The consumption data from each event is listed below. Complete the missing data in the report, and then help Jackson answer the questions that follow:

	Number of Guests Served	Beer Cost	Wine Cost	Spirit Cost	Total Cost	Cost per Guest
June 07	250	$500	$400	$600		
June 14		650	1,225		2,875	5.75
June 21	400	525	1,000	675		
Total						

a. What do you think should be Jackson's "best estimate" of the cost to the Club of providing a 4-hour hosted bar at weddings?

b. If Jackson seeks to ensure a 20% beverage cost, what should be his selling price, per guest, for a 4-hour hosted bar?

c. Would you recommend Jackson charge half of the amount in the answer in part b. for a 2-hour hosted bar? Explain your answer.

9. One criticism of both the food cost percentage and contribution margin methods of determining menu price is that both are based primarily on the cost of "food" and ignore the cost of labor. In many foodservice operations, however, the cost of labor equals or even exceeds the cost of food. Do you foresee the cost of labor playing an increasing role in the calculation of menu prices? Explain your answer.

Chapter 7

MANAGING THE COST OF LABOR

OVERVIEW

This chapter details the techniques used to control costs by establishing and monitoring labor cost standards. The factors that affect labor productivity, as well as methods for improving labor productivity, are presented. This chapter teaches you how to schedule employees based on established labor standards, and how to compute a labor cost percentage and other commonly used measures of labor productivity.

Chapter Outline

LEARNING OUTCOMES

At the conclusion of this chapter, you will be able to:
- Identify the factors that affect employee productivity.
- Develop labor standards and employee schedules used in a foodservice operation.
- Analyze and evaluate actual labor utilization.

LABOR EXPENSE IN THE HOSPITALITY INDUSTRY

*H*aving the correct amount of food and beverage products on hand to serve your guests is important. Knowing how those products should be prepared is vital also. Consider the case of Pauline. She manages the cafeteria of a large urban hospital. Both hospital staff and patients' visitors, who constitute the majority of her guests, have good things to say about the quality of her food. They complain often, however, about the slowness of her cafeteria line, the dirty tables during the busy lunch hour, and the frequent running out of items at the salad bars. Pauline often feels that she needs more employees. She knows, however, that her current staff is actually larger than it was a few years ago. Of course, she also serves more guests each day. Her question is "Do I have the right number of employees scheduled at the right times for the number of guests I anticipate today?" Unfortunately, Pauline is so busy "helping" her employees get through the meal periods that there seems to be little time for thinking about and planning the strategies and techniques she needs to apply if she is to solve her labor-related customer service problems.

In years past, when labor was relatively inexpensive, Pauline might have responded to her need for more workers by simply hiring more employees. Today's foodservice manager, however, does not have that luxury. In the current tight and increasingly costly labor market, you must learn the supervisory skills needed to maximize the effectiveness of your staff and the cost control skills required to evaluate their effort.

In some foodservice establishments, the cost of labor actually exceeds the cost of food and beverage products. Today's competitive labor market indicates that, in the future, foodservice managers will find it even more difficult to recruit, train, and retain an effective team of employees. Therefore, the control of labor expenses takes on a greater level of importance than ever before. In some sectors of the foodservice industry, a reputation for long hours, poor pay, and undesirable working conditions has caused quality employees to look elsewhere for a more satisfactory job or career. It does not have to be that way, and it is up to you to help ensure that in your organization it is not. When labor costs are adequately controlled, management has the funds necessary to create desirable working conditions and pay a wage that will attract the very best employees. In every service industry, better employees mean better guest service and, ultimately, better profits.

■ LABOR EXPENSE DEFINED

Payroll is the term generally used to refer to the salaries and wages you pay your employees. **Labor expense** includes salaries and wages, but it also includes other labor-related costs such as the following:

1. FICA (Social Security) taxes, including taxes due on employees' tip income
2. FUTA (Federal unemployment taxes) and state unemployment taxes
3. Workers' compensation
4. Group life insurance
5. Health insurance, including:
   Medical
   Dental
   Vision
   Disability
6. Pension/retirement plan payments
7. Employee meals
8. Employee training expenses
9. Employee transportation
10. Employee uniforms, housing, and other benefits
11. Vacation/sick leave/personal days
12. Tuition reimbursement programs
13. Employee incentives and bonuses

Not all operations will incur all of the costs listed. Some operations will have additional labor costs. You can be sure, however, that regardless of the facility you manage, you will incur some labor-related expenses in addition to wages and salaries (payroll costs). The critical question you must answer is, "How much should I spend on payroll and labor expense to deliver the quality of products and service that I feel is appropriate?" Before you can hope to answer that question, it is important that you fully understand the individual components that make up payroll and labor expense.

■ PAYROLL

Payroll refers to the gross pay received by an employee in exchange for his or her work. That is, if an employee earns $10.00 per hour and works 40 hours for his or her employer, the gross paycheck (the employee's paycheck before any mandatory or voluntary deductions) would be $400 ($10.00 per hour × 40 hours = $400). This amount is considered a payroll expense.

If the employee earns a salary, that salary amount is also a payroll expense. A **salaried employee** generally receives the same income per week or month regardless of the number of hours worked. Thus, if a salaried employee is paid $700 per week when he or she works a complete week, we consider that $700 to be part of the payroll expense. Salaried employees are actually more accurately described as **exempt employees** because their duties, responsibilities, and level of decisions make them "exempt" from the overtime provisions of the federal government's Fair

Labor Standards Act (FLSA). Exempt employees do not receive overtime for hours worked in excess of 40 per week and are expected by most organizations to work whatever hours are necessary to accomplish its goals.

FUN ON THE WEB!

Designation of employees who can (and who cannot) be considered to be exempt employees is governed by the U.S. Department of Labor and the Fair Labor Standards Act (FSLA). Minimum allowable salary levels are also determined by this department. To learn more about exempt employees, go to: **www.dol.gov** and click "Wages."

FIXED PAYROLL VERSUS VARIABLE PAYROLL

When you manage a foodservice facility, you must make choices regarding the number and type of employee you will hire to help you serve your guests. Some employees are needed simply to open the doors for the minimally anticipated business. **Minimum staff** is used to describe the least number of employees, or payroll dollars, needed to operate a facility or department within the facility. For example, this may include one manager, one server, and one cook. The cost of providing payroll to these three individuals is called a minimum-staff payroll.

Suppose, however, that you anticipate much greater volume on a given day. The increased number of guests expected means that you must have more cooks, more servers, added cashiers, more dish room personnel, and, perhaps, more supervisors to handle the additional workload. Clearly, these additional staff positions create a work group that is far larger than the minimum staff but is of a size that you feel is needed to adequately service the anticipated number of guests.

Some managers confuse the minimum-staff concept with that of fixed payroll and variable payroll. **Fixed payroll** refers to the amount an operation pays in salaries. This amount, in most cases, is fixed because it remains unchanged from one pay period to the next unless the individual receiving the pay separates employment from the organization. **Variable payroll** consists of those dollars paid to hourly employees. Thus, variable payroll is the amount that "varies" with changes in sales volume. Generally, as you anticipate increased volume levels in your facility, you may need to add additional hourly and, sometimes, salaried employees. The distinction between fixed and variable labor is an important one; you may have little control over your fixed labor expense, whereas you may have nearly 100% control over the variable labor expenses that are above your minimum-staff levels.

■ LABOR EXPENSE

Labor expense refers to the total of all costs associated with maintaining your workforce. As such, labor expense is always larger than payroll expense. As the cost of providing employee benefits increases or employment taxes go up, labor expense will increase, even if payroll expense remains constant.

Most foodservice operators have total control over their payroll expense. It is, therefore, often referred to as a "controllable" labor expense. Other labor expenses, over which an operator has little or no control, are called "noncontrollable" labor expenses. These expenses include items such as federal- or state-mandated payroll-related taxes, insurance premiums, and mandatory retirement plan payments. In reality, however, you can exert some control over these noncontrollable labor expenses, such as a foodservice manager who works very hard to ensure a well-trained workforce in a safe environment and achieves, thereby, a lower rate on workers' compensation, accident, and health insurance for his or her employees.

In this chapter, we deal primarily with payroll-related expenses. This is in keeping with the concept that these are the most controllable of labor-related expenses, and the ones most managers will evaluate when they are called upon to control labor expenses.

To determine how much labor is needed to operate your business, you must be able to determine how much work each employee can perform. If too few employees are scheduled to work, poor service and reduced sales can result, because guests may go elsewhere. If too many employees are scheduled, payroll and other labor expenses will be too high, resulting in reduced profits. The best solution to this challenge is to know how many employees are needed given the estimated number of guests you will serve. To determine this number of employees, you must have a clear idea of the productivity of each of your employees. Simply put, **productivity** is the amount of work performed by an employee in a fixed period of time.

EVALUATING LABOR PRODUCTIVITY

*T*here are many ways to assess labor productivity. In general, productivity is measured in terms of the **productivity ratio** as follows:

$$\frac{\text{Output}}{\text{Input}} = \text{Productivity Ratio}$$

To illustrate, assume a restaurant employs 4 servers to serve 60 guests. Using the productivity ratio formula, the output is guests served, the input is servers employed, as follows:

$$\frac{60 \text{ Guests}}{4 \text{ Servers}} = 15 \text{ Guests per Server}$$

This formula demonstrates that, for each server employed, 15 guests can be served. The productivity ratio is 1 server per 15 guests (1/15) or, stated another way, 15 guests to 1 server (15 to 1).

There are several ways of defining foodservice output and input; thus, there are several types of productivity ratios. Some of these are presented later in this chapter. All of these productivity ratios can be helpful in determining the answer to the key question, "How much should I spend on labor?" The answer, however, is even more complicated than it might seem at first. In the preceding example, you know that, on average, 1 server can serve 15 guests. But how many guests will a slow server serve? How about your best server? How much do you pay our most productive server? Your least productive? Are you better off scheduling your best server if you anticipate 20 guests or should you schedule two of your slower servers? How can you help the slower server become an above-average server? At what cost? These are the types of questions that must be answered daily if you are to effectively manage payroll costs, and they can be managed. Foodservice operators must develop their own methods for managing payroll because every foodservice unit is different. Consider the differences between managing payroll costs at a small, quick-service food kiosk in a shopping mall and a large banquet kitchen in a 1,000-room convention hotel. Although the actual methods may vary, it is always true that payroll costs can and should be managed.

MAINTAINING A PRODUCTIVE WORKFORCE

*B*efore we discuss how to establish and use productivity ratios, it is important to understand the factors that make employees more productive and, thus, directly affect productivity. The following are ten key employee-related factors that affect employee productivity:

Ten Key Factors Affecting Employee Productivity

1. Employee selection
2. Training
3. Supervision
4. Scheduling
5. Breaks
6. Morale
7. Menu
8. Convenience versus scratch preparation
9. Equipment/tools
10. Service level desired

■ EMPLOYEE SELECTION

Choosing the right employee from the beginning is vitally important in developing a highly productive workforce. Good foodservice managers know that proper selection procedures go a long way toward establishing the kind of workforce that can be both efficient and effective. This involves matching the right employee with the right job. The process begins with the development of the job description.

JOB DESCRIPTION

A **job description** is a listing of the tasks that must be accomplished by the employee hired to fill a particular position. For example, in the case of a room service delivery person in a large hotel, the tasks might be listed as indicated on the job description shown in Figure 7.1. A job description should be maintained for every position in the foodservice operation. From the job description, a job specification can be prepared.

■ **FIGURE 7.1** Job Description

Job Description

Unit Name: Thunder Lodge Resort   **Position Title: Room Service Delivery Person**

PRIME TASKS:

1. Answer telephone and monitor online site to receive guest orders

2. Set up room service trays in steward area

3. Deliver trays to room, as requested

4. Remove tray covers upon delivery

5. Remove soiled trays from floors

6. Maintain guest check control

7. Balance room service cash drawer

8. Clean room service setup area at conclusion of shift

9. Other duties, as assigned by supervisor

10.

11.

12.

Special Comments: Hourly rate excludes tips. Uniform allowance is $45.00 per week

Salary Range: $9.00–$11.25/hour   Signature: Matt V.

■ **FIGURE 7.2** Job Specification

Job Specification

Unit Name: Thunder Lodge Resort   Position Title: Room Service Delivery Person

Personal Characteristics Required:

1. Good telephone skills; speaks clearly, easily understood English

2. Ability to operate point of sale (POS) systems

3. Detail oriented

4. Pleasant personality

5. Discreet

Special Comments: Good grooming habits are especially important in this position as employee will be a primary guest contact person.

Job Specification Prepared By: Matt V.

JOB SPECIFICATION

A **job specification** is a listing of the personal characteristics needed to perform the tasks contained in a particular job description. Figure 7.2 shows the job specification that would match the job description in Figure 7.1.

As can be seen, this position requires a specific set of personal characteristics and skills. When a room service delivery person is hired, the job specification requirements must be foremost in management's mind. If the job specs do not exist or are not followed, it is likely that employees may be hired who are simply not able to be highly productive. Each employee must bring either the skills necessary to do the job or the ability to acquire those skills. It is your role to develop and maintain both job descriptions and job specifications so that employees know what their jobs are and so that you know the characteristics that your employees must have, or be trained in, to do their jobs well. When actually beginning to select employees for your vacancies, you will likely use one or more of the following selection aids:

1. Applications
2. Interviews
3. Preemployment testing
4. Background/reference checks

APPLICATIONS

The employment application is a document completed by the candidate for employment. It will generally list the name, address, work experience, and related information of the candidate. It is important that each employment candidate for a given position be required to fill out in person, or online, an identical application, and that an application be on file for each candidate who is ultimately selected for the position.

INTERVIEWS

From the employment applications submitted, you will select some candidates for the interview process. It is important to realize that the types of questions that can be asked in the interview are highly regulated. As a result, job interviews, if improperly performed, can subject an employer to significant legal liability. If a candidate is not hired based on his or her answer to—or refusal to answer—an inappropriate question, that candidate has the right to file a lawsuit. What questions can and cannot be asked? The Equal Employment Opportunity Commission suggests that all employers consider the following three questions in deciding whether to include a particular question on an employment application or in a job interview:

1. Does this question tend to screen out minorities or females?
2. Is the answer needed to judge this individual's competence for performance of the job?
3. Are there alternative, nondiscriminatory ways to judge the person's qualifications?

In all cases, questions asked both on the application and in the interview should focus on the applicant's job skills and nothing else.

PREEMPLOYMENT TESTING

Preemployment testing is a common way to help improve employee productivity. In the hospitality industry, preemployment testing will generally fall into one of the following categories:

1. Skills tests
2. Psychological tests
3. Drug screening tests

Skills tests can include activities such as drink production for bartenders, computer application tests for those involved in using word processing or spreadsheet tools, or food production tasks for cooks and chefs. **Psychological testing** can include personality tests, tests designed to predict performance, or tests of mental ability.

Preemployment drug testing is used to determine if an applicant uses drugs. Such testing is allowable in most states, and it can be a very effective tool for reducing insurance rates and potential employee liability issues. It is permissible to ask an applicant if he or she uses drugs. It is also allowable to ask candidates if they are willing to submit to a voluntary drug test as a condition of employment. Of course, potential employees have a right to refuse to submit to a drug screening test, just as you have a right to insist that all prospective employees submit to such a test. The important point to remember is that, if you are using drug screening, it must be used on all employees and not just those you may suspect of drug use. To selectively, rather than uniformly, require drug screening could place you and your organization in legal jeopardy if you were subject to charges of discrimination.

A drug-free workplace tends to attract better-quality employment candidates, with the resulting impact of a higher-quality workforce and greater productivity. Most hospitality companies find that drug testing as a preemployment screening device not only boosts employee productivity but reduces job-related accidents as well.

BACKGROUND/REFERENCE CHECKS

Increasingly, hospitality employers are utilizing background checks prior to hiring employees in selected positions. Common verification points include the following:

- Name
- Social Security number
- Address history
- Dates of past employment and duties performed
- Education/training
- Criminal background
- Credit history

Background checks, like preemployment testing, can leave an employer subject to litigation if the information secured during a check is false or is used in a way that violates employment law. In addition, if the information is improperly disclosed to third parties, it could violate the employee's right to privacy. Not conducting background checks on some positions can, however, subject the employer to potential litigation under the doctrine of **negligent hiring**, that is, a failure on the part of an employer to exercise reasonable care in the selection of employees. When background checks are performed, a candidate for employment should be required to sign a consent form authorizing you to conduct the background check.

In the past, employment references were a very popular tool for managers to use in the screening process. In today's litigious society, however, accurate ones are much more difficult to obtain. Although many organizations still seek information from past employers about an employee's previous work performance, few sophisticated companies will divulge such information. To help minimize the risk of litigation related to reference checks, it is best to secure the applicant's permission in writing before contacting an ex-employer. Even with such authorization, however, many employers are reluctant to give out information about former employees. Verification of application entries such as dates of employment and duties performed can be helpful to you in making decisions about the potential "fit" and, thus, productivity of a potential employee.

The advertising for, interviewing of, and selection of the right employee for the right job is a specialized area of human resources, and you will often be able to rely on a human resources department in your organization for assistance when undertaking this important task. Selection of employees is, in the final analysis, critically important in creating a productive workforce in your facility.

■ TRAINING

Perhaps no area under your control holds greater promise for increased employee productivity related to current employees than improvement through training. In fact, the human being is the only asset you can expand without spending money. In too many cases, however, training in the hospitality industry is poor or almost nonexistent. Highly productive employees have been well-trained employees, and, frequently, employees with low productivity are poorly trained. Every position in a foodservice operation should have a specific, well developed, and ongoing training program. Effective training will improve job satisfaction and instill in employees a sense of well-being and accomplishment. It will also reduce confusion, product waste, and loss of guests. In addition, supervisors find that a well-trained workforce is easier to manage than one in which the employees are poorly trained. An additional advantage of a well-trained workforce is that management will be more effective because of reduced stress, in terms of both work completion and interpersonal relationships.

Effective training begins with a good orientation program. An **orientation program** simply prepares a worker for success on his or her job. The following list includes some of the concerns that most employees have when they start a new job. You should identify which items are relevant to your new employees and take care to provide information in each area, in written or verbal form.

Orientation Program Information

1. Payday
2. Annual performance review
3. Probationary period
4. Dress code
5. Telephone call policy
6. Smoking policy
7. Uniform allowance
8. Disciplinary system
9. Educational assistance
10. Work schedule
11. Mandatory meetings
12. Tip policy
13. Transfers
14. Employee meal policy
15. Sexual harassment policy
16. Lockers/security
17. Jury duty
18. Leave of absence

19. Maternity leave
20. Alcohol/drug policy
21. Employee assistance programs
22. Tardy policy
23. Sick leave policy
24. Vacation policy

25. Holidays and holiday pay
26. Overtime pay
27. Insurance
28. Retirement programs
29. Safety/emergency procedures
30. Grievance procedures

Most employees truly want to do a good job for their employer. To achieve this, most employees look forward to and enjoy participating in training sessions. Managers who like to train tend to find themselves with motivated employees. Managers who, on the other hand, dislike or can find no time for training usually encounter less productive, less motivated individuals.

Training programs need not be elaborate. They must, however, be continual. Hospitality companies can train in many different areas. Some training seeks to influence attitudes and actions, for example, when training to prevent work-related harassment is presented. In other cases, training may be undertaken to assist employees with stress or other psychologically related job aspects. In most cases, however, the training you will be responsible for as a unit manager is task training. **Task training** is the training undertaken to ensure an employee has the skills to meet productivity goals. The development of a training program for any task involves the following:

1. Determine how the task is to be done.
2. Plan the training session.
3. Present the training session.
4. Evaluate the session's effectiveness.
5. Retrain at the proper interval.

DETERMINE HOW THE TASK IS TO BE DONE

Often, jobs can be done in more than one way. An employee making a salad may elect to clean carrots prior to washing the lettuce, or the reverse, with no effect on the total amount of time it takes to prepare the salad. In other areas, for example, in taking table service orders on a guest check, management may have very specific procedures that must be followed so that both cooks and cashiers can receive the guest's order and process it properly. When management has determined how a task should be completed, that method should be made part of the training program and should be strictly maintained unless a better method can be demonstrated. If this is not done, employees will find that "anything goes," and product consistency, along with service levels, will vary tremendously.

Employees watch management very carefully. If management is not diligent in the enforcement of standard operating procedures (SOP), employees may perform tasks in a manner that is easiest for them. This may not be the manner that is best for your operation. This is not to underestimate the value of employee input in job design. They should certainly have input into the execution of a task, but once management has made the decision to follow a certain procedure, it must be communicated and enforced. This enforcement is best done through a positive approach. Managers should focus less on people who are "doing it wrong" than on those who are "doing it right." Positive reinforcement and praise, as well as rewarding employees for a job well done, are powerful management tools because most employees truly want to be recognized by management for that good job.

PLAN THE TRAINING SESSION

Like any other important management task, the training session must be planned. This includes asking and appropriately answering the following questions:

1. Who should be trained?
2. Who should do the training?
3. Where should the training occur?
4. When should the session occur?
5. What tools, materials, or supplies are needed to conduct the session?
6. What should the length of the session be?
7. How frequently should the sessions occur?
8. How and where will the attendance and completion records regarding each training session offered be kept?

Good training sessions are the result of a need felt by management to train personnel matched with a management philosophy that training is important. Taking time to effectively plan the training session is a good way for you to let employees know that you take the training process seriously. Whether the training session is self-paced, an interactive program delivered via the Internet, a DVD, a video, a hands-on demonstration, a group discussion, or a lecture-style presentation, time spent planning the session is time well spent.

PRESENT THE TRAINING SESSION

Many managers feel that they have no time for training. But management is about teaching, encouraging, and coaching. You must find the time. Managers interested in the long-term success of their operations and employees will set aside time each week to conduct training. Some managers maintain that all of the training in their unit must be **OJT** (on-the-job training). They feel that structured training either takes too long or is inappropriate. In nearly all cases this is incorrect and is a major cause of the rather low rate of productivity so prevalent in parts of the hospitality industry.

The best training sessions are presented with enthusiasm and an attitude of encouragement. Make sure that training is presented not because employees "don't know" but because management wants them to "know more." Involve employees in the presentation of training exercises. Seek their input in the sessions. Ask questions that encourage discussion, and always conclude the sessions on a positive note.

A brief, but effective, outline for each session could be as follows:

1. Tell the employees what you hope to teach them and why.
2. Present the session.
3. Reemphasize the main points and discuss why they are important.
4. Ask for questions to ensure understanding.

EVALUATE THE SESSION'S EFFECTIVENESS

There is a saying in education that "if the student hasn't learned, then the teacher hasn't taught." This concept, when applied to hospitality training, implies that simply presenting a training session is not enough. Training should result in change. Either employees improve and gain new skills, knowledge, or information, or they have not learned. If you are to know which of these is the case, you must evaluate the training session. This can be as simple as observing employee behavior (to test skill acquisition) or as detailed as preparing written questions (to test knowledge retention).

Posttraining evaluation should also be directed at how the sessions were conducted. Were they too long? Were they planned well? Were they delivered with the appropriate attitude? The evaluation of training is as important as its delivery. Both the content of the session and the delivery itself should be evaluated. The bottom line, of course, is changed behavior. A workforce that is trained well is more productive. In fact, employees who are well trained are more productive, are more highly motivated, and provide better service to guests.

RETRAIN AT THE PROPER INTERVAL

Few 35-year-old foodservice managers could walk into a room, sit down, and pass, with a good grade, the algebra final they took in high school some 18 or so years earlier. Why is that? The answer is not that they did not learn algebra. Clearly, they knew the answers at one time. Humans, however, do not learn and then remain stagnant. We learn, unlearn, and relearn on a regular basis. The telephone number we knew so well 10 years ago is now gone from memory. The friend or teacher's name we knew well at one time and felt we would never forget is forgotten. In the same way, employees who are well trained in an operation's policies and procedures need to be constantly reminded and updated if their skill levels are to remain high. Performance levels can decline because of a change in the operational systems you have in place or changes in equipment used. When this is true, you must retrain your employees. Nearly every operating foodservice manager has had a conversation like this:

Supervisor: "Alex, I thought I told you to . . . ."

Alex: "I did!"

Supervisor: "Yes, you did it, but you did it wrong. That's not how we do it here!"

Alex: "I thought it was but I guess I forgot! I'll get it right next time."

Supervisor: "Good! Make sure you do!"

The point is that, without a regular retraining program, Alex will not get it right the next time. It matters little whether Alex never got the correct training or whether he got it at one point in time but has now forgotten what he learned. Conversations like this are a sure sign that effective training sessions are not in place.

Training a workforce is one, if not the best, method of improving employee productivity. Effective training costs a small amount of time in the short run, but pays off extremely well in dollars in the long run. Managers who have risen to the top in the hospitality industry have some specific characteristics and traits. Chief among these is their desire to teach and encourage their employees and, thus, get the best results from each and every one of them.

■ SUPERVISION

All employees require proper supervision. This is not to say that all employees desire to have someone tell them what to do. Proper supervision means assisting employees in improving productivity. In this sense, the supervisor is a helper and facilitator who provides assistance. Supervising should be a matter of assisting employees to do their best, not just identifying their shortcomings. It is said that employees think one of two things when they see their boss approaching:

1. Here comes help!

or

2. Here comes trouble!

For those supervisors whose employees feel that the boss is an asset to their daily routine, productivity gains are remarkable. Supervisors who see their position as one of power, or who see themselves as taskmasters, can only rarely maintain the quality workforce necessary to compete in today's competitive market. It is important to remember that it is the employee, not management, who services the guest. When supervision is geared toward helping employees, the guest benefits, and, thus, the operation benefits. This is why it is so important for managers to be **on the floor,** in other words, in the dining area, during meal periods. The foodservice manager is, in the final analysis, the individual in the best position to see what must be done to satisfy the guest. This means being where the action is when meals are served. Greeting guests, solving bottleneck problems, maintaining food quality, and ensuring excellent service are all tasks of the foodservice manager during the service period. When employees see that management is committed to customer service and is there to assist employees in delivering that service, their productivity will improve. Again, most employees want to please both the guest and the boss. When both can be pleased at once, productivity rises. If employees feel that they can satisfy only the guest or the operation, difficulties will arise.

Consider, for example, the employee who has been instructed to serve one 2-ounce portion of tartar sauce with a particular fried lake perch dinner. When she does so, she finds that 80% of the guests request a second portion of the tartar sauce. If management does not respond to this consumer demand and adjust the portion size, the employee is faced with a difficult choice: "Do I satisfy management (serve one portion) or the guest (serve two portions)?" Situations such as this one can, and do, occur, but they must be addressed by management. Good managers do this by involving themselves closely with the work of their employees.

This does not mean that the supervisor does the employees' work but, rather, that employees know that they can go to management with their problems or, better yet, that they can say, "Here comes help" (not trouble!) when they see the boss approaching.

■ SCHEDULING

Even with highly productive employees, poor employee scheduling by management can result in low productivity ratios. Consider the example in Figure 7.3, where management has determined a schedule for pot washers in a unit that is open for three meals per day.

In Schedule A, four employees are scheduled for 32 hours at a rate of $8.00 per hour. Payroll, in this case, is $256 per day (32 hours/day × $8.00/hour = $256/day). Each shift, breakfast, lunch, and dinner, has two employees scheduled.

In Schedule B, three employees are scheduled for 24 hours. At the same rate of $8.00 per hour, payroll is $192 per day (24 hours/day × $8.00/hour = $192/day). Wages, in this case, are reduced by $64 ($256 − $192 = $64), and further savings will be realized due to reduced benefits, employee meal costs, and other labor-related expenses. Schedule A assumes that the amount of work to be done is identical at all times of the day. Schedule B covers both the lunch and the dinner shifts with two employees but assumes that one pot washer is sufficient in the early-morning period as well as very late in the day.

■ FIGURE 7.3 Two Alternative Schedules

Schedule A

	7:30 to 8:30	8:30 to 9:30	9:30 to 10:30	10:30 to 11:30	11:30 to 12:30	12:30 to 1:30	1:30 to 2:30	2:30 to 3:30	3:30 to 4:30	4:30 to 5:30	5:30 to 6:30	6:30 to 7:30	7:30 to 8:30	8:30 to 9:30	9:30 to 10:30	10:30 to 11:30
Employee 1	■	■	■	■	■	■	■	■								
Employee 2	■	■	■	■	■	■	■	■								
Employee 3									■	■	■	■	■	■	■	■
Employee 4									■	■	■	■	■	■	■	■

Total Hours = 32

Schedule B

	7:30 to 8:30	8:30 to 9:30	9:30 to 10:30	10:30 to 11:30	11:30 to 12:30	12:30 to 1:30	1:30 to 2:30	2:30 to 3:30	3:30 to 4:30	4:30 to 5:30	5:30 to 6:30	6:30 to 7:30	7:30 to 8:30	8:30 to 9:30	9:30 to 10:30	10:30 to 11:30
Employee 1	■	■	■	■	■	■	■	■								
Employee 2					■	■	■	■	■	■	■	■				
Employee 3									■	■	■	■	■	■	■	■

Total Hours = 24

■ **FIGURE 7.4** Effect of Scheduling on Productivity Ratios

Number of Pots to Be Washed	Number of Pot washers Scheduled	Productivity Ratio
600	4	150 pots/washer
600	3	200 pots/washer

When scheduling is done to meet projected demand, productivity ratios will increase. If production standards are to be established and monitored, management must do its job in ensuring that employees are scheduled only when needed to meet the sales or volume anticipated. Returning to our formula for computing the productivity ratio, assume that 600 pots are to be washed and that four rather than three pot washers are scheduled to work. Figure 7.4 shows the effect on the productivity ratio of different scheduling decisions.

Proper scheduling ensures that the correct number of employees is available to do the necessary amount of work. If too many employees are scheduled, productivity ratios will decline. If too few employees are scheduled, customer service levels may suffer or necessary tasks may not be completed on time or as well as they should be.

Work in a foodservice operation tends to occur in peaks and valleys, and the foodservice manager is often faced with uneven demands regarding the number of employees needed. Different days of the week may require different levels of staffing. In a hotel restaurant, for example, the slow period might be a weekend when most business travelers are at home rather than in the hotel. In an upscale restaurant, on the other hand, the slow period may be during the week with volume picking up on the weekends. For the weekend increase in business, the manager might hire part-time employees to handle the higher volume. To further complicate matters, some operations are faced with seasonal variations. In a college dining hall, the summers may be slow, whereas a beach resort may be extremely busy during that time. The manager at the beach resort might hire seasonal employees to meet increased demand. Demand can also vary from hour to hour because people in the United States tend to eat in three major time periods. In some restaurants with a busy lunch, 5 cooks and 15 servers may be necessary. At 3:00 in the afternoon at the same restaurant, one cook and one server may find themselves with few guests to serve.

Scheduling efficiency during the day can often be improved through the use of the **split-shift,** a technique used to match individual employee work shifts with peaks and valleys of customer demand. In using a split shift, the manager would require an employee to work a busy period, for example, lunch, be off in the afternoon, and then return for the busy dinner period.

Employee scheduling in the hospitality industry is difficult. It is important, however, that it be done well. Productivity standards help the foodservice operator match workload to the number of employees required.

■ BREAKS

Employees simply cannot work at top speed for eight hours straight. They have both a physical and mental need for breaks from their work. These breaks give them a chance to pause, collect their thoughts, converse with their fellow employees, and, in general, prepare for the next work session. Employees who are given frequent, short breaks will outproduce those who are not given any. It simply makes no sense, then, for management to behave as if they begrudge their staff the breaks that are so beneficial to the organization, as well as to the employee. As management, the foodservice supervisor must determine both the frequency and the length of designated breaks. In some cases, especially regarding the employment of students and minors, both federal and state law may mandate breaks for employees; as a manager, you will need to know these laws.

■ MORALE

Employee morale is not often mentioned in a discussion about controlling foodservice costs. Yet, as experienced managers will attest, it is impossible to overestimate the financial value of a highly motivated employee or crew. Although it is a truism that employees motivate themselves, it is also true that effective managers can create an environment that makes it easy for employees to want to be motivated. History is filled with examples of groups who have achieved goals that seemed impossible because they were highly motivated. Serving people should be fun. It should be exciting. If this sense of fun and excitement can be instilled in each employee, work also becomes fun and exciting.

Volumes have been written about the manner in which managers can create a highly motivated workforce. It is the authors' opinion, however, that work groups with high morale share a common trait. In general, these groups work for a manager or management team that has the following characteristics:

1. A vision has been created.
2. The vision is constantly communicated to employees.
3. The vision is shared and embraced by both management and employees.

Creating a vision is nothing more than finding a "purpose" for the workforce. Any manager who communicates that the purpose for a pot washer is simply to clean pots cannot expect to have a fired-up, turned-on employee. Yet, pot washers can have high morale. They can be a critical part of management's overall purpose for the work crew. Consider, for purposes of illustration, some of the following techniques you could use to communicate a customer service vision to pot washers:

1. If your unit has been, as it should be, free from cases of foodborne illness, part of the credit goes to your pot washing staff. Recognize them for this achievement on a quarterly basis.
2. Conduct regular "pot washing station inspections." Score the area for cleanliness on a scale of 1 to 100. Present each pot washer with a certificate when the area score exceeds 90. If it does not exceed 90, increase training until it does!
3. Recognize your "best" pot washer(s) at an annual employee recognition luncheon or dinner for:
   a. Best attendance
   b. Best productivity
   c. Cleanest work area
   d. Most improved
   e. Most thorough
   f. Most often in proper uniform
   g. Safest worker
4. Include a pot washer on your safety committee. Publicly recognize all committee members on a regular basis.
5. Make it a point to go to the pot washing area on a daily basis to thank those employees for a job well done. Emphasize the importance of their efforts.
6. Encourage food production employees (your pot washers' customers) to take the time to thank the pot washers for their contribution to the food production process.

If the purpose or vision that management creates is only financial profit for the organization or owners, employees will rarely share the vision, even if it is strongly communicated. If management's vision, however, includes the vital importance of each employee, each employee can share that vision. This vision might be to be the number-one unit in sales volume, the unit with the highest percentage sales increase, or the unit with the lowest food cost or most meals served. A shared purpose between management and employee is important for the development and maintenance of high morale. It is just not enough for management to feel that employees should be "glad to have a job." This type of attitude by management results in high employee turnover and lost productivity.

Employee turnover can be high in some sections of the hospitality industry. By some estimates, it exceeds 200% per year. You can measure your turnover by using the following formula:

$$\frac{\text{Number of Employees Separated}}{\text{Number of Employees in Workforce}} = \text{Employee of Turnover Rate}$$

For example, assume that you have a total of 50 employees in your foodservice operation. In the past year, you replaced 35 employees. Your turnover rate is computed as follows:

$$\frac{35 \text{ Employees Separated}}{50 \text{ Employees in Workforce}} = 70\% \text{ Turnover Rate}$$

Separated is the term used to describe employees who have either quit, been terminated, or in some other manner have "separated" themselves from the operation. The number of employees in the workforce is computed by adding the number of employees at the beginning of the accounting period to the number of employees at the end of the accounting period and dividing the sum by two. The number of employees in the workforce, then, refers to the average number of people employed by the operation during a given time period.

Some foodservice operators prefer to distinguish between voluntary separation and involuntary separation. A **voluntary separation** is one in which the employee made the decision to leave the organization. This may be due, for example, to retirement, a better opportunity in another organization, or relocation to another state. An **involuntary separation** is one in which management has caused the employee to separate from the organization. This may have been, for example, firing the employee because of poor attendance or violation of procedures or policy or a result of a reduction in the workforce. Some managers want to know the amount of turnover that is voluntary compared to involuntary. For example, excessively high voluntary turnover rates may be a signal that wages and salaries are too low to keep your best employees. High involuntary turnover rates may mean that employee screening and selection techniques need to be reviewed and improved.

If it is your preference, you can modify the turnover formula to create these two ratios:

Involuntary Employee Turnover Rate

$$= \frac{\text{Number of Employees Involuntarily Separated}}{\text{Number of Employees in Workforce}}$$

Voluntary Employee Turnover Rate

$$= \frac{\text{Number of Employees Voluntarily Separated}}{\text{Number of Employees in Workforce}}$$

Whether separation is involuntary or voluntary, turnover is expensive. Employee turnover costs you in terms that are both actual and hidden. Actual costs, such as those involved in advertising the vacancy, relocation costs, interviewing and training time, and record keeping, are easy to determine. The hidden costs are harder to quantify but can cost dearly in an operation with high turnover rate. Increased dishroom breakage may result as a new ware washer learns the job. A new server may provide slower customer service, or a new cook may cause an increase in improperly prepared food. Good foodservice managers calculate and closely monitor their turnover rates. High turnover rates mean trouble. Low rates mean that employees feel good about the operation they work for.

To counteract the turnover syndrome, management can decide to be smart. It can seek to create job satisfaction by providing a healthy environment and wholesome working conditions. It can develop and train a strong and loyal workforce that will be willing and committed to work under many different conditions, some pleasant, some less so. If the understanding between management and the workforce is established over time, on good faith, the relationship will transcend and exceed the monetary value attached to the job and allow for the establishment of a committed, dependable, and permanent staff. In those cases, the kind of environment that yields high employee productivity and morale and reduced turnover rates will also result in your staff providing excellent service to your guests.

■ MENU

A major factor in employee productivity is the foodservice operation's actual menu. The items that you elect to serve on your menu will have a profound effect on your employees' ability to produce the items quickly and efficiently.

In general, the more variety of items a kitchen is asked to produce, the less efficient that kitchen will be. Of course, if management does not provide the guest with enough choices, loss of sales may result. Clearly, neither too many nor too few menu choices should be offered. The question for management is, "How many are too many?" The answer depends on the operation, the skill level of employees, and the level of menu item variety management feels is necessary to properly service the guests.

Menus that continuously expand are costly in many ways. The quick-service unit that elects to specialize in hamburgers can prepare them quickly and efficiently. If the same restaurant decides to add pizza, tacos, salads, tofu wraps, and fried chicken strips, its management may find that not only are employees less productive but also guests are confused as to what the operation really is. Again, the dilemma management faces is to serve the widest variety possible but not so many things as to markedly reduce employee productivity.

Although the number of items produced is important, so is the type of item. Obviously, a small diner with one deep-fat fryer will have production problems if the day's specials are fried fish, fried chicken, and a breaded fried vegetable platter! Menu items must be selected to complement the skill level of the employees and the equipment available to produce the menu item. Most foodservice operations change their menu fairly infrequently. Print costs are often high, and restaurateurs are reluctant to radically change their product offerings. Thus, it is extremely important that the initial menu items selected by management are items that can be prepared efficiently and well. If this is done, productivity rates will be high, and so will guest satisfaction.

■ CONVENIENCE VERSUS SCRATCH PREPARATION

Few, if any, foodservice operators today make all of their menu items from scratch. Indeed, there is no real agreement among operators as to what "scratch" or "on-site" cooking truly is. Canned fruits, frozen seafood, and ready-to-bake pastries are examples of foods that would not be available to many guests if it were not for the fact that they were processed to some degree before they were delivered to the foodservice operator's door. At one time, presliced white bread was considered a convenience item. Today, of course, this is considered a staple. Some foods, such as canned cheese sauce, can be modified by an operator to produce a unique item. This can be done by the addition of special ingredients according to the standardized recipe, with the intent of creating a product served only by that foodservice operation.

The decision of whether to "make" or "buy" involves two major factors. The first is, of course, product quality. In general, if an operation can make a product that is superior to the one it can buy from a supplier, it should produce that item. The second factor, product cost, is also a major issue for management. It is possible that management determines that a given menu item can be made in-house and that it is a superior product. The cost of preparing that product, however, may be so great that it is simply not cost effective to do so. Fortunately, convenience products are becoming more quality driven and less expensive due to advances in technology and increased competition among the major food suppliers.

Consider the situation that would arise if you managed a quick-service Mexican restaurant. One of the items that you use is frijoles, or cooked pinto beans, which are seasoned and mashed. Assume that you use 50 edible portion (EP) pounds of these beans per day. You can buy the beans in a can for 80 cents per pound. Your cost per pound with the canned product includes only the cost of the beans. In addition, you would incur the labor cost required to open the cans and heat the beans, as well as the cost of cooking fuel.

If you were to consider making the frijoles from scratch, your food cost would go down to 36 cents per pound (the price of the dried pinto beans), a savings of over 50%. The complete story, however, can only be viewed when you consider the labor required to produce the frijoles. Figure 7.5 details the hypothetical costs involved in the decision that you must make, assuming a usage of 50 pounds of product per day and a labor cost of $8.00 per hour to both cook the beans and clean up the production process.

As you can see in this example, you would experience a reduction in your cost of food if you made the frijoles from scratch but an increase in the cost of labor

■ **FIGURE 7.5**   Frijoles: 50 Pounds

Component	Cost of Convenience Product	Cost of Scratch Product
Beans	$40.00 ($0.80/lb.)	$18.00 ($0.36/lb.)
Seasoning	0	2.00
Labor	8.00 (1 hour)	32.00 (4 hours)
Fuel	1.40	4.40
Total Cost	49.40	56.40

because your own employees must now complete the cooking process. In the case of frijoles, your decision may well be to purchase the convenience item rather than make it from scratch because the overall cost would be less.

Management, often in consultation with kitchen production staff, must resolve make-or-buy decisions. It is important to note, however, that these decisions affect both food *and* labor costs. One cannot generally achieve food cost savings without expending additional labor dollars. Conversely, when a manager elects to buy rather than make an item from scratch, food costs tend to rise but labor costs should decline. In general, productivity in your operation will rise when you elect to buy, rather than make from scratch, any item that you cannot produce efficiently. This may be due to specialized skills required, as is the case with some purchased bakery items, or it could simply be a case of your supplier having the tools and equipment necessary to do a time-consuming task at a great savings to you, such as the case of buying a prechopped, frozen onion.

In many cases, convenience items will save you significant money by reducing your overall labor costs. Productivity of your staff will increase. It is important, however, that you not fall into the trap of electing to buy more convenience-type items without reducing your labor expenditures. When that happens, you lose in terms of both high food costs and higher than required labor costs, thus causing your labor productivity ratios to decrease.

■ EQUIPMENT/TOOLS

In most cases, foodservice productivity ratios have not increased as much in recent years as have those of other businesses. Much of this is due to the fact that ours is a labor-intensive, not machine-intensive, industry. In some cases, equipment improvements have made kitchen work much easier. Slicers, choppers, and mixers have replaced human labor with mechanical labor. However, robotics and automation are not yet a part of our industry in any major way. Nonetheless, it is critical for you to understand the importance of a properly equipped workplace to improve productivity. This can be as simple as understanding that a sharp knife cuts more quickly and better than a dull one or as complex as deciding which Internet service will be used to provide communication links to the 1,000 stores in a quick-service restaurant chain. In either case, management must ask itself a fundamental question: "Am I providing my employees with the tools necessary to do their job effectively?" The key word in that question is "effectively." If the proper tools are provided but they are mounted at the wrong height, placed in the wrong location, or unavailable at the right time, the tools will not be used effectively. Similarly, if the proper tools are provided but employees are not adequately trained in their use, productivity gains will not occur. It is part of your job to provide your employees with the tools they need to do their jobs quickly and effectively.

■ SERVICE LEVEL DESIRED

It is a fact that the average quick-service employee can serve more guests in an hour than the best server at an exclusive French-style restaurant. The reason for this is quite obvious. In the quick-service situation, speed, not total service rendered, is of the utmost importance. In the French-style restaurant, service is to be more elegant and the total service rendered is of a much higher level. Thus, when you vary service levels, you also vary employee productivity ratios. In the past, foodservice managers focused very heavily on speed of service. Although that is still important today, many operators are finding that guests expect and demand higher levels of service than ever before. If this trend continues, one could expect that foodservice productivity levels will tend to go down. To prevent this from happening, foodservice operators will need to become very creative in finding ways to improve employee productivity in other areas (for example, through training and improved morale) so that these "savings" can be used to provide the higher level of customer service demanded by today's sophisticated foodservice consumer.

Now that we have discussed some of the factors that impact employee productivity and what management can do to affect them, we return to the question of knowing "how many employees are needed" to effectively operate the foodservice unit. As previously stated, the key to answering that question lies in developing productivity standards for the foodservice unit. There are many measures of employee productivity. Next, you will learn about the most popular of these and examine their weaknesses and strengths. In the final analysis, the best productivity measure for any unit you manage is the one that makes the most sense for your unique operation.

FUN ON THE WEB!

For government information regarding labor issues and laws in the United States, explore the U.S. Department of Labor Web site at **www.dol.gov.** Review the "Find It" list. You will find information on minimum wage and overtime pay, family and medical leave, employment discrimination, and much more.

MEASURING CURRENT LABOR PRODUCTIVITY

*T*here are a variety of ways to measure productivity in the hospitality industry. We examine six of them, as follows:

1. Labor cost percentage
2. Sales per labor hour
3. Labor dollars per guest served
4. Guests served per labor dollar
5. Guests served per labor hour
6. Revenue per available seat hour (RevPASH)

■ LABOR COST PERCENTAGE

A commonly used measure of employee productivity in the foodservice industry is the labor cost percentage. The labor cost percentage is computed as follows:

$$\frac{\text{Cost of Labor}}{\text{Total Sales}} = \text{Labor Cost \%}$$

It is important to realize that there are several ways to define cost of labor. You should select the one that makes the most sense for your own operation. Cost of labor, as previously mentioned, includes both payroll and total labor costs. To measure productivity, you may elect, for example, to include only payroll costs and not total labor costs. This approach makes sense if, for example, in your operation you have the ability to control only your payroll and not total labor costs. In a like manner, some managers elect to include the cost of management when computing their labor cost percentage, whereas others do not. Again, the most important point is that you should compute a labor cost percentage that makes sense for your operation. Remember, however, that when comparing your labor cost percentage with those of other similar units, it is important that you make sure both your unit and the one you are comparing use the same formula for your computations. If you do not, your comparisons will not accurately reflect true differences between the units.

Controlling the labor cost percentage is extremely important in the foodservice industry because it is the most widely used measure of productivity and, thus, is often used to determine the effectiveness of a manager. If labor cost percentage increases, management may be held accountable and penalized. A labor cost percentage that increases too much may result in management turnover, even if, as in many cases, the management did not want to turn over!

■ FIGURE 7.6   Roderick's 4-Week Labor Cost % Report

Week	Cost of Labor	Sales	Labor Cost %
1	$ 7,100	$18,400	38.6%
2	8,050	21,500	37.4
3	7,258	19,100	38.0
4	6,922	24,800	27.9
Total	29,330	83,800	35.0

Labor cost percentages are easy to compute and analyze. Consider the case of Roderick, a foodservice manager in charge of a table service restaurant in a year-round theme park. The unit is popular and has a $20 per guest check average. Roderick uses only payroll (wages and salaries) when determining his overall labor cost percentage because he does not have easy access to the cost of taxes and benefits provided to his employees. These labor-related expenses are considered by Roderick's supervisor to be noncontrollables and thus are beyond Roderick's immediate influence. Roderick has computed his labor cost percentage for each of the last four weeks using the labor cost percentage formula. His supervisor has given Roderick a goal of 35% for the four-week period. Roderick feels that he has done well in meeting that goal. Figure 7.6 shows Roderick's four-week performance.

Roderick's supervisor, Madeline, is concerned because she received many comments in week 4 regarding poor service levels in Roderick's unit. As she analyzes the numbers in Figure 7.6, she sees that Roderick exceeded his goal of a 35% labor cost in weeks 1 through 3 and then reduced his labor cost to 27.9% in week 4. Although the monthly overall average of 35% is within budget, she knows all is not well in this unit. Roderick elected to reduce his payroll in week 4, and yet it is clear from the negative guest comments that, at a 27.9% labor cost, service to guests suffers. That is, too few employees were on staff to provide the necessary guest attention. Unfortunately, one disadvantage of using an overall labor cost percentage is that it can hide daily or weekly highs and lows. As in Roderick's case, labor costs were too high the first three weeks, too low the last week, but acceptable overall. Recall that the total labor cost of 35% indicates that, for each dollar of sales generated, 35 cents is paid to the employees who assisted in generating those sales.

Using the labor cost percentage formula and the (Total row) data from Figure 7.6, Roderick's Labor Cost % is calculated as:

$$\frac{\text{Cost of Labor}}{\text{Total Sales}} = \text{Labor Cost \%}$$

or

$$\frac{\$29,330}{\$83,800} = 35\%$$

■ **FIGURE 7.7** Roderick's 4-Week Revised Labor Cost % Report

			(Includes 5% Raise)		
Week	Original Cost of Labor	5% Raise	Total Cost of Labor	Sales	Labor Cost %
1	$ 7,100	$ 355.00	$ 7,455.00	$18,400	40.5%
2	8,050	402.50	8,452.50	21,500	39.3
3	7,258	362.90	7,620.90	19,100	39.9
4	6,922	346.10	7,268.10	24,800	29.3
Total	29,330	1,466.50	30,796.50	83,800	36.8

In many cases, a targeted labor cost % is viewed as a measure of employee productivity and, to some degree, management's skill in controlling labor costs. The labor cost percentage does, however, have some limitations as a measure of productivity. Notice, for example, what happens to this measure of productivity if all Roderick's employees are given a 5% raise in pay. If this were the case, Roderick's labor cost percentages for last month would be calculated as shown in Figure 7.7.

Note that labor now accounts for 36.8% of each dollar sales value. It is important to realize that Roderick's workforce did not become less productive because they got a 5% increase in pay. Labor cost percentage varies with changes in the price paid for labor. When the price paid for labor increases, labor cost percentage increases. When the price paid for labor decreases, labor cost percentage goes down. Because of this, using labor cost percentage alone to evaluate workforce productivity can be misleading.

To see another example of the limitations of labor cost percentage as a complete measure of productivity, consider the effect on labor cost percentage of increasing the selling prices of your products. Return to the data in Figure 7.6 and assume that Roderick's unit raised all menu prices by 5% prior to the beginning of the month. Figure 7.8 shows how an increase of this size in selling prices would affect the labor cost percentage.

Note that increases in selling price (assuming no decline in guest count or buying behavior) will result in decreases in the labor cost percentage. Alternatively, lowering the selling price without increasing total revenue generally results in increased labor cost percentage. Although labor cost percentage is easy to compute and widely used, it is difficult to use as a measure of productivity over time because it depends on labor dollars spent and sales dollars received for its computation. Even in relatively noninflationary times, wages do increase and menu prices are adjusted upward. Both activities affect labor cost percentage but not worker productivity. In addition, institutional foodservice settings, which have no sales figures to report, find that it is not easily possible to measure labor productivity using labor cost percentage because they generally calculate and report guest counts or meals served rather than sales dollars earned.

■ **FIGURE 7.8** Roderick's 4-Week Revised Labor Cost % Report

Week	Cost of Labor	Original Sales	5% Selling Price Increase	Total Sales	Labor Cost %
			(Includes 5% Increase in Selling Price)		
1	$ 7,100	$18,400	$ 920	$19,320	36.7%
2	8,050	21,500	1,075	22,575	35.7
3	7,258	19,100	955	20,055	36.2
4	6,922	24,800	1,240	26,040	26.6
Total	29,330	83,800	4,190	87,990	33.3

■ SALES PER LABOR HOUR

It has been said that the most perishable commodity any foodservice operator buys is the labor hour. When not productively used, it disappears forever. It cannot be "carried over" to the next day like an unsold head of lettuce or a slice of turkey breast. Indeed, when one considers the items that a foodservice operator sells as the result of both food products and labor added to those products, the importance of effectively using each labor hour paid for is very clear. It is for this reason that some foodservice operators prefer to measure labor productivity in terms of the amount of sales generated for each labor hour used. The formula for computing this measure of labor productivity is as follows:

$$\frac{\text{Total Sales}}{\text{Labor Hours Used}} = \text{Sales per Labor Hour}$$

Labor hours used is simply the sum of all labor hours paid for by management in a given sales period. Consider Roderick's labor usage as presented in Figure 7.9.

■ **FIGURE 7.9** Roderick's 4-Week Sales per Labor Hour

Week	Sales	Labor Hours Used	Sales per Labor Hour
1	$18,400	943.5	$19.50
2	21,500	1,006.3	21.37
3	19,100	907.3	21.05
4	24,800	865.3	28.66
Total	83,800	3,722.4	22.51

Sales per labor hour ranged from a low of $19.50 in week 1 to a high of $28.66 in week 4. Operators who compute sales per labor hour do so because they feel it is a better measure of labor productivity than the labor cost percentage. Indeed, although sales per labor hour will vary with changes in menu selling price (as does the labor cost percentage), it will not vary based on changes in the price paid for labor. In other words, increases and decreases in the price paid per hour of labor will not affect this productivity measure. On the negative side, however, sales per labor hour neglects to consider the hourly amount paid to employees per hour to generate the sales. A foodservice unit paying its employees an average of $8.00 per hour could, using this measure of productivity, have the same sales per labor hour as a similar unit paying $10.00 for each hour of labor used. Obviously, the manager paying $8.00 per hour has created a lower cost, yet equally productive, workforce if the sales per labor hour used are the same in the two units.

Sales per labor hour, however, is useful in some situations. Consider, for example, the decision you could face as the food and beverage director of a private golf course/country club. One of the services you would like to offer your members is beverage service while golfers are on the course. The question you must answer is, "How many beverage carts should I place on the golf course at any given time of the day and week to adequately serve the club's members?" Too few beverage carts will result in thirsty, unserved golfers, whereas too many carts will cause the club to incur excessive labor costs. In this situation, you would want to monitor your beverage cart sales per labor hour and make determinations on the number of carts that you should use at various times to ensure cost-effective, quality service.

It is relatively easy to compute total sales per labor hour used because both the numerator and the denominator of the formula are generated on a very regular basis. However, depending on the record-keeping system employed, it may be more difficult to determine total labor hours used than total labor dollars spent. This is especially true when large numbers of employees are salaried rather than hourly employees. Remember that the efforts of both salaried and hourly employees should be considered when computing a facility's overall sales per labor hour used.

■ LABOR DOLLARS PER GUEST SERVED

Had Roderick preferred, he might have measured his labor productivity in terms of the labor dollars per guest served. The formula for this measure is as follows:

$$\frac{\text{Cost of Labor}}{\text{Guests Served}} = \text{Labor Dollars per Guest Served}$$

Using Roderick's data, the labor dollars per guest served computation would be as shown in Figure 7.10.

■ **FIGURE 7.10**   Roderick's 4-Week Labor Dollars per Guest Served

Week	Cost of Labor	Guests Served	Labor Dollars per Guest Served
1	$ 7,100	920	$7.72
2	8,050	1,075	7.49
3	7,258	955	7.60
4	6,922	1,240	5.58
Total	29,330	4,190	7.00

In this example, the labor dollars expended per guest served for the four-week period would be computed as follows:

$$\frac{\$29,330}{4,190} = \$7.00$$

Using this measure of productivity, it is fairly easy to see why Roderick experienced guest complaints during the fourth week of operation. Note that in the first three weeks, he "supplied" his guests with more than $7.00 of guest-related labor costs per guest served, but in the fourth week that amount fell to less than $6.00 per guest. As is the case with labor cost percentage, labor dollars per guest served is limited in that it will vary based on the price paid for labor.

■ GUESTS SERVED PER LABOR DOLLAR

A variation on the formula of labor dollars per guest served is to reverse the numerator and denominator to create a new productivity measure, that is, guests served per labor dollar. The formula for this measure of productivity is:

$$\frac{\text{Guests Served}}{\text{Cost of Labor}} = \text{Guests Served per Labor Dollar}$$

Had Roderick wanted to, his productivity data could have been as presented in Figure 7.11.

In this situation, Roderick served for the four-week average a total of 0.143 guests for each labor dollar expended. It is important to note, however, that cost of labor in this case represents all the labor required to serve the guests. This includes cooks, servers, dishwashers, and Roderick himself. It is, therefore, not surprising that each dollar spent services less than one complete guest. As a measure of productivity, guests served per labor dollar expended has advantages. It is relatively easy to compute and can be used by foodservice units, such as institutions,

■ **FIGURE 7.11**   Roderick's 4-Week Guests Served per Labor Dollar

Week	Guests Served	Cost of Labor	Guests Served per Labor Dollar
1	920	$ 7,100	0.130
2	1,075	8,050	0.134
3	955	7,258	0.132
4	1,240	6,922	0.179
Total	4,190	29,330	0.143

that do not routinely record dollar sales figures. When the number of guests to be served stays fairly constant, it can be a good measure of productivity. In addition, this measure is relatively easy to compute because you are very likely to get records on total guests served on a daily basis, as well as total payroll amounts each time payroll is paid.

If the number of guests anticipated varies widely, this measure of productivity will vary widely also, despite management's conscientious efforts at forecasting. Of course, that is true of even the best measures of labor productivity.

■ GUESTS SERVED PER LABOR HOUR

Guests served per labor hour is a powerful measure of productivity. Had Roderick elected to use this labor assessment method, he would compute it as follows:

$$\frac{\text{Guests Served}}{\text{Labor Hours Used}} = \text{Guests Served per Labor Hour}$$

The formula of guests served per labor hour is especially useful because it has neither sales figures nor labor expense figures in its computation. That means it is free from variations due to changes in the price paid for labor and from fluctuations due solely to changes in menu selling prices. Guests served per labor hour is a true measure of productivity, not a measure (like the earlier ones you learned about!) of either cost and productivity or sales and productivity. Guests served per labor hour is powerful in its ability to measure productivity gains across time due to changes that are unrelated to selling price or wages. It is extremely useful in comparing similar operating units in areas with widely differing wage rates or selling prices and is, thus, popular with multiunit corporations comparing one operational unit to another. It is also useful in comparing dissimilar facilities with similar wages and selling prices because it helps identify areas of weakness in management scheduling, employee productivity, facility layout and design, or other factors that can affect productivity.

■ **FIGURE 7.12**   Roderick's 4-Week Guests Served per Labor Hour

Week	Guests Served	Labor Hours Used	Guests Served per Labor Hours
1	920	943.5	0.975
2	1,075	1,006.3	1.068
3	955	907.3	1.053
4	1,240	865.3	1.433
Total	4,190	3,722.4	1.126

Had Roderick elected to evaluate his workforce productivity through the use of the guests served per labor hour formula, his data might have looked as shown in Figure 7.12.

As the data show, Roderick's guests served per labor hour figure ranges from a low of 0.975 guests per hour (week 1) to a high of 1.433 guests per hour (week 4). The average for the four-week period is 1.126 guests served per labor hour (4,190 guests served/3,722.4 hours used = 1.126 guests per labor hour).

Managers who use guests served per labor hour as a measure of productivity generally do so because they like the focus of emphasizing service levels and not just reducing costs. However, it may be more difficult and time consuming to compute this measure of productivity because you must compute the number of labor hours used as well as make decisions on how to define a guest. For example, in an outdoor café, a guest who orders a cup of coffee is indeed a guest, but he or she requires much less service than one who consumes a full meal. Unless you decide differently, however, the guests served per labor hour productivity measure treats these two guests in the same manner.

Consider The Costs

"You wanted to see me, sir?" said Francis to the clearly agitated guest seated at the six-top table in the corner of Chez Lapin, the upscale French Bistro-style restaurant that Francis managed.

"I've been waiting 10 minutes for my waiter to bring us our check. And as slow as he's been, it will probably take another 10 minutes to process my credit card. I just want to pay and leave. The food was fine, but this is ridiculous!"

"I'm really sorry, sir. I'll find your server," replied Francis, as he glanced around the dining room. As he did, he noticed several unbussed tables that were littered with dirty dishes, as well as the hostess stand where the line of guests waiting to be seated hadn't gotten any smaller in nearly an hour.

When Francis entered the kitchen looking for the disgruntled guest's server, he was surprised to see several of the line cooks relaxing on the production line.

"How's it going back here tonight?" asked Francis, as he glanced around the kitchen.

"No problems. Just waiting for the orders to come in boss," replied Sasha, the sous chef in charge of the production line. "We're keeping up easily."

Assume that all of the workers at Chez Lapin are well trained and highly motivated:

1. Do you think the servers are likely doing their best to provide good service to the restaurant's guests? If you believe so, then why was the guest in this scenario unhappy?

2. What do you think is the cause of a consistently long line of waiting diners when there are numerous vacant, but unbussed, tables in the dining room?

3. The sous chef in this case said, "We're keeping up easily." Do you think that means they are being very efficient and, thus, very productive? Explain your answer.

■ REVENUE PER AVAILABLE SEAT HOUR (REVPASH)

The final assessment of productivity that you should know about is also the newest. Dr. Sheryl E. Kimes of Cornell University has developed and advocated the continual evaluation of **Revenue per Available Seat Hour (RevPASH)** as a way to measure the efficiency with which commercial restaurants manage their operations. RevPASH helps managers evaluate how much guests buy and how quickly they are served. It does so primarily by assessing the duration of guests' dining experiences. Duration is simply the length of time customers sit at a table.

Although you will not generally have the ability to directly control the menu items your guests will purchase, the time it takes them to eat, or how long they linger at their table after eating, RevPASH can give you a good idea of the speed at which your kitchen produces food and your service personnel deliver it. To calculate RevPASH, you must be able to identify the number of diners you serve each hour, as well as the amount these guests spend (revenue). Typically, this information can be easily retrieved from your operation's point of sale (POS) system. In addition, you must know the number of dining room seats available to your guests as well as the number of hours those seats were available. The formula for this measure of productivity is:

$$\frac{\text{Revenue}}{\text{Available Seat Hours}} = \text{Revenue per Available Seat Hour (RevPASH)}$$

To illustrate, assume that Roderick's operation had 100 seats and that it was open for dinner from 5:00 p.m. to 10:00 p.m. Figure 7.13 shows the revenue his operation generated during each of the hours he was open last Friday.

■ **FIGURE 7.13** Revenue per Available Seat Hour (RevPASH)

				For: Last Friday Night
Hour	Avialable Seats	Guests Served	Revenue	RevPASH
4–5 p.m.	0	0	0	0
5–6 p.m.	100	25	$ 1,500	$ 15.00
6–7 p.m.	100	75	3,700	$ 37.00
7–8 p.m.	100	100	5,200	$ 52.00
8–9 p.m.	100	100	5,150	$ 51.50
9–10 p.m.	100	100	4,800	$ 48.00
10–11 p.m.	0	0	0	0
Total	500	400	$ 20,350.00	$ 40.70
% Seats Sold = 400/500 = 80%				

Roderick calculates the total Available Seat Hours in his operation simply by multiplying the number of seats available for guests times the number of hours these seats are available (Available Seats × Hours of Operation = Available Seat Hours). Note that, on average, Roderick fills 80% of his seats at a RevPASH of $40.70. His operation is most efficient from 7:00 p.m. to 10:00 p.m. as can be determined by a higher than average ($40.70) RevPASH for each of these hours. If Roderick could add incentives to attract or move diners to earlier times (5:00 p.m. to 6:00 p.m.), or perhaps stay open later (10:00 p.m. to 11:00 p.m.), an increase in his profit potential could be considerable. Also, note that if Roderick could increase his seat turnover (i.e., in one hour serve 120 guests in 100 seats), RevPASH could also increase significantly. Note that RevPASH does not directly utilize the price paid for labor in its evaluation of operational efficiency. Managers using this measure, however, gain valuable information about when the operation's labor needs are greatest and can use that information to efficiently schedule workers for each hour the operation is serving guests.

It is widely believed that work really does magically expand to meet (and often exceed!) the number of people available to do the job, and so measures of productivity must be available to guide management in making productivity assessments. Figure 7.14 summarizes the six productivity measures discussed in this text and lists some advantages and disadvantages associated with each. You may select one or more of the measures described previously or create your own measure. In most cases, it is recommended that you monitor your labor cost percentage (the easiest measure to compute) and at least one other measure of productivity if you are truly serious about controlling labor-related expenses.

■ **FIGURE 7.14** Productivity Measures Summary

Measurement	Advantages	Disadvantages
Labor Cost % = $\dfrac{\text{Cost of Labor}}{\text{Total Sales}}$	1. Easy to compute 2. Most widely used	1. Hides highs and lows 2. Varies with changes in price of labor 3. Varies with changes in menu selling price
Sales per Labor Hour = $\dfrac{\text{Total Sales}}{\text{Labor Hours Used}}$	1. Fairly easy to compute 2. Does not vary with changes in the price of labor	1. Ignores price per hour paid for labor 2. Varies with changes in menu selling price
Labor Dollars per Guests Served = $\dfrac{\text{Cost of Labor}}{\text{Guests Served}}$	1. Fairly easy to compute 2. Does not vary with changes in menu selling price 3. Can be used by non–revenue-generating units	1. Ignores average sales per guest and, thus, total sales 2. Varies with changes in the price of labor
Guests Served per Labor Dollar = $\dfrac{\text{Guests Served}}{\text{Cost of Labor}}$	1. Fairly easy to compute 2. Does not vary with changes in menu selling price 3. Can be used by non–revenue-generating units	1. Ignores average sales per guest and, thus, total sales 2. Varies with changes in the price of labor
Guests Served per Labor Hour = $\dfrac{\text{Guests Served}}{\text{Labor Hours Used}}$	1. Can be used by non–revenue-generating units 2. Does not change due to changes in price of labor or menu selling price 3. Emphasizes serving guests rather than reducing costs	1. Time consuming to produce 2. Ignores price paid for labor 3. Ignores average sales per guest and, thus, total sales
RevPASH = $\dfrac{\text{Revenue}}{\text{Available Seat Hours}}$	1. Measures overall efficiency in seating and selling products to guests 2. Identifies most and least efficient serving periods 3. Assesses how much guests buy and how long it takes to serve them their selections	1. Most suitable for commercial operations 2. Varies with changes in menu selling price 3. Does not utilize the price paid for labor in its calculation 4. Requires a detailed data collection/reporting system

■ SIX-COLUMN DAILY PRODUCTIVITY REPORT

Many operators, upon selecting a productivity measure, prefer to compute that measure on a daily, rather than on a weekly or monthly, basis. This can easily be done by using a six-column form similar to the one introduced in Chapter 3.

A six-column form for Roderick's restaurant sales and labor cost in week 1 is presented in Figure 7.15.

To show how it could be used to maintain any productivity measure, consider the labor cost percentage (Cost of Labor/Total Sales = Labor Cost %). Amounts in the Today columns are divided to create the Labor Cost % Today column, just as the amounts in the To Date columns are divided to create the Labor Cost % To Date column.

■ **FIGURE 7.15** Six-Column Labor Cost %

Unit Name: **Roderick's**　　　Date: **1/1–1/7**

| Weekday | Cost of Labor | | Sales | | Labor Cost % | |
	Today	To Date	Today	To Date	Today	To Date
1	$ 800	$ 800	$ 2,000	$ 2,000	40.0%	40.0%
2	880	1,680	1,840	3,840	47.8	43.8
3	920	2,600	2,150	5,990	42.8	43.4
4	980	3,580	2,300	8,290	42.6	43.2
5	1,000	4,580	2,100	10,390	47.6	44.1
6	1,300	5,880	4,100	14,490	31.7	40.6
7	1,220	7,100	3,910	18,400	31.2	38.6
Total	7,100		18,400		38.6	

Roderick's daily labor cost percentage during week 1 ranged from a low of 31.2% (day 7) to a high of 47.8% (day 2). The labor cost percentage for the week was 38.6%. Again, you can see the effect of averaging highs and lows when using measures of labor productivity. Any of the six productivity-related measures can be calculated on a daily basis using a modification of the six-column form. Figure 7.16 details the method to be used to establish six-column forms for each of the six productivity measures presented in this chapter. When using the six-column report, it is important to remember that the To Date column value, on any given day, is always the sum of the values of all the preceding Today columns, including the current day.

■ **FIGURE 7.16** Six-Column Labor Productivity Form

Measure of Productivity	Columns 1 & 2	Columns 3 & 4	Columns 5 & 6
Labor Cost % = Cost of Labor / Total Sales	Cost of Labor Today Cost of Labor to Date	Sales Today Sales to Date	Labor Cost % Today Labor Cost % to Date
Sales per Labor Hour = Total Sales / Labor Hours Used	Sales Today Sales to Date	Labor Hours Used Today Labor Hours Used to Date	Sales per Labor Hour Today Sales per Labor Hour to Date
Labor Dollars per Guest Served = Cost of Labor / Guests Served	Cost of Labor Today Cost of Labor to Date	Guests Served Today Guests Served to Date	Labor Dollars per Guest Served Today Labor Dollars per Guest Served to Date
Guests Served per Labor Dollar = Guests Served / Cost of Labor	Guests Served Today Guests Served to Date	Cost of Labor Today Cost of Labor to Date	Guests Served per Labor Dollar Today Guests Served per Labor Dollar to Date
Guests Served per Labor Hour = Guests Served / Labor Hours Used	Guests Served Today Guests Served to Date	Labor Hours Used Today Labor Hours Used to Date	Guests Served per Labor Hour Today Guests Served per Labor Hour to Date
Revenue Per Available Seat Hour = Revenue / Available Seat Hours	Revenue (Sales) Today Revenue (Sales) to Date	Available Seat Hours Today Available Seat Hours to Date	RevPASH Today RevPASH to Date

■ DETERMINING COSTS BY LABOR CATEGORY

Because of the various approaches used to measure effectiveness, it is not surprising that many operators find a single measure of their labor productivity is insufficient for their needs. Consider the case of Otis, the owner and operator of a restaurant called the Squirrel Flats Diner, which services both backpacking tourists and loggers taking a break from work at the nearby logging camp. Otis's sales last month were $100,000. His labor costs were $30,000. Thus, his labor cost percentage was 30% ($30,000/$100,000 = 0.30). Otis, however, knows more about his labor cost percentage than the overall number alone tells him. Figure 7.17 shows the method Otis uses to compute his overall labor cost percentage.

Note that Otis divides his labor expense into four distinct labor subcategories. Production includes all those individuals who are involved with preparing the food Otis sells. Service includes all the servers and cashiers involved in delivering the food to guests and receiving guest payments. Sanitation consists of the individuals responsible for ware washing and after-hour cleanup of the establishment. Management includes the salaries of Otis's two supervisors.

By establishing four labor categories, Otis has a better idea of where his labor dollars are spent than if only one overall figure had been used. Just as it is often helpful to compute more than one food cost percentage, it is helpful to calculate more than one labor cost percentage. Notice in Figure 7.17 that the sum of Otis's four labor cost percentage subcategories equals the amount of his total labor cost percentage:

$$12\% + 9\% + 3\% + 6\% = 30\%$$

You may establish any number of labor subcategories that make sense for your own unique operation. Of course, you can apply any measure of labor productivity to these labor subcategories, just as you would the overall total. The important

---

■ **FIGURE 7.17** Labor Cost % for Squirrel Flats Diner

Time Period: 1/1–1/31   Sales: $100,000

Labor Category	Cost of Labor	Labor Cost %
Production	$12,000	12%
Service	9,000	9
Sanitation	3,000	3
Management	6,000	6
Total	30,000	30

points for you to remember when determining labor productivity measures by sub-category are:

1. Be sure to include all the relevant data, whether dollars spent, hours used, sales generated, or guests served.
2. Use the same method to identify the numerator and denominator for each category.
3. Compute an overall total to ensure that the sum of the categories is consistent with the overall total.

Keep these points in mind as you examine Figure 7.18, which details Otis's second measure of labor productivity. He has selected guests served per labor dollar as a supplement to his computation of labor cost percentage. Otis feels that this second measure helps him determine his effectiveness with guests without losing sight of the total number of dollars he spends on payroll expense. The formula he uses for this computation is:

$$\frac{\text{Guests Served}}{\text{Cost of Labor}} = \text{Guests Served per Labor Dollar}$$

Each labor category in Figure 7.18 yields a different guests served per labor dollar figure. As could be expected, when labor dollars in a category are low, guests served per labor dollar in that category is relatively high. This is clearly demonstrated in the Sanitation category of Figure 7.18. When labor dollars expended are high, as in the Total category, guests served per labor dollar is lower. With the exception of RevPASH, each of the measures of labor productivity presented in this chapter can be categorized in any logical manner that is of value to management. The purpose of computing numbers such as these is, of course, that they are valuable in developing staff schedules and estimating future payroll costs. Assume, for

---

■ **FIGURE 7.18**   Guests Served per Labor Dollar for Squirrel Flats Diner

Guests Served: 25,000 _____   Time Period: 1/1–1/31 _____

Labor Category	Cost of Labor	Guests Served Per Labor Dollar
Production	$12,000	2.083
Service	9,000	2.778
Sanitation	3,000	8.333
Management	6,000	4.167
Total	30,000	0.833

example, that one month Otis finds his labor cost percentage has exceeded his goal of 30%. By computing his guests served per labor dollar subcategory values, Otis can quickly see exactly where he has exceeded his goal and, thus, where he needs to make adjustments. In addition, if Otis knows, for example, that next month he is projecting 30,000 guests, he can estimate his labor costs for each subcategory. By following the rules of algebra and adding the word "estimated," the guests served per labor dollar formula can be restated as follows:

$$\frac{\text{Number of Estimated Guests Served}}{\text{Guests Served per Labor Dollar}} = \text{Estimated Cost of Labor}$$

From the data in Figure 7.18 and using the Production subcategory as an example, Otis estimates his production labor costs in a month where 30,000 guests are anticipated as follows:

$$\frac{30,000}{2.083} = \$14,402.30$$

Using this estimation method, Otis knows his production-related costs for the month should be $14,402.30. Using the same estimated cost of labor formula, Otis can project and budget different labor costs for each of his subcategories, as well as his overall total. Using this information, Otis can prepare an employee schedule that uses the planned for amount of payroll cost and no more.

MANAGING PAYROLL COSTS

*E*ssentially, the management of payroll costs is a four-step process, which includes:

Step 1. Determine productivity standards.

Step 2. Forecast sales volume.

Step 3. Schedule employees using productivity standards and forecasted sales volume.

Step 4. Analyze results.

■ STEP 1. DETERMINE PRODUCTIVITY STANDARDS

The first step in controlling payroll costs is to determine productivity standards for your operation. A **productivity standard** is defined simply as your view of what constitutes an appropriate productivity ratio in your foodservice operation. Thus, a productivity standard might be, as in this case, a particular labor cost percentage, a specific number of guests served per labor dollar expended, or any other predetermined productivity ratio you want to utilize. In other words, you must find the answers to the questions of how long it should take an employee to do a job and how many employees it takes to do the complete job.

It was previously stated that a productivity ratio measures the units of output, such as sales revenue achieved or the number of guests served or meals served, relative to the units of input, such as the number of employees on duty, the number of hours worked, or the number of available seats. Productivity standards represent what you reasonably expect in the way of output per unit of labor input. Assume, for example, that a cafeteria manager knows that a well-trained, motivated cashier can total seven guest trays per minute during a busy lunch period. Actual payment for these meals will be made at another station at the conclusion of the meal. Seven trays (output) per one labor minute (input) would be the productivity standard for a cashier totaling trays in this operation. If the manager knew (or could accurately estimate) the number of guests who would go through the line, he or she could estimate the "minutes" of total cashier time needed to service these guests.

A productivity standard, then, is simply management's expectation of the productivity ratio of each employee. Establishing productivity standards for every employee is an essential management task and the first step in controlling payroll costs.

Thus far, we have discussed some methods of measuring current productivity ratios based on historical sales and expense data. This tells you where you are in relation to productivity, but it does not say where you should be. To illustrate this concept, assume that you have decided to buy and operate a franchise unit within a themed steakhouse chain. Currently, four units of the same chain exist in your immediate geographic area, which has been designated a district by the **franchisor**, the entity responsible for selling and maintaining control over the franchise brand's name.

The area franchise representative who monitors labor productivity by using labor cost percentage has shared the following data with you, as shown in Figure 7.19.

■ FIGURE 7.19 Labor Cost % Summary

Unit Description	Labor Cost %
Unit 1	34.1%
Unit 2	35.5
Unit 3	34.3
Unit 4	35.2
District Average	34.8
Company Average	34.0
Industry Average	35.5

The figures for units one to four represent labor cost percentages in those franchise steakhouse units in your district. The district average is the unweighted mean of those four units. Company average refers to the overall labor cost percentage in the steakhouse chain that you are joining. Industry average refers to the average labor cost percentage reported by theme-style steakhouses of the type similar to the one you will own and operate.

Using the data presented in Figure 7.19, you could begin to establish your own desired productivity measures and goals. Your restaurant is not yet open; you therefore face the problem of not having historical data from your own unit to help you. Of course, this is always the case when opening new restaurants, but it is also true when significantly changing the theme, decor, or menu of an existing restaurant. Using your own judgment and the information you do have available, you could choose to use as your goal the lowest labor cost percentage (unit one); the highest (unit two); the district, company, or industry average; or even some other number not included in this listing. Any of these numbers could become your target, or ideal, labor cost percentage. In the final analysis, you must use whatever data you have available, as well as your own insight, to establish an appropriate productivity standard for your operation. Productivity standards are typically based on the following types of information:

1. Unit history
2. Company average
3. Industry average
4. Management experience
5. A combination of two or more of the above

In this case, you might choose to begin with a 35% labor cost as one of your productivity standards. This figure is close to the district average (34.8%) and is likely an aggressive, but realistic, goal for your first year. As mentioned previously, you would likely want to choose at least one more measure of productivity to help you monitor your labor efficiency. In the years to come, you would want to effectively manage the factors that affect productivity, carefully monitor your actual productivity using the productivity measures you select, and then establish a goal that is both realistic and attainable.

■ STEP 2. FORECAST SALES VOLUME

Sales volume forecasting (examined in Chapter 2), when combined with established labor productivity standards, allows you to determine the number of employees needed to effectively service your guests. All foodservice units must forecast volume if they are to supply an adequate number of employees to service that volume. This forecasting may be done in terms of either sales dollars or number of guests to be served.

An important, but frequently misunderstood, distinction must be made between forecasting sales volume and forecasting the number of employees needed

■ FIGURE 7.20 Ted's Coffee Shop Staffing Guide

Number of Guests Anticipated	Number of Servers Needed
1–30	1
31–60	2
61–90	3
91–120	4

to service that volume. The distinction is simply that, as a manager, you will view guests coming to your operation in "block" fashion, that is, in groups at a time. Employees, on the other hand, are added to your schedule one individual at a time and, thus, will significantly affect productivity measures. A brief example will make this clear. Ted owns a small shop that sells only specialty coffees. His service staff productivity standard is one server for each 30 guests. Thus, he schedules his employees as shown in Figure 7.20.

When 30 or fewer guests are expected, Ted needs only one server on duty. In effect, each time a block of 30 guests is added, Ted must add another server. Thus, if Ted anticipates 40 guests one day and 50 the next, no change in staff is necessary. That is, an addition of 10 extra guests does not dictate the addition of another server. On the other hand, if Ted anticipates 60 guests one day and 70 the next, an additional staff person is required because Ted has introduced a new block of guests.

It does not matter how much of the new block actually arrives; Ted has staffed for all of it. He hopes, of course, that all or nearly all of the block will arrive because this will keep his cost per guest served lower. If only a small portion of the block comes, Ted's cost per guest served will, of course, rise unless he takes some action to reduce his labor-related expense.

■ STEP 3. SCHEDULE EMPLOYEES USING PRODUCTIVITY STANDARDS AND FORECASTED SALES VOLUME

Forecasting sales volume is important to cost control because it begins to take management out of the past and present and allows it to project into the future and significantly influence what will happen then. To illustrate how established productivity standards (Step one) are combined with sales forecasts (Step two) to develop employee schedules (Step three), consider Darla, the foodservice director at Langtree, a private college enrolling a high percentage of female students. Darla is responsible for operating both a dormitory feeding situation and an open snack bar/cafeteria. The dormitory, Geier Hall, houses 1,000 young women. The snack bar/cafeteria, called Lillie's, is open to all students, staff, and faculty of the school. Darla is committed to controlling her labor-related expense. As such, she has carefully monitored her past labor productivity ratios, those of other similar schools, and national averages. In addition, she has considered the facilities she operates, the skill level and morale of her workforce and the impact of her aggressive training program on her future productivity. Considering all of these factors, Darla has determined that Lillie's snack bar/cafeteria should be able to operate at a labor cost of 30% of gross sales. In the dormitory, where guest counts, but no dollar sales figures, are kept on a daily basis, she has decided that her labor productivity measure should be established in terms of guests served per labor hour. Her goal is a ratio of 30 to 1, that is, 30 guests served per labor hour expended. Darla may now establish her labor cost expense budget in terms of both dollars (Lillie's) and labor hours used (Geier Hall).

Look at Figure 7.21 to see how Darla would establish her labor budget for Lillie's using her productivity standards, her sales forecast, and the labor cost percentage formula you have already learned. Remember that the labor cost percentage formula is defined as:

$$\frac{\text{Cost of Labor}}{\text{Total Sales}} = \text{Labor Cost \%}$$

If you include the words "forecasted," "standard," and "budget" and then apply the rules of algebra, the labor cost percentage formula can be restated as follows:

$$\text{Forecasted Total Sales} \times \text{Labor Cost \% Standard} = \text{Cost of Labor Budget}$$

Thus, budgeted cost of labor in the preceding formula becomes Darla's targeted labor expense budget. To determine, for example, her targeted labor expense budget in week 1, Darla would compute the amount as follows:

$$\$6,550 \times 30\% = \$1,965$$

■ **FIGURE 7.21** Labor Budget for Lillie's Snack Bar Using Labor Cost %

Time Period	Forecasted Total Sales	Labor Cost % Standard	Cost of Labor Budget
Week 1	$ 6,550	30%	$1,965
Week 2	6,850	30	2,055
Week 3	6,000	30	1,800
Week 4	8,100	30	2,430
Total	27,500	30	8,250

■ **FIGURE 7.22** Labor Budget for Geier Hall Using Guests Served per Labor Hour

Time Period	Forecasted Number of Guests Served	Guests Served per Labor Hour Standard	Labor Hour Budget
Week 1	20,000	30 guests/hour	666.7
Week 2	18,600	30 guests/hour	620.0
Week 3	18,100	30 guests/hour	603.3
Week 4	17,800	30 guests/hour	593.3
Total	74,500	30 guest/hour	2,483.3

Figure 7.22 illustrates how Darla would establish a budget for total number of labor hours used to service Geier Hall. Recall that, in this food facility, sales refers to the number of guests served rather than dollars, and this is reflected in Darla's sales forecast. Also remember that the guests served per labor hour formula is defined as:

$$\frac{\text{Guests Served}}{\text{Labor Hours Used}} = \text{Guests Served per Labor Hour}$$

If you include the words "forecasted," "standard," and "budget" and follow the rules of algebra, the guests served per labor hour formula can be restated as follows:

$$\frac{\text{Forecasted Number of Guests Served}}{\text{Guests Served per Labor Hour Standard}} = \text{Labor Hour Budget}$$

Using week one in Figure 7.22 as an example, the computation would be:

$$\frac{20,000}{30} = 666.7$$

Note that in Figures 7.21 and 7.22, Darla could have varied her weekly productivity standard and still have produced a four-week budget. In other words, on weeks when volume was high, she could have elected to reduce her desired labor cost % or increase the guests served per labor hour standard. This can be a logical course of action if the operator feels that increased volume can have the effect of reducing the cost percentage of fixed labor or can increase the number of guests served per labor hour by staff persons in specific positions, such as cashiers, managers, and so on. Experience tells Darla, however, that, in her case, a standard labor productivity ratio that remains unchanged across the four weeks is her best option.

From the labor budgets she developed, Darla can now schedule her production people in terms of dollars to be spent for labor (Lillie's) or labor hours to be used

■ FIGURE 7.23   Weekly Labor Hour Budget for Geier Hall

Day	Forecasted Number of Guests Served	Guests Served per Labor Hour Standard	Labor Hour Budget
1	3,000	30 guests/hour	100.0
2	2,900	30 guests/hour	96.7
3	2,900	30 guests/hour	96.7
4	2,850	30 guests/hour	95.0
5	3,000	30 guests/hour	100.0
6	2,700	30 guests/hour	90.0
7	2,650	30 guests/hour	88.3
Total	20,000	30 guests/hour	666.7

(Geier Hall). She must be careful to schedule employees only when they are needed. To do this, she must forecast her volume in time blocks smaller than one-day segments. Perhaps, in her case, volume should be predicted in three periods (breakfast, lunch, and dinner) in the dormitory, and in one- or two-hour blocks in her snack bar/cafeteria.

To see how Darla might schedule her dormitory staff during week 1 of her four-week projection, assume that Darla's weekly projection of sales volume for Geier Hall is as presented in Figure 7.23.

On any given day, Darla can match her volume projections with budgeted hours or dollars. To see exactly how she would use this information to determine her employees' schedules, let us examine day 1 in Figure 7.23, a day when Darla projects 3,000 guests (meals) served and 100 labor hours needed. She knows that she should "spend" no more than 100 total hours for labor on that day. She also knows, from recording her productivity ratio in the past (Figure 7.24), where she has spent her labor hours in prior time periods. Thus, Darla should invest approximately 60 hours

■ FIGURE 7.24   Recap of Percentage of Total Usage by Category

Geier Hall	
Labor Category	% of Total
Production	60%
Service	30
Management	10
Total	100

■ **FIGURE 7.25** Recap of Guests Served per Labor Hour

Labor Category	Geier Hall		
	Forecasted Number of Guests Served	Labor Hour Standard	Budgeted Guests Served per Labor Hour
Production	3,000	60	50
Service	3,000	30	100
Management	3,000	10	300
Total	3,000	100	30

(100 hours available × 0.60 average usage) for production employees, 30 hours for service employees, and 10 hours of management time for Monday if she is to stay within her labor budget while providing an adequate number of workers in each of the three categories of labor she monitors regularly.

Presented in a different way, Darla knows that, to stay within her labor goals, each labor category will have its own unique guest served per labor hour ratio, as noted in Figure 7.25. It is important to note that, although guests served per labor hour varies by labor category, the overall total yields 30 guests per labor hour used, which is Darla's productivity standard. Darla's employee schedule for the production area on Monday might look as shown in Figure 7.26.

Because employee schedules are based upon the number of hours to be worked or dollars to be spent, an employee schedule recap form similar to the one in Figure 7.26 can be an effective tool in a daily analysis of labor productivity. Labor is purchased on a daily basis; labor costs should, therefore, be monitored on a daily basis. The labor schedule should be modified as needed during the day. This constant adjustment is a key to the quick-service industry's profitability because schedule modifications by good managers in this segment of the industry are implemented hourly, not daily! In other words, if customer demand is lower than expected, employees can be released from the schedule to reduce costs. If volume is higher than expected, additional employees should be available on an "as needed" basis.

Some foodservice managers practice an **on-call** system whereby employees who are off duty are assigned to on-call status. This means that these employees can be contacted by management on short notice to cover for other employees who are absent or to come to work if customer demand suddenly increases. State laws vary regarding the compensation that must be paid to these on-call employees; thus, managers who use this method should know about existing state laws and their own company policies regarding the practice before it is implemented.

Other managers practice a **call-in** system. In this arrangement, employees who are off-duty are required to check in with management on a daily basis to see if the predicted sales volume is such that they may be needed. This is a particularly good way to make rapid changes in staffing because of unforeseen increases in projected sales volume.

■ **FIGURE 7.26** Employee Schedule

Unit Name: **Geier Hall**			Date: **Monday 1/1**	
Labor Category: **Production**	Shift: A.M. & P.M.		Labor Budget: **60 hours**	

Employee Name	Schedule	Hours Scheduled	Rate	Total Cost
Sally S.*	6:00 a.m.–2:30 p.m.	8	N/A	N/A
Tom T.*	6:30 a.m.–3:00 p.m.	8		
Steve J.*	8:00 a.m.–4:30 p.m.	8		
Abhijit S.*	10:00 a.m.–6:30 p.m.	8		
Janice J.	7:00 a.m.–11:00 a.m.	4		
Susie T.	6:30 a.m.–10:30 a.m.	4		
Peggy H.	10:30 a.m.–1:30 p.m.	3		
Marian D.	2:00 p.m.–5:00 p.m.	3		
Larry M.*	11:00 a.m.–7:30 p.m.	8		
Ahmed D.*	1:00 p.m.–7:30 p.m.	6		
Total		60	N/A	N/A

*Includes 30-minute meal break.

Overtime, which must be paid at a higher than average rate, should generally be held to a minimum and should require documented management approval before it is authorized. In the case of Geier Hall, the Rate and Total Cost columns in Figure 7.26 are not computed because, in this unit, they are not part of the productivity measure (remember that guests served per labor hour relies on neither cost of labor nor sales revenue for its computation). They would, of course, be filled out when determining the cost of the schedule for Lillie's snack bar because, in that unit, it is labor dollars, not hours used, that is the integral part of the productivity standard. In all cases, an employee schedule, reviewed on a daily basis, should be established for each unit, labor category, and individual. It is critical to match labor usage with projected volume.

■ STEP 4. ANALYZE RESULTS

Darla has done a good job of using established labor standards and volume projections in building her employee schedule. To complete the job of managing labor-related expense, she should analyze her results. Figure 7.27 details the

■ **FIGURE 7.27** Labor Recap for Lillie's Actual versus Budgeted Labor Cost

| Week | Sales | | | Labor Cost | | | Labor Cost % | |
	Budgeted	Actual	% of Budget	Budgeted	Actual	% of Budget	Budgeted	Actual
1	$ 6,550	$ 6,400	98%	$1,965	$1,867	95%	30%	29%
2	6,850	7,000	102	2,055	2,158	105	30	31
3	6,000	6,000	100	1,800	1,980	110	30	33
4	8,100	7,600	94	2,430	2,430	100	30	32
Total	27,500	27,000	98	8,250	8,435	102	30	31

budgeted and actual results of the operation of Lillie's for the first four weeks of the year.

To determine the percentage of budget, the following formula, introduced in Chapter 1, is used:

$$\frac{\text{Actual Amount}}{\text{Budgeted Amount}} = \% \text{ of Budget}$$

Note that total sales were somewhat less than budgeted (98%), whereas total labor cost dollars were somewhat higher than budgeted (102%). Consequently, labor cost % was somewhat higher than anticipated, in other words, a 31% actual result compared to a 30% budget percentage. Notice also that, when sales are projected perfectly (week 3) but labor is overspent, the actual labor cost % will be too high (33%). Conversely, when labor costs are exactly as budgeted (week 4) but sales volume does not reach the estimate, labor cost percent will similarly be too high (32%).

It may seem that a 1% variation in overall labor cost percentage is insignificant. In fact, in this case it represents $185 ($8,435 actual – $8,250 budgeted = $185). However, if a foodservice company achieved sales of $30,000,000 per year, 1% would represent $300,000 per year in cost overrun! Small percentages can add up. What constitutes a significant budget variation can only be determined by management. Darla may well want to review standard scheduling techniques with her supervisors because she exceeded her budgeted labor cost in two of the four weeks shown. In Darla's case, $185 may well be a significant budget variation.

When referring to labor costs, some foodservice operators use the term **standard cost**—that is, the labor cost needed to meet established productivity standards—rather than budgeted cost. If productivity standards are used to establish budgeted labor costs, then, of course, the two terms are synonymous. It is important, however, not to confuse the concept of standard labor cost with that of standard food cost. A simple example will help to explain the difference. Assume that

■ **FIGURE 7.28** Ten-Point Labor Schedule Checklist

1. Monitor historical operational data (or alternative data if historical data are not available).
2. Identify productivity standards.
3. Forecast sales volume.
4. Determine budgeted labor dollars or hours.
5. Divide monthly budget into weekly budgets.
6. Divide weekly budget into daily budgets.
7. Segment daily budget into meal period budgets.
8. Build schedule based on the budget.
9. Analyze service levels during schedule period.
10. Reassess and adjust productivity standards as needed.

a restaurant serves each of four guests a flat iron steak for dinner. If the restaurant had ten such steaks in the refrigerator and six remain at the end of the meal period, the food standard of one per guest has been maintained. Assume also, however, that these four guests are the only customers of the night and that labor staffing was established based on five guests. In this case, the standard cost, or budget, was not met in terms of guests served or perhaps dollar sales, yet management is in control. To further make the point, if one flat iron steak were missing, our food standard would be off by 10% (one steak/ten total). This would represent a serious loss of food product control. In our labor example, our forecast was off by 20% (one guest short/five total projected), yet the variation is not due to lack of management control. In the case of labor, we are still within reasonable budget, though we may vary greatly from the standard.

For this reason, the authors prefer the term **budgeted labor** rather than **standard labor**. Labor standards will always vary a bit unless guest counts can be predicted perfectly, which, of course, is rarely the case. We can, however, compare budgeted labor expense with actual results to determine if the reasons for the variation from budget are valid and acceptable to management. The complete process for establishing the labor schedule is summarized in the checklist contained in Figure 7.28.

REDUCING LABOR-RELATED COSTS

If through your analysis you find that labor costs are too high, problem areas must be identified and corrective action must be taken. If the overall productivity of your work group cannot be improved, other action must be taken. The approaches you can take to reduce labor-related costs, however, are different for fixed-payroll costs than for variable costs. Figure 7.29 indicates actions that can be taken to reduce

FIGURE 7.29 Reducing Labor-Related Expenses

Labor Category	Action
Fixed	1. Improve worker productivity.
	2. Increase sales volume.
	3. Combine jobs to eliminate fixed positions.
	4. Reduce wages paid to the fixed-payroll employees.
Variable	1. Improve worker productivity.
	2. Schedule appropriately to adjust to changes in sales volume.
	3. Combine jobs to eliminate variable positions.
	4. Reduce wages paid to the variable employees.

labor-related expense in each of these two categories. Notice that you can only decrease variable expense by increasing productivity, improving the scheduling process, eliminating employees, or reducing wages paid. Fixed expense can be reduced (as a percentage of revenue) by increasing sales volume. In all cases, however, the foodservice operation gains when increases in productivity mean that wages can remain high and, in fact, increase.

■ EMPLOYEE EMPOWERMENT

One way of increasing employee productivity, and thus reducing labor-related expense, is through employee empowerment. This results from a decision by management to fully involve employees in the decision-making process as far as guests and the employees themselves are concerned.

The shortage of skilled labor, shrinking numbers of qualified applicants, and increased competition from other industries all force management in the hospitality industry to act and think creatively when attempting to secure a productive workforce. Contrary to what custom has dictated in the past, the workforce today is not as amenable to "forced" labor as in years past. Today's employees realize that there is more to life than work. They expect more from life than a 50-plus-hour workweek with little time left for family and friends. Blind allegiance to an organization with the likelihood of being dismissed when management is in a squeeze is no longer the norm. Employees seek job satisfaction in addition to their pay. Salaries and wages must be acceptable and fair, but it has become critical that management show its human, compassionate side and provide for its employees those amenities that make life gentler, smoother, and more gratifying. Employees make demands, and management, frequently often unable to offer more money, often finds itself in a position where it has to come up with incentives of a different sort. In addition to creating a good working environment and providing competitive benefits, progressive managers have found that one way of increasing employee productivity, and thus reducing related expense, is through the use of employee empowerment. **Empowerment** refers simply to the fact that, whereas it was once customary for management to make all decisions regarding every facet of the operational aspects of its organization and present them to its employees as inescapable facts to be accomplished, employees are now being given the "power" to get involved. They are being empowered to make decisions concerning themselves and, most important, the guests—the bread and butter of the hospitality industry. Employees, generally, work closely with guests. They see and observe, they talk to guests, they hear and listen to complaints, they can appease guests, and when called upon to do so, they can find remedies to fix problem situations.

Many guest-related problems in the hospitality industry could be easily solved if employees were given the power to make it "right" for the guest. Management has found in many cases that, through a well-planned and consistently delivered training program, and by giving their employees a share in the decision-making process, they are nurturing a loyal and committed workforce that is supportive of management and willing to go the extra mile. Employee empowerment, which has been discussed in the hospitality industry primarily in terms of its positive effect on employees and guests, can also be of great assistance in freeing management to concentrate on running the business while allowing employees to service the guests. It has been said that management gets the quality of workforce it deserves. That is, managers who care little about the welfare of their employees get employees who care little for the welfare of the organization. Those managers, on the other hand, who demonstrate real care and concern for their employees and do their best to meet their needs as well as those of the guest, find employees who return that care and concern to the organization.

Green and Growing!

Consumers are increasingly aware that when they support businesses committed to sustainability, their dollars make an impact socially and environmentally. As a result, influential and leading-edge thinkers concerned about society and the environment seek out companies that share their health, social, and environmental interests and priorities. So committed are they that they are, on average, willing to spend 20% more than the typical guest for products that conform to their values and lifestyle.

In a similar manner, environmentally conscious workers are increasingly becoming aware that a company's care for the environment most often is also reflected in its care for its employees. As a result, companies espousing genuine commitment to the environment attract a more committed and, as a result, higher-quality staff. These workers tend to value health, the environment, social justice, personal development, and sustainable living. They want to contribute their efforts to companies that share those values, and their numbers are growing.

Do you have to be "certified" as green to attract these environmentally conscious employees? That is, do you have to be a "perfect" green facility? No. But you cannot just pretend that you are, either. Workers easily see beyond false claims of care, in part because they share information so freely and easily via Web pages, twitters, blogs, and chat rooms. The more environmentally friendly, socially responsible, and healthy you are known to truly be, the easier it will be for prospective employees who share these goals to find you—because they *are* looking.

FUN ON THE WEB!

Monthly journals and daily Web briefings are important sources of management information. The Society for Human Resource Management (SHRM) is a great source of human resource management information. You can visit the Web site at: **www.shrm.org.**

While you are there, browse the bookstore. Also consider a daily reading of the "HR News" column.

Technology Tools

As labor costs continue to increase, and as labor cost management becomes increasingly important to the profitability of restaurateurs, the tools available to manage these costs have significantly improved and increased as well.

Current software programs enable you to manage and control labor costs by helping you perform the following tasks:

1. Maintain employment records, such as:
   a. Required employment documents (i.e., applications, I-9s, W-2s, etc.)
   b. Tax data
   c. Pay rates
   d. Earned vacation or other leave time
   e. Department/cost center affiliation
   f. Benefits eligibility
   g. Training records
2. Conduct and record the results of on-line or computer-based training programs.
3. Compute voluntary and involuntary employee turnover rates by department.
4. Track employee lost days due to injury/accident.
5. Maintain employee availability records (requested days off, vacation, etc.).
6. Develop employee schedules and interface employee schedules with time clock systems.
7. Monitor overtime costs.
8. Maintain job descriptions and specifications.
9. Develop and maintain daily, weekly, and monthly productivity reports, including:
   a. Labor cost percentage
   b. Sales per labor hour
   c. Labor dollars per guest served

> d. Guests served per labor dollar
>
> e. Guests served per labor hour
>
> f. Optimal labor costs based on actual sales achieved
>
> 10. Interface an employee scheduling component with forecasted sales volume software in the POS system.

Fun on the Web!

Innovation in management tools that involve software programming is not always aimed toward larger companies. To view a payroll assistance program developed for smaller operations, including restaurants, go to: **www.paycycle.com.**

Apply What You Have Learned

Teddy Fields is the Kitchen Manager at the Tanron Corporation International Headquarters. The facility he helps manage serves 3,000 employees per day. Teddy very much needs an additional dishwasher and is interviewing Wayne, an excellent candidate with five years of experience who is now washing dishes at the Roadway restaurant. Teddy normally starts his dishwashers at $9.00 per hour. Wayne states that he makes $10.00 per hour, a rate that is higher than all but one of Teddy's current dishwashers. Wayne states that he will not leave his current job to take a "pay cut."

1. Should Teddy offer to hire Wayne at a rate higher than most of his current employees? Why or why not?

2. Assume you answered "No" to question one above, what would you say to Wayne?

3. Assume you answered "Yes" to question one above, what would you say to your current dishwashing employees if in the future Wayne shared his pay information with them?

Key Terms and Concepts

The following are terms and concepts discussed in the chapter that are important for you as a manager. To help you review, please define the terms below:

Labor expense	Minimum staff	Productivity ratio
Payroll	Fixed payroll	Job description
Salaried employee	Variable payroll	Job specification
Exempt employee	Productivity	Skills test

Psychological testing	Split shift	Franchisor
Preemployment drug testing	Separated	On-call
Negligent hiring	Voluntary separation	Call-in
Orientation program	Involuntary separation	Standard cost
Task training	Revenue per Available	Budgeted labor
OJT	Seat Hour (RevPASH)	versus standard
On the floor	Productivity	labor
	standard	Empowerment

Test Your Skills

Complete the Test Your Skills exercises by placing your answers in the shaded boxes and answering the questions as indicated.

1. Rosa is the manager of a fine-dining Italian restaurant in a large Midwest city. She has experienced high turnover with her hourly employees over the past several months because they say that she isn't paying competitive wages. More employees have threatened to leave if she doesn't give them a raise. She has determined that she can compete with local restaurants if she raises the hourly wage from $8.00 per hour to $8.50, a 6.25% increase. Rosa is concerned about what this will do to her labor cost percentage. Her current labor cost is 35%, and she feels that 38% is the highest labor cost ratio she can maintain and still make a profit. Using last month's data, help Rosa calculate the effect of a 6.25% increase in wages. Can she give the employees what they want and still make a profit?

Week	Original Cost of Labor	Raise in Dollars	Total Cost of Labor	Sales	Labor Cost %
1	$10,650			$27,600	
2	12,075			32,250	
3	10,887			28,650	
4	10,383			37,200	
Total					

2. Jennifer operates Joe Bob's Bar-B-Q Restaurant. She specializes in beef brisket and blackberry cobbler. Her operation is very popular. The following data are taken from her last month's operation. She would like to establish labor standards for the entire year based on last month's figures because she believes that month represents a good level of both customer service and profitability for her operation. Jennifer has an average guest check of $12 and an overall average payroll cost of $8 per hour.

a. Use Jennifer's last month's operating results to calculate the following productivity standards: labor cost percentage, sales per labor hour, labor dollars per guest served, guests served per labor dollar, and guests served per labor hour. (Spreadsheet hint: Use the ROUND function to two decimal places for "Guests Served per Labor Hour" because you will use it in part c.)

Operating Results for Joe Bob's		
Week	Number of Guests Served	Labor Hours Used
1	7,000	4,000
2	7,800	4,120
3	7,500	4,110
4	8,000	4,450
Total	30,300	16,680

Calculate:

Average Guest Check	$12.00
Average Wage Paid per Hour	$ 8.00
Total Sales	
Total Labor Cost	

Productivity Measurement	Productivity Standard
Labor Cost Percentage	
Sales per Labor Hour	
Labor Dollars per Guest Served	
Guests Served per Labor Dollar	
Guests Served per Labor Hour	

b. Jennifer has subdivided her employees into the following categories: meat production, bakery production, salad production, service, sanitation, and management. She wants to develop a sales per labor hour standard for each of her labor categories. She believes this will help her develop future labor budgets based on forecasted sales. Help Jennifer calculate this standard based on her current usage of labor hours.

Labor Category	% of Labor Hours Used	Labor Hours	Sales per Labor Hour
Meat Production	25%		
Bakery Production	15%		
Salad Production	10%		
Service	20%		
Sanitation	20%		
Management	10%		
Total	100%		

c. Now that Jennifer has calculated her productivity standards, she would like to use them to develop a labor hours budget for each day next week. She has forecasted 8,000 guests, and she wants to use the guests served per labor hour standard that was calculated in part a. Use this information to develop a labor hours budget for Jennifer.

Day	Forecasted Number of Guests Served	Guests Served per Labor Hour Standard	Labor Hours Budget
1	900		
2	925		
3	975		
4	1,200		
5	1,400		
6	1,600		
7	1,000		
Total	8,000		

3. Mikel owns Mikel's Steak House, a popular dining establishment just outside of town on a busy state highway. Mikel uses labor cost % as his productivity measure, but he has been calculating it only once per month. Since his monthly costs have been higher than he expected, Mikel has decided that he needs a daily measure of his labor cost % to better control his costs.

    a. Calculate Mikel's daily labor cost % using the six-column daily productivity report, which follows.

Six-Column Labor Cost Percentage							
Unit Name: Mikel's Steak House				Date: 3/1–3/7			
	Cost of Labor			Sales		Labor Cost %	
Weekday	Today	To Date	Today	To Date	Today	To Date
1	$ 950		$2,520			
2	1,120		2,610			
3	1,040		2,720			
4	1,100		2,780			
5	1,600		3,530			
6	1,700		4,100			
7	1,300		3,910			
Total						

    b. Mikel wants to keep his labor cost % at 37%. Given the results of his six-column daily productivity report for the first week of March, will he be able to achieve his labor cost % standard if he continues in the same manner for the remainder of the month? If not, what actions can he take to reduce both his fixed and his variable labor-related expenses?

4. Jeffrey operates a high-volume, fine-dining restaurant called the Baroness. His labor productivity ratio of choice is guests served per labor hour. His standards for both servers and buspersons are as follows:

Servers = 10 Guests per Labor Hour
Buspersons = 25 Guests per Labor Hour

On a busy day, Jeffrey projects the following volume in terms of anticipated guests. His projections are made in 1-hour blocks. Determine the number of labor hours Jeffrey should schedule for each job classification for each time period.

How often in the night should Jeffrey check his volume forecast to ensure that he achieves his labor productivity standards and, thus, is within budget at the end of the evening? (Spreadsheet hint: Format "Server Hours Needed" and "Busperson Hours Needed" to one decimal place.)

Volume/Staff Forecasting for Saturday: The Baroness			
Time	Forecasted Number of Guests Served	Server Hours Needed	Busperson Hours Needed
11:00–12:00	85		
12:00–1:00	175		
1:00–2:00	95		
2:00–3:00	30		
3:00–4:00	25		
4:00–5:00	45		
5:00–6:00	90		
6:00–7:00	125		
7:00–8:00	185		
8:00–9:00	150		
9:00–10:00	90		
10:00–11:00	45		
Total	1,140		

5. Steve is in trouble. He has never been a particularly strong labor cost control person. He likes to think of himself more as a "people person." His boss, however, believes that Steve must get more serious about controlling labor costs or he will make Steve an unemployed people person! Steve estimates his weekly sales and then submits that figure to his boss, who then assigns Steve a labor budget for the week. Steve's operating results and budget figures for last month are presented below.

a. Compute Steve's % of budget figures for both sales and labor cost. Also, compute Steve's budget and actual labor cost percentages per week and for the five-week accounting period.

Operating Results: Steve's Airport Deli								
							For Weeks 1–5	
	Sales			Labor Cost		Labor Cost %		
Week	Budget	Actual	% of Budget	Budget	Actual	% of Budget	Budget	Actual
1	$2,500	$2,250		$ 875	$ 900			
2	1,700	1,610		595	630			
3	4,080	3,650		1,224	1,300			
4	3,100	2,800		1,085	1,100			
5	2,600	2,400		910	980			
Total								

b. Do you feel that Steve has significant variations from budget? Why do you think Steve's boss assigned Steve a lower labor cost % goal during week 3? How do you feel about Steve's overall performance? What would you do if you were Steve's boss? If you were Steve?

6. Jordan is the new western regional manager for The Lotus House, an Asian buffet restaurant chain. Her territory consists of 12 stores in four states. Last week she received the following data from her stores. Compute Jordan's labor cost by store, by state, and for her region.

	Sales	Cost of Labor	Labor Cost%
California			
Store 1	$ 91,000.00	$34,500.00	
Store 2	$106,500.00	$38,750.00	
Store 3	$ 83,500.00	$31,500.00	
Total			
Oregon			
Store 1	$ 36,800.00	$12,250.00	
Store 2	$ 61,000.00	$18,750.00	
Store 3	$ 52,000.00	$17,500.00	
Total			
Washington			
Store 1	$ 47,500.00	$14,750.00	
Store 2	$ 46,500.00	$15,000.00	
Store 3	$ 45,500.00	$15,000.00	
Total			
Nevada			
Store 1	$ 53,000.00	$17,250.00	
Store 2	$ 56,000.00	$18,500.00	
Store 3	$ 55,100.00	$17,250.00	
Total			
Region			

Can Jordan compute the average labor cost percentage for her region by summing the labor cost percentages of the four states and dividing by four? Why or why not? How is the overall labor cost percentage for her region computed?

7. Ravi Shah is the food and beverage director at the St. Andrews Golf Course and Conference Center. The facility is a popular place for weddings and Ravi finds that on many Friday and Saturday nights the banquet space at St. Andrews is completely booked. That is good news, but Ravi also finds that Allisha, the one full-time (paid $20.00 per hour) employee he has utilized as a supervisor for the banquet area is averaging 15 hours overtime per week.

   Ravi is considering three alternative courses of action. They are:

   1. Maintain the status quo and pay Allisha for 55 hours per week.
   2. Create a salaried position, schedule the employee who holds the position 55 hours per week, and pay that individual $50,000 per year.
   3. Split the job into two part-time positions of 30 and 25 hours per week and pay these employees $22.50 per hour.

Assume the following:

- Overtime is paid at 1.5 times the normally paid rate.
- The operation's benefit package for part-time employees is 20% of the wages paid to them.
- The operation's benefit package for full-time employees is 35% of the wages paid to them.
- All full-time and part-time employees at the supervisor level or above receive two weeks paid vacation per year.

   Which of these three courses of action will cost the facility the most money? The least? If you were Ravi, which of these alternatives would you implement? Why?

	Hours Worked	Pay per Hour	Pay per Week	Weeks in a Year	Pay before Benefits	Benefits	Annual Pay with Benefits
Alternative 1							
Total							
Alternative 2							
Alternative 3							
Total							

8. Luis manages Havana, a 150-seat full-service restaurant featuring Cuban and other Caribbean-style menu items. His restaurant is open for dinner from 5:00 p.m. to 11:00 p.m. Luis was excited to read, in one of the industry publications to which he subscribes, an article explaining RevPASH. In the past, Luis used labor cost % to create his allowable labor cost budget. Luis now wants to calculate RevPASH, as well as continue to use labor cost % to establish his *hourly* allowable labor cost budget. He has created a form (below) to calculate each of these measures.

Luis is a good manager. When his dining room is slower, he encourages his servers to aggressively sell appetizers and desserts to increase his check average. When the restaurant is very busy, he encourages his servers to stress the quick turn of tables to minimize guest wait times and maximize the number of guests that can be served. As a result, and based on his historical records, when he serves 100 or fewer guests per hour, the restaurant achieves a $20.00 per guest check average. When 101–150 guests are served per hour, the check average drops to $18.00 per guest. When over 150 guests are served per hour, Havana achieves a $16.00 per guest check average.

Consider Luis's forecast, shown in the following, of the number of guests he will serve this coming Friday night, and then calculate his forecasted RevPASH for each hour he will be open. Next, help him know how much he can spend for labor for each hour he will be open. Assume Luis's target is a 30% labor cost at all times. (Spreadsheet hint: Calculate Total Check Average *after* Total Revenue and Total Guests Served have been calculated.)

Havana Forecast for:						This FRIDAY Night
Hour	Available Seats	Guests Served	Check Average	Revenue	RevPASH	Allowable Cost Based on 30% Labor Cost
5–6 p.m.		50				
6–7 p.m.		100				
7–8 p.m.		150				
8–9 p.m.		175				
9–10 p.m.		125				
10–11 p.m.		75				
Total						
% Seats Sold =						

a. What percentage of his total seats available does Luis believe he will fill on Friday night? What overall check average does he estimate he will achieve?

b. What would be Luis's forecast for his hourly and overall RevPASH on this day?

c. What would be Luis's labor budget for each hour his restaurant will be open, as well as the total amount that could be spent for labor that night?

d. What are some specific steps Luis might take to improve his RevPASH on Friday's from 5–6 p.m.? From 8–9 p.m.?

9. In this chapter you learned about the importance of employee training when seeking to improve worker productivity. The old foodservice adage that "Training doesn't cost—it pays!" is true. With creative thinking, even the cost of acquiring quality training materials can be made very reasonable. Assume you were the Director of Foodservices for a school district that included 20 elementary, middle, and high schools. You seek to provide training to the 100 foodservice employees working in your district. Identify five specific steps you could take to identify and secure low-cost training materials that could be utilized at a minimum "cost-per-employee" to be trained.

Chapter 8

CONTROLLING OTHER EXPENSES

OVERVIEW

T his chapter explains the management of foodservice costs that are neither food, beverage, nor labor. These costs can represent 15%, or even more, of an operation's sales revenue and must be controlled if your financial goals are to be achieved in the operation you manage. The chapter teaches how to identify the costs you can control, as well as those that are considered to be noncontrollable expenses. In addition, it details how to express other expenses in terms of both other expenses per guest served and other expenses as a percentage of sales revenue.

Chapter Outline

- Managing Other Expenses
- Fixed, Variable, and Mixed Other Expenses
- Controllable and Noncontrollable Other Expenses
- Monitoring Other Expenses
- Reducing Other Expenses
- Technology Tools
- Apply What You Have Learned
- Key Terms and Concepts
- Test Your Skills

LEARNING OUTCOMES

At the conclusion of this chapter, you will be able to:
- Categorize Other Expenses in terms of being fixed, variable, or mixed.
- Classify individual Other Expenses as either controllable or noncontrollable
- Compute Other Expense costs in terms of both cost per guest and percentage of sales.

MANAGING OTHER EXPENSES

*F*ood, beverage, and payroll expenses represent the greatest cost areas you will encounter as a foodservice manager. There are, however, additional operating expenses you must pay that are neither food, beverage, nor labor. These **other expenses** can account for a significant amount of the total cost of operating your foodservice unit. They include a variety of items, such as administrative costs, utility bills, the repair and maintenance of equipment, insurance, and property taxes and mortgage payments if a building is owned, and rent or lease payments if it is not.

Controlling other expense costs will be just as important to your success as controlling food, beverage, and payroll expenses. Remember that the profit margins in many restaurants can be small. Thus, the control of all costs is critically important. Even in those situations that are traditionally considered nonprofit, such as hospitals, nursing homes, and educational institutions, all costs must be controlled because dollars that are wasted in the foodservice area are not available for use in other areas of the institution.

You must look for ways to control all of your expenses, but sometimes the environment in which you operate will act upon your facility to influence some of your costs in positive or negative ways. An excellent example of this is in the area of energy conservation and waste recycling. Energy costs are one of the other expenses examined in this chapter. In the past, serving water to each guest upon arrival in a restaurant was simply **standard operating procedure (SOP)** for many operations. The rising cost of energy has caused many foodservice operations to implement a policy of serving water on request rather than with each order, or of selling bottled water in lieu of "free" tap water. Guests have found these changes quite acceptable, and the savings in the expenses related to warewashing costs, equipment usage, energy, cleaning supplies, as well as labor are significant. In a similar vein, many operators today are finding that recycling fats and oils, cans, jars, and paper can be good not only for the environment but also for their bottom line. Recycling these items reduces your cost of routine garbage and refuse disposal, and, in some communities, the recycled materials themselves have a cash value.

FUN ON THE WEB!

Look up the following site for ideas on how to cut other expenses through energy conservation, source reduction, and recycling.

www.use-less-stuff.com. This is a great place to learn about source reduction, packaging, and waste reduction. Especially note their Use Less Stuff (ULS) report. Also browse through this site for reports, articles, and links to other interesting sites.

An other expense can constitute almost anything in the foodservice business. If your restaurant is a floating ship, periodically scraping the barnacles off the boat is an "other expense." If an operator is serving food to oil field workers in Alaska, heating fuel for the dining rooms and kitchen is an other expense, and probably a very large one! If a company has been selected to serve food at the Olympics in a foreign country, airfares for its employees may be a significant other expense.

Each foodservice operation will have its own unique list of required other expenses. It is not possible, therefore, to list all imaginable expenses that could be incurred by the foodservice operator. It is possible, nonetheless, to group them into categories that make them easier to manage and understand. Napkins, straws, paper cups, and plastic lids, for example, might all be listed under the heading paper supplies, whereas stir sticks, coasters, tiny plastic swords, small paper umbrellas, and the like used in a cocktail lounge might be grouped under the listing bar supplies. Credit card processing fees, Internet access costs, and the cost of ink cartridges for printers could be grouped under the listing of administrative costs.

If cost groupings are used, they should make sense to the operator and should be specific enough to let the operator know what is in the category. Although some operators prefer to make their own groups, the categories used in this text come from the Uniform System of Accounts for Restaurants (USAR). The categories may be identified either by name, such as paper supplies, or by number, such as category 7420. The Uniform System of Accounts for Restaurants lists categories both by name and by number. For the purpose of our discussion, titles alone will suffice.

The different types of other expenses that can be incurred by a foodservice operation are varied, but a large number of them are identified in the USAR. The following pages list many of the other expenses associated with the four major USAR expense groupings, some of which include sub-groupings to provide managers even more information. These major groups are:

1. Costs related to food and beverage operations
2. Costs related to labor
3. Costs related to facility maintenance
4. Occupancy costs

■ COSTS RELATED TO FOOD AND BEVERAGE OPERATIONS

Direct Operating Expenses

Uniforms	Auto and truck expenses
Laundry and dry cleaning	Cleaning supplies
Linen rental	Paper supplies
Linen	Guest supplies
China and glassware	Bar supplies
Silverware	Menus and wine lists
Kitchen utensils	Contract cleaning

Exterminating

Flowers and decorations

Parking lot expenses

Licenses and permits

Banquet expenses

Other operating expenses

Music and Entertainment

Musicians

Professional entertainers

Mechanical music

Contracted wire services

Piano rental and tuning

Films, records, tapes, and sheet music

Programs

Royalties to ASCAP, BMI, and SESAC

Booking agents fees

Meals served to musicians

Marketing

Selling and promotion
 Sales representative service
 Travel expense on solicitation
 Direct mail
 Telephone used for advertising and
  promotion
 Complimentary food and beverage
  (including gratis meals to customers)
 Postage
 Advertising
 Newspapers
 Magazines and trade journals
 Circulars, brochures, postal cards,
  and other mailing pieces
 Outdoor signs
 Radio and television

 Programs, directories, and guides
 Preparation of copy, photographs,
  etc.

Public relations and publicity
 Civic and community projects
 Donations
 Souvenirs, favors, treasure
  chest items

Fees and commissions
 Advertising or promotional
  agency fees

Research
 Travel in connection with research
Outside research agency
 Product testing

Utility Services

Electric current

Electric bulbs

Water

Removal of waste

Natural Gas

Other fuels

Administrative and General Expenses

Office stationery, printing, and supplies

Data processing costs

Postage

Telegrams and telephone

Dues and subscriptions

Traveling expenses

Insurance—general

Commissions on credit card charges

Provision for doubtful accounts

Cash over (or short)

Professional fees

Protective and bank pickup services

Bank charges

Miscellaneous

Internet Access (not currently in USAR; added by authors)

■ COSTS RELATED TO LABOR

Employee Benefits

FICA

Federal unemployment tax

State unemployment tax

Workers' compensation

Group insurance

State health insurance tax

Welfare plan payments

Pension plan payments

Accident and health insurance premiums

Life insurance premiums

Employee meals

Employee instruction and education expenses

Employee Christmas and other parties

Employee sports activities

Medical expenses

Credit union

Awards and prizes

Transportation and housing

■ COSTS RELATED TO FACILITY MAINTENANCE

Repairs and Maintenance

Furniture and fixtures

Kitchen equipment

Office equipment

Refrigeration

Air conditioning

Plumbing and heating

Electrical and mechanical

Floors and carpets

Buildings

Parking lot

Gardening and grounds maintenance

Building alterations

Painting, plastering, and decorating

Maintenance contracts

Autos and trucks

Other equipment and supplies

■ OCCUPANCY COSTS

Rent

Rent—minimum or fixed

Percentage rent

Ground rental

Equipment rental

Real estate taxes

Personal property taxes

Other municipal taxes

Franchise tax

Capital stock tax

Partnership or corporation license fees

Insurance on building and contents

Interest

Notes payable

Long-term debt

Other

Depreciation

Buildings

Amortization of leasehold

Amortization of leasehold improvements

Furniture, fixtures, and equipment

Although there are many ways to assess other expenses, two considerations of these costs are particularly useful for the foodservice manager. Managers may consider if the Other Expense cost they are evaluating is:

1. Fixed, variable, or mixed
2. Controllable or noncontrollable

FUN ON THE WEB!

If your restaurant plays background music, hosts live bands or Karaoke nights, or even allows DJs, your facility will be required to pay artists royalties for the music your guests hear. The following groups represent those who produce music. Go to their Web sites to see how and why you will interact with them.

www.ascap.com. ASCAP is a membership association of over 200,000 U.S. composers, songwriters, lyricists, and music publishers of every kind of music. Through agreements with affiliated international societies, ASCAP also represents hundreds of thousands of music creators worldwide.

www.bmi.com. BMI is an American performing rights organization that represents more than 300,000 songwriters, composers, and music publishers in all genres of music. The non–profit-making company collects license fees on behalf of the American and international artists that it represents.

www.sesac.com. SESAC was founded in 1930, making it the second-oldest performing rights organization in the United States. SESAC's repertory, once limited to European and gospel music, has diversified to include today's most popular music, including R&B/hip-hop, dance, rock classics, country, Latina, contemporary Christian, jazz, and the television and film music of Hollywood.

FIXED, VARIABLE, AND MIXED OTHER EXPENSES

As a foodservice manager, some of the costs you will incur will stay the same each month, whereas others will vary. For example, if you elect to lease a building to house a restaurant and cocktail lounge you want to operate, your lease payment will likely be such that you pay the same amount for each month of the lease. In other instances, the amount you pay for an expense will vary based on the success of your business. Expenses you incur for paper cocktail napkins used at the cocktail lounge in your restaurant, for example, will increase as the number of guests you serve increases and decrease as the number of guests you serve decreases. As an effective cost control manager, it is important to recognize the difference between costs that are fixed and those that vary with sales volume.

A **fixed expense** is one that remains constant despite increases or decreases in sales volume. A **variable expense** is one that generally increases as sales volume increases and decreases as sales volume decreases. A **mixed expense** is one that has properties of both a fixed and a variable expense. To illustrate all three of these expense types, consider Jo Ann's Hot Dogs, a midsize, freestanding restaurant outside a shopping mall, where Jo Ann sells upscale Chicago-style hot dogs.

Assume that Jo Ann's average sales volume is $136,000 per month. Assume also that rent for her building and parking spaces is fixed at $8,000 per month. Each month, Jo Ann computes her rent as a percentage of total sales, using the following standard cost percentage formula:

$$\frac{\text{Other Expense}}{\text{Total Sales}} = \text{Other Expense Cost \%}$$

In this case, the other expense category she is interested in looking at is rent; therefore, the formula becomes:

$$\frac{\text{Rent Expense}}{\text{Total Sales}} = \text{Rent Expense\%}$$

Jo Ann has computed her rent expense % for the last six months. The results are shown in Figure 8.1.

Note that Jo Ann's rent expense % ranges from a high of 6.67% (February) to a low of 4.88% (May), yet it is very clear that rent itself was a constant, or fixed, amount of $8,000 per month. Thus, rent, in this lease arrangement, is considered to be a fixed expense. It is important to note that, although the dollar amount of her rent expense is fixed, the rent % declines as volume increases. Thus, the rent payment as a percentage of sales or cost per item sold is not constant. This is true because as sales volume increases, the number of guests contributing to rent expense also increases, thus it takes a smaller dollar and percentage amount of each guest's sales revenue to generate the $8,000 that Jo Ann needs to pay her rent.

■ **FIGURE 8.1** Jo Ann's Fixed Rent

For Period: 1/1–6/30

Month	Rent Expense	Sales	Rent %
January	$8,000	$121,000	6.61%
February	8,000	120,000	6.67
March	8,000	125,000	6.40
April	8,000	130,000	6.15
May	8,000	164,000	4.88
June	8,000	156,000	5.13
6-Month Average	8,000	136,000	5.88

It makes little sense for Jo Ann to be concerned about the fact that her rent expense % varies by a great amount based on the time of the year. If Jo Ann is comfortable with the six-month average rent percentage (5.88%), she is in control of and managing her other expense category called rent. If Jo Ann feels that her rent expense % is too high, she has only two options. She must increase sales, and thereby reduce her rent expense %, or she must negotiate a lower monthly rental with her landlord. When rent, or any type of other cost, is fixed the expense as expressed by the percentage of sales will vary with sales volume. The total amount of the expense, however, is not affected by sales volume.

Some restaurant lease arrangements are based on the sales revenue an operator achieves in the leased facility. Assume, for example, that Jo Ann has a lease arrangement of this type, requiring Jo Ann to pay 5% of her monthly sales revenue as rent. If that were the case, Jo Ann's monthly lease payments would be completely variable, as shown in Figure 8.2. Note that the dollar amount of Jo Ann's rent, in

■ **FIGURE 8.2** Jo Ann's Variable Rent

For Period: 1/1–6/30

Month	Sales	Rent %	Rent Expense
January	$121,000	5.00%	$6,050
February	120,000	5.00	6,000
March	125,000	5.00	6,250
April	130,000	5.00	6,500
May	164,000	5.00	8,200
June	156,000	5.00	7,800
6-Month Average	136,000	5.00	6,800

■ **FIGURE 8.3** Jo Ann's Mixed Rent

For Period: 1/1–6/30

Month	Sales	Fixed Rent Expense	1% Variable Rent Expense	Total Rent Expense
January	$121,000	$5,000	$1,210	$6,210
February	120,000	5,000	1,200	6,200
March	125,000	5,000	1,250	6,250
April	130,000	5,000	1,300	6,300
May	164,000	5,000	1,640	6,640
June	156,000	5,000	1,560	6,560
6-Month Average	136,000	5,000	1,360	6,360

---

this case, varies a great deal. It ranges from a low of $6,000 (February) to a high of $8,200 (May). The percentage of her sales revenue that is devoted to rent, however, remains constant at 5%.

A third type of lease that is common in the hospitality industry illustrates the fact that some other expenses are mixed, that is, there is both a fixed and a variable component to this type of expense. Figure 8.3 demonstrates such a lease type. In it, Jo Ann pays a flat lease amount of $5,000 per month plus 1% of total sales revenue.

In this arrangement, a major portion ($5,000) of Jo Ann's lease is fixed, whereas a smaller amount (1% of revenue) varies based on sales revenue. Mixed expenses of this type are common and include items such as some energy costs, garbage pickup, cell phone use, some franchise fees, and other expenses where the operator must pay a base amount and then additional amounts as usage or sales volume increases.

In summary, the total dollar amount of fixed expenses does not vary with sales volume, whereas the total dollar amount of variable expenses changes as volume changes. As a percentage of total sales, however, a fixed-expense % decreases as sales increase, and a variable-expense % does not change. A mixed expense has both fixed and variable components; therefore, as sales increase, the mixed-expense % decreases while total mixed expense increases. Figure 8.4 shows how fixed, variable, and mixed expenses are affected as sales volume increases.

A convenient way to remember the differences between fixed, variable, and mixed expenses is to consider a napkin holder and napkins on a cafeteria line. The napkin holder is a fixed expense. One holder is sufficient whether you serve 10 guests at lunch or 100 guests. The napkins themselves, however, are a variable expense. As you serve more guests (if each guest takes one napkin), you will incur a greater paper napkin

■ **FIGURE 8.4**   Fixed, Variable, and Mixed Expense Behaviors as Sales Volume Increases

Expense	As a Percentage of Sales	Total Dollars
Fixed Expense	Decreases	Remains the Same
Variable Expense	Remains the Same	Increases
Mixed Expense	Decreases	Increases

expense. The cost of the napkin holder and napkins, if considered together, would be a mixed expense. For some very large restaurant chains, it makes sense to separate some mixed expenses into their fixed and variable components, whereas smaller operations may elect, as in the case of the napkin holder and napkins, to combine these expenses. The company you work for may make the choice of how you account for other expenses, or you may be free to consider other expense costs in a manner you feel is best for your own operation.

Effective managers know they should not categorize fixed, variable, or mixed costs in terms of being either "good" or "bad." Some expenses are, by their very nature, related to sales volume. Others are not. It is important to remember that the goal of management is not to reduce but to increase variable expenses in direct relation to increases in sales volume. Expenses are required if you are to service your guests. In the example of the paper napkins, it is clear that management would prefer to use 100 napkins at lunch rather than 10. As long as the total cost of servicing guests is less than the amount spent, expanding the number of guests served will not only increase variable other expenses but increase profits as well. Thus, increasing variable costs is desirable if management increases them in a way that makes sense for both the operation and the satisfaction of the guest.

As we saw in the case of labor expense (Chapter 7), the concept of fixed, variable, and mixed expense is quite useful. Normal variations in expense percentage that relate only to whether an expense is fixed, variable, or mixed should not be of undue concern to management. It is only when a fixed expense is too high or a variable expense is out of control that management should act. This is called the concept of **management by exception.** That is, if the expense is within an acceptable variation range, there is no need for management to intervene. You must take corrective action only when operational results are outside the range of acceptability. This approach keeps you from overreacting to minor variations in expense, but allows you to monitor all important activities.

Examples of other fixed foodservice expenses can include the areas of advertising (outdoor sign rentals), utilities (such as the cost of utilizing light bulbs in rest rooms), employee benefits (employee-of-the-month prizes), repairs and maintenance (parking lot paving), and the interest due on some types of business loans. Many foodservice operation other expenses, however, are directly related to sales volume, and, thus, management has some ability to control the cost of these items.

CONTROLLABLE AND NONCONTROLLABLE OTHER EXPENSES

*I*t is useful to consider other expenses in terms of their being fixed, variable, or mixed, but it is also useful to consider some expenses in terms of their being controllable or noncontrollable. Consider the case of Steve, the owner of a neighborhood tavern/ sandwich shop. Most of Steve's sales revenue comes from the sale of beer, sandwiches, and his special pizza.

Steve is free to decide on the monthly amount he will spend on advertising. Advertising expense, then, is under Steve's direct control and is considered to be a controllable expense. Some of his other expenses, however, are not under his control. The licenses needed to sell selected products are a familiar form of a noncontrollable expense. The state in which Steve operates charges a liquor license fee to all those operations that serve alcoholic beverages. If his state increases the liquor license fee, Steve is required to pay the additional fee. In this situation, the alcoholic beverage license fee would be considered a noncontrollable expense, that is, an expense beyond Steve's immediate control.

As an additional example, assume that you own a franchised quick-service unit that sells takeout chicken. Your store is part of a nationwide chain of such stores. Each month, your store is charged a $500 advertising and promotion fee by the regional headquarters' office. The $500 is used to purchase television advertising time for your chain. This $500 charge, as long as you own the franchise, is a noncontrollable operating expense.

A **noncontrollable expense**, then, is one that the foodservice manager can neither increase nor decrease. A **controllable expense** is one in which decisions made by the foodservice manager can have the effect of either increasing or reducing the expense. Management has some control over controllable expenses, but of course has little or no control over noncontrollable expenses. Other examples of noncontrollable expenses include some insurance premiums, property taxes, interest on debt, and depreciation. In every one of these cases, the foodservice operator will find that even the best control systems will not reduce the specific expense. As a manager, you should focus your attention on controllable, rather than noncontrollable, expenses. In all likelihood, it is your ability to manage controllable expenses that will most influence how your cost control-related administrative abilities are evaluated.

MONITORING OTHER EXPENSES

*W*hen managing other expenses, two control and monitoring alternatives are available to you. They are:

1. Other expense cost %
2. Other expense cost per guest

Each alternative can be used effectively in specific management situations, thus it is important for you to understand both.

As you learned earlier in this chapter, the other expense cost % is computed as follows:

$$\frac{\text{Other Expense}}{\text{Total Sales}} = \text{Other Expense Cost \%}$$

Thus, for example, in a situation where a restaurant you operate incurs an advertising expense of $5,000 in a month, serves 10,000 guests, and achieves sales of $78,000 for that same month, you would compute your advertising expense percentage for that month as follows:

$$\frac{\$5,000}{\$78,000} = 6.4\%$$

The other expense cost per guest is computed as follows:

$$\frac{\text{Other Expense}}{\text{Number of Guests Served}} = \text{Other Expense Cost per Guest}$$

In this example and using the preceding formula, you would compute your advertising expense cost per guest as follows:

$$\frac{\$5,000}{10,000} = \$0.50$$

As we have seen, the computation required to calculate the other expense percentage requires that the other expense category be divided by total sales. In many cases, this approach yields useful management information. In some cases, however, this computation alone may not provide adequate information; therefore, using the concept of other expense cost per guest can be very useful. To illustrate, consider the following example: Scott operates Chez Scot, an exclusive, fine-dining establishment in a suburban area of a major city. One of Scott's major other expenses is linen. He uses both tablecloths and napkins. Scott's partner, Joshua, believes that linen costs are a variable operating expense and should be monitored through the use of a linen cost % figure. In fact, says Scott's partner, records indicate that the linen cost % has been declining over the past five months; therefore, current control systems must be working. As is evident in Figure 8.5, the linen cost % has indeed been declining over the past five months.

Scott, however, is convinced that there are control problems. He has monitored linen costs on a cost per guest basis. His information is presented in Figure 8.6, and it validates Scott's concern. There is indeed a control problem in the linen area.

Figures 8.5 and 8.6 both show that a linen control problem does exist; yet Figure 8.6 shows it most clearly because it is plain that linen cost per guest has risen from $1.06 in January to its May high of $1.22.

Chez Scot is enjoying increased sales ($68,000 in January vs. $74,000 in May), but its guest count is declining (2,566 in January vs. 2,305 in May). The check

■ **FIGURE 8.5** Chez Scot Linen Cost %

Month	Total Sales	Linen Cost	Cost %
January	$ 68,000	$ 2,720	4.00%
February	70,000	2,758	3.94
March	72,000	2,772	3.85
April	71,500	2,753	3.85
May	74,000	2,812	3.80
Total	355,500	13,815	3.89

average has obviously increased. This is a good sign because it indicates that each guest is buying more food. The fact that fewer guests are being served should, however, result in a decrease in demand for linen and, thus, a decline in linen cost. In fact, on a per-person basis, linen costs are up. Scott is correct to be concerned about possible problems in the linen control area.

Calculating other expense cost per guest may also be useful in a situation where the foodservice manager receives no sales figures. Consider a college dormitory feeding situation where paper products such as cups, napkins, straws, and lids are placed on the serving line to be used by the students while eating their meals.

In this case, Juanita, the cafeteria manager, wonders whether students are taking more of these items than is normal. The problem is, of course, that she is not exactly sure what "normal" usage is when it comes to supplying paper products to her students. Juanita belongs to an industry trade association that asks its members to supply annual cost figures to a central location where they are tabulated and reported back to the membership. Figure 8.7 shows the tabulations from five colleges in addition to those from Juanita's unit.

Juanita has computed her paper products cost per student for the year and has found it to be higher than at P. University and the University of T., but lower than O. University, C. State University, and A. State University. Juanita's costs appear to

■ **FIGURE 8.6** Chez Scot Linen Cost per Guest

Month	Linen Cost	Number of Guests Served	Cost per Guest
January	$ 2,720	2,566	$1.06
February	2,758	2,508	1.10
March	2,772	2,410	1.15
April	2,753	2,333	1.18
May	2,812	2,305	1.22
Total	13,815	12,122	1.14

■ **FIGURE 8.7** Average Paper Product Cost

Institution	Cost of Paper Products	Number of Students	Paper Product Cost per Student
O. University	$140,592	8,080	$17.40
C. State University	109,200	6,500	16.80
P. University	122,276	7,940	15.40
University of T.	184,755	11,300	16.35
A. State University	61,560	3,600	17.10
5-University Average	123,676.60	7,484	16.53
Juanita's Institution	77,220	4,680	16.50

■ **FIGURE 8.8** Six-Column Cost of Paper Products

Juanita's Institution					Date: 4/1–4/8	
	Other Expense Cost		Number of Guests Served		Cost per Guest	
Weekday	Today	To Date	Today	To Date	Today	To Date
Monday	$ 145.50	$ 145.50	823	823	$0.18	$0.18
Tuesday	200.10	345.60	751	1,574	0.27	0.22
Wednesday	417.08	762.68	902	2,476	0.46	0.31
Thursday	0	762.68	489	2,965	0	0.26
Friday	237.51	1,000.19	499	3,464	0.48	0.29
Saturday	105.99	1,106.18	375	3,839	0.28	0.29
Sunday	0	1,106.18	250	4,089	0	0.27
Monday	157.10	1,263.28	841	4,930	0.19	0.26
Total	1,263.28		4,930		0.26	

be in line in the paper goods area. If, however, Juanita hopes to reduce paper products cost per student even further, she could, perhaps, call or arrange a visit to either P. University or the University of T. to observe their operations or purchasing techniques.

The other expense cost per guest formula is of value when management believes it can be helpful or when lack of a sales figure makes the computation of other expense cost % impossible. Figure 8.8 presents a six-column form that is useful in tracking both daily and cumulative cost per guest figures. It is maintained by inserting Other Expense Cost and Number of Guests Served in the first two sets of columns. The third set of columns, Cost per Guest, is obtained by using the other expense cost per guest formula.

Green and Growing!

Increasingly, foodservice managers are finding that creative "green" initiatives benefit their operations in many ways, including those that reduce other expenses. "Trayless dining" is just such an example. In study after study, college foodservice operators find that when serving trays are removed from cafeteria lines, diners take less food (because they only want to carry what they know they will eat). In typical cases, trayless operations experience a 30–50% reduction in food and beverage waste (and in the long run, a likely reduction in the "waist" lines of students!).

Without trays to wash, water consumption is also decreased. In fact, one large foodservice operator reports that trayless dining saves about 200 gallons of water for every 1,000 meals served by reducing the number of trays and dishes that must be washed. The result is a decrease in other expenses, such as water, utilities, and cleaning products. Of course, the removal of trays doesn't just eliminate waste and save money. It also fits into popular campus themes of green living and sustainability, making trayless dining an excellent example of a win-win-win situation for operators, those they serve, and the environment.

REDUCING OTHER EXPENSES

*O*ther expenses can be broken down into four distinct areas; it can be helpful to consider these same four areas when developing strategies for reducing overall other expense costs. It is important to remember that each foodservice manager faces his or her own unique set of other expenses. A restaurant on a beach in southern Florida may well experience the expense of hurricane insurance. A similar restaurant in Kansas would not. Each foodservice operation is unique. Effective operators are those who are constantly on the lookout for ways to reduce unnecessary additions to any of their other expense categories.

1. REDUCING COSTS RELATED TO FOOD AND BEVERAGE OPERATIONS

In many respects, some of these other expenses should be treated like food and beverage expenses. For instance, in the case of cleaning supplies, linen, uniforms, and the like, products should be ordered, inventoried, and issued in the same manner used for food and beverage products. In general, fixed costs related to food and beverage operations can only be reduced when they are measured as a percentage of total sales. This is done, of course, by increasing the total sales figure. Reducing total variable cost expenses is generally not desirable because, in fact, each additional sale will bring additional variable expense. In this case, although total variable expenses may increase, the positive impact of the additional sales on fixed costs will serve to reduce the overall other expense percentage.

To see how this occurs, let's examine a shaved-ice kiosk called Igloo's located in the middle of a small mall parking lot. Figure 8.9 demonstrates the impact of volume increases on both total other expense and other expense cost %. In this example, some of the other expenses related to food and beverage operations are fixed and others are variable. The variable portion of other expense, in this example, equals 10% of gross sales. Fixed expenses equal $150.

FUN ON THE WEB!

Rising utility costs concern everyone who manages a food service operation. Energy conservation is not only good for your country; it's also good for your operation's bottom line. The "Energy Star for Small Business" program is free to use and provides you access to unbiased information about energy-efficient technologies and services. For more information, visit: **www.energystar.gov/smallbiz.**

■ **FIGURE 8.9** Igloo's Fixed and Variable Other Expenses

Sales	Fixed Expense	Variable Expense (10%)	Total Other Expense	Other Expense Cost %
$ 1,000	$150	$ 100	$ 250	25.00%
3,000	150	300	450	15.00
9,000	150	900	1,050	11.67
10,000	150	1,000	1,150	11.50
15,000	150	1,500	1,650	11.00

Variable expense shown in Figure 8.9 increases from $100 to $1,500, but total other expense percentage drops from 25% of sales to 11% of sales. Thus, to reduce the percentage of these costs that are related to food and beverage operations, increases in sales are quite helpful! If all other expenses related to food and beverage operations were 100% variable, however, this strategy would not have the effect of reducing other expense cost % because the dollar amount of other expenses would increase proportionately to volume increases (recall the napkins example!) and, as a result, total other expense cost % would be unchanged.

Consider The Costs

"The piece looks great, but tell me about the prices one more time," said Nigel, the manager of the Old Dublin Pub. Nigel was talking to Alice Petoskey, the sales representative for Image Custom Printing.

Nigel had asked Alice for a quote on producing a flyer that would advertise the pub's St. Patrick's Day festivities to be held in just one month. Nigel planned to offer special menu items on that day as well as discounted prices on the Irish-made beers he offered on tap. He had also arranged to hire a band to play traditional Irish music. He was now considering how best to advertise the event and all of the special activities he had planned at the pub on that day.

He and Alice were discussing prices for printing the beautiful flyer Alice's company had designed for him.

"Okay," replied Alice, "there is a one-time design and set-up fee of $300.00, no matter how many pieces we print. After that fee, they are $0.50 per copy if you buy 1 to 1,000 copies, $0.40 per copy if you buy 2,000 to 5,000 copies, and, like I was telling you, the best deal for you is if you buy 10,000. Then the price per copy goes down to only $0.25!

1. What would Nigel's total payment to Alice's company be if he purchases 1,000 flyers? 5,000 flyers? 10,000 flyers? Use the table below to help you with your answer.

Number of Copies	Cost per Copy	Set-Up-Fee	Total Cost

2. What additional flyer-related costs will Nigel incur if he decides to purchase the advertising flyers from Alice?

3. Assume you are Nigel. What additional and potentially lower-cost advertising alternatives would you want to consider prior to agreeing to buy the flyers from Alice's company?

■ **FIGURE 8.10** Typical Energy Usage Pattern

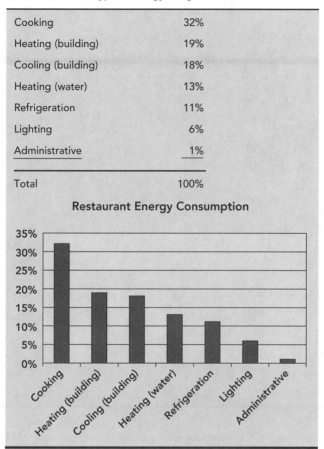

Cooking	32%
Heating (building)	19%
Cooling (building)	18%
Heating (water)	13%
Refrigeration	11%
Lighting	6%
Administrative	1%
Total	100%

Restaurant Energy Consumption

Utility services costs are an important subcategory of other expenses related to food and beverage operations. To produce their menu items, serve, and clean up, restaurants typically use thousands of gallons of water, consume significant amounts of natural gas (generally used for cooking and water heating), and utilize a large number of **kilowatt hours (kwh)**—the measure of electrical usage—each month.

Like food and labor costs, energy usage costs can be controlled. This process starts by understanding just where your restaurant uses its energy. Although the building heating and cooling costs incurred by a restaurant in Alaska will be different than those of a restaurant in Arizona, the usage pattern shown in Figure 8.10 is a typical one. Your utility costs can (and should) be controlled, and learning and teaching your staff about the information in Figure 8.11 is a good way to start the process.

■ **FIGURE 8.11** Ten Commonsense Energy Tips for Restaurateurs

1. Turn It Off
   • Turn off lights, cooking equipment, and exhaust fans when they are not being used.
   • Activate the standby mode for office equipment, in-house computers, and printers to effectively put these pieces of equipment "to sleep" when not in use.
2. Keep It Closed
   • Keep refrigerator doors closed.
   • Keep back doors, if any, to the kitchen closed to minimize heat and cooling loss.
3. Turn It Down
   • Set air-conditioning units at 76°F (24.5°C) for cooling.
   • Set heating systems at 68°F (20°C) for heating.
   • Reduce the temperature of your hot water heater (where appropriate).
   • Adjust heating/cooling temperature settings when you close your operation for the night.
4. Vent It
   • Use ceiling fans to help recirculate dining room air.
   • Retrofit exhaust hoods with both low and high speed fans in dishroom areas and in food preparation and cooking areas.
5. Change the Bulbs
   • Replace incandescent bulbs with fluorescent. They use 75% less electricity and last 10 times as long.
   • Install photocell light sensors (motion detectors) where appropriate (storage areas and the like) to activate lighting only when needed.
6. Watch the Water
   • Run dishwashers only when they are full.
   • Replace/repair leaking faucets immediately.
   • Insulate all hot water pipes.
   • Install "water-saver" spray nozzles in dish areas.
7. Cook Right
   • Stagger preheat times for equipment to minimize surcharges for high energy use.
   • Bake during off-peak periods.
   • Idle cooking equipment (between meal periods) at reduced temperatures where appropriate.
8. Seal It
   • Caulk and weather-strip cracks and openings around doors, windows, vents, and utility outlets.
   • Check freezer, refrigerator, and walk-in seals and gaskets for cracks or warping. Replace as needed.
9. Maintain It
   • Change air filters on a regular basis (monthly during peak heating and cooling seasons).
   • Clean grease traps on ventilation equipment.
   • Clean air-conditioner and refrigeration condenser/evaporator coils at least every three months.
   • Oil, lube, clean, and repair equipment as needed to maximize operating efficiency.
10. Get Help
   • Take advantage of any advisory services offered by your local utility company and governmental agencies.
   • Talk to your *heating, ventilation, and air-conditioning (HVAC)* repair person for tips on minimizing energy and maintenance costs with your particular HVAC system. It's like getting a free energy management consultant!

2. REDUCING COSTS RELATED TO LABOR

As you learned in Chapter 7, some labor-related expenses can be considered partially fixed and some partially variable. To help reduce other expense costs related to labor, it is necessary for you to eliminate wasteful labor-related expense. Examples include the cost of advertising, hiring, and training new employees resulting from excessive employee turnover. It also means implementing cost-reducing hiring practices, such as preemployment drug screening that may result in lower health insurance premiums for employees if these benefits are provided. Proper employment practices also impact the workers' compensation and unemployment tax rates you may pay. Remember that, in many states, the rate you pay for these two insurance programs is determined, in part, by your history of work-related injuries and employment separations. Careful hiring and training of employees will reduce the costs associated with workers' compensation claims and unemployment compensation. They will thus save you money and reduce your other expenses related to labor.

Conversely, operators who attempt to reduce other expenses related to labor too much, such as by not providing adequate health care, retirement savings programs such as 401(k)s, or sick leave benefits, will find that the best employees prefer to work elsewhere. This leaves the operator with a less productive workforce than would otherwise be possible. In many ways, employees will be your most valuable assets. Effective management is not magic. If your employees feel they are treated fairly, they will be motivated to do their best. If they do not, they will not. Reducing employee benefits while attempting to retain a well-qualified workforce is simply management at its worst!

FUN ON THE WEB!

Record keeping is one of the most important aspects of a preventive maintenance program. To see one company's software developed to help you record and plan preventive maintenance activities, go to **www.maintsmart.com**.

3. REDUCING COSTS RELATED TO EQUIPMENT MAINTENANCE

Any skilled craftsman knows that keeping his or her tools clean and in good working order will make them last longer and perform better. The same is true for foodservice facilities. A properly designed and implemented preventive maintenance program can go a long way toward reducing equipment failure and, thus, decreasing equipment and facility-related costs. Proper care of mechanical

■ **FIGURE 8.12** Equipment Inspection Report

Unit Name: <u>Your Restaurant</u>			Time Period: <u>1/1–1/31</u>
Item Inspected	Inspection Date	Inspected By	Action Recommended
A. Refrigerator #6	1/1	D.H.	Replace gasket
B. Fryer	1/7	D.H.	Inspected, no maintenance needed
C. Ice Machine	1/9	D.H.	Drain, de-lime
D.			
E.			

equipment not only prolongs its life but also actually reduces operational costs. As prices for water, gas, and other energy sources needed to operate facilities continue to rise, you must implement a facility repair and maintenance program that seeks to discover and treat minor equipment and facility problems before they become major problems.

One way to help ensure that costs are as low as possible is to use a competitive-bid process before awarding contracts for services you require. For example, if you hire a carpet cleaning company to clean your dining room carpets monthly, it is a good idea to annually seek competitive bids from new carpet cleaners. This can help to reduce your costs by ensuring that the carpet cleaner you select has given you a price that is competitive with other service providers. In the area of maintenance contracts, for areas such as the kitchen or for mechanical equipment, elevators, or grounds, it is recommended that these contracts be bid at least once per year. This is especially true if the dollar value of the contract is large.

Air-conditioning, plumbing, heating, and refrigerated units should be inspected at least yearly, and kitchen equipment, such as dishwashers, slicers, and mixers, should be inspected at least monthly for purposes of preventive maintenance. A form such as the one in Figure 8.12 is useful in this process.

Some foodservice managers operate facilities that are large enough to employ their own facility maintenance staff. If this is the case, make sure these employees have copies of the operating and maintenance manuals of all equipment. These documents can prove invaluable in the reduction of equipment and facility-related operating costs.

Technology Tools

Those expenses that are related to neither food nor labor were introduced in this chapter. Depending upon the specific foodservice operation, these costs can represent a significant portion of the operations total expense requirements. As a result, controlling these costs is just as important as controlling food- and labor-related costs. Software and hardware that can be purchased to assist in this area include applications that relate to:

1. Assessing and monitoring utilities cost
2. Minimizing energy costs via the use of motion-activated sensors
3. Managing equipment maintenance records
4. Tracking marketing costs/benefits
5. Menu and promotional materials printing hardware and software
6. Analysis of communications costs (telephone tolls)
7. Analysis of all other expense costs on a per-guest basis
8. Analysis of all other expense costs on a "cost per dollar sale" basis
9. Comparing building/contents insurance costs across alternative insurance providers
10. Software designed to assist in the preparation of the income statement, balance sheet, and the statement of cash flows
11. Income tax management
12. Income tax filing

The unique needs of an individual restaurant will heavily influence which other expense–related software packages would be helpful. At the minimum, most independent operators should computerize their records related to taxes at all levels to ensure accuracy, safekeeping, and timeliness of required filings.

FUN ON THE WEB!

Energy management is important, especially for larger operations. Advancements in software and hardware make this an area where operators can truly save on other expenses. To view one company's innovative product offerings in this area, go to **www.lodgingtechnology.com/html/frabo.html.**

4. REDUCING OCCUPANCY COSTS

Occupancy costs refer to those expenses incurred by the foodservice unit that are related to the occupancy of and payment for the physical facility it occupies.

For the foodservice manager who is not the owner, the majority of occupancy costs will be noncontrollable. Rent, taxes, and interest on debt are real costs but are beyond the immediate control of the unit manager. However, if you own the facility you manage, occupancy costs are a primary determinant of both profit on sales and return on dollars invested. If your occupancy costs are too high because of unfavorable rent or lease arrangements or due to excessive debt load, you may face extreme difficulty in generating profits. Food, beverage, and labor costs can only be managed to a point; beyond that, efforts to reduce costs can result in decreased product quality, guest service, and satisfaction. If occupancy costs are unrealistically high, no amount of effective cost control can help "save" the operation's profitability.

Total other expenses in an operation can range from 5% to 15% or more of the unit's gross sales. These expenses, although sometimes considered minor expenses, can be extremely important to overall operational profitability. This is especially true in a situation where the number of guests you serve is fixed, or nearly so, and the prices you are allowed to charge for your products is fixed also. In a case such as this, your ability to control all other expenses is vital to your success.

Apply What You Have Learned

Hyewon Kim owns her own catering business. She provides her full-time employees with good health insurance benefits. Part-time employees do not receive the benefit. This year, Hyewon's health insurer advises Hyewon that health, dental, and vision insurance rates for her employees will increase an average of 25% next year.

Hyewon had planned on giving both full- and part-time employees a wage increase on January 1, but finds that the increased cost of the health care premiums for her full-time employees will take all of the funds she had budgeted for the wage increases.

1. If you were Hyewon, would you give your part-time employees a wage increase? If so, how?

2. What specific types of employees value health insurance coverage as much or more than a higher hourly pay rate?

3. What steps can Hyewon take next year to help control her health insurance coverage costs? For example, one company drew international attention for its new policy of refusing to allow its employees to use tobacco (smoke) while at work or while off the job. Random testing for tobacco use was instituted and those found to have violated the policy were terminated. The company maintained the policy was a way to help curtail rising health care costs and employees who disagreed with the policy were free to quit. Opponents claimed the company was infringing on their employees' rights to engage in lawful behavior when they were off the job. Do you agree with the company's policy? What other types of health-adverse behaviors might employers seek to monitor in the future? Should they do so?

Key Terms and Concepts

The following are terms and concepts discussed in the chapter that are important for you as a manager. To help you review, please define the terms below:

Other expenses
SOP
Fixed expense
Variable expense
Mixed expense

Management by
   exception
Noncontrollable expense
Controllable expense
kwh

heating, ventilation, and
   air-conditioning
   (HVAC)
401(k)
Occupancy costs

Test Your Skills

Complete the Test Your Skills exercises by placing your answers in the shaded boxes and answering the questions as indicated.

1. Susie operates a restaurant in the ski resort town of Asvail. She has decided to group her Other Expense categories in terms of either fixed expense or variable expense. Place an X in the Variable Expense column for those expenses that vary with sales volume. For expenses that do not vary with sales, place an X in the Fixed Expense column.

Other Expenses	Variable Expense	Fixed Expense
Linen rental		
Piano rental		
Ice		
Insurance		
Pension plan payments		
Snow shoveling fees (parking lot)		
Paper products		
Kitchen equipment lease (mixer)		
Long-term debt payment		
Real estate tax		

2. Tutti owns a fine-dining restaurant in a suburb of a major coastal city. Last year, her sales were not as high as she would have liked. To help increase her sales volume, Tutti decided to hire a sales consultant, Tina Boniner, to help bring in more customers. Tutti hired Tina on a trial basis for the first six months of the year. Tina was paid a fixed fee of $1,000 per month and a commission of 1% of sales. At the end of June, Tutti wants to evaluate whether she should hire Tina for the next six months. Calculate Tutti's sales consultant cost %.

Mixed Expense—Sales Consultant					
					For Period: 1/1–6/30
Month	Sales	Fixed Fee	1% Variable Expense	Total Expense	Cost %
January	$ 81,000				
February	80,000				
March	88,000				
April	92,000				
May	110,000				
June	108,000				
6-Month Average					

a. Tutti has decided that she cannot spend more than 2.2% of total sales for Tina's services. Based on the six-month average cost %, can Tutti afford to hire Tina for another six months?

b. Last year's average monthly sales for the first six months was $80,000. Based on this year's sales data, has Tina done a good job at increasing sales? Should she be hired again?

3. John owns and operates the End Zone Steakhouse. He would like to turn the operation over to his son Zeke, a graduate of Spartacus High School. Zeke, however, has no foodservice background. Zeke would like to prove that he can effectively operate the restaurant and that he would be good at controlling costs. Operating cost categories for the restaurant, in terms of Other Expenses, are as follows. Place an X in the Controllable column for those operating expenses that Zeke could control. If he could not control the cost, place an X in the Noncontrollable column.

Other Expenses	Controllable	Noncontrollable
Real estate tax		
Menu printing		
Professional musicians		
Interest on long-term debt		
Charitable donations		
Cleaning supplies		
Flowers and decorations		
Licenses and permits		

4. Shanna operates a lounge in an extremely popular downtown convention hotel. The hotel regularly operates around the 80% occupancy mark, and its lounge, Luigi's, is very often filled to capacity. On weeks when business at the hotel is slower, Shanna attempts to build local sales by scheduling a variety of popular bands to play on the stage. She must select one band to play on Saturday night, six weeks from now, when the hotel is not busy. She has kept records of the costs and sales volume of the last four bands she has booked.

   a. Compute both band expense % and cost per guest served. Based on the cost % of the bands, which one should Shanna select for booking?

Expense % and Cost per Guest Served—Bands						
Unit Name: Luigi's Lounge						
Date	Band	Band Expense	Lounge Sales	Cost %	Number of Guests Served	Cost per Guest Served
1/1	Tiny and the Boys	$1,400	$11,400		1,425	
2/1	Shakin' Bill and the Billfolds	1,900	12,250		1,980	
3/1	La Noise	2,000	12,000		2,005	
4/1	The Hoppers	2,000	10,250		2,100	

b. Would your answer change if you knew Shanna charged a $5.00 cover charge to enter the lounge on the nights she has a band, and that the cover charge is reported separately from the lounge sales? If so, which band would you choose?

Date	Band	Number of Guests Served	Cover Charge per Guest	Total Cover Charges	Lounge Sales	Total Sales
1/1	Tiny and the Boys	1,425			$11,400	
2/1	Shakin' Bill and the Billfolds	1,980			$12,250	
3/1	La Noise	2,005			$12,000	
4/1	The Hoppers	2,100			$10,250	

5. Marjorie runs a 200-seat, white-tablecloth restaurant in an upscale neighborhood. Since her guests expect her tablecloths and napkins to be really white, she sends her linens to a local laundry service daily. The laundry service charges her by the piece. She wants to keep track of her laundry cost per guest to see if she can use the information to control her laundry costs better. Help her complete her six-column cost per guest report. She has budgeted $0.60 per guest on average. How is she doing at controlling her costs?

Six-Column Cost per Guest—Laundry Service						
Unit Name: Marjorie's					Date: 5/1–5/7	
	Laundry Service Cost		Number of Guests Served		Cost per Guest	
Weekday	Today	To Date	Today	To Date	Today	To Date
1	$225		400			
2	204		375			
3	200		350			
4	240		425			
5	275		450			
6	300		500			
7	230		420			
Total						

6. Josiam operates the foodservice at Springdale Valley school system. He has just been informed by City Power, the electrical company in his area, that the rate per kilowatt hour (kwh) for the school system's kitchens will be rising from $0.085 per kwh to $0.092 per kwh beginning next academic year (September). Based on last year's bill, what was each kitchen's electricity usage? Assuming no operating changes, how much more will be spent next year?

School	Electricity Cost Last Year	Number of kwh Used Last Year	Cost per kwh Estimate Next Year	Estimated Electricity Cost for Next Year
Springdale Elementary	$ 6,800.00		0.092	
Jefferson Elementary	$ 7,650.00		0.092	
Clinton Middle School	$10,200.00		0.092	
Tri-Valley High School	$12,750.00		0.092	
Total	$37,400.00		0.092	

a. Who are some of Josiam's best resources for discovering ways to limit electricity usage in the kitchens?

7. Enrique has located the perfect spot for his restaurant. It is 3,000 square feet in the local mall, and the mall managers have given him the following monthly lease options:

   Option 1: Pay a flat fee of $2.00 per square foot per month

   Option 2: Pay a flat fee of $3,000 per month and 5% of food sales.

   Enrique estimates that his sales for the coming year will be as follows. Calculate the monthly lease amount for both options. Which lease option should Enrique choose? Why?

| Month | Sales Forecast | Option 1 | | | Option 2 | | |
		No. of Square Feet	Flat Fee per Square Foot	Monthly Lease $	Flat Fee per Month	Five % of Sales	Monthly Lease $
Jan	$ 65,000						
Feb	55,000						
Mar	65,000						
April	70,000						
May	80,000						
June	70,000						
July	70,000						
Aug	85,000						
Sept	90,000						
Oct	95,000						
Nov	110,000						
Dec	135,000						
Total							

8. Libbey Hocking is the owner of the Hummingbird, an all-organic restaurant featuring fresh salads and a variety of vegetarian entrée dishes. As part of a dining room redesign, she is replacing all of the glassware in her 100-seat restaurant. Libbey would like to purchase 40 dozen glasses. Her glassware vendor has offered her similarly styled glassware at three different quality levels. The highest quality glassware would cost Libbey $50.00 per dozen. The average life expectancy of these glasses is 1,000 uses before they either break or chip. A lower priced, mid-quality glass sells for $35.00 per dozen and has an expected life of 750 uses. The least expensive glasses sell for $26.00 per dozen and have an expected life of 500 uses. Help Libbey get more information to assess her best purchase choice by completing the following product cost comparison worksheet. (Spreadsheet hint: format the "Per Use Cost" column to five decimal places.).

Hummingbird's Glassware Purchase Worksheet							
Product Durability	Price per Dozen	Number of Dozens	Total Cost	Total Number of Glasses	Per Glass Cost	Estimated Uses Per Glass	Per Use Cost
Highest							
Middle							
Lowest							

a. Based on cost per use only, which quality glass should Libbey purchase?

b. What non–purchase price factors might influence Libbey's choice of glassware?

c. If you were Libbey, which product alternative would you select? Explain your answer.

9. The cost of maintaining a Web site is increasingly considered to be an expense that can be justified by many foodservice operations. Name some specific "Other Expense" costs that could be reduced through the use of an operation's website if it were properly designed and utilized.

Chapter 9

ANALYZING RESULTS USING THE INCOME STATEMENT

OVERVIEW

This chaptzer explains what you will do to analyze the cost effectiveness of your operation. It teaches you how to read and use the income statement, a financial document that is also known as the profit and loss (P&L) statement. It explains techniques used to analyze your sales volume as well as expense levels, including food, beverage, labor, and other expenses. Finally, the chapter shows you how to review the income statement to analyze your profitability.

Chapter Outline

At the conclusion of this chapter, you will be able to:
* Prepare an income (profit and loss) statement.
* Analyze sales and expenses using the P&L statement.
* Evaluate a facility's profitability using the P&L statement.

INTRODUCTION TO FINANCIAL ANALYSIS

*F*ar too many foodservice managers find that they collect information, fill out forms, and enter and receive numbers from their computers with little regard for what they should do with all these data. Some have said that managers often make poor decisions because they lack information, but when it comes to the financial analysis of a hospitality operation, the opposite is usually true. Foodservice managers, more often than not, find themselves awash in numbers! It is an important part of your job to sift through this information and select for analysis those numbers that can shed light on exactly what is happening in your operation. Among other things, you will want to know:

How much money did we take in?

How much did we spend?

How much profit was made?

This information is necessary to effectively operate your business. It also may be required by groups that are directly or indirectly involved with the financial operation of your facility. For example, local, state, and federal financial records relating to taxes and employee wages have to be submitted to the government on a regular basis. In addition, records showing the financial health of an operation may have to be submitted to new suppliers to establish credit worthiness. If a foodservice operation has been established with both operating partners and investors, those owners and investors will certainly require accurate and timely updates that focus on the financial health of the business. Owners, stockholders, and investment bankers may all have an interest in the day-to-day efficiency and effectiveness of management. For each of these groups, and, of course, for the foodservice organization's own management, an accurate examination of operational efficiency is critical.

As a professional foodservice manager, you will be very interested in examining your cost of doing business. Documenting and analyzing sales, expenses, and profits is sometimes called **cost accounting,** but a more appropriate term for the process is **managerial accounting,** a term that reflects the importance managers place on this process. In this text, we use the term managerial accounting when referring to documenting, analyzing, and managing sales, expenses, and profit data.

It is important for you to be aware of the difference between **bookkeeping,** the process of simply recording and summarizing financial data, and the actual analysis of that data. As an example, a point of sale (POS) system can be programmed to provide data about food and beverage sales per server. Management can, if it wishes, track, per shift, the relative sales effort of each service employee. If this is done with the goal of either increasing the training of the less productive server or rewarding the most productive one, the POS system has, in fact, added information that is valuable and has assisted in the unit's operation. If, on the other hand, information describing server effectiveness is dutifully recorded on a daily basis, filed away or sent to a regional office, and is then left to collect dust, the POS system has actually harmed the operation by taking management's time away from the more important task of running the business. It has converted the manager's role from that of cost analyst to one of a book (record) keeper only. This type of situation must be avoided at all cost; you need to maximize your effectiveness by being in the production area or dining room during high-service periods rather than in the office "catching up" on your paperwork.

Bookkeeping is essentially the summarizing and recording of data. Managerial accounting involves the summarizing, recording, and, most important, the analysis of those data. As a professional foodservice manager, you are also a managerial accountant!

You do not have to be a certified management accountant (CMA) or a certified public accountant (CPA) to analyze data related to foodservice revenue and expense. This is not meant to discount the value of an accounting professional, who can assist a manager. It is important to establish, however, that it is the professional foodservice manager, not an outside expert, who is most qualified to assess the effectiveness of the foodservice team in providing the service levels desired by management and in controlling production-related costs. The analysis of operating data, a traditional role of the accountant, must also be part of your role as manager. The process is not complex and, in fact, is one of the most fun and creative aspects of a foodservice manager's job.

It is important to recognize that a good foodservice manager is, in fact, a manager first and not an accountant. It is also important, however, for you to be able to read and understand financial information and be able to converse intelligently and confidently with the many parties outside your operation who will read and use the information produced by accountants. This information will be crucial to your operation's overall health and success. It can also provide the needed data that will assist you to sharpen the quality of your management decisions. It is also important to remember that, by federal law, it is an operation's management (not its accountants) that is called upon to verify the accuracy of the financial data it reports. In the past, some managers in some industries have fraudulently reported their financial information, thus the United States Congress, in 2002, passed the **Sarbanes-Oxley Act (SOX).** Technically known as the Public Company Accounting Reform and Investor Protection Act, the law provides criminal penalties for those found to have committed accounting fraud. Sarbanes-Oxley (SOX) covers a whole range of corporate governance issues, including the regulation of those who are assigned the task of verifying a company's financial health. Ultimately, Congress determined that a company's implementation of proper financial reporting techniques is not merely good business, it is the law, and violators are subject to fines or even prison terms!

FUN ON THE WEB!

The 2002 Sarbanes-Oxley Act became law to help rebuild public confidence in the way corporate America governs its business activities. The Act has far-reaching implications for the tourism, hospitality, and leisure industry. To examine an overview of its provisions, and to see a product designed to help companies stay in compliance with it, go to **www.vigilar.com/sol_compliance_sarbanes_oxley.html.**

UNIFORM SYSTEM OF ACCOUNTS

*F*inancial reports related to the operation of a foodservice facility are of interest to management, stockholders, owners, creditors, governmental agencies, and, often, the general public. To ensure that this financial information is presented in a way that is both useful and consistent, a **uniform system of accounts** has been established for many areas of the hospitality industry. The National Restaurant Association, for example, has developed the *Uniform System of Accounts for Restaurants (USAR)*. Uniform systems of accounts also exist for hotels, clubs, nursing homes, schools, and hospitals. Each system seeks to provide a consistent and clear manner in which managers can record sales, expenses, and the overall financial condition for their specific organizations. Sales categories, expense classifications, and methods of computing relevant ratios are included in the uniform systems of accounts. These uniform systems are typically available from the national trade associations involved with each hospitality segment.

It is important to note that the uniform systems of accounts are guidelines, not a mandated methodology. Small foodservice operations, for example, may use the **Uniform System of Accounts for Restaurants** in a slightly different way than will large operations. In all cases, however, operators who use the uniform system of accounts "speak the same language," and it is truly useful that they do so. If operators prepared financial records in any manner they wished, it is unlikely that the many external audiences who must use them could properly interpret the reports. Thus, effective managers secure a copy of the appropriate uniform system of accounts for their operations and become familiar with its basic formats and principles.

FUN ON THE WEB!

Look at the following site to review *The Uniform System of Accounts for the Lodging Industry.*

www.ei-ahla.org. Search for "Uniform System of Accounts for the Lodging Industry 10th Revised Edition" to see a synopsis of the book and place an order.

INCOME STATEMENT (USAR)

*T*he **income statement** is a summary report that describes the sales achieved, the money spent on expenses, and the resulting profit generated by a business in a specific time period. It is popularly referred to as the **profit and loss (P&L) statement.** It is a manager's most important tool for cost control. Properly designed P&L statements show revenue and expense at a level of detail deemed best by managers after reviewing the appropriate uniform system of accounts (i.e., restaurant, hotel, club or other industry segment).

The word profit can mean many things; therefore, the profit and loss statement can be somewhat confusing if you are not familiar with it. To see why, assume that someone asked you how much money you "made" on your last job. You could answer by telling the amount of gross earnings you achieved (your pay before taxes), or you could just as accurately answer by telling your net earnings (after-tax earnings) or "take-home" pay. In either case, you would be accurately communicating the amount that you earned but the two answers you would provide would be very different. In a similar manner, some operators consider profit to be what they earn before they pay taxes, whereas other managers reserve the term for their after-tax earnings. A precise definition of exactly what is meant by the term "profit" must be established for each P&L statement if it is to be helpful and communicate information accurately. In all cases, however, one purpose of the P&L statement is to identify **net income,** which is the profit generated after all appropriate expenses of the business have been paid.

Figure 9.1 details P&L statements for two years for Joshua's Inc., a foodservice complex that includes a cocktail lounge, two dining areas, and banquet space. Joshua's **fiscal year,** that is, his year established for accounting purposes, begins on October 1 and concludes on September 30 of the next year. This fiscal year coincides with the beginning of his busy season and, thus, gives him a logical starting point. As can be seen in Figure 9.1, last year Joshua's generated $2,306,110 in total sales and achieved a net income of $101,772. This year, when the corporation generated total sales revenue of $2,541,206, Joshua achieved a net income of $114,923. The question Joshua must ask himself, of course, is, "How good is this performance?"

■ **FIGURE 9.1** Joshua's Income Statement (P&L)

Joshua's Inc. Last Year versus This Year				
	Last Year	%	This Year	%
SALES:				
Food	$1,891,011	82.0%	$2,058,376	81.0%
Beverage	415,099	18.0	482,830	19.0
Total Sales	2,306,110	100.0	2,541,206	100.0
COST OF SALES:				
Food	712,587	37.7	767,443	37.3
Beverage	94,550	22.8	96,566	20.0
Total Cost of Sales	807,137	35.0	864,009	34.0
GROSS PROFIT:				
Food	1,178,424	62.3	1,290,933	62.7
Beverage	320,549	77.2	386,264	80.0
Total Gross Profit	1,498,973	65.0	1,677,197	66.0
OPERATING EXPENSES:				
Salaries and Wages	641,099	27.8	714,079	28.1
Employee Benefits	99,163	4.3	111,813	4.4
Direct Operating Expenses	122,224	5.3	132,143	5.2
Music and Entertainment	2,306	0.1	7,624	0.3
Marketing	43,816	1.9	63,530	2.5
Utility Services	73,796	3.2	88,942	3.5
Repairs and Maintenance	34,592	1.5	35,577	1.4
Administrative and General	66,877	2.9	71,154	2.8
Occupancy	120,000	5.2	120,000	4.7
Depreciation	41,510	1.8	55,907	2.2
Total Operating Expenses	1,245,383	54.0	1,400,769	55.1
Operating Income	253,590	11.0	276,428	10.9
Interest	86,750	3.8	84,889	3.3
Income Before Income Taxes	166,840	7.2	191,539	7.5
Income Taxes	65,068	2.8	76,616	3.0
Net Income	101,772	4.4	114,923	4.5

Prepared By: L. Dopson

It is important to note that each operation's P&L statement could look slightly different. All of them, however, typically take a similar approach to reporting revenue and expense. Note that, although the detail is much greater, the layout of Joshua's P&L is similar in structure to the abbreviated P&L presented as Figure 1.3. Both statements list revenue first, then expense, and finally the difference between the revenue and expense figures. If this number is positive, it represents a profit. If expenses exceed revenue, a loss, represented by a negative number or a number in brackets, is shown. Operating at a loss is, for reasons lost in history, often referred to as operating "in the red" or "shedding red ink." Regardless of the color of the ink, operating at a loss can cause an operator to shed a few tears!

To help ensure that your operation does not produce a loss, you need to know some important components of the *Uniform System of Accounts for Restaurants*. The USAR can best be understood by dividing it into three sections: (1) gross profit, (2) operating expenses, and (3) nonoperating expenses. Referring to Figure 9.1, the gross profit section consists of the Sales through Total Gross Profit entries, the operating expenses section covers Operating Expenses through Operating Income entries, and the nonoperating expenses section includes Interest through Net Income entries. These three sections are arranged on the income statement from most controllable to least controllable by the foodservice manager.

The **gross profit section** consists of food and beverage sales and those food and beverage related costs that can and should be controlled by the manager on a daily basis. The majority of this book is devoted to controlling these items. The **operating expenses section** is also under the control of the manager but on a weekly or monthly basis (with the exception of wages, which can be controlled daily). To illustrate, consider the Repairs and Maintenance category. Although repairs will be needed when equipment breaks down, maintenance is typically scheduled on a monthly basis. The manager can control, to some extent, how employees use the equipment, but he or she cannot control or predict the breakdown of equipment when it occurs. The third section of the USAR is the **nonoperating expenses section.** It is this section that is least controllable by the foodservice manager. For example, interest paid to creditors as part of short-term or long-term debt repayment is due regardless of the ability of the manager to control day-to-day operating costs.

Furthermore, taxes are controlled by the government; to paraphrase Benjamin Franklin, the only sure things in life are death and taxes. So, the foodservice manager has little control over the amount of money "Uncle Sam" gets every year. Knowing what the three sections of the income statement contain allows you to focus on those things over which you have the most control as a foodservice manager. This book helps you to focus on these controllable areas so that you can better manage your time and make the most out of your efforts to control costs.

Note also that each revenue and expense category in Figure 9.1 is expressed both in terms of its whole dollar amount and its percentage of total sales. All ratios are calculated as a percentage of total sales <u>except</u> the following:

- Food costs are divided by food sales.
- Beverage costs are divided by beverage sales.

• Food gross profit is divided by food sales.
• Beverage gross profit is divided by beverage sales.

Food and beverage items use their respective food and beverage sales as the denominator so that these items can be evaluated separately from total sales. Food costs and beverage costs are the most controllable items on the income statement; thus Joshua needs to separate these sales and costs out of the aggregate and evaluate these items more carefully. Notice also that Joshua's accountant presents this year's P&L statement along with last year's; this can help Joshua make comparisons and analyze trends in his business.

Another facet of the uniform system of accounts that you should know is the supporting schedule. The income statement as shown in Figure 9.1 is an **aggregate statement.** This means that all details associated with the sales, costs, and profits of the foodservice establishment are summarized on the P&L statement. Although this summary gives the manager a one-shot look at the performance of the operation, the details are not included directly on the statement. These details can be found in **supporting schedules.** Each line item on the income statement should be accompanied by a schedule that outlines all of the information that the manager needs to know to operate the business successfully. For example, Direct Operating Expenses could have an accompanying schedule that details costs incurred in uniforms, laundry and linen, china and glassware, silverware, etc. These expenses can also be broken down by percentage of total direct operating expenses. In addition, the supporting schedule should have a column in which notes can be taken regarding the costs.

Figure 9.2 is an example of a schedule that would accompany Joshua's Income Statement shown in Figure 9.1. Note that the Total Direct Operating Expenses, $132,143 in the schedule, is taken directly from this year's Direct Operating Expenses on the income statement. The type of information and the level of detail that are included on the schedules are left up to the manager, based on what is appropriate for the operation. The schedules are used to collect the information needed to break down sales or costs and determine problem areas and potential opportunities for improving each item on the income statement.

The P&L statement is one of several documents that can help evaluate profitability. The P&L statement alone, however, can yield important information that is critical to the development of future management plans and budgets. The analysis of P&L statements is a fun and very creative process if basic procedures are well understood. In general, managers who seek to uncover all that their P&L will tell them undertake the following areas of analysis. Using the data from Figure 9.1, each of these areas will be reviewed in turn.

1. Sales/volume
2. Food expense
3. Beverage expense
4. Labor expense
5. Other expense
6. Profits

■ **FIGURE 9.2** Direct Operating Expenses Schedule

Type of Expense	Expense	% of Direct Operating Expenses	Notes
Uniforms	$ 13,408	10.15%	
Laundry and Linen	40,964	31.00	
China and Glassware	22,475	17.01	Expense is higher than budgeted because china shelf collapsed on March 22.
Silverware	3,854	2.92	
Kitchen Utensils	9,150	6.92	
Kitchen Fuel	2,542	1.92	
Cleaning Supplies	10,571	8.00	
Paper Supplies	2,675	2.02	
Bar Expenses	5,413	4.10	
Menus and Wine Lists	6,670	5.05	Expense is lower than budgeted because the new wine supplier agreed to print the wine lists free of charge.
Exterminating	1,803	1.36	
Flowers and Decorations	9,014	6.82	
Licenses	3,604	2.73	
Total Direct Operating Expenses	132,143	100.00	

ANALYSIS OF SALES/VOLUME

As discussed earlier in this text, foodservice operators can measure sales in terms of either dollars or number of guests served. In both cases, an increase in sales volume is usually to be desired. A sales increase or decrease must, however, be analyzed carefully if you are to truly understand the revenue direction of your business. Consider the sales portion of Joshua's P&L statement, as detailed in Figure 9.3.

■ **FIGURE 9.3** Joshua's P&L Sales Comparison

Sales	Last Year	% of Sales	This Year	% of Sales
Food Sales	$1,891,011	82.0%	$2,058,376	81.0%
Beverage Sales	415,099	18.0	482,830	19.0
Total Sales	2,306,110	100.0	$2,541,206	100.0

Based on the data from Figure 9.3, Joshua can compute his overall sales increase or decrease using the following steps:

Step 1. Determine sales for this accounting period.

Step 2. Calculate the following: this period's sales minus last period's sales.

Step 3. Divide the difference in Step 2 by last period's sales to determine percentage variance.

For Joshua, the percentage variance is as indicated in Figure 9.4. To illustrate the steps outlined using total sales as an example, we find:

Step 1. $2,541,206

Step 2. $2,541,206 − $2,306,110 = $235,096

Step 3. $235,096/$2,306,110 = 10.2%

It appears that Joshua has achieved an overall increase in sales of 10.2%. There are several ways total sales could have increased in the current year:

1. The same number of guests at a higher check average
2. More guests at the same check average
3. More guests at a higher check average
4. Fewer guests at a much higher check average

To determine precisely which of these alternatives was responsible for the total sales increase, Joshua must use a sales adjustment technique.

Assume, for a moment, that Joshua raised prices for food and beverage by 5% at the beginning of this fiscal year. If this was the case, and he wishes to determine fairly his sales increase, he must consider the impact of that 5% menu price increase.

■ **FIGURE 9.4** Joshua's P&L Sales Variance

Sales	Last Year	This Year	Variance	Variance %
Food Sales	$1,891,011	$2,058,376	$167,365	+8.9%
Beverage Sales	415,099	482,830	67,731	+16.3
Total Sales	2,306,110	2,541,206	235,096	+10.2

■ **FIGURE 9.5** Joshua's P&L Sales Comparison with 5% Menu Price Increase

Sales	Last Year	Adjusted Sales (Last Year × 1.05)	This Year	Variance	Variance %
Food Sales	$1,891,011	$1,985,561.60	$2,058,376	$ 72,814.40	+3.67%
Beverage Sales	415,099	435,853.95	482,830	46,976.05	+0.78
Total Sales	2,306,110	2,421,415.50	2,541,206	119,790.50	+4.95

The procedure he would use to adjust sales variance to include known menu price increases is as follows:

Step 1. Increase prior-period (last year) sales by amount of the price increase.

Step 2. Subtract the result in Step 1 from this period's sales.

Step 3. Divide the difference in Step 2 by the value of Step 1.

Thus, in our example, Joshua would follow the steps outlined previously to determine his real sales increase. In the case of total sales, the procedure would be as follows:

Step 1. $2,306,110 × 1.05 = $2,421,415.50

Step 2. $2,541,206 − $2,421,415.50 = $119,790.50

Step 3. $119,790.50/$2,421,415.50 = 4.95%

Figure 9.5 details the results that are achieved if this 5% adjustment process is completed for all sales areas. Joshua's total sales figure would be up by 4.95% if he adjusted it for a 5% menu price increase. Thus, although Joshua's overall sales did increase significantly this year, approximately half of the increase was due to increased menu prices.

There is still more, however, that the P&L can tell Joshua about his sales. If he has kept accurate guest count records, he can compute his sales per guest figure (see Chapter 2). With this information, he can determine whether his sales are up because he is serving more guests or because he is serving the same number of guests but each one is spending more per visit or because some of both has occurred. In fact, if each guest is spending quite a bit more per visit, Joshua may even have experienced a decrease in total guest count yet still achieved an increase in total sales. If this were the case, he would want to know about it because it may be quite unrealistic to assume that revenue will continue to increase over the long run if the number of guests visiting his establishment is declining.

■ OTHER FACTORS INFLUENCING SALES ANALYSIS

In some foodservice establishments, other factors must be taken into consideration before sales revenue can be accurately analyzed. Consider the situation you would face if you owned a restaurant across the street from a professional basketball

■ **FIGURE 9.6** Hot Dog! Sales Data

	Last Year	This Year	Variance	Variance %
Total Sales (October)	$17,710	$17,506	$−204	−1.2%
Number of Operating Days	22 days	21 days	1 day	
Average Daily Sales	$ 805	$833.62	$28.62	+3.6

stadium. If you were to compare sales from this May to sales generated last May, the number of home games in May for this professional team would have to be determined before you could make valid conclusions about guest count increases or decreases. Also, if a foodservice facility is open only Monday through Friday, the number of operating days in two given accounting periods may be different for the facility. When this is the case, percentage increases or decreases in sales volume must be based on average daily sales, rather than the total sales figure.

To illustrate this, consider Hot Dog!, a hot dog stand that operates in the city center Monday through Friday only. In October of this year, the stand was open for 21 operating days. Last year, however, because of the number of weekend days in October, the stand operated for 22 days. Figure 9.6 details the comparison of sales for the stand, assuming no increase in menu selling price this year compared with last year.

At first glance, it appears that October sales this year are 1.2% lower than last year, but in reality, average daily sales are up 3.6%! Are sales for October up or down? Clearly, the answer must be qualified in terms of monthly or daily sales. For this reason, effective foodservice managers must be careful to consider all of the relevant facts before making determinations about sales direction.

Every critical factor must be considered when evaluating sales revenue, including the number of operating meal periods or days; changes in menu prices, guest counts, and check averages; and holidays and special events. Only after carefully reviewing all details can you truly know whether your sales are going up or down.

ANALYSIS OF FOOD EXPENSE

*I*n addition to sales analysis, the P&L statement, whether created weekly, monthly, or annually, provides information about other areas of operational interest. For the effective foodservice manager, the analysis of food expense is a matter of major concern. Figure 9.7 details the food expense portion of Joshua's P&L as detailed in the food expense schedule.

It is important to remember that the numerator of the food cost % equation is cost of food sold, whereas the denominator is total food sales rather than total food and beverage sales. With total cost of food sold this year of $767,443, and total food sales of $2,058,376, the total food cost % is 37.3% ($767,443/ $2,058,376 = 37.3%).

■ **FIGURE 9.7** Joshua's P&L Food Expense Schedule

	Last Year	% of Food Sales	This Year	% of Food Sales
Food Sales	$1,891,011	100.0%	$2,058,376	100.0%
Cost of Food Sold				
Meats and Seafood	$ 297,488	15.7	$ 343,063	16.7%
Fruits and Vegetables	94,550	5.0	127,060	6.2
Dairy	55,347	2.9	40,660	2.0
Baked Goods	16,142	0.9	22,870	1.1
Other	249,060	13.2	233,790	11.4
Total Cost of Food Sold	712,587	37.7	767,443	37.3

A food cost percentage can be computed in a similar manner for each subcategory of food. For instance, the cost percentage for the category Meats and Seafood for this year would be computed as follows:

$$\frac{\text{Meats and Seafood Cost}}{\text{Total Food Sales}} = \text{Meats Cost Seafood Cost \%}$$

or

$$\frac{\$343,063}{\$2,058,376} = 16.7\%$$

At first glance, it appears that Joshua has done well for the year and that his total cost of goods sold expense has declined 0.4%, from 37.7% overall last year to 37.3% this year. This is true. Closer inspection, however, indicates that, although the categories Dairy and Other showed declines, Meats and Seafood, Fruits and Vegetables, and Baked Goods showed increases.

Figure 9.8 shows the actual differences in food cost percentage for each of Joshua's food categories. Although it is true that Joshua's overall food cost percentage is down by 0.4%, the variation among categories is quite significant. It is clearly to his benefit to subcategorize food products so that he can watch for fluctuations within and among groups rather than merely monitor his overall increase or decrease in food costs. Without such a breakdown of categories, he will not know exactly where to look if costs get too high.

Sometimes, food costs rise because too much food is held in inventory, resulting in excessive product loss. It would be helpful for Joshua to determine how appropriate the inventory levels are for each of his product subgroups so that he can adjust the inventory sizes if needed. To do this, Joshua must be able to compute his food inventory turnover.

■ FIGURE 9.8   Joshua's P&L Variation in Food Expense by Category

Category	Last Year %	This Year %	Variance
Meats and Seafood	15.7%	16.7%	+1.0%
Fruits and Vegetables	5.0	6.2	+1.2
Dairy	2.9	2.0	−0.9
Baked Goods	0.9	1.1	+0.2
Other	13.2	11.4	−1.8
Total Cost of Food Sold	37.7	37.3	−0.4

■ FOOD INVENTORY TURNOVER

Inventory turnover refers to the number of times the total value of inventory has been purchased and replaced in an accounting period. Each time the cycle is completed once, we are said to have "turned" the inventory. For example, if you normally keep $100 worth of oranges on hand at any given time and last month's usage of oranges was $500, you would have replaced your orange inventory five times that month. The formula used to compute inventory turnover is as follows:

$$\frac{\text{Cost of Food Consumed}}{\text{Average Inventory Value}} = \text{Food Inventory Turnover}$$

Note that it is cost of food consumed, rather than cost of food sold, that is used as the numerator in this ratio. This is because all food inventories should be tracked so that you can better determine what is sold, wasted, spoiled, pilfered, or provided to employees as employee meals.

Stated another way, inventory turnover is a measure of how many times the inventory value is purchased and sold to guests. In the foodservice industry, we are, of course, interested in high inventory turnover as it relates to increased sales. It simply makes sense that if a 5% profit is made on the sale of an inventory item, we would like to sell (turn) that item as many times per year as possible. If the item were sold from inventory only once per year, one 5% profit would result. If the item turned 10 times, a 5% profit on each of the 10 sales would result. However, you have to be sure that a high inventory turnover is caused by increased sales and not by increased food waste, food spoilage, or employee theft.

To compute his inventory turnover for each of his food categories, Joshua must first establish his average inventory value for each food category. The average inventory value is computed by adding the beginning inventory for this

■ **FIGURE 9.9**   Joshua's P&L Average Inventory Values

Inventory Category	This Year Beginning Inventory	This Year Ending Inventory	Average Inventory Value
Meats and Seafood	$16,520	$14,574	$15,547
Fruits and Vegetables	1,314	846	1,080
Dairy	594	310	452
Baked Goods	123	109	116
Other	8,106	9,196	8,651
Total	26,657	25,035	25,846

period to the ending inventory for this period and dividing by two, using the following formula:

$$\frac{\text{Beginning Inventory Value} + \text{Ending Inventory Value}}{2}$$
$$= \text{Average Inventory Value}$$

From his inventory records, Joshua creates the data recorded in Figure 9.9.

To illustrate the computation of average inventory value, note that Joshua's Meats and Seafood beginning inventory for this year was $16,520, whereas his ending inventory for that category was $14,574. His average inventory value for that category is $15,547 [($16,520 + $14,574)/2 = $15,547]. All other categories and the total average inventory value are computed in the same manner.

Now that Joshua has determined the average inventory values for his food categories, he can compute the inventory turnovers for each of these. As you recall from Chapter 3, cost of food consumed is identical to cost of food sold when no reduction is made in cost as a result of employee meals. That is the case at Joshua's facility because he charges employees full price for menu items that he sells to them as employee meals. Therefore, employee meals are included in regular food cost because a normal food sales price is charged for these meals. Figure 9.10 shows the result of his computation using the food inventory turnover formula for this year.

To illustrate, Joshua's Meats and Seafood inventory turnover is 22.1 ($343,063/$15,547 = 22.1). That is, Joshua purchased, sold, and replaced his meat and seafood inventory, on average, 22 times this year. Note that all other food categories and the total inventory turnover are computed in the same manner. Note also that in categories such as fruits and vegetables, dairy, and baked goods, the turnovers are very high, reflecting the perishability of these items. Joshua's overall inventory turnover is 29.7.

If Joshua's *target* inventory turnover for the year was 26 times (every two weeks), then he should investigate why his actual inventory turnover is higher. It could be because of his increase in sales, which is a good sign of his restaurant's

■ **FIGURE 9.10** Joshua's P&L Food Inventory Turnover

Inventory Category	Cost of Food Consumed	Average Inventory	Inventory Turnover
Meats and Seafood	$343,063	$15,547	22.1
Fruits and Vegetables	127,060	1,080	117.6
Dairy	40,660	452	90.0
Baked Goods	22,870	116	197.2
Other	233,790	8,651	27.0
Total	767,443	25,846	29.7

performance. Or it could be due to wastage, pilferage, and spoilage. Alternatively, if his inventory turnover was less than 26 times per year, it could be due to lower sales or overstocking of inventory. Joshua could be buying excess inventory at a bulk discount (which is an intentional management decision to save money), or he might be purchasing too much due to poor inventory management. He should use inventory turnover analysis to help him determine how he can more effectively control his product costs in the future.

ANALYSIS OF BEVERAGE EXPENSE

Joshua's P&L (Figure 9.1) indicates beverage sales for this year of $482,830. With total sales of $2,541,206, beverages represent 19% of Joshua's total sales ($482,830/$2,541,206 = 19%). Also from Figure 9.1, beverage costs for this year are $96,566; thus, Joshua's beverage cost percentage, which is computed as cost of beverages divided by beverage sales, is 20% ($96,566/$482,830 = 20%). To completely analyze this expense category, Joshua would compute his beverage cost percentage, compare that to his planned or targeted expense, and compute a beverage inventory turnover rate using the same formulas as he did for his food products.

If an operation carries a large number of rare and expensive wines, its beverage inventory turnover rate is relatively low. Conversely, those beverage operations that sell their products primarily by the glass are likely to experience inventory turnover rates that are quite high. The important concept here is to compute the turnover rates at least once per year (or more often if needed) to gauge whether inventory sizes should be increased or decreased. High beverage inventory turnovers accompanied by frequent product outages may indicate inventory levels that are too low, whereas low turnover rates and many slow-moving inventory items may indicate the need to reduce beverage inventory levels.

Figure 9.1 shows that last year's beverage cost percentage was 22.8% ($94,550/$415,099 = 22.8%). A first glance would indicate that beverage costs have been reduced, not in total dollars spent, sales were higher this year than last year, but in percentage terms. In other words, a beverage cost % of 22.8% last year versus 20% this year indicates a 2.8% overall reduction.

Assume, for a moment, however, that Joshua raised drink prices by 10% this year over last year. Assume also that Joshua pays, on average, 5% more for beverages this year compared with last year. Is his beverage operation more efficient this year than last year, less efficient, or the same? To determine the answer to this important question in the beverage or any other expense category, Joshua must make adjustments to both his sales and his cost figures. Similar to the method for adjusting sales, the method for adjusting expense categories for known cost increases is as follows:

Step 1. Increase prior-period expense by amount of cost increase.

Step 2. Determine appropriate sales data, remembering to adjust prior-period sales, if applicable.

Step 3. Divide costs determined in Step 1 by sales determined in Step 2.

Thus, in our example, Joshua's beverage expense last year, adjusted for this year's costs, would be $94,550 × 1.05 = $99,277.50.

His beverage sales from last year, adjusted for this year's menu prices, would be $415,099 × 1.10 = $456,608.90.

His last year's beverage cost percentage, adjusted for increases in this year's costs and selling prices, would be computed as follows:

$$\frac{\$99,277.50}{\$456,608.90} = 21.7\%$$

In this case, Joshua's real cost of beverage sold has, in fact, declined this year, although not by as much as he had originally thought. That is, a 21.7% adjusted cost for last year versus a 20% cost for this year equals a reduction of 1.7%, not 2.8% as originally determined.

All food and beverage expense categories must be adjusted in terms of both costs and selling price if effective comparisons are to be made over time. When older foodservice managers remember back to the time when they purchased hamburger for $0.59 per pound, it is important to recall that the 1/4 -pound hamburger they made from it may have sold for $0.59 also! The 25% resulting product cost percentage is no different from today's operator paying $3.00 a pound for ground beef and selling the resulting 1/4-pound burger for $3.00. Notice that it is not possible to compare efficiency in food and beverage usage from one time period to the next unless you are making that comparison in equal terms. As product costs increase or decrease and as menu prices change, so, too, will food and beverage expense percentages change. As an effective manager, you must determine if variations in product percentage costs are caused by real changes in your operation or simply by differences in the price you pay for your products as well as your selling prices for those products.

ANALYSIS OF LABOR EXPENSE

From Figure 9.1, it is interesting to note that, although the total dollars Joshua spent on labor increased greatly from last year to this year, his labor cost percentage increased only slightly. This was true in the Salaries and Wages category as well as the Employee Benefits category. Recall that whenever your labor costs are not 100% variable costs, increasing sales volume will help you decrease your labor cost percentage, although the total dollars you spend on labor will increase. The reason for this is simple. When total dollar sales volume increases, fixed labor cost percentages will decline. In other words, the dollars paid for fixed labor will consume a smaller percentage of your total revenue. Thus, as long as any portion of total labor cost is fixed (manager's salaries, for example), increasing volume will have the effect of reducing labor cost percentage. Variable labor costs, of course, will increase along with sales volume increases, but the percentage of revenue they consume should stay constant.

When you combine a declining percentage (fixed labor cost) with a constant percentage (variable labor cost), you should achieve a reduced overall percentage, although your total labor dollars expended can be higher. Serving additional guests may cost additional labor dollars. That, in itself, is not a bad thing. In most foodservice situations, you want to serve more guests. If labor expenses are controlled properly, you will find that an increase in the number of guests and sales will result in an appropriate increase in the labor costs required to service those guests. You must be careful, however, to always ensure that increased costs are appropriate for increases achieved in sales volume.

Remember, too, that declining costs of labor are not always a sign that all is well in a foodservice unit. Declining costs of labor may be the result of significant reductions in the number of guests served. If, for example, a foodservice facility produces poor-quality products and gives poor service, guest counts can be expected to decline, as would the cost of labor required to service those guests who do remain. Labor dollars expended by management would decline, but it would be an indication of improper, rather than effective, management. An effective foodservice manager seeks to achieve declines in operational expense because of operational efficiencies, not reduced sales.

Figure 9.11 details the labor cost portion of Joshua's P&L. Note that all the labor-related percentages he computes are based on his total sales, that is, the

■ **FIGURE 9.11** Joshua's P&L Labor Cost

Labor Cost	Last Year	% of Total Sales	This Year	% of Total Sales
Salaries and Wages	$641,099	27.8%	$714,079	28.1%
Employee Benefits	99,163	4.3	111,813	4.4
Total Labor Cost	740,262	32.1	825,892	32.5

combination of his food and beverage sales. This is different from computing expense percentages such as food and beverage because food cost percentage is determined using food sales as the denominator and beverage cost percentage computations use beverage sales as a denominator. Thus, Joshua's salaries and wages expense % for this year is computed as follows:

$$\frac{\text{Salaries and Wages Expense}}{\text{Total Sales}} = \text{Salaries and Wages Expense}\%$$

or

$$\frac{\$714,079}{\$2,541,206} = 28.1\%$$

A brief examination of the labor portion of Joshua's P&L would indicate an increase in both dollars spent for labor and labor cost percentage. Just as adjustments must be made for changes in food and beverage expenses before valid expense comparisons can be made, so too must adjustments be made for changes, if any, in the price an operator pays for labor. In Joshua's case, assume that all employees were given a **cost of living adjustment (COLA)**, or raise, of 5% at the beginning of this year. This, coupled with an assumed 10% menu price increase, would indeed have the effect of changing overall the labor cost % even if labor productivity did not change.

From Figure 9.11, Joshua can see that his actual labor cost % increased from 32.1% last year to 32.5% this year, an increase of 0.4%. To adjust for the changes in the cost of labor and his selling prices, if these indeed occurred, Joshua uses the techniques previously detailed in this chapter. Thus, based on the assumption of a 5% increase in the cost of labor and a 10% increase in selling price, he adjusts both sales and cost of labor, using the same steps as those employed for adjusting food or beverage cost percentage, and computes a new labor cost for last year as follows:

Step 1. Determine sales adjustment: $2,306,110 × 1.10 = $2,536,721

Step 2. Determine total labor cost adjustment: $740,262 × 1.05 = $777,275.10

Step 3. Compute adjusted labor cost percentage: $777,275.10/$2,536,721 = 30.6%

As can be seen, last year Joshua's P&L would have indicated a 30.6% labor cost percentage *if* he had operated under this year's increased labor costs and selling prices. This is certainly an area that Joshua would want to investigate. The reason is simple. If he were exactly as efficient this year as he was last year, and if he assumed a 10% menu price increase and a 5% labor cost increase, Joshua's cost of labor for this year should have been computed as follows:

This Year's Sales × Last Year's Adjusted Labor Cost %
= This Year's Projected Labor Cost

or

$2,541,206 0.306 = $777,609.03

Put in another way, if Joshua were just as efficient with his labor this year as he was last year, he would have expected to spend 30.6% of sales for labor this year, given his 5% payroll increase and 10% menu price increase. In actuality, Joshua's labor cost was $48,282.96 higher ($825,892 actual this year − $777,609.04 projected = $48,282.96). A variation this large should obviously be of concern to Joshua and should be examined closely.

Increases in payroll taxes, benefit programs, and employee turnover can all affect labor cost percentage. Although, for our example, we assumed that employee benefits (including payroll taxes, insurance, etc.) increased at the same 5% rate as did salaries and wages, these are, of course, different expenses and may increase at rates higher or lower than salary and wage payments to employees. Indeed, one of the fastest-increasing labor-related costs for foodservice managers today is the cost of health insurance benefit programs. These programs are needed to attract the best employees to the hospitality industry, but they are expensive.

Controlling and evaluating labor cost is an important part of your job as a hospitality manager. In fact, many managers feel it is more important to control labor costs than product costs because, for many of them, labor and labor-related costs comprise a larger portion of their operating budgets than do food and beverage product costs.

ANALYSIS OF OTHER EXPENSE

*A*n analysis of other expenses should be performed each time the P&L is produced. Figure 9.12 details other expenses from Joshua's P&L statement.

Joshua's other expenses consist of both operating expenses (excluding salaries and wages and employee benefits) and nonoperating items, and he must review these carefully. In Joshua's operation, these costs have increased from last year's levels. Note that his Repairs and Maintenance category is also higher this year than it was last year. This is one area in which he both expects and approves a cost increase. It is logical to assume that kitchen repairs will increase as a kitchen ages. In that sense, a kitchen is much like a car. Even with a good preventative maintenance program, Joshua does not expect an annual decline in kitchen repair expense. In fact, he would be somewhat surprised and concerned should this category be smaller this year than in the previous year because his sales were higher and probably caused more wear and tear on his kitchen equipment. In the same way, his contributions to his state and national association political action funds, charged to Administrative and General expense, were up significantly. This is due to Joshua's belief that he, as part of the hospitality industry, needs to make his voice heard to his local and national political leaders. Joshua is a strong believer in taking a leadership role in his association on the local, state, and national levels. Indeed, one of his goals is to someday serve on the board of his national association! He knows that membership in that organization gives him a voice straight to the nation's lawmakers and policymakers.

■ **FIGURE 9.12** Joshua's P&L Other Expenses

Other Expenses	Last Year	% of Total Sales	This Year	% of Total Sales
Operating Expenses (excluding salaries and wages and employee benefits)				
Direct Operating Expenses	$122,224	5.3%	$132,143	5.2%
Music and Entertainment	2,306	0.1	7,624	0.3
Marketing	43,816	1.9	63,530	2.5
Utility Services	73,796	3.2	88,942	3.5
Repairs and Maintenance	34,592	1.5	35,577	1.4
Administrative and General	66,877	2.9	71,154	2.8
Occupancy	120,000	5.2	120,000	4.7
Depreciation	41,510	1.8	55,907	2.2
Nonoperating Expenses				
Interest	$ 86,750	3.8%	$ 84,889	3.3%
Income Taxes	65,068	2.8	76,616	3.0

An analysis of other expenses proves difficult for Joshua because he is not sure how he compares with others in his area or with operations of a similar nature. For comparison purposes, he is, however, able to use industry trade publications to get national averages on other expense categories. One helpful source Joshua can use is an annual publication, *The Restaurant Industry Operations Report*, published by the National Restaurant Association and prepared by Deloitte & Touche (it can be ordered through **www.restaurant.org**). For operations that are a part of a corporate chain, unit managers can receive comparison data from district and regional managers, who can chart performance against those of other units in the city, region, state, and nation.

Consider The Cost

"Wow!" I can't believe the size of the electricity bill this month," said Wendy. She was talking to Matt, the assistant manager of the Aussie Steakhouse in Phoenix, Arizona, where Wendy served as general manager.

"Is it higher than last month?" asked Matt.

"It's a lot higher," replied Wendy. "I thought it would be a little higher because it was really hot last month."

"So our usage was up?" asked Matt.

"Yes," said Wendy, "and the rate per kilowatt hour we pay is up from last year, too. It seems like that rate goes up a little more every year."

"Is the bill so high it will affect our monthly bonus?" asked Matt. "I hope not," he continued, "because we had a great month last month, and I was really counting on the extra money in my next check."

"I don't know," said Wendy. "Let me get the calculator and we'll see."

1. What would be the likely effect on both the dollar amount and the percent of sales reported on the monthly P&L of the Aussie Steakhouse if there were:

   a. An increase in the amount of electricity used in the restaurant?
   b. An increase in the cost per unit (kilowatt hour) of the electricity consumed?
   c. An increase in the number of guests served by the restaurant?

2. In this scenario it appears that if the cost of other expenses in this restaurant is too high, its managers may not achieve their monthly bonus. Do you believe the cost of electricity is a controllable or noncontrollable operating expense?

3. Regardless of your answer to the previous question, what are at least three specific actions Wendy and Matt could take to minimize the future impact on their P&L of rising electricity costs?

ANALYSIS OF PROFITS

As can be seen in Figure 9.1, profits for Joshua's, Inc., refer to the net income figure at the bottom of the income statement. Joshua's net income for this year was $114,923, or 4.5% of total sales, and his total sales for this year were $2,541,206. His profit percentage using the **profit margin** formula is as follows:

$$\frac{\text{Net Income}}{\text{Total Sales}} = \text{Profit Margin}$$

or

$$\frac{\$114,923}{2,541,206} = 4.5\%$$

Profit margin is also known as **return on sales (ROS).** For the foodservice manager, perhaps no number is more important than ROS. This percentage is often considered to be the most telling indicator of a manager's overall effectiveness at generating revenues and controlling costs in line with forecasted results. Although it is not possible to state what a "good" ROS figure should be for all restaurants, industry averages, depending on the specific segment, range from 1% to over 20%.

Some operators prefer to use operating income (see Figure 9.1) as the numerator for profit margin instead of net income. This is because interest and income taxes are considered nonoperating expenses (because they cannot truly be "managed" by a manager) and, thus, are not truly reflective of a manager's ability to generate a profit. Although ROS is important, it is also important to recognize that you ultimately will bank "dollars" and not "percentages." Clearly, a manager whose operation nets a 15% ROS on sales of $2,000,000 is going to generate more profits than a manager who nets a 20% ROS on sales of $500,000.

Joshua's ROS results this year represent an improvement over last year's figure of $101,772, or 4.4% of total sales. Thus, he has shown improvement both in the dollar size of his net income and in the size of net income as related to total sales. He realizes, however, that increased sales, rather than great improvements in operational efficiency, could have caused this progress because his sales volume this year was greater than his sales volume last year. To analyze his profitability appropriately, he should determine how much of his revenue increase was due to increased menu prices as opposed to increased guest count or check average.

Joshua can compute the variance in his net income by subtracting net income last year from net income this year as follows:

$$\text{Net Income This Year} - \text{Net Income Last Year} = \text{Variance}$$
$$\text{or}$$
$$\$114,923 - \$101,772 = \$13,151$$

Joshua can then compute his net income variance percentage as follows:

$$\frac{\text{Net Income This Year} - \text{Net Income Last Year}}{\text{Net Income Last Year}} = \text{Percentage Variance}$$
$$\text{or}$$
$$\frac{\$114,923 - \$101,772}{\$101,772} = 12.9\%$$

An alternative, and shorter, formula for computing the percentage variance is as follows:

$$\frac{\text{Variance}}{\text{Net Income Last Year}} = \text{Percentage Variance}$$
$$\text{or}$$
$$\frac{\$13,151}{\$101,772} = 12.9\%$$

Another way to compute the percentage variance is to use a math shortcut, as follows:

$$\frac{\text{Net Income This Year}}{\text{Net Income Last Year}} - 1 = \text{Percentage Variance}$$

or

$$\frac{\$114,923}{\$101,772} - 1 = 12.9\%$$

How much of this improvement is due to improved operational methods versus increased sales will depend, of course, on how much Joshua actually did increase his sales relative to increases in his costs. Monitoring selling price, guest count, sales per guest, operating days, special events, and actual operating costs is necessary for accurate profit comparisons. Without knowledge of each of these areas, the effective analysis of profits becomes a risky proposition.

Green and Growing!

Some foodservice operators think that adopting a sustainable, or "green," operations viewpoint inevitably means putting planet before profit. They would argue that businesses can survive only if they put profits first so that is where their focus should be. In the long run, of course, an organization's purpose must include a focus on *both* profit and planet. It is true that an unprofitable business will not stay in business long. It is also true that "planet friendly" management yields many positive financial outcomes for businesses, as well as for the health of the local communities these businesses count on to support them.

For example, the simple act of buying local (to minimize transportation costs and environmental impact) produces an additional reward: community connection. Buying local creates relationships with those who produce food and keeps money flowing through a local economy, resulting in a healthier community.

There are additional positive outcomes from the local food movement. For example, as more hospitality businesses use local, seasonal, sustainably raised food, more fresh fruits and vegetables may be consumed, resulting in positive nutrition and health impacts within the community. The long-term result may be a reduction in healthcare costs. Perceptive foodservice operators now clearly recognize that profits, planet, and people all benefit from an operation's green commitment.

Technology Tools

This chapter introduced the concept of management analysis as it relates to sales, expenses, and profits. In this area, software is quite advanced, and there are many tools available to assist you. The best of these will help you:

1. Analyze operating trends (sales and costs) over management-established time periods.
2. Analyze food and beverage costs.
3. Analyze labor costs.
4. Analyze other expenses.
5. Analyze profits.
6. Compare operating results of multiple profit centers within one location or across several locations.
7. Interface with an operation's point of sales (POS) system or even incorporate it completely.
8. "Red flag" areas of potential management concern.
9. Evaluate the financial productivity of individual servers, day parts, or other specific time periods established by management.
10. Compare actual to budgeted results and compute variance percentages as well as suggest revisions to future budget periods based on current operating results.

FUN ON THE WEB!

There are few areas of foodservice management advancing more rapidly than the ones described in this chapter. To see how one very progressive software development company is integrating the rapid advancements of technology tools with the practical needs of foodservice managers, go to **www.menusoft.com.**

Apply What You Have Learned

*T*erri Settles is a registered dietitian (RD). She supervises five hospitals for Maramark Dining Services, the company the hospitals have selected to operate their foodservices. Her company produces a monthly and annual income statement for each hospital.

1. Discuss five ways in which income statements can help Terri do her job better.
2. What would a hospital do with "profits" or surpluses made in the foodservice area?
3. What effect will "profit" or "loss" have on the ability of Terri's company to continue to manage the foodservices for these hospitals?

Key Terms and Concepts

The following are terms and concepts discussed in the chapter that are important for you as a manager. To help you review, please define the terms below:

Cost accounting
Managerial accounting
Bookkeeping
Sarbanes-Oxley Act
 (SOX)
Uniform system of
 accounts
Income statement

Profit and loss (P&L)
 statement
Net income
Fiscal year
Gross profit section
 (of the USAR)
Operating expenses
 section (of the USAR)

Nonoperating expenses
 section (of the USAR)
Aggregate statement
Supporting schedules
Inventory turnover
COLA
Profit margin
Return on sales (ROS)

Test Your Skills

Complete the Test Your Skills exercises by placing your answers in the shaded boxes and answering the questions as indicated.

1. Lucir manages a German restaurant in a large western city. The owner wants to know how well Lucir did this year at generating sales, controlling costs, and providing a profit. The owner promised Lucir that he would give her a raise if she increased return on sales (profit margin) by at least 1%. Complete Lucir's P&L. Should she receive a raise?

Lucir's P&L

SALES:	Last Year	%	This Year	%
Food	$2,647,415		$2,675,889	
Beverage	498,119		965,660	
Total Sales				
COST OF SALES:				
Food	855,104		1,074,420	
Beverage	104,005		115,879	
Total Cost of Sales				
GROSS PROFIT:				
Food	1,792,311		1,601,469	
Beverage	394,114		849,781	
Total Gross Profit				
OPERATING EXPENSES:				
Salaries and Wages	769,319		785,487	
Employee Benefits	118,996		122,994	
Direct Operating Expenses	146,669		145,357	
Music and Entertainment	2,767		8,386	
Marketing	52,579		69,883	
Utility Services	88,555		97,836	
Repairs and Maintenance	41,510		39,135	
Administrative and General	80,252		78,269	
Occupancy	144,000		132,000	
Depreciation	49,812		61,498	
Total Operating Expenses				
Operating Income				
Interest	104,100		93,378	
Income Before Income Taxes				
Income Taxes	235,146		343,150	
Net Income				

2. Faye manages Faye's Tea Room in a small suburban town. She sells gourmet food and a variety of teas. This year, Faye increased her selling prices by 5%, and she increased her wages by 10%. Faye's condensed P&L follows. Help her calculate her variance and variance % from last year to this year. Use her adjusted sales and labor cost to provide a more accurate picture of her performance this year. Do not put any answers in the shaded boxes.

Faye's Condensed P&L

	Last Year	Adjusted Sales and Labor (for last year)	This Year	Variance	Variance %
Sales	$1,865,000		$2,315,000		
Cost of Food	615,450		717,650		
Cost of Labor	540,850		671,350		
Other Expenses	428,950		486,150		
Total Expenses					
Profit					

3. a. Rudolfo owns Rudolfo's Italian Restaurante in the Little Italy section of New York City. He wants to compare last year's costs to this year's costs on his food expense schedule to see how he performed in each food category. Help Rudolfo complete his schedule.

Rudolfo's Food Expense Schedule

	Last Year	% of Food Sales	This Year	% of Food Sales
Food Sales	$2,836,517		$3,087,564	
Cost of Food Sold				
Meats and Seafood	$ 386,734		$ 445,982	
Fruits and Vegetables	122,915		165,178	
Dairy	71,951		52,858	
Baked Goods	20,985		29,731	
Other	323,778		303,927	
Total Cost of Food Sold				

b. In addition to calculating the food cost % for each of his food categories, Rudolfo wishes to calculate his inventory turnover for the year. Rudolfo's inventory turnover target for this year was 32 times. Did he meet his target? If not, what may have caused this? (Assume that cost of food sold, part a., and cost of food consumed, part b., are the same for Rudolfo's.)

Rudolfo's Food Inventory Turnover

Inventory Category	This Year Beginning Inventory	This Year Ending Inventory	Average Inventory Value	Cost of Food Consumed	Inventory Turnover
Meats and Seafood	$21,476	$17,489		$445,982	
Fruits and Vegetables	1,708	1,015		165,178	
Dairy	772	372		52,858	
Baked Goods	160	131		29,731	
Other	10,538	11,035		303,927	
Total					

4. Jaymal is director of club operations for five military bases in Florida. He has just received year-end income statements for each. Information from the revenue and labor portion of those statements is shown below. Jaymal wants to use the current year's data to create next year's budget. Assume that Jaymal is happy with his labor productivity in each unit and that both wages and revenue in each will increase 2% next year. Calculate how much Jaymal should budget for revenue and labor in each unit. Also, calculate what Jaymal's labor cost % will be for each unit if he meets his budget.

	This Year's Results		Next Year's Budget		
Location	This Year's Cost of Labor	This Year's Revenue	Projected Cost of Labor	Projected Revenue	Projected Labor Cost %
Pensacola	$ 285,000	$ 980,500			
Daytona	197,250	720,000			
Fort Myers	235,500	850,250			
Tampa	279,750	921,750			
Miami	1,190,250	3,720,000			

5. Ron MacGruder is senior vice president of acquisitions for Yummy Foods. Yummy is a large multinational food service company. It owns over 2,000 restaurants. Among its famous brands are a chain of pizza parlors, a Mexican carryout group, a chain of fried chicken stores, and a large group of fried fish stores. Ron is constantly on the lookout for growing food service concepts that could be purchased at a fair price and added to the Yummy group. One such concept that is currently available for sale is a small but expanding group of upscale Thai restaurants called Bow Thais. The current owners wish to sell the 17-unit chain and retire to Florida. They proudly point to the fact that both their sales and profits have increased in each of the last three years. Revenue has more than doubled this year compared to two years ago. Profits have risen from just $600,000 two years ago to over $1,000,000 this year. The summary P&Ls they have supplied to Ron indicate the following:

Two Years Ago	
Revenue	$ 6,500,000
Profit	$ 600,000
Last Year	
Revenue	$ 9,900,000
Profit	$ 800,000
This Year	
Revenue	$13,500,000
Profit	$ 1,010,000

Assume that two years ago, the Bow Thais chain consisted of 6 units. One year ago it consisted of 12 units, and this year it consists of 17 units. Develop a summary P&L for each of Bow Thais's last three years showing revenue, expense, and profit. Next compute a "per unit" revenue, expense, profit, and profit margin level for each of the three years for which you have data. Would you advise Ron to buy the company? Why or why not?

	Revenue	Expense	Profit	No. of Units	Revenue per Unit	Expense per Unit	Profit per Unit	Profit Margin %
2 Years Ago	$ 6,500,000		$ 600,000					
Last Year	9,900,000		800,000					
This Year	13,500,000		1,010,000					

6. Basil Bakal is the newly appointed food and beverage director at Telco Industries. Telco creates and markets software programs developed for use with iPods. The company has 500 employees and operates its own cafeteria and executive dining room, where it daily offers free lunches to all employees. Basil's cafeteria serves between 375 and 425 lunches per day. Approximately 50 more meals per day are served in the Executive Dining Room. Basil has created his own modified version of a P&L for use in his operation. Calculate the percentages of meals served in the cafeteria and executive dining room and the costs per meal served, and then answer the questions that follow.

Telco Industries Food Services Department		
	Meals Served Last Year	% Of Total Meals Served
NUMBER OF MEALS SERVED:		
Cafeteria	104,250	
Executive Dining Room	12,150	
Total Served		
	Total Cost $	Per Meal Cost$
COST OF SALES:		
Cafeteria	$248,750	
Executive Dining Room	48,450	
Total Cost of Sales		
OPERATING EXPENSES:		
Salaries and Wages	244,440	
Employee Benefits	61,110	
401(k) Match	25,350	
Administrative and General Expense	46,669	
China/Glass Replacement	12,767	
Paper Products	52,579	
Other Direct Operating Expenses	46,669	
Utilities	96,000	
Repairs and Maintenance	21,510	
Equipment Rental	1,500	
Total Operating Expenses		

a. How much more did it cost (cost of sales) Basil to serve a meal in the executive dining room than it did in the employee cafeteria? Why do you think that would be so?

b. Basil's modified P&L combines all wage and salary-related costs when calculating cost per meal served. Why do you think he elected not to allocate labor costs between the two serving areas? How could he do so?

c. Assume you were on the board of directors of Telco. How would decide how much more money you should allocate to Basil's area next year to account for rising food prices? Who would you expect to provide you with the information you need to make an informed decision about the appropriate size of the increase?

7. In this chapter you learned that a P&L statement is used to report revenue, expense, and profit. In many cases, noncommercial foodservice operators, such as those responsible for schools, colleges and universities, and health care facilities, including retirement complexes, nursing homes, as well as hospitals, are severely restricted in their ability to increase their revenues. This is so because the operating budgets of many such facilities are fixed annually based upon the number of meals estimated to be served. Also, such facilities do not seek to earn a "profit" in the traditional sense of the word. In these noncommercial operations, however, the preparation and thoughtful analysis of monthly P&L statements is still considered essential. Why do you believe this is so?

Chapter 10

PLANNING FOR PROFIT

OVERVIEW

This chapter shows you how to analyze your menu so you can identify which individual menu items contribute most to your profits. In addition, it teaches you how to determine the sales dollars and volume levels you must achieve to break even and to generate a profit in your operation. Finally, the chapter shows you how to establish an operating budget and presents techniques you can use to monitor your effectiveness in staying within your budget.

Chapter Outline

- Financial Analysis and Profit Planning
- Menu Analysis
- Cost/Volume/Profit Analysis
- The Budget
- Developing the Budget
- Monitoring the Budget
- Technology Tools
- Apply What You Have Learned
- Key Terms and Concepts
- Test Your Skills

LEARNING OUTCOMES

At the conclusion of this chapter, you will be able to:
- Analyze a menu for profitability.
- Prepare a cost/volume/profit (break-even) analysis.
- Establish a budget and monitor performance to the budget.

FINANCIAL ANALYSIS AND PROFIT PLANNING

*I*n addition to analyzing the profit and loss (P&L) statement, you should also undertake a thorough study of three areas that will assist you in planning for profit. These three areas of analysis are:

1. Menu analysis
2. Cost/volume/profit (CVP) analysis
3. Budgeting

Whereas menu analysis concerns itself with the profitability of the menu items you sell, CVP analysis deals with the sales dollars and volume required by your foodservice unit to avoid an operating loss and to make a profit. The process of budgeting allows you to plan your next year's operating results by projecting sales, expenses, and profits to develop a budgeted P&L statement.

Some foodservice operators "hope for profit" instead of "planning for profit." Although hoping is an admirable pursuit when playing the lottery, it does little good when managing a foodservice operation. Smart managers know that planning is the key to achieving the cost and profit goals that will keep them in business.

MENU ANALYSIS

*E*ffective managers want to know the answer to a basic operational question: "How does the sale of a particular menu item contribute to the overall success of my operation?" The answer to such a question can sometimes be provided by applying mathematics, but numbers are only one component of menu analysis. There are others to consider.

Consider the case of Danny, who operates a successful family restaurant, called The Mark Twain, in rural Tennessee. The restaurant has been in his family for three generations. One item on the menu is mustard greens with scrambled eggs. It does not sell often, but both mustard greens and eggs are ingredients in other, more popular items. Why does Danny keep the item in a prominent spot on the menu? The answer is simple and has little to do with finance. The menu item was Danny's grandfather's favorite. As a thank-you to his grandfather, who started the business and inspired Danny to become service and guest oriented, the menu item survives every menu reprint.

Menu analysis, then, is about more than just numbers. It involves marketing, sociology, psychology, and a good deal of emotion. Remember that guests respond best not to weighty financial analyses, but rather to menu item descriptions, placement on the physical menu, price, and current popularity. Although the financial analysis of a menu is indeed done "by the numbers," you must realize that those numbers are just one part, but an important part, of the total menu analysis picture.

For the serious foodservice manager, the analysis of a menu deserves special study. Many components of the menu, such as pricing, layout, design, and copy, play an important role in the overall success of a foodservice operation. The foodservice manager who does not seek to understand how a menu truly works is akin to the manager who does not seek to understand the essential components of a good cup of coffee! If you investigate the menu analysis methods that have been widely analyzed and used in recent times, you will find that each seeks to perform a menu analysis using one or more of the following operational variables with which you are familiar:

- Food cost percentage
- Popularity
- Contribution margin
- Selling price
- Variable expenses
- Fixed expenses

Although there are many variations, three of the most popular systems of menu analysis are shown in Figure 10.1. They represent the three major philosophical approaches to menu analysis. The **matrix analysis** referenced in Figure 10.1 provides a method for comparisons between menu items. A matrix allows menu items to be placed into categories based on whether they are above or below overall menu item averages for factors such as food cost %, popularity, and contribution margin.

■ **FIGURE 10.1** Three Methods of Menu Analysis

Method	Variables Considered	Analysis Method	Goal
1. Food cost %	a. Food cost % b. Popularity	Matrix	Minimize overall food cost %
2. Contribution margin	a. Contribution margin b. Popularity	Matrix	Maximize contribution margin
3. Goal value analysis	a. Contribution margin % b. Popularity c. Selling price d. Variable cost % e. Food cost %	Algebraic equation	Achieve predetermined profit % goals

Each approach to menu analysis has its proponents and detractors, but an understanding of each will help you as you attempt to develop your own philosophy of menu analysis.

■ FOOD COST PERCENTAGE

Menu analysis that focuses on food cost percentage is the oldest and most traditional method used. When analyzing a menu using the food cost percentage method, you are seeking menu items that have the effect of minimizing your overall food cost percentage. The rationale for this is that a lowered food cost percentage leaves more of the sales dollar to be spent for other operational expenses. A criticism of the food cost percentage approach is that items that have a higher food cost percentage may be removed from the menu in favor of items that have a lower food cost percentage, but when purchased by guests, these items also contribute fewer dollars to overall profit.

To illustrate the use of the food cost percentage menu analysis method, consider the case of Maureen, who operates a steak and seafood restaurant near the beach in a busy resort town. Maureen sells seven items in the entrée section of her menu. The items and information related to their cost, selling price, and popularity for a one-week period in January are presented in Figure 10.2.

■ FIGURE 10.2   Maureen's Menu Analysis Worksheet

Date: 1/1–1/7

Menu Item	Number Sold	Selling Price	Total Sales	Item Cost	Total Cost	Item Contribution Margin	Total Contribution Margin	Food Cost %
Strip Steak	73	$17.95	$ 1,310.35	$ 8.08	$ 589.84	$ 9.87	720.51	45%
Coconut Shrimp	121	16.95	2,050.95	5.09	615.89	11.86	1,435.06	30
Grilled Tuna	105	17.95	1,884.75	7.18	753.90	10.77	1,130.85	40
Chicken Breast	140	13.95	1,953.00	3.07	429.80	10.88	1,523.20	22
Lobster Stir-Fry	51	21.95	1,119.45	11.19	570.69	10.76	548.76	51
Scallops/Pasta	85	14.95	1,270.75	3.59	305.15	11.36	965.60	24
Beef Medallions	125	15.95	1,993.75	5.90	737.50	10.05	1,256.25	37
Total	700		11,583.00		4,002.77		7,580.23	
Weighted Average	100	16.55	1,654.71	5.72	571.82	10.83	1,082.89	35

The numbers in the rows of Figure 10.2 are calculated as follows:

Individual Menu Item Rows:

Sold and Selling Price can be obtained from a POS system.

Total Sales = # Sold × Selling Price

Item Food Cost can be obtained from a standardized recipe cost sheet.

Total Food Cost = # Sold × Item Food Cost

Item Contribution Margin = Selling Price − Item Food Cost

Total Contribution Margin = # Sold × Item Contribution Margin

Food Cost % = Total Food Cost/Total Sales *or* Item Food Cost/Selling Price

Total Row:

The totals in the # Sold, Total Sales, Total Food Cost, and Total Contribution Margin columns are calculated by simply adding the numbers in those columns.

Average/Weighted Average Row:

Do the weighted average calculations in the following order:

AVERAGE/WEIGHTED AVERAGE	CALCULATION
Average # Sold	700 Total # Sold/7 menu items = 100
Average Total Sales	11,583.00 Total Sales/7 menu items = 1,654.71
Weighted Average Selling Price	1,654.71 Average Total Sales/100 Average # Sold = 16.55
Average Total Food Cost	4,002.77 Total Food Cost/7 menu items = 571.82
Weighted Average Item Food Cost	571.82 Average Total Food Cost/100 Average # Sold = 5.72
Average Total Contribution Margin (CM)	7,580.23 Total CM/7 menu items = 1,082.89
Weighted Average Item Contribution Margin (CM)	1,082.89 Average Total CM/100 Average # Sold = 10.83
Weighted Average Food Cost %	571.82 Average Total Food Cost/1,654.71 Average Total Sales = 35%

To analyze her menu using the food cost percentage method, Maureen separates her items based on two variables:

1. Food cost percentage
2. Popularity (number sold)

Maureen's overall food cost is 35%, so she considers any individual menu item with a food cost percentage above 35% to be High in food cost percentage, whereas any menu item with a food cost below 35% will be considered Low. In a similar way, with a total of 700 entrées served in this accounting period and seven possible menu choices, each menu item would sell 700/7, or 100 times, if all were equally popular. Given that fact, Maureen determines that any item that sold more than

100 times during this week's accounting period will be considered High (above average) in popularity, whereas any item selling less than 100 times will be considered Low (below average) in popularity. Having made these determinations, Maureen produces a matrix labeled as follows:

		Popularity	
		Low	High
Food Cost %	High	1 High food cost % Low popularity	2 High food cost % High popularity
	Low	3 Low food cost % Low popularity	4 Low food cost % High popularity

Based on the number sold and food cost percentage data in Figure 10.2, Maureen can classify her menu items in the following manner:

Square	Characteristics	Menu Item
1	High food cost % Low popularity	Strip steak, lobster stir-fry
2	High food cost % High popularity	Grilled tuna, beef medallions
3	Low food cost % Low popularity	Scallops/pasta
4	Low food cost % High popularity	Coconut shrimp, chicken breast

Note that each menu item can be placed in one, and only one, square. Using the food cost percentage method of menu analysis, Maureen would like as many menu items as possible to fall within square 4. These items have the characteristics of being low in food cost percentage but high in guest acceptance. Thus, both coconut shrimp and chicken breast have below-average food cost percentages and above-average popularity. When developing a menu that seeks to minimize food cost percentage, items in the fourth square are highly desirable because the low food cost percentage of the individual items helps keep the operation's overall food cost percentage low and the items sell well. These items are, of course, kept on the menu. They should be well promoted and have high menu visibility. Promote them to your best guests and take care not to develop and attempt to sell a menu item that is similar enough in nature that it could detract from the sales of these items. The characteristics of the menu items that fall into each of the four matrix squares are unique and, thus, should be managed differently. Because of this, items that fall into each individual square require a special marketing strategy, depending on their matrix location. These strategies can be summarized as shown in Figure 10.3.

■ **FIGURE 10.3** Analysis of Food Cost Matrix Results

Square	Characteristics	Problem	Marketing Strategy
1	High food cost %, Low popularity	Marginal due to both high product cost and lack of sales	a. Remove from the menu. b. Consider current food trends to determine if the item itself is unpopular or if its method of preparation is. c. Survey guests to determine current wants regarding this item. d. If this is a high-contribution-margin item, consider reducing price and/or portion size.
2	High food cost %, high popularity	Marginal due to high product cost menu	a. Increase price. b. Reduce prominence on the menu. c. Reduce portion size. d. "Bundle" the sale of this item with one that has a lower cost and, thus, provides better overall food cost %.
3	Low food cost %, Low popularity	Marginal due to lack of sales	a. Relocate on the menu for greater visibility. b. Take off the regular menu and run as specials. c. Reduce menu price. d. Eliminate other unpopular menu items in order to increase demand for this one.
4	Low food cost %, high popularity	None	a. Promote well. b. Increase visibility on the menu.

It can be quite effective to use the food cost percentage method of menu evaluation. It is fast, easy to calculate, and time-tested. Remember that if you achieve too high a food cost percentage, you run the risk that not enough percentage points will remain to generate a profit on your sales.

In spite of its popularity, the food cost percentage analysis method has limitations. For example, most foodservice operators would say it is better to achieve a 20% food cost than a 40% food cost. Consider, however, a chicken dish that sells for $5.00 and costs you just $1.00 to make. This item yields a 20% food cost ($1.00/$5.00 = 20%), and there are $4.00 ($5.00 − $1.00 = $4.00) remaining to pay for the labor and other expenses of serving this guest. Compare that to the same guest buying a steak for $10.00 that costs you $4.00 to make. Your food cost percentage would be 40% ($4.00/$10.00 = 40%). In this case, however, there would be $6.00 ($10.00 − $4.00 = $6.00) remaining to pay for the labor and other expenses of serving this guest. Clearly in this example it would be better to sell more steak than chicken, despite the steak's higher food cost percentage. For this reason, many operators prefer to analyze their menus using a contribution margin matrix.

■ CONTRIBUTION MARGIN

When analyzing a menu using the contribution margin approach, the operator seeks to produce a menu that maximizes the overall contribution margin. Recall from Chapter 6 that **contribution margin per menu item** is defined as the amount that remains after the product cost of the menu item is subtracted from the item's selling price. Contribution margin is the amount that you will have available to pay for your labor and other expenses and to keep for your profit. Thus, from Figure 10.2, if an item on Maureen's menu, such as strip steak, sells for $17.95 and the product cost for the item is $8.08, the contribution margin per menu item would be computed as follows:

Selling Price − Product Cost = Contribution Margin per Menu Item

or

$17.95 − $8.08 = $9.87

When contribution margin is the driving factor in analyzing a menu, the two variables used for the analysis are contribution margin and item popularity. To illustrate the use of the contribution margin approach to menu analysis, the data in Figure 10.2 are again used. In this case, Maureen must again separate her items based on high or low popularity. Doing so gives the same results as those obtained when using the food cost percentage method; thus, any item that sells 700/7, or 100 times, or more is considered to be a high-popularity item, whereas any menu choice selling less than 100 times would be considered low in popularity. Some menu experts maintain that any menu item that achieves at least 70% of the average number sold be considered a high-popularity menu item, whereas those that sell below 70% of the average should be considered low-popularity. We will be using the average number of items sold (in this case, 100 items) for our calculations.

When computing average contribution margin for the entire menu, Maureen must follow two steps. First, to determine the total contribution margin for the menu, the following formula is used:

Total Sales − Total Product Costs = Total Contribution Margin

or

$11,583.00 − $4,002.77 = $7,580.23

Because 700 total menu items were sold, you can determine the average contribution margin per item using the following formula:

$$\frac{\text{Total Contribution Margin}}{\text{Number of Items Sold}} = \text{Average Contribution Margin per Item}$$

or

$$\frac{\$7,580.23}{700} = \$10.83$$

To develop the contribution margin matrix, you proceed along much the same lines as with the food cost percentage matrix. In this case, average item popularity is 100 and average item contribution margin is $10.83. The matrix is developed as follows:

Popularity

		Low	High
		1	**2**
Contribution Margin	High	High Contribution Margin Low Popularity	High Contribution Margin High Popularity
		3	**4**
	Low	Low Contribution Margin Low Popularity	Low Contribution Margin High Popularity

Maureen now classifies her menu items according to the contribution margin matrix in the following manner:

Square	Characteristics	Menu Item
1	High Contribution Margin Low Popularity	Scallops/Pasta
2	High Contribution Margin High Popularity	Coconut Shrimp, Chicken Breast
3	Low Contribution Margin Low Popularity	Strip Steak, Lobster Stir-Fry
4	Low Contribution Margin High Popularity	Grilled Tuna, Beef Medallions

Again, each menu item can be placed in one, and only one, matrix square. Using the contribution margin method of menu analysis, Maureen would like as many of her menu items as possible to fall within square 2, that is, high contribution margin and high popularity. From this analysis, Maureen knows that both coconut shrimp and chicken breast yield a higher than average contribution margin. In addition, these items sell very well. Just as Maureen seeks to give high menu visibility to items with low food cost percentage and high popularity when using the food cost percentage method of menu analysis, she seeks to give that same visibility to items with high contribution margin and high popularity when using the contribution margin approach.

Each of the menu items that fall in the other squares requires a special marketing strategy, depending on its square location. These strategies are summarized as shown in Figure 10.4.

A frequent, and legitimate, criticism of the contribution margin approach to menu analysis is that it tends to favor high-priced menu items over low-priced ones because higher-priced menu items, in general, tend to have the highest contribution margins. Over the long term, this can result in sales techniques and menu placement decisions that tend to put in the guest's mind a higher check average than the operation may warrant or desire. This may not be desirable at all. Alternatively, the successful menu strategy related to McDonald's $1.00 value menu items (these prices have not changed in the last decade) is certainly not one of maximizing contribution margin.

The selection of either food cost percentage or contribution margin as a menu analysis technique is really an attempt by the foodservice operator to answer the following questions:

- Are my menu items priced correctly?
- Are the individual menu items selling well enough to warrant keeping them on the menu?
- Is the overall profit margin on my menu items satisfactory?

■ **FIGURE 10.4** Analysis of Contribution Margin Matrix Results

Square	Characteristics	Problem	Marketing Strategy
1	High contribution margin Low popularity	Marginal due to lack of sales	a. Relocate on menu for greater visibility. b. Consider reducing selling price.
2	High contribution margin High popularity	None	a. Promote well. b. Increase prominence on the menu.
3	Low contribution margin Low popularity	Marginal due to both low contribution margin and lack of sales	a. Remove from menu. b. Consider offering as a special occasionally, but at a higher menu price.
4	Low contribution margin High popularity	Marginal due to low contribution margin	a. Increase price. b. Reduce prominence on the menu. c. Consider reducing portion size.

Some users of the contribution margin method of menu analysis refer to it as **menu engineering** and classify the squares used in the analysis with colorful names. The most common of these are "Plow horses" (square 1) because these items have high contribution margins but are less popular, "Stars" (square 2), because these items are popular and also have high contribution margins, "Dogs" (square 3) because these have low contribution margins and are not popular, and "Puzzles" or sometimes "Challenges" (square 4) because these menu items are highly popular but return lower than average contribution margins to the operator.

The use of matrix menu analysis is, the authors believe, overly simplistic for use in today's increasingly sophisticated foodservice operations. Because of the limitations of matrix analysis, neither the matrix food cost nor the matrix contribution margin approach is tremendously effective in analyzing menus. This is the case because, mathematically, the axes on the matrix are determined by the mean (average) of food cost percentage, contribution margin or sales level (popularity). When this is done, some items will always fall into the less desirable categories. This is so because, in matrix analysis, high food cost percentage, for instance, really means food cost percentage above that operation's **average**. Obviously, then, some items must fall below the average regardless of their contribution to operational profitability. Eliminating the poorest items only shifts other items into undesirable categories. To illustrate this significant drawback to matrix analysis, consider the following example. Assume that Homer, one of Maureen's competitors, sells only four items, as follows:

Homer's No. 1 Menu

Item	Number Sold
Beef	70
Chicken	60
Pork	15
Seafood	55
Total	200
Average sold	50 (200/4)

Homer may elect to remove the pork item because its sales range is below the average of 50 items sold. If Homer adds turkey to the menu and removes the pork, he could get the following results:

Homer's No. 2 Menu

Item	Number Sold
Beef	65
Chicken	55
Turkey	50
Seafood	30
Total	200
Average sold	50 (200/4)

As can be seen, the turkey item drew sales away from the beef, chicken, and seafood dishes and did not increase the total number of menu items sold. In this case, it is now the seafood item that falls below the menu average. Should it be removed because its sales are below average? Clearly, this might not be wise. Removing the seafood item might serve only to draw sales from the remaining items to the seafood replacement item. Obviously, the same type of result can occur when you use a matrix to analyze food cost percentage or contribution margin. As someone once stated, half of us are below average in everything. Thus, the matrix approach, because of its format, inherently forces some items to be below average.

An additional and increasingly relevant criticism of both the food cost percentage and contribution margin analysis methods relates to the fact that the results of both are determined by the price operators pay for food. As increasing numbers of operators find they pay more for labor to produce their menu items than for the food to make them, some question any menu analysis system that ignores labor and other important costs. How, then, can an operator answer questions related to price, sales volume, and overall profit margin? One answer is to avoid the overly simplistic and ineffective matrix analysis and employ all, or even part, of a more effective method of menu analysis called goal value analysis.

FUN ON THE WEB!

Because it is fairly simple to do so, some companies have included menu analysis components in their POS software systems. To view the offerings of one such company that seeks to help users identify menu "Winners and Losers," go to **www.costguard.com/sales.**

■ GOAL VALUE ANALYSIS

Goal value analysis was introduced by Dr. David Hayes (www.pandapros.com) and Dr. Lynn Huffman (Texas Tech University) in an article titled "Menu Analysis: A Better Way" (Hayes & Huffman, 1985), published by the respected and refereed hospitality journal *The Cornell Quarterly*. Ten years later, at the height of what was known as the "value pricing" (i.e., extremely low pricing strategies used to drive significant increases in guest counts) debate, the effectiveness of goal value analysis was again proved in a second article, "Value Pricing: How Low Can You Go?" (Hayes & Huffman, 1995), which was also published in *The Cornell Quarterly*. Ultimately, the system was reviewed and its usefulness expanded by Dr. Lea Dopson of the University of North Texas.

Goal value analysis uses the power of an algebraic formula to replace less sophisticated menu averaging techniques. Before the widespread introduction of computerized spreadsheet programs, some managers found the computations required to use goal value analysis challenging. Today, however, such computations are easily made. The advantages of goal value analysis are many, including ease of use, accuracy, and the ability to simultaneously consider more variables than is possible with two-dimensional matrix analysis. Mastering the power of goal value analysis can truly help you design menus that are effective, popular, and, most important, profitable.

Goal value analysis is used to evaluate each menu item's food cost percentage, contribution margin, and popularity. Unlike the two previous analysis methods introduced, however, it includes the analysis of the menu item's nonfood variable costs as well as its selling price. Returning to the data in Figure 10.2, we see that Maureen has an overall food cost % of 35%. In addition, she served an average of 100 guests per menu item at an entrée check average of $16.55. If we knew about Maureen's overall fixed and variable costs, we would know a great deal more about the profitability of each of Maureen's menu items. Goal Value Analysis evaluates that profitability information.

One difficulty encountered when seeking to evaluate a menu item's profitability is that the assignment of nonfood variable costs to individual menu items can be a challenge. The issue is complex. It is very likely true, for example, that different items on Maureen's menu require differing amounts of labor to prepare. For instance, the strip steak on her menu is purchased precut and vacuum-sealed. Its preparation simply requires opening the steak package, seasoning the steak, and placing it on a broiler. The lobster stir-fry, on the other hand, is a complex dish that requires cooking and shelling the lobster, cleaning and trimming the vegetables, then preparing the item when ordered by quickly cooking the lobster, vegetables, and a sauce in a wok. Thus, the variable labor cost of preparing the two dishes is very different. It is assumed that Maureen responds to these differing costs by charging more for a more labor-intensive dish and less for one that is less labor intensive. Other dishes require essentially the same amount of labor to prepare; thus, their variable labor costs have less impact on individual menu item's selling prices. Because that is true, for analysis purposes, most operators find it convenient to assign variable costs to individual menu items based on their *average* labor and other variable costs. For example, if labor and other variable costs are 30% of total sales, all menu items may be assigned that same variable cost percentage of their selling price.

For the purpose of her goal value analysis, Maureen determines her total variable costs. These are all the costs that vary with her sales volume, excluding the cost of the food itself. She computes those variable costs from her P&L statement (see Chapter 9) and finds that they account for 30% of her total sales. Using this information, Maureen assigns a variable cost of 30% of selling price to each menu item.

Having compiled the information in Figure 10.2, Maureen can use the algebraic goal value formula to create a specific target, or goal value, for her entire menu, and then use the same formula to compute the goal value of each individual menu item. Menu items that achieve goal values higher than that of the menu's overall goal value will contribute greater than average profit percentages. As the goal value for an item increases, so too does its profitability percentage. Assuming that Maureen's average food cost %, average number of items sold per menu item, average selling price (check average), and average variable cost % all meet the overall profitability goals of her restaurant, each individual menu item's goal value can be analyzed to assess that item's contribution to profits. The goal value formula is as follows:

$$A \times B \times C \times D = \text{Goal Value}$$

where

A = 1.00 − Food Cost %
B = Item Popularity
C = Selling Price
D = 1.00 − (Variable Cost % + Food Cost %)

Note that A in the preceding formula is really the contribution margin *percentage* of a menu item, and D is the percentage amount available to fund fixed costs and provide for a profit after all variable costs (including food) are covered.

Maureen uses this formula to compute the goal value of her overall menu and finds that:

A	× B	× C	× D		= Goal Value
(1.00 − 0.35) × 100 × $16.55 × [1.00 − (0.30 + 0.35)]					= Goal Value
			or		
0.65	× 100 × $16.55 × 0.35				= 376.5

According to this formula, any menu item whose goal value equals or exceeds 376.5 will achieve profitability that equals or exceeds that of Maureen's overall menu. The computed goal value carries no unit designation; that is, it is neither a percentage nor a dollar figure because it is really a numerical target or score. Figure 10.5 details the goal value data Maureen needs to complete a goal value analysis on each of her seven individual menu items.

Figure 10.6 details the results of Maureen's goal value analysis. Note that she has calculated the goal values of her menu items and listed them in order of highest to lowest goal value. She has also inserted her overall menu goal value in the appropriate rank order.

■ FIGURE 10.5   Maureen's Goal Value Analysis Data

Item	Food Cost % (in decimal form)	Number Sold	Selling Price	Variable Cost % (in decimal form)
Strip Steak	0.45	73	$17.95	0.30
Coconut Shrimp	0.30	121	16.95	0.30
Grilled Tuna	0.40	105	17.95	0.30
Chicken Breast	0.22	140	13.95	0.30
Lobster Stir-Fry	0.51	51	21.95	0.30
Scallops/Pasta	0.24	85	14.95	0.30
Beef Medallions	0.37	125	15.95	0.30

■ **FIGURE 10.6** Goal Value Analysis Results

Rank	Menu Item	A	B	C	D	Goal Value
1	Chicken Breast	0.22	140	$13.95	0.30	731.2
2	Coconut Shrimp	0.30	121	16.95	0.30	574.3
3	Scallops/Pasta	0.24	85	14.95	0.30	444.3
4	Beef Medallions	0.37	125	15.95	0.30	414.5
	Overall Menu (Goal Value)	*0.35*	*100*	*$16.55*	*0.30*	*376.5*
5	Grilled Tuna	0.40	105	17.95	0.30	339.3
6	Strip Steak	0.45	73	17.95	0.30	180.2
7	Lobster Stir-Fry	0.51	51	21.95	0.30	104.2

Note that the grilled tuna falls slightly below the profitability of the entire menu, whereas the strip steak and lobster stir-fry fall substantially below the overall goal value score. Should these two items be replaced? The answer, most likely, is no if Maureen is satisfied with her current target food cost percentage, profit margin, check average, and guest count. Every menu will have items that are more or less profitable than others. In fact, some operators develop items called **loss leaders**. A loss leader is a menu item that is priced very low, sometimes even below total costs, for the purpose of drawing large numbers of guests to the operation. If, for example, Maureen has the only operation in town that serves outstanding lobster stir-fry, that item may, in fact, contribute to the overall success of the operation by drawing people who will buy it, whereas their fellow diners may order items that are more profitable.

The accuracy of goal value analysis is well documented. Used properly, it is a convenient way for management to evaluate the profitability, sales volume, and pricing characteristics of menu items. Because all of the values needed for the goal value formula are readily available, management need not concern itself with puzzling through endless decisions about item replacement.

Items that do not achieve the targeted goal value tend to be deficient in one or more of the key areas of food cost percentage, popularity, selling price, or variable cost percentage. In theory, all menu items have the potential of reaching the goal value. Management may, however, determine that some menu items can best serve the operation as loss leaders, an approach illustrated by the continued use of "value" menu items by leading chains in the **Quick Service Restaurant** (QSR) segment.

To better understand goal value analysis, consider the formula results for Maureen's strip steak:

Strip Steak

$$
\begin{aligned}
A \quad &\times B \times C \quad\quad \times D &&= \text{Goal Value} \\
(1.00 - 0.45) &\times 73 \times \$17.95 \times [1 - (0.30 + 0.45)] &&= \text{Goal Value} \\
0.55 \quad &\times 73 \times \$17.95 \times 0.25 &&= 180.2
\end{aligned}
$$

This item did not meet the goal value target. Why? There can be several answers. One is that the item's 45% food cost is too high. This can be addressed by reducing portion size or changing the item's recipe or garnish; these actions could have the effect of reducing the food cost % and, thus, increasing the A value (see Chapter 5). A second approach to improving the goal value score of the strip steak is to work on improving the B value, that is, the number of times the item is sold. This may be done through improved placement on the menu, increased merchandising, or, because it is one of the more expensive items on the menu, incentives to wait staff for upselling this item.

Variable C, menu price, is in line with the rest of the menu but could be adjusted upward. Of course, any upward price adjustments in C may well result in declines in the number of items sold (B value)! Increases in the menu price will also have the effect of decreasing the food cost % and the variable cost % of the menu item (and increasing the contribution margin). This is because selling price (sales) is the denominator of the food cost % and variable cost % equations. Obviously, the changes you undertake as a result of menu analysis are varied and can be complex. As you gain experience in knowing the tastes and behavior of your guests, however, your skill in menu-related decision making will quickly improve.

Sophisticated users of the goal value analysis system can, as suggested by Lendal Kotschevar, in *Management by Menu, Fourth Edition* (Kotschevar and Withrow, 2007), modify its formula to increase its accuracy and usefulness even more. In the area of variable costs, a menu item might be assigned a low, medium, or high variable cost. If overall variable costs equal 30%, for example, management may choose to assign a variable cost of 25% to those items with very low labor costs attached to them, 30% to others with average labor costs, and 35% to others with even higher costs. This adjustment affects only the D variable of the goal value formula and can be accommodated quite easily.

Goal value analysis will also allow you to make better decisions more quickly. This is especially true if you know a bit of algebra and realize that anytime you determine a desired goal value and know any three of the four variables contained in the formula, you can solve for the fourth unknown variable by using goal value as the numerator and placing the known variables in the denominator. Figure 10.7 shows you how to solve for each unknown variable in the goal value formula.

To illustrate how the information in Figure 10.7 can be used, let's return to the information in Figure 10.6 and assume that, after Maureen talks with many of her customers, she feels the 12-ounce strip steak she is offering may be too large for her typical guest and that is why its popularity (B value) is low. Thus, Maureen elects to take three actions:

1. She reduces the portion size of the item from 12 ounces to 9 ounces, resulting in a reduction in her food cost from $8.08 to $6.10.

2. Because she knows her guests will likely be hesitant to pay the same price for a smaller steak, she also reduces the selling price of this item by $1.00 to $16.95. She feels that this will keep the strip steak from losing any popularity resulting from the reduction in portion size. Her new food cost percentage for this item is 36% ($6.10/$16.95 = 36%).

■ **FIGURE 10.7** Solving for Goal Value Unknowns

Known Variables	Unknown Variables	Method to Find Unknown
A, B, C, D	Goal Value (GV)	$A \times B \times C \times D$
B, C, D, GV	A	$\dfrac{GV}{B \times C \times D}$
A, C, D, GV	B	$\dfrac{GV}{A \times C \times D}$
A, B, D, GV	C	$\dfrac{GV}{A \times B \times D}$
A, B, C, GV	D	$\dfrac{GV}{A \times B \times C}$

3. Since the labor required to prepare this menu item is so low, she assigns a below-average 25% variable cost to its D value.

Maureen now knows three of the goal value variables for this item and can solve for the fourth. Maureen knows her A value (1.00 − 0.36), her C value ($16.95), and her D value [1.00 − (0.25 + 0.36)]. The question she would ask is this, "Given this newly structured menu item, how many must be sold to make the item achieve the targeted goal value and thus contribute to profits?" The answer requires solving the goal value equation for B, the number sold. From Figure 10.7, recall that, if B is the unknown variable, it can be computed by using the following formula:

In this case:

$$\frac{\text{Goal Value}}{A \times C \times D} = B$$

Thus:

$$\frac{376.5}{(1.00 - 0.36) \times \$16.95 \times [1.00 - (0.25 + 0.36)]} = B$$

$$89 = B$$

According to the formula, 89 servings of strip steak would have to be sold to achieve Maureen's target goal value. An easy, alternativee way to determine the effects of changes made to menu items is to use an Excel spreadsheet. Once you put the formulas in a spreadsheet, it is then easy to see how changes made to food costs, number of items, selling prices, and variable costs affect the goal values.

Goal value analysis is also powerful because it is not, as is matrix analysis, dependent on past performance to establish profitability but can be used by management to establish future menu targets. You can use it to establish a desired food cost percentage, target popularity figure, selling price, or variable cost percentage. To explain, assume that Maureen wishes to achieve a greater profit margin and a

$17.00 entrée average selling price for next year. She plans to achieve this through a reduction in her overall food cost to 33% and her other variable costs to 29%. Her overall menu goal value formula for next year, assuming no reduction or increase in guest count, would be as follows:

A	$\times$ B	$\times$ C	$\times$ D	= Goal Value
$(1.00 - 0.33)$	$\times$ 100	$\times$ $17.00	$\times$ $[1.00 - (0.29 + 0.33)]$	= Goal Value
		or		
0.67	$\times$ 100	$\times$ $17.00	$\times$ 0.38	= 432.8

Thus, each item on next year's menu should be evaluated with the new goal value in mind. It is important to remember, however, that Maureen's actual profitability will be heavily influenced by sales mix. Thus, all pricing, portion size, and menu placement decisions become critical. Note that Maureen can examine each of her menu items and determine whether she wishes to change any of the item's characteristics to meet her goals. It is at this point that she must remember that she is a foodservice operator and not merely an accountant. A purely quantitative approach to menu analysis is neither practical nor desirable. Menu analysis and pricing decisions are always a matter of experience, skill, insight, and educated predicting because it is difficult to know in advance how changing any one menu item may affect the sales mix of the remaining items.

COST/VOLUME/PROFIT ANALYSIS

Each foodservice operator knows that some accounting periods are more profitable than others. Often, this is because sales volume is higher or costs are lower during certain periods. The ski resort that experiences tremendous sales during the ski season but has a greatly reduced volume or may even close during the summer season is a good example. Profitability, then, can be viewed as existing on a graph similar to Figure 10.8.

The x axis represents the number of covers sold in a foodservice operation. The y axis represents the costs/revenues in dollars. The Total Revenues line starts at zero because if no covers are sold, no dollars are generated. The Total Costs line starts farther up the y axis because fixed costs are incurred even if no covers are sold. The point at which the two lines cross is called the **break-even point.** At the break-even point, operational expenses are exactly equal to sales revenue. Stated in another way, when sales volume in your operation equals the sum of your total variable and fixed costs, your break-even point has been reached. Below the break-even point, costs are higher than revenues, so losses occur. Above the break-even point, revenues exceed costs, so profits are made. Most operators would like to know their break-even point on a daily, weekly, or monthly basis. In effect, by

■ FIGURE 10.8 Cost/Volume/Profit Graph

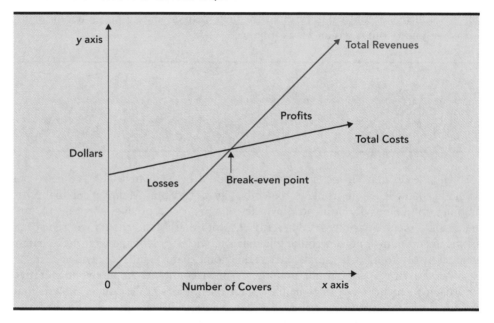

determining the break-even point, the operator is answering the question: "How much sales volume must I generate before I begin to make a profit?"

Beyond the break-even point, you will want to answer another question: "How much sales dollars and volume must I generate to make my desired profit level?" To answer this question, you must conduct a **cost/volume/profit (CVP) analysis.** A CVP analysis helps predict the sales dollars and volume required to achieve desired profit (or break even) based on your known costs.

The answer to these questions may be found either by constructing a CVP graph or by arithmetical calculation. Although there are advantages to both methods, the arithmetical calculation is typically the most accurate. The CVP calculations can be done on either the dollar sales volume required to break even or achieve the desired profit, or the number of guests (covers) that must be served to break even.

Consider the case of Jennifer, who operates an Asian restaurant. Based on her income statement and sales records from last month, Jennifer has converted her P&L statement to a **contribution margin income statement,** as shown in Figure 10.9. A contribution margin income statement simply shows P&L items in terms of sales, variable costs, contribution margin, fixed costs, and profit.

As discussed in Chapter 8, foodservice expenses can generally be classified as either fixed or variable. Of course, some expenses have both a fixed and a variable component and, thus, in reality, are mixed. For the purpose of engaging in a CVP analysis, however, it is necessary for the operator to assign costs to either a fixed or a variable category, as Jennifer has done. In addition, the **contribution margin for her overall operation** is defined as the dollar amount that contributes to covering fixed

■ FIGURE 10.9 Contribution Margin Income Statement

Jennifer's			
Total Sales	$125,000	Sales per Guest	$12.50
Variable Costs	50,000	Guests Served	10,000
Contribution Margin	75,000		
Fixed Costs	60,000		
Before-Tax Profit	15,000		
Taxes (40%)	6,000		
After-Tax Profit	9,000		

costs and providing for a profit. Contribution margin is calculated for Jennifer's as follows:

Total Sales − Variable Costs = Contribution Margin

or

$125,000 − $50,000 = $75,000

Jennifer can also view her contribution margin income statement in terms of per-unit (guest) and percentage sales, variable costs, and contribution margin, as shown in Figure 10.10.

Notice the box in Figure 10.10 that includes per unit (guest) and percentage calculations for sales per guest (selling price, (SP)), variable costs (VC), and contribution margin (CM). Note also that fixed costs are not calculated as per unit or as a percentage of sales. This is because fixed costs do not vary with sales volume increases.

■ FIGURE 10.10 Contribution Margin Income Statement with per-Unit and
Percentage Calculations

Jennifer's			
Total Sales	$125,000		
Variable Costs	50,000	**Per Unit (Guest)**	**Percentage**
Contribution Margin	75,000	SP $12.50	100%
		VC 5.00	40
Fixed Costs	60,000	CM 7.50	60
Before-Tax Profit	15,000	Guests Served = 10,000	
Taxes (40%)	6,000		
After-Tax Profit	9,000		

To calculate these numbers, the following steps apply:

Step 1. Divide total sales, variable costs, and contribution margin by the number of guests served (units) to get per-unit (guest) values:

$$\frac{SP}{Unit} = \frac{\$125{,}000}{10{,}000 \text{ Units}} = \$12.50$$

$$\frac{VC}{Unit} = \frac{\$50{,}000}{10{,}000 \text{ Units}} = \$5.00$$

$$\frac{CM}{Unit} = \frac{\$75{,}000}{10{,}000 \text{ Units}} = \$7.50$$

$$\frac{SP}{Unit} - \frac{VC}{Unit} = \frac{CM}{Unit}$$

$$\$12.50 - \$5.00 = \$7.50$$

Step 2. Divide VC/Unit by SP/Unit, and CM/Unit by SP/Unit to get percentage values:

$$SP\% = 100\%$$

$$VC\% = \frac{\$5.00}{\$12.50} = 40\%$$

$$CM\% = \frac{\$7.50}{\$12.50} = 60\%$$

$$SP\% - VC\% = CM\%$$

$$100\% - 40\% = 60\%$$

Once Jennifer's P&L statement has been converted to a contribution margin income statement and per-unit values and percentages have been calculated, she can determine her operational break-even point and the sales required to achieve her desired profit. She wants to do this based both on dollar sales and on the number of guests (units) required to be served.

To determine the dollar sales required to break even, Jennifer uses the following formula:

$$\frac{\text{Fixed Costs}}{\text{Contribution Margin }\%} = \text{Break-Even Point in Sales}$$

or

$$\frac{\$60{,}000}{0.60} = \$100{,}000$$

Thus, Jennifer must generate $100,000 in sales per month before she begins to make a profit. At a sales volume of less than $100,000, she is operating at a loss. In terms of the number of guests that must be served to break even, Jennifer uses the following formula:

$$\frac{\text{Fixed Costs}}{\text{Contribution Margin per Unit (Guests)}} = \text{Break-Even Point in Guests Served}$$

or

$$\frac{\$60,000}{\$7.50} = 8,000 \text{ Guests (Covers)}$$

Now assume that Jennifer has decided that next month she will plan for $12,000 in after-tax profits. To determine sales dollars and covers to achieve her after-tax profit goal, Jennifer uses the following formula:

$$\frac{\text{Fixed Costs} + \text{Before-Tax Profit}}{\text{Contribution Margin \%}} = \text{Sales Dollars to Achieve Desired After-Tax Profit}$$

Jennifer knows that her after-tax-profit goal is $12,000, but the preceding formula calls for before-tax profit. To convert her after-tax profit to before-tax profit, Jennifer must compute the following:

$$\frac{\text{After-Tax Profit}}{1-\text{Tax Rate}} = \text{Before-Tax Profit}$$

or

$$\frac{\$12,000}{1 - 0.40} = \$20,000$$

Now that Jennifer knows her before-tax profit goal of $20,000, she can calculate the sales dollars needed to achieve her targeted after-tax profit as follows:

$$\frac{\text{Fixed Costs} + \text{Before-Tax Profit}}{\text{Contribution Margin \%}} = \text{Sales Dollars to Achieve Desired After-Tax Profit}$$

or

$$\$60,000 + \mathbf{\$20,000/0.60} = \$133,333.33$$

Thus, Jennifer must generate $133,333.33 in sales to achieve her desired after-tax profit of $12,000. In terms of calculating the number of guests that must be served to make her profit, Jennifer uses the following formula:

$$\frac{\text{Fixed Costs} + \text{Before-Tax Profit}}{\text{Contribution Margin per Unit (Guest)}} = \text{Guests to Be Served to Achieve Desired After-Tax Profit}$$

or

$$\frac{\$60,000 + \$20,000}{\$7.50} = 10,666.67 \text{ Guests (Covers); round up to 10,667 Guests}$$

Notice that the number of guests was rounded up from 10,667.67 to 10,667. You *must always* round the number of guests *up* because (1) a guest (person) does not exist as a fraction, and (2) it is better to slightly overstate the number of guests to achieve break-even or desired profits than to understate the number and risk a loss or reduce profit. It is better to be safe than sorry!

Also note that once you round the number of guests up to 10,667, you should adjust the total sales dollars to reflect this. Thus, 10,667 × $12.50 = $133,337.50 sales dollars to achieve the desired after-tax profit is more accurate than $133,333.33, which you calculated using CM%. The variation in these two sales dollar levels is due to rounding. This difference is minimal and may not warrant adjustment unless an exact sales dollar amount is required based on number of guests.

When calculating sales and covers needed to achieve break-even and desired after-tax profits, you can easily remember which formulas to use if you know the following:

1. Contribution margin % is used to calculate sales dollars.
2. Contribution margin per unit is used to calculate sales volume in units (guests).

Once you fully understand the CVP analysis concepts, you can predict any sales level for break-even or after-tax profits based on your selling price, fixed costs, variable costs, and contribution margin. You can also make changes in your selling prices and costs to improve your ability to break even and achieve desired profit levels. This is where menu pricing and cost control concepts covered in this text come into play. As you make changes in your control areas, you will be able to manage your operation efficiently so that losses can be prevented and planned profits can be achieved.

■ LINKING COST/VOLUME/PROFIT ANALYSIS WITH GOAL VALUE ANALYSIS

Cost/volume/profit analysis is used to establish targets for the entire operation, whereas goal value analysis evaluates individual menu items against those operational targets. Goal value analysis is based on the operational goals in terms of food cost, other variable costs, selling price, and number of covers. If, for example, the cost/volume/profit analysis suggests that covers needed to generate desired profits will not likely be achieved, costs should be evaluated. If food and labor costs are reduced to generate a more reasonable sales figure in cost/volume/profit analysis by increasing contribution margin, then those changes affect the desired food and variable costs in goal value analysis. In addition, desired selling price (check average) and number of covers in goal value analysis should be set based on results from cost/volume/profit analysis. Therefore, the two analyses can be strategically linked, as follows:

Cost/Volume/Profit Analysis	Goal Value Analysis
Food cost % from contribution margin income statement	Food cost % goal
Guests served to achieve desired after-tax profit	Total average number of covers per menu item goal
Selling price	Selling price goal
Labor and other variable cost % from contribution margin income statement	Variable cost % goal

Consider Priscilla's Mexican Restaurant in a major metropolitan area in north Texas. Priscilla, the restaurant's owner, conducted a cost/volume/profit analysis and goal value analysis for the month of June (30 days). Figure 10.11 shows how her cost/volume/profit analysis links with her goal value analysis. The following table shows the specific links between Priscilla's two analyses (see also bolded numbers in Figure 10.11).

Cost/Volume/Profit Analysis	Priscilla's CVP	Goal Value Analysis	Priscilla's GV
Food cost % from contribution margin income statement	32%	Food cost % goal	32%
Guests served to achieve desired after-tax profit	18,334/30 days = 611	Total average number of covers per menu item goal	611/7 menu items = 87
Selling price	$15.00	Selling price goal	$15.00
Labor and other variable cost % from contribution margin income statement	28%	Variable cost % goal	28%

By looking at these two analyses, you can learn how the overall goals of the operation affect menu item profitability. Conversely, you can see how changes you make to menu items affect the overall profitability of the operation.

Information in this section was obtained from L. Dopson (2004), "Linking Cost-Volume-Profit Analysis with Goal Value Analysis in the Curriculum Using Spreadsheet Applications," *The Journal of Hospitality Financial Management* 12(1), 77–80.

■ MINIMUM SALES POINT

Every foodservice operator should know his or her break-even point. The concept of minimum sales point is related to this area. *Minimum sales point (MSP)* is the

■ **FIGURE 10.11** Linking Cost/Volume/Profit with Goal Value Analysis

Priscilla's Mexican Restaurant - June

	Per Unit (Guest)	Percentage
SP	$15.00	100%
VC	9.00	60%
CM	6.00	40%

CVP Analysis

Fixed costs	$ 90,000.00	
Desired after-tax profit	$ 12,000.00	
Tax rate	40%	
Before-tax profit	$ 20,000.00	
Break-even point in guests served	15,000.0	Rounded up = 15,000
Break-even point in sales dollars	$225,000.00	
Guests served to achieve desired after-tax profit	18,333.3	Rounded up = **18,334**
Sales dollars to achieve desired after-tax profit	$275,010.00	

Contribution Margin Income Statement for June

Units Sold		18,334	
Revenues		$275,010.00	100.00%
Food Cost		$ 88,003.20	**32.00%**
Labor & Other Variable Costs		$ 77,002.80	**28.00%**
Total Variable Costs		$165,006.00	60.00%
Contribution Margin		$110,004.00	40.00%
Fixed Costs		$ 90,000.00	
Before-Tax Profit		$ 20,004.00	7.27%
Taxes		$ 8,001.60	
After-Tax Profit		$ 12,002.40	4.36%
Total average number of covers/night	611	Average number of covers/item	87

Goal Value Analysis Data

Item	Food Cost % (in decimal form)	Number Sold	Selling Price	Variable Cost % (in decimal form)
Fajita Plate	38%	86	$18.13	28%
Grande Dinner	35%	116	$17.41	28%
Menudo	25%	48	$12.16	28%
Mexican Salad	24%	75	$13.91	28%
Burrito Dinner	28%	73	$15.66	28%
Chimichanga Dinner	33%	97	$17.41	28%
Enchilada Dinner	26%	131	$10.41	28%
Overall Menu (Goal Value)	*32%*	*87*	*$15.00*	*28%*

Goal Value Analysis Results

Item	Food Cost % (in decimal form)	Number Sold	Selling Price	Variable Cost % (in decimal form)	Goal Value
Grande Dinner	35%	116	$17.41	28%	485.7
Enchilada Dinner	26%	131	$10.41	28%	464.2
Chimichanga Dinner	33%	97	$17.41	28%	441.3
Mexican Salad	24%	75	$13.91	28%	380.6
Burrito Dinner	28%	73	$15.66	28%	362.2
Overall Menu (Goal Value)	*32%*	*87*	*$15.00*	*28%*	*355.0*
Fajita Plate	38%	86	$18.13	28%	328.7
Menudo	25%	48	$12.16	28%	205.7

sales volume required to justify staying open for a given period of time. At sales levels below the MSP, the operation is not profitable. At sales levels above the MSP, enough revenue is being taken in to make a contribution to profits. The information needed to calculate the MSP is:

1. Food cost %
2. Minimum payroll cost needed for the time period
3. Variable cost %

Fixed costs are eliminated from the calculation because, even if the volume of sales equals zero, fixed costs still exist and must be paid. Consider the situation of Richard, who is trying to determine whether he should close his steakhouse at 10:00 p.m. or 11:00 p.m. Richard wishes to compute the sales volume necessary to justify staying open the additional hour. He can make this calculation because he knows that his food cost equals 40%, his minimum labor cost to stay open for the extra hour equals $150, and his variable costs (taken from his P&L statement) equal 30%. In calculating MSP, his Food Cost % + Variable Cost % is called his **minimum operating cost.** Richard applies the MSP formula as follows:

$$\frac{\text{Minimum Labor Cost}}{1 - \text{Minimum Operating Cost}} = \text{MSP}$$

$$\text{or}$$

$$\frac{\text{Minimum Labor Cost}}{1 - (\text{Food Cost \%} + \text{Variable Cost \%})} = \text{MSP}$$

In this case, the computation would be as follows:

$$\frac{\$150}{1 - (0.40 + 0.30)} = \text{MSP}$$

$$\text{or}$$

$$\frac{\$150}{1 - 0.70} = \text{MSP}$$

$$\text{or}$$

$$\frac{\$150}{0.30} = \text{MSP}$$

$$\text{thus}$$

$$\$500 = \text{MSP}$$

If Richard can achieve a sales volume of $500 in the 10:00 p.m. to 11:00 p.m. time period, he should stay open. If this level of sales is not feasible, he should consider closing the operation at 10:00 p.m. Richard can also use MSP to determine the hours his operation is most profitable. Of course, some operators may not have the authority to close the operation, even when remaining open is not very profitable. Corporate policy, contractual hours, promotion of a new unit, competition, and other factors must all be taken into account before the decision should be made to modify operational hours.

THE BUDGET

In most managerial settings, you will be responsible for preparing and maintaining a **budget** for your foodservice operation. This budget, or financial plan, will detail the operational direction of your unit and your expected financial results.

The techniques used in managerial accounting will show you how close your actual performance conformed to your budget, and will provide you with the information you need to make changes to your operational procedures or budget. This will ensure that your operation achieves the goals of your financial plan. It is important to note that the budget should not be a static document. It should be modified and fine-tuned as managerial accounting presents data about sales and costs that affect the direction of the overall operation.

For example, if you own a dance club featuring Latin music, and you find that a major competitor in your city has closed its doors, you may quite logically determine that you want to increase your estimate of the number of guests who will come to your club. This would, of course, affect your projected sales revenue, your costs, and your profitability. Not to do so might allow you to meet and even exceed your original sales goals but would ignore a significant event that very likely will affect your financial plan for the club.

In a similar manner, if you are the manager of a delicatessen specializing in salads, sliced meats, and related items, and you find through your purchase orders that the price you pay for corned beef has tripled since last month, you must adjust your budget or you will find that you have no chance of staying within your food cost guidelines. Again, the point is that the foodservice budget should be closely monitored through the use of managerial accounting, which includes the thoughtful analysis of the data this type of accounting provides.

Just as the P&L tells you about your past performance, the budget is developed to help you achieve your future goals. In effect, the budget tells you what must be done if predetermined profit and cost objectives are to be met. In this respect, you are attempting to modify the profit formula, as presented in Chapter 1. With a well-thought-out and attainable budget, your profit formula would change from:

Revenue − Expense = Profit

to

Budgeted Revenue − Budgeted Expense = Budgeted Profit

To prepare the budget and stay within it ensures your results. Without such a plan, you must guess how much to spend and how much sales you should anticipate. The effective foodservice operator builds his or her budget, monitors it closely, modifies it when necessary, and achieves the desired results. Yet, many operators do not develop a budget. Some say that the process is too time consuming. Others feel that a budget, especially one shared with the entire organization, is too revealing. Budgeting can also cause conflicts. This is true, for example, when dollars budgeted for new equipment must be used for either a new kitchen stove or a new beer-tapping system. Obviously, the kitchen manager and the beverage manager may hold different points of view on where these funds would best be spent!

Despite the fact that some operators avoid budgets, they are extremely important. The rationale for having and using a budget can be summarized as follows:

1. It is the best means of analyzing alternative courses of action and allows management to examine alternatives prior to adopting a particular one.

2. It forces management to examine the facts regarding what must be done to achieve desired profit levels.

3. It provides a standard for comparison, which is essential for good controls.

4. It allows management to anticipate and prepare for future business conditions.

5. It helps management to periodically carry out a self-evaluation of the organization and its progress toward its financial objectives.

6. It provides a communication channel whereby the organization's objectives are passed along to its various departments.

7. It encourages department managers who have participated in the preparation of the budget to establish their own operating objectives and evaluation techniques and tools.

8. It provides management with reasonable estimates of future expense levels and serves as an instrument for setting proper prices.

9. It identifies time periods in which operational cash flows may need to be supplemented from other sources.

10. It communicates realistic financial performance to owners, investors, and the operation's managers.

Budgeting is best done by the entire management team, for it is only through participation in the process that the whole organization will feel compelled to support the budget. Foodservice budgets can be considered as one of three main types:

1. Long-range budget
2. Annual budget
3. Achievement budget

■ LONG-RANGE BUDGET

The **long-range budget** is typically prepared for a period of three to five years. Although its detail is not great, it does provide a long-term view about where the operation should be going. It is also particularly useful in those cases where additional operational units may increase sales volume and accompanying expense. Assume, for example, that you are preparing a budget for a corporation you own. Your corporation has entered into an agreement with an international franchise company to open 45 cinnamon bun kiosks in malls across the United States and Canada. You will open a new store approximately every month for the next four years. To properly plan for your revenue and expense in the coming four-year period, a long-range budget for your company will be necessary.

■ ANNUAL BUDGET

The annual, or yearly, budget is the type most operators think of when the word budget is used. As it states, the **annual budget** is for a one-year period or, in some cases, one season. This would be true, for example, in the case of a summer camp that is open and serving meals only while school is out of session and campers are attending, or a ski resort that opens in late fall but closes when the snow melts.

It is important to remember that an annual budget need not follow a calendar year. In fact, the best time period for an annual budget is the one that makes sense for the operation. A college foodservice director, for example, would want a budget that covers the time period of a school year, that is, from the fall of one year through the spring of the next. For a restaurant whose owners have a fiscal year different from a calendar year, the annual budget may coincide with either the fiscal year or the calendar, as the owners prefer.

It is also important to remember that an annual budget need not consist of 12 one-month periods. Although many operators prefer one-month budgets, some prefer budgets consisting of 13 28-day periods, whereas others use quarterly (three-month) or even weekly budgets to plan for revenues and costs throughout the budget year.

■ ACHIEVEMENT BUDGET

The **achievement budget** is always of a shorter range, perhaps a month or a week. It provides current operating information and, thus, assists in making current operational decisions. A weekly achievement budget might, for example, be used to predict the number of gallons of milk needed for this time period or the number of servers to be scheduled on Tuesday night.

DEVELOPING THE BUDGET

*S*ome managers think it is very difficult to establish a budget, and so they simply do not do it. Creating a budget is not that complex. You can learn to do it and do it well. To establish any type of budget, you need to have the following information available:

1. Prior-period operating results
2. Assumptions of next-period operations
3. Goals
4. Monitoring policies

To examine how prior-period operating results, assumptions of next-period operations, and goals drive the budgeting process, we will consider the case of Levi, who is preparing the annual foodservice budget for his 100-bed extended-care facility.

■ PRIOR-PERIOD OPERATING RESULTS

Levi's facility serves patient meals to an average occupancy of 80%, and he serves approximately 300 additional meals per day to staff and visitors. His department is allotted a flat dollar amount by the facility's administration for each meal he serves. His operating results for last year are detailed in Figure 10.12. Patient and additional meals served were determined by actual count. Revenue and expense figures were taken from Levi's income (P&L) statements at the year's end. It is important to note that Levi must have this information if he is to do any meaningful profit planning. Foodservice unit managers who do not have access to their operating results are at a tremendous managerial disadvantage. Levi has his operational summaries and the data that produced them. Because he knows how he has operated in the past, he is now ready to proceed to the assumptions section of the planning process.

■ ASSUMPTIONS OF NEXT-PERIOD OPERATIONS

If Levi is to prepare a budget with enough strength to serve as a guide and enough flexibility to adapt to a changing environment, he must factor in the assumptions he and others feel will affect his operation. Although each management team will arrive at its own conclusions given the circumstances of its own operation, in this example, Levi makes the following assumptions regarding next year:

1. Food costs will increase by 3%.

2. Labor costs will increase by 5%.

3. Other expenses will rise by 10% due to a significant increase in utility costs.

■ **FIGURE 10.12** Levi's Last-Year Operating Results

Patient Meals Served: 29,200   Revenue per Meal: $3.46

Additional Meals Served: 109,528

Total Meals Served: 138,728

	Amount	Percentage
Total Department Revenue	$480,000	100%
Cost of Food	192,000	40%
Cost of Labor	153,600	32%
Other Expenses	86,400	18%
Total Expenses	432,000	90%
Profit	48,000	10%

4. Revenue received for all meals served will be increased by no more than 1%.

5. Resident occupancy of 80% of facility capacity will remain unchanged.

Levi makes these assumptions after discussions with his suppliers and union leaders, after review of his own records, and, most important, by his sense of the operation itself. In the commercial sector, when arriving at assumptions, operators must also consider new or diminished competition, changes in traffic patterns, and national food trends. At the highest level of foodservice management, assumptions regarding the acquisition of new units or the introduction of new products will certainly affect the budget process. As an operator, Levi predicts items 1, 2, and 3 by himself, whereas his supervisor has given him input about items 4 and 5. Given these assumptions, Levi can establish operating goals for next year.

Green and Growing!

Budgeting for utility costs is one of a foodservice operator's biggest challenges. This is due to both the instability of energy prices and the impact of the weather on usage. Both of these factors should lead cost-conscious and planet-conscious managers to consider all possible strategies for reducing energy usage. For many operators, these strategies should include:

1. Investigating the installation of smart lighting systems that automatically turn off lights when storage areas are vacant.

2. Replacing all incandescent lighting with an appropriate type of electric discharge lamp (such as fluorescent, mercury vapor, metal halide, or sodium) wherever possible.

3. Using dual-flush, low-flow, or waterless toilets to reduce water waste.

4. Installing low-flow faucet aerators on all sinks to cut water usage by as much as 40%—from a standard 4 gallons per minute to a cost-saving 2.5 gallons a minute.

5. Implementing an effective preventive maintenance program for all cooking equipment, including frequent and accurate temperature recalibrations.

6. Reducing waste disposal costs by implementing effective source reduction plans as well as pre- and post-production recycling efforts.

The benefits to implementing strategies such the preceding are twofold. They will improve an operation's bottom line and reduce its carbon footprint. Those results are good news for a business's P&L, and they directly benefit the business's current, as well as its future, customers.

■ ESTABLISHING OPERATING GOALS

Given the assumptions he has made, Levi can now determine actual operating goals for the coming year. He will establish them for each of the following areas:

1. Meals served
2. Revenue

3. Food costs

4. Labor costs

5. Other expenses

6. Profit

MEALS SERVED

Given the assumption of no increase in patient occupancy, and in light of his results from last year, Levi budgets to prepare and serve 29,200 patient meals. He feels, however, that he can increase his visitor and staff meals somewhat by being more customer-service driven and by offering a wider selection of lower calorie and lighter items on the facility's cycle menu. He decides, therefore, to raise his goal for additional meals from the 109,528 served last year to 115,000 for the coming year. Thus, his budgeted total meals to be served will equal 144,200 meals (29,200 + 115,000 = 144,200).

REVENUE

Levi knows that his total revenue is to increase by only 1%. His revenue per meal will thus be $3.46 × 1.01 = $3.49. With 144,200 meals to be served, Levi will receive $503,258 (144,200 × $3.49 = $503,258) if he meets his meals-served budget.

FOOD COSTS

Levi is planning to serve more meals, so he expects to spend more on food. In addition, he assumes that this food will cost, on average, 3% more than last year. To determine a food budget, Levi computes the estimated food cost for 144,200 meals as follows:

1. Last Year's Food Cost per Meal = Last Year's Cost of Food/Total Meals Served = $192,000/138,728 = $1.38

2. Last Year's Food Cost per Meal + 3% Estimated Increase in Food Cost = $1.38 × 1.03 = $1.42 per Meal

3. $1.42 × 144,200 Meals to Be Served This Year = $204,764 Estimated Cost of Food This Year

LABOR COSTS

Levi is planning to serve more meals, so he also expects to spend more on the labor cost required to prepare and serve the extra meals. In addition, he assumes that this labor will cost, overall, 5% more than last year. To determine a labor budget, Levi computes the estimated labor cost for 144,200 meals to be served as follows:

■ **FIGURE 10.13** Levi's Budget for Next Year

Patient Meals Budgeted: 29,200   Budgeted Revenue per Meal: $3.49

Additional Meals Budgeted: 115,000

Total Meals Budgeted: 144,200

	Amount	Percentage
Total Budgeted Revenue	$503,258	100.0%
Budgeted Expenses		
Cost of Food	204,764	40.7%
Cost of Labor	168,714	33.5%
Other Expense	95,040	18.9%
Total Expense	468,518	93.1%
Profit	34,740	6.9%

1. Last Year's Labor Cost per Meal = Last Year's Cost of Labor/Total Meals Served = $153,600/138,728 = $1.11 per Meal

2. Last Year's Labor Cost per Meal + 5% Estimated Increase in Labor Cost = $1.11 × 1.05 = $1.17 per Meal

3. $1.17 × 144,200 Meals to Be Served This Year = $168,714 Estimated Cost of Labor This Year

OTHER EXPENSES

Levi assumes a 10% increase in other expenses, and, thus, they are budgeted as last year's amount plus an increase of 10%. Thus, $86,400 × 1.10 = $95,040.

Based on his assumptions about next year, Figure 10.13 details Levi's budget summary for the coming 12 months.

PROFIT

Note that the increased costs Levi will be forced to bear, when coupled with his minimal revenue increase, will cause his profit to fall from $48,000 for last year to a projected $34,740 for the coming year. If this is not acceptable, Levi must either increase his revenue beyond his assumption or look to his operation to reduce costs.

Levi has now developed concrete guidelines for his operation. Since his supervisor approves his budget as submitted, Levi is now ready to implement and monitor his new budget.

MONITORING THE BUDGET

An operational plan has little value if management does not use it. In general, the budget should be monitored and analyzed in each of the following three areas:

1. Revenue
2. Expense
3. Profit

■ REVENUE ANALYSIS

If revenue falls below projected levels, the impact on profit can be substantial. Simply put, if revenues fall far short of projections, it may be difficult or even impossible for you to meet your profit goals. If revenue consistently exceeds your projections, the overall budget must be modified or the expenses required to produce the increased sales will soon exceed the originally predicted amounts. Effective managers compare their actual revenue to budgeted revenue on a regular basis.

Increases in operational revenue should result in proportional increases in variable expense budgets. Fixed expenses, of course, need not be adjusted for increases in revenue. For those foodservice operations with more than one meal period, monitoring budgeted sales volume may mean monitoring each period. Consider the case of Rosa, the night (p.m.) manager of a college cafeteria. She feels that she is busier than ever, but her boss, Lois, maintains that there can be no increase in Rosa's labor budget because the overall cafeteria sales volume is exactly in line with budgeted projections. Figure 10.14 shows the complete story of the sales volume situation at the college cafeteria after the first six months of their fiscal year. Note that the year is half (or 50%) completed at the time of this analysis.

■ **FIGURE 10.14** College Cafeteria Revenue Budget Summary

			Time Period: <u>First 6 Months</u>
Meal Period	**Annual Budget**	**Actual YTD**	**% of Budget**
A.M.	$480,500	$166,698	35%
P.M.	350,250	248,677	71
Total	830,750	415,375	50

Based on the sales volume she generates, Rosa should have an increase in her labor budget for the p.m. meal period. The amount of business she is generating in the evenings is substantially higher than budgeted. Note that she is one-half way through her budget year, but has already generated 71% of the annual revenue forecasted by the budget. This, however, does not mean that the labor budget for the entire cafeteria should be increased. In fact, the labor budget for the a.m. shift should likely be reduced because those dollars are more appropriately needed in the evening meal period.

Some foodservice operators relate revenue to the number of seats they have available in their operation. As a result, they sometimes budget based on **sales per seat,** the total revenue generated by a facility divided by the number of seats in the dining area(s). The size of a foodservice facility affects both total investment and operating costs, therefore this can be a useful number. The formula for the computation of sales per seat is as follows:

$$\frac{\text{Total Sales}}{\text{Available Seats}} = \text{Sales per Seat}$$

To illustrate this, assume that, if Rosa's cafeteria has 120 seats, her p.m. sales per seat thus far this year would be as follows:

$$\frac{\$248,677}{120} = \$2,072.31$$

The a.m. sales per seat, given the same number of seats, would be computed as follows:

$$\frac{\$166,698}{120} = \$1,389.15$$

As can be seen, Rosa's sales per seat are much higher than that of her a.m. counterpart. Of course, part of that may be due to the fact that evening menu items in the cafeteria may sell for more, on average, than do breakfast and lunch items.

Some commercial foodservice operators relate revenue to the number of square feet their operations occupy. These operators budget revenues based on a **sales per square foot** basis. This is a very common approach in shopping centers and malls where occupation costs are determined in large degree by the number of square feet a foodservice operation leases from the space's owner. The computation is quite similar to that used in Rosa's sales per seat calculation. The formula of sales per square foot is as follows:

$$\frac{\text{Total Sales}}{\text{Total Square Footage Occupied}} = \text{Sales per Square foot}$$

When sales volume is lower than originally projected, management must seek ways to increase revenue or reduce costs. As stated earlier, one of management's main tasks is to generate guests, whereas the staff's main task is to service these guests to the best of their ability. There are a variety of methods used for increasing sales volume, including the use of coupons, increased advertising, price discounting, and specials. For the serious foodservice manager, a thorough study of the modern techniques of foodservice marketing is mandatory if you are to be ready to meet all the challenges you will face.

■ EXPENSE ANALYSIS

Effective foodservice managers are careful to monitor operational expense because costs that are too high or too low may be cause for concern. Just as it is not possible to estimate future sales volume perfectly, it is also not possible to estimate future expense perfectly; some expenses will vary as sales volume increases or decreases. To know that an operation spent $800 for fruits and vegetables in a given week becomes meaningful only if we know what the sales volume for that week was. Similarly, knowing that $500 was spent for labor during a given lunch period can be analyzed only in terms of the amount of sales achieved in that same period. To help them make an expense assessment quickly, some operators elect to utilize the **yardstick method** of calculating expense standards so determinations can be made as to whether variations in expenses are due to changes in sales volume or other reasons, such as waste or theft.

To illustrate the yardstick method, consider the case of Marion, who operates a college cafeteria during nine months of the year in a small southeastern city. Marion has developed both revenue and expense budgets. His problem, however, is that variations in revenue cause variations in expense. This is true in terms of food products, labor, and other expenses. As a truly effective manager, he wishes to know whether changes in his actual expenses are due directly to these variations in revenues or due to inefficiencies in his operation. To begin his analysis, Marion establishes a purchase standard for food products using a seven-step model.

Developing Yardstick Standards for Food

Step 1. Divide total inventory into management-designated subgroups, for example, meats, produce, dairy, and groceries.

Step 2. Establish dollar value of subgroup purchases for prior accounting period.

Step 3. Establish sales volume for the prior accounting period.

Step 4. Determine percentage of purchasing dollar spent for each food category.

Step 5. Determine percentage of revenue dollar spent for each food category.

Step 6. Develop weekly sales volume and associated expense projection. Compute % cost to sales for each food grouping and sales estimate.

Step 7. Compare weekly revenue and expense to projection. Correct if necessary.

■ **FIGURE 10.15** Marion's College Cafeteria Food Data

		Last School Year (9 Months)
Total Sales: **$450,000**		Average Sales per Month: **$50,000**
Purchases		
Meats	$ 66,600	
Fish/Poultry	36,500	
Produce	26,500	
Dairy	20,000	
Groceries	18,300	
Total	167,900	

To develop his yardstick standards for food, Marion collects data from last year as shown in Figure 10.15.

Assuming that Marion has created a revenue estimate of $52,000 per month for this year and that he was satisfied with both last year's food cost percentage and profits, he can now follow the steps outlined previously to establish his yardstick standards for food. Marion estimates a weekly sales volume of $52,000/4, or $13,000, for this year.

Marion's Yardstick Standards for Food

Step 1. Meats
Fish/Poultry
Produce
Dairy
Groceries

Step 2.
Meats	$ 66,600
Fish/Poultry	36,500
Produce	26,500
Dairy	20,000
Groceries	18,300
Total	167,900

Step 3. $450,000 total revenue in prior period (9 months)

Step 4.
Meats	$ 66,600/167,900 =	39.7%
Fish/Poultry	36,500/167,900 =	21.7
Produce	26,500/167,900 =	15.8
Dairy	20,000/167,900 =	11.9
Groceries	18,300/167,900 =	10.9
Total	167,900	100.0

Step 5.
Meats	$ 66,600/450,000 =	14.8%
Fish/Poultry	36,500/450,000 =	8.1
Produce	26,500/450,000 =	5.9

Dairy	20,000/450,000 = 4.4
Groceries	18,300/450,000 = 4.1
Total	167,900 37.3%

Step 6.

Category	% Cost to Total Cost	% Cost to Total Sales	Weekly Sales Estimate				
			$11,000	$12,000	$13,000	$14,000	$15,000
Meat	39.7%	14.8%	$1,628	$1,776	$1,924	$2,072	$2,220
Fish/Poultry	21.7	8.1	891	972	1,053	1,134	1,215
Produce	15.8	5.9	649	708	767	826	885
Dairy	11.9	4.4	484	528	572	616	660
Groceries	10.9	4.1	451	492	533	574	615
Total	100.0	37.3	4,103	4,476	4,849	5,222	5,595

Note that, to compute the data for Step 6, you must multiply % cost to total sales by the weekly sales estimate. When using the sales estimate of $13,000 for a week, for example, the meat budget would be computed as follows:

$$0.148 \times \$13{,}000 = \$1{,}924$$

Fish/poultry would be computed as follows:

$$0.081 \times \$13{,}000 = \$1{,}053$$

Step 7. Analysis

Marion can now compare his budgeted expense with actual performance over several volume levels. In a week in which sales volume equals $14,000, for example, Marion expects that total meat used for that period, according to his yardstick measure, will equal approximately $2,072 ($14,000 × 14.8% = $2,072). If his usage exceeds $2,072 for the period, he knows exactly where to direct his attention. Using the yardstick system, Marion can easily monitor any expense over any number of differing volume levels. The yardstick method of purchase estimation is especially helpful for those operations that experience great variation in sales volume. An operation that has a slow season and a busy season, for instance, may find that the use of this method is quite helpful in monitoring expenses.

DEVELOPING YARDSTICK STANDARDS FOR LABOR

Just as Marion used the yardstick method to estimate food expense at varying sales volume levels, he can also use it to estimate labor cost expenditures at those various levels. To develop a labor yardstick, he follows these steps:

Step 1. Divide total labor cost into management-designated subgroups, for example, servers, cooks, ware washers, and bartenders.

Step 2. Establish dollar value spent for each subgroup during the prior accounting period.

Step 3. Establish sales volume for the prior accounting period.

Step 4. Determine percentage of labor dollar spent for each subgroup.

Step 5. Determine percentage of revenue dollar spent for each labor category.

Step 6. Develop weekly sales volume and associated expense projection. Compute % cost to sales for each labor category and sales estimate.

Step 7. Compare weekly revenue and expense to projection. Correct if necessary.

Marion collected labor-related data from last year's operation as shown in Figure 10.16.

It is important to note that Marion can develop a labor yardstick based on guests served, labor hours worked, or, as is his preference here, labor cost percentage. To develop the labor standard based on labor cost percentage, Marion follows the seven-step process outlined below.

Marion's Yardstick Standards for Labor

Step 1. Management
Food Production
Service
Sanitation

Step 2. Management $ 40,000
Food Production   65,000
Service   12,000
Sanitation   18,000
Total   135,000

Step 3. $450,000 total revenue in prior period (9 months)

■ **FIGURE 10.16** Marion's College Cafeteria Labor Data

	Last School Year (9 Months)
Total Sales: $450,000	Average Sales per Month: $50,000
Labor Costs	
Management $ 40,000	
Food Production 65,000	
Service 12,000	
Sanitation 18,000	
Total 135,000	

Step 4. Management $ 40,000/135,000 =   29.6%
Food Production   65,000/135,000 =   48.2
Service   12,000/135,000 =   8.9
Sanitation   18,000/135,000 =   13.3
Total   135,000   100.0%

Step 5. Management $ 40,000/450,000 =   8.9%
Food Production   65,000/450,000 =   14.4
Service   12,000/450,000 =   2.7
Sanitation   18,000/450,000 =   4.0
Total   135,000   30.0%

Step 6.

Category	% Cost to Total Cost	% Cost to Total Sales	Weekly Sales Estimate				
			$11,000	$12,000	$13,000	$14,000	$15,000
Management	29.6%	8.9%	$ 979	$1,068	$1,157	$1,246	$1,335
Food Production	48.2	14.4	1,584	1,728	1,872	2,016	2,160
Service	8.9	2.7	297	324	351	378	450
Sanitation	13.3	4.0	440	480	520	560	600
Total	100.0	30.0	3,300	3,600	3,900	4,200	4,545

Note that, to compute the data for Step 6, Marion must multiply % cost to total sales by his weekly sales estimate. Using the sales estimate of $13,000, for example, the management portion of the budget would be computed as follows:

$$0.089 \times \$13,000 = \$1,157$$

The food production cost expense estimate, based on the same weekly sales, would be computed as follows:

$$0.144 \times \$13,000 = \$1,872$$

Step 7. Analysis

It is now easy for Marion to identify exactly where his labor variations, if any, are to be found.

The yardstick method may, of course, be used for any operational expense, be it food, labor, or one of the many other expenses you will incur. Today, the use of spreadsheet formulas allows those operators familiar with them to easily calculate their estimated expenses at any level of actual revenue. In all cases, however, you must monitor your actual expenditures as they relate to budgeted expenditures, while keeping changes in sales volume in mind.

Consider the Costs

Sophia Lancaster is the registered dietitian (RD) responsible for all dietary services at Parker Meridian Memorial Hospital. Her operation consists of two departments. The first, and largest, is patient feeding. It consists of the tray line staff and the majority of her food production staff. The second department is the public cafeteria, which includes special dining areas for hospital staff and a large dining area for visitors. Each year, she submits to her supervisor an annual labor expense budget broken down by month for each department.

On June 1, and after four months of consideration and planning, Sophia and her staff were excited to implement a new public cafeteria menu. The response from hospital visitors was excellent. The dining room staff reported that there were many positive comments about the food selected for the new menu, and the production staff reported a 25% increase in the amount of food prepared for cafeteria service. Sophia had only budgeted for a 5% sales increase because of the new menu, so she was very happy.

On July 7, when Sophia's assistant, Jason, brought her the financial reports for the month of June, he was concerned. "I think we are in big trouble, Boss," he said. "We spent a lot more on cafeteria labor last month than we budgeted!"

1. What do you think is the cause of Sophia's labor budget overage in the cafeteria?

2. Do you think that going "over" budget in this situation is a good thing or a bad thing? Why?

3. If you were Sophia, would you re-examine your cafeteria labor budget for future operating periods? Why or why?

■ PROFIT ANALYSIS

As business conditions change, changes in the budget are to be expected. This is because budgets are based on a specific set of assumptions and if these assumptions change, so too will the budgets. Assume, for example, that you budgeted $1,000 in January for snow removal from the parking lot attached to the restaurant you own in New York state. If unusually severe weather causes you to spend $2,000 for snow removal in January instead, the assumption (normal levels of snowfall) was incorrect and the budget will be incorrect as well.

Ultimately, budgeted profit levels must be realized if an operation is to provide adequate returns for owner and investor risk. Consider the case of James, the operator of a foodservice establishment with excellent sales but below-budgeted profits. James budgeted a 5% profit on $2,000,000 of sales; thus, $100,000 profit ($2,000,000 $\times$ 0.05 = $100,000) was planned. At year's end, however, James achieved only $50,000 profit, or 2.5% of sales ($50,000/$2,000,000 = 2.5%). If the operation's owners feel that $50,000 is an adequate return for their risk, James' professional services may be retained. If they do not, he may lose his position, even though the operation is profitable. Remember that your goal is not merely to generate a profit, but rather to generate budgeted profit. In most cases, you will be rewarded only when you meet this goal because a primary purpose of management is to generate the profits needed to continue the business. Budgeting for these profits is a fundamental step in the process. Analyzing the success of achieving budget forecasts is of tremendous managerial concern. If profit goals are to be met, safeguarding your operational revenue is critical. It is to that task that we turn our attention in the next chapter. The proper collection and accounting for guest payment of services is one of the final steps in a successful food and beverage cost control system.

FUN ON THE WEB!

Look up the following sites to review and obtain copies of books related to foodservice accounting and cost control: **www.amazon.com**, **www.borders.com**, and **www.barnesandnoble.com**.

Search these sites using key words, such as food and beverage management, food and beverage cost control, menu pricing, budgeting, menu design, hospitality accounting, hospitality managerial accounting, and restaurant management.

Technology Tools

This chapter introduced the concepts of conducting individual menu item analysis and identifying a break-even point for your operation. When this break-even point is known, an effective operational budget can be produced. The chapter concluded with a discussion of the importance of developing and monitoring a budget. Although menu analysis software is often packaged as part of a larger program and is somewhat limited, software designed for overall break-even analysis and budgeting is readily available. Software in this area is available to help you:

1. Evaluate item profitability based on:
   a. Food cost percentage
   b. Popularity
   c. Contribution margin
   d. Selling price
2. Conduct menu matrix analysis.
3. Perform break-even analysis.
4. Budget revenue and expense levels.
5. Budget profit levels.

6. Assemble budgets based on days, weeks, months, years, or other identifiable accounting periods.

7. Conduct performance to budget analysis.

8. Maintain performance to budget histories.

9. Blend budgets from multiple profit centers (or multiple units).

10. Perform budgeted cash flow analysis.

For commercial operators, it is simply not wise to attempt to operate an effective foodservice unit without a properly priced menu and an accurate budget that reflects estimated sales and expense levels.

Apply What You Have Learned

Ananda Fields is the CEO of a company that operates a very large number of quick-service restaurants. Recently, competitors have been increasing sales at their restaurants at a faster rate than Ananda's. Joseph Smiley, vice president of operations, is encouraging Ananda to introduce a new line of higher priced, higher quality, and higher contribution margin items to increase sales and improve profits. Sonya Miller, her vice president for marketing, is recommending that Ananda introduce a "value" line of products that would be priced very low but significantly increase traffic to the stores.

1. Do you think more customers would be attracted using Joseph's recommendation or Sonya's?

2. What factors would cause Ananda to choose one menu recommendation over the other?

3. What impact will Ananda's menu decision have on the image projected by her stores? What can she do to influence this image?

Key Terms and Concepts

The following are terms and concepts discussed in the chapter that are important for you as a manager. To help you review, please define the terms below:

Matrix analysis
Contribution margin per
  menu item
Menu engineering
Goal value analysis
Loss leaders7
Quick Service Restaurant
  (QSR)
Break-even point

Cost/volume/profit
  (CVP) analysis
Contribution margin
  income statement
Contribution margin for
  overall operation
Minimum sales point (MSP)
Minimum operating
  cost

Budget
Long-range budget
Annual budget
Achievement budget
Sales per seat
Sales per square foot
Yardstick method

Test Your Skills

Complete the Test Your Skills exercises by placing your answers in the shaded boxes and answering the questions as indicated.

1. Boniso operates Boniso's Mexican Restaurant in an urban area in the South. He has worked hard at setting up cost control systems, and he is generally happy with his overall results. However, he is not sure if all of his menu items are providing profitability for his restaurant. He decides to use food cost matrix and contribution margin matrix analyses to study each of his menu items.

   a. Complete his Menu Analysis Worksheet.

Menu Analysis Worksheet

Menu Item	Number Sold	Selling Price	Total Sales	Item Cost	Total Cost	Item Contribution Margin	Total Contribution Margin	Food Cost %
Fajita Plate	147	$12.95		$4.92				
Enchilada Dinner	200	9.95		3.48				
Menudo	82	6.95		1.74				
Mexican Salad	117	7.95		2.39				
Chalupa Dinner	125	8.95		2.51				
Burrito Dinner	168	9.95		3.25				
Taco Dinner	225	5.95		1.55				
Total								
Weighted Average								

b. Using the results of Boniso's menu analysis worksheet (in part a), place each menu item in its appropriate square in the following matrices.

Food Cost Matrix

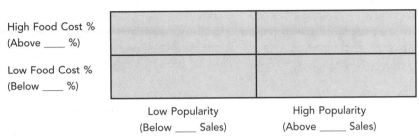

High Food Cost %
(Above _____ %)

Low Food Cost %
(Below _____ %)

Low Popularity
(Below _____ Sales)

High Popularity
(Above _____ Sales)

Contribution Margin Matrix

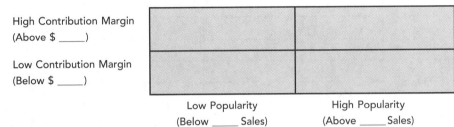

High Contribution Margin
(Above $ _____)

Low Contribution Margin
(Below $ _____)

Low Popularity
(Below _____ Sales)

High Popularity
(Above _____ Sales)

2. Garikai is a manager at Boniso's Mexican Restaurant (from the previous exercise), and he believes that goal value analysis, rather than Boniso's matrix analysis, is a better way to study the profitability of his menu items.

a. Using the following goal value analysis data, help Garikai analyze the restaurant's menu items.

Goal Value Analysis Data				
Item	Food Cost % (in decimal form)	Number Sold	Selling Price	Variable Cost % (in decimal form)
Fajita Plate	0.38	147	$12.95	0.28
Enchilada Dinner	0.35	200	9.95	0.28
Menudo	0.25	82	6.95	0.28
Mexican Salad	0.30	117	7.95	0.28
Chalupa Dinner	0.28	125	8.95	0.28
Burrito Dinner	0.33	168	9.95	0.28
Taco Dinner	0.26	225	5.95	0.28
Overall Menu (Goal Value)	0.32	152	8.95	0.28

After computing the following goal values, sort (in descending rank order) by goal value. Be sure to include the overall menu in the appropriate rank order. Spreadsheet hint: Calculate the Goal Values by placing the ENTIRE Goal Value formula for each item in the Goal Value column as follows: (1 − Food Cost %) × Item Popularity × Selling Price × (1 − (Variable Cost % + Food Cost %)). The table will not sort correctly if partial calculations for Goal Value exist in columns A, B, C, or D. For example, DO NOT calculate (1−Food Cost %) in the A column or (1−(Variable Cost % + Food Cost %)) in the D column.

Goal Value Analysis Results					
Item	"A" Food Cost % (in decimal form)	"B" Number Sold	"C" Selling Price	"D" Variable Cost % (in decimal form)	Goal Value

b. After analyzing his menu items, Garikai believes he can improve the chalupa dinner by lowering the selling price to $8.55. He believes that this lower price will increase the number of chalupa dinners sold to 150. However, the change in price will increase both his food cost % and variable cost % to 29% for the chalupa dinner. If he makes these changes, will the chalupa dinner meet or exceed the overall menu goal value? Should Garikai make these changes?

Results of Changes Made to Chalupa Dinner					
Item	"A" Food Cost % (in decimal form)	"B" Number Sold	"C" Selling Price	"D" Variable Cost % (in decimal form)	Goal Value
Chalupa Dinner					

3. Eunice manages a Thai restaurant in a primarily Asian section of a major West Coast city. She is interested in determining dollar sales and number of guests needed to break even and to generate her desired profits. Her check average (selling price) is $16.00, her variable cost per unit (guest) is $5.60, and her fixed costs are $170,000.

a. Complete the following grid and determine her before-tax profit.

	Per Unit (Guest)	Percentage
SP		
VC		
CM		

Fixed costs	$170,000.00
Desired after-tax profit	24,000.00
Tax rate	40%
Before-tax profit	_____

b. Using the information from part a., calculate the following numbers. (Spreadsheet hint: Use the ROUNDUP function for "Rounded up—Break-even point in guests served" and "Rounded up—Guests served to achieve desired after-tax profit.")

Break-even point in
  sales dollars   _____

Break-even point in
  guests served   _____   Rounded up = _____

Sales dollars to achieve
  desired after-tax profit   _____

Guests served to achieve
  desired after-tax profit   _____   Rounded up = _____

c. Based on her calculations, Eunice doesn't think that she can attract as many guests as she needs to achieve her desired after-tax profit. Therefore, she has decided to make some changes to improve her situation. Due to these changes, she has been able to reduce her selling price by $1.00, decrease her variable cost % by 5%, and lower her fixed costs by $5,000. After these changes, what are Eunice's sales dollars and guests served to achieve her after-tax profit? Complete the following grid and calculations. (Spreadsheet hint: Use the ROUNDUP function for "Rounded up—Guests served to achieve desired after-tax profit.")

	Per Unit (Guest)	Percentage
SP		
VC		
CM		

Fixed costs _____
Sales dollars to achieve desired after-tax profit _____
Guests served to achieve desired
    after-tax profit _____ Rounded up = _____

4. Sinqobile manages a restaurant in an East Coast city that specializes in African-American cuisine. She has compiled her sales and cost data from last year, and she wants to develop a budget for this year. She has projected the following increases for this year:

Projected Increases
Meals served   = 3%
Selling price per meal = 2%
Cost of food   = 5%
Cost of labor   = 10%
Other expenses   = 2%

Using this information, help Sinqobile complete her budget.

	Last Year	Budget
Meals Served	122,000	
Selling Price per Meal	$ 12.50	

Last year's food cost per meal: _____

Last year's food cost per meal + estimated increase: _____

Estimated cost of food this year: _____

Last year's labor cost per meal: _____

Last year's labor cost per meal + estimated increase: _____

Estimated cost of labor this year: _____

	Last Year $	Last Year %	Budget $	Budget %
Revenue	$1,525,000.00			
Cost of Food	610,000.00			
Cost of Labor	488,000.00			
Other Expenses	245,760.00			
Total Expenses	1,343,760.00			
Profit	181,240.00			

The owner of the restaurant has requested that Sinqobile make at least 10% profit for this year. Based on her budget figures, is she likely to meet this goal? If not, what can she do to achieve a 10% profit?

5. Sitabiso manages an executive dining room in an office building of a major food manufacturing company. Her sales, on average, run between $17,000 and $21,000 per week. She has decided to use yardstick standards for labor to predict labor costs for varying sales levels. With these data, she can determine if variations in her expenses are due to changes in sales volume or other reasons, such as waste or theft. She has compiled information from last year to help her predict her weekly labor costs. Using this information, help Sitabiso complete her yardstick standards for labor. (Spreadsheet hint: Use the ROUND function for % Cost to Total Sales column. Also, round to 3 decimal places, e.g., 0.123 or 12.3%.)

Yardstick Standards for Labor

Total sales: $900,000   Average Sales per Month: $75,000
Labor costs:
  Management $ 84,000
  Food production   143,000
  Service   27,600
  Sanitation   34,200
  Total   288,800

Category	% Cost to Total Cost	% Cost to Total Sales	Weekly Sales Estimate				
			$17,000	$18,000	$19,000	$20,000	$21,000
Management							
Food Production							
Service							
Sanitation							
Total							

6. Toni Lamazza is developing next year's foodservice budget for the Springdale school system, consisting of 17 different schools in a two-county area. Toni knows the revenue she will get from the School Board, but is not sure how much the Board will give her to pay for anticipated increases in employee benefits. Complete the chart below to help Toni determine the amount employee benefits can increase and still allow her to show a budget surplus.

    At what level of employee benefit cost increase will Toni have a "break-even" budget? How much would her surplus/deficit be if benefits increase by 20%?

	Current Budget	Budget with Employee Benefits Increases			
		5% Increase	10% Increase	15% Increase	20% Increase
Revenue	$7,000,000	$7,000,000	$7,000,000	$7,000,000	$7,000,000
Cost of Food	$2,095,000	$2,095,000	$2,095,000	$2,095,000	$2,095,000
Cost of Payroll	$3,700,000	$3,700,000	$3,700,000	$3,700,000	$3,700,000
Cost of Employee Benefits	$ 700,000				
Other Expenses	$ 400,000	$ 400,000	$ 400,000	$ 400,000	$ 400,000
Total Costs	$6,895,000				
Budget Surplus/Deficit	$ 105,000				

7. J. D. McAllister is really happy. He has just succeeded in securing a $2,000,000 bank loan with a variable percentage interest rate to build his dream restaurant. J. D.'s loan is for 25 years, and it carries an interest rate that is set at 7% for the first year (this year). Thus, his first year's monthly interest payments will be $14,136. An experienced restaurateur, J. D. has prepared the following annual budget for this year.

Annual Budget for This Year

Total Sales $2,046,000.00

Variable Costs
Food   429,660.00
Beverage   257,796.00
Labor   572,880.00
Other Variable Costs   171,864.00
Total Variable Costs   1,432,200.00

Fixed Costs (excluding loan repayment)   239,568.00
Loan Repayment (7% interest)   169,632.00
Total Fixed Costs   409,200.00

Before-Tax Profit   204,600.00
Taxes (40%)   81,840.00
After-Tax Profit   122,760.00

J. D.'s interest rate will likely vary over the life of the loan because it is tied to the "prime" interest rate established by the Federal Reserve Board (part of the federal government). Assume the "Fed" actions increase interest rates next year by 1/2%, and as a result J. D.'s interest rate moves to 7.5%. Due to the increase, his new monthly loan repayment will be $14,780.

Assume that his total variable cost % and fixed costs (excluding the increased loan repayment) will be the same next year, and his check average (selling price) will be $20 per cover. With the higher mortgage payment, what sales dollars and number of guests served will J. D. need to achieve next year to maintain the same number of after-tax profit dollars as he budgeted for this year?

	Per Unit (Guest)	Percentage
SP		
VC		
CM		

Fixed Costs (excluding loan repayment)   _____
Loan Repayment (7.5% interest)   _____
Total Fixed Costs   _____
Desired after-tax profit   _____
Tax rate   _____
Before-tax profit   _____

Sales dollars to achieve desired after-tax profit   _____
Guests served to achieve desired after-tax profit   _____

8. The Wheatfield Valley golf course has been owned by the Miley family for two generations. Currently it is managed by Cyrus Miley, a graduate of State University, where he majored in hospitality management. Last year was a good one for the food and beverage department at the golf course. Now Cyrus is preparing next year's operating budget. He has gathered a great deal of information to help him prepare the best budget possible. After carefully analyzing that information, Cyrus predicts that next year the course will experience:

- A 5% increase in food sales.
- A 3% increase in beverage sales.
- No change in food or beverage product cost percentage.
- Salaries and wages will increase 4.5%.
- Benefits will increase 10%.
- An increase of 2.5% in each Other Expense category except for Occupancy cost and Depreciation. His accountant states that those two categories will be unchanged.
- Interest payments of $1,000 per month
- Tax payments that are estimated to be 25% of income before income taxes.

Calculate this year's operating percentages for the food and beverage department on the budget worksheet provided, and then, using his assumptions about next year, create Cyrus's new operating budget in dollars and percentages.

The Wheatfield Valley Golf Course F&B Department Budget Worksheet for Next Year				
	This Year Actual $	%	Next Year Budget $	%
SALES:				
Food	173,250.00			
Beverage	56,750.00			
Total Sales	**230,000.00**	100.00%		
COST OF SALES:				
Food	58,250.00			
Beverage	9,375.00			
Total Cost of Sales	**67,625.00**			
GROSS PROFIT:				
Food	115,000.00			
Beverage	47,375.00			
Total Gross Profit	**162,375.00**			
OPERATING EXPENSES:				
Salaries and Wages	36,250.00			
Employee Benefits	6,200.00			
Direct Operating Expenses	8,275.00			
Outing Rentals	1,600.00			
Beer Cart Expense	3,325.00			
Utility Allocation	5,975.00			
Kitchen Repair and Maintenance	1,750.00			
Administrative and General	6,375.00			
Occupancy	15,000.00			
Depreciation	4,200.00			
Total Operating Expenses	**88,950.00**			
Operating Income	**73,425.00**			
Interest	12,000.00			
Income Before Income Taxes	**61,425.00**			
Income Taxes	15,356.25			
Net Income	**46,068.75**			

9. Menu analysis is typically associated with commercial foodservice operators who charge individual selling prices for their menu items. In many cases, however, noncommercial foodservice operators receive a fixed amount of money per guest served regardless of the menu items selected by the guest. Those managers in charge of foodservice in a college dormitory cafeteria are one such example. Despite the differences in how they charge for the items they serve, managers in both commercial and noncommercial operations are concerned about guest acceptance of the menu items they offer. Identify and then compare or contrast at least two other areas of concern shared by menu planners in the commercial and noncommercial segments of the foodservice industry. How does the menu analysis process address these issues?

Chapter 11

MAINTAINING AND IMPROVING THE REVENUE CONTROL SYSTEM

OVERVIEW

This chapter will teach you the principles of revenue control, which includes protecting your sales revenue from external and internal threats of theft. This chapter will also teach you how to establish an effective revenue security system, which includes an extensive series of checks and balances and helps you protect your revenue from the time it is collected from your guests to the time it is deposited in your bank and properly spent.

Chapter Outline

- Revenue Security
- External Threats to Revenue Security
- Internal Threats to Revenue Security
- Developing the Revenue Security System
- The Complete Revenue Security System
- Technology Tools
- Apply What You Have Learned
- Key Terms and Concepts
- Test Your Skills

LEARNING OUTCOMES

At the conclusion of this chapter, you will be able to:
- Identify internal and external threats to revenue.
- Create effective countermeasures to combat internal and external theft.
- Establish and monitor a complete and effective revenue security system.

REVENUE SECURITY

*I*n Chapter 1 you learned that Revenue − Expenses = Profit. A close examination of that formula has led some foodservice operators to state that 50% of their time should be focused on managing revenue and 50% on managing expenses. This is reasonable because all the cost control systems you can develop will be of little use if you are unable to collect the revenue generated by your restaurant, deposit that revenue into your bank account, and spend it only on legitimate expenses. Errors in revenue collection or distribution can come from simple employee mistakes or, in some cases, outright theft by either guests or employees. An important part of your job is to devise revenue security systems that protect your funds or revenue, whether in the form of cash, checks, credit or debit card receipts, coupons, meal cards, or any other method of guest payment.

In its simplest form, revenue control and security is a matter of matching products sold with funds received. Thus, an effective revenue security system ensures that the following five formulas reflect what really happens in your foodservice operation:

1. Documented Product Requests = Product Issues
2. Product Issues (by the kitchen) = Guest Charges
3. Total Charges = Sales Receipts
4. Sales Receipts = Sales (bank) Deposits
5. Sales Deposits = Funds Available to Pay Legitimate Expenses (called Accounts Payable)

The potential for guest or employee theft or fraud exists in all of the preceding areas, so it is important for you to remain alert to irregularities that can help you know if either is taking place.

To illustrate problems that could occur, assume that you own a chain of 10 coffee/dessert shops. You call your units The Pie Parlor. You sell freshly baked gourmet pies of many varieties, all for the same price of $2 per slice or $15 for a whole pie. A whole pie consists of eight slices. In addition, you sell coffee for $2 per cup. Assume that Figure 11.1 details your sales record on a Monday for unit 6, which is one of your 10 stores. If you have in place a good system of controlling your revenue, you should have total receipts (revenue) of $1,400 for January 1 at this unit. If, in fact, at the conclusion of the day you have only $1,300 in actual revenue, a security problem exists, not perhaps in the control of products but rather in the control of receipts. If you were short $100 in revenue per day for each of your 10 units, and you were open 360 days per year, your revenue loss for the year would be a staggering $360,000 ($100 × 10 × 360 = $360,000)!

There are several reasons why you might have a revenue shortage. An examination of the potential problems you might be facing will be helpful as we proceed to examine revenue security systems designed to address these issues. Revenue security problems can exist in either of the following areas:

1. External threats to revenue security
2. Internal threats to revenue security

■ **FIGURE 11.1** Sales Record

Unit Name: The Pie Parlor #6			Date: 1/1
Item	Number Sold	Selling Price	Total Sales
Apple Pie			
Slices	60	$ 2.00	$ 120.00
Whole	11	15.00	165.00
Pumpkin Pie			
Slices	40	2.00	80.00
Whole	14	15.00	210.00
Cherry Pie			
Slices	75	2.00	150.00
Whole	5	15.00	75.00
Peach Pie			
Slices	25	2.00	50.00
Whole	10	15.00	150.00
Coffee	200	2.00	400.00
Total			$1,400.00

EXTERNAL THREATS TO REVENUE SECURITY

*B*oth guests and employees can be threats to revenue. As a result, your facility could have lost sales revenue because of guests defrauding your foodservice operators. This activity can take a variety of forms, and a very common one is for a guest to **walk, or skip, the bill** or guest check. Guests are said to have walked, or skipped, a check when they consume products but then leave the foodservice operation without paying the bill. This type of theft is not generally present in, for example, a quick-service restaurant (QSR) where payment is collected before, or at the same time, the food is given to the guest.

In cases where a guest is in a busy dining room, however, it is quite possible for one or more members of a dining party to slip outside while the server is busy with other guests. In any case, the loss of revenue to your business can be substantial if you do not take the necessary steps to reduce this type of theft. The fact is, in a busy restaurant it can sometimes be relatively easy for a guest or an entire party to leave without settling their bill unless everyone on your staff is extremely vigilant. To help reduce this type of guest theft, implementation of the steps in Figure 11.2 is suggested.

■ **FIGURE 11.2** Steps to Reduce Guest Walks, or Skips

1. If the custom of your restaurant is that guests order and consume their food prior to your receiving payment, instruct servers to present the bill for the food promptly when the guests have finished.
2. If your facility has a cashier in a central location in the dining area, have that cashier available and visible at all times.
3. If your facility operates in such a manner that each server collects for his or her own guest's charges, instruct the servers to return to the table promptly after presenting the guest's bill to secure a form of payment.
4. Train employees to be observant of exit doors near restrooms or other areas of the facility that may provide an unscrupulous guest the opportunity to exit the dining area without being easily seen.
5. If an employee sees a guest leave without paying the bill, management should be notified immediately.
6. Upon approaching a guest who has left without paying the bill, the manager should ask if the guest has inadvertently "forgotten" to pay. In most cases, the guest will then pay the bill.
7. Should a guest still refuse to pay or flee the scene, the manager should note the following on an incident report:
   a. Number of guests involved.
   b. Amount of the bill.
   c. Physical description of the guest(s).
   d. Vehicle description if the guests flee in a car, as well as the license plate number if possible.
   e. Time and date of the incident.
   f. Name of the server(s) who actually served the guest.
8. If the guest is successful in fleeing the scene, the police should be notified. In no case should your staff members or managers be instructed to attempt to physically detain the guest. The potential liability resulting from an employee hurt in such an attempt would be far greater than the value of a single skipped food and beverage bill.

It is, of course, also possible that a guest truly forgets to settle his or her bill and leaves the establishment without paying. However, if many of your guests walked their bills on your day of $1,400 sales in our Pie Parlor example, you would, of course, find that the products had indeed been consumed, but the money in your cash drawer would not equal the sales value of the pie and coffee products issued by the kitchen to the waitstaff and then served to the guests.

In addition to skipping a bill, another form of external theft you must be aware of is that used by the quick-change artist. A **quick-change artist** is a guest who, having practiced the routine many times, attempts to confuse the cashier; in his or her confusion, the cashier gives the guest too much change. For example, a guest who should have received $5 in change may use a confusing routine to secure $15. To prevent this from happening, you must train your cashiers well and instruct them to notify management immediately if there is any suspicion of attempted fraud to your operation through quick-change routines by a guest.

Another form of external theft involves guests who pay with personal checks but do not have enough money available in their bank accounts to cover the check amounts. Although most foodservice operations no longer accept personal checks, those that do should employ an external company to provide check verification services. In most cases, these companies do not actually certify that there are sufficient funds in the bank to complete a checking transaction, but rather they notify the foodservice operator if that particular checking account or individual has had difficulty in the past in covering checks written on that account. If a particular check writer has a history of writing checks from accounts containing funds insufficient to cash the check, most operators would refuse to accept additional checks written by that individual.

If you do agree to accept checks, you will likely experience some loss. That is, despite your best efforts, some checks you accept will inevitably be returned to you because the accounts on which they were written had **nonsufficient funds (NSF)**, or not enough money, in them to allow the checks to be cashed. Costs experienced from this type of loss, like all other costs, must be reflected in your menu prices. It is imperative, however, that guest theft of this type be kept to an absolute minimum.

FUN ON THE WEB!

Look at the following site to see an example of a company that provides businesses personal check verification and check guarantee services: **www.checkcare.com.** Click "Verification Program" to learn more about this important product offering.

An additional form of external theft that you must guard against is that of a guest using counterfeit money. **Counterfeit money** is an imitation of currency intended to be passed off fraudulently as real money. Counterfeit money used by guests will not be honored as legal currency by banks. Therefore, counterfeit money deposited by a restaurant manager will result in the ultimate loss of revenues if the perpetrator is not caught. You will have an exercise in the Test Your Skills section of this chapter that will help you identify counterfeit money.

■ USE OF CARDS AS BILL PAYMENT

In our society, fewer and fewer consumers carry large amounts of cash, and many facilities are reluctant to accept personal checks. Thus, most foodservice operations (including QSR), now accept a variety of "plastic" forms of bill payment. Since the 1960s, credit cards and travel and entertainment (T&E) cards have been the most common form of plastic guest payment at most restaurants. Today, debit cards are increasingly used by guests to pay their bills.

Also known as "bank" cards, **credit cards** are simply a system by which banks loan money to consumers as the consumer makes purchases. The loans typically carry interest. Merchants such as restaurants and hotels accepting the cards for payment are charged a fee (by the banks) for the right to allow their customers to pay by credit card. Examples of credit cards are Visa and MasterCard.

Travel and entertainment (T&E) cards are a payment system by which the card issuer collects full payment from the card users on a monthly basis. These card companies do not typically assess their users interest charges. Rather they rely on larger fees collected from the merchants who accept the cards to make their profits. Examples of T&E cards are American Express (Amex) and Diners Club. In some cases, the fees charged by T&E card issuers are so high restaurateurs do not accept them.

Increasingly, **debit cards** are an extremely popular form of guest payment. In this system, the funds needed to cover the user's purchase are automatically transferred from the user's bank account to the entity issuing the debit card. As with bank cards and T&E cards, merchants accepting debit cards are assessed a fee for the right to do so.

If restaurant managers are to ensure that they collect all of the money they are due from payment card companies, they must effectively manage the **interface** (electronic connection) between the various payment card issuers and their restaurant. That interface is provided by the restaurant's **merchant service provider (MSP)**. An MSP plays an important role as the restaurant's coordinator/manager of payment card acceptance and funds collection.

It is important to understand that payment card issuers as well as MSP who are assisting restaurants do so for a price. The card issuer will charge the restaurant a fee and the MSP will charge a variety of fees, including setup fees, per transaction fees, programming fees, statement fees, and fees related to managing the card interface. These interface-related fees may include equipment purchase charges (or leases) and connectivity fees.

In most cases, restaurants have little option but to accept the most popular of payment cards. The MSP selected, however, will vary and so will the amount of fees they charge. Overall, the MSP generally keeps 10 to 20 percent of all the fees you will pay, and the card company (Visa, MasterCard, and others) receives the balance. At the end of the month, you will get a statement displaying the total transactions and the various fees you paid (because the fees are withdrawn by the MSP before your revenue is deposited in your account).

It is important to remember that maintaining the quality of relationship between your MSP and the restaurant's revenue is just as important as maintaining adequate control over the cash your restaurant accepts. This is so because a restaurant accepting payment cards does not actually "receive" immediate cash from its card sales but, rather, it will be credited via **electronic funds transfer (EFT)** the money it is due after all fees have been paid. If a restaurant's POS/MSP interface is faulty or mismanaged the result can be slow processing, increased errors, omissions, and even disappearing sales!

Unfortunately, the number of stolen and fraudulent payment cards in use today is very high. It is, therefore, important for the foodservice operator to check the validity of the payment card before accepting it for payment. The federal government has passed a law prohibiting the fraudulent use of credit cards. Individuals who fraudulently use credit cards in interstate commerce to obtain goods or services of $1,000 or more in any given year could be subject to fines of up to $10,000 and prison terms of up to 10 years; yet payment card fraud continues.

Fortunately, payment card security has come a long way since the early introduction of these cards. Today, payment cards are issued with three-dimensional designs, magnetic strips, encoded numbers, card holder photos, and other features that reduce the chance of guest fraud as well as theft of the card user's personal information by unscrupulous employees. In addition, today's electronic payment card verification (interface) systems are fast, accurate, and designed to reduce the chances of loss by your business.

To ensure that you can collect your money from the MSP that administers your account, your staff will be required to follow the specific procedures of the various payment card companies. If you agree to accept credit, T&E, and debit cards for payment, you should become very familiar with the procedures required by each card issuer and follow them carefully. To enhance your chances of collecting your money from these companies and to reduce the risk of fraudulent card use, insist that your staff follow the steps in Figure 11.3.

■ **FIGURE 11.3 Credit and Debit Card Verification**

1. Confirm that the name on the card is the same as that of the individual presenting the card for payment. Drivers' licenses or other acceptable forms of identification can be used.
2. Examine the card for any obvious signs of alteration.
3. Confirm that the card is indeed valid, that is, check to see if the card has expired or is not yet in effect.
4. Compare the signature on the back of the card with the one produced by the guest paying with the card.
5. The employee processing the charge should initial the credit card receipt.
6. Carbon paper, if used, should be destroyed.
7. Credit card charges that have not yet been processed should be kept in a secure place to limit the possibility that they could be stolen.
8. Do not issue cash in exchange for credit card charges.
9. Do not write in tip amounts for the guest. These should be supplied by the guest only unless the "tip" is, in truth, a mandatory service charge and that fact has been communicated in advance to the guest.
10. Tally credit card charges on a daily basis, making sure to check that the preceding procedures have been followed. If they have not, corrective action should immediately be taken to ensure compliance.

FUN ON THE WEB!

Look at the following sites to see examples of credit card companies that you can use to provide payment services for your operation.

www.totalmerchant-ca.com. Click "Set up a retail/restaurant, hotel or wireless account," and then click "Restaurants and hotels" to find merchant account rates and fees.

www.novusnet.com. Scroll down, click "Information for Merchants," and then click "Information for Merchants" again to review the benefits of accepting Discover Cards in your operation.

www.americanexpress.com. Click "Merchants" to discover reasons why you should consider accepting American Express cards in your operation.

www.visa.com. Click "United States," and then click "Merchants/Accepting Visa" to learn about the benefits and services that Visa offers to restaurants.

www.mastercard.com. Click "United States," and then click "Merchant Services" to get information about the benefits and services that MasterCard can offer.

INTERNAL THREATS TO REVENUE SECURITY

*M*ost foodservice employees are honest, but some are not. In addition to protecting your revenue from unscrupulous guests, you must protect it from those few employees who may attempt to steal the revenue your facility has earned from sales. Cash is the most readily usable asset in a foodservice operation, and it is a major target for dishonest employees. In general, theft from service personnel is usually not a matter of removing large sums of cash at one time because this is too easy for management to detect. Rather, service personnel may use a variety of techniques to cheat an operation of a small amount at a time.

One of the most common server theft techniques involves the omission of recording the guest's order. If, in our Pie Parlor example, a guest ordered both pie and coffee, but the pie sale was not recorded, you would find that a piece of pie was missing, but no record of sale was ever made. In this situation, the server might have chosen to charge the guest and keep the revenue from the piece of pie, or the server might have attempted to build favor with the guest by not charging for the product at all. Theft of this type is especially prevalent in bars. As an old bartending story goes: "A guest walks into a bar that sells drinks for $5, has four drinks, and places $20 on the counter as he leaves. The bartender then turns to the facility manager and says, 'Hey, that guy didn't pay for his drinks, but he left a great tip!'" The manager, of course, is not amused. The point, however, is that all sales must be recorded if management is to develop a system that matches products sold to revenue received. Complete revenue control is a matter of developing the checks and balances necessary to ensure that the value of products sold and the amount of revenue received equal each other.

To understand how server theft could occur in your operation, it is important to know your options in recording sales. In the least effective option, no record is made of the sale at all. Guests are simply told how much they owe by the server. This system is frequently seen in the small snack-bar type operations found during intermission at high school musicals and plays, Little League ballparks, and various fund-raising events. Although inexpensive to implement, obviously, this approach is ineffective. Servers can misrepresent the amount they charged guests, and no historical record of sales is available to help you make decisions in the future. This system should never be used by professional foodservice managers.

A second, and improved, approach is to require a written guest check recording each sale. A **guest check** is simply a written record of what the guest purchased and how much the guest was charged for the item(s). The use of paper or electronic guest checks is standard in the industry because guest checks also serve as the way employees take guest orders and communicate the orders to those employees responsible for filling them. A rule when using guest checks is that no food or beverage should be issued to a server unless the server first records the sale on a guest check.

Dishonest employees can still abuse some types of guest check systems. For example, assume one of your guests at the Pie Parlor orders peach pie and coffee. The server writes the order on a paper guest check and as required, submits the order for filling. The server then collects the revenue due from the sale. If the used guest check is not identifiable by number, or is returned to the server, the same guest check could be used one hour later for another guest who orders peach pie and coffee. The server could then keep the money from the second sale, and, at the end of the day, your operation would find itself short on revenue relative to product used. To prevent fraud of this type, you must have a system of guest check controls in place so that each check can be used only once and is subsequently put under the safekeeping of management. It should not be possible, for example, for a server to submit a guest check that had previously been used and keep a blank one. If used, paper guest checks should be recorded by number and then safely stored or destroyed, as management policy dictates. Modern point of sale (POS) systems assign unique numbers to each guest check they create. This POS feature eliminates duplicate guest check fraud and is one of the main reasons even the smallest of foodservice operations should utilize an electronic POS system.

It is important to note that most guests do not know (or even care!) if the guest check presented to them is actually theirs or belongs to someone else. This could be the case, for example, in pay-one-price buffets, where it is the number of guests served, rather than individual menu items selected, that determine the guest's total bill. In fact, in many cases, if the guest check is accurate in terms of total charges and items ordered, guests may have no way of knowing if they are paying their own bill or someone else's.

Another method of service personnel fraud is one in which the server gives the proper guest check to the guest, collects payment, and destroys the guest check but keeps the money. In this case, you would find that the money you collected equaled the sum of the guest checks you have, but, of course, the actual amount of product you served would not be equal to that indicated on the guest checks. For this reason, POS systems operate on a precheck/postcheck system for guest checks.

In a **precheck/postcheck system,** the dining room server writes guest orders on a piece of paper for subsequent entry into a POS terminal called a *user work station*. The terminal records the items ordered and then displays the order in the production area. In some systems, the order may even be printed in the production area. Increasingly, this method of entering guest orders can be accomplished in one step instead of two. Handheld and wireless at-the-table order entry devices now allow servers (and guests in some cases!) to enter precheck orders directly into an operation's POS system. This direct data entry system is fast, and it eliminates mistakes made when transferring handwritten guest orders to the POS system.

Regardless of how the prechecked guest check is created, kitchen and bar personnel are, in this system, prohibited from issuing any products to the server without a uniquely numbered, prechecked guest check. When the guest is ready to leave, the cashier retrieves the prechecked guest check and prepares a postcheck bill for the guest to pay. The postcheck total includes the charges for all of the prechecked items ordered by the guest. The guest then pays the bill. In a precheck/postcheck system, products ordered by the guest, prechecked by the server, and issued by the kitchen or bar should match the items and money collected by the cashier.

There can be reasons why initial prechecked sales totals do not match the amount of money collected by the cashier. Many times, guests place orders and then change their minds, adding or subtracting from their original orders. In other cases, an ordered item may be returned by a guest and, depending upon the reason for the item's return, the guest may not be charged for it. For these types of reasons, the question of who can make deletions (voids, returns, reductions) to a prechecked guest check is a potential security concern to the restaurant manager and should be closely controlled.

Not all service personnel are dishonest, of course, but POS systems are especially designed to prevent dishonest employees from committing theft and fraud. It is important to remember, however, that even sophisticated POS systems hold the potential for employee fraud. Consider, for example, the precheck/postcheck POS system that requires a server to enter his or her password before allowing that server to precheck items. In this case, an unscrupulous server who discovers another server's password could use that password to defraud the operation and then blame the fraud on the unsuspecting server. Regardless of the weaknesses that can exist in them, today's POS systems, properly used and managed, are a tremendous asset in helping to reduce server theft.

FUN ON THE WEB!

The POS systems available to foodservice operators range from the very simple to the highly sophisticated. To see one POS company's range of products, go to **www.micros.com**. When you arrive, click "Industries" and then select "Restaurants" to view this vendor's varied product line.

To view additional systems, Google "POS Restaurants" in the **www.google.com** search field.

■ CASHIER THEFT

In some operations, servers act as their own cashiers; in others, the server function and cashier function fall to different individuals. Regardless of the system in place, when a cashier is responsible for the collection of money, several areas of potential fraud can exist. For example, the cashier may collect payment from a guest but destroy the record of the sale.

Another method of cashier theft involves failing to finalize a sale recorded on the precheck and pocketing the money. To prevent such theft, management must have systems in place to identify open checks during and after each server's work shift. **Open checks** are those that have been used to authorize product issues from the kitchen or bar but that have not been added to the operation's sales total. Unless all open checks are ultimately closed out and presented to guests for payment, the value of menu items issued will not equal the money collected for those items.

In addition to theft of your own business financial assets, the hospitality industry affords some employees the opportunity to defraud guests as well. Some techniques include:

- Charging guests for items not purchased, then keeping the overcharge.
- Changing the totals on payment card charges after the guest has left or entering additional payment card charges and pocketing the cash difference.
- Incorrectly adding legitimate charges to create a higher than appropriate total, with the intent of keeping the overcharge.
- Purposely shortchanging guests when giving back change, with the intent of keeping the extra change.
- Charging higher than authorized prices for products or services, recording the proper price, and then keeping the overcharge.

The totals of guest checks rung on the POS during a predetermined period are electronically tallied, so management can compare the sales recorded by the POS with the money actually contained in the cash drawer. For example, a cashier working a shift from 7:00 a.m. to 3:00 p.m. might have recorded $1,000 in sales during that time period. If that were in fact the case, and if no errors in handling change occurred, the cash drawer should contain the $1,000 in sales revenue (in addition to the amount that was in the drawer at the beginning of the shift). If it contains less than $1,000, it is said to be **short**; if it contains more than $1,000, it is said to be **over**. Cashiers rarely steal large sums directly from the cash drawer because such theft is easily detected, but management must make it a policy that any cash shortages or overages will be investigated. Some managers believe that only cash shortages, not overages, need to be monitored. This is not the case. Consistent cash shortages may be an indication of employee theft or carelessness and should, of course, be investigated. Cash overages, too, may be the result of sophisticated theft by the cashier. Essentially, a cashier who is defrauding an operation because he or she knows that management does not investigate overages may remove $18.00 from a cash drawer, but falsify sales records by $20.00. The result is a $2.00 cash "overage"!

If the POS system has a void key, a dishonest cashier could enter a sales amount, collect for it (and keep the cash), and then void (erase) the sale after the guest has departed. In this way, total sales would equal the amount of the cash drawer. To prevent this, management should insist that all voids be performed by a supervisor or at least be authorized by management on an individual basis. In addition, because POS systems record the number and the time at which voids are performed, these, too, should be monitored by management. As well, servers should be required to account for all open guest checks at the end of their work shifts.

Another method of cashier theft involves the manipulation of complimentary meals or meal coupons. Assume, for example, that at your Pie Parlor you have produced and distributed a large number of guest coupons good for a free piece of pie. If the cashier has access to these coupons, it is possible to collect the money from a guest who does not have a coupon and then add a coupon to the cash drawer and simultaneously remove sales revenue equal to the value of the coupon. A variation on this theme is for the cashier to declare a check to be complimentary after the guest has paid the bill. In cases like this, the cashier would again remove sales revenue from the cash drawer in an amount equal to the "comped" check. This kind of fraud can be prevented by denying cashiers access to unredeemed cash value coupons and by requiring special authorization from management to "comp" guest checks.

■ BONDING

Even if you have controls that make internal theft difficult, the possibility of significant fraud still exists. Consequently, some companies protect themselves from employee dishonesty by bonding their employees. **Bonding** is simply a matter of management purchasing an insurance policy against the possibility that an employee(s) will steal.

Through the process of bonding an employer can be covered for the loss of money or other property sustained through dishonest acts of a "bonded" employee. Bonding can cover many types of acts including larceny, theft, embezzlement, forgery, misappropriation, or other fraudulent or dishonest acts committed by an employee, alone or in collusion with others. Essentially, a business can select from several bonding options. These are:

- Individual—covers one employee (for example, a restaurant's bookkeeper)
- Position—covers all employees in a given position (for example, all bartenders or all cashiers)
- Blanket—covers all employees

If an employee has been bonded and an operation can determine that he or she was indeed involved in the theft of a specific amount of money, the operation will be reimbursed for the loss by the bonding company. Although bonding will not completely eliminate theft, it is relatively inexpensive and well worth the cost to ensure that all employees who handle cash or other forms of operational revenue are bonded. Because the bonding company may require detailed background information on employees prior to agreeing to bond them, it is also an excellent preemployment check to verify an employee's track record in prior jobs.

■ **FIGURE 11.4 Common Methods of Theft by Service Employees**

- Omits recording the guest's order and keeps the money
- Uses the same guest check more than once
- Destroys the guest check or voids the sale but keeps the money
- Enters another server's password in the POS and keeps the money
- Fails to finalize sale and keeps the money
- Charges guests for items not purchased and then keeps the overcharge
- Changes the totals on payment card charges after the guest has left
- Enters additional payment card charges and pockets the cash difference
- Incorrectly adds legitimate charges to create a higher than appropriate total, with the intent of keeping the overcharge
- Purposely shortchanges guests when giving back change, with the intent of keeping the extra change
- Charges higher than authorized prices for products or services, records the proper price, and then keeps the overcharge.
- Adds a coupon to the cash drawer and simultaneously removes sales revenue equal to the value of the coupon
- Declares a check to be complimentary after the guest has paid the bill
- Engages in collusion between two or more employees to defraud the operation

The scenarios discussed in this chapter do not list all possible methods of revenue loss, but it should be clear that you must have a complete revenue security system if you are to ensure that all products sold generate sales revenue that finds its way into your bank account. It is important to remember that even good revenue control systems present the opportunity for theft if management is not vigilant or if two or more employees conspire to defraud the operation (**collusion**). Figures 11.4 and 11.5 summarize common methods of theft and ways of minimizing theft discussed in this chapter.

■ **FIGURE 11.5 Common Methods to Minimize Theft by Service Employees**

- Require a written guest check recording each sale
- Assign unique numbers to each guest check created
- Use a precheck/postcheck system
- Do not allow employees to share POS passwords
- Close out open checks
- Monitor overs/shorts
- Perform voids by supervisor only
- Deny cashiers access to unredeemed cash value coupons
- Require special authorization from management to "comp" guest checks
- Develop a system of checks and balances
- Bond employees (acquire an insurance policy against employee theft)

"The beauty of our system," said Phil Larson, "is that you can monitor the actions of all your employees and all your managers."

Phil was talking to Gene Monteagudo, chief operating officer for Fazziano's Fast Italian Kitchens, a chain of 150 casual dining and carryout Italian food restaurants. Gene had called POS-Video Security, the company Phil represented, because, for the second time this year, one of Gene's regional managers had discovered a case of employee/manager collusion. Working together, the employee and manager stole revenue from their restaurant by manipulation of their unit's POS system.

"I'm pretty sure I see how your company's product would have detected our most recent theft problem, but go over it one more time," said Gene.

"Okay, Gene, I'd be glad to," said Phil. "Essentially, our new system goes beyond traditional surveillance methods by synchronizing the video with the data mined from your POS system to create detailed, customized video reports. Potentially fraudulent activity such as manager overrides, coupons or comps, or even a cash drawer being open for too long, is tracked and the corresponding video surveillance can be searched by transaction number. Data reports and streaming video, both real time and stored, can be accessed securely on a PC or handheld device via a Web browser."

"So, for example," replied Gene, "when a sales void occurs, your system identifies the portion of videotape that was recording at the time of the void and would then allow my regional managers to view just that portion of the video so they could see what was going on in the store at the precise time of that transaction."

"Exactly," said Phil.

1. What types of employee fraud do you think could be uncovered utilizing the technology offered by POS-Video Security's new product?

2. Do you think that the behavior of most dishonest cashiers and managers would be changed if they knew their actions were being video recorded?

3. What issues should Gene consider as he evaluates the potential benefits to be gained from the purchase of an advanced technology control system such as the one offered by Phil's company?

We now turn our attention to the development of an effective revenue control system. It may not be possible to prevent all types of theft, but a good revenue control system should help you determine if, in fact, a theft has occurred and establish ways to prevent losses in your operation.

DEVELOPING THE REVENUE SECURITY SYSTEM

*A*n effective revenue security system will help you accomplish the following five important tasks:

1. Verification of product issues
2. Verification of guest charges

3. Verification of sales receipts

4. Verification of sales deposits

5. Verification of accounts payable

You must consider each of these five areas when developing your total revenue security system. In many cases, each foodservice operation you manage will have a different manner of both selling products and accounting for revenue. It is useful, however, to view the revenue control system for any unit in terms of these five key points and how they relate to each other. In an ideal world, a product would be sold, its sale recorded, its selling price collected, the funds deposited in the foodservice operation's bank account, and the cost of providing the product would be paid for, all in a single step. Rapid advances in the area of computers and "smart" cards are making this a near reality for more foodservice operators each day. The following example from the grocery industry helps illustrate just how this works.

A grocery store customer uses his or her bank-issued debit card when buying a frozen entrée dinner. The cashier, in this instance, uses a scanner to read the bar code printed on the frozen entrée dinner. The following actions then take place:

- The amount the shopper owes the store is recorded in the POS system and the sale itself is assigned a tracking number (verification of product issued/sold).
- The sale amount is displayed for the guest who is asked to confirm its correctness; if it is correct, a receipt is printed for the shopper (verification of guest charge).
- The store POS system records the amount of the sale as well as the form of payment used by this shopper (verification of sales receipt).
- The shopper's debit card number is attached to this specific sales tracking number and a transfer of funds takes place from the shopper's account to that of the grocery store (verification of sales deposit).
- The funds on deposit in the grocery store's bank account are available to pay for the purchase of additional frozen entrée dinners (verification of accounts payable).

Of course, not all foodservice operations have the technological sophistication to duplicate the system described in our grocery store example. Foodservice operators should, however, adapt the technology they currently have available to the development of good revenue control systems.

In all cases, the foodservice manager should have a thorough understanding of how the revenue security system works and, thus, what is required to maintain it. To illustrate the five-step process of revenue security, consider the situation of Faris, who operates a Lebanese restaurant in New York City. Faris considers his restaurant to be a family-oriented establishment. It has a small cocktail area and 100 guest seats in the dining room. Total revenue at Faris's exceeds $1 million per year. When he started the restaurant, he did not give a tremendous amount of thought to the design of his revenue control system because he was in the restaurant at all times. Due to his success, however, he spends more and more of his time developing a second restaurant and, thus, needs both the security of an adequate revenue security system and the ability to review it quickly to evaluate the sales levels in his original store. Thus, Faris has begun to develop a revenue security system, concentrating on the following formula:

Product Issues = Guest Charges = Sales Receipts = Sales Deposits
= Funds Available for Accounts Payable

Faris knows that the first goal he must achieve is that of verifying his product sales.

■ STEP 1. VERIFICATION OF PRODUCT ISSUES

The key to verification of product issues in the revenue security system is to follow one basic rule: *No product shall be issued from the kitchen or bar unless a permanent record of the issue is made.*

In its simplest terms, this means that the kitchen should not fill any server request for food unless that request has been documented in this step of the control system. In some restaurants, the server request for food or beverages will take the form of a multicopy, written guest check, designed specifically for the purpose of revenue control. When this is the case, the top copy of this multicopy form would generally be sent to the kitchen or bar. The guest check, in this case, becomes the documented request for the food or beverage product. For those operations utilizing a POS system, the "guest check" consists of an electronic record of product issues. When this is the case, a guest's order information is viewed by the production staff on a computer terminal, or, in other cases, the POS system prints a hard copy of the order for use by the production staff. In this case, the software within the computer keeps the permanent record of the request. In every case, however, there should be a permanent documented order that authorizes the kitchen to prepare food or the bar to prepare a drink. In a quick-service restaurant also, no food should be given to the guest unless that sale has been recorded. If a foodservice operation elects to supply its employees with meals during work shifts, these meals, too, should be recorded in the system.

In the bar, this principle of verifying all product sales is even more important. Bartenders should be instructed never to issue a drink unless that drink has first been recorded in the POS system. This should be the procedure, even if the bartender is working alone.

This rule regarding product issuing is important for two reasons. In the first place, requiring a permanent documented order ensures that there is a record of each product sale. Second, this record of product sales can be used to verify both proper inventory usage and product sales totals. Faris enforces this basic rule by requiring that no menu item be served from his kitchen or the bar without the sale first being entered into his POS system.

If his verification of product sales system is working correctly, Faris will find that the following formula should hold true:

Documented Product Requests = Product Issues

Experienced foodservice operators know that it is possible for employees to issue products *without* a document product request when:

1. Two or more employees work together to defraud the operation. Collusion of this type can be discovered when managers have a system in place to carefully count the number of items removed from inventory and then compare that number to the number of products that were actually issued.

2. A single employee (such as a bartender working alone) is responsible for both making and filling the product request. In this case also, managers will uncover this type of fraud when they carefully compare the number of items (or servings) removed from inventory with the number of recorded product requests.

■ STEP 2. VERIFICATION OF GUEST CHARGES

When the production staff is required to prepare and distribute products only in response to a properly documented request, it is critical that those documented requests result in charges to the guest. It makes little sense to enforce a verification of product issues step without also requiring the service staff to ensure that guest charges match these requests. This concept can be summarized as follows: ***Product issues must equal guest charges.***

There are a variety of ways this can be achieved. If managers use manually generated guest checks as a primary control device, the managerial goal is to ensure that product issues equal guest check totals. If they do, all issued products will result in appropriate charges to the guest. Figure 11.6 is a sample of a guest check that could be in use at Faris's. Note that the check is numbered on both the top and the bottom, or guest receipt portion.

If guest checks are used as a control device, it is important to remember that the numbers on the checks are of no operational value if the checks are not tightly controlled. Each guest check must be accounted for, and employees must know that they will be held responsible for each check they are issued. This is because an unscrupulous employee could present a guest check for payment to a guest, then destroy the check and keep the money. For this reason, "lost" guest checks should always be accounted for. To keep track of the checks issued to service personnel, managers use a guest check control form. Figure 11.7 is an example of such a form that could be used at Faris'.

Note that this form recognizes that some guest checks can be lost or destroyed. When using the guest check system of verifying guest charges, you must be aware of these incidents when they occur and must investigate when it is determined that

■ FIGURE 11.6   Sample Guest Check

				Check Number	
		Faris'		Phone #: 123-4567	

Date	Table	Server	Guests	Check Number 123456	
Items Ordered					Price
Subtotal					
Tax					
Gratuity					
Total					

Guest Receipt

Date	Table	Server	Guests	Check Number 123456	Total

a check is missing. Each lost or destroyed check should be "approved" by management. That is, management should know why and how each missing check came to be missing!

A POS system simplifies the task of guest check control by creating a unique transaction number (guest check) for each server request. That is, a documented request for products generates, within the POS system, a guest check that is matched to that request. Guest checks cannot be "lost" on purpose, because the POS keeps a record of each transaction, as well as attempts by employees to request a product, receive it from the kitchen or bar, and then "void" (subtract) the charge from the guest's bill. Guest check control is another significant advantage enjoyed by operators who utilize their POS systems properly.

■ **FIGURE 11.7** Sample Guest Check Control Form

Faris'

Date: 1/1   Shift: Lunch

Check Numbers Issued			Check Numbers Returned				
From	To	Issued To	From	To	Checks Used	Checks Accounted for	Number Missing
00001	00100	Beth	00055	00100	45	44	1
00101	00200	Sally	00130	00200	70	70	0
00201	00300	Gerry	00264	00300	36	36	0

Unaccounted Checks:

Check Number	Issued To	Explanation	Manager's Initials
00035	Beth	Torn by accident	D.K.H.

When properly implemented, this second step of the revenue control system will result in the following formula:

$$\text{Product Issues} = \text{Guest Charges}$$

Faris has now implemented two key revenue control principles. The first one is that no product can be issued from the kitchen or bar unless the order is documented; the second one is that all guest charges must match product issues.

With these two systems in place, Faris can deal with many problems. If, for example, a guest has "walked" his or her check, the operation would have a duplicate record of the transaction. The POS would have recorded which products were sold to this guest, which server sold them, and perhaps additional information, such as the time of the sale, the number of guests in the party, and, of course, the sales value of the products. The POS system Faris utilizes also ensures that service personnel do not attempt to write one item on the guest check but charge the guest a higher or lower price. This would be possible in a manual check system, and those operators who utilize such systems must perform a periodic audit of checks to help detect this type of fraud.

To complete this aspect of his control system, Faris implements a strict policy regarding the documentation of employee meals. This has the added advantage of giving him a monthly total of the value of employee meals. Recall that he needs this figure to accurately compute his cost of food sold. Faris is now ready for the next major component in a revenue security system, that is, the actual collection of guest payment.

■ STEP 3. VERIFICATION OF SALES RECEIPTS

Sales receipts, as defined in this step, refer to actual revenue received by the cashier or other designated personnel, in payment for products served. In Faris's case, this means all sales revenue from his restaurant and lounge. This essential principle can be summarized as follows: ***Both the cashier and a member of management must verify sales receipts.*** Verifying sales receipts is more than a simple matter of counting cash at the end of a shift. In fact, cash handling, although it is an important part of the total sales receipt reconciliation, is only one part of the total sales receipt verification system.

To illustrate this, consider Figure 11.8, the form Faris uses to verify his total sales receipts. The form indicates that both the cashier and a supervisor make the sales receipt verification. Although this will not prevent possible collusion by this pair, it is extremely important that sales receipt verification be a two-person process.

Faris wishes to ensure that the amount of cash and checks in his cash drawer, as well as his payment card charges, matches the dollar amount that he has charged his guests. If this is so, he has accounted for all of his sales receipts, given that he has controlled both product issues and guest charges. As you can see, the form presented in Figure 11.8 details both the guest charges recorded in the POS system and the money Faris has collected.

In most operations, individual guest charges are recorded only in the POS system. This is the case, for example, in a cafeteria or QSR, where food purchases are totaled and paid for at the same time. It is also true in any operation using a precheck/postcheck POS system. In such instances, the POS system provides an accurate total of guest and other charges. Receipts collected should equal these charges. In those operations still using a manual guest check system, the sum of the individual check totals (charges to guests) should equal the amount of revenue (receipts) collected.

If Faris's revenue security system is working properly, he knows that the following formula should be in effect:

Total Charges = Sales Receipts

Note that the function of Figure 11.8 is to require Faris's staff to reconcile total charges with actual revenue (sales receipts). Overages or shortages are entered

■ **FIGURE 11.8** Sales Receipt Report

		Faris'	
			Performed By:
Date: 1/1			Cashier: Tammi F.
Shift: Dinner			Supervisor: Faris L.
Revenue per Guest Check			
Guest check totals		$7,500.00	
Service charges		450.00	
Tax		618.00	
Total guest check revenue			$8,568.00
Receipts			
Charge cards			
VISA		893.00	
MasterCard		495.00	
Discover		1,200.00	
American Express		975.00	
Total charge card receipts		3,563.00	
Cash			
Twenties and larger	$4,840.00		
Tens	1,480.00		
Fives	240.00		
Ones	196.00		
Change	68.20		
Total cash	6,824.20		
Less: Bank	500.00		
Tip-outs	1,320.00		
Net cash receipts		5,004.20	
Net total receipts			8,567.20
Variance check revenue to net receipts			$ (0.80)

and, if they exceed predetermined allowable limits, are investigated by management. Service charges, the second entry on the form, are special charges assessed to guests. Faris assesses a service charge of 15% on all parties larger than eight persons. Hotels often assess a service charge on all food and beverages sold in their meeting spaces. Notice also that total charges consist of all sales, service charges, and taxes. This is the total amount of revenue the operation should have received on this date. Sales receipts refer to all forms of revenue, such as cash, checks (if accepted), and payments made by credit or debit cards. In addition, note that Faris must subtract the value of his starting cash bank and any tip-outs, or gratuities, due to service personnel. These gratuities are typically added to payment card vouchers by the guest, but paid out to the service personnel by management either in cash or in their paychecks; such income is taxable to the server.

Note also that Figure 11.8 has a space to indicate cash overages and shortages (variance of total charges to net total receipts). It will be up to you, as the manager, to determine the level of variance you are comfortable with as far as this reconciliation is concerned. Some foodservice operators allow no variance whatsoever. Others routinely ignore minor variances. The level of variance that is tolerated is greatly affected by the method of guest payment collection that is in place. In general, there are five basic payment arrangements in use in typical foodservice operations. They are as follows:

1. Guest pays cashier.
2. Guest pays at the table.
3. Guest pays service personnel, who pay cashier.
4. Guest pays service personnel, who have already paid cashier.
5. Guest is direct billed.

GUEST PAYS CASHIER

In this situation, a common one in the hospitality industry, losses can occur primarily due to guest walks. This collection system works best in quick-service and cafeteria settings where a guest does not actually receive his or her food or beverage until the bill has been paid. It works less well in a busy table service restaurant where a cashier may simply be too preoccupied to notice whether each individual who has consumed a product has indeed paid the bill before leaving. Only a few guests are dishonest, but these few will account for some walked checks in this collection system. In addition, under this system, cashiers could collect guest payments, void records of the payments, and claim guests had walked their bills.

GUEST PAYS AT THE TABLE

In this system, servers present guest bills and collect payment at the guests' tables. Wireless technology is utilized to directly connect handheld payment acceptance devices with the operation's POS system. This increasingly popular payment system is often favored by guests using bank cards to pay their bills because it is fast and because with this approach the guest's payment card is never out of the guest's sight during the payment process. As a result, the chance for a foodservice employee to defraud the customer through **credit card skimming** is greatly reduced. Skimming is the theft of credit card information used in an otherwise legitimate transaction. It is typically done by a dishonest employee, such as a server or bartender, who has easy access to a guest's payment card information. In the most common case, the employee secretly records the guest's name, credit card number and the 3 or 4 digit security code number found on the back of the card. This information is later used to make unauthorized purchases on that guest's payment card.

Foodservice managers also like pay at the table systems because they are fast, accurate, and in most cases their MSP charges lower credit card processing fees when guests swipe cards and use pin numbers instead of signatures for payment authorization. This system works best in operations where a large percentage of guests pay by credit or debit card. It works less well when large numbers of customers pay with cash because in that situation, each server must carry individual cash banks needed for holding payments and for making change.

GUEST PAYS SERVICE PERSONNEL, WHO PAY CASHIER

In this situation, the server simply presents the bill to the guest and then accepts payment (payment card or cash), which is taken to the cashier for processing. Under this system, the guest's change is returned by the service personnel along with the receipt, if appropriate. An advantage of this system is that it is more difficult for guests to walk their checks because it is easier for servers to watch their own tables than it is for a cashier to observe an entire dining room. A second advantage is that the guest is not required to stand in line to pay his or her bill during a busy period. A disadvantage of the system is that guests may have to wait longer than desired to settle their bill if service personnel do not notice when they are finished with their meal. This can be the case especially when the operation is very busy.

GUEST PAYS SERVICE PERSONNEL, WHO HAVE ALREADY PAID CASHIER

This method of payment, also known as working with individual cash drawers or cash banks, is popular in some restaurants and many beverage operations. In this scenario, each server begins his or her shift with a predetermined cash bank, which either is his or her own or is issued by management. As the kitchen or bar fills guest orders, the service personnel purchase these products from the kitchen or bar and use their own bank to fund the purchase. The server will then collect final payment from the guest. In this manner, each server is responsible for the total of his or her bank only because all food and beverages were purchased at the time they were issued.

In some beverage operations, a record is made of each drink issued to an individual server. Funds equal to the sales value of those drinks are then collected from the server at the conclusion of his or her shift rather than having the bartender and server settle their cash accounts after each drink is issued because, in a very busy operation, this would require much time and effort. Using this system, where the guest pays the service personnel who have already "paid" the cashier, management has less concern regarding the cash overages or shortages of each server's bank because all products are paid for at the time they are issued (or collected at the end of the shift). It is important to note, however, that this collection system is not under direct management control. Service personnel can defraud guests, and guest checks can be walked without management's knowledge. In addition, employees may resent this system because it makes them personally responsible for guest walks, instead of the operation itself sharing some of the risk.

GUEST IS DIRECT BILLED

In some situations, guests are not billed immediately upon finishing their meal, beverages, or reception. This is often the case in hotel food and beverage operations as well as those restaurants with banquet facilities. When this is the case, credit-worthy guests are sent a bill for the value of the products they have consumed after their event is over. When this form of billing is employed, it is important that the invoice accurately reflects all guest charges. Consider, for example, the case of Faris, who agrees to provide a wedding banquet. The guest who arranged the event guarantees a count of 90 guests, but on the evening of the dinner, 100 guests actually attend. The guest should be billed for 100 if all were served, and payment by the guest should reflect that. In this manner, the principles of revenue control are still in place; that is, guest charges should equal revenue collected. Figure 11.9 is an example of a banquet event order/invoice (guest check) that Faris could use to bill customers.

■ **FIGURE 11.9** Banquet Event Order/Invoice

Faris'   Date 1/1

Banquet Event Order/Invoice

Day of Event: _____   Date of Event: _____

Time of Event: _____ to _____   Time Ready By: _____

Type of Event: _____   Location: _____

Expected Count: _____   Guaranteed Count: _____   Final Count: _____

Organization Hosting Event: _____

Organization Contact Person: _____

Organization Address: _____

Organization Telephone: _____   Fax: _____   E-mail: _____

Price: _____   Tax: _____   Service Charge: _____%

Deposit Amount: _____   Deposit Received: _____

Total Amount Due: _____   Payment Due Date: _____

Menu	Setup (Style of Room, A/V)
	Linen
Wines/Liquors	Decor/Flowers

Signature of Guest: _____   Date: _____

Signature of Manager: _____   Date: _____

Accounts receivable is the term used to refer to guest charges that have been billed to the guest but not yet collected. Too high an accounts receivable amount should be avoided because the foodservice operation has paid for the products consumed by the guest and the labor to serve the products but has not yet collected from the guests for these. In addition, collecting money after a guest has left your operation can be more difficult as time passes. For these reasons, you must be diligent in promptly collecting accounts receivable.

SPECIAL REVENUE COLLECTION SITUATIONS

In some cases, variations on the five payment systems presented can be put in place. For example, consider the drink ticket, or coupon, often sold or issued in hotel reception areas for use at cocktail receptions. These coupons should be treated as if they were cash, for, in fact, they are its equivalent. Thus, those individuals who are selling the coupons should not be the same ones as those dispensing the beverages. In addition, the collected drink coupons should equal the number of drinks served. The recording form required to verify this will vary, based on each operation's drink price policy, but such a record should be developed and used.

A second special pricing situation is the reduced-price coupon. Coupons are popular in the hospitality industry and can take a variety of forms, such as 50% off a specific purchase, "buy-one-get-one-free" promotions, or a program whereby a guest who buys a predetermined number of meals gets the next one free. In all of these cases, the coupon should be treated as its cash equivalent because, from a revenue control perspective, these coupons are like cash.

With his guest charges, including taxes and service charges, reconciled to sales receipts, Faris now moves to Step 4 of the revenue security process.

■ STEP 4. VERIFICATION OF SALES DEPOSITS

It is strongly recommended that only management make the actual bank deposit of daily sales revenue. A cashier or other clerical assistant may complete the deposit slip, but management alone should bear the responsibility for monitoring the actual deposit of sales. This concept can be summarized as follows: *Management must personally verify all bank deposits.*

This involves the actual verification of the contents of the deposit and the process of matching bank deposits with actual sales. These two numbers obviously should match. That is, if you deposit Thursday's sales on Friday, the Friday deposit should match the sales amount of Thursday. If it does not, you have experienced some loss of revenue that has occurred after your cashier has reconciled sales receipts to guest charges. **Embezzlement** is the term used to describe employee theft where the embezzler takes company funds he or she was entrusted to keep and diverts them to personal use. Embezzlement is a crime that often goes undetected for long periods of time because many times the embezzler is a trusted employee. Falsification of, or destroying, bank deposits is a common method of embezzlement. To prevent this activity, you should take the following steps to protect your deposits:

1. Make bank deposits of cash and checks daily if possible.

2. Ensure that the person preparing the deposit is not the one making the deposit—unless you or the manager do both tasks. Also, ensure that the individual making the daily deposit is bonded.

3. Establish written policies for completing *bank reconciliations*, the regularly scheduled comparison of the business's deposit records with the bank's acceptance records. Payment card funds transfers to a business's bank account should be reconciled each time they occur. Increasingly, cash and payment card reconciliations can be accomplished on a daily basis via the use of online banking features.

4. Review and approve written bank statement reconciliations at least once each month.

5. Change combinations on safes periodically and share the combinations with the fewest employees possible.

6. Require that all cash handling employees take regular and uninterrupted vacations on a regular basis so that another employee can assume and uncover any improper practices.

7. Employ an outside auditor to examine the accuracy of deposits on an annual basis.

If verification of sales deposits is done correctly and no embezzlement is occurring, the following formula should hold true:

$$\text{Sales Receipts} = \text{Sales Deposits}$$

■ STEP 5. VERIFICATION OF ACCOUNTS PAYABLE

Accounts payable, as defined in this step, refers to the legitimate amount owed to a vendor for the purchase of products or services. The basic principle to be followed when verifying accounts payable is: *The individual authorizing the purchase should verify the legitimacy of the vendor's invoice before it is paid.*

Vendor payments are an often overlooked potential threat to the security of a restaurant's revenue. Of course, a restaurant should pay all of its valid expenses. However, both external vendors and the restaurant's employees can attempt to defraud a foodservice operation through the manipulation of invoices.

For example, consider again the case of Faris. One day, he receives an invoice for fluorescent light bulbs. The invoice is for over $400 dollars, yet the invoice lists only two dozen bulbs as having been delivered. This is clearly a large overcharge. Faris is not familiar with this specific vendor, but the delivery slip included with the invoice was, in fact, signed (six weeks ago) by his receiving clerk. Quite likely, in this case, Faris and his operation are the victims of a bogus invoice scam by the vendor and that scam threatens his facility's revenue.

Businesses, churches, and fraternal and charitable organizations are routinely targeted for invoice payment scams. The typical supplier scam involves goods or services that you would routinely order. These include items such as copier paper, toner and maintenance supplies, equipment maintenance contracts, or classified advertising. Dishonest suppliers can take advantage of weaknesses in an organization's purchasing procedures or of unsuspecting employees who may not be aware of their fraudulent practices. In addition, the supplies delivered by these bogus firms are most often highly overpriced and of poor quality.

In a revenue system that is working properly, the following formula should be in effect:

$$\text{Sales Deposits} = \text{Funds Available for Accounts Payable}$$

Funds available for accounts payable should, of course, only be used to pay legitimate expenses that result from a purchase that can be verified by authorized personnel within the hospitality operation.

AVOIDING VENDOR SCAMS

You can protect your revenue from vendors who would attempt to defraud you. Here are steps you can take:

1. **Know your rights.** If you receive supplies or bills for services you didn't order, don't pay, and don't return the unordered merchandise. You may treat unordered merchandise as a gift.

2. **Assign designated buyers and utilize purchase orders at all times.** For each legitimate order, the designated employee should issue a purchase order, electronic or written, to the supplier with an authorized signature and a purchase order number.

3. **Check the documentation before paying bills.** When merchandise arrives, the receiving employee should verify that it matches the buyer's purchase order, paying special attention to the vendor's invoice price, brands, and quantity. If everything is in order, the employee should send a copy of the delivery invoice to the individual or department responsible for accounts payable.

4. **Train your staff.** Train everyone in the restaurant who may answer the telephone how to respond to telemarketers. Advise employees who are not authorized to order supplies and services to say, "I'm not authorized to place orders. If you want to sell us something, you must speak to the person who is authorized."

Finally, to help reduce revenue loss due to unscrupulous suppliers and unwitting employees, buy only from vendors you know and trust. Employees who are authorized to buy should be skeptical of unsolicited telephone or in-person sales calls and should be made to feel comfortable saying "No!" to high-pressure sales tactics.

THE COMPLETE REVENUE SECURITY SYSTEM

If he follows the steps outlined in the preceding pages, Faris will have now completed the development of his revenue security system. Its five key principles are as follows:

1. No product shall be issued from the kitchen or bar unless a permanent record of the issue is made.
2. Product issues must equal guest charges.
3. Both the cashier and a member of management must verify sales receipts.
4. Management must personally verify all bank deposits.
5. Management or the individual authorizing the purchase should verify the legitimacy of the vendor's invoice before it is paid.

It is possible to develop and maintain a completely manual revenue control system. That is, each of the five major components of the revenue control system described in this chapter could be instituted without the aid of a computer or even a cash register. In today's world, however, such an approach is both wasteful of time and suspect in accuracy. The simple fact is that the amount of information you need to effectively operate your business grows constantly. Guest dining choices, vendor pricing, inventory levels, payroll statistics, and revenue control are simply a few of the issues involving the huge amount of data collection and manipulation your business demands.

Fortunately, inexpensive POS systems that can help you easily and quickly assemble the data you need to make good management decisions are readily available. It is dangerous, however, for a foodservice manager to expect that a POS system will "bring" control to an operation. That happens rarely! A POS system will, however, take good control systems that have been carefully designed by management and add to them in terms of speed, accuracy, or additional information. If you hope to improve your revenue security or any other cost control system in the operation, your POS system will be of immense value. If, however, your operation has no controls and you are not committed to the control process, your POS will simply become a high-tech adding machine, used primarily to sum guest purchases and nothing more. Properly selected and utilized, however, POS systems play a crucial role in the implementation of a complete revenue security system.

Green and Growing!

In most foodservice operations, the use of sophisticated information technology (IT) systems continues to grow. Operators can purchase POS systems designed to gather and analyze more operational and customer-related data than ever before.

These same POS systems provide an excellent example of how companies seeking to reduce energy consumption and become more environmentally responsible can do so in every area of their operations. Considering the purchase of a "green" POS system means choosing energy-efficient systems designed for upgradability, expandability, and long life. By using energy-efficient POS equipment for longer periods of time, operating costs are reduced and landfill waste lessened. Green-oriented operators can also insist that POS system manufacturers do their part by utilizing sustainable shipment packaging materials. For example, by switching from Styrofoam packaging to recycled and reusable paper packaging, the average packaging footprint can be reduced by an estimated 50 percent.

Some recently introduced POS solutions consume less energy than a standard 100-watt light bulb! Efficiency advancements such as these help operators save money from high energy costs, while also helping to relieve the stress of excess energy consumption on the environment. When foodservice operators "grow green" by purchasing refurbished computer equipment for use in their cost and revenue control systems, they may be able to save even more money. Both of these approaches to POS system implementation (choosing new or refurbished equipment) allow operators to aggressively pursue their profit goals in an environmentally friendly fashion.

Technology Tools

In this chapter, the principles of revenue control were introduced. In years past, the manual counting of money and balancing of cashier drawers was time consuming and, in most cases, very tedious. With the advent of credit and debit card sales, the process has become easier, but its importance has not diminished. Protecting sales revenue from external and internal threats of theft requires diligence and attention to detail. The POS software and specialized hardware now on the market that can help in this area includes those that:

1. Maintain daily cash balances from all sources, including those of multiunit and international operations.
2. Reconcile inventory reductions with product issues from kitchen.
3. Reconcile product issues from kitchen with guest check totals.
4. Reconcile guest check totals with revenue totals.
5. Create over and short computations by server, shift, and day.
6. Balance daily bank deposits with daily sales revenue and identify variances.
7. Maintain database of returned checks.
8. Maintain accounts receivable records.
9. Maintain accounts payable records.
10. Maintain records related to the sale and redemption of gift cards.
11. Interface back office accounting systems with data compiled by the operation's POS system.
12. Interface budgeting software with revenue generation software.
13. Create income statements, statements of cash flows, and balance sheets.

It is important to note that interfacing (electronically connecting) the various software programs you select is very helpful. For example, a program that forecasts sales revenue and also supplies that data to the software program you are using to schedule labor hours needed will be more effective and helpful to you than one that does not directly connect to the scheduling feature. In a similar manner, a software program that compares sales recorded on the POS with daily bank deposits is preferable to one that does not connect these two independent but correlated functions.

Apply What You Have Learned

Donald Wright worked for 15 years as a snack bar cashier for the Sports Arena managed by Stanley Harper's company. Donald had twice won the company's "Employee of the Year" award, and Stanley considered Donald a valued and trusted employee who had, on many occasions, performed above and beyond the call of duty.

Stanley was surprised when newly installed video surveillance equipment confirmed that Donald, despite rules against it, had, on several occasions, given free food and beverages to friends of his who had visited the arena.

On the advice of the company's human resources representative, Stanley is documenting, in writing, his decision on handling the situation.

1. Assume you are Stanley, and draft a letter to Donald indicating the consequences of his actions.

2. Do you believe an employee caught defrauding his/her employer should ever be given a second chance? If so, under what circumstances?

3. What impact will Stanley's decision in this case have if, in the future, other employees are caught stealing?

Key Terms and Concepts

The following are terms and concepts discussed in the chapter that are important for you as a manager. To help you review, please define the terms below:

Walk, or skip, (the bill)

Quick-change artist

Nonsufficient funds (NSF)

Counterfeit money

Credit cards

Travel and Entertainment (T&E) cards

Debit cards

Interface

Merchant service provider (MSP)

Electronic funds
transfer (EFT)

Guest check

Precheck/postcheck
system

User work station

Open check

Short

Over

Bonding

Collusion

Credit card skimming

Accounts receivable

Embezzlement

Bank reconciliation

Accounts payable

Test Your Skills

Complete the Test Your Skills exercises by placing your answers in the shaded boxes and answering the questions as indicated.

1. Trisha Sangus manages a large hotel. Recently, her hotel controller identified a problem in one of the hotel dining rooms. Essentially, one of the evening cashiers was voiding product sales after they had been rung up on the POS, and then removing an equal amount of money from the cash drawer so that the drawer balanced at the end of the shift. What procedures would you recommend to Trisha to prevent a further occurrence of this type of incident? Assume that a precheck/postcheck guest check system is in place.

2. Counterfeit money is a problem for all U.S. businesses, including those in the hospitality industry. The U.S. Department of Treasury has developed educational aids to assist managers who must train those who handle cash. To do so, they have compiled information that is critical in the detection of imitation currency and coins.

   Go to this U.S. Secret Service site to learn about how to detect counterfeit money: **www.treas.gov/usss.** Under "Investigations" click "Know Your Money," and then click "How to Detect Counterfeit Money" to learn more about this threat to revenue security. When you are done, prepare a training session appropriate for cashiers who may routinely be responsible for the detection of counterfeit money. Include a memo to your cashiers detailing what they should actually do if they suspect a bill is counterfeit.

3. Mary Margaret and Blue are the owners/operators of an extremely upscale bakery goods boutique, and they are interested in a complete asset control system that includes protection of both products and revenue. Identify two control devices/procedures that they could implement to help them control revenue security in the following areas, and explain your reason for choosing each.

   a. Product issues

   b. Guest charges

   c. Sales receipts

   d. Sales deposits

   e. Accounts payable

4. Each of the following payment methods allows for potential employee and/or guest theft. Assume that Debbie operates a semiprivate country club where club members and the general public may purchase products in a variety of settings. Specify at least two potential methods of theft for each of the following, as well as a description of the specific procedures Debbie should implement to prevent such theft.

   a. Guest pays cashier

   b. Guest pays at table

   b. Guest pays service personnel, who pay cashier

   c. Guest pays service personnel, who have already paid cashier

   d. Guest is direct billed

   Which system would you favor using?

5. Denise Cronin operates a quick-service sandwich restaurant in a busy section of a major downtown area. Last week, the POS system in Denise's operation reported the following guest charges, and Denise, upon verifying cash on hand at the end of each day, generated the following sales receipts. Determine Denise's daily and weekly overage and shortage amounts.

   Does Denise have a cash control problem? How often in a day do you believe Denise should balance her sales receipts with her guest charges? Why?

Day	Sales Receipts	Guest Charges	Over/(Short)
Monday	$3,587.74	$3,585.28	
Tuesday	$3,682.22	$3,693.35	
Wednesday	$3,120.35	$3,110.54	
Thursday	$2,985.01	$3,006.27	
Friday	$4,978.80	$4,981.50	
Saturday	$6,587.03	$6,588.82	
Sunday	$1,733.57	$1,737.93	
Total			

6. Allison Holmes has just been promoted to the job of Regional Beverage Manager at Appleboy's Restaurants. Her district includes six successful units. In one unit, Allison suspects that Ron, the restaurant manager, and Tony, the bar manager, have collaborated to defraud their restaurant by serving cash-paying guests at the bar, not ringing up the sales, and then splitting the revenue collected from those guests.

   Since the unit's cash drawers are always in balance, no one has previously investigated the possibility of employee theft in this unit. What are some indications of such fraudulent activity that would lend support to Allison's suspicions? How would you suggest Allison find out if she is actually correct?

7. Kathy, the general manager, was shocked to discover that the thief in her successful seafood restaurant was Dan, her own dining room supervisor. Dan had used his detailed knowledge of weaknesses in the POS data monitoring system Kathy had designed to void legitimate sales after the fact and thus defraud the restaurant out of an average of $800.00 in revenue per day, every day, for the past six months. When finally confronted, Dan confessed to the thefts, citing a gambling problem as the reason for his actions.

   The information below details Kathy's reported revenue, food cost, labor cost, other costs, and profit for the past 180 days. Calculate the potential financial performance in dollars and percentages her restaurant would have achieved had it not been for Dan's actions. (Spreadsheet hint: Food Cost, Labor Cost, and Other Costs will be the same for Actual $ and Potential $.)

Kathy's Restaurant Performance

Revenue Stolen				
	Actual %	Actual $	Potential $	Potential %
Revenue	100.0%	1,566,000		
Food Cost	37.0%			
Labor Cost	29.0%			
Other Costs	26.5%			
Profit	7.5%			

   a. How much profit in dollars did Kathy lose because of Dan's fraudulent activities (difference between potential and actual)?

   b. How much profit percent did Kathy lose because of Dan's fraudulent activities (difference between potential and actual)?

   c. List three things that Kathy could have done to minimize the potential for Dan's illegal activity.

8. Sometimes it can be difficult to determine whether errors made in the payment of an operation's bills (when they are uncovered by an audit) represent intentional fraud or simply are mistakes resulting from an employee's poor training or lack of knowledge. Assume an audit uncovered duplicate invoice payments made to three different food vendors. The payments were made to them by the individual in your operation who is responsible for accounts payable. What specific action would you take to determine whether the individual's mistakes were intentional or simply exposed other weaknesses in your accounts payable system?

Chapter 12

GLOBAL DIMENSIONS OF COST CONTROL

OVERVIEW

Tasty food sold at a fair price is appreciated by consumers all around the world. Today, people in many countries enjoy the local consumption of "globally popular" menu items produced and sold by successful international hospitality companies. If you work in the area of food and beverage cost control, the challenges of multinational operations are many. In this chapter you will learn how professionals responsible for controlling and analyzing food and beverage costs can effectively manage their businesses, regardless of the number of countries in which they operate.

Chapter Outline

- Multinational Foodservice Operations
- Managing in a Global Economy
- Cost Control Challenges in Global Operations
- The Final Word
- Apply What You Have Learned
- Key Terms and Concepts
- Test Your Skills

LEARNING OUTCOMES

At the conclusion of this chapter, you will be able to:

- Recognize the increasingly important role international expansion plays on the growth of foodservice companies.
- Identify important challenges faced by all foodservice professionals who are responsible for managing their company's international business operations.
- Determine how operational, cultural, financial, and technological challenges can affect the cost control–related activities of international foodservice managers.

MULTINATIONAL FOODSERVICE OPERATIONS

*F*or those professionals working in the restaurant business, the global expansion of their industry really should come as no surprise. Travel, tourism, and the sampling of international cuisines have historically been integral parts of the hospitality industry. As cooking methods and menu items that are very popular in one culture are introduced to another culture, it is not surprising that their popularity often expands. Examples in the foodservice industry are many. Perhaps two of the best known U.S. examples are Coca Cola, the Atlanta, Georgia–based soft drink company, and the QSR (quick-service restaurant) franchisor and restaurant operator McDonald's, headquartered in Oak Brook, Illinois.

Founded in 1886, Coca Cola is the world's leading manufacturer, marketer, and distributor of nonalcoholic beverage concentrates and syrups. In 1906, Coca Cola opened its first international bottling plants in Canada, Cuba, and Panama. Today, Coca Cola sells more than 400 brand-name products in over 200 countries. In fact, over 70% of the company's income is now generated outside of the United States.

Ray Kroc opened the first McDonald's restaurant in Des Plaines, Illinois in 1955. Today, McDonald's restaurants are operated in over 115 countries worldwide and serve more than 50 million customers per day. McDonald's operates or franchises more than 13,500 restaurants in the United States and nearly twice that many more outside the United States.

Although Coca-Cola and McDonald's are among the best known, many other foodservice companies now operate in the international market and the number doing so increases each year. Burger King, Wendy's, Hilton, Dave and Busters, Hooters, T.G.I. Friday's, Mrs. Fields, Dunkin Donuts, Baskin Robbins, Pizza Hut, Marriott, Taco Bell, Aramark, TCBY, and Rainforest Cafe are just a few examples of the increasingly large number of U.S.-based restaurant companies expanding internationally. Increasingly, those foodservice professionals working in hotels and contract foodservices are being given assignments in their companies' expanding international divisions.

MANAGING IN A GLOBAL ECONOMY

*E*xperienced restaurateurs know that it is difficult to ensure consistency of menu item preparation, cost control, and profitability when operating multiple restaurants within the United States. The issues associated with ensuring consistency in these areas are often greatly increased for those companies and managers operating restaurants (many of which may be located thousands of miles from the corporation's home office) in foreign countries. Regardless of the difficulties involved, however, most companies want to exercise a specific level of control over their international operations. The control may be quite significant or it may be advisory in nature only. Despite variations in the control-related goals of an international business, one or more of its employees will be given the responsibility of monitoring and (usually) expanding the international aspect of the business.

If your career in the hospitality industry lasts for very many years, it is highly likely that, at some point, you will work with (or start!) a company that does business internationally. As a professional in the hospitality industry, there are a variety of reasons why you might be assigned the responsibility of controlling and monitoring costs in one or more of your company's international operations. These include the following:

- Your education and past work history give you the experience you need to succeed in the job.
- No local staff (in the foreign country) is currently qualified to assume the responsibility.
- Your responsibilities include the training of local staff.
- Local persons are being trained for positions and will ultimately replace you, but they are not yet qualified to assume 100% responsibility.
- Your employer wants to instill a global perspective in you (and other managers).
- It is in the company's best long-term interest to improve the cultural understanding between managers and employees in the company's various international components.
- An international assignment is considered an integral part of your professional development process.
- There is an interest in obtaining tighter administrative control over a foreign division or addressing and correcting a significant problem.
- There are property start-up, operating, or other issues that require long-term onsite management direction to properly address the issues.

Regardless of the reason for your international assignment, you are likely to face unfamiliar situations on a variety of fronts. Experienced **expatriate** (a citizen of one country who is working in another country) managers and those whose offices are located in their home country but who travel extensively to their foreign assignments report that they sometimes confront issues in one or more of the following areas:

- Language
- Local Government Entities
- Facilities
- Employees
- Suppliers

■ LANGUAGE

Despite the fact that they may know how to speak a foreign language fairly well, many U.S. managers still report that difficulty in translation can result in problems in other areas of the foodservice operation. Although English is widely spoken in many parts of the world, in many cases it will not be the primary language of a restaurant's employees, and thus expatriate managers must be sensitive to the variety of issues language barriers and the direct translation of languages may present.

An excellent example of this can be found in the "Finger Lickin' Good" slogan that was made popular in the United States by Kentucky Fried Chicken. The slogan works well in English, but in Chinese its direct translation is "Eat Your Fingers Off!" Other instances of misunderstanding abound and virtually every manager working in the international arena can relate one or more instances of a language misunderstanding and the resulting humorous (or very serious) difficulty.

■ LOCAL GOVERNMENT ENTITIES

Americans (as well as those from other countries) are justly proud of their form of government, but it does not follow that the rest of the world will duplicate the American form of government. As a result, the democratic style of open government that has shaped the understanding of many foodservice managers may simply not be present in some foreign countries. Routine items such as operating permits and permissions to do business may be slower in coming than in the United States. As well, local customs may dictate that money, paid directly or indirectly to governmental officials, accompany the granting of these permissions.

■ FACILITIES

In many cases, a restaurant's popularity is tied closely to the type of equipment or facility it requires for the production of its most popular menu items. When these key facility-related objects are missing, because repair service or spare parts are not readily available, the results can be disastrous. For example, imagine a McDonald's with a fryer that needs to be repaired, a Dairy Queen with a malfunctioning "Blizzard" machine, or a Rain Forest Café with a defective sound system. You can easily see how the character (and popularity) of those restaurants would be significantly and negatively altered if one or more critical pieces of equipment were unavailable for a significant amount of time.

In many cases, foodservice operators will find it more difficult to build, service, and maintain their physical facilities in foreign countries. This is especially true if the company has not identified a dependable, cost-effective, and local service representative for the building they occupy or the major equipment they utilize.

FUN ON THE WEB!

Finding reliable service and repair for foodservice equipment is always an issue. This is even truer for those operators whose restaurants are located in less populated areas of the world or in areas where service is hard to obtain. Fortunately, some quality companies do offer virtually "worldwide" sales and service. To view one such company, go to **www.hobartcorp.com.** Click "Service," then click "Locations," and then click "Outside the U.S." to view a list of the international sales and service centers maintained by this foodservice equipment and consulting company.

■ EMPLOYEES

The local labor force that is available to international managers can vary greatly from one area of the world to another. In addition, the expectations management may have for its workers and the expectations these workers have for management can also differ widely. These differences can take on a variety of forms. For example, Figure 12.1 details the amount of paid vacation earned by employees (who have worked at least one year) in several different countries in which U.S. companies typically do business.

The quality of available training and the sheer availability of qualified numbers of employees are other potentially problematic issues in many areas of the world. In addition, employee attitudes toward gender equality, appropriate dress, work ethic, religious tolerance, and the rights of minorities are all areas that may present significant trials to you as an international foodservice manager seeking to design and implement a successful cost control program.

■ SUPPLIERS

The actual operation of an international foodservice unit can be challenging for a variety of reasons. Among these is the potential unreliability of the unit's food supply chain. A dependable **supply chain** is essential. If, for example, a restaurant specializes in a menu item that utilizes sour cream, a safe and dependable source for this dairy product will need to be available locally. Alternatively, if a restaurant is dependent upon a unique product that is prepared in another location, frozen, and then shipped to the unit, a dependable refrigerated storage and delivery company will likely be of critical importance if a high level of food quality is to be maintained.

COST CONTROL CHALLENGES IN GLOBAL OPERATIONS

*W*ith the number of potential difficulties confronting global restaurant operators, it is not surprising that complex issues directly related to food and beverage cost control are also frequently encountered. To quote one experienced foodservice professional, when it comes to managing costs in the international arena, "It's not as easy as it looks, and it doesn't look that easy!"

Because food and beverage cost control is the title and the single topic of this text, it is appropriate to examine, in detail, how the control of cost is affected by some of the global issues identified in this chapter. It is also important for you to learn how foodservice professionals operating internationally can address these

■ **FIGURE 12.1** Annual Earned Vacation Time

Country	Vacation Time Earned
Argentina	14 calendar days
Australia	No law, but 4 weeks is standard
Belgium	20 days with premium pay
Bulgaria	20 business days
Canada	At least 2 weeks, as determined by provincial law
Chile	15 days
China	0
Czech Republic	4 weeks
France	5 weeks
Germany	4 weeks
Hong Kong	7 days
Hungary	20 days
Ireland	4 weeks
Israel	14 days
Italy	Mandated vacation, length determined by employment contract
Japan	10 days paid time off
Mexico	6 days
Poland	18 days
Puerto Rico	15 days
Saudi Arabia	15 days
Singapore	7 days
South Africa	21 consecutive days
South Korea	10 days
Spain	30 days
Sweden	5 weeks
Taiwan	7 days
The Netherlands	4 weeks
Turkey	12 days
UK	EC directive (4 weeks annual leave)
Ukraine	24 calendar days
U.S.	No national requirement. Two weeks is common but not mandatory.
Venezuela	15 paid days

issues. One convenient way to view international cost control–related challenges is by categorizing them as one of the following types:

- Operational challenges
- Cultural challenges
- Financial challenges
- Technological challenges

■ OPERATIONAL CHALLENGES

Operationally, the cost control issues encountered by expatriate hospitality managers can be related to what is done, when things are done, and exactly how things are done. For example, although U.S. companies are accustomed to the **day parts** that have traditionally been defined as the breakfast, lunch, and dinner periods, in other countries the names for, and the times of, these day parts may vary significantly. The type and amounts of foods traditionally eaten during these day parts may differ considerably as well. Some operational differences you will encounter if you have an international work assignment will be minor, and the adjustments you must make will be easy; other will be more complex.

For example, most hospitality managers from the United States or Canada would not be all that surprised to learn, and adjust to the fact that, in Germany, mayonnaise is an extremely popular topping for pommes frites (French fries). These same managers, however, might find it a bit more challenging to master the fine points of efficiently producing the "McAloo Tikki Burger," The McAloo Tikki is a breaded potato & peas patty that is flavored with a special spice mix, fresh tomato slices, and onion served on a toasted bun. It is offered by McDonald's restaurants in India in deference to Hindu religious injunctions against the consumption of beef and the Muslim prohibition against the eating of pork. It is worth noting too that, in India, separate cooks and cooking areas are another local operational practice. To assure customers of their commitment to separating vegetarian from nonvegetarian menu items, green aprons and a separate production area identify those workers preparing vegetarian items, whereas red aprons are used by those workers preparing nonvegetarian items in their own production area. Some McDonald's customers in India may, like their German counterparts, enjoy mayonnaise with their fries, but the McDonald's restaurants in India serve a vegetarian version of mayonnaise made without eggs.

From operational differences to advertising/marketing issues (does a ".11 kilogramer" sound as appetizing to you as a "$^1/_4$ pounder"?), companies doing business internationally will find that, in many cases, they must adapt to local customs, traditions, and tastes. For those managers who have learned food production techniques using the **British Imperial** (U.S. Standard) measurement system of ounces, pounds, gallons, and tablespoons, converting recipes and purchasing standards to the metric system can often seem challenging. Although the British completed their official conversion to the metric system in 1995 (although interestingly, beer is still sold by the pint and speed limits must be posted in miles per hour!) the U.S. tradition of training food production workers (including managers) via the Imperial system of

■ **FIGURE 12.2** British Imperial to Metric and Metric to British Imperial Conversions*

Conversions by Volume

1 teaspoon	= 5 milliliters (ml)		
1 tablespoon	= 15 ml		
2 tablespoons	= 1 U.S. fluid ounce	= 30 ml	
$\frac{1}{4}$ cup	= 2 fluid ounces	= 60 ml	
$\frac{1}{2}$ cup	= 4 fluid ounces	= 120 ml	
1 cup	= 8 fluid ounces	= 235 ml	
1 U.S. pint	= 16 fluid ounces	= 2 cups	= 470 ml
1 U.S. quart	= 4 cups	= .946 Liters	
1 Liter	= 34 ounces	= 1.06 quarts = 4.23 cups or 4 cups plus 3 $\frac{1}{2}$ tablespoons	
1 milliliter	= .001 or 1/1000 liters		

Conversions by Weight (Mass)

1 ounce	= $\frac{1}{16}$ pound = 28.34 grams	
1 pound	= 454 grams	
1 gram	= .035 ounces	
1 kilogram	= 2.2 pounds	

*In some cases the numbers have been rounded to a whole number that can be easily measured.

weights and measures continues. Most American managers still do not regularly produce new recipes using a metric measurement system. If you were trained in food production and recipe cost calculation using the Imperial (or the metric) system, you can use the information detailed in Figure 12.2 to help you convert amounts from one system to the other.

FUN ON THE WEB!

Even when you know the Imperial-to-metric conversion ratios, it can be very time-consuming to make the conversions necessary to cost out a menu item and generate a recipe that can be used to create a quality product. Fortunately, many Web sites can be of assistance in the process. To view one impressive site that can be utilized for recipe conversions, go to **www.chefdesk.com**.

When you arrive, click "Chef's Calculators," located on the home page. As you will see, this free site provides easy-to-use tools for making quantity recipe conversions and for calculating recipe costs.

Guest preferences and food production issues are not the only operational topics of concern to multinational restaurant operators. Other important areas that can be greatly affected include:

- Marketing
- Menu planning
- Pricing
- Safety standards
- Purchasing
- Receiving
- Beverage production and service
- Equipment selection and maintenance
- Utility (natural resource) management

Green and Growing!

A commitment to "green" operations is good for business as well as for the planet. According to Pacific Gas and Electric's Food Service Technology Center, 80 percent of the $10 billion annual energy bill for the commercial foodservice sector is expended by inefficient food cooking, holding and storage equipment. Energystar, the U.S. government-operated Web site devoted to energy efficiency reports that the average foodservice operator who invests strategically can cut his or her utility costs 10 to 30 percent without sacrificing service, quality, style, or comfort. On its Web site, Energystar also points out that "the money you save on operating costs adds to what you get to keep, so saving 20% on energy operating costs can increase your profit as much as one-third."

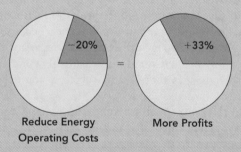

Reduce Energy   More Profits
Operating Costs

Source: www.energystar.gov

Globally, green initiatives mean more profits for foodservice companies as well as a lessened negative impact on the environment. The bottom line is clear; a commitment to sustainable operations simply makes good sense for the future of the foodservice industry and the future of the planet.

FUN ON THE WEB!

Foodservice companies operating internationally increasingly recognize that Green initiatives are important in countries all across the globe. Greenbiz.com is the Web site for the Green Business Network, a group of large and small businesses who share an interest in sustainable operations. This site will help you stay abreast of international environment-related legislation that directly affects foodservice operators. To view the site, go to **www.Greenbiz.com**.

When you arrive, enter "Restaurants" in the search field to review green initiatives taken by forward thinking leaders in the international foodservice industry, as well as legislative actions taken by governments shaping sustainability efforts in their own countries.

■ CULTURAL CHALLENGES

In addition to the large number of potentially difficult operating issues expatriate managers may encounter, there are a wide variety of cultural issues that can significantly affect your cost control efforts in an international setting. For expatriate managers to be successful, it is critical that they understand the culture of the country in which they are working. **Culture** can be defined as the customary beliefs, social forms, and characteristic traits of a racial, religious, or social group. The local culture must be not only understood but respected as well.

Some cultural issues may require expatriate managers to reexamine their personal views of fairness and even morality. For example, assume that you, as a restaurant manager in a foreign country, pay wages that are considered to be very good in that country but that are significantly less (in U.S. dollars paid per hour) than those granted to workers in the United States who are doing the same job. Some observers would say your restaurant is providing valuable local jobs at fair wages; others might accuse your company of injustice because of the disparity in wage rates paid. Add to this challenge the fact that, in many cultures, it is traditional to pay men more than women for doing identical work and you can easily see the type of cultural challenges that you may face if you accept an international work assignment.

It is beyond the scope of this text to address and comment on all of the issues of wage equality, gender inequity, and business variations due to culture that may be experienced by expatriate managers. It is important for all U.S. managers to remember, however, that "our" way is rarely the "only" way to operate. Those expatriate managers who succeed best do so by demonstrating the real respect and understanding for local culture that is most often missing in less successful international managers.

Cultural clashes can occur between a restaurant's managers and its workers, but they also can and do frequently occur between employee groups within the operation who do not share identical cultures. Similar to employee groups in the United States, employee groups in restaurants operated internationally may not be of a homogeneous culture. As a manager, it will be your responsibility to ensure the smooth operation of your facilities by fairly addressing the issues that may arise between groups such as these. Serving as the leader of divergent groups is always demanding, and experienced expatriate managers know that the process can be challenging. Utilizing the following guidelines, however, can help you effectively meet those challenges.

Foster an environment that encourages open discussion. Keep lines of communication open. When employees feel comfortable discussing potential problem areas, many of these problems disappear.

Encourage interaction. It is frequently the case that those who do not know each other well do not understand each other well. Although it may sometimes seem natural for groups of similar individuals to associate primarily within their group, an important part of your job may include actively encouraging members of diverse groups to work together to better know and understand each other.

Celebrate diversity. Gene Monteagudo, former international market director for Aramark Services, was fond of the saying "We do not have to be twins to be brothers." The fact that individuals from diverse cultures may believe and behave differently can be very healthy for any organization that understands the positive synergy that can result from combining the strengths of its employees' diverse cultures.

Foster a healthy understanding of group identity. Remind workers that pride in your own group's values, attitudes, and beliefs does not mandate disrespect for the values, attitudes, and beliefs of others. In addition, make it clear that criticism of one group by members of another group is not an effective way to elevate the status of the group doing the criticizing.

Model appropriate behavior. As the manager you are also the leader and your employees will look to you to "practice what you preach." Tolerance and genuine acceptance of others must be one of your own professional characteristics, and it should be visibly displayed.

Consider The Cost

"We open our two new plants in Reynosa next year," said Bill Richardson, vice president of operations for Tech-Mar Manufacturing. "We love the work you do for us here in our U.S. operations and feel our partnership will be just as successful in Mexico."

Bill was talking to Ellen Luros, president of Luros Associates, a foodservice management company that had, for the past five years, been providing in-plant foodservices for Tech-Mar, an auto parts supplier whose client list included General Motors and Ford.

Bill had just laid out for Ellen the size and operational hours envisioned for the two new Tech-Mar manufacturing facilities to be located in Reynosa, Mexico, a city of 500,000 residents located just across the border from McAllen, Texas.

"I'm sure we will do a good job for you," replied Ellen.

"We're excited about the new manufacturing facilities we have built, and we recognize the importance to our success of a well-run and cost-effective employee meal program. It's good to have an experienced partner like you ready to help us ramp up!" said Bill.

1. Assume this is Luros Associates' first contract to operate foodservice outside the United States. What challenges will Ellen likely face as she selects the foodservice managers currently in her company who will help operate the new Mexican facilities? What challenges will she face choosing new managers?

2. What menu development and food production–related challenges do you think Ellen may encounter as her company begins operations in Reynosa? How will these affect her managers' cost control efforts?

3. Do you think Ellen and any other managers currently employed by her will encounter culture-related operational challenges in the new plants? Where would you advise her to go to learn more about how she and her managers might best address those challenges?

■ FINANCIAL CHALLENGES

To illustrate some of the ways in which the global economy affects financial reporting in the foodservice industry, consider the challenges and opportunities facing Carlos Magana. Carlos is the Southern Region Director of Operations for El Pollo Salsa, a restaurant chain with units in the United States, Caribbean, Mexico, Brazil, and other South American countries. He oversees 100 company-owned stores. One of Carlos's most important tasks is to accurately report and then analyze the financial performance of his restaurants. It is a fundamental principle of accounting that the financial results of a business should be reported in an identifiable **monetary unit.** A monetary unit is simply defined as a specific and recognized currency denomination. Typically, financial statements are prepared in the currency of the country in which the business is based. Thus, in Carlos's case, the U.S. dollar is the monetary unit used for preparing his financial statements.

At first it might appear easy to ensure that financial summaries are prepared in the currency denomination used by the company whose records are being reported, but in reality, fulfilling the monetary unit reporting principle can be quite complex. Consider that Carlos operates restaurants internationally and his restaurants' sales are reported as follows:

- Sales in his American restaurants are reported in U.S. dollars.
- Sales in his Mexican restaurants are reported in Mexican pesos.
- Sales in his Brazilian restaurants are reported in Brazilian reals.
- Sales in his Dominican Republic restaurants are reported in Dominican Republic pesos.
- Sales in his Bolivian restaurants are reported in Bolivian bolivianos.
- Sales in his Aruban restaurants are reported in Aruban florins.

The reporting of cash sales in his restaurants, although complex, is relatively straightforward. Credit, debit, and bank card sales (which constitute a large portion of many restaurants' total sales) create further complications because the company's merchant service provider (see Chapter 11) must apply an **exchange rate** (to convert the value of one currency to another) before the funds can be credited to the main El Pollo Salsa bank account. Thus, a guest's credit card payment to an El Pollo Salsa restaurant in the Dominican Republic resort area of Punta Cana will be recorded in one monetary unit (the Dominican Republic peso) and then, before an appropriate amount is deposited in the El Pollo Salsa bank account in Miami, it will be converted (by the card processor) to U.S. dollars.

It is clear that Carlos faces challenges when it comes to reporting his actual revenue and expenses (in U.S. dollars) and ensuring the accuracy of his own merchant service provider's conversion rate calculations. Fortunately for Carlos, easy access to the Internet provides him with the ability to quickly compute his own currency conversion rates (for cash sales) and to monitor (online) the currency exchange rate calculations used by his merchant service provider.

FUN ON THE WEB!

Knowing about currency exchange rates is critical to those international foodservice operators affected by fluctuations in those exchange rates. When it started in 1995, OANDA was the first to make comprehensive currency exchange information available over the Internet. Since then, OANDA rates have become the conversion standard for many corporations and tax authorities. To have some fun and see how OANDA currency conversion tables help managers compute constant currency rates, go to **www.oanda.com**.

Choose "FXConverter" when you arrive and you can access the exchange rates for 164 different currencies.

FUN ON THE WEB!

Generally, international restaurant operators are not paid in local currency but rather via payment cards that include credit, debit, bank, and entertainment cards. Many of these are issued internationally. Because of the increased use of these cards, restaurants should be set up to accept virtually all of them. However, finding a merchant service provider who can do so can be difficult. To see the Web site for a European (Scotland) merchant service provider that specializes in international card processing and currency conversion, go to **www.worldpay.com**. Click "About Us" to learn more about how merchant service providers can help restaurants that accept customer payments in multiple currencies.

■ TECHNOLOGICAL CHALLENGES

As you now know, it is very important for an expatriate manager to address and understand issues related to international operations and the local cultures of those individuals actually operating the international restaurants. As a professional managing operations across the globe, however, it is important to recognize that the sphere that is changing most rapidly (and thus will demand much continued attention and analysis) is related to technology and information (data) management.

The rate of technological change experienced by global hospitality managers is not likely to lessen in the coming years. As a result, foodservice managers working anywhere in the world will continue to face technology-related challenges to cost control. These challenges will vary based upon the country or region in which a foodservice operation is located but can usually be related to one of the two following issues:

1. Choosing currently available advanced technology products
2. Monitoring developments in cost control-related technology

CHOOSING CURRENTLY AVAILABLE ADVANCED TECHNOLOGY PRODUCTS

There are large numbers of advanced technology products that directly assist those managers operating foodservice facilities in multiple countries.

It would be impossible to describe in one chapter (even briefly!) all the ways new technologies affect professional foodservice managers and the way these managers do business. Technological advances occur almost daily and thus choosing currently available products and monitoring the introduction of new ones are both important parts of every foodservice professional's job. The specific technology-related tools managers select will vary based upon their industry segment, but the issues these managers must consider when making their selections are very similar. These include:

- Cost
- Complexity
- System warrant/maintenance
- Upgrading
- Reliability

COST

Cost plays an important role in the decision of how much technology a group of facilities can afford. When it is possible to demonstrate that the technology-related purchase will pay for itself (such as in reduced labor or product cost) relatively quickly, the decision to buy can be an easy one. Often, however, it is complex to identify actual savings. It is also important to recognize that labor-saving devices in countries where labor costs are high may make good economic sense; however, the same product may not be cost-justifiable in countries where labor costs are lower. Your technology vendors can be helpful in this area, but remember that their ultimate goal is to sell their products. Remember also that technology is simply a tool to be used by you and your staff. If the cost of the tool exceeds its value to your operations it likely should not be purchased.

COMPLEXITY

Some technology systems are so advanced that their implementation and routine operation requires very high levels of skill. This skill level may be readily available in the work forces of some countries but lacking in others. A recipe conversion software package, for example, may require knowledge of both computer entry and basic cooking skills. If your staff is not sophisticated enough in all of your locations to use the technology you purchase, difficulties can arise. Fortunately, these type of difficulties can be reduced or eliminated through the implementation of thorough training programs.

SYSTEM WARRANTY/MAINTENANCE

Because technology items are machines, they need routine maintenance and can break down. When they do, it will be critical that you receive quality repair service in a timely manner and at a fair price. This can be difficult unless the technology vendor has dependable service providers in all of the countries in which their products are used. As a result, if a technology product is purchased for international implementation the warranty for the product must be carefully reviewed. Items of particular importance to you will be:

1. A listing of precisely which items are covered under the terms of the warranty
2. The length of the warranty
3. The allowable charges for repair service for nonwarranted items
4. Expected response time of the service/repair technicians

Item 4 is of particular importance to international operators. Many standard warranties specify 24-hour response time to service problems. Imagine, however, that the POS system you have installed in one of your busiest (but somewhat remote) locations goes down on a busy Friday evening. You certainly would want it repaired in less than 24 hours! In some cases, however, it is simply unrealistic to assume that international service can be obtained as rapidly as service in the technology provider's home country. In all cases, this is an issue to address before, not after, a technology-related purchase that you will be implementing across a large geographic area.

UPGRADING

It is difficult to predict what new technological developments may occur in the future, but advancements that are compatible with your current system will likely prove to be less expensive than those that require completely new software, hardware, or communication devices. Because this is so, many operators prefer to work with larger, more established technology vendors, because these organizations generally will ensure that advancements in their products are compatible with the products they already have marketed. Smaller and newer technology companies may offer some features that are desirable, but their systems may be subject to complete obsolescence if newer technology makes the old systems incompatible with newer hardware, software, or systems offered by alternative vendors.

RELIABILITY

Where reliability is concerned, there are two areas of importance. These are the reliability of the product or service and the reliability of the vendor. To help ensure that you select a product or service that is reliable, insist that your potential vendor share with you a list of current customers who can be contacted for information about the reliability of the products they have purchased. This is especially important for those international operators seeking to interface (electronically connect to share data) the equipment in their individual units with a central location or home office. Vendor reliability is also very important. There is no consideration that is more consequential when electing to integrate a new technology cross-culturally than the quality of the vendor supplying that technology.

FUN ON THE WEB!

For most restaurateurs, the selection of a POS system is a critical part of their overall cost control program. This is especially so when financial reporting compatibility across countries and languages is important. To view the Web site of Kanecal, a company that specializes in POS systems designed for use internationally, go to **www.kanecal.net**.

■ MONITORING DEVELOPMENTS IN COST CONTROL TECHNOLOGY

It is simply not possible to know about every software, hardware, or communication advance that could directly affect your international business. You can, however, stay abreast of the commercial application of these advances, and it is important that you do. Your choices for continuing education in this area are varied, but most foodservice managers can choose from one or more of the following methods:

- Trade shows/professional associations
- Publications
- Current vendors
- Competitive vendors
- Your own organization

TRADE SHOWS/PROFESSIONAL ASSOCIATIONS

As a hospitality professional, you will likely elect to join one or more **professional trade associations.** These associations typically serve the certification, educational, social, and legislative goals of their members. Such associations hold annual gatherings and invite exhibitors who sell products and services of interest to interact with their members at trade shows. These trade shows bring together a variety of vendors, all of whom are interested in exhibiting their latest product offerings. Trade shows are an extremely efficient way to see the product offerings of a large number of vendors in a very short time.

Many trade associations also have both state and local chapters, some of which will host their own trade shows. Some of the largest of these associations, as well as their Internet locations, are listed in "Fun on the Web!" below.

FUN ON THE WEB!

Visit these association sites to find out when and where they will be holding their next trade shows.

Association	Web Address
National Restaurant Association	www.restaurant.org
American Hotel and Lodging Association	www.ahla.com
American Dietetic Association	www.eatright.com
Dietary Managers Association	www.dmaonline.org
American Culinary Federation	www.acfchefs.org
Club Managers Association of America	www.cmaa.org
American School Foodservice Association	www.asfsa.org
National Association of Catering Executives	www.ienace.org
Hospitality Financial and Technology Professionals	www.hftp.org
International Hotel and Restaurant Association	www.ih-ra.com

On a local level, chambers of commerce and professional service organizations often hold meetings and schedule speakers who can update you on the newest business applications of technology. Membership in these organizations is generally well worth its modest cost.

PUBLICATIONS

Regularly reading about the hospitality industry will not only make you a better manager but also keep you abreast of the latest technological trends. In many cases, technology and its application have become such a large part of the editorial interest of these publications that a special technology editor is employed to monitor technological changes that could be of interest to the publication's readers. Some printed publications are distributed free to qualified members of the hospitality industry, whereas others are not. Many publications that are available on the Internet (and these are increasing in number yearly) require only that the reader supply a valid e-mail address.

CURRENT VENDORS

Your current supplier of software, hardware, or communications systems should be a valuable source of free information. All of these vendors will make improvements in their products because competition and the desire to grow drive their development efforts. An added advantage of working with your current technology suppliers is the fact that the new systems they develop are likely to be compatible with those systems you already have and maintain. This can reduce staff training time and the errors that sometimes come with new system implementation. In addition, your current vendors may be more competitive when pricing their new offerings because, in most cases, they would very much like to retain your current and future international business.

COMPETITIVE VENDORS

Your current vendors can certainly inform you of their own efforts, but competition in the area of cost control–related products and services is robust and getting stronger. Whether your interest is software, hardware, or communications, identifying your current vendor's strongest and best competitors is a good way to monitor advances in technology. At minimum, annual visits, either in person or by telephone, can help you quickly identify improvements in procedures and features that your own vendor may have overlooked or dismissed. Don't hesitate to contact small vendors you may see advertised in publications or exhibiting at trade shows. Often, these start-up companies offer the most innovative and cutting-edge programs available. Conversely, their small size may limit their ability to adequately service your account. In any case, they can be a source of tremendous information and are well worth monitoring.

YOUR OWN ORGANIZATION

For those managers employed by an international or national chain or a large company, the parent organization can be an excellent source for information about changing management tools. Often, large international companies will produce newsletters, conduct in-service training, or hold regularly scheduled conventions that can be a source of information on changing technology. All of these resources should be monitored and utilized if they are available to you. As a wise professional, you know that you must continually be aware of changes in technology and committed to implementing the best and most cost effective of these changes so that your business and your career will continue to flourish. Advances in technological capabilities will continue to change the world and the hospitality industry as well. When these advances help you to better manage your business, you, your employees, and, most important, your guests are all beneficiaries.

THE FINAL WORD

The control of costs is critically important to a successful business. In this book you have learned about many of the cost control principles and practices you will utilize throughout your career. It is important to recognize, however, that truly effective managers are careful to pay as much attention to their customers (an external focus) as they do to their own operations (an internal focus). These managers know that it is a mistake to confuse cost efficiency with business effectiveness. The difference is clear and can be illustrated by a simple example. Consider the foodservice operator who built a successful restaurant chain based upon the popularity of a single menu item. Through hard work, conscientious cost control, and superior managerial skills, the company enjoyed great success. Its customers' tastes, however, began to change. As a result fewer and fewer came to this company's restaurants. In response, the company increased its cost control efforts, becoming extremely efficient (cost effective) at providing the original menu item. Unfortunately, the number of customers served by the company continued to decline. The problem, of course, was that this company became even better at doing the wrong thing!

The best cost control managers know that their businesses will survive only if they carefully consider what their customers want to buy now and what they will want to buy in the future. Cost-effectively doing what your customers do not care about is a sure sign of a business that will not long be in business. Experience shows that a company's excessive focus on the internal cost of operations can sometimes lead directly to an unwarranted focus on cost containment. More often than not, this is then followed by excessive cost cutting and a negative impact on its customers' perceptions of value received for prices paid. As a talented cost control professional, you can readily recognize there is only so much expense that can be cut and controlled before a hospitality business runs the risk of compromising product or service quality. Successful cost control professionals never compromise either product or service quality. To be truly successful, it is important for you to understand that you have two primary tasks. These are the professional implementation of effective cost control procedures a continual focus on your customers. You have mastered the material in this book, and you are now well prepared to accomplish both of these tasks! Best wishes from the authors in all you do!

Apply What You Have Learned

Beyonce Powers is director of North American operations for ARADEXO, a U.S.-based foodservice management company that has just secured the contract to provide foodservices for the 2014 Winter Olympic Games to be held in Sochi, Russia. As the leading foodservice provider at the games, ARADEXO will serve more than 3.5 million meals over a two-month period (which includes not only the Olympics but also the Paralympic Games) in the Olympic Village. At the peak, the company will serve over 100,000 meals per day. Beyonce has been placed in charge of coordinating her company's Olympic efforts. A big challenge will be finding enough skilled workers to do all the cooking because ARADEXO will need 6,000 kitchen staff members to prepare all the different types of foods it will be required to serve.

Bess Haley, Beyonce's boss and the CEO of ARADEXO, has instructed Beyonce to ensure that the company makes the most of this important opportunity. As Bess put it, "I want the world to see how well we can perform, but at the same time I want to make sure we make this a profitable venture. I know you can do both!"

1. Of the management issues in a global economy presented in this chapter, which do you feel will be experienced by Beyonce as she leads her company's Olympic feeding efforts?

2. Of the four cost control–related challenges presented in this chapter, which do you feel will be the most critical challenge Beyonce will face? Why?

3. Assume you are Beyonce. How important would it be for you to physically attend the 2014 Olympic Games? Explain your answer.

Key Terms and Concepts

The following are terms and concepts discussed in the chapter that are important for you as a manager. To help you review, please define the terms below:

Expatriate
Supply chain
Day parts

British Imperial
  (measurement system)
Culture
Monetary unit

Exchange rate
Professional trade
  association

Test Your Skills

Complete the Test Your Skills exercises by answering the questions as indicated.

1. Assume that you were an expatriate food and beverage manager for an international hotel company that operated a 5-Star resort in a nation with a very modest standard of living. How would you respond to local newspaper criticism that your company was creating more damage to the area's environment than it was contributing positively to the local economy?

2. One of the most significant changes in the American hospitality industry in the past two decades has been the introduction of the drive-through window in the quick-service restaurant (QSR) segment. Analyze this development in terms of its dependence on the automobile. Do you think the drive-thru feature will be important in all countries in which these QSR operate? Defend your answer.

3. Increasingly, American companies are using advances in technology, such as monitors and surveillance cameras, to both observe and reduce employee theft and to help ensure the safety and security of their assets. Placement of these devices in food and beverage storage, production, and, in some cases, service areas has become commonplace. Assume that in your company you are responsible for maintaining such surveillance systems in all of your U.S. and international operations. How would you respond to a European guest who protested to you that he or she resented being videotaped while dining?

4. Advances in technology are often associated with improvements in production-related cost control issues, such as food and beverage preparation, purchasing, storage, and inventory. Technological advances, however, also influence human resource management. Identify three ways you believe technology advancements will influence how individuals across the globe will seek jobs and how employers will find them.

5. As a foodservice professional, what do you feel are your responsibilities to ensure the operations you manage minimize their carbon footprints in their international operations? Would your feelings change if you operated in a country in which yours was the only company committed to green initiatives? Explain your position.

6. The restaurant industry is fortunate to have an additional resource for professional development that exists in only a few other industries. It is called the National Restaurant Association Educational Foundation, and it offers a variety of continuing education opportunities. Its products and services can be accessed at **www.nraef.org**. Visit the site, and then identify at least five programs they offer that could help international foodservice operators better control their costs and increase their profitability.

7. Many organizations implement green initiatives because of the potential for increased profitability that will ultimately be measured on their P&L statements. Would you implement a worthwhile green initiative that you knew would *not* increase profits but rather would unquestionably reduce them? What specific factors would influence your decision to undertake an initiative of this type?

8. In some countries, the culture is very different from that of an expatriate manager's home culture. The impact of such differences can vary among managers. For example, assume you were offered a foodservice cost control–related position in a country whose culture reflected very significant differences in the rights afforded to women and men. How would you personally determine if such an assignment were right for you?

GLOSSARY

Acceptance hours. The hours of the day in which an operation is willing to accept food and beverage deliveries.

Accounting period. A period of time, that is, hour, day, week, or month, in which an operator wishes to analyze revenue and expenses.

Accounts payable. The legitimate amount owed to a vendor for the purchase of products or services.

Accounts receivable. The term used to refer to guest charges that have been billed to the guest but not yet collected.

Achievement budget. A forecast or estimate of projected revenue, expense, and profit for a period of a month or a week. It provides current operating information and, thus, assists in making current operational decisions.

Aggregate statement. Summary of all details associated with the sales, costs, and profits of a foodservice establishment.

Alcoholic beverages. Those products that are meant for consumption as a beverage and that contain a significant amount of ethyl alcohol. They are classified as beer, wine, or spirits.

Annual budget. A forecast or estimate of projected revenue, expense, and profit for a period of one year.

AP. See As purchased.

AP weight required. As-purchased amount necessary to yield the desired EP weight. AP required is computed as EP required divided by yield percentage.

As needed. A system of determining the purchase point by using sales forecasts and standardized recipes to decide how much of an item to place in inventory so that no more than the absolute minimum of needed inventory level is secured from the vendor.

As purchased (AP). This term refers to the weight or count of a product as delivered to the foodservice operator.

Attainable product cost. That cost of goods sold figure that should be achievable given the product sales mix of a particular operation.

Auditors. Those individuals responsible for reviewing and evaluating proper operational procedures.

Average. The value arrived at by adding the quantities in a series and dividing the sum of the quantities by the number of items in the series. Often referred to as mean.

Average sales per guest. The mean amount of money spent per customer during a given financial accounting period. Often referred to as check average.

Back of the house. The kitchen production area of a foodservice establishment.

Bank reconciliation. The regularly scheduled comparison of the business's deposit records with the bank's acceptance records.

Beer. A fermented beverage made from grain and flavored with hops.

Beginning inventory. The dollar value of all products on hand at the beginning of the accounting period. This amount is determined by completing a physical inventory.

Best price. The lowest price that meets the requirements of both the foodservice operation and its vendor.

Beverage costs. The costs related to the sale of alcoholic beverages.

Bid sheet. A form used to compare prices among many vendors in order to select the best prices.

Bin card. An index card (or line on a spreadsheet) that details additions to and deletions from given product's inventory level.

Blood alcohol content (BAC). A measure of the level of alcohol existing in the blood of a person who has been drinking alcoholic beverages. Each state sets its own allowable limit of BAC for establishing intoxication of motor vehicle drivers.

Bonding. Purchasing an insurance policy to protect the operation in case of employee theft.

Bookkeeping. The process of recording and summarizing financial data.

Break-even point. The point at which operational expenses are exactly equal to sales revenue.

British Imperial. (U.S. Standard) Imperial measurement system of weights and measures including ounces, pounds, gallons, tablespoons, etc.

Broken case. A case of beverage products in which several different brands or products make up the contents of the case.

Budget. A forecast or estimate of projected revenue, expense, and profit for a defined accounting period. Often referred to as plan.

Budgeted labor. Planned labor costs for a defined accounting period.

Bundling. The practice of selecting specific menu items and pricing them as a group, in such a manner that the single menu price of the group is lower than if the items in the group were purchased individually.

Business dining. Food is provided as a service to the company's employees either as a no-cost (to the employee) benefit or at a greatly reduced price.

Call-in. A system whereby employees who are off duty are required to check in with management on a daily basis to see if the predicted sales volume is such that they may be needed.

Call liquors. Those spirits that are requested (called for) by a particular brand name.

Carbon footprint. A term used to describe a measure of the impact human activities have on the environment in terms of the amount of greenhouse gases (carbon dioxide) produced.

Carryover. A menu item prepared for sale during a meal period but carried over for use in a different meal period.

Category food cost percentage. A food cost percentage computed on a portion of total food usage. Categories include meat, seafood, dairy, produce, and so on.

Check average. See Average sales per guest.

Cherry picker. A customer who buys only those items from a supplier that are the lowest in price among the supplier's competition.

COLA. See Cost of living adjustment.

Collusion. Two or more employees conspire to defraud the operation.

Comp. Short for the word complimentary, which refers to the practice of management giving a product to a guest without a charge. This can be done for a special customer or as a way of making amends for an operational error.

Contract price. A price mutually agreed upon by supplier and operator. This price is the amount to be paid for a product or products over a prescribed period of time.

Contribution margin. The profit or margin that remains after product cost is subtracted from an item's selling price.

Contribution margin for overall operation. The dollar amount that contributes to covering fixed costs and providing for a profit.

Contribution margin income statement. A financial summary that shows P&L items in terms of sales, variable costs, contribution margin, fixed costs, and profit.

Contribution margin per menu item. The amount that remains after the product cost of the menu item is subtracted from the item's selling price.

Controllable expense. An expense in which the decisions made by the foodservice manager can have the effect of either increasing or reducing the expense.

Control states. States that regulate the sale of alcoholic beverages by direct control and sale of the products by the state.

Convenience foods. Food products that are pre-prepared in some fashion. Also referred to as ready foods.

Cost. See Expense.

Cost accounting. See Managerial accounting.

Cost of food consumed. The actual dollar value of all food used, or consumed, by the operation.

Cost of food sold. The dollar amount of all food actually sold, thrown away, wasted, or stolen.

Cost of living adjustment (COLA). A term used to describe a raise in employee pay.

Cost per guest. A method of analyzing costs that uses the total expense and total number of guests served to establish an actual cost of servicing each guest.

Cost/volume/profit (CVP) analysis. Method that helps predict the sales dollars and volume required to achieve desired profit (or break-even) based on known costs.

Count. Term used to designate size. Size as established by number of items per pound or number of items per container.

Counterfeit money. An imitation of currency intended to be passed off fraudulently as real money.

Credit cards. Cards in a payment system by which banks loan money to consumers as the consumer makes purchases. The loans typically carry interest.

Credit card skimming. Theft of credit card information used in an otherwise legitimate transaction.

Credit memo. An addendum to the vendor's delivery slip (invoice) that reconciles differences between the delivery slip and the purchase order.

Culture. The customary beliefs, social norms, and characteristic traits of a racial, religious, or social group.

Cycle menu. A menu that is in effect for a predetermined length of time, such as 7 days or 14 days.

Daily inventory sheet. A form that lists the items in storage, the unit of purchase, and the par value. It also contains the following columns: on hand, special order, and order amount.

Daily menu. A menu that changes every day.

Day parts. In the United States, breakfast, lunch and dinner periods.

Debit cards. Cards in a payment system by which the funds needed to cover the user's purchase are automatically transferred from the user's bank account to the entity issuing the debit card.

Desired profit. The profit that an owner seeks to achieve on a predicted quantity of revenue.

Draft beer. The term used to identify beer products sold in a keg.

Dramshop laws. The term used to describe a series of legislative acts that, under certain conditions, holds businesses and, in some cases, individuals, personally responsible for the actions of guests who consume excessive amounts of alcoholic beverages. These "laws" shift the liability for acts committed by an individual under the influence of alcohol from that individual to the server or operation that supplied the intoxicating beverage.

Edible portion (EP). This term refers to the weight or count of a product after it has been trimmed, cooked, and portioned.

Edible portion cost (EP cost). The cost of an item after cooking, trimming, portioning, or cleaning. It represents the cost based on product yield.

Electronic funds transfer (EFT). Provides for the electronic payment and collection of money and information. EFT is safe, secure, efficient, and less expensive than paper check payments and collections.

Embezzlement. Theft by an employee who takes company funds he or she was entrusted to keep and diverts them to personal use.

Employee meals. Free or reduced-cost meals that are employee benefits and are labor-related, not food-related, costs.

Empowerment. Giving employees the power to make decisions.

Empty for full system. The bartender is required to retain empty liquor bottles, and then each empty liquor bottle is replaced with a full one at the beginning of the next shift. The empty bottles are then either broken or disposed of, as local beverage law requires.

Ending inventory. The dollar value of all products on hand at the end of the accounting period. This amount is determined by completing a physical inventory.

Environmental sustainability A variety of earth-friendly practices and policies designed to meet the needs of the present population without compromising the ability of future generations to meet their own needs.

EP. See Edible portion.

Ethics. The choices of proper conduct made by an individual in his or her relationships with others.

Exchange rate. Conversion of the value of one currency to another.

Exempt employees. Salaried employees whose duties, responsibilities, and level of decisions make them "exempt" from the overtime provisions of the federal government's Fair Labor Standards Act (FLSA). Exempt employees do not receive overtime for hours worked in excess of 40 per week and are expected by most organizations to work whatever hours are necessary to accomplish its goals.

Expatriate. A citizen of one country who is working in another country.

Expense. The price paid to obtain the items required to operate the business. Often referred to as cost.

Extended price. The price per unit multiplied by the number of units. This refers to a total unit price on a delivery slip or invoice.

FIFO. See First-in, first-out.

First-in, first-out (FIFO). Term used to describe a method of storage in which the operator intends to sell his or her oldest product before selling the most recently delivered product.

Fiscal year. Start and stop dates for a 365-day accounting period. This period need not begin in January and end in December.

Fixed average. The average amount of sales or volume over a specific series or time period; for example, first month of the year or second week of the second month.

Fixed expense. An expense that remains constant despite increases or decreases in sales volume.

Fixed payroll. Those dollars spent on employees such as managers, receiving clerks, and dietitians whose presence is not generally directly dependent on the number of guests served.

Food cost percentage. The portion of food sales that was spent on food expenses.

Food costs. The dollar costs associated with actually producing the menu item(s) a guest selects.

401(k). A retirement plan in which employees are allowed to contribute money before taxes are assessed.

Franchisor. The entity responsible for selling and maintaining control over the franchise brand's name. (Alternative spelling: franchiser.)

Free-pouring. Pouring liquor from a bottle without carefully measuring the poured amount.

Fresh-dated. A food package upon which a date is stamped to indicate the freshness of its contents.

Freezer burn Deterioration in product quality resulting from poorly wrapped or stored items at freezing tempertures.

Goal value analysis. A menu pricing and analysis system that compares goals of the foodservice operation to performance of individual menu items.

Goods available for sale. The sum of the beginning inventory and purchases. It represents the value of all food that was available for sale during the accounting period.

Gross profit section (of the USAR). First portion of the income statement (Uniform System of Accounts for Restaurants) that consists of food and beverage sales and those food and beverage related costs that can and should be controlled by the manager on a daily basis.

Guest check. A written record of what was purchased by the guest and how much the guest was charged for the item(s).

Guest count. The number of individuals served in a defined time period.

Half bottle (wine). A bottle of wine that is approximately one-half the size of the standard 750 ml wine bottle.

Head size. The amount of space on the top of a glass of beer that is made up of foam. Thus, a glass of beer with one inch of foam on its top is said to have a one-inch head.

House wine. The term used to indicate the type of wine to be served in the event a specific brand-name product is not requested by the guest as well as those named wines offered by the glass.

HVAC. Heating, ventilation, and air-conditioning.

Hydrometer. An instrument used to measure the specific gravity of a liquid.

Ideal expense. Management's view of the correct or appropriate amount of expense necessary to generate a given quantity of sales.

Income. Net income. See Profit.

Income statement. A summary report that describes the sales achieved, the money spent on expenses and the resulting profit generated by a business in a specific time period.

Ingredient room. A storeroom or section of a storeroom where ingredients are weighed and measured according to standardized recipes, and then delivered to the appropriate kitchen production area.

Interface. Electronic connection for the purpose of sharing data.

Inventory turnover. The number of times the total value of inventory has been purchased and replaced in an accounting period.

Inventory valuation sheet. A form that documents all inventory items, the quantity on hand, and the unit value of each item.

Involuntary separation. Management causes the employee to separate from the organization (fires the employee).

Issuing. The process of supplying food or beverage products from storage by management for use in an operation.

Jigger. A bar device used to measure predetermined quantities of alcoholic beverages. Jiggers usually are marked in ounces and fractions of an ounce, for example, 1 ounce or 1½ ounces.

Job description.   A listing of the tasks to be performed in a particular position.

Job specification.   A listing of the personal skills and characteristics needed to perform those tasks pertaining to a particular job description.

Just-in-time.   See As needed.

Keg beer.   See Draft beer.

Kilowatt hours.   The measure of electrical usage.

KWH.   See Kilowatt hours.

Labor costs.   See Labor expense.

Labor expense.   All expenses (costs), including salaries, wages, and other labor-related costs such as FICA taxes, health insurance, etc., required to maintain a workforce in a foodservice operation.

Last-in, first-out (LIFO).   Term used to describe a method of storage in which the operator intends to sell his or her most recently delivered product before selling the older product.

License states.   States that regulate the sale of alcoholic beverages by the licensing of establishments.

LIFO.   See Last-in, first-out.

Loss leader.   A menu item that is priced very low for the purpose of drawing large numbers of customers to the operation.

Long-range budget.   A forecast or estimate of projected revenue, expense, and profit for a period of three to five years.

Management by exception.   If an expense is within an acceptable variation range, there is no need for management to intervene. Management takes corrective action only when operational results are outside the range of acceptability.

Managerial accounting.   The process of documenting and analyzing sales, expenses, and profits. Sometimes referred to as cost accounting.

Matrix analysis.   A method for comparisons between menu items. A matrix allows menu items to be placed into categories based on whether they are above or below overall menu item averages for factors such as food cost %, popularity, and contribution margin.

Mean.   See Average.

Menu engineering.   A common name for the contribution margin method of matrix menu analysis. Menu specials. Menu items that will appear on the menu and be removed when they are either consumed or discontinued. These daily or weekly specials are an effort to provide variety, take advantage of low-cost raw ingredients, utilize carryover products, or test market potential of new menu items.

Merchant service provider (MSP).   MSP is the restaurant's coordinator/manager of payment card acceptance and funds collection, and it provides the electronic connection between payment card issuers and their merchants.

Metered bottle.   Dispensing unit that delivers a predetermined portion of product.

Minimum operating cost.   Food Cost % plus Variable Cost % used in calculating minimum sales point.

Minimum order requirement.   The smallest order, usually expressed in dollar value, that can be placed with a vendor who delivers.

Minimum sales point (MSP).   The sales volume required to justify staying open for a given period of time.

Minimum staff.   The term used to designate the least number of employees, or payroll dollars, required to operate a facility or department within the facility.

Mixed expense.   An expense that has properties of both a fixed and a variable expense.

Monetary unit.   A specific and recognized currency denomination, for example, U.S. dollar, British pound, Japanese yen.

MSP.   See Minimum sales point.

Negligent hiring.   Failure on the part of an employer to exercise reasonable care in the selection of employees.

Net income.   The profit realized after all expenses and appropriate taxes for a business have been paid.

Noncontrollable expense.   An expense that the foodservice manager can neither increase nor decrease.

Nonoperating expenses section (of the USAR).   Covers Interest through Net Income on the Uniform System of Accounts for Restaurants income statement. It is this section that is least controllable by the foodservice manager.

Nonsufficient funds (NSF).   Not enough money in a bank account to allow a check to be cashed.

Occupancy costs.   Expenses related to occupying and paying for the physical facility that houses the foodservice unit.

OJT.   See On-the-job training.

On-call.   A system whereby selected employees who are off duty can be contacted by management on short notice to cover for other employees who are absent or to come to work if customer demand suddenly increases.

On the floor.   In the dining area.

On-the-job training (OJT).   A method of training in which workers are training while they actually are performing their required tasks.

Open bar.   A bar in which no charge for an individual drink is made to the customer, thus establishing an all-you-can-drink environment. Sometimes referred to as a hosted bar.

Open check.   Check that has been used to authorize product issues from the kitchen or bar, but that has not been added to the operation's sales total.

Operating expenses section (of the USAR).   Covers Operating Expenses through Operating Income on the Uniform System of Accounts for Restaurants income statement. Consists of expenses under the control of the manager on a weekly or monthly basis.

Opportunity cost.   The cost of forgoing the next best alternative when making a decision. For example, with two choices, A and B, both having potential benefits or returns, if A is chosen, then the potential benefits from choosing B are lost.

Orientation program.   A program usually held during the first week of an employee's job that provides information about important items such as dress code, disciplinary system, tip policy, lockers/security, sick leave policy, and retirement programs.

Other expenses.   The expenses of an operation that are neither food, beverage, nor labor.

Over. Term used when the total amount of money in a cash drawer is more than the total amount of money that should be there based on sales receipts.

Oxidation. A process that occurs when oxygen comes in contact with bottled wine, resulting in a deterioration of the wine product.

P&L. See Profit and loss statement.

Padded inventory. The term used to describe the inappropriate activity of adding a value for nonexisting inventory items to the value of total inventory in an effort to understate actual costs.

Par level. A system of determining the purchase point by using management-established minimum and maximum allowable inventory levels for a given inventory item.

Payroll. Total wages and salaries paid by a foodservice operation to its employees. Also referred to the gross pay received by an employee in exchange for his or her work.

Percent. The number "out of each hundred." Thus, 10 percent means 10 out of each 100. This is computed by dividing the part by the whole.

Percentage variance. The change in sales, expressed as a percentage, that results from comparing two operating periods.

Percent selecting. A formula for determining the proportion of people who will buy a given menu item from a list of menu choices.

Performance to budget. The percent of the budget actually spent on expenses.

Perpetual inventory. An inventory control system in which additions to and deletions from total inventory are noted as they occur.

Perpetual inventory card. A bin card that includes the product's price at the top of the card, allowing for continual tracking of the quantity of an item on hand and its price.

Physical inventory. An inventory control system in which an actual or physical count and valuation of all inventory on hand is taken at the close of each accounting period.

Plan. See Budget.

Plate cost. The sum of all product costs included in a single meal (or plate) served to a guest.

PO. See Purchase order.

Point of sale (POS) system. A system for controlling hospitality operations' cash and product usage by using a computer processor and, depending on the size of the operation, additional computer hardware, communication devices, and/or software.

Popularity index. The percentage of total guests choosing a given menu item from a list of menu alternatives.

POS. See Point of sale.

Precheck/postcheck system. System in which products ordered by the guest, recorded by the server, and issued by the kitchen or bar should match the items and money collected by the cashier. Predicted number to be sold. The quantity of a specific menu item likely to be sold given an estimate of the total number of guests expected.

Preemployment drug testing. A preemployment test used to determine if an applicant uses drugs. Such testing is allowable in most states, and can be a very effective tool for reducing insurance rates and potential employee liability issues.

Premium liquors. Expensive call liquors.

Price blending. The process of assigning prices based on product groups for the purpose of achieving predetermined cost objectives.

Price comparison sheet. A listing of several vendors' bid prices on selected items that results in the selection of a vendor, based on the best price.

Price spread. The difference in price on a menu between the lowest and highest priced item of a similar nature.

Price/value relationship. The guests' view of how much value they are receiving for the price they are paying.

Productivity. The amount of work performed by a worker in a set amount of time.

Productivity ratio. This formula refers to the total unit output divided by the total unit input.

Productivity standard. Management's expectation of the productivity ratio of each employee. Also, management's view of what constitutes the appropriate productivity ratio in a specificfoodservice operation.

Product mix. See Sales mix.

Product request log. A record of guest beverage requests that are not currently available.

Product specification. A detailed description of an ingredient or menu item. Also referred to as a spec.

Product yield. The amount of product remaining after cooking, trimming, portioning, or cleaning.

Professional trade associations. Associations that typically serve the certification, educational, social, and legislative goals of its members. Such associations hold annual gatherings, and, in conjunction with these meetings, they invite exhibitors who sell products and services of interest to interact with their members at trade shows.

Profit. The dollars that remain after all expenses have been paid. Often referred to as net income.

Profit and loss (P&L) statement. See Income statement.

Profit margin. This formula refers to net income divided by total revenues. Also referred to as return on sales.

Projected sales. Sales that may be determined by either dollar sales or customer count. Projected sales are established by using sales histories and other knowledge the operator may have that could impact total volume. They are predictions of future sales volume.

Psychological testing. Preemployment testing that can include personality tests, tests designed to predict performance, or tests of mental ability.

Pull date. Expiration date on beverage products, usually beers, after which they should not be sold.

Purchase order (PO). A listing of products requested by the purchasing agent. The purchase order lists various product information, including quantity ordered and price quoted by the vendor.

Purchase point. The point in time when an item held in inventory reaches a level that indicates it should be reordered.

Purchases. The sum cost of all food purchased during the accounting period. Determined by adding all properly tabulated invoices for the accounting period.

QSR. See Quick Service Restaurant. **Quick-change artist.** A guest who, having practiced the routine many times, attempts to confuse the cashier so that the cashier, in his or her confusion, will give the guest too much change.

Quick Service Restaurant. A foodservice operation that offers a limited menu and is designed for the convenience of customers who want their food fast.

Ready foods. See Convenience foods.

Recipe ready. A recipe ingredient that is cleaned, trimmed, cooked, and generally completed, save for its addition to the recipe.

Recodable electronic locks. A locking system that allows management to issue multiple keys and to identify precisely the time an issued key was used to access the lock, as well as to whom that key was issued.

Refusal hours. Those hours of the day in which an operation refuses to accept food and beverage deliveries.

Reporting period. The process of reporting a time period for which records are being maintained. This may be of the same duration as an accounting period.

Requisition. When a food or beverage product is requested from storage by an employee for use in an operation.

Return on sales (ROS). Often referred to as profit margin. This formula refers to net income divided by total revenues. ROS can also be stated in whole dollar terms.

Revenue. The term used to indicate the dollars taken in by the business in a defined period of time. Often referred to as sales.

Revenue Per Available Seat Hour (RevPASH). A measure of how much guests buy and how quickly they are served, calculated as dividing revenue by available seat hours.

Revenue versus price. Revenue means the amount spent by all guests, while price refers to the amount charged to one guest.

Rolling average. The average amount of sales or volume over a changing time period, for example, the last ten days or the last three weeks.

ROS. See Return on sales.

Safety stock. The extra amount above working stock of an ingredient kept on hand to meet higher than anticipated demand.

Salaried employee. An employee who receives the same income per week or month regardless of the number of hours worked.

Sales. See Revenue.

Sales forecast. A prediction of the number of guests to be served and the revenues they will generate in a defined, future time period.

Sales history. A record of sales achieved by an operator in a given sales outlet during a specifically identified time period.

Sales mix. The series of consumer-purchasing decisions that result in a specific food and beverage cost percentage. Sales mix affects overall product cost percentage any time menu items have varying food and beverage cost percentages.

Sales per seat. The total revenue generated by a facility divided by the number of seats in the dining area.

Sales per square foot.   The total revenue generated by a facility divided by the number of square feet the business occupies.

Sales to date.   The resulting number when adding today's daily sales to the sales of all prior days in the reporting period.

Sales variance.   An increase or decrease from previously experienced or predicted sales levels.

Sales volume.   The number of units sold.

Sarbanes-Oxley Act (SOX).   Technically known as the Public Company Accounting Reform and Investor Protection Act, the law provides criminal penalties for those found to have committed accounting fraud. SOX covers a whole range of corporate governance issues including the regulation of those who are assigned the task of verifying a company's financial health.

Separated.   The term used to describe employees who have either quit, been terminated, or in some other manner have left their place of employment.

Shelf life.   The period of time an ingredient or menu item maintains its freshness, flavor, and quality while in storage.

Short.   Term used when the total amount of money in a cash drawer is less than the total amount of money that should be there based on sales receipts.

Shorting.   When the vendor is unable to deliver the quantity of item ordered for the appointed delivery date.

Skills tests.   Preemployment tests such as drink production for bartenders, computer application tests for those involved in using word processing or spreadsheet tools, or food production tasks for cooks and chefs.

Skip.   See Walk.

SOP.   See Standard operating procedure.

Source reduction.   Techniques used by food manufacturers and wholesalers to reduce product packaging waste.

Spec.   See Product specification.

Spirits.   Fermented beverages that are distilled to increase the alcohol content of the product.

Split (wine).   A bottle of wine that is approximately one-quarter the size of the standard 750 ml wine bottle.

Split shift.   A scheduling technique used to match individual employee work shifts with the peaks and valleys of customer demand.

Spotter.   An individual employed by management for the purpose of inconspicuously observing bartenders and waitstaff in order to detect any fraudulent or policy-violating behavior.

Standard cost.   The labor cost needed to meet established productivity standards. Also called standard labor.

Standard labor.   See Standard cost.

Standardized recipe.   The procedures to be used for consistently preparing and serving a given menu item.

Standardized recipe cost sheet.   A record of the ingredient costs required to produce an item sold by a foodservice operation.

Standard menu.   A fixed menu that stays the same day after day.

Standard operating procedure (SOP).   Term used for the way something is done in normal business operations.

Supply chain. The distribution system that gets products from the primary source (i.e., grower) to the foodservice operation.

Supporting schedules. List of all details associated with each line item on the income statement.

Tapped keg. A draft beer container (keg) that has been opened.

Task training. The training undertaken to ensure an employee has the skills to meet productivity goals.

Tip-on (menu). Smaller menu segments intented to influence impulse buying that are attached to more permanent menus.

Total bar system. A system that combines sales information with product dispensing information to create a complete revenue and product management system.

Travel and entertainment (T&E) cards. Cards in a payment system by which the card issuer collects full payment from the card users on a monthly basis. These card companies do not typically assess their users' interest charges.

Twenty-eight-day-period approach. Accounting method that divides a year into 13 equal periods of 28 days each.

Two-key system. A system to control access to storage areas.

Uniform systems of accounts. Standardized sets of procedures used for categorizing revenue and expense in a defined industry, for example, Uniform System of Accounts for Restaurants (USAR).

User work station. A computer terminal used only to ring up food and beverage orders.

Value pricing. The practice of reducing prices on selected menu items in the belief that total guest counts will increase to the point that total sales revenue also increases.

Variable expense. An expense that generally increases as sales volume increases and decreases as sales volume decreases.

Variable payroll. Those dollars expended on employees whose presence is directly dependent on the number of guests served. These employees include servers, bartenders, and dishwashers, for example. As the number of guests served increases, the number of these individuals required to do the job also increases. As the number of guests served decreases, variable payroll should decrease.

Vintage. The specific year(s) of production for a wine.

Vintner. Wine producer.

Voluntary separation. An employee makes the decision to leave the organization.

Walk. A term used to describe a customer who has consumed a product, but leaves the foodservice operation without paying the bill. Also known as a skip.

Waste percentage. This formula is defined as product loss divided by AP weight and refers to product lost in the preparation process.

Weighted average. An average that weights the number of guests served and how much each has spent during a given financial accounting period.

Well liquors. Those spirits that are served by an operation when the customer does not specify a particular brand name.

Wine. A fermented beverage made from grapes, fruits, or berries.

Wine list. A menu of wine offerings.

Working stock. The amount of an ingredient you anticipate using before purchasing that item again

Yardstick method. Method of calculating expense standards so determinations can be made as to whether variations in expenses are due to changes in sales volume or other reasons such as waste or theft.

Yield percentage. This formula is defined as one minus waste percentage and refers to the amount of product available for use by the operator after all preparation-related losses have been taken into account.

Yield test. A procedure used to determine actual EP ingredient costs. It is used to help establish actual costs on a product that will experience weight or volume loss in preparation.

BIBLIOGRAPHY

A

Adams, Deborah. *Management Accounting for the Hospitality Industry: A Strategic Approach*. London, England: Cassell Academic, 1997.

American Hotel and Motel Association. *Uniform System of Accounts for the Lodging Industry, 10th ed.* Orlando, FL: Educational Institute of the American Hotel and Motel Association, 1996.

Asch, Allen B. Hospitality *Cost Control: A Practical Approach*. Upper Saddle River, NJ: Prentice Hall, 2005.

B

Bell, Anthea. *History of Food*. Blackwell Publishers, 1994.

Brown, Alton. *I'm Just Here for the Food*. Stewart. Tabori & Chang Publishers, 2002.

C

Chaban, Joel. *Practical Foodservice Spreadsheets With Lotus 1-2-3*. New York: John Wiley & Sons, Inc., 1997.

Club Managers Association of America (Editor). *Uniform System of Financial Reporting for Clubs*. Dubuque, IA: Kendall/Hunt Publishing Co., 2003.

D

DeFranco, Agnes L. and Pender B. M. Noriega. *Cost Control in the Hospitality Industry*. Upper Saddle River, NJ: Prentice Hall, Inc., 2000.

Deloitte & Touche, LLP. *Uniform System of Accounts for Restaurants, 7th ed.* Washington, DC: National Restaurant Association, 1996.

Dittmer, Paul R. and J. Desmond Keefe. *Principles of Food, Beverage, and Labor Cost Controls, 8th ed.* Hoboken, NJ: John Wiley & Sons, Inc., 2006.

Dopson, Lea R. and Hayes, David K. *Managerial Accounting for the Hospitality Industry*. Hoboken, NJ: John Wiley & Sons, Inc., 2008.

Douglas, Robert B. *The Food Service Managers Guide to Creative Cost Cutting and Cost Control: Over 2001 Innovative and Simple Ways to Save Your Food Service Operation Thousands by Reducing Expenses.* Ocala, FL: Atlantic Publishing Groups, Inc., 2006.

Drysdale, John A. and Jennifer Adams Aldrich. *Profitable Menu Planning, 4th ed.* Upper Saddle River, NJ: Prentice Hall, Inc., 2008.

F

Feinstein, Andrew Hale and John M. Stefanelli. Purchasing: *Selection and Procurement for the Hospitality Industry, 7th ed.* Hoboken, NJ: John Wiley & Sons, Inc., 2007.

Foster, Dennis L. *Food and Beverage: Operations, Methods, and Cost Controls.* New York: Glencoe/McGraw-Hill, 1994.

G

Gisslen, Wayne. *Essentials of Professional Cooking.* Hoboken, NJ: John Wiley & Sons, Inc., 2004.

Gisslen, Wayne. *Professional Cooking, 6th ed.* Hoboken, NJ: John Wiley & Sons, Inc., 2007.

Grossman, Harold J. *Guide to Wine Beer and Spirits, 7th ed.* Hoboken, New York: John Wiley & Sons, Inc., 1983.

Gudmundsen, Lynn. *Math for Life and Food Service.* Upper Saddle River, NJ: Prentice Hall, Inc., 2002.

Guilding, Chris. *Financial Management for Hospitality Decision Makers (Hospitality, Leisure and Tourism).* Woburn, MA: Butterworth-Heinemann, 2002.

H

Haines, Robert. *Math Principles for Food Service Occupations.* Albany, NY: Delmar Publishing, 1995.

Hales, Jonathan A. *Accounting and Financial Analysis in the Hospitality Industry (Butterworth-Heinemann Hospitality Management Series).* Burlington, MA: Butterworth-Heinemann, 2005.

Hayes, David K. and Lynn M. Huffman. (1985). "Menu Analysis, A Better Way" *Cornell Hotel and Restaurant Administration Quarterly,* 25(4), 64–70.

Hayes, David K. and Lynn M. Huffman. (1995). Value Pricing: How Low Can You Go? *Cornell Hotel and Restaurant Administration Quarterly,* 36(1), 51–56.

Hayes, David K. and Ninemeier, Jack D. *50 One-Minute Tips for Recruiting Employees: Finding the Right People for Your Organization.* Menlo Park, CA: Crisp Learning, 2001.

Hayes, David K. and Ninemeier, Jack D. *50 One-Minute Tips for Retaining Employees: Building a Win-Win Environment.* Menlo Park, CA: Crisp Learning, 2001.

Hug, Richard J. and Marshall C. Warfel. *Menu Planning and Merchandising, 2nd ed.* Berkeley, CA: McCutchan Publishing Corp., 1997.

J

Jagels, Martin. *G. Hospitality Management Accounting, 9th ed.* Hoboken, NJ: John Wiley & Sons, Inc., 2007.

K

Katsigris, Costas, Mary Porter, and Chris Thomas. *The Bar and Beverage Book, 4th ed.* Hoboken, NJ: John Wiley & Sons, Inc., 2007.

Keiser, James, Frederick J. Demicco, and Robert N. Grimes. *Contemporary Management Theory: Controlling and Analyzing Costs in Foodservice Operations, 4th ed.* Upper Saddle River, NJ: Prentice Hall, Inc., 2000.

Keister, Douglas C. *Food and Beverage Control, 2nd ed.* Upper Saddle River, NJ: Prentice Hall, Inc., 1990.

Knight, John Barton, and Lendal H. *Kotschevar. Quantity Food Production, Planning, and Management, 3rd ed.* New York: John Wiley & Sons, Inc., 2000.

Kotschevar, Lendal H. and Diane Withrow. *Management by Menu, 4th ed.* Hoboken, NJ: John Wiley & Sons, Inc., 2008.

Kotschevar, Lendal Henry, and Richard Donnelly. *Quantity Food Purchasing, 5th ed.* Upper Saddle River, NJ: Prentice Hall, Inc., 1998.

L

Labensky, Sarah R. *Applied Math for Food Service.* Upper Saddle River, NJ: Prentice Hall, Inc., 1998.

Lipinski, Robert A., Kathie Lipinski, and Kathleen Lipinski (Contributor). *Professional Beverage Management.* New York: John Wiley & Sons, Inc., 1996.

Lynch, Francis T. *The Book of Yields: Accuracy in Food Costing and Purchasing, 7th ed.* Hoboken, NJ: John Wiley & Sons, Inc., 2008.

M

Marvin, B. From Turnover to Teamwork: *How to Build and Retain a Customer-Oriented Foodservice Staff.* New York: John Wiley & Sons, Inc., 1994.

McVety, Paul J., Susan Desmond Marshall, and Bradley J. Ware. *The Menu and the Cycle of Cost Control.* Dubuque, IA: Kendall/Hunt Publishing Company, 1997.

McVety, Paul J., Bradley J. Ware, and Claudette Lévesque. *Fundamentals of Menu Planning, 2nd ed.* New York: John Wiley & Sons, Inc., 2001.

Miller, Jack E. and David V. Pavesic (Contributor). *Menu Pricing & Strategy, 4th ed.* New York: John Wiley & Sons, Inc., 1997.

N

Ninemeier, Jack D. *Planning and Control for Food and Beverage Operations.* Orlando, FL: Educational Institute of the American Hotel and Motel Association, 2004.

O

Ojugo, Clement and Todd Rymer. *Practical Food and Beverage Cost Control.* Albany, NY: Delmar Publishing, 1998.

P

Pavesic, David V. *Labor Cost: 25 Keys to Profitable Success (Restaurant Manager's Pocket Handbook Series).* New York: Lebhar-Friedman Books, 1999.

Pavesic, David V. *Purchasing and Inventory: 25 Keys to Profitable Success (Restaurant Manager's Pocket Handbook Series).* New York: Lebhar-Friedman Books, 1999.

Pavesic, David V. and Paul Magnant. *Fundamental Principles of Restaurant Cost Control, 2nd ed.* Upper Saddle River, NJ: Prentice Hall, Inc., 2005.

R

Reid, Robert D. and David C. Bojanic. *Hospitality Marketing Management, 4th ed.* Hoboken, NJ: John Wiley & Sons, Inc., 2006.

Roberts, Phil, Deborah Henckel (Illustrator), and Andrea Steward (Contributor). *Turn the Tables on Turnover: 52 Ways to Find, Hire, and Keep the Best Hospitality Employees.* Denver, CO: Pencom, 1995.

Roberts, Phil, T. J. McDonald, and Jim Sullivan. *Playing Games at Work: 52 Best Incentives, Contests, and Rewards for the Hospitality Industry.* Denver, CO: Pencom, 1994.

S

Sanders, Edward E. and Timothy H. Hill. *Foodservice Profitability: A Control Approach, 2nd ed.* Upper Saddle River, NJ: Prentice Hall, Inc., 2000.

Schmidgall, Raymond S. *Hospitality Industry Managerial Accounting, 6th ed.* Orlando, FL: Educational Institute of the American Hotel and Motel Association, 2006.

Schmidgall, Raymond S., David K. Hayes, and Jack D. Ninemeier. *Restaurant Financial Basics.* New York: John Wiley & Sons, Inc., 2002.

Schmidt, Arno. *Chef's Book of Formulas, Yields, and Sizes.* New York: John Wiley & Sons, Inc., 2003.

Spears, Marion C. and Sharon Morcos. *Foodservice Procurement: Purchasing for Profit.* Upper Saddle River, NJ: Prentice Hall, Inc., 1998.

INDEX